GOOD FICTION GUIDE

GOOD FICTION GUIDE

edited by
Jane Rogers

Consultant Editor
Hermione Lee

Assistant Editors
Mike Harris, Douglas Houston

OXFORD
UNIVERSITY PRESS

OXFORD
UNIVERSITY PRESS

Great Clarendon Street, Oxford OX2 6DP

Oxford University Press is a department of the University of Oxford.
It furthers the University's objective of excellence in research, scholarship,
and education by publishing worldwide in
Oxford New York

Athens Auckland Bangkok Bogotá Buenos Aires Calcutta
Cape Town Chennai Dar es Salaam Delhi Florence Hong Kong Istanbul
Karachi Kuala Lumpur Madrid Melbourne Mexico City Mumbai
Nairobi Paris São Paulo Singapore Taipei Tokyo Toronto Warsaw
with associated companies in Berlin Ibadan

Oxford is a registered trade mark of Oxford University Press
in the UK and in certain other countries

Published in the United States
by Oxford University Press Inc., New York

Introduction © Jane Rogers 2001
Compilation © Jane Rogers and Oxford University Press 2001
Text © Oxford University Press 2001
The moral rights of the author have been asserted
Database right Oxford University Press (maker)

First published 2001

British Library Cataloguing in Publication Data
Data available

Library of Congress Cataloging in Publication Data
Data available

ISBN 0–19–210021–1

1 3 5 7 9 10 8 6 4 2

Typeset in Minion
by Graphicraft Limited, Hong Kong
Printed and bound by
TJ International, Padstow, Cornwall

Contents

Introduction

Jane Rogers

This is a book for anyone who likes reading fiction. The aim behind it is to offer information—and enthusiasm—about over a thousand authors, and over five thousand books. We've set out to do this in two ways; first, in thirty-four short essays introducing different areas or genres of fiction, each by a different writer with a special interest in that field. And secondly, in the longer part of the book, by one thousand-plus individual author entries which aim to give a flavour of each writer's work, recommendations of which books to read, and suggestions about other writers whose work is similar.

Books are promoted to us endlessly, through adverts, reviews, adaptations, through glossy attention-grabbing covers in bookshops, and wild claims on jacket sleeves. They are set texts for exams; they are hyped by prizes and awards; or they are written by celebrities. But in the end, every reader knows, probably the single most compelling reason for picking up a book which is new to you, is when a friend tells you, 'Read this, it's really good.'

This guide sets out to do exactly that. Each of the essayists has picked out their twelve favourite fiction books (in all the world) in their particular area—in order to explain and pass on their passion for those books. Many of the essayists are themselves novelists in the field they describe—Michael Dibdin writes on **Crime**, Nigel Williams on **Humour**, Michèle Roberts on **France**, E. A. Markham on the **Caribbean**, Aritha van Herk on **Canada**; others are novelists writing about branches of fiction which they know and love as readers rather than practitioners (Livi Michael on **Science fiction**, Robert McCrum on **Adventure**). In all the essays, and indeed the individual author entries, the notion of one reader recommending books to another is central.

I should make it clear from the start that this is a *fiction* guide, encompassing both literature and popular fiction. There are a number of excellent literature guides already in existence; the best of course being Margaret Drabble's peerless *Oxford Companion to English Literature*. There are several good guides to contemporary literature available, my personal favourite being Peter Parker's thorough and fascinating *The Reader's Companion to 20th Century Writers*. But this book aims to cover popular and genre fiction, as well as classics and contemporary literary fiction. It aims to cover (sketchily, I admit, but to my knowledge there is no other guide that even makes the attempt) international fiction, not just the classics like Dostoevsky and Flaubert, but more recent foreign-language writers in translation—Süskind, Sebald, Calvino, Fuentes, Maryse Condé, Naguib Mahfouz, Venedikt Yerofeev, and many more. We are attempting to cover the full range of fiction because most readers love different kinds of books at different times. Or at the same time, come to that. A bag of holiday reading might happily contain Tolstoy, Georgette Heyer, Elmore Leonard, Frank Herbert and Nadine Gordimer. Snobbery in reading is the most pointless thing. And we don't buy or borrow books according to the nationality of the author—if they're available in English and we like the sound of them, we read them. For a general fiction guide to cut out fiction in translation seems arbitrary and narrow-minded.

Most of this book's contributors are writers; I am a writer. Before I was a writer, I was a reader. Being a reader, an obsessive devourer of books, an honest critic, and a passionate defender, is part of the make-up of most writers, and for this reason I think they write well about books. I have worked hard to free the guide from academic jargon and critical theory. I have sometimes bullied contributors into using plainer language, and stating things more straightforwardly, than perhaps they would have liked. This is because books are for everybody. I dislike the mystique some academics create around literature; and on written English, my guiding star is Orwell: 'Good prose is like a window pane.'

Each essayist's 'top twelve' is entirely his or her own choice, and as the essays have come in, I've had first-hand experience of how this *Guide* should work: I've rejoiced to find favourite books recommended, been outraged by omissions of equally good writers, and been tempted into entirely new areas of fiction by the enthusiasms of essayists. (I had never read a Western in my life before, but Lee Clark Mitchell has shown me what I'm missing. Then there's recent Russian fiction to tackle . . .) Many readers will want to pick a quarrel with these 'top twelves'—as those of us editing the essays have frequently done. I was horrified to find that in Richard Francis' wonderfully concise and eloquent overview of fiction from the United States, he made no mention of John Updike—who in my view is the best living American writer. Well, Richard doesn't rate him so highly. (And you *can* always turn to the Updike author entry, which I have written myself.) Consultant editor Hermione Lee, upon reading Lesley Glaister's particular and lovingly described choices in **Short stories**, noted in the margin, 'Heartbroken no Elizabeth Bowen!' Bowen did, as a result, find her way into Lesley's essay, but often authors that were argued over did not. I was disturbed to find no Camus or Stendhal in **France**, but utterly seduced by Michèle Roberts's delightful reader's meander through the country's history and geography. Assistant editor Mike Harris wanted to know what Angela Carter was doing in **Social issues** when Elizabeth Gaskell and George Gissing were missing—but Valentine Cunningham's wide-ranging essay has its own agenda. And Camus, Stendhal, Gaskell, and Gissing, can all be found in the author entries section. The point about the subject essays is that they are based on personal taste—they are here to lead readers to new books by putting those books in a context and explaining why the essayists rate them so highly: and, of course, the essays are here to be argued with. How, in a list of twelve books, can you cover a genre, a country, a continent?

Which brings me to the whole vexed question of which authors are featured in the author entries, and which are not. Battles have raged over which authors should be included here, but the selection process has been guided by certain principles. Authors are *in* if their books are well known; they must be still in print, or must be so seminal to the development of a genre, or so dear to a particular contributor's heart, that they have won me over by sheer passion and persistence. (Any out-of-print titles recommended here are titles which contributors hope and believe should be brought back into print; and most of them are still available through libraries.) Authors are *in* if they have been particularly strong sellers over the years, or if they have featured recently within the Public Libraries list of most-borrowed authors—that seemed to me to be a pretty good guide to popularity. That doesn't mean we've been prepared to recommend any old rubbish; there *are* popular writers who have been excluded on the grounds that no one involved in this project could find it in their heart to recommend them (the best example being Mills and Boon romances). I hope and believe that readers of **Romance** will find suggestions to interest them in Elizabeth Buchan's wide-ranging essay, and by reading on from the writers she recommends.

Another difficulty in deciding who to include is the question of new or only recently established writers. When I drew up the original author list, Arundhati Roy was unpublished—now she is a Booker Prize winner. There will be other rising stars whom I've missed, who will seem to be glaring omissions by the time this guide is published; and there will, sadly and inevitably, be writers here whose books disappear from print and library shelves with horrible speed. Established authors covered here continue to produce new novels; many of them, inconsiderately, not long after entries on them have been completed. Keeping up to date on a project like this means running to stay on the spot; in the end, I think, with all its defects and omissions, this must be regarded as a snapshot of fiction in English at the opening of the twenty-first century.

The scope of the book is also deliberately limited because it had to be possible to get it into one volume. A decision was taken early on not to cover children's fiction, which is well covered elsewhere. But it seemed important to cover fiction for teens, that crucial point where avid readers suddenly can't find anything they like any more. This has been addressed by Adèle Geras, whose own books for teens are much admired.

Limits have also had to be imposed on the amount of foreign fiction we could include. When the idea of essays on fiction in translation was first raised, many more were suggested than just **France, Russia**, and **Germany**. Of course there should be an essay on Spanish fiction, on Italian, on South American —but we simply don't have space. South America has, at least partly, been covered in Carol Birch's excellent overview of **Magic realism**, but for the others the best we could do was to include individual author entries from those countries. Likewise, we have limited ourselves strictly to fiction; not because the only good books are fiction, but because one guide can't hope to do everything.

There are overlaps; not only between authors recommended in the essays, and the individual entries on those authors—but also between some of the essays. This is because of the huge areas of overlap between genres of fiction; it is entirely possible for a novel to be romantic, historical, and crime, for example. In particular you will find overlap between **Spy** and **Adventure** (not surprisingly), and **Crime** and **Thrillers**. My interest in using these labels is to help readers to find what they like; it is never to be prescriptive, nor to suggest that it is a good idea to slap labels on books. Many of the best books entirely defy categorization, they cross genres from murder mystery to love-story, they include elements of great literature, pot-boiling narrative, melodramatic cliffhangers, and characters varying from psychologically complex to caricature (and I'm only talking about one book here; admittedly, though, it is *The Brothers Karamazov*). It has become fascinating to see how certain favourite books crop up over and over again, nominated in different genre or subject areas; books which are favourites many times over—Dickens tops the list, closely followed by Tolstoy and Salinger. (Turn to Dickens; the seven essays where he is recommended are listed at the end of the entry.)

I know we won't have got it all right; despite the fact that the original list of 1,000 authors (now grown to 1,120) was checked by reviewers, librarians, authors, editors, and academics. I know there will be fascinating and important writers who are missed off—and that there will be some writers here you may think don't deserve to be. I regret any omissions; it is human fallibility rather than anything more sinister, and I am the person to blame. But I hope that the catholic spread of authors and types of books recommended here will make it clear that this is not a reflection of any one individual's taste. Though there are many authors here whose work I love, there are also many whom I have not read, and a significant number whose books I dislike. And the same goes for my consultant and assistant editors. If we succeed in making you want to read new books, even if you disagree with us along the way, then we will have succeeded in our aim.

Writers of author entries were encouraged to concentrate on their favourite books by the writers they describe, and were given the freedom to include biographical information where it seemed important, or to use their wordage simply to concentrate on describing the novels. Thus there is rather more variation between author entries than in a standard reference book; I hope the idiosyncrasy of the entries will lead readers into the enthusiasms of individual contributors.

There are no lists of titles in the author entries, because any library or book-shop catalogue can provide that; every title mentioned in this book is described, even if only briefly. And for that reason contributors of author entries were asked, in general, to limit their recommendations to a maximum of five titles per entry, working on the assumption that if readers read and like these five, they are perfectly capable of discovering that writer's other titles on their own. The 📖 symbol takes you to authors to follow on with. These have been chosen either for similarities of subject matter or style, or because they offer an earlier or later historical example of that genre or treatment of that theme; or, occasionally, because they provide an interesting contrast. All the suggested recommendations for further reading are names of authors featured in this book, so if, for example, you have read and enjoyed Graham Greene, it is possible to read the entries on each of the authors recommended after his entry, in order to decide which you may prefer. Again, the suggestions for further reading are endlessly open to argument. Sometimes rather less good authors will be followed by recommendations to read on to more interesting ones. That should not be seen as an insult to the recommended authors; no one is suggesting all recommendations are of the same literary quality as the books they follow. Conversely, sometimes a writer considered great may be followed by a recommendation to read a less-well-known author, who is recommended, not for being the *same*, but for treating some aspect of the great writer's work in an interesting way of his or her own.

All titles are followed by date of first publication; if first publication was in a foreign language, it is the date of first publication in that language. For books published serially, the dates of publication of first and last chapters are given (e.g. 1866–9).

There are many people who are due thanks for their hard work and help with this guide; in particular, Angus Phillips, whose brainchild it was when he was working at Oxford University Press as commissioning editor. He persuaded me to take it on, and together we thrashed out what it would be. Since then I have had invaluable help from my consultant editor, Hermione Lee, my assistant editor, Mike Harris, from Douglas Houston, assistant editor in the early stages, from my current editor at OUP, Vicki Rodger, and from all the essayists and author-entry writers, whose names and initials are below. I would like to pay a special tribute here to Tony Tanner, whose teaching inspired me as an undergraduate, and who sadly died in December 1998, very shortly after sending me his excellent essay on **The sea**.

Author entries are initialled, since this is a book about personal taste and personal recommendation; it does not set out to be objective. For plot summaries, author biographies, lists of prize-winners, and academic analysis, there are other places a reader can look (although much of that information is also here). For books which I hope are clearly described, by readers with likes and dislikes, for readers with likes and dislikes: Reader, read on.

Contributors

SHERRY ASHWORTH (SA), novelist. *See author entry.*

KARIN BAMBOROUGH (KB), director of an independent film and TV company, and a visiting professor and external examiner in screenwriting, film production, and the moving image.

CAROL BIRCH (CB), novelist and critic. *See author entry.*

SOPHIE BREESE (SB), freelance researcher, editor and writer. Previous work includes a lecturership in English at Harris Manchester College, University of Oxford. Currently working in the Middle East.

ELIZABETH BUCHAN, novelist. *See author entry.*

WAYNE BURROWS (WB), journalist and poet. Contributor to *The Big Issue in the North*; poems published in *Poetry Wales*, *Sheffield Thursday*, and the Seren anthology *The Bloodstream*.

LESLEY CHAMBERLAIN, writer. Works on Russian themes, including fiction: *In a Place Like That* (1998), travel: *Volga Volga* (1995), and autobiography: *In the Communist Mirror* (1990).

ANTHONY CHENNELLS, Associate Professor of English, University of Zimbabwe. Co-editor of *Emerging Perspectives on Dambudzo Marechera* (1999).

SHIRLEY CHEW, Professor of Commonwealth and Postcolonial Literatures, University of Leeds. Co-editor of *Translating Life: Studies in Transpositional Aesthetics* (1999).

RITA CHRISTIAN, Senior Lecturer in Caribbean Literature, University of North London.

NICHOLAS CLEE (NC), Editor, *The Bookseller*. Member of the judging panels of the Booker Prize (1993) and of the Encore Award (1997).

GLADYS MARY COLES (GC), poet and biographer. Works include *Leafburners* (1986), *The Glass Island* (1992), and *The Land Within* (1999). Biographer of Mary Webb and president of the Mary Webb Society. Lecturer in Writing, Liverpool John Moores University and University of Liverpool.

MICHAEL COX, Senior Commissioning Editor, Oxford University Press. Co-editor of *The Oxford Book of English Ghost Stories* (1986), editor of *The Oxford Book of Twentieth-Century Ghost Stories* (1996), and biographer of M. R. James.

PATRICIA CRAIG, reviewer, and editor of anthologies including the *Oxford Books of Ireland*, *English Detective Stories*, *Travel Stories*, and *Modern Women's Stories*.

VALENTINE CUNNINGHAM, Professor of English Language and Literature, University of Oxford; Senior English Fellow, Corpus Christi College, Oxford. Latest book: *Victorian Poetry and Poetics: An Anthology* (Blackwell).

EDMUND CUSICK (EC), poet and lecturer in Imaginative Writing, John Moores University, formerly Lecturer in English Literature at the University of Wales. Poetry includes *Gronw's Stone: Voices from the Mabinogion* (1997).

JAN DALLEY, Literary Editor of the *Financial Times*. Author of *Diana Mosley: A Life* (1999) and various translations including *The Book of Proust* (1988).

MICHAEL DIBDIN, novelist. *See author entry.*

MARTIN EDWARDS (ME), novelist. Author of the Harry Devlin series of crime novels, including *All the Lonely People* (1991) and *First Cut Is the Deepest* (1999).

RICHARD FRANCIS (RF), novelist and biographer. *See author entry.*

MAUREEN FREELY, writer. Novels include *Mother's Helper*, *The Life of the Party*, *The*

Stork Club, Under the Vulcania, and *The Other Rebecca.* Non-fiction: *Pandora's Clock, What About Us?,* and *The Parent Trap.* Lecturer at the University of Warwick. Regular contributor to the *Guardian,* the *Observer,* the *Sunday Times,* the *Daily Mail,* and the *Independent.*

ADÈLE GERAS (AG), children's novelist and poet. *See author entry.*

LESLEY GLAISTER (LG), novelist. *See author entry.*

BEN HARKER (BH) is currently working as a lecturer at the University of York. He has recently completed a PhD about contemporary American fiction.

MIKE HARRIS (MH) is a script-writer and theatre director who works in radio drama, touring theatre, theatre in education, large-scale community plays and TV. He is a senior lecturer on the MA in Writing at Sheffield Hallam University.

CHRISTOPHER HART (CH), novelist, journalist, and Literary Editor of the *Erotic Review.* Previous works include *The Harvest* (1999) and *The Venetian Carnival* (2000).

ARITHA VAN HERK, novelist and Professor of Canadian Literature and Creative Writing, University of Calgary, Canada. Her latest works of fiction are *Restlessness, Places Far From Ellesmere,* and *No Fixed Address.* Her ficto-criticism is collected in *In Visible Ink* and *A Frozen State.*

DOUGLAS HOUSTON (DH), writer and researcher. Books of verse include *With the Offal Eaters* (1986) and *The Hunters on the Snow* (1994).

TREVOR HOYLE (TH), novelist. *See author entry.*

MICHAEL HULSE, poet, critic, and translator of German literature (Goethe, Wassermann, Jelinek, Sebald, etc.). Poetry includes *Eating Strawberries in the Necropolis* (1991). Co-editor of *The New Poetry* (1993) and, since 1999, of the literary quarterly *Stand.*

MAXIM JAKUBOWSKI (MJ), novelist and *Guardian* columnist. Editor of numerous anthologies in the crime and erotica field. Recent novels include *The State*

of Montana (1998) and *On Tenderness Express* (2000).

DICKIE JAMES (DJ) has taught Philosophy and Cultural Studies at Staffordshire University and for the Workers Educational Association. She is a voluntary sector manager, training consultant, and freelance writer.

CAROL JOYNER (CJ), PhD student, QMW College, University of London. The thesis considers space in Contemporary American Bi-Cultural writers.

GODFREY KEARNS (GK), Lecturer in English and American Studies at University of Manchester, currently working on a book on Steinbeek.

HERMIONE LEE (HL), Goldsmith's Professor English Literature and Fellow of New College, Oxford. Previous work includes *Virginia Woolf* (1996), *Elizabeth Bowen* (1981, 1999), and *Willa Cather: A Life Saved Up* (1989).

E. A. MARKHAM (EM), Professor of Creative Writing at Sheffield Hallam University. His publications include 6 collections of poetry and the novel *Marking Time.* He has edited the *Penguin Book of Caribbean Short Stories,* and his collected short stories are due out in 2001.

ANDREW MCALLISTER (AM), reviewer and editor. Previous work includes *The Objectivists* (1996), a critical anthology of modernist poetry in the 1930s.

ROBERT MCCRUM, novelist and literary editor. *See author entry.*

VAL MCDERMID (VM), novelist. *See author entry.*

LIVI MICHAEL (LM), novelist. *See author entry.*

LEE CLARK MITCHELL, Professor of English, Princeton University. Previous works include *Witnesses to a Vanishing America: The Nineteenth-Century Response* (1981), *Determined Fictions: American Literary Naturalism* (1989), *The Photograph and the American Indian* (1994), and *Westerns: Making the Man in Fiction and Film* (1996).

JENNY NEWMAN (JN), novelist. Previous works include *The Faber Book of Seductions* (1988), *Women Talk Sex: Autobiographical*

Writing on Sex, Sexuality and Sexual Identity (1992), *Going In* (1995) and *Life Class* (2000).

TRACEY O'ROURKE (TO), poet and tutor in Creative Writing at Sheffield Hallam University.

RA PAGE (RP), journalist. Edited *The City Life Book of Manchester Short Stories* (1999).

IAN POPLE (IP) works at the University of Manchester. Previous works include *The Glass Enclosure* (1996) and *An Introduction to Text and Discourse Analysis* (1998).

SARAH RIGBY (SR), Editor at Carcanet Press, Manchester.

MICHÈLE ROBERTS, novelist and poet. *See author entry.*

JANE ROGERS (JR), novelist and television dramatist. *See author entry.*

KATE SAUNDERS, novelist and journalist. Previous works include *Night Shall Overtake Us* (1993), *Lily-Josephine* (1998), and *The Belfry Witches* series for children (1999–2000).

MICHAEL SHEA, novelist and businessman. Former diplomat, Press Secretary to The Queen, and currently member of the Independent Television Commission. Author of 23 books of fiction and nonfiction, including *Spindoctor* and *Spinoff.*

TOM SHIPPEY (TS), Chair of Humanities, Saint Louis University. Books include *The Road to Middle-Earth* (1992), *The Oxford Book of Fantasy Stories* (1994), and *J. R. R. Tolkien: Author of the Century* (2000).

FELICITY SKELTON (FS), short story writer and lecturer in creative writing. Previous work includes a collection of short stories *Eating a Sandwich* (1999).

JULES SMITH (JS), literary critic. Works include *Art, Survival and So Forth* (2000). Also contributed to *The Oxford Companion to Twentieth-Century Literature in English* (1996) and *The New Dictionary of National Biography.*

CATH STAINCLIFFE (CS), novelist. Founder member of Murder Squad, crime fiction collective; visit the web site at www.murdersquad.co.uk. *See author entry.*

JOHN SUTHERLAND, Lord Northcliffe Professor of Modern English Literature at University College London. His books include *Thackeray at Work, Where was Rebecca Shot?*, and *The Literary Detective.* He has also edited titles for Oxford World's Classics.

TONY TANNER was a Fellow of King's College, Cambridge and the first Professor of American Literature at the University of Cambridge. His *City of Words: American Fiction 1950–70* introduced English readers to American experimental fiction of that period; his other works of criticism include *Adultery in the Novel: Contract and Transgression* (1979) and *Jane Austen* (1986).

TRUDI TATE (TT), Visiting Professor in English at Goethe University, Frankfurt and member of Clare Hall, Cambridge. Works include *Modernism, History and the First World War* (1998).

BOYD TONKIN, Literary Editor of the *Independent* since 1996 and former literary editor of the *New Statesman.* Judge of the Booker Prize for Fiction, 1999; convenor and judge of the *Independent*/Arts Council Foreign Fiction Prize.

AILEEN LA TOURETTE (AT), novelist and Lecturer in Imaginative Writing, Liverpool John Moores University. Previous works include *Nuns and Mothers* (1984) and *Cry Wolf* (1986).

RACHEL VAN RIEL and OLIVE FOWLER (RV) create resources for readers and the reading industry including *Opening the Book—Finding a Good Read* (1996), *The Reading Group Toolbox* (2000) and openingthebook.com.

SUE VICE (SV) is Reader in English Literature at the University of Sheffield. She is the author of *Introducing Bakhtin* (1997) and *Holocaust Fiction* (2000).

EMILY WEYGANG (EW) is working on the final stages of her doctoral thesis on South African Literature in the 1950s, University of York.

NIGEL WILLIAMS, novelist and playwright. *See author entry.*

SUBJECT ESSAYS

Adventure

Robert McCrum

The classic adventure story is Robert Louis Stevenson's *Treasure Island*. Stevenson's thrilling first paragraph, an exquisitely crafted single sentence, which could profitably adorn the seminar rooms of any number of American campus writing schools, is a model of how to hook the reader's attention with the promise of drama to come.

> Squire Trelawney, Dr Livesey, and the rest of these gentlemen having asked me to write down the whole particulars about Treasure Island, from the beginning to the end, keeping nothing back but the bearings of the island, and that only because there is still treasure not yet lifted, I take up my pen in the year of grace 17—, and go back to the time when my father kept the 'Admiral Benbow' inn, and the brown old seaman with the sabre cut first took up his lodging under our roof.
>
> I remember . . .

Treasure Island was published in 1883. Victorian England was then the centre of the greatest, most far-flung empire the world had ever known, covering almost a quarter of the globe. Its newspapers were full of imperial adventure stories (many of them featuring the activities of heroic Scots) in exotic parts of the world, from 'darkest Africa' to the uncharted Antipodes. It's somehow apt that *Treasure Island*, which was originally entitled 'The Sea Cook', should have been written by a young Scot whose family had designed lighthouses to protect seafarers navigating the rocky seas around the British Isles. Stevenson understood that a first-class adventure story needed a cast of credible, but also lovable, villains. In addition to the gripping tale young Jim Hawkins has to tell of the recovery of Captain Flint's treasure, Stevenson populates his tale with a cast of extraordinary characters, some of whom passed straight into the culture: Long John Silver, Blind Pew, Israel Hands, and Ben Gunn.

Stevenson said that his book was 'for boys'. Many of these came from the great Victorian public schools, Rugby, Marlborough, Winchester, Eton, and Harrow, harsh private educational institutions set up to supply classically trained young men for colonial service. For many years, until the turn of the century, the greatest 'adventure stories' found an enthusiastic audience in these schools because the adventure novel reflected the drama of empire quite explicitly. Some splendid examples of late-Victorian adventure are to be found in the works of Rider Haggard, a fine, once-popular writer now unjustly neglected.

Haggard, who was a close friend of Rudyard Kipling, had a worldwide readership for his adventure stories which were notable chiefly for weird invention and spellbinding narrative. The most famous are *She* (1887) and *King Solomon's Mines* (1886) which combine story-telling verve with Haggard's fascination for African landscape, primitive society, wildlife, and the mysterious tribal past.

Haggard was a literary craftsman with many imitators. Another late-Victorian adventure writer, now almost forgotten, was G. A. Henty, a former journalist whose military-historical series, which includes *With Clive in India* (1884) and *Under Drake's Flag* (1883), dramatize the imperial saga through the eyes of a series of young English boys who find themselves caught up in a decisive historical moment. Henty did not flinch from expounding the virtues of empire and his adventures rely on the glorification of mainly male, historical figures, backed up by a strong narrative, and a good line-up of supporting characters spiced with plenty of historical verisimilitude.

Both Henty and Haggard came from a metropolitan world of amateur public school imperialists. Another *fin de siècle* adventure writer, Anthony Hope, in real life the successful lawyer A. H. Hawkins, represents the last gasp of the Victorian adventure story. Hope's *The Prisoner of Zenda* (1894) is set in 'Ruritania' with splendid villains, a virtuous heroine, and a swashbuckling English gentleman-hero.

By the turn of the century, the adventure story had become sufficiently established as a genre to attract the attention of serious novelists. Joseph Conrad's *Lord Jim* (1900) is, from this perspective, an imperial adventure story with a high moral purpose. Jim, who might have stepped from the pages of a Henty novel, is the chief mate on board the *Patna*, a poorly manned ship carrying a party of pilgrims in Eastern waters. Jim is young, idealistic, a dreamer of heroic deeds. When, in a storm, the *Patna* threatens to sink, the officers decide to escape in one of the few lifeboats. Jim refuses to follow their cowardly example, but at the last minute his resolve weakens and he joins them. The ship does not sink and the pilgrims are rescued. But Jim remains haunted by his moment of weakness and searches for ways to find redemption. Much of the narrative is told by an observer, Marlow, who is also the central figure in Conrad's masterpiece *Heart of Darkness* (1899).

The dramas of empire lost their shine with the Boer War, but in the first decade of the new century the threat of war with Germany mesmerized people's attention and found its way into the adventure writing of the time. Now the threat to the empire, for so long concentrated in exotic villains in faraway lands, could be located across the North Sea, in the Kaiser's Germany and his expanding navy of fearsome battleships. Erskine Childers, who was eventually to be shot for his support of the Irish republican movement, was the first to capitalize on this British nationalist neurosis with his masterpiece *The Riddle of the Sands* (1903), in which two amateur yachtsmen sailing in the Baltic uncover German preparations for an invasion of England.

Another young writer who captured the public mood and successfully dramatized the fear of a war with Germany was John Buchan who wrote *The Thirty-Nine Steps* while recovering from flu in 1915. Here too the plot turns on the unmasking of a dangerous invasion plot by unscrupulous foreigners, a device that came to feature in many twentieth-century thrillers. Buchan, who went on to write *Greenmantle* (1916) and *Mr Standfast* (1918), became the interwar writer of adventure stories *par excellence*.

When the Great War actually came, the thrill of imperial adventure came to a sticky end in the mud and horror of Flanders. Once the war was over, there was no longer much taste for derring-do. In the 1920s and 1930s, then, this kind of fiction became transmuted into something more realistic and contemporary. It never lost sight of its duty to entertain. One writer, whose father was a headmaster of an English public school, whose education was full of Haggard, Henty, and Childers, and who was actually related to Stevenson, was Graham Greene. By the end of his life, Greene had been elevated (by his publisher, Penguin) to the status of 'greatest living English writer', but his work was always rooted in the adventure story. He acknowledged this explicitly in the novels he called 'entertainments', the first of which, *Stamboul Train* (1932), was a subtle reworking of many of the elements described so far.

Greene went on to write many novels of far greater moral consequence, but adventure lies at the heart of his best work, much of which is set in former British colonies and exotic foreign parts: Sierra Leone—*The Heart of the Matter* (1948); Vietnam—*The Quiet American* (1955); the Congo—*A Burnt-Out Case* (1961); Mexico—*The Power and the Glory* (1940).

Another adventure writer, almost a contemporary of Greene, but badly overshadowed by him, was Eric Ambler, who died as recently as 1998. His work is characterized by all those qualities—strong narrative drive, intelligent writing, and powerful atmosphere—that are the hallmark of the classic adventure story. *The Mask of Dimitrios* (1939) is among Ambler's finest yarns, the story of a crime novelist holidaying in Istanbul who is drawn into a spiralling world of assassination and double-dealing. Ambler's fictional world is no longer located in the outposts of the British empire, but closer to home in the Europe of the pre-Second World War dictators. Ambler's work prefigured and certainly influenced a generation of spy-thriller writers, from Len Deighton and Philip Kerr to John Le Carré and Jack Higgins.

Elsewhere, the adventure story languished. None has matched the literary imagination (or genius) of Stevenson or Haggard. The genre passed into the hands of pulp entertainers of whom the most distinguished, Nevil Shute, is remembered (and still in print) for books like *No Highway* (1948), a gripping tale of suspense concerning the effect of metal fatigue on a mid-flight transatlantic passenger jet. Shute was always concerned with contemporary issues— his last work, *On the Beach* (1957), is a post-nuclear apocalyptic tale set in his native Australia—and it was this focus that also inspired the immensely popular writings of Arthur Hailey, whose implausible, best-selling yarn *Airport* (1968) was also made into a blockbusting film. Shute and Hailey, in turn, have many imitators, from Wilbur Smith to Desmond Bagley.

Truer to the Victorian idea of the adventure story, however, are the page-turning works of Bernard Cornwell (whose '*Sharpe*' series of historical adventures is set during the Napoleonic Wars) and the historically meticulous, comic novels of George MacDonald Fraser, whose hero, first seen in *Flashman* (1969), cuts a swathe through the opposite sex and imperial history alike.

See also ROBERT MCCRUM

See also SPY

Top Twelve

ROBERT LOUIS STEVENSON, *Treasure Island* (1883)

G. A. HENTY, *With Clive in India* (1884)

H. RIDER HAGGARD, *King Solomon's Mines* (1886)

ANTHONY HOPE, *The Prisoner of Zenda* (1894)

JOSEPH CONRAD, *Lord Jim* (1900)

ERSKINE CHILDERS, *The Riddle of the Sands* (1903)

JOHN BUCHAN, *The Thirty-Nine Steps* (1915)

GRAHAM GREENE, *Stamboul Train* (1932)

ERIC AMBLER, *The Mask of Dimitrios* (1939)

NEVIL SHUTE, *No Highway* (1948)

ARTHUR HAILEY, *Airport* (1968)

BERNARD CORNWELL, *Sharpe's Eagle* (1981)

Africa

Anthony Chennells

For over four hundred years Africa has been precisely imaged in the European mind. The Sahara is extended south to make a continent of sand-dunes and oases and at some point in the eighteenth century tropical rain forests replace the deserts. More recently, tourist promotions and television reports have competed with one another for the authentic image of Africa: luxurious safaris across the game-covered plains are placed alongside the civilian casualties of famines brought on by Africa's many wars and droughts. Quaint 'tribal' Africans laid on for a tourist adventure, and starving Africans as objects of world philanthropy, serve to confirm older impressions of African passivity: they were either being enslaved or were waiting for a missionary to point them towards the true god, the settler to teach them the dignity of labour, or the entrepreneur to draw them into the world economy. Only as savages rejecting divine grace and civil order were Africans ever represented as agents of their own destiny.

Of course Africans were never passive and Africa's enormous diversity of climates produced widely different cultures with complex theologies and philosophies and technological, medical, and scientific systems appropriate to widely different material needs. The African literature produced prolifically over the last forty years is evidence of the opposite of silent passivity. One of my favourite early modern African novels, the Nigerian Chinua Achebe's *Arrow of God* (1964), opposes images of African disorder with highly ritualized festivals which celebrate the interaction of a spiritual order and the demands of an agricultural economy. Such an account could easily result in fictionalized anthropology or become a celebration of pre-colonial Africa as a Golden Age. But while Achebe traces the tragedy of a man who underestimates the power of the new colonial dispensation, he also shows a society divided between power-hungry factions. Nor are beliefs fixed in past practice; the novel debates the sources of moral authority. Achebe refuses to be dogmatic and the reader has to draw his or her own conclusions from the story itself.

Most of Africa's written fiction was produced either just before or since the decolonization of Africa, and consequently colonialism, anti-colonial resistance, and the often tyrannical regimes which replaced the colonial state have been important subjects. One of the most interesting of these novels is Ngugi wa Thiong'o's *A Grain of Wheat* (1967) which is set immediately before and during the celebration of Kenyan independence. While the brutalities of colonialism are attacked, people who opposed it are not shown as uncomplicatedly heroic. Ngugi's later novels reveal a greater disillusionment with the path independent Kenya has been led along. The ruthless élite are agents to international capitalism and allow foreign domination to continue but Ngugi never loses his faith in the capacity for resistance by the mass of the people. The most ambitious of these later novels, *Petals of Blood* (1977), is on one level a detective story but on another displaces the Christian conception of human history moving towards a New Jerusalem with a secular myth of a country moving through socialism towards true democracy.

Ngugi wrote his later novels in Gikuyu, believing it to be politically, socially, and culturally vital that African writers write in local languages. These works were soon translated into English, as were the great Francophone novels of the late 1950s and 1960s. The Senegalese writer Sembene Ousmane's most famous novel, *God's Bits of Wood* (1960), provides a useful contrast with Ngugi's and Achebe's contention that the retrieval of a people's cultural memory is an important mode of anti-colonial resistance. Sembene makes no attempt to return to a pre-colonial past but instead centres *God's Bits of Wood* on the historic strike on the Dakar–Bamako railway line in 1948. The colonial railway has forged the workers of the novel into a new class who transcend Senegal's pre-colonial ethnicities. Through the strike a new consciousness grows in both the men strikers and the women, who in having to forage for food, discover in themselves a forgotten capacity for militancy.

Sembene was an orthodox Marxist when he wrote the novel and few other African novelists share his view that African culture is richer if it is open to foreign cultural influences. The Francophone novelist Mongo Beti uses satire to show how French colonialism ignored the profundity of religious beliefs and the complexity of social organization in pre-colonial Cameroon. Beti's *The Poor Christ of Bomba* (1956) satirizes the naïvety of a young Christian boy who by the end has learned that people turn to Christianity in the hope that the institutional church will stand between them and an oppressive colonial state, while in *Mission to Kala* (1958) the tables are turned on a boy educated at a colonial secondary school. He discovers that his education has detached him from any context while his family has been educated into a culture which shapes their relationships, and satisfies both their material and spiritual needs.

Another novel which examines pre-colonial culture with respect is Charles Mungoshi's *Waiting for the Rain* (1975). Mungoshi is a Zimbabwean and this, his first novel, was written when Zimbabwe was still Rhodesia. By telling the story from differing points of view, Mungoshi is able to register something of the alienation of people under settler rule. At one extreme is the grandfather who is concerned only that his family remain faithful to tradition; at the other extreme his grandson Lucifer believes that personal fulfilment is possible for him only by going abroad. The novel is open-ended, refusing the dogmatism of cultural nationalism, while recognizing the danger to Africa's self-esteem if it looks at the West with uncritical admiration. Ayi Kwei Armah's *Fragments* (1970) develops this last idea. Ghanaian culture in this novel is a culture of dependency incapable of creating meaning in the lives of Ghanaians. The families in the novel are literally dependent on the 'been-to', the relative who has travelled to Europe or America, who will enrich his family with First World wealth.

An often repeated observation about colonial Africa is that women were doubly oppressed both as blacks and as women. This is largely confirmed by women writers. The Egyptian novelist Nawal El Saadawi's powerful *God Dies by the Nile* (1974), written in Arabic, shows the local officials of a small Nile town despising the peasants but regarding young peasant girls as being at their disposal. These petty tyrants appropriate for themselves the authority which properly belongs to God. Only through the violence of an older woman is this blasphemous connection broken. Another ambitious feminist novel is Tsitsi Dangarembga's *Nervous Conditions* (1988). Instead of taking women as a group, the novel traces the lives of five women who range from illiterate to highly educated and from marginalized peasant to a girl whose formative years have been spent in England. The novel shows that only when speaking on their own behalf will women escape both colonial and patriarchal control.

Several men have also written sympathetically about the condition of women in African countries. In Nuruddin Farah's *Sardines* (1981) the traditional sub-ordination of Somali women to men echoes Somalia's political dictatorship which tries to impose conformity through terror. The cosmopolitan scepticism of the main woman character subverts the beliefs of cultural traditionalists, self-serving lackeys of the dictator, a naïve African-American and an Italian communist, the last two claiming that the regime represents whatever their different ideologies want Africa to mean. Farah seems to suggest that since both traditional clans and modern regimes are corrupt, the only collective from which people will derive strength is the western-type nuclear family.

African literature includes the work of many whites since whites have lived and written in South Africa for over three hundred years. Of all these books J. M. Coetzee's *Waiting for the Barbarians* (1980) may seem a curious choice since it is not set in any particular country or time. But this story of a magistrate serving his empire on its frontier is deeply informed by apartheid's use of terror and mind control to make groups of people, both white and black, play their allotted roles. The magistrate discovers that his passivity has made him a collaborator with evil, and so arbitrary is the designation 'barbarian' to describe people beyond the empire's frontier that by the end of the novel, the magistrate himself is a barbarian as far as the empire's police are concerned.

My final choice is again from Zimbabwe when it was still Rhodesia. Doris Lessing's African short stories, published in two volumes as *Collected African Stories* (1973), manage to show not only something of the racism of Rhodesian settler society, but also the diversity of the colonists. Despite the independence they showed in emigrating from England and South Africa, race inevitably became an issue for such people and they allowed themselves to be pressed into a racist conformity.

An entry of this length can only skim the surface of African literature in English, but will, I hope, convey something of the power and the variety with which the continent's writers speak about their own familiar realities.

Top Twelve

Mongo Beti, *The Poor Christ of Bomba* (1956; trans. 1971)

Sembene Ousmane, *God's Bits of Wood* (1960; trans. 1970)

Chinua Achebe, *Arrow of God* (1964)

Ngugi wa Thiong'o, *A Grain of Wheat* (1967) and *Petals of Blood* (1977)

Ayi Kwei Armah, *Fragments* (1970)

Doris Lessing, *This was the Old Chief's Country* and *The Sun Between their Feet*, volumes 1 and 2 of *Collected African Stories* (1973)

Nawal El Saadawi, *God Dies by the Nile* (1974; trans. 1985)

Charles Mungoshi, *Waiting for the Rain* (1975)

J. M. Coetzee, *Waiting for the Barbarians* (1980)

Tsitsi Dangarembga, *Nervous Conditions* (1988)

Australia & New Zealand

Jane Rogers

Australian and New Zealand fiction has a distinctive flavour. Partly it must be down to the physical qualities of Australasia; vast deserts and mountain ranges, surrounded by a fringe of farmland and cities, flanked by sand and sea; a continent composed entirely of islands, as remote from its colonizer as it is possible to be—with the opposite seasons, even the opposite day and night. A country where not so long ago schoolchildren reading English books were offered visions of themselves as 'on the other side of the world'.

No wonder Australian writers felt the need to flee to Europe; to join English writers in the mother country where landscapes were wet and green (not dry and red), where art and culture were seen to be valued; where publishers could be found. This passionate rejection of Australia is vividly described in Christina Stead's *For Love Alone* (1944) as the heroine almost starves herself to death scraping together a fare to Europe, where she would 'perhaps suffer every misery, but she would know life'. Stead herself left Australia at 26, and lived in both Britain and the United States, physically distancing herself from the land she sprang from and yet, in her writing, never losing her uniquely Australian vision. She finally returned to Australia forty years later.

So what is this 'Australian' quality, this distinctive flavour? Other countries have been English colonies, have had wild and difficult frontiers, have histories of appalling indifference and cruelty to the original owners of the land, have a rich mixture of emigrant cultures. What is different about the Aussie/New Zealand brand? How can one sum up the literature of a continent in a sentence? Henry Lawson, making a case for the Australian-ness of Australian fiction in the 1890s, declared: 'We have nothing in common with English people except our language.' I'll stick my neck out and say I think directness is one of its qualities; a willingness to get straight in there and tackle big issues, big ideas; a willingness to open up the heart; and alongside directness, a degree of self-criticism and self-questioning which prevents the directness from being brash. This self-questioning has often been seen as a negative quality—as in the famous 'cultural cringe'—yet it is often, in the fiction, something which makes the writer demand even greater rigour from him/herself; it is the enemy of complacency and hypocrisy.

The clearest example of this is also the first; Miles Franklin's *My Brilliant Career* (1901), written when the author was 16, and describing the life of an energetic, imaginative young woman trapped in a narrow life of grinding poverty on her parents' outback station—and then moved to the richer, kindlier setting of her grandmother's farm. She turns her beady eye on everything and everyone around her, analysing, describing, pronouncing; and then suffers utterly endearing fits of self-doubt and self-hatred. Needless to say, Franklin fled to Europe as soon as she could (not least to escape the notoriety her book had brought her). So too did Katherine Mansfield, born in New Zealand in 1888, whose first collection of stories *In A German Pension* (1911) is set in Germany. The narrator of those wickedly funny stories is clearly Antipodean, with her inner confidence, her debunking of pomposity and hypocrisy, and then her pangs of social guilt, her good-girl attempts to play the game. In later stories Mansfield meticulously dissects moods and motivations, with an ever-ready eye for her characters' self-delusions and hypocrisy.

Christina Stead's masterpiece *The Man Who Loved Children* (1940) is set in the United States but the central character is based on her own Australian father —and indeed the book is set almost entirely in a private world, the tempestuous, hilarious, tragic world of family, where an egotistical, self-serving father, Sam, dominates the lives of his children with his love, his treats, his baby-talk, and his projects (painting the house, boiling up fish oil). Their mother, the poisonous, wrecked, indebted Hetty, maintains her fierce opposition from the safety of her room. In this book Stead dares to push at love (parental, filial, sexual) until it is manifested as hate; her examination of family emotions and dynamics are more intimate and penetrating—and more devastatingly accurate—than any other writer I can think of.

Patrick White, the only Australian to win the Nobel Prize for Literature, studied and wrote in Britain as a young man but returned to Australia after the war, and his books embrace Australian landscape and history in a way that Mansfield and Stead do not. In *Voss* (1957) the obsessed explorer leads his team towards dusty death in a landscape where only the Aborigines know how to live; in *The Tree of Man* (1956) Stan and his wife Amy carve a homestead in the bush and plant their fragile lives. White is interested in frontiers, difficult territories, boundaries, and ways (including those beyond the merely physical —psychic and spiritual ways) of crossing them. Again, that mixture of direct-ness and self-questioning; the confidence to write about the biggest questions. If I was forced to reduce the subject-matter of White's great *œuvre* into one phrase, it would have to be, What is the meaning of life? All his characters approach, circle, beat themselves like moths against that question; and then, in his very style, the circumlocutory sentences, the odd movements, the heaps of qualifying phrases that shade in and dab towards meaning—in his very style is incorporated that self-doubt, that vastly intelligent caution. Janet Frame's work also pushes at the boundaries between interior and exterior worlds, and explores madness with a forthright, often humorous, energy; and yet also with a heart-breaking acceptance of the powerlessness of those judged (as she at times has been) insane.

Elizabeth Jolley is an interesting Australian writer; born in England, she didn't even move to Australia till she was 36. But her work is self-avowedly Australian, and it shows in the confidence and self-confessed insecurity of her heroines, both when treated humorously as in *Foxybaby* (1984), or in darker tone, in a book like *The George's Wife* (1993) where the narrator circles her life in search of meaning. Jolley herself, when asked to typify an Australian writer, commented on the emigrant experience of many Australians: 'As well as the effects of the sights and sounds of the strange new country there has been the uneasiness of being the stranger, the newcomer.' The new arrivals are outsiders—but the second and third generation Australians also write as outsiders, outsiders from Europe, with all the sharp-eyed, take-nothing-for-granted, shocking honesty of outsiders.

Helen Garner is a generation away from Elizabeth Jolley but her self-confident, self-destructive female characters are from the same stable—only they have grown up in the 1960s, and are able to apply political analysis and justification to their contradictory impulses. Like Stead, Garner takes her scalpel uncomfortably close to the heart of relationships and family. Seen in the context of Australia and New Zealand, Keri Hulme is not a weird intrusion into the staid lists of Booker Prize winners; her marvellously energetic book *The Bone People* (1984) is absolutely rooted in place and history, taking in Maori culture alongside 1960s' feminism and—again—the biggest questions.

Thomas Keneally is the Australian writer who perhaps fits least easily into my categorizations; he is so prolific and his work is so wide-ranging in terms of subject, that it's hard to pin him down. Although he's best known for *Schindler's Ark* (1982), about the manufacturer who saved his Jewish workforce from the camps, he has written books set in and engaging vividly with Australian history, including *The Playmaker* (1987) and *The Chant of Jimmie Blacksmith* (1972). These are among my favourites of his. Peter Carey has played games with Australian history (*Illywhacker*, 1985, *Oscar and Lucinda*, 1988) before returning to straight historical fiction in *Jack Maggs* (1997). Although *The Unusual Life of Tristan Smith* (1994) is set in an imaginary world, which parallels the First/Third world divisions of our own, the book has those qualities of confidence and loss, of boldly tackling huge ideas, and of outsiderness, which seem to me quintessentially Australian. David Malouf has written lovingly of

Australia, its heat, its quality of light, and in *Harland's Half Acre* (1984) describes a haunting and memorable world. The land is a marvellously vivid presence in much Australian fiction, and is often (as here) used to explore other values, other meanings than those offered by Western civilization.

Tim Winton's *Cloud Street* (1991) is a happy book to end with; a big family saga, where openness and innocence are provided by Fish, a brain-damaged boy who can never grow old, and where damage and despair and humour proliferate in a great warm tangle around him. Winton won't push things as far as Stead or Garner, he won't make you so uncomfortable; but there is a joyous confidence in this sprawling novel. There are a hundred other books to recommend—Australian fiction richly repays exploration.

See also JANE ROGERS

Top Twelve

MILES FRANKLIN, *My Brilliant Career* (1901)

KATHERINE MANSFIELD, *The Stories of Mansfield* (Collected edition, 1984)

CHRISTINA STEAD, *The Man Who Loved Children* (1940)

PATRICK WHITE, *Riders in the Chariot* (1961)

JANET FRAME, *Faces in the Water* (1961)

ELIZABETH JOLLEY, *Miss Peabody's Inheritance* (1983)

HELEN GARNER, *The Children's Bach* (1984)

KERI HULME, *The Bone People* (1984)

DAVID MALOUF, *Harland's Half Acre* (1984)

THOMAS KENEALLY, *The Playmaker* (1987)

PETER CAREY, *Oscar and Lucinda* (1988)

TIM WINTON, *Cloud Street* (1991)

Black and white

Rita Christian

Twentieth-century fiction in America, Europe, Africa, and Asia has all been much concerned with racial themes and issues, from Camus to Ralph Ellison, from Primo Levi to Alice Walker. This essay takes a specific area of fiction dealing with such themes, and looks at some favourite examples.

Caribbean and African-American writers of fiction have always been pre-occupied with racial themes. This, I believe, is due to their similar histories of enslavement and colonization. In the Caribbean the variety of races thrown together has created a melting-pot, and Caribbean writers often tend to focus on racial prejudice and colour hierarchies; while many African-American writers tend to examine the link between race and economics. Because African-Americans have been subject to some of the worst forms of political, social, and educational deprivation as well as grinding poverty, these experiences are often manifested in their fiction. The writer has, more often than not, lived the experience.

My first recommendation is James Weldon Johnson's *The Autobiography of an Ex-colored Man* (1912). Johnson's novel tells the story of a light-skinned African-American who, until one of his teachers refers to him as a 'nigger', believes he is white. Despite this, he grows up to discover pride in his African origins, race, and colour. However, the story takes an interesting turn when the narrator-protagonist decides to pass himself off as a white businessman because of his 'Italian like appearance' which gives him entry into the white man's world. At the end of the novel, he freely admits to having 'sold his birthright for a mess of potage', by choosing an easier life which would otherwise have been fraught with racial hatred and prejudice in America in the early part of this century.

Race and racial conflict is ever present in the novels of Edgar Mittelholzer, the Guyanese writer who is hailed as a pioneer of the modern Caribbean novel. Mittelholzer's ancestry was both Teutonic and African and he was to carry a sense of inferiority because of his African ancestry all his life. A number of Mittelholzer's characters seem to be imbued with his own ideas of good and evil: the evil which he was convinced stemmed from contamination due to racial mixing. This conflict is reflected in his writing where white is represented as good and black as evil. *Corentyne Thunder* (1941), his first novel, is set in the Corentyne region of Guyana. It is the story of an Indian family. Here we are presented with the racial stereotype of the Indian in the Caribbean: miserly penny-pinching Ramgolal, who waters down the milk before selling it. He eats badly, walks around in rags and keeps his children short of money. The notion of good and evil is manifested in his grandson, Geoffrey, a brilliant young man whose father is English and whose mother is Ramgolal's daughter. In the character of Geoffrey, Mittelholzer demonstrates his own views on racial mixing, for one witnesses not only pragmatism inherited from his European father, but also his peasant sensibility from his Indian mother's side.

Mittelholzer's *A Swarthy Boy* (1963) is an autobiographical novel, focusing on a young boy growing up in colonial British Guyana where colour determined one's social class. The novel charts Mittleholzer's formative years during which he suffered dreadfully because of his 'swarthy' complexion. The fact that he was dark-skinned compared to his sibling and was constantly reminded of this by his relatives contributed greatly to his own fragmented inner self. This ever-present conflict within Mittelholzer probably contributed to his suicide in later life.

Toni Morrison's *The Bluest Eye* (1970) examines racial issues in a sensitive and poignant way. It tells the tragic story of Pecola Breedlove. Set in Ohio in the 1940s, *The Bluest Eye* looks at the structure of American society where blacks are at the bottom of the economic ladder and where poverty is synonymous with colour. Pecola Breedlove, a little black girl, prays every night to have blue eyes like the little white girls of her neighbourhood. If she were white her mother would love her as she does the white children that she cares for. Morrison's novel leads us into a nightmarish world of the black underclass of American society.

This is also true of Richard Wright's *Native Son*. It was first published in 1940 and gained the author almost instant notoriety. Wright depicts his protagonist, Bigger, as a young man brought up in the ghetto who harbours an almost obsessive hatred of whites, and who is very much the product of a brutal and racist society. He portrays Bigger as the stereotypical young 'nigger' whose killing of a white woman can only be perceived as sexually motivated. A novel as dramatic as it is disturbing, but well worth reading.

Black Shack Alley (1950) is an autobiographical novel set in Martinique in the 1930s. Joseph Zobel aptly shows through the eyes of young Jose, the protagonist, the startling divisions between the rich plantation owning bekes (the local whites) and the overwhelming masses of poor blacks who work on the plantation for a pittance. Jose grows up with an increasing awareness of the realities of life for blacks in a French colonial society.

Samuel Selvon's *The Lonely Londoners* (1956) is a humorous novel, dealing with post-war migration to Britain mainly from the English-speaking Caribbean. The reader will enjoy 'hanging out' with Galahad in Bayswater and 'liming' with the boys and Moses in his room on a Sunday morning. Despite the light-hearted camaraderie and apparent easy-going lifestyle of the characters, the harsh realities of everyday life in London are also vividly highlighted. As they all try to make ends meet, cope with racism and appalling job prospects, and battle with the unfamiliar English weather, each episode in this realistic novel is brought strikingly to life by Selvon's clever use of language.

My next recommendation takes us back to the Caribbean, this time to Belize. Zee Edgell's novel, *Beka Lamb* (1982), is the story of the coming of age of the young heroine, Beka, whose development into womanhood is set within the context of Belize's struggle for independence. Edgell's novel looks at the changing political situation in a small colony where education offers the black Belizean students an alternative to domesticity. Education, on the other hand, also means embracing European values and lifestyles. Beka's convent education forces her to adapt and conform to the standards of a culture which conflicts with her own local creole culture. Edgell also shows the tragic results associated with attempts to cross the race barrier, in a black girl's relationship with Emilio, a young man of Spanish origins.

Set both in Haiti and New York, *Breath, Eyes, Memory* (1994) is the first novel by Haitian-born Edwidge Danticat which focuses on the relationship between three generations of Haitian women. We also get a glimpse of life under the brutal Duvalier regime. Migration to New York is perceived as an opportunity for a better life; however, this poses its own problems of racial prejudice and harassment as all Haitian migrants are treated with suspicion and blamed for spreading AIDS.

For another novel which gives a different perspective on race, I suggest Danticat's most recent novel, *The Farming of Bones* (1997). Sensitively and movingly written, it is a demonstration of racial prejudice against Haitians living in the Dominican Republic. Based on historical events both in Haiti and the Dominican Republic—two countries sharing the same land mass divided by a border—it deals with the massacre of Haitian labourers by Dominican troops in 1937. Because of their lighter skin many Dominicans tend to view their darker-skinned Haitian neighbours as inferior. The novel examines the persecution of a group of people, and it particularly shows how racial prejudice affects the lives of Amabelle, a young Haitian maid, and her lover Sebastian who has also come to the Dominican Republic from Haiti to work in the canefields. The author examines the existence of a people who are persecuted simply for being Haitian but who are willing to work hard doing menial jobs in a country where they are not really welcome. But it is Danticat's writing that gives the novel its appeal.

My next recommendation, *In Another Place, Not Here* (1996), is Dionne Brand's first novel and is set both in Canada and the Caribbean. As a Caribbean woman writer exiled in Canada, Brand's novel examines issues of racial oppression and the struggle for equality in Canada as well as the fight against exploitation of the working class in the Caribbean. Brand highlights problems of sexism and racism which affect black people, in particular, black women in Canadian society.

We return to Guyana in the 1970s to examine racial tension between the African-Guyanese population and the Indo-Guyanese in Oonya Kempadoo's novel, *Buxton Spice* (1998). This is a novel about growing up in Guyana and is set against the backdrop of a country in decline and undergoing severe political and economic changes. It also examines the racial tension between the two most prominent racial groups in Guyana.

See also AFRICA, CARIBBEAN, INDIA, UNITED STATES OF AMERICA

Top Twelve

JAMES WELDON JOHNSON, *The Autobiography of an Ex-colored Man* (1912)

EDGAR MITTELHOLZER, *Corentyne Thunder* (1941) and *A Swarthy Boy* (1963)

RICHARD WRIGHT, *Native Son* (1940)

JOSEPH ZOBEL, *Black Shack Alley* (1950)

SAMUEL SELVON, *The Lonely Londoners* (1956)

TONI MORRISON, *The Bluest Eye* (1970)

ZEE EDGELL, *Beka Lamb* (1982)

EDWIDGE DANTICAT, *Breath, Eyes, Memory* (1994) and *The Farming of Bones* (1997)

DIONNE BRAND, *In Another Place, Not Here* (1996)

OONYA KEMPADOO, *Buxton Spice* (1998)

Canada

Aritha van Herk

While readers might expect Canadian fiction to be about canoeing or the wilderness, they are more likely to discover urban landscapes, complex characters, and psychological tension. Canadian writing is as varied as the country's multicultural, multiracial, and multigeographical dimensions. Readers will encounter many voices and styles, as well as a sweep of thematic concerns, some of them indeed focused on Canada's enormous geography, but overall a mosaic of echoes and ethnicities.

Among many excellent Canadian writers, Margaret Atwood is arguably the best known. Her first novel, *The Edible Woman* (1969), is one of the earliest to examine food, anorexia, and self-esteem. A wittily acerbic autopsy of the gaps between men and women, it is Atwood's funniest work. *The Handmaid's Tale* (1985), a chilling evocation of reproductive technology as political tool, is set in a dystopic future where women have no role except to breed. It is both Atwood's most frightening and most skilful novel. The tone is so perfectly managed that readers will feel the hair rising on the backs of their necks. Atwood achieves that pitch again in *Alias Grace* (1996), a historical and psychological retelling of the life of Grace Marks, a nineteenth-century Ontario servant woman charged with murdering her employer.

From a host of potential names, including Mordecai Richler and Robertson Davies, Hugh McLennan could be designated Canadian literature's long-time patriarch. The Halifax explosion of 1917, when a munitions ship blew up in the harbour (the biggest man-made explosion before Hiroshima) is compellingly depicted in his *Barometer Rising* (1941). *Two Solitudes* (1945) examines shifting French–English viewpoints through a cast of characters who represent those two political entities. But if McLennan's writing is respected, the work of Canada's literary matriarch, Margaret Laurence, is loved. Laurence's fiction depicts women both confined by and escaping small prairie towns. The best of her novels, *The Stone Angel* (1964), brilliantly evokes the thoughts of an old woman facing death, and, 'rampant with memory', reviewing her life. *A Jest of God* (1966), which was made into the movie, *Rachel, Rachel*, celebrates a woman's rejection of duty as she discovers sexual pleasure. It is the most complex and intriguing of Laurence's novels. Laurence's fiction is compellingly realistic in its portrayal of human pride and redemption, and her stories depict women's physical and emotional desires without coyness or restraint.

Carol Shields is part of the Canadian tradition of powerful women writers. *The Stone Diaries* (1993) follows the extraordinary life of an ordinary woman, her sudden pleasures and rare disappointments. Its male counterpart novel, *Larry's Party* (1996), traces the maze-like obsessions of Larry, from his work to his penis and his health. Both stories are rich with texture and detail. Just as remarkable but far less well known are Shields' short stories, especially the collection *Various Miracles* (1989).

Another superb short-story writer, Alice Munro, details the ambivalent dreams of women searching for validation. *The Progress of Love* (1986) and *Open Secrets* (1994) collect intricate, almost photographically realistic stories that test the limits of secrets and shame. Similarly, expatriate writer Mavis Gallant's *The Selected Stories* (1997) demonstrate outsiderhood and alienation. Gallant and Munro are renowned for their amazing virtuosity, yet their writing is so beautifully transparent that readers enter their stories as easily as walking through a door. Many Canadian short-story writers merit attention, including especially Audrey Thomas's *The Wild Blue Yonder* (1990), and Sandra Birdsell's *Agassiz Stories* (1987). This list merely scratches the surface.

Historical novels set out to describe the world's wider canvas, often choosing moments important to Canada's national story. *Burning Water* (1980), by George Bowering, reconstructs the voyages of Captain George Vancouver as he mapped Canada's west coast, redrawing, too, the role of the writer in relation to his subject. John Steffler's *The Afterlife of George Cartwright* (1992) details that eighteenth-century English trader's complicity in the colonization and genocide of the Labrador native people. In *The Whirlpool* (1986) Jane Urquhart characterizes the compelling force of historical Niagara Falls, with its suicides and its honeymooners, its poets and its scavengers. Her novel *Away* (1994) chronicles the physical and emotional voyage of nineteenth-century Irish immigrants to Canada with exquisite compassion.

Timothy Findley's novels combine history and mythology. *Famous Last Words* (1981) reinvents Ezra Pound's Hugh Selwyn Mauberley, who writes a subversive testament to the horror of war. *Not Wanted on the Voyage* (1984) is the story of Noah's ark and the flood that obliterates the world in Genesis. Told through the perspective of Noah's wife and her blind cat, it is a remarkable novel about human complicity with death and destruction.

History enjoys a tantalizing presence in Michael Ondaatje's novels. *The English Patient* (1992), set in an Italian villa at the end of the Second World War, uses the sensuous details of a love-story as a contrast to the terrifying dictates and duties of victory. *In the Skin of a Lion* (1987), which celebrates the workers and immigrants who built the growing city of Toronto in the 1920s, is possibly the most powerful of all historical novels written in Canada. Full of physical detail, it makes the city of Toronto a living, breathing fictional presence.

It is to be expected that a nation of immigrants will be shaped by that experience, and one of the greatest markers of Canadian literature is its ethnic diversity. Multiple origins give rise to a cacophony of voices, haunted by the ghosts who accompany them to their new places of settlement. Included in that diversity are powerful stories from Canada's many aboriginal peoples. Tomson Highway's *Kiss of the Fur Queen* (1998) describes the terrible effect of residential schools on First Nations children. Thomas King's *Green Grass, Running Water* (1993) rewrites European mythology from an Indian point of view. Many races rainbow Canadian fiction's horizons. Dionne Brand's *In Another Place, Not Here* (1996) dances between Toronto and the Caribbean. Joy Kogawa's depiction of the displacement and humiliation of the Japanese in the Second World War is unforgettably rendered in *Obasan* (1981), while Hiromi Goto's *Chorus of Mushrooms* (1994) investigates a more contemporary Japanese-Canadian experience. Sky Lee's *Disappearing Moon Café* (1990) orchestrates the development of Vancouver's Chinatown. Rohinton Mistry's *A Fine Balance* (1996) is steeped in the marginalities of the Parsi diaspora. Anita Badami's *Tamarind Mem* (1997) moves characters between the Indian railway system and Canada. Such a list might seem a bewildering smorgasbord, but there is not one immigrant story, but many; not one racist experience, but many; no single aboriginal mythology, but many.

Canada's many geographical regions suggest a spatial diversity as well. Robert Kroetsch rewrites the tall tales of western and northern Canadian bar-rooms. In the magic realist *What the Crow Said* (1978), a community plays host to a series of mythical events, from flood and fire to endless winter. This is the best, the most wildly imaginative novel written about the weather in Canadian literature. In Kroetsch's *Alibi* (1983) a collector roams the world in search of the perfect spa, and finally finds both peace and rejuvenation. Geography prompts strange tales indeed. In the crevasses of the Columbia Icefields in the Rocky Mountains, Thomas Wharton's *Icefields* (1995) comes face to face with angels. David Adams Richards uses New Brunswick to show his characters' inarticulate frustrations in *Nights Below Station Street* (1988), and Wayne Johnson, in *The Colony of Unrequited Dreams* (1998) portrays a Newfoundland as eccentric as its history. These are but a few representative novels, for every region of Canada has developed a literary vernacular singular to that area, and writers are creating fictions to match.

Then there are bizarre novels, oddities that refuse to belong anywhere. Leonard Cohen's *Beautiful Losers* (1966), as might be expected from the king of deep-throated song, is a quest novel in search of the erotics of sainthood. Marian Engel's *Bear* (1976) is a short, brilliant parable about a woman's love-affair with a bear—yes, a real and not metaphorical love-affair with a real bear. The deformed, crippled, and mutilated characters in Barbara Gowdy's *We So Seldom Look on Love* (1992) are enticingly grotesque. And for sheer comic relief, there is little to compare with Suzette Mayr's lament for the loneliness of old age, *The Widows* (1998). Some of these novels are well known and some ignored, but they describe a parabola of incredible temptations.

Last but not least trail two inimitable children, children who have been a part of Canadian literature for years. W. O. Mitchell's description of a boy growing up on the prairie and learning the exquisite ripples of sadness and loss, *Who has Seen the Wind* (1947), merits multiple rereadings. And Anne of L. M. Montgomery's classic *Anne of Green Gables* (1908), the story of an imaginative red-headed orphan who invents stories and who loves trouble, is possibly the best loved of any Canadian character. Anne is a reader's delight, and a passport to a literature where such heroines are commonplace, and where wonderful, engaging fiction is a part of a country's character.

Top Twelve

L. M. MONTGOMERY, *Anne of Green Gables* (1908)

MARGARET LAURENCE, *The Stone Angel* (1964)

LEONARD COHEN, *Beautiful Losers* (1966)

MARIAN ENGEL, *Bear* (1976)

ROBERT KROETSCH, *What the Crow Said* (1978)

TIMOTHY FINDLEY, *Not Wanted on the Voyage* (1984)

MARGARET ATWOOD, *The Handmaid's Tale* (1985)

JANE URQUHART, *The Whirlpool* (1986)

MICHAEL ONDAATJE, *In the Skin of a Lion* (1987)

SKY LEE, *Disappearing Moon Café* (1990)

CAROL SHIELDS, *The Stone Diaries* (1993)

SUZETTE MAYR, *The Widows* (1998)

Caribbean

E. A. Markham

With its rich literary heritage—French, Spanish, Dutch, and oral—Caribbean literature is not best served by focusing on one tradition to the exclusion of others; talking about the English literature of the Caribbean might seem to legitimize certain old colonial arrangements which still disfigure the region. Also, it limits literary cross-cultural discussion that may be valuable. An example: Jean Rhys's 1966 novel *Wide Sargasso Sea*—the story of the first Mrs Rochester, the mad wife in Charlotte Brontë's *Jane Eyre* (1847)—offers fascinating glimpses of aspects of British and Caribbean society. But when we encounter the Guadeloupean Maryse Condé's *Winward Heights*, a 1995 reworking of Emily Brontë's *Wuthering Heights* (1847), that, with the Jean Rhys, might provoke an equally productive cross-Caribbean cultural discussion. With that proviso, let us look at the fiction produced in the Anglophone Caribbean.

The literary critic Kenneth Ramchand in *The West Indian Novel and Its Background* (1970) famously reminded us that people in the region before, say, 1930 had, among other privations, to endure a 'life without fiction'. That meant in part that the ability to read was limited to the few, and the habit of reading was undeveloped. The 1920s saw the growth of national consciousness, and the establishment of literary journals which provoked a readership and necessary encouragement for local writers. The first novelist of note was the Jamaican Herbert G. de Lisser (1878–1944), described as being of 'mixed descent'. His two most enduring books have proved to be *Jane's Career* (1914) and *The White Witch of Rosehall* (1929). The first charts the progress of a young Jamaican woman from country to town and the compromises she is led to make in a rapacious Kingston environment. *The White Witch of Rosehall* is an exotic romance, and an absorbing read.

After de Lisser came Claude McKay (1890–1948), also from Jamaica, who migrated to the United States in 1912, and was to be associated with the Harlem Renaissance. His *Home to Harlem* (1928) was a best-seller and his other novels and stories won critical praise. McKay travelled widely, as far afield as Russia, and was the first West Indian writing in English to gain an international reputation.

The novels of the Beacon group in Trinidad, followed: Alfred Mendes' *Pitch Lake* (1934) and *Black Faunus* (1935) and C. L. R. James's *Minty Alley* in 1936. These social realist novels sought to capture a West Indian (as opposed to colonial) perspective of the everyday world in which they lived. By the late 1940s and early 1950s the novel as political statement manifested itself strongly in the work of Vic Reid and Roger Mais, both Jamaicans. V. S. Reid's *New Day* (1949) is a historical novel, the first, perhaps, to present the emancipated slave in terms other than as something victimized and oppressed. Reid's *The Leopard* (1958) is overtly set against the background of Kenya's 'Mau Mau' struggle. Roger Mais, in novels like *The Hills were Joyful Together* (1953), evokes the life of squalor of the 'yard' and hints at a possible avenue of escape through rastafarianism. Edgar Mittelholzer (1909–65) from Guyana won critical attention with *A Morning at the Office* (1950), a novel set in Trinidad which teases out the absurdities inherent in a race- and class-conscious society. His *Kaywana* trilogy (1952–4), an epic treatment of a Guyanese family from the seventeenth to the twentieth century, was a popular success.

The writers that followed, from 1950 to 1970, are sometimes referred to as the first 'Great Wave'. George Lamming's *In the Castle of my Skin* (1953), Samuel Selvon's second novel, *The Lonely Londoners* (1956), V. S. Naipaul's biting social comedies leading up to his masterpiece, *A House for Mr Biswas* (1961), Wilson Harris's *Palace of the Peacock* (1960), all of Jean Rhys, including *Wide Sargasso Sea*, which made her reputation—signalled the coming of age of West Indian fiction. *In the Castle of my Skin* is in one sense about childhood and growing up in rural Barbados. The richly textured prose seemed to reflect the boy's maturing consciousness with a sensitivity not encountered before on this scale in a home-grown subject. Lamming's work is radical, but maintains its literary integrity, even while it invites us to challenge the relation between colonized and colonizer.

V. S. Naipaul and Samuel Selvon are East Indians from Trinidad and, although the work of both issues from a comic impulse, Naipaul comes over as the more (relentlessly) bitter satirist. He is an elegant writer with a loathing for most things West Indian. *A House for Mr Biswas* is the portrait of an East Indian family in Trinidad in the process of creolization. Naipaul's is a literary family; his father, Seepersad, younger brother, Shiva, and nephew, Neil Bissoondath, are all published writers. Unlike V. S. Naipaul, Samuel Selvon identifies himself with the folk tradition and has been much imitated. Selvon's novels and stories contain a similar gallery of comic types, but they are presented with indulgence rather than scorn. In *The Lonely Londoners* we encounter the portraits, both comic and poignant, of Caribbean migrants new to England. ('Boy, you black like midnight,' says one of the 'boys', on seeing one of the new arrivals to England. He takes another look at the newcomer's impressive blackness. 'No, you more like Five Past Twelve.') This pioneering book breaks the taboo of relegating dialect (now called Nation Language) to characters of inferior social rank or private moments of stress or intimacy, and makes it the narrating voice.

Of other writers mentioned above Wilson Harris is the most unusual. He comes from Guyana and is therefore assumed not to have the 'island mindset' of other West Indians. (He shares a certain panoramic vision with his Guyanese contemporary, the artist Aubrey Williams, whose paintings enliven many a Caribbean book-jacket.) Harris's hallucinatory technique seeks to reconnect fragments of history, long severed. His many short novels demand care and vigilance from the reader. In his first and best-loved book, *Palace of the Peacock*, we witness a river journey in the interior of the country, a journey that might have happened in the past, or might be happening in the future (or the present). On board are representatives of the Amerindian and the African—past and present.

By the 1970s the themes of West Indian fiction seemed to be set: childhood and growing up, often in a rural setting; the evils of class and colour-consciousness; revisiting the plantation/slave experience; the experience of life as a migrant. Among the many who contributed to the story were Garth St Omer (St Lucia), Roy Heath (Guyana/London), and Michael Anthony and Earl Lovelace, both of Trinidad. Anthony's lyrical talent comes through in novels and stories about growing up in rural Trinidad such as *Green Days by the River* (1973). Lovelace is probably one bridge to the new wave, even though two of his novels appeared in the 1960s. His 1979 novel about carnival, *The Dragon Can't Dance*, juggles with the possibilities of heroism and self-betrayal among the poor in a Trinidad slum yard. His prize-winning *Salt* (1996), investing the 'folk' with a sense of history, has added to his reputation.

And so to the present: one challenge now is against type-casting. The short-story writers are among the most adventurous, and their most exciting work is collected in *The Penguin Book* (1996) and *The Oxford Book* (1999) *of Caribbean Short Stories*. Olive Senior's *Discerner of Hearts* (1995, stories) shows her to be ever more adventurous in the formal aspects of story-telling. True, novels about slavery and the plantation system proliferate (Caryl Phillips and Fred D'Aguiar have written particularly fine ones); but there is also Phillips's *The Nature of Blood* (1997) that explores themes of race and history through a largely non-Caribbean context.

Erna Brodber (Jamaica) and Jamaica Kincaid (Antigua/USA) share a prose style akin to poetry. Brodber's appearance in 1980 with *Jane and Louise will Soon Come Home* and Kincaid's early stories, *At the Bottom of the River* (1983) mark them out as unusual stylists. A different sort of stylist is Michelle Cliffe

(Jamaica/USA). Her *No Telephone to Heaven* (1987) takes on the stock themes of colonization and race, but by eschewing naturalism, makes it all seem fresh.

Four names to end with: Pauline Melville, Andrea Levy, David Dabydeen, and Lawrence Scott. Melville, from Guyana/Britain, manages to blend the magical and quotidian and portray a world of risk and adventure that we recognize instantly as our own. *Shape-Shifter* (1990, stories) and *The Ventriloquist's Tale* (1997) are required reading. Andrea Levy (b.1966, Jamaican/British) in her second novel, *Every Light in the House Burnin'* (1994), shows the new black British generation to be intimate with her English surroundings; and surprises us with the effects that still can be achieved in a naturalistic mode. David Dabydeen in his fourth novel, *A Harlot's Complaint* (1999), breaks free from the racial stereotyping, his central narrator being an African—presented with empathy by this writer of Indian heritage. And Lawrence Scott's *Aelred's Sin* (1998) is a novel about homoeroticism which is both courageous and beautifully written.

Top Twelve

GEORGE LAMMING, *In the Castle of my Skin* (1953)

SAMUEL SELVON, *The Lonely Londoners* (1956)

V. S. NAIPAUL, *Miguel Street* (1959)

WILSON HARRIS, *Palace of the Peacock* (1960)

JEAN RHYS, *Tigers are Better-Looking* (1968)

EARL LOVELACE, *The Dragon Can't Dance* (1979)

JAMAICA KINCAID, *At the Bottom of the River* (1983)

PAULINE MELVILLE, *Shape-Shifter* (1990)

OLIVE SENIOR, *Discerner of Hearts* (1995)

E. A. MARKHAM (ed.), *The Penguin Book of Caribbean Short Stories* (1996)

CARYL PHILLIPS, *The Nature of Blood* (1997)

LAWRENCE SCOTT, *Aelred's Sin* (1998)

Childhood

Jan Dalley

Before Charles Dickens children were scarcely seen or heard in novels, and never in a central role: Dickens placed them in the centre of the stage. Particularly through his boy-heroes in the eponymous novels *Oliver Twist* (1837–9), *Nicholas Nickleby* (1838–9), and *David Copperfield* (1849–50), and through perhaps the greatest of all, Pip in *Great Expectations* (1860–1), he wrote brilliantly and accessibly about children's perceptions and feelings, and truly saw the world through their eyes. He became the supreme chronicler of children's experience in the nineteenth century, in these magnificent works.

Each of these novels sees its child-hero pass through all sorts of misery, deprivation, and vicissitude before the comforting ending comes; it was presumably the hard circumstances of Dickens's own childhood that made him feel this theme so deeply and revisit it so often. His children are real, and we feel them to be real—unlike the idealized children in many of the sentimental novels the Victorian age also produced. Some of the most famous of these were written for crusading purposes, such as Charles Kingsley's *The Water-Babies* (1863), for instance, about the terrible lives of the child chimney-sweeps. This is a glutinous though well-meaning fable that is nearly unreadable now, even if the lives it describes are still heart-rending.

In fact, the great literature of childhood is not for the faint-hearted, and certainly not for those in search of comfort-reading. Happy families are not the stuff of fiction, and novels about children's experience usually pivot around childhood miseries rather than idyllic memories, broken families rather than warm and comforting ones. Orphans, sad and lonely children, neglected and unwanted children, appear time and again in the fiction classics, as do children we would now consider 'abused'—as Dickens's David Copperfield was by a sadistic stepfather. It is a modern fallacy that widespread family breakdown was a phenomenon of the second half of the twentieth century: although divorce was far less frequent in previous eras, high death-rates meant that a very large number of children lost one or both parents, remarriage and step-relations were common, and a dislocated upbringing equally so. Many children's lives were less safe and stable than now. While the most wretched were on the streets, expected to fend for themselves, the slightly better-off might be dispatched to harsh schools which had no holidays, sent to live with strangers, apprenticed very young, or simply ignored. Work began early, and was often extremely hard. Even for the well-to-do life was sometimes brutal. (Thomas Hughes's *Tom Brown's Schooldays* (1857), for instance, described the vicious regime at a famous public school as vividly as Dickens told of the horrors of Dotheboys Hall in *Nicholas Nickleby*.) Dickens's child-protagonists are unusual because they are essentially alone, without family. More usually, novels about children are—for obvious reasons—novels about families. Quite a few of the classic plots rely on the notion of 'breeding'—good blood or bad, nature always winning out over nurture. Heathcliff, the romantic anti-hero of Emily Brontë's *Wuthering Heights* (1847), was a gipsy waif picked up on the streets of Liverpool; despite kind Mr Earnshaw's attempts to bring the boy up as one of his own, Heathcliff is the agent of havoc and tragedy. It's an idea which persists into the next century, when children's untamed nature and capacity for evil are central to Richard Hughes's *A High Wind in Jamaica* (1929) and become the driving force behind William Golding's *Lord of the Flies* (1954), in which groups of stranded children grow increasingly violent and eventually murderous towards each other. Golding's is one of the greatest novels about children, but also one of the darkest parables about human nature in modern literature. Another brilliant study of the savage in the child is Roddy Doyle's *Paddy Clarke Ha Ha Ha* (1993), in which young boys commit a killing.

Previous centuries treated children differently, we know, and allowed customs we would now consider extraordinary—for instance, the practice of giving away a child from a numerous but hard-up family to be brought up by a wealthier, often childless relative or acquaintance. This happened to one of Jane Austen's brothers, and although her novels do not focus on childhood, they show us a good deal about contemporary experience, even in a much more comfortable social world than Dickens's. In *Emma* (1816), for instance, the young people (we would now call them teenagers, although neither the word nor the concept had been invented then) are either motherless (Emma herself), illegitimate and unwanted (Harriet Smith), or dislocated from family in other ways (both Jane Fairfax and Frank Churchill).

Perhaps it was no coincidence that *Emma* was remade into a modern film, *Clueless*, about scatty, affluent teenagers. A more modern child-heroine was created by Henry James, whose uncharacteristic *What Maisie Knew* (1897) is a short, brilliant story of family collapse seen through the eyes of a watchful little girl, a precocious child made lonely, despite her comfortable circumstances, by the mysteries of adult unhappiness. A very different watchful child, at the end of the twentieth century, is Esther Freud's young heroine in *Hideous*

Kinky (1992). Similarly buffeted by emotional forces over which she has no control, she tells of growing up in a fractured family in the craziness of the 1960s, and though Freud writes very enjoyably, with pace and wry humour, the childish pain is never far beneath the surface.

Esther Freud's novel is at least partly autobiographical, and this impulse has produced some of the great works about childhood and adolescence: from Ireland James Joyce's *A Portrait of the Artist as a Young Man* (1914–15), from Australia Miles Franklin's *My Brilliant Career* (1901), and from Britain Jeanette Winterson's *Oranges are Not the Only Fruit* (1985), which describes an upbringing with dour, religious adoptive parents. From the United States, J. D. Salinger's inimitable *The Catcher in the Rye* (1951), whose hero, Holden Caulfield, probably counts as the world's first literary teenager (just as James Dean is credited with that title in the movies), must hold pride of place as the novel of adolescence.

Freud and Salinger share a kind of wacky humour, an attitude that deals with difficulties through laughter, the hallmark of many modern accounts of growing pains. Of these, the most successful is Sue Townsend's *The Secret Diary of Adrian Mole aged 13¾* (1982), which treats spots and blushes and teenage crushes with hilarity. For high humour in a different time and a different social milieu, Nancy Mitford's brilliant comic study of her own eccentric family, remade in fiction as the Radletts, makes her 1945 novel *The Pursuit of Love* one of the century's comic masterpieces, as well as a superb and pitiless portrait of family relationships and the trials of growing up.

In all these, however, it's hard to find a novel to recommend which looks back on a childhood bathed in calm and happiness. Childhood stories written for children may be full of picnics and ponies, pets, and pear-trees; those written about children are not. Memoirs hold more luminous light—Laurie Lee's *Cider with Rosie* (1959), or Gerald Durrell's *My Family and Other Animals* (1956) come to mind, as do Roald Dahl's *Boy* (1984) and *Going Solo* (1986). In the world of fiction, perhaps Alain-Fournier's *Le Grand Meaulnes* (1913), sometimes translated as *The Lost Domain*, conveys best the bitter-sweet tang of youth, the innocent passions of friendship and exploration, the sense of mystery within safe boundaries.

Top Twelve

Charles Dickens, *Great Expectations* (1860–1)
Henry James, *What Maisie Knew* (1897)
Miles Franklin, *My Brilliant Career* (1901)
Alain-Fournier, *Le Grand Meaulnes* (1913)
James Joyce, *A Portrait of the Artist as a Young Man* (1916)
Nancy Mitford, *The Pursuit of Love* (1945)
J. D. Salinger, *The Catcher in the Rye* (1951)
William Golding, *Lord of the Flies* (1954)
Sue Townsend, *The Secret Diary of Adrian Mole aged 13¾* (1982)
Jeanette Winterson, *Oranges are Not the Only Fruit* (1985)
Esther Freud, *Hideous Kinky* (1992)
Roddy Doyle, *Paddy Clarke Ha Ha Ha* (1993)

Classics

John Sutherland

However well-read, one always feels ill-read. There are familiar ways of dealing with nervousness on the subject. 'Have you read the latest Salman Rushdie?' someone asks. 'I *know* it', one replies, without specifying whether that means 'I've scrutinized the text from cover to cover and could go head-to-head with Magnus Magnusson' or (more likely) 'I've seen it on display in Waterstone's window'. With classics, as the Italian writer, Italo Calvino, notes (in *Why Read the Classics?*, 1999), one never says one is 'reading' *War and Peace*, or whatever. One is always 'rereading' the work. Too shame-making to have reached adult years and still not have got round to Tolstoy. For all its fame in academic circles, David Lodge's parlour game 'Humiliation' (you win by *not* having read as many classics as your competitor) has never caught on. We lie about drinking, sex, but most of all about the good books we've (not) read.

The canon of classics will endure, whether we read them or not. Unlike best-sellers, they do not depend on our fickle tastes. What then can the classics do for us? Reading them will not, depend on it, make us healthy, wealthy, nor even wise (least of all wise, forget that Leavisite fantasy). Calvino offers the barest of inducements: 'the only reason that can be adduced in their favour is that reading the classics is always better than not reading them.' It's as good a starting-point as any.

'Classic Fiction' is not a literary genre as such. It is best understood as a publishers' and retailers' category, dependent, at a pre-commercial level, on cumulative critical judgements confirmed over long tracts of time. The best that has been written anywhere, at any time. Incontrovertibly great books. All-time winners. Books every educated person should have read. Take your pick.

The history of classic reprints in England can be conveniently begun with the Aldine series of reprints in the early nineteenth century. It continued with Henry Bohn's mid-century 'Standard Library' of cheaply produced 'British Classics' and culminated at the end of the century with Ernest Rhys's 'Everyman Library' imprint (marketed with great success in the twentieth century by the publisher Dent). In the twentieth century, the brand leaders were 'World's Classics' (eventually an OUP line) and, in the 1940s, 'Penguin Classics'. What all these 'cheap luxury' lines aimed at was to mimic, at a cost 'Everyman' could afford, the eighteenth-century English gentleman's library.

The most recent mutation in classic reprinting began with the 'Penguin English Library' (now 'Penguin Classics') in the early 1960s. These were budget-priced paperbacks, pictorially jacketed, complete with introduction, textual and explanatory notes. Penguin's innovation was strikingly successful and inspired in the 1970s the revival of a similarly formatted 'World's Classics' (now 'Oxford World's Classics') from OUP. Later still, in the 1980s and 1990s, came rejuvenated 'Everyman' lines (soft- and hardcover) and the ultra-cheap 'Wordsworth Classics'. The British consumer of the third millennium enjoys a veritable Aladdin's Cave of classic reprints. At least five competing editions of *Jane Eyre* (1847), to take one example, will be found in most well-stocked bookstores—all under a tenner and most under a fiver. Click onto Amazon and you will have your choice of a dozen competing editions of most of the works judged by our culture to be 'classic'.

There are many such works; the Penguin and Oxford World's Classics catalogues list some 600–700 titles. Selecting the dozen best books from so many best books is necessarily a captious exercise. I have used as my criterion or filtering device books by authors who have achieved epithetic status. That is to say, literature which has given us useful adjectives whose meaning we grasp even if we have never read the works in question. They are: Austenish, Dickensian, Flaubertian, Homeric, Jamesian, Lawrentian, Quixotic, Rabelaisian, Swiftian, Tolstoyan, Trollopian, Wertherian.

What does the term 'Austenish' evoke in the mind's eye? Charlotte Brontë's observation about the author of *Pride and Prejudice* (1813) creating her miniature and perfect designs on two inches of ivory (or two reels of Merchant–Ivory); 'Janeites' rereading the six novels once a year; Gwyneth Paltrow's neck. Start with *Emma* (1816), the most Austenish of them all. If you haven't read it before, I envy you the delights of the first reading.

'Dickensian' has been much invoked by politicians recently to describe the condition of the homeless in London streets—a scandal given added poignancy by the fine revisionary *Oliver Twist* (1837–9) created by Alan Bleasdale and shown by ITV in December 1999. How gloomy the Great Inimitable would be to discover human beings *still* sleeping rough under Hungerford Bridge. Read *Oliver Twist* and judge for yourself whether we have progressed as an urban civilization over the last one hundred and sixty years. Dickens's 'social problem' fiction remains painfully topical.

'Flaubertian' invokes for most of us the novelist's masterpiece, *Madame Bovary* (1857). A fanatic stylist (something that can be apprehended even in translation), Flaubert considered it a good day's work if he inserted a comma into his narrative in the morning and removed it in the evening. Emma Bovary, who discovers in adultery all the platitudes of marriage, is a twenty-first century woman before her time. Flaubert's scathing satire of rural-provincial life is a welcome antidote to Ambridgean sentimentalities about country life.

'Homeric' recalls Troy—love, war, heroism. *The Iliad* and *The Odyssey* record the hero's pilgrimages to battle and back home again. Which are useful (though certainly not essential) preparation for James Joyce's *Ulysses* (1922), a book which every person in our unheroic age who considers him/herself civilized should read—even if, as Joyce threatened, it requires a lifetime to do it properly. If you finish early, you can get started on *Finnegans Wake* (1928–37).

'Jamesian', like 'Flaubertian', invokes ideas of virtuosic technique. For James, 'how to tell it' was the great issue confronting the novelist. The subtlest and most accessible exercise in his mastery as a narrator is found in *What Maisie Knew* (1897), a story of great complexity refracted through the innocent eye of a little (but sophisticated) girl. Short as a novella, it is rich in texture as grand opera. A classic to be sipped, like old wine.

Until *Lady Chatterley's Lover* (1928) was acquitted in November 1960, the Penguin Classics *The Iliad* and *The Odyssey* were Britain's bestselling postwar paperbacks. *Lady Chatterley* outsold Homer in two years. Doubtless many early purchasers were disappointed by Lawrence's 'erotic classic'. But *Lady Chatterley's Lover* contains the essence of 'Lawrentianism' (the novel as the 'bright book of life'), and marked out new boundaries for post-1960 English fiction. The classic 'landmark' novel.

'Quixotic' is, of all these epithets, the one most commonly used by those of us who could know nothing of the novel other than that the hero is driven mad by reading romances, tilts at windmills, and has a fat servant called Sancho Panza. Yet the archetypal forms of all British comic fiction can be traced back to the anti-romance of *Don Quixote of La Mancha* (1605) and his misadventures. Own it, even if you don't read it. Who knows, you may get washed up on a desert island.

'Rabelaisian' (like 'Chaucerian') evokes pre-puritan, medieval bawdy. The notion of the hero in François Rabelais's *Pantagruel* (1533), is 'a being who induces thirst in others'—thirst for strong liquor, that is. Rabelais creates fiction that satisfies our animal appetites. This book and its sequel *Gargantua* (1534)— the story of Pantagruel's father—are sometimes incredibly filthy, but always clever and—even after four hundred years—side-splittingly funny. Classics from what Henry James would call the *enfance* of European literature.

Swift is funny too, but 'savage' and lean in his narrative forms (the rogue never hazards a metaphor, as Dr Johnson observed). Savagery and civilization are the theme of his masterwork, the fourth book of *Gulliver's Travels* (1726), the quintessence of 'Swiftianism'. Read it, but do not expect it to enhance your love of your fellow man. You may even wish you were a horse.

'Tolstoyan' suggests a kind of super-green 'back to nature' earthiness of the author's late-life philosophical treatises. The fiction is something else. Read *Anna Karenina* (1873–7), a story of loveless marriage and unhappy adultery besides which every English and most French novels of the century look juvenile. A classic for grown-ups.

Nothing is more English than the *Barchester* sequence of novels. The 'Trollopian' world is safe, insular, comic; as appetizing as a side of British beef, as a contemporary American admirer put it. (In those days, the world admired British beef—and Trollope.) The necessary work for those coming to the 47-strong Trollope *œuvre* is *Barchester Towers* (1857). Mrs Proudie's 'Unhand it, sir!' remains the funniest line in all Victorian fiction.

Goethe's *The Sorrows of Young Werther* (1774) was the first true European best-seller, precipitating a sales and imitative mania. Young men adopted 'Wertherian' yellow trousers, in tribute to their hero, moped horribly, and committed suicide like lemmings (many, like Werther, botching the job badly). Half-way between a curio and a classic, the novel earns its place in any list of favourite classics.

Top Twelve

FRANÇOIS RABELAIS, *Pantagruel* (1533) and *Gargantua* (1534).

MIGUEL DE CERVANTES SAAVEDRA, *Don Quixote of La Mancha* (1605, 1615)

JONATHAN SWIFT, *Gulliver's Travels* (1726)

J. W. VON GOETHE, *The Sorrows of Young Werther* (1774)

JANE AUSTEN, *Emma* (1816)

CHARLES DICKENS, *Oliver Twist* (1837–9)

GUSTAVE FLAUBERT, *Madame Bovary* (1857)

ANTHONY TROLLOPE, *Barchester Towers* (1857)

LEO TOLSTOY, *Anna Karenina* (1873–7)

HENRY JAMES, *What Maisie Knew* (1897)

JAMES JOYCE, *Ulysses* (1922)

D. H. LAWRENCE, *Lady Chatterley's Lover* (1928)

Crime

Michael Dibdin

The other day, I read a report in the local newspaper of the American city where I live. A 19-year-old youth who had just split up with his girlfriend went home and took his father's revolver, returned to the girl's house, and murdered her and a friend she had called over to talk about the break-up.

No, actually I made that up (never trust a crime writer), but if you read a headline like that, what would interest you most about the story? The drama, the violence, the blood and gore? Or would you be more intrigued by the killer's state of mind, his perceived motives and deranged attempts at self-justification? Or . . . Or, suppose the person under arrest was actually innocent. Suppose that a jealous rival or psychopathic sibling, knowing about the break-up with the accused's girlfriend, had set up the killing to frame him.

One way of looking at crime fiction is as a mixture consisting, in varying proportions, of these three areas of interest, which we might label the Sensational, the Psychological, and the Cerebral. The invention of this power-ful cocktail can be dated and attributed as precisely as that of the steam engine. The time was the 1840s, and the inventor the American writer Edgar Allan Poe. Poe is now more usually thought of in connection with the horror or Gothic genres, but two of his tales featuring Auguste Dupin—'The Murders in the Rue Morgue' and 'The Purloined Letter'—reveal to the highest extent the power of the sensational and cerebral aspects of the genre, while another, 'The Tell-Tale Heart', is a chilling psychological study of a murderer's mind.

The only aspect of the genre which Poe did not touch, except to mock it, was the one centred on the official investigations of a police detective. These form the basis of *The Moonstone* (1868) by Wilkie Collins, a contemporary of Dickens, which is the earliest and perhaps supreme example of crime fiction aspiring to the level of 'mainstream' literature. But it was only much later that the police procedural came into its own, perhaps as a result of the success of the television series based on the books by Georges Simenon featuring the Parisian detective Maigret. Later writers who have exploited this sub-genre with success include Reginald Hill, Ed McBain, James McClure, Ian Rankin, and Ruth Rendell in her Inspector Wexford series. The stylized hyper-violence of James Ellroy's work appeals to many, although not to me.

But until the First World War, the gifted amateur had the field almost entirely to himself, most notably in the personage of Sherlock Holmes and his plodding sidekick and amanuensis Dr Watson. Conan Doyle's creation owed much to Poe's Dupin, but soon surpassed his model to establish himself as the most famous fictional detective ever. He appears in four volumes of stories, of which the first two are generally considered to be the best, but to my mind it is a late novel which is probably Doyle's supreme achievement. *The Hound of the Baskervilles* (1902) is a gripping, atmospheric story in which Holmes is off-stage for much of the time, reappearing just in time to reveal the nature and origin of the spectral hound which has been terrorizing the Baskerville family.

Up to this point, the central contest in crime fiction had been between the criminal and the detective. It was sometimes fairly clear who the guilty party was; the question was how he was to be prevented or brought to justice. All this changed in the work of Agatha Christie, where the struggle between criminal and detective becomes subordinate to the true contest, which takes place between author and reader. Christie and her contemporaries in the so-called Golden Age of English crime writing (roughly 1920–40) in effect said to the reader: 'I'm going to tell you about a murder in such a way that you won't be able to guess who did it or how until I reveal it, and you'll then wonder why on earth you didn't see it all along.'

This form of literary conjuring trick had a successful career which is now effectively over, there being only so many plot devices which can be used to flummox the increasingly sophisticated reader. Perhaps the most famous example is *The Murder of Roger Ackroyd* (1926); among my other favourites are *The ABC Murders* (1936) and the devilishly cunning *And Then There Were None* (1941). After Dame Agatha, reading most of the other practitioners of the 'whodunit' strikes me as like drinking champagne that has gone flat, but the work of Dorothy L. Sayers and Ngaio Marsh, Josephine Tey and Marjorie Allingham has many admirers, as do the elaborately facetious concoctions of Michael Innes and Edmund Crispin. The best modern exemplars of the form are perhaps Colin Dexter and P. D. James.

Meanwhile, across the Atlantic, Raymond Chandler and Dashiell Hammett were setting about an utterly different conception of crime fiction. The essential point is, as Chandler finely said of Hammett, they 'gave murder back to the kind of people that commit it for reasons, not just to provide a corpse'. We might add that by virtue of their often imitated but never equalled style, they made crime writing once and for all a question of *writing*.

People will argue for ever about which is Chandler's greatest novel, with most favouring *Farewell, My Lovely* (1940) or *The Big Sleep* (1939). My own vote would go to the relatively late *The Long Goodbye* (1953), but all Chandler's work, including the short stories he wrote for the so-called 'pulp magazines', is well worth investigating. Hammett's entire output is of the same high quality; my personal favourite is the perennially popular *The Maltese Falcon* (1930). If you like these, try James M. Cain (*Double Indemnity*, 1936; *The Postman Always Rings Twice*, 1934) and Cornell Woolrich, a.k.a. William Irish (*Phantom Lady*, 1942). Interestingly, these titles are among the very few novels which have inspired an equally successful film.

For a modern take on Chandler's Los Angeles, you could try Walter Mosley's *Easy Rawlins* series (e.g. *A Red Death*, 1991), but the authors who can best sustain stylistic comparison with these giants are George V. Higgins (*The Friends of Eddie Coyle*, 1972) and the prolific Elmore Leonard, who combines elements of the police procedural and the John Wayne western with meticulously-researched settings and spare, punchy dialogue. One of his best books is *Freaky Deaky* (1988), which displays all the above in the context of a fiendishly tortuous plot.

The work of Chandler and Hammett has spawned a massive sub-genre with the professional private detective as hero(ine), and all tastes are catered for. There are male and female private investigators, gay and lesbian private investigators, black and Asian private investigators. For some reason, most of the best writers seem to be women (perhaps goaded on by Chandler and Hammett's perceived misogyny). In its native America, this category is represented by such names as Sara Paretsky, Sue Grafton, Marcia Muller, and Patricia Cornwell, with Carl Hiaasen providing a welcome touch of humour. In Britain, the work of Liza Cody and Val McDermid stands out. The field has also inspired numerous parodies.

At the same time, in Britain, a contemporary of Chandler and Hammett was renewing the genre in his own way. *Malice Aforethought* (1931) by Francis Iles starts with the startling sentence: 'It was not until several weeks after he had decided to murder his wife that Dr Bickleigh took any active steps in the matter.' This is one of the earliest and best examples of the 'inverted' crime story, where the identity of the murderer is known from the beginning, and the interest lies in why he did it and how—or whether—he will be caught.

In the traditional whodunnit, character rarely amounted to more than a set of Cluedo cards; if everyone has to be a potential suspect, we cannot be allowed to get to know them in any depth. In the inverted form, personality is the key to crime, as evidenced in the work of Patricia Highsmith. The opening chapters of *Strangers on a Train* (1950) have never been surpassed in this regard: no spray-on blood or cheap thrills, just a sense of dread and of converging destinies. Equally remarkable is *The Talented Mr Ripley* (1955), in which Highsmith not only reveals the murderer's identity, motives, and intentions, but has the reader cheering him on in horrified collusion. Highsmith's ability to make the darkest forms of behaviour seem natural, even seductive, has been immensely influential, notably in the work of Barbara Vine, Minette Walters, and John Harvey.

This article is about crime fiction—as opposed to non-fiction, or 'true crime' —but an exception must be made for Truman Capote's self-styled 'non-fiction novel' *In Cold Blood* (1966). Capote had read Patricia Highsmith, and there are many echoes of her eerily affectless, detached style in this dramatized re-creation of the brutal and pointless murders of an entire family on a Kansas farm in 1959. Although based strictly on fact, Capote's book employs many of the conventions of crime fiction, and provides fascinating insights into the workings of this ever-popular genre.

See also MICHAEL DIBDIN

See also THRILLERS

Top Twelve

ARTHUR CONAN DOYLE, *The Hound of the Baskervilles* (1902)

DASHIELL HAMMETT, *The Maltese Falcon* (1930)

FRANCIS ILES, *Malice Aforethought* (1931)

AGATHA CHRISTIE, *And Then There Were None* (1941)

WILLIAM IRISH, *Phantom Lady* (1942)

RAYMOND CHANDLER, *The Long Goodbye* (1953)

PATRICIA HIGHSMITH, *The Talented Mr Ripley* (1955)

GEORGE V. HIGGINS, *The Friends of Eddie Coyle* (1972)

P. D. JAMES, *An Unsuitable Job for a Woman* (1972)

BARBARA VINE, *A Dark-Adapted Eye* (1986)

CARL HIAASEN, *Double Whammy* (1987)

ELMORE LEONARD, *Freaky Deaky* (1988)

Family saga

Sherry Ashworth

In the preface to *The Forsyte Saga* (1922) John Galsworthy remarks of his title: 'the word Saga might be objected to on the ground that it connotes the heroic.' How the mighty have fallen! At the start of the twenty-first century, in literary circles, the word 'saga' is, if not exactly contemptuous, belittling. We have Aga sagas, even lager sagas, and of course, family sagas. For most of us, the label 'family saga' brings to mind a long, possibly rather trashy, put-on-the-kettle-and-put-your-feet-up good read. Fortunately, family saga is much, much more than that.

The great Victorian novels generally aren't family sagas. There are families, but they are static entities, they are given. The novels focus on the hero or heroine and their struggles for autonomy. It is only in the century post-Freud, when family dynamics have been deemed worthy of serious interest, and we accept more than ever that upbringing is a significant factor in forming and destroying character, that the family has been seen organically, and can be the subject of the novel. And what a rich, infinitely fascinating subject it is.

The first substantial and successful family saga of the twentieth century is indubitably John Galsworthy's *The Forsyte Saga*. It begins with the novel *The Man of Property* (1906) and runs on through *In Chancery* (1920), *To Let* (1921), and numerous others. Galsworthy's setting is London, his period is late-Victorian England, and his family come from the prosperous, property-acquiring, upper-middle classes who live in or around Hyde Park. Galsworthy's novels are informed by a satiric vision; he is particularly interested and delighted by the limitations of the Forsytes, their money-grubbing ways and their bafflement in the face of Art. The novels are worth reading for the study of the relationship between Soames and Irene alone. What also motivates Galsworthy as a writer is the creation of the whole world that the Forsyte family inhabits—it is beautifully realized.

The first serious, literary saga, I suggest, is comprised of the companion novels *The Rainbow* (1915) and *Women in Love* (1920) by D. H. Lawrence. These concern the Brangwen family and in every respect they conform to the conventions of family saga: they are concerned with three generations, the setting is specific in time and place (the beginning of the twentieth century, Nottinghamshire), and the structure of the books is episodic. We follow the story of Tom and his marriage to the Polish refugee Lydia, the courtship of his nephew Will to Anna, and the quest of their daughters Ursula and Gudrun for a soulmate/lover. Lawrence's uncomfortably accurate psychological insight, the insistent rhythms of his prose and his desire to shock his reader mean he will never be forgotten, and will always be an irritant, either to the respectable classes or feminist critics. A family saga not to be missed!

For light relief, look at the novels of Mazo de la Roche. She was a Canadian, whose novel *Jalna* (1927) inspired sixteen others, chronicling the affairs of the Whiteoak family from generation to generation. Like her own family, they own a farm in Ontario, and there are, not surprisingly, lush descriptions of the countryside. Set and written in the first half of the twentieth century, there is a period charm to the novels, with characterization which is a little predictable.

For a startling contrast to Galsworthy's irony, go to R. F. Delderfield's *God is an Englishman* (1970). The title is more politically incorrect than the novel itself, which charts the setting up of the Swann family business, a nationwide road transport network, competing with the railways. The novel presents a tender and moving central relationship between the hero and his wife. It is set in nineteenth-century England—one can almost hear the national anthem playing faintly in the background. In fact, Delderfield has written a Victorian novel, leisurely, panoramic, and long. The saga continues in three further novels. As an antidote to Delderfield's patriotism, move straight to Vikram Seth's *A Suitable Boy* (1993), a family saga set in post-independence India and based on Seth's own family. Family relationships are explored deftly and tenderly. This is one of the most accessible of sagas, and is tremendously wide-ranging in its appeal, being neither simplistic nor pretentious. Its digressions into Indian politics are not untypical of family saga, because writers often wish to give their family a socio-political setting, class being a significant factor in the formation of family values.

This is also very true of Isabel Allende. Her novel, *The House of the Spirits* (1985), is a family saga with a difference, the difference being magic realism. Allende's humour, her astonishing imagination, and detailed knowledge of her background make this novel a masterpiece, the best literary family saga there is. It is set in a mythical South American country and spans the whole of the twentieth century, but focuses particularly on the way politics and the class system impinge on the life of her family, or indeed, families, for there are two, one upper, one lower caste. The novel opens with the short life of the beautiful Rosa—a mermaid—and moves on to her younger sister Clara, who is to be the matriarch of the saga—one who can communicate with the spirits.

For a stark contrast of setting, move on to the English Elizabeth Jane Howard's *The Cazalet Chronicle*, which incorporates *The Light Years* (1990), *Marking*

Time (1991), *Confusion* (1993), and *Casting Off* (1995). These also attempt to move between classes as they include the narrative viewpoints of servants as well as the 'upstairs' characters in her family group. The many interior mind-scapes in the novels give the books a literary feel. The novels move slowly and focus on the personal lives and inner conflicts of the characters, while evoking the period around the Second World War in Sussex. This is no nostalgic portrait—Howard is often drawn to examine the darker side of life, and the ways in which a family can be dysfunctional.

The same is not true of Rosamunde Pilcher. Her saga *The Shell Seekers* (1987) is a shameless romanticization of England, English middle-class values, and the English country garden. All the clichés are there, together with strong, silent heroes and women doing all the cooking. Nevertheless, it's a likeable novel and a good read, but ought to be taken in conjunction with Zoe Fairbairns' *Stand We at Last* (1983), the first and only feminist saga. The author obeys the conventions of the genre while writing feelingly about real women's lives, but interestingly there is the same exhilarating sense of progress apparent that exists in Delderfield. This is because both writers feel they are charting a period when history is being made.

As yet another contrast to Pilcher, look at Maisie Mosco's trilogy starting with the novel *Almonds and Raisins* (1979). This is another twentieth-century set-in-England best-seller saga, but with a difference. The family are Jewish immigrants to Manchester, and thus class issues are seen from a new perspective. The family-saga format works particularly well when the family in question has a specific problem—in this case, establishing itself in a new country. On reflection, perhaps the first true family saga is the Old Testament itself, where the same description applies. Family sagas continue to sell steadily and please readers. A contemporary author who has done well in the genre is Harry Bowling, who writes Cockney sagas, set in the East End of London and beginning in the late nineteenth century. His novels are page-turners—they're the sort of good-natured not-too-depressing books you might choose to give someone recovering from flu! They read rather like soap opera, with quick-change scenes and a scattering of cliffhangers. This is most definitely not a criticism; the quality of the writing is high and the books are successfully entertaining.

The last word must go to the novelist who has created the anti-family saga, Kate Atkinson. *Behind the Scenes at the Museum* (1995) is set in Yorkshire, and also covers four generations of women, but is constructed so as to unpeel, layer by layer, the truth about families that we prefer to keep hidden, and in the process reveals the family as a dark beast, rather than the clannish, self-serving, ultimately triumphant animal of de la Roche and Delderfield. Her writing is witty, she captures place and time with tremendous accuracy yet succeeds in writing a novel which is both best-seller and a challenging read.

Thus it is that family saga is far more than just genre fiction—the family is, I suggest, a worthy subject for a novel, possibly the best subject of all. Some family sagas affirm social survival; others show the stifling claustrophobia of the family unit and so focus instead on the development of character. All of us have emerged undamaged or otherwise from families and our curiosity about them and the way they work will never be sated. This is why the family saga has such universal success.

See also SHERRY ASHWORTH

Top Twelve

JOHN GALSWORTHY, *The Man of Property* (1906)

D. H. LAWRENCE, *The Rainbow* (1915)

MAZO DE LA ROCHE, *Jalna* (1927)

R. F. DELDERFIELD, *God is an Englishman* (1970)

MAISIE MOSCO, *Almonds and Raisins* (1979)

ZOE FAIRBAIRNS, *Stand We At Last* (1983)

ISABEL ALLENDE, *The House of the Spirits* (1985)

ROSAMUNDE PILCHER, *The Shell Seekers* (1987)

ELIZABETH JANE HOWARD, *The Light Years* (1990)

HARRY BOWLING, *Gaslight in Page Street* (1991)

VIKRAM SETH, *A Suitable Boy* (1993)

KATE ATKINSON, *Behind the Scenes at the Museum* (1995)

Fantasy

Tom Shippey

Fantasy fiction was established in modern times as a popular genre, for most readers, by the works of J. R. R. Tolkien. Tolkien's two classics, *The Hobbit* (1937) and the three volumes of *The Lord of the Rings* (1954–5), created the format of extensive adventures set in a world similar to that of ancient legend and fairy-tale, and populated by creatures such as elves, dwarves, trolls, wizards, and talking dragons, as well as hobbits and humans. The success of these two works inspired a whole series of emulators, who responded to the Tolkienian format while contributing often powerful imagination of their own.

Of these the most distinguished are Stephen Donaldson, whose two trilogies *The First* and *Second Chronicle of Thomas Covenant the Unbeliever* began with *Lord Foul's Bane* (1977); David (and later Leigh) Eddings, with four sequences including the five volume *Malloreon* begun by *Guardians of the West* (1987), and the *Elenium* series begun by *The Diamond Throne* (1989); and Robert Jordan, whose *Wheel of Time* sequence began with *The Eye of the World* (1990). All three authors are actively writing at present, and the works mentioned above are only a sample. One of Donaldson's most creative strokes was to make his central hero a leper, whose health, as in legend, is bound up with the health of the magic land to which he finds himself transported. Eddings meanwhile is distinguished by a pervasive humour; Jordan's sequence is the most ambitious to date in size and scope.

Other writers in the 'epic fantasy' mode (a label which is often disputed) include Tad Williams, whose *The Dragonbone Chair* (1988) and its successors, published in Britain in two volumes as *Siege* and *Storm* (both 1994), present in some ways an ironic reversal of Tolkien, in which the forces of 'good' prove less reliable than in their predecessor; and Terry Brooks, whose first book in the *Shannara* series, *The Sword of Shannara* (1977) sticks very close to Tolkien indeed. Michael Scott Rohan has produced two trilogies, the *Winter of the World* sequence starting from *The Anvil of Ice* (1986) and the *Spiral* sequence begun by *Chase the Morning* (1990); he is perhaps the best of Tolkien's successors at integrating his knowledge of early legend into his own narratives. 'State of the art' in epic fantasy is meanwhile represented by George R. R. Martin's *Song of Ice and Fire* series, projected as six volumes, of which the first two appeared as *A Game of Thrones* (1996) and *Clash of Kings* (1998).

Determined attempts to strike out in new directions, meanwhile, have come from Michael Swanwick, whose *The Iron Dragon's Daughter* (1993) opens unforgettably in a fairyland munitions factory staffed by changeling slaves, one of whom manages to escape in the Iron Dragon itself, a kind of fairyland intelligent bomber; and by Tim Powers, whose most recent works, such as *Last Call* (1992) and *Expiration Date* (1995) are best described as occult thrillers set in a modern United States infiltrated by magi and ghost-eaters.

Some of the most exciting and readable fantasy currently available how-ever comes from authors whose careers began before the Tolkien revival, in a tradition which goes back to the short-lived American fantasy magazines of the first half of the twentieth century. The best of these is Jack Vance, who began a sequence set in a very far future with *The Dying Earth* (1950), and continued it through *The Eyes of the Overworld* (1966) and *Cugel's Saga* (1983). More recently his *Lyonesse* trilogy (*Lyonesse I, II*, and *III*, 1983–9) is set in a Dark Age land now lost beneath the Atlantic. One of Vance's major characteristics is a mordant humour, combined with fantastic invention: his imagined worlds are the most unforgettable yet created.

A close rival to Vance is Avram Davidson, whose work (like Vance's) has varied between fantasy and science fiction. The lead character of his *The Phoenix and the Mirror* (1969) is the Roman poet Virgil, here seen not as the author of the *Aeneid* but as Vergil the arch-magician of medieval legend, contesting not with trolls and orcs but with gargoyles and manticores. An excellent set of linked stories, set with prescient gloom in a happy alternative-universe Yugoslavia on the edge of break-up, is Davidson's *The Enquiries of Doctor Eszterhazy* (1975); Eszterhazy functions as a kind of Balkan Sherlock Holmes whose cases invari-ably involve the supernatural.

Going back still further into the popular American fantasy tradition, one should note the work of authors who made their mark in the 1930s, in particu-lar Robert E. Howard. Howard has had major posthumous success through his invention of 'Conan the Barbarian', the hero of the Arnold Schwarzenegger film. He completed only one full novel in this sequence, *Conan the Conqueror* (in book form, 1950), but many of his early magazine stories have been col-lected, completed, and continued by other authors; the barbarian hero entering civilization has become a fantasy cliché.

At least one of Howard's continuators has however found his own voice and his own worlds, Lyon Sprague de Camp. In collaboration with Fletcher Pratt, de Camp created the *Incomplete Enchanter* sequence, in which a group of modern American university dons find themselves able to enter one imagined world after another (that of the Norse *Elder Edda*, of Edmund Spenser's *Faerie Queene*, of the Finnish *Kalevala*, etc.), and to succeed in them through their rather imperfect scientific understanding of the rules of magic. The series was collected almost fifty years after its original publication as *The Intrepid Enchanter* (UK) or *The Complete Compleat Enchanter* (USA), both 1989. De Camp also created a solo sequence set in another 'world where magic works' in the *Novaria* novels, begun by *The Goblin Tower* (1968), and partly collected as *The Reluctant King* (1985). Another author of the same generation, Fritz Leiber, developed a switch on the Howardian 'barbarian' motif with a hero-pair, Fafhrd the gigantic Northerner partnered with the defter and shrewder 'Gray Mouser'. They occupy a series of tales set in and around the wicked metropolis Lankhmar, of which the only full novel is *The Swords of Lankhmar* (1968), in which intelligent rats threaten to take over the city.

The most distinguished continuator of this mode is Michael Shea, who began, with Vance's permission, by writing a sequel to *The Eyes of the Overworld* above, *A Quest for Simbilis* (1974); but went on to produce the brilliant, if gruesome, *In Yana, the Touch of Undying* (1985). Two further variations of the 'world where magic works' theme are Poul Anderson's *Operation Chaos* (1971), and Randall Garrett's *Too Many Magicians* (1967). Both are set in the present, but in worlds where events have taken a different course so that magic has developed rather than science. Anderson's is an at times grim fable of world war, Garrett's by contrast set in a happier, still-feudalized world, where the hero is again a Sherlock Holmes figure, accompanied not by Dr Watson but by an Irish sorcerer, Master Sean.

The whole epic fantasy genre has meanwhile been transposed into comedy by Terry Pratchett, whose *Discworld* sequence is now up to twenty volumes. The first of these, *The Colour of Magic* (1983), began with parody of several of the authors above (Howard, Leiber, Tolkien), but the sequence then created its own momentum, with several interlinked groups of characters recurring in repeated volumes. Pratchett makes fun of epic fantasy conventions, but with a deep knowledge and love of the genre.

The fantasy genre has had room, however, for many less readily classifiable authors. T. H. White's *The Once and Future King* (1958) retells the Arthurian story with an extraordinary blend of humour and anachronism, starting from Arthur's childhood (about which all early legends are silent). While C. S. Lewis is best known in fantasy for his children's *Narnia* sequence, his 'fairy-tale for adults', *That Hideous Strength* (1945), forms a kind of bridge between Orwellian science fiction and Arthurian re-creation; in it the sorcerer Merlin is brought back from his enchanted sleep to thwart a new if diabolically inspired technological tyranny.

Finally, Ursula Le Guin's *Earthsea* quartet, which opens with *A Wizard of Earthsea* (1968) is aimed at a teenage market, but like both White's and Tolkien's work 'grows up' as it progresses. Her later novel *Threshold* (published in Britain as, *Us the Beginning Place*, both 1980) is one of the best of modern 'window' stories, in which modern characters step though a gate of some kind into another world: in Le Guin's story, to meet and slay a dragon, and so to gain the confidence to fight the dragons of our own real world. A similar motif is found in Alan Garner's *Red Shift* (1973), also aimed at teenage readers, as is Diana Wynne Jones's *Fire and Hemlock* (1984), a retelling of the ballad of Tam Lin and the Elf-Queen in a strongly contemporary context.

Top Twelve

C. S. LEWIS, *That Hideous Strength* (1945)

J. R. R. TOLKIEN, *The Lord of the Rings* (1954–5)

T. H. WHITE, *The Once and Future King* (1958)

AVRAM DAVIDSON, *The Phoenix and the Mirror* (1969)

STEPHEN R. DONALDSON, *Lord Foul's Bane* (1977)

URSULA LE GUIN, *Earthsea Quartet* (1968–90)

DIANA WYNNE JONES, *Fire and Hemlock* (1984)

MICHAEL SHEA, *In Yana, the Touch of Undying* (1985)

JACK VANCE, *Lyonesse II: The Green Pearl* (1985)

LYON SPRAGUE DE CAMP AND FLETCHER PRATT, *The Intrepid Enchanter (published in the USA as The Complete Compleat Enchanter)* (1989)

MICHAEL SWANWICK, *The Iron Dragon's Daughter* (1993)

GEORGE R. R. MARTIN, *A Game of Thrones* (1996)

Film adaptations

Mike Harris

People who go on to read a novel after first seeing the screen adaptation frequently complain that the original (especially if it's a classic) is slower and
'heavier' than the film it inspired, and it usually is. Someone who first made
acquaintance with Shakespeare through Baz Luhrmann's excellent, action-
packed, streetwise but distinctly slimline version of *Romeo and Juliet* (1996)
will most certainly find the Bard's script both wordier and slower-paced.

Conversely, people who read and love novels are wont to complain that
screen adaptations (especially of classics) are superficial because they change or
miss out key story-lines or visualize characters and locations differently. How
could they not? Tolstoy's great novel *War and Peace* (1863–9) ran for nearly
eight hours in Sergei Bondarchuk's brilliant 1968 adaptation. But the 1,500 pages
of the book itself would take a fast reader at least *50 hours* to get through. Even
allowing for the greater visual economy of their medium, film adapters just
have to make cuts.

So why bother making adaptations at all? And why should we watch them?
And if we like watching them, why we should we bother with the book afterwards? Beginning to answer all that involves taking a quick glance at a 100-
year-old relationship between film and prose fiction that is both complicated
and symbiotic.

Many of the great nineteenth-century novels were serialized in magazines
before they appeared as books. These novels are frequently adapted for screen.
That's not a coincidence. If these writers wanted their readers to keep coming
back they had to capture their interest at the beginning of every episode and
leave them in suspense at the end. To do this they resorted to attention-
grabbing tricks as old as story-telling, but developed them into a sophisticated
narrative form that used the actions of protagonists in extreme or sensational
situations not only to sustain interest, excite emotion, and create suspense but
to explore character, social values, and moral choices.

A few decades later the first silent movie producers had to maintain a similarly massive output whilst inventing a medium from scratch, and they looked
to earlier forms (principally stage melodramas, short stories, and novels) for
lots of cheap, off-the-peg content. Between 1896 and 1915 for example, there
were at least 56 adaptations of Dickens, 6 *Jane Eyre*s, 10 *Uncle Tom's Cabin*s,
9 *Dr Jekyll*s and umpteen Thomas Hardys. As films got longer and audiences

more sophisticated, film companies began buying in writers. These were not infrequently novelists soaked in the conventions of nineteenth-century classics. None more so than Thomas Hardy himself, who was employed to edit story-captions for several of the many silent adaptations of his books. These writers naturally took the narrative form of the novel and—whether adapting existing texts or inventing entirely new screenplays—developed it for a visual medium that could communicate action, emotion, and character more economically. They then used that medium, just as the novel did, to explore character, social values, and moral choices, but for a world-wide audience of exploited urban workers who didn't have the leisure time for reading books.

At the same time cameramen and directors were remembering the great descriptive passages of prose fiction—for example that wonderful moving crane shot over the whole of London at the start of Dickens's *Bleak House* (1853), or the fast intercutting between two story-lines that adds pace and tension to the climax of Tolstoy's *Anna Karenina* (1873–7) or the tracking, panning, close-ups, flashbacks, and chaotic crowd scenes to be found in Thackeray, Zola, Hugo, and hundreds of lesser writers—and steadily transformed these into the basic vocabulary and grammar of film.

Then, as films became more culturally acceptable, and novelists employed as screenwriters used their ill-gotten gains to subsidize further novel writing, the techniques originally borrowed from the novel by film (but in it given greater pace and visual emphasis) were re-absorbed into prose fiction. So successfully and completely was this done that when (to take two examples more or less at random) Jean-Paul Sartre cuts rapidly back and forth between half-a-dozen developing narratives in *The Reprieve* (1945), or Roddy Doyle writes *The Commitments* (1988) almost entirely in racy idiomatic dialogue interspersed with the briefest of scene-setting, it is possible that neither is fully aware of the debt they owe to film, but no surprise that both books were remade into successful screen dramas. Conversely, when Hollywood guts classic novels on the grounds of slow pace or a lack of narrative hooks, they are obliviously (and ironically) applying rules derived ultimately from their authors.

None of this means, of course, that there aren't plenty of bad films made from great books. Fortunately, there are just as many great films made from bad books. David Lean's *Bridge on the River Kwai* (1957) takes a nasty xeno-phobic novel by Pierre Boulle and turns it into a visually stunning, moving satire on military honour and imperial pretensions. It would be impossible to even begin to list here the number of dime novels made into film westerns that have both moral dignity and visual grandeur, but start with John Ford's *Stagecoach* (1939). The same goes for the pulp detective stories transformed by Hollywood into brooding masterpieces of 1940s' film noir. The best of these writers—for example Raymond Chandler and Dashiell Hammett—wrote screenplays as well, and put the lessons they learnt into great books that were in turn transformed back into great films like *The Big Sleep* (1946) and *The Maltese Falcon* (1941).

Occasionally, a good book is turned into an even better film. C. S. Forester's prose original of John Huston's *The African Queen* (1951) is a good enough page-turner but it unfortunately lacks the on-screen chemistry of Humphrey Bogart, playing the drunken tug-captain, and Katharine Hepburn's teetotal, sexually repressed missionary, learning to love each other whilst running the rapids and torpedoing a German warship.

Then again, good books often turn into equally good films. Visconti's *Death in Venice* (1971) captures exactly the mood of Thomas Mann's limpid, poignant novella about an ageing homosexual (played magnificently by Dirk Bogarde) obsessed with an angelically beautiful boy. And David Lean's *Great Expectations* (1946) might have cut a lot of the plot and half the characters from Dickens but it matched the original's brooding atmosphere, affecting sentimentality, and imaginative energy, and played it in public images twenty foot high.

This sheer scale, in combination with the shared immediacy of the cinema experience, can give a film adaptation a powerful edge, no matter how good the prose original. The violence in Stanley Kubrick's *A Clockwork Orange* (1971) is no worse than in Anthony Burgess's dystopian novel, and the amoral pleasure taken in it by the teenage protagonist no less. But it was Kubrick's version that provoked the moral panic that caused Kubrick to withdraw his film in this country during his lifetime, and it is his images that stay in the mind, not Burgess's prose.

A film adaptation doesn't have to include a single word of dialogue, scene, or location from the original but can still gain from and illuminate it. Coppola's great film *Apocalypse Now* (1979) shares only the names of two characters and its theme with Joseph Conrad's equally great novel *Heart of Darkness* (1899). One is set in Vietnam during the 1970s, the other in the Belgian Congo before the First World War. Conrad's protagonist goes up river into the jungle to rescue Kurtz. Coppola's CIA assassin travels to kill him. Both works of art create an atmosphere that is simultaneously dangerous and surreal. Both delve deep into the heart of chaos and evil. To suggest that one was better or worse than the other would be absurd.

At the other end of the spectrum, a romantic college movie like *Ten Things I Hate about You* (1999) demonstrates how to breathe life into a stale and entirely trivial film-genre with an intelligent script that wittily acknowledges its debt to a greater literary original, in this case Shakespeare's *The Taming of the Shrew*. The debt can go the other way too. Choderlos de Laclos's wonderful but little-read eighteenth-century epistolary novel *Les Liaisons dangereuses* (1782), was brought to the top of the bookshop piles by Stephen Frears's wickedly faithful 1988 film adaptation, *Dangerous Liaisons*, in which Glenn Close plays the tragic procurer to John Malkovich's doomed seducer of Michelle Pfeiffer's tantalizing virtue.

Finally, there is the interesting case of films that do cheapen and simplify, that excise virtually all the ideas from their literary source, add hokey tunes, stupid dancing animals, and sentimentalize everything beyond all recognition, and are so different from the original book you wouldn't recognize it, but still produce wonderful popular art. The Disney cartoon version of Kipling's *The Jungle Book* (1967) is my example of this strange phenomenon. You will no doubt have your own . . .

Top Twelve

Stagecoach (1939)—JOHN FORD (from the story by Ernest Haycox)

The Big Sleep (1946)—HOWARD HAWKS (from Raymond Chandler's novel)

Great Expectations (1946)—DAVID LEAN (from Charles Dickens's novel)

The African Queen (1951)—JOHN HUSTON (from C. S. Forester's novel)

Bridge on the River Kwai (1957)—DAVID LEAN (from Pierre Boulle's novel)

The Jungle Book (1967)—DISNEY (from Rudyard Kipling's story collection)

War and Peace (1968)—SERGEI BONDARCHUK (from Leo Tolstoy's novel)

Death in Venice (1971)—LUCHINO VISCONTI (from Thomas Mann's novella)

A Clockwork Orange (1971)—STANLEY KUBRICK (from Anthony Burgess's novel)

Apocalypse Now (1979)—FRANCIS FORD COPPOLA (from Joseph Conrad's novel *Heart of Darkness*)

Dangerous Liaisons (1988)—STEPHEN FREARS (from Christopher Hampton's theatrical adaptation of the Choderlos de Laclos novel)

Romeo and Juliet (1996)—BAZ LUHRMANN (from William Shakespeare's play)

France

Michèle Roberts

One way into reading French literature is to think of yourself going on holiday to France. To begin with you might choose a favourite city like Paris, tried and tested on weekend hops, easily accessible, full of famous landmarks. As well as visiting the great historic sites you'd want to make time for the classics of contemporary life: shopping and nightclubbing. Later on you might start wanting to branch out a bit, going south perhaps, exploring the countryside and the coast. You travel from desire, following instinct and whim to some extent, armed with maps and restaurant guides perhaps, even with campsite or hotel bookings, or making for a *gite* you have rented, but none the less open to adventures on the way, able to stop and browse whenever you choose. You're guided by appetite and chance as much as by the recommendations of friends, and your experience of the holiday is all the richer because of the spice of uncertainty, of unexpected encounters and treats.

So it is with French books. You might start with some of the famous novels of the nineteenth century and try reading them against their modern counterparts. You might want to compare city novels with country novels, for the capital and the provinces remain quite distinct in culture, despite being increasingly linked by modern technology. With the help of a few signposts, you make your own pattern of reading. What follows here, then, is a suggestion or two to start you off. It certainly isn't comprehensive and it does not pretend to be authoritative.

If you are lucky enough to be able to combine your reading of French writers with an actual trip to France, then it is great fun to match the writers to the places you are visiting. The best guide to writing in and about France that I have ever read is the *Traveller's Literary Companion to France* by John Edmondson. Accessible and entertaining, this not only gives you biographies of the writers born in or associated with the different regions of France, plus maps, photographs, and indexes of authors and places, but also includes over a hundred and twenty extracts from books. So, for example, if you were mooching around Normandy, you could, with the help of this guide, track the movements of the great nineteenth-century short-story writer and novelist Guy de Maupassant, who set many of his works in the pays de Caux and its coastal resorts of Étretat and Le Havre. Maupassant's work is often seen as cynical, harshly critical of the bourgeoisie, misanthropic, even misogynistic.

So, for a revelation about what he's capable of, try reading *A Woman's Life* (*Une vie*; 1883). This tells a simple story, creating a surprisingly tender and compassionate portrait of a young woman growing up in the clifftop country-side inland from Fécamp, recounting the heart-breaking tale of how she is gradually stripped of everything and reduced to penury. Her honeymoon in Corsica, and her discovery of sexual pleasure, are beautifully described.

Still in Normandy, you could try Maupassant's mentor Gustave Flaubert, famous for his dissection of the materialism and illusions of provincial life in his masterpiece *Madame Bovary* (1857). Of course poor Madame Bovary has to die at the end. To please his close woman friend, the great best-selling novelist George Sand, Flaubert wrote his novella, *A Simple Heart* (1877). In this short work, he drops his harshly moralizing persona to give us the touching figure of the servant Félicité and the consolation she finds in a stuffed parrot. *Flaubert's Parrot* (1984) by Julian Barnes brings us up to date on Flaubert, detailing a quest to Flaubert's home at Croisset and the little Rouen museum which contains a stuffed parrot. Barnes's novel is like a love-letter to Flaubert, mixing travelogue, history, and lists, and deploying thriller techniques, and is both very funny and remarkably elegantly written.

George Sand (pseudonym of Amandine-Aurore-Lucille Dupin), in her day, was far more famous than Flaubert. Like many modern woman writers, she wrote for her contemporaries rather than aiming at literary immortality. Some of her novels have dated, but try a late one, *Marianne* (1876), which was per-haps inspired by her love for Flaubert. It is a charming story which examines the love between a nature-loving young woman and her philosopher-tutor. Sand wrote evocatively about country life in the Berry, the département in which she grew up, for example in *The Master Pipers* (1853), which combines themes of rustic life, love, and revolution.

All these writers kept one foot in the provinces, which nurtured them, and one in Paris, where they did their business deals. Typical of this is (Sidonie-Gabrielle) Colette, who is like George Sand in that she was a tremendously popular writer who is also acclaimed as a fine stylist. Colette, who flourished in the 1920s and 1930s, wrote about the Burgundy countryside in her racy series of Claudine novels, and about high and low life in Paris. To sample her writing, try *The Vagabond* (1910), about an actress on the road travelling from one music-hall venue to the next, dealing with problems of love and sex and iden-tity along the way. It remains as fresh as though it were written yesterday. More recently, contemporary novelist Sylvie Germain has captured acutely the time-less qualities of life in what's called *la France profonde*; the wild, mysterious centre, a harsh region of mountains and forests. Germain's novels are poetic and jewelled as fairy stories. Try *Days of Anger* (1989), which mixes melodrama and a French sort of magic realism to convey themes of murder and revenge.

A completely different take on life in contemporary France is provided by Michel Houellebecq, whose novel *Whatever* (1994) satirizes urban disaffection and alienated youth, technology and psychobabble. The book is very bleak, sharp, and easy to read. Nothing could be further from the rural idylls described by George Sand, which is why it's worth reading. A female perspective on our complicated age is given by another young writer, Marie Darrieussecq. She made her name with the funny and sexy *Pig Tales* (1996) and followed this up with *My Phantom Husband* (1999)—what a woman does when the man in her life disappears. Again, this is tough, clever, and smooth to read. If it's accessibility plus strong story-telling you're after then I'd recommend Jean Rouand. The landscape this time is that of the Loire-Atlantique, and the narratives of *Fields of Glory* (1990) and *Of Illustrious Men* (1993) follow a family saga, from the male point of view, from the First World War onwards.

French writing of course includes writing in creole by authors from the former colonies who are proud to be black and not Parisian, a growth area of terrific vitality and originality. Writers translated into English include Patrick Chamoiseau from Martinique and Maryse Condé from Guadeloupe. Condé's *I, Tituba* (1986) is a gripping account of the involvement of a former slave in the Salem witch trials, written in the accessible style of historical romance.

See also MICHÈLE ROBERTS

Top Twelve

GEORGE SAND, *Marianne* (1876)

GUSTAVE FLAUBERT, *A Simple Heart* (in *Three Tales*, 1877)

GUY DE MAUPASSANT, *A Woman's Life* (1883)

COLETTE, *Claudine at School* (1900) and *The Vagabond* (1910)

MARYSE CONDÉ, *I, Tituba—Black Witch of Salem* (1986)

SYLVIE GERMAIN, *Days of Anger* (1989)

JEAN ROUAND, *Fields of Glory* (1990) and *Illustrious Men* (1993)

MICHEL HOUELLEBECQ, *Whatever* (1994)

MARIE DARRIEUSSECQ, *Pig Tales* (1996) and *My Phantom Husband* (1999)

Germany

Michael Hulse

In 1895, the year in which his masterpiece *Effi Briest* was published, Germany lost its great novelist of the late nineteenth century, Theodor Fontane. Observing the new nation (united in 1871 under Prussian leadership), Fontane had taken his amiably ironic scalpel to the fledgeling Reich's foundation myths, the gulf between its conservative and progressive instincts, and its class and gender conflicts. The first great novel of the new twentieth century came from one of Fontane's profoundest admirers, Thomas Mann: *Buddenbrooks* (1901) is a searching portrait of three generations of a patrician family in a proud old Hanseatic city (transparently Mann's own birthplace, Lübeck), recognizing both the qualities and the shortcomings of the wealthy upper middle class. Deft in its characterization, generous and shrewd in its portrayal of milieu and its human sympathies, *Buddenbrooks* also began Thomas Mann's lifelong exploration of the conflicting claims of artistic imperative and social circumstance, a theme later pursued in numerous novellas and above all in the great novels *The Magic Mountain* (1924) and *Doctor Faustus* (1947). His Nobel Prize (1929) and, through years of exile, his active opposition to the Nazi regime, gave him a commanding influence internationally. (His brother Heinrich was also an acclaimed novelist, with rather more streetwise bite.)

One contemporary frequently applauded by Thomas Mann was Jakob Wassermann, who at times shared aspects of Mann's subject matter. *Christian Wahnschaffe* (1919) looks at a younger generation's rejection of the moneyed elders' *mores* in favour of a more spiritual life. (The same conflict occurs in other guises in the works of Hermann Hesse.) As a Jew, Wassermann could not but be conscious of his outsider role in a German nation which paid only lip-service to principles of assimilation, and his novel *Caspar Hauser* (1908) stands as a great metaphor for social outcasts of every description. It concerns the celebrated case of a 'wild boy' who appeared in Nuremberg in 1828, clearly in his late teens but unable to speak more than a single sentence—'I want to be a rider like my father.' The historical Hauser had been kept in a dark cell since early infancy, and speculation was rife that this was a great dynastic crime, that he was perhaps an illegitimate son of Napoleon—and the speculation was further fuelled by the youth's murder. Wassermann's love of Dostoevsky but also of cloak-and-dagger yarns makes this a compelling account of society's problems with those on its impenetrable fringes.

But the great Jewish writer of the first quarter century was born in Prague as a citizen of that xenophobic patchwork state, the Austro-Hungarian Empire. Franz Kafka's stories and novels can also be read as elaborately mournful allegories of the Jewish experience. The universality of *Metamorphosis* (1915), *The Trial* (1925), and *The Castle* (1926), though, lies in Kafka's subtle and profound understanding of the nature of individual alienation from a world bewilderingly unsympathetic and indeed hostile. If the adjective 'Kafkaesque' has entered many languages to describe a somewhat grotesque exploration of identity *in extremis*, that is because these parables of life in a society increasingly institutionalized, faceless, and menacing have struck an unpleasantly familiar chord with readers world-wide.

The achievements of Franz Kafka, in a life closed prematurely by tuberculosis, belong very much to that new order of society superseding the old which is glimpsed only on the fringes of Mann and Wassermann. The First World War left Germany a changed nation: the Kaiser abdicated, the major cities were racked by a series of revolts in the post-war months, and as the dust of peace settled it became clear that this world of perceived humiliation, reparations payments, the crippled veterans of an army popularly thought undefeated and betrayed by the politicians—and then, as the short-lived Weimar Republic wore on, of inflation, rising unemployment, political instability, and factional thuggery—was a world transformed for ever. *All Quiet on the Western Front* (1929) placed Erich Maria Remarque alongside Barbusse, Graves, and a select few other prose writers who recorded the sorry carnage of the war once called 'great'.

In the same year as that classic of anti-war literature appeared, Alfred Döblin published *Berlin Alexanderplatz*, the story of Franz Biberkopf, adrift in the teeming city after release from prison, turning to drink and a prostitute for comfort, falling in with criminals and with the rising Nazi movement. This was the seedy metropolitan Germany of Brecht's plays and Otto Dix's paintings, and novels by another highly gifted writer, Joseph Roth, a Germany that bore little resemblance to that which Thomas Mann had commemorated not thirty years before.

Meanwhile, in Austria Robert Musil charted the eclipse of the old order in his immensely long, sprawling masterpiece *The Man without Qualities* (1930–43). Its action is confined to the year 1913–14, and a major strand in the plot concerns preparations to celebrate the seventieth anniversary of the ageing Austro-Hungarian emperor's accession in 1918, the year in which, as the reader knows, that empire ceased to exist. Musil's novel also shares with Döblin's an Austro-German obsession of the interwar years: sex crime.

The twelve ignoble years of the Nazi Third Reich drove many writers into exile, silenced others, and transformed the literary landscape in Germany and Austria. From the infamous book-burning of 1933 (at which the works of every author I've mentioned so far were consigned to the flames) to the smouldering ruins of May 1945, the totalitarian dictatorship ensured that any spirit resembling critical, liberal pluralism was expunged from the literature officially tolerated. After the defeat of the Axis powers and the return of the soldiers and evacuated civilians to the bombed-out cities, what became known as a literature of the rubble (*Trümmerliteratur*) made its tentative appearance, with Heinrich Böll's stories and early novels expressing the desolate, taciturn hardihood of the returnees. But it was left to Böll's fellow Nobel laureate Günter Grass, more than a decade after the Second World War had ended, to publish the first masterpiece of the newly democratic (West) Germany. *The Tin Drum* (1959) swiftly became a global best-seller, not least because of what George Steiner called 'the power of that bawling voice to drown the siren-song of smooth oblivion, to make the Germans—as no writer did before—face up to their monstrous past.' Told by a dwarf now confined to a mental asylum, the novel is staggering in its detail and its imaginative range, and with it Grass single-handedly established European magic realism.

Swiss literature is often overlooked when German-language writing is discussed, but two post-war authors both equally at home in drama and fiction put it emphatically on the map: Friedrich Dürrenmatt and Max Frisch. While the former turned to fiction chiefly for the relaxation of writing crime stories, Frisch explored the century's obsessive dilemma of identity in *I'm Not Stiller* (1954) and produced other fiction of distinction before publishing, towards the end of his life, one of the most inspiring and delightful novels of recent decades, highly acclaimed in the United States: *Man Appears in the Holocene* (1979). A gentle inquiry into the nature of knowledge and of human frailty, it centres upon an old man on an isolated mountainside in the Ticino region as he struggles to determine what he can really feel sure of remembering or knowing.

The diversity of fiction in German in the closing two decades of the twentieth century is well illustrated by four extraordinary performances by an East German, an Austrian, a West German, and a West German resident for more than half his life in England. The East German (the term is just, for the forty-year German Democratic Republic left its mark on her every sentence) is Christa Wolf, whose writings turn time and again to the vexed relation of individual to collective identity. *No Place on Earth* (1981) records an imaginary meeting in 1804 between two troubled writers, each later to commit suicide, and through their conversation explores the male and female principles and the nature of creation in dark times. The Austrian is Elfriede Jelinek, a writer outspokenly uncomfortable with her troublesome country. *The Piano Teacher* (1983) explores the love-hate relation between Erika Kohut and her mother, and Kohut's fascination with the seamy side of Vienna. The West German is Patrick Süskind, whose *Perfume* (1985), a murder story set in eighteenth-century France, is a stylistic and imaginative *tour de force*. The best-selling German novel worldwide since *The Tin Drum*, it symbolized the arrival of a new generation of German writers more concerned to tell a powerful story than to examine the nation's historical guilt or the teething troubles of democracy through the years of student revolt and of terrorism.

And finally, the German writer long resident in England is W. G. Sebald, whose idiosyncratically melancholy narratives, a teasing blend of fact and fiction, won a wide readership either side of the Atlantic as the century closed. His master-piece, *The Emigrants* (1993), is among many other and more important things an unspoken rebuke to those German writers (and others) who would consider reunification in 1990 as setting a triumphalist full stop to the probing of the painful past. It consists of four brief lives of Jewish people who left Germany, and through the re-creation of the circumstances of those lives it evokes bygone times that can never return. Arresting for its graceful language, its elegiac compassion, and its meditative sensitivities, it marks a mature and responsible closing to a century of writing from a troubled and troubling nation.

Top Twelve

THOMAS MANN, *Buddenbrooks* (1901)

JAKOB WASSERMANN, *Caspar Hauser* (1908)

FRANZ KAFKA, *The Castle* (1926)

ERICH MARIA REMARQUE, *All Quiet on the Western Front* (1929)

ALFRED DÖBLIN, *Berlin Alexanderplatz* (1929)

ROBERT MUSIL, *The Man without Qualities* (1930–43)

GÜNTER GRASS, *The Tin Drum* (1959)

MAX FRISCH, *Man Appears in the Holocene* (1979)

CHRISTA WOLF, *No Place on Earth* (1981)

ELFRIEDE JELINEK, *The Piano Teacher* (1983)

PATRICK SÜSKIND, *Perfume* (1985)

W. G. SEBALD, *The Emigrants* (1993)

Glamour

Kate Saunders

The Glamour novel, at the time of writing, is in eclipse. The Zeitgeist is inner fulfilment rather than outer show, and this particular sub-genre of romantic fiction deals in breathtaking excess. Stakes are always high here, and emotions searing. There should be moments of pure melodrama—for instance, the central scene in Shirley Conran's *Lace* (1993), in which a young model asks the four heroines: 'Which one of you bitches is my mother?' Unwieldy tracts of history must be skimmed for the juicy bits, and recast in tabloid headlines. It is more than putting the plums at the top of the cake. The point about Glamour fiction is that it is all plums. Fame is global, fortunes are massive, passions are volcanic —and my dear, the clothes—'At a state dinner at the White House she was the most resplendent figure there, only 22 years old, wearing pale lilac satin from Dior and emeralds that had once belonged to Empress Josephine' (Judith Krantz, *Scruples*, 1978); 'The men looked much more glamorous than the women this evening, gaudy peacocks in their different tail coats, red with grey-blue facings for the West Cotchester Hunt, red with crimson for the neighbouring Gatheram Hunt, dark blue with buff for the Beaufort' (Jilly Cooper, *Rivals*, 1988).

Krantz and Cooper are, for my money, the queens of this genre. Krantz, whose ground-breaking *Scruples* appeared back in 1978, can be said to have invented it, or at least set the boundaries. The Glamour novel rode high in the 1980s, when 'aspiration' was an acceptable euphemism for old-fashioned greed. Female readers in search of escapist entertainment wanted more than the feisty kitchenmaids and mill-girls of Catherine Cookson; more than the virginal young things in the typical Mills and Boon romance, which tradition-ally kept the bedroom door closed.

We wanted it all—love, money, success, clothes, jewels, houses, cars. And if a writer had taken the trouble to invent an incredibly sexy hero, we wanted to see him put through his paces. Where could we sigh over fabulous descriptions of designer sex, before Judith Krantz ripped the bedroom door off its hinges, and made sexual passion a vital element of the feminine best-seller? Women had written explicitly about sex before, but Krantz arguably invented aspira-tional sex, where orgasms are always seismic and men are rendered helpless by desire—sex, in fact, as part of a whole, desirable lifestyle package. 'Life-style' was itself an 1980s concept, and the Glamour novel belongs firmly in the era of Reagan and Thatcher.

Judith Krantz followed *Scruples* with the equally successful *Princess Daisy* (1980), a glittering farrago of Russian aristos, old money, and hidden twin sisters. In Britain, the above-mentioned *Lace* rode high in the best-seller lists. The journalist Celia Brayfield, who claimed to have assisted with large sections of Conran's book, successfully went independent with her own piece of Glamour fiction, *Pearls* (1998). Sally Beauman, also a journalist, famously sold her novel *Destiny* (1988) for £1 million. These books, of a type popularly known as 'Shopping and Fucking', attracted enormous advances from glamour-hungry publishers, and this fact took the glitzy mythology a stage further. As far as an aspiring female public were concerned, writing about incredible amounts of glamour had admitted the authors themselves to the charmed circle they were writing about. There was a teasing hint, when you bought one of these gaudily packaged paperbacks, that some of the hyperbole might rub off.

No publishing phenomenon is entirely new, of course, and the Glamour novel is a direct descendant of the so-called 'Silver Fork' novels of the 1830s and 1840s; conventional marriage-broking dramas in which plots are drowned in luxurious detail. Then as now, they were widely regarded as ludicrous by the literary establishment. Dickens parodies the genre in *Nicholas Nickleby* (1839), when he has the virtuous Kate Nickleby reading a novel called *The Lady Flabella* to her snobbish but vulgar employer, Mrs Wititterly:

At this instant, while the Lady Flabella yet inhaled that delicious fragrance by holding the mouchoir to her exquisite, but thoughtfully-chiselled nose, the door of the boudoir (artfully concealed by rich hangings of silken damask, the hue of Italy's firmament) was thrown open ... two valets-de-chambre, clad in sumptuous liveries of peach-blossom and gold ... presented, on a golden salver gorgeously chased, a scented billet.

It was an easy style to send up. 'There was not a line in it,' comments Dickens, 'which could, by the most remote contingency, awake the smallest excitement in any person breathing.' As the author of *The Lady Flabella* might have said, *plus ça change*. Then as now, Glamour fiction was critically despised because it was specifically aimed at women, and usually written by women. It is still broadly true that novels catering to female fantasies have a lower intellectual status than escapist fiction for men or children.

At its best, however, the Glamour novel has an extravagance, gusto, and richness of invention that is very appealing. It is a form without pretension— the one exclusive enclosure it does not aspire to join is the canon of Western Literature. It is significant that its leading exponents, including Krantz and Cooper, began as successful journalists. The form demands a high gloss of professionalism. As novelists, they never lose sight of the fact that they are in the business of entertainment.

For Krantz, in her first and best novel *Scruples*, the main attractions are obscene amounts of money, and Hollywood fame discussed with gossipy intensity. For Cooper, over on the other side of the Atlantic, the headline is social class—the reader is invited to admire houses and objects that money alone cannot buy, because they have a patina of poshness several centuries deep. The stark cultural differences between these two novelists, however, are only highlighted by their similarities. The Glamour novel sticks to a time-honoured romantic template. The heroine must still end up in the arms of the right hero. No matter how much Bollinger has been licked out of her navel by Olympic-standard studs along the way, true love is still monogamous and eternal. Krantz's Bostonian beauty Billy Ikehorn ends *Scruples* married and pregnant—her husband's Oscar is only the cherry on the cake. Cooper's dewy Taggie O'Hara wins and tames the handsome beast of a hero, Rupert Campbell-Black.

The road to romantic fulfilment has remained basically unchanged since Jane Eyre fell into the arms of Mr Rochester, but the Glamour novel placed new landmarks along the way. A Glamour heroine ought to be a successful businesswoman in her own right, before winning the man who will free her from the burden of making her own money (fun for a while, like making your own chutney—but who wants to do it for ever?). Art is about conflict, and the heroine's progress should not be too easy. There should be a Cinderella-ish element in her meteoric rise. Krantz's Billy Ikehorn starts out not poverty-stricken, like one of Cookson's poor girls, but enormously fat. Cooper's sweet Taggie O'Hara is dyslexic, and despised by her flighty mother.

In its heyday, the Glamour novel understood and defined the new demands of the 1980s female escapist. Fantasies change as time passes, and the best-sellers of the late 1990s are far more likely to concern struggling single women, in more ordinary jobs, worrying that they will never get a husband until they are too old to have babies (see Helen Fielding's *Bridget Jones' Diary*, 1996, and Jane Green's *Mr Maybe*, 1999). This sharp move away from Glamour is neatly illustrated by the subsequent careers of Judith Krantz and Jilly Cooper. In the early 1990s, Krantz produced *Scruples Two*, a sequel to her masterpiece. In the first book, Billy Ikehorn seeks fulfilment by starting a Beverly Hills shop called 'Scruples' which sells the very best that money can buy. The sequel, rather sadly, finds her selling style to the masses via a catalogue. How are the mighty fallen —from Harrods to Next. Jilly Cooper, with her teeming plots and exuberant humour, is still riding high in the best-seller lists. But as her most recent book, *Score!* (1999) shows, she is retreating further into the absurd. The sheer silliness of the antics (murderers in underground tunnels, beloved dogs appearing as ghosts) masks a realization that conspicuous consumption alone will not grab the reader's interest.

When writers of Glamour fiction survive and prosper, it is because they have the intelligence to adapt the form to contemporary tastes. Rosie Thomas and Penny Vincenzi, both mega-selling writers of the 1980s, were even more popular in the late 1990s; playing down the glitz and melodrama in favour of more emotional realism. But excess is never out of fashion for long. And when it comes back, it will bring in its wake a new generation of Glamour novels, formulated to fit the times.

Top Six

JUDITH KRANTZ, *Scruples* (1978)

JILLY COOPER, *Rivals* (1988)

SALLY BEAUMAN, *Destiny* (1988)

ROSIE THOMAS, *Bad Girls, Good Women* (1988)

PENNY VINCENZI, *Old Sins* (1992)

SHIRLEY CONRAN, *Lace* (1993)

The reduced list reflects **Glamour***'s fading appeal; it is difficult to find any good new Glamour novels to recommend*

Historical

Boyd Tonkin

Thirty years or so ago, the historical novel had dropped below the horizon of respectable attention. The romantic gestures that thrilled Victorian readers had dwindled into the folderol of swashbucklers and bodice-rippers in pulp fiction, kitsch movies and television serials. Before long, a host of gleeful parodists from *Monty Python* to *Blackadder* would deliver the *coup de grâce* to this risible style. Period romances by the likes of Daphne du Maurier, Georgette Heyer, and Jean Plaidy still packed lending-library shelves, and in the classroom historical yarns never lost their cachet. Authors such as Rosemary Sutcliff were still creating children's classics that repaid visits from adult readers. But among literary novelists it was only the relatively recent events of the Second World War that led to the choice of a broad historical canvas. In the early 1960s Olivia Manning and Evelyn Waugh both completed ambitious triptychs about the impact of that war on private and public life: respectively, *The Balkan Trilogy* (1960–5) and the *Sword of Honour* (1952–61) sequence. Apart from this recent history, however, history (for serious novelists) was a no-go area.

Yet, by the century's end, historical fiction commanded a prestige and acclaim unknown since its heyday. As I write, *Captain Corelli's Mandolin* (1994) by Louis de Bernières, a period romance whose methods and motifs Walter Scott himself could have grasped at a glance, has just sold its millionth copy. Around a quarter of the titles that have appeared on the Booker Prize shortlists since 1975 count as historical novels of one brand or other. And the response to Toni Morrison's harrowing account of American slavery and its aftermath, *Beloved* (1987), has helped to make her the most popular Nobel literature laureate in decades.

What accounts for this sudden about-turn, and why did the genre fall so far? The form first took wing around 1800, in the wake of the French Revolution. European writers shared a consciousness of revolutionary change, a new fascination with their medieval and Renaissance past and a craving for larger-than-life heroes and villains on the scale of Napoleon himself. These streams converged into a taste for exotic tales of epoch-making conflict set in the near or distant past. On the back of this fashion, Sir Walter Scott, who published twenty-five *Waverley* novels from 1814 to 1832, became one of the earliest cultural superstars. Because he more or less patented the conventions of historical romance, Scott suffered most from their later exhaustion. But he stands squarely at the source of period fiction, and a novel such as *Ivanhoe* (1819)—honest Saxons versus haughty Normans, with Robin Hood himself in a cameo role—takes the reader right to the corny, colourful heart of all those later pastiches.

Nourished by an age of revolution, the historical novel tilted towards moments of conflict and transformation. In Victor Hugo's evergreen *The Hunchback of Notre Dame* (1831), a character shakes a book at the cathedral towers and shouts 'This will kill that!' When Charles Dickens came to tackle the French Revolution itself in *A Tale of Two Cities* (1859), his scene-painting summed up the Victorian ambivalence towards the gore and glitter of the past: 'It was the best of times, it was the worst of times.'

Massacres aside, most nineteenth-century novelists still thought that history told a tale of hard-won progress and enlightenment. Nostalgia seldom dominates the form, certainly not in a portrayal of stifling dogma as bleakly realistic as Nathaniel Hawthorne's great account of Puritan bigotry in colonial New England, *The Scarlet Letter* (1850). As the century wore on, however, a few writers began to inspect the past and see a mess instead of a moral. No historical mess ever looked more thrillingly decadent—or more minutely researched—than the ancient Carthage of Gustave Flaubert's *Salammbô* (1862), a pioneer in the sensation-sodden treatment of the pre-Christian world that continues to this day. For most of Flaubert's peers, history did lead somewhere and mean something, however murky its message. The novelist who grappled most heroically with the question of how the vast forces of change may make or break an individual fate was Leo Tolstoy. His Napoleonic epic, *War and Peace* (1863–9), ranks for many critics as simply the greatest nineteenth-century novel: proof of just how central the historicizing impulse was to fiction at this time.

As a new century loomed, scepticism took root. Serious fiction turned towards the conflicts of the present, or the dark places of the soul. The historical novel drifted downmarket as genres past their prime will often do. Only Robert Louis Stevenson, who mastered the tricks of the trade in works such as *Kidnapped* (1886), pointed a way ahead with his sombrely brilliant, unfinished *Weir of Hermiston* (1896). A sword-and-breeches romp such as Baroness Orczy's *The Scarlet Pimpernel* (1905) could still enchant a wide public, but the form as a whole had forfeited its place at fiction's top table.

Decades of disdain ensued. As the Victorians became a laughing-stock, so did their favourite story-telling modes. Virginia Woolf's gender-bending, century-hopping fantasia *Orlando* (1928) is, in part, a sparkling burlesque of the costumed clichés that filled the reading of her girlhood. Yet Robert Graves's gripping chronicles of Imperial intrigue (*I, Claudius* and *Claudius the God*, 1934) proved that ancient Rome and Greece remained a rich storehouse of darkly glamorous tales. Good writers such as Mary Renault and Allan Massie would later carry on the toga-and-tunic line.

As a whole, historical novels only regained a place in the critical sun, along with other Victorian styles, in the later 1960s. (In the English-speaking world at least: a one-off masterpiece came out of Sicily in the mid-1950s, with Giuseppe di Lampedusa's *The Leopard*, 1958. In Britain, it was John Fowles's *The French Lieutenant's Woman* (1969) that forged a template for new period fiction as it grafted a knowing modern narrator onto nineteenth-century romance. To the era of high modernism, period fiction looked merely silly. In our own, post-modern age, the past opens up again but only if we keep a self-conscious eye on the way we plunder it. Thus a witty, gently ironic voice steers even such a virtuoso reconstruction as Timothy Mo's novel of the British in Hong Kong, *An Insular Possession* (1986). Elsewhere, the Fowlesian switch between past and present narratives has served other writers well as in A. S. Byatt's *Possession* (1990), with its nimble interweaving of Victorian poetic passion and modern academic rivalry.

Once again, fine novelists can focus on epochs of trauma and transformation. The prolonged agony of the slave trade, the carnage of the trenches in the First World War, and of the Holocaust in the Second: these culture-shaping events marked late twentieth-century novelists as deeply as the trail of blood from the Bastille to Waterloo had their forebears. If Toni Morrison's *Beloved* (1987) can stand as a paradigm of the slave-era narrative, Pat Barker's *Regeneration* trilogy (1991–5) shows what becomes of First World War history when a late-century talent—laconic, feminist, irreverent but compassionate—gets to work on it. As for the Second World War, some critics claim that fiction will always make light of its crimes. Certainly, Thomas Keneally's *Schindler's Ark* (1982) impresses so much because its account of the high-living entrepreneur who saved Jews from the death camps cleaves so closely to the documentary record. Yet, with time, even some aspects of this war became a vehicle for a more playful art—nowhere better than in the erotic and satirical sidelights of Michael Ondaatje's *The English Patient* (1992).

Now, history and 'heritage' have grown into a leisure pursuit for millions. In this climate, the period novel can again entertain as well as edify. No contemporary writer has more devoted fans than Patrick O'Brian, whose vivid sequence of maritime yarns returns to the fountainhead of British historical fiction—the Napoleonic wars. The same epoch sets the stage for *Black Ajax* (1997), a glorious prize-fighting romance from the finest modern comic writer to scour the past for plots: George MacDonald Fraser.

Knowing humour has become an essential feature of the genre. Today's readers will have watched more *Blackadder* than they have swallowed Walter Scott. Julian Rathbone's clever Saxons-versus-Normans romp, *The Last English King* (1997), admits as much in its sly anachronistic gags. So historical fiction must now wear its period drag with an ironic grin. Yet this self-scrutinizing wit has not destroyed the form. On the contrary: it has helped to save it. History is bunk, jeered that arch-modernist, Henry Ford. But Ford is now history, while E. L. Doctorow's spellbinding mosaic of the tycoon and his times, *Ragtime* (1975), keeps his presence alive, and in better nick than any Model-T. Although the butt of mockery for most of a century, the historical novelist has enjoyed the last, and longest, laugh.

Top Twelve

WALTER SCOTT, *Ivanhoe* (1819)

NATHANIEL HAWTHORNE, *The Scarlet Letter* (1850)

CHARLES DICKENS, *A Tale of Two Cities* (1859)

LEO TOLSTOY, *War and Peace* (1863–9)

ROBERT LOUIS STEVENSON, *Weir of Hermiston* (1896)

VIRGINIA WOOLF, *Orlando* (1928)

ROBERT GRAVES, *I, Claudius* and *Claudius the God* (1934)

JOHN FOWLES, *The French Lieutenant's Woman* (1969)

E. L. DOCTOROW, *Ragtime* (1975)

TONI MORRISON, *Beloved* (1987)

PAT BARKER, *Regeneration* trilogy (1991–5)

GEORGE MACDONALD FRASER, *Black Ajax* (1997)

Humour

Nigel Williams

There is sometimes a section called 'humour' in bookshops. It's usually full of books (often illustrated) that are specifically designed to make people laugh. I always find such books rather sad. One of the nicest things about really great humorous story-tellers is that they usually don't consciously try and make you chuckle. It's simply that the way they see the world somehow makes the rest of us tune in to its absurdity. And often they surprise us into being moved or angered—perhaps because the best kind of laughter always lays you open to feeling.

Which is why I shall start with *David Copperfield* (1849–50). As well as being the wonderfully exciting story (based on Dickens's own life) of a young boy surviving a cruel stepfather, bullying contemporaries, and the betrayals of friendship, it also has some of the best running gags in all of our literature. And they perfectly illustrate how Dickens can be serious and funny at the same moment. Every time Mrs Micawber, referring to her improvident but lovable husband, says 'I will *never* desert Micawber!' we laugh again—not only because we recognize an all-too-familiar type of melodramatic Mum but also because, with each repetition of the joke, her lack of awareness of the fact that deserting the old rogue is precisely what she would like to do becomes more obvious and more touching. The other classic that makes me laugh out loud is *Tom Jones* (1749), Henry Fielding's tale of an orphan, brought up by the kindly Squire Allworthy, who displays one of the most important features generally associated with comic characters—an inability to keep his hands off the opposite sex.

The eighteenth century is not usually thought of as a time when people laughed out loud—it specializes in pointed elegance and wit. But they didn't spend all their time sneering at each other from the opposite ends of formal gardens. *Gulliver's Travels* (1726) is still one of the funniest books in the language, especially if, like me, you like lavatory jokes. Johnson said that once you had got the idea—that a normal-sized human moves first through a world of miniature Lilliputians and then through the land of Brobdingnagian giants—there wasn't much more to the book. He was wrong. Swift was a master of inspired nonsense, such as the section in the book where he describes two groups of Lilliputians quarrelling over which end to break open their boiled eggs. If you enjoy this side of his writing, dip into some of his shorter pieces, especially *A Meditation Upon a Broomstick* (1710), a hilarious send-up of pompous moralizing.

Swift was of course Irish, and, perhaps because they have never been encumbered by Roman logic, the Irish have always been masters of comedy. Under the pen-name of Flann O'Brien, an Irish civil servant turned journalist called Brian O'Nolan wrote several comic masterpieces, of which you might try *At Swim-Two-Birds* (1939) and *The Third Policeman* (1967). It was O'Brien who invented the wonderful idea that a man who spent too much time on a bicycle might well turn into one. My favourite of his, however, was originally written in the Irish language and is called, in English translation, *The Poor Mouth* (1941; translated 1973), an expression which is used about those people (do we not all know some of them?) who think exaggerating the hard circumstances of their life will win them a large and sympathetic audience. If you enjoy parody you could also try Stella Gibbons' *Cold Comfort Farm* (1932), a deadpan look at rural melodrama, or the American Terry Southern's *Candy* (1958), a hilarious send-up and endorsement of that staple of the Internet—pornography.

The other American choice on my list (although I love Mark Twain he never raises more than a smile) is *Catch-22* (1961) by Joseph Heller. Set on an American bombing base in the Second World War it manages to twist logic so cleverly that you find yourself howling with laughter at something as obscene and pointless as a war that destroyed millions of lives. Among the scores of wonderfully funny characters, we should perhaps single out Milo Minderbender, an entrepreneur of genius who sees mass bombing as just another business opportunity. We British don't have many books that use humour to face up to issues as important as this. One that does is *Animal Farm* (1945) by George Orwell, written just after the war that Heller describes. Originally turned down by London publishers (including T. S. Eliot) who were afraid of offending the Soviet Union, it is a short satirical fable about a group of animals who kick out their farmer-boss and set up their own free community. It is based very precisely on events in Russia and Europe from the revolution of 1917 down to the Yalta agreement at the end of the Second World War, in which Roosevelt, Stalin, and Churchill agreed to carve up the so-called civilized world between them. Detailed knowledge of the history is not necessary to enjoy this; the wonderfully drawn animal characters, including a splendid cart-horse called Boxer, would be funny even if Joe Stalin had never existed.

The heart of English humour, though, is whimsy and nonsense, of a peculiarly harmless kind—nowhere better expressed than in Lewis Carroll's *Alice's Adventures in Wonderland* (1865). Carroll, a mathematics don at Oxford, sends his heroine down a hole after a white rabbit with a fob watch and into a world where logic of a very special kind holds sway. Faced by events that are, in her own words 'curiouser and curiouser' and, like Gulliver, never entirely sure how big or small she is going to be, Alice manages to assert herself against characters as strange as a playing-card Queen who keeps trying to behead everybody. The obstacles in her path may not seem as frightening as giants or enemy bombers but the laughter she provokes is still liberating. Nearly all of the English School of comic fiction manages this trick of making the apparently ordinary—a passing animal, a leaf falling on a child's face—suddenly of tremendous significance. In *Three Men in a Boat* (1889) by Jerome K. Jerome, a fictionalized account of a camping trip up the Thames by three young men, the characters wrestling for hours with a tin of pineapple they are unable to open assumes the dimensions of one of the Labours of Hercules. In *Uncle Dynamite* (1948) by P. G. Wodehouse, the leading character is so traumatized by the prospect of an innocuous welcome-home committee that he ducks under the seat of his train compartment to avoid it, and in *The Mating Season* (1949) by the same author, the prospect of spending time with the son of his fearsome Aunt Agatha (*'She is a thug!'*) makes Bertie Wooster tremble like a man facing immediate execution. In *Scoop* (1938) by Evelyn Waugh (surely one of the funniest books of the century), the hero William Boot takes a journalistic expedition to Africa so seriously and so wrongfootedly that he tries to order a consignment of cloven sticks from a London department store in order to send messages by, from, and to the local natives. You will come out of all these books with a seriously altered sense of scale.

Waugh himself said that so-called 'escapist' literature should not be looked down upon, since it was often offering the reader escape from prison. He put Wodehouse in the category of writers offering this service to the reader but the lines of Wodehouse's humour are so classic—Jeeves and Wooster are straight out of Goldoni—that he almost manages to fool you into thinking he has some important purpose in mind. There is, however, some stuff that may look as if it belongs on the 'Humour' shelves—about which I was so unkind at the beginning of this article—but, because of the sheer skill of the writing or the miraculous liveliness of the central character, is in fact as good a class of nonsense as you will find anywhere. In a strong field I would suggest *The Secret Diary of Adrian Mole aged 13¾* (1982) by Sue Townsend, a small masterpiece in the tradition of the Grossmiths' *Diary of a Nobody* (1892) and Geoffrey Willans' inspired *Down with Skool* (1953; reprinted with three other Molesworth books in a collected edition, 1999). Its central character, Molesworth, has glasses, no dress sense, a 'grate friend' called Peason, and a classmate who goes under the name of Fotherington Thomas—a youth given to running about the games pitch squeaking 'hullo birds hullo sky!' 'He is', as Molesworth says, 'utterly wet and a weed' but it is hard to dislike him. And utterly impossible to take against the small, grubby boy who introduces him to us.

See also NIGEL WILLIAMS

Top Twelve

JONATHAN SWIFT, *Gulliver's Travels* (1726)

HENRY FIELDING, *Tom Jones* (1749)

CHARLES DICKENS, *David Copperfield* (1849–50)

LEWIS CARROLL, *Alice's Adventures in Wonderland* (1865)

JEROME K. JEROME, *Three Men in a Boat* (1889)

EVELYN WAUGH, *Scoop* (1938)

FLANN O'BRIEN, *The Poor Mouth* (1941)

GEORGE ORWELL, *Animal Farm* (1945)

P. G. WODEHOUSE, *Uncle Dynamite* (1948)

JOSEPH HELLER, *Catch-22* (1961)

SUE TOWNSEND, *The Secret Diary of Adrian Mole aged 13¾* (1982)

GEOFFREY WILLANS, *Molesworth* (1999)

India

Shirley Chew

India has sixteen official languages and, compared to the major literatures which exist in, for example, Hindi, Bengali, Urdu, Tamil, and Malayalam, Indian fiction in English is a newcomer to the literary scene. Its beginnings are usually linked to the publication of R. K. Narayan's first novel, *Swami and Friends* (1935), Mulk Raj Anand's *Untouchable* (1935), and Raja Rao's *Kanthapura* (1938). The 1930s was also a time when India's struggle for freedom from British rule was gathering momentum under the leadership of Gandhi. The novel as a literary form borrowed from the West was used by these Indian writers and their successors as a vehicle of social and political inquiry. It also served as the means by which the non-native reader could be carried across into the world of the text.

Untouchable describes a day in the life of a teenage latrine cleaner, and the ill-treatment he has to put up with as an outcaste. *Kanthapura* is an exuberant retelling, at once celebratory and elegiac, of the impact of Gandhi and the freedom movement on a small village in south India. The story-teller, a loquacious grandmother, is the repository of Kanthapura's history; and, woven into her rich account of actual events, legends, and myths are the overwhelming changes brought about through the influence of Moorthy, an educated young villager and a follower of Gandhi. Rao in this novel experiments in lively fashion with form and language, translating the idiom and rhythms of Kannada into English, and oral narrative into scripted fiction.

Unlike Anand and Rao, Narayan's concerns are not overtly political or social. He is best known for Malgudi, his fictional version of a small south Indian town and the setting of all his stories (with the exception of *The Grandmother's Tale*, 1993); for his bright canvas of nervy, self-conscious, and resourceful characters, and for his humanist vision. As well as sharp and intimate depictions of everyday life, Narayan's novels are imaginative reworkings of Hindu myths and philosophical concepts. The novel *The Guide* (1958) relates the familiar tale of a con man turned swami. In this particular case, Raju—shopkeeper, tourist guide, impresario, gaolbird—is transformed by the collective will of his simple followers into a holy man who can be expected, through his penance, to bring rain to the drought-stricken land. Along the way, questions are raised regarding the true nature of detachment (is Raju altogether selfless in undergoing the fast or is he indulging in another instance of play-acting?), of free will (should

Raju be regarded as the author of his own fate or as merely a participant in *lila*, the 'sport' of the World Soul?), and of *dharma* or duty (is Raju no more than trickster, or is he, through his several roles, fulfilling his duty in life which is clearly to guide, whether the people he is involved with are tourists or the spiritually helpless?).

On 15 August 1947 India became independent but the nation's triumph was marred by the sectarian violence which attended the Partition of the sub-continent. Khushwant Singh's *Train to Pakistan* (1956) recounts the tragedy as it befalls Mano Majra, a tiny village close to the frontier between India and Pakistan. The narrative moves on two levels: first, a realistic account of the rising tensions and hostilities among the Sikh and Muslim villagers who, until that moment, have lived peaceably together; second, a symbolic shadowing forth, through images of the river choked with dead bodies and the silent trains packed with carnage, of the unspeakable horror of the catastrophe.

The 1950s onwards saw the rise to prominence of women novelists: Kamala Markandaya, whose first book, *Nectar in a Sieve* (1954), treats of the plight of the landless poor in the face of natural disasters and capitalist exploitation; Attia Hosain whose *Sunlight on a Broken Column* (1961) counterpoints in intricate ways the public demand for *swaraj* (self-rule) in the 1930s and the private aspirations of Laila, a young Muslim woman, towards self-definition; and Ruth Prawer Jhabvala who, living in India from 1951 to 1976, transmutes her personal dilemmas as an expatriate into ironic comedy and satire. *A New Dominion* (1973) exposes in incisive ways the complicity of foreign visitors and local gurus in the fabrication of a spiritual India.

A dominant theme in the work of more recent writers is the retrieval of the past through self-conscious revisioning of history and myth. The spur to memory is often an unexpected crisis. This could be domestic, such as the unwelcome arrival of Nanda Kaul's granddaughter at her hilltop retreat in Anita Desai's *Fire on the Mountain* (1977) and the alleged business malpractices of Jaya's husband in Shashi Deshpande's *That Long Silence* (1988). Or it could be national in magnitude, such as the Emergency of 1975–7, which led to the reappraisal of the nation state in Nayantara Sahgal's *Rich Like Us* (1983). The process of preserving, destroying, and re-creating is realized in a most sensitive and complex form in Anita Desai's *Clear Light of Day* (1980) as the two sisters, Bim and Tara, return again and again to crucial moments in their lives in the old Delhi house, remaking them into patterns different yet complementary; and remaking themselves, too, in ways that extricate them from some of the ghosts of the past, and leave revealed their new-found maturity. Domestic plot mirrors national event in Amitav Ghosh's *The Shadow Lines* (1988), and to retrace the steps which led up to the death of the narrator's uncle, Tridib, is to uncover along the way the communal riots which overran Calcutta and Dhaka in 1964. It is also to question the divisive force of nationalism, and the invisible yet inexorable lines that such a force lays down between peoples and communities.

Along with *Rich Like Us* and *The Shadow Lines*, Vikram Seth's *A Suitable Boy* (1993) seeks to re-imagine the nation. In this voluminous, many stranded, and very readable work, the private life of passion, marriage-making, and family affairs is subject to critical examination along with the national story. The General Election of 1952 returned Congress to power but it is a Congress resting largely on its reputation as a force for freedom from foreign rule, and lacking in the integrity and the vision needed to lead the new India into the second half of the century. What is conceivable in private conduct—for example, the principled manner in which Lata goes about choosing a husband —does not seem possible in the larger sphere of public affairs, given the stranglehold of tradition and vested interests.

Today, a good number of the Indian novelists writing in English live outside India. As an emigrant from India and a newcomer in 'England, where I live, and Pakistan, to which my family moved against my will', the condition of migrancy is central to Salman Rushdie's aesthetic. How is it possible, from a distance and straddling so many different cultures, to write about India? *Midnight's Children* (1981) is an amazing display of the multiplicity of which Saleem, the narrator, is at once the victim and the celebrant. Should he approach his material as autobiography or history? Pursue the tale in realistic fashion or exploit its 'fantastic heart'? Narrate the story orally to Padma or write it out for the shadowy reader waiting behind her? No sooner has a narrative genre or convention been fixed upon than it is subverted, and the impression is given of Saleem manipulating his multicultural resources with gusto even as they continually threaten to overwhelm him.

A writer who has made her home in the United States, Bharati Mukherjee has in *The Middleman and Other Stories* (1989) created a full canvas of dis-placed characters—Indian, Filipino, Sri Lankan, Vietnamese, Italian, Caribbean, Chinese—all seeking in energetic ways to shape life to their own purposes. The familiar cultural baggage is not so easily shaken off, however, and some of the most poignant moments in these stories occur when characters are suspended between different and irreconcilable worlds: the Indian wife, for example, who is startled to see herself standing 'shameless' before an image in the mirror of her own nakedness; and the political refugee from Afghanistan who is unable to find the words to speak of the scars on his back.

Indian fiction in English continues to be as diverse and robust as it has been since the 1930s. Among the new and talented writers publishing today, mention has to be made of Githa Hariharan, whose stories in *The Art of Dying* (1993) are inimitable in combining precise social observation and surreal transformations; Amit Chaudhuri, whose *Afternoon Raag* (1993) is distinguished for its beautifully distilled prose; and Arundhati Roy, whose *The God of Small Things* (1997) is wonderfully powerful in its celebration of passion and in its social criticism.

Top Twelve

Raja Rao, *Kanthapura* (1938)

Khushwant Singh, *Train to Pakistan* (1956)

R. K. Narayan, *The Guide* (1958)

Attia Hosain, *Sunlight on a Broken Column* (1961)

Ruth Prawer Jhabvala, *A New Dominion* (1973)

Anita Desai, *Clear Light of Day* (1980)

Salman Rushdie, *Midnight's Children* (1981)

Nayantara Sahgal, *Rich Like Us* (1983)

Shashi Deshpande, *That Long Silence* (1988)

Amitav Ghosh, *The Shadow Lines* (1988)

Bharati Mukherjee, *The Middleman and Other Stories* (1989)

Vikram Seth, *A Suitable Boy* (1993)

Ireland

Patricia Craig

Irish fiction proper could be said to begin with Maria Edgeworth's sprightly *Castle Rackrent* of 1800, which concerns itself with 'the manners of the Irish Squires, before the Year 1782'. As a dissection of profligacy and imprudence, satirically framed, this work stands alone; and its central emblem, the ramshackle 'big house' itself, sparked off an entire tradition in Irish writing which continues up to the present in the work of authors such as Jennifer Johnston and Caroline Blackwood. Edgeworth never again matched the exuberance and inventiveness of her first novel—and it wasn't until late in the century that a recognizably modern note began to be struck by other writers, like George Moore, or Somerville and Ross in their admired novel *The Real Charlotte* (1894). Moore's stories in *The Untilled Field* (1903) are constructed with great artistry, and, by analysing priestly interference in secular affairs, pinpoint a crucial social problem.

George Moore got to grips with the moral climate of the day; James Joyce, who followed him, beginning with *Dubliners* in 1914, and going on to further illuminate his native city in *A Portrait of the Artist as a Young Man* (1914–15) and *Ulysses* (1922), revolutionized not only Irish writing, but literature in general, by turning his disenchantment with the country to a formidable literary purpose. Joyce is so colossal a presence in twentieth-century literature that it took some time before his successors in Ireland could get him into perspective. Those who were heavily influenced by him include Samuel Beckett (*More Pricks Than Kicks*, 1934), and Flann O'Brien (a.k.a. Brian O'Nolan and Myles na Gopaleen), whose best-known novel, *At Swim-Two-Birds* (1939), with its key elements of parody, high comedy, and Celtic convolution, is distinctly Joycean. Its successor, the wonderfully satirical *The Poor Mouth* (written in Irish in 1941 and not translated until 1973) pokes fun at excessive Irishness. Joyce's contemporary James Stephens's best-known work, *The Crock of Gold* (1912), is a fantasy of considerable sophistication and charm, as well as being pointed in its social criticisms; still in a minor key, in the same year, came George A. Birmingham's ingenious and comic narrative of the Home Rule crisis, *The Red Hand of Ulster*.

The dramatic events of the early twentieth century—the 1916 Rising, the War of Independence, the Civil War—were quickly enshrined in contemporary fiction. Ex-freedom fighters like the Corkmen Sean O'Faolain and Frank O'Connor drew on their own experiences of guerrilla warfare in their earliest story collections

(*Midsummer Night Madness*, 1932, and *Guests of the Nation*, 1931, respectively), before going on to epitomize the new Ireland in stories poised between comedy and poignancy (O'Connor), or abounding in grace, vigour, and complexity (O'Faolain). From *A Purse of Coppers* (1937) on, O'Faolain's breeziness and urbanity acted, in a sense, to subvert the provincial inertia and downbeat Catholicism of his Irish settings. With these authors, and their contemporaries O'Donnell and O'Flaherty, you're conscious of a certain disenchantment with the revolution which failed to produce a better, more progressive or just society. The Donegal novelist Peadar O'Donnell—also an ex-revolutionary— goes in for authenticity and gusto in his portrayals of remote communities of the north-west, while taking a stand against all forms of action, including republican action, not grounded in proper socialist principles. His *Adrigoole* (1928) is a powerful story—based on a true incident—of death by starvation, in the twentieth century; and in *The Big Windows* (1955) the title phrase stands for enlightenment of outlook, embodied in an island woman who, on marrying, comes to live among the mountains. Liam O'Flaherty, an Aranman, is best remembered for his novel *The Informer* (1925; filmed by John Ford in 1935), and for his historical trilogy beginning with *Famine* (1937). He writes with energy and directness.

From the other side—the Anglo-Irish side, and in the 'Big House' mode established by Maria Edgeworth—comes Elizabeth Bowen's *The Last September* (1929), a novel of the Black and Tan war, composed with striking subtlety and edginess, and ending with the burning by republicans of a great house, Danielstown (a fictional counterpart of Bowen's Court, which survived). Julia O'Faolain, in the Bowen tradition, has an ambitious novel, *No Country for Young Men* (1980), about political violence and the recovery of the past.

The Belfast novelist Michael McLaverty got off to an impressive start with *Call My Brother Back* (1939)—a child's-eye view of the disturbances of 1921, and a work of great economy and lucidity—and followed it up with *Lost Fields* (1942) which tells you all you want to know about Belfast street life, customs, and privations. John O'Connor's single novel, *Come Day—Go Day* (1948) does the same for Co. Armagh, though in a more high-spirited manner. Sam Keery's *The Last Romantic Out of Belfast* (1984) is a vivid, impressionistic account of a Northern Irish upbringing in the 1930s and 1940s.

The decade of the 1940s is generally held to be a rather dreary, backward-looking era in Irish life and literature; but Sean O'Faolain and Peadar O'Donnell (successive editors of the lively journal *The Bell*) kept the spirit of protest in fine fettle, and novels such as Patrick Kavanagh's *Tarry Flynn* (1948)—a pungent recreation of Co. Monaghan life—and Mervyn Wall's hilarious fantasies set in medieval, monastic Ireland, *The Unfortunate Fursey* (1946) and its sequel, appeared to temper the monotony. In 1955 came Brian Moore's first novel, *The Lonely Passion of Judith Hearne*, about a spinster and incipient alcoholic, in which the author's exasperation with his native city, Belfast, fuels a narrative of considerable dynamism. Moore's other Belfast novels, *The Feast of Lupercal* (1958), *The Emperor of Ice Cream* (1965), and *Lies of Silence* (1990) make equally compelling reading. (The last, written as comic realism, is still the most striking evocation of wartime Belfast in existence.)

Puritan Ireland, you might say, was in its last throes by the early 1960s; and writers such as John McGahern (*The Dark*, 1965), John Montague (in his collection of stories, *Death of a Chieftain*, 1964), and Edna O'Brien (*The Country Girls*, 1960) were responding in various heartening ways to the changing social climate. The ebullient Benedict Kiely, whose collection of stories, *A Journey to the Seven Streams*, came out in 1963, continued to exercise his ragbag imagination in the celebration of distinctive localities and idiosyncratic characters—though his tone turns darker with *Proxopera* (1977), which deals with the degradation of republicanism, as evinced by the Provisional IRA's campaign of violence. Certain old themes were appearing in new guises—the 'big house', for example, which gets a deadpan and very funny airing in Caroline Blackwood's *Great Granny Webster* (1977), is presented symbolically, and engagingly, in Jennifer Johnston's *The Gates* (1973), and surfaces in colourful, dense and surreal form in John Banville's *Birchwood* (1973). Molly Keane's *Good Behaviour* (1981)—her first novel for over twenty years—turns mistreatment, disappointment and entrapment (all in a big house setting) into the blackest of black comedies. Turning to provincial Ireland—this, in the hands of William Trevor, a master of the ironic and oblique, appears in its most invigorating incarnation. The title story from Trevor's 1972 collection *The Ballroom of Romance* has become something of a national archetype, while his later novels and stories—in particular, *Fools of Fortune* (1983) and *The News from Ireland* (1986)—engage to the full with historical and social pressures.

If Ireland, north and south, has finally caught up with the modern world, in ways both encouraging and dispiriting, this is being reflected in literature at all levels. The very popular Roddy Doyle (*The Snapper*, 1990) gains his effects from an onslaught of cunning and insouciance in Dublin's post-war housing estates, with an overlay of charm slapped on top of these qualities for good measure. More dispassionate than Dublin's new streetsmart fiction is Colm Toibin's *The Heather Blazing* (1992), about commitment to Ireland and its history—a familiar theme, but tellingly recharged here. Jennifer Johnston's *The Old Jest* (1979), set in 1920 and dealing with a young girl's involvement in

Ireland's business, displays the author's customary style which is beautifully balanced between delicacy and bravado. If you like a sparky tone, you might try Clare Boylan (*Holy Pictures*, 1983); or if you're more drawn to 'strange, sad lives' then Deirdre Madden (*One by One in the Darkness*, 1996) is the one for you. Dermot Healy's *A Goat's Song* (1993), which contains some crucial Irish oppositions, such as north and south, Protestant and Catholic, is intensely felt and evocative. Maurice Leitch (*The Liberty Lad*, 1965) and Glenn Patterson (*Burning Your Own*, 1988) have both contributed to the literature of communal psychic disorder. Seamus Deane's first novel, *Reading in the Dark* (1996), details an exceptionally pungent Derry upbringing. And with intriguing newcomers such as Anne Enright (*The Wig My Father Wore*, 1995) and Robert McLiam Wilson (*Eureka Street*, 1996) playfully extending the scope, you have to concede that the whole field of Irish fiction remains in a thriving state.

Top Twelve

MARIA EDGEWORTH, *Castle Rackrent* (1800)

JAMES STEPHENS, *The Crock of Gold* (1912)

JAMES JOYCE, *A Portrait of the Artist as a Young Man* (1914–15)

PEADAR O'DONNELL, *Adrigoole* (1928)

ELIZABETH BOWEN, *The Last September* (1929)

SEAN O'FAOLAIN, *A Purse of Coppers* (1937)

FLANN O'BRIEN, *The Poor Mouth* (1941)

EDNA O'BRIEN, *The Country Girls* (1960)

BRIAN MOORE, *The Emperor of Ice Cream* (1965)

CAROLINE BLACKWOOD, *Great Granny Webster* (1977)

JENNIFER JOHNSTON, *The Old Jest* (1979)

WILLIAM TREVOR, *The News From Ireland* (1986)

Magic realism

Carol Birch

The term magic realism was originally applied to French and German surrealist artists in the 1920s. The Cuban writer Alejo Carpentier was the first to use it in relation to fiction, in the prologue to *The Kingdom of This World* (1949), his novel about the Haitian Revolution. In this, Carpentier fused realism with Afro-Caribbean folk traditions to convey a history of oppression and slavery, a world in which reason appears to have broken down. Carpentier's novel made time fluid, synchronous, and looping rather than linear. Magic realism was, he claimed, 'exclusive to the Americas', arising from the singular history of the New World, the only sane response in the face of overwhelming insanity being to spin off into the dream-sense of wild imaginings and make of it something profound and uplifting.

Granted, magic realism has seen a remarkable flowering in Latin America, but when we look at its typical elements—myth, dream, religion, the fantastic and absurd—it's clear that the thing itself is as old as time and as widespread as story-telling. What distinguishes magic realism from straightforward fantasy is that its roots are firmly in this world. The great otherworlds—Narnia, Gormenghast, Ringworld—are pure fantasy. Magic realism builds an alternative reality upon recognizable foundations—Moscow, London, India—but strangely moulds and bends them, affording the magical elements the same status as the mundane. Elements of magic realism turn up in writers from Dickens to Steinbeck. It thrives on chaos. For this reason it has lent itself readily as the voice of the colonized, the uprooted, and oppressed. Fractured realities, however, can take any number of forms.

Franz Kafka's *The Trial* (1925) is magic realism. A true classic of alienation with its famous opening: 'Someone must have been telling lies about Joseph K., for without having done anything wrong he was arrested one fine morning,' *The Trial* is always sinister and often nightmarish. K. is never told what he's supposed to have done but is guilty by dint of his very existence. Human life is an insoluble enigma, the world absurd and menacing, existence pointless. K.'s story is told in sharp, measured prose, as is *The Unbearable Lightness of Being* (1984), by another Czech writer, Milan Kundera. Though set in Prague just after the Soviet invasion, this derives its power less from politics than philosophical sophistication. Taking as its starting-point Nietzsche's theory of eternal return, it unfolds the erotic, gently meandering tale of Tomas and

Tereza, a philandering surgeon and his wife. Kundera confronts the nihilism of Kafka and pushes through to the weightlessness of acceptance.

The same techniques, of dislocation and the endless recurrence of events in a version of time that is whole and round rather than fixed and linear, can be used in an aptly unlimited number of ways. Take *The Master and Margarita*, in which the Devil, a man called Woland, appears in Moscow with his familiars, a monstrous cat and a naked girl. All hell breaks loose, literally. Inexplicably, in the midst of the madness Woland takes under his wing the Master and Margarita, a writer in an asylum and the woman he loves. Mikhail Bulgakov wrote this under Stalinist oppression between 1928 and 1938. It was not published till thirty years after his death. The symbolism is clear when one learns that Stalin for some reason protected Bulgakov at a time when writers were being persecuted. Chaotic, garish, and violent, *The Master and Margarita* is a dazzling nightmare.

Similarly unrestrained and energetic is Salman Rushdie, who uses magic realist techniques to express the mingling of east and west. Saleem Sinai, in *Midnight's Children* (1981) epitomizes the post-colonial voice. One of the thousand and one children born at midnight on the dawn of India's independence, Saleem tells stories which teem and multiply in an anarchic cocktail of history, myth, and popular culture. As a liberating device for the writer, magic realism is wonderfully efficient; any law can be broken. A master lawbreaker is Gabriel García Márquez. Like Rushdie a born story-teller, Márquez is humorous, gentle, and humane. *One Hundred Years of Solitude* (1967) relates the history of the mythical Colombian shanty town of Macondo, home of the mystical Buendia family, for whom ghosts are real and time exists as in dreams, obeying no laws.

Chilean writer Isabel Allende is often compared to Márquez. *The House of the Spirits* (1985) tells the Trueba family saga up to the period after the Chilean coup in 1973, in which Allende's own uncle was assassinated. Patriarchy here is represented by the conservative Esteban Trueba, spirit and intuition by his telepathic wife Clara. Allende's perspective is staunchly feminist and deeply romantic, qualities found with darker, more sinister tones in Angela Carter's work. Carter loved fairy-tales and retold them lushly and brilliantly in *The Bloody Chamber* (1979). Melanie, the orphaned adolescent heroine of *The Magic Toyshop* (1967) is also in a fairy-tale, though it masquerades as 'melancholy, down-on-its-luck South London'. Sent from the country to live in the house of her frightening Uncle Philip and his bullied family, dumb Aunt Margaret and two red-haired Irish brothers, Melanie's sexual awakening takes place in a quaint, nightmarish world, rich in Gothic and Freudian tints. Eroticism is well served by magic realism. Leopold Bloom's sado-masochistic fantasies in *Ulysses* (1922) are essentially magic realism, as is the scene that concludes Carlos Fuentes' *Terra Nostra* (1975), in which the sex act becomes a startlingly literal fusion of two bodies, and exaggeration overflows into an image of cosmic procreation that sends us spinning back to Genesis.

In fact, if you are at all interested in magic realism, *Terra Nostra* is crucial reading. It is a vast erudite book, rich, poetic, and mystical. Here time has thrown off all constraints. History is scrambled: Philip II of Spain marries Elizabeth Tudor, a boy falls into the Seine and is washed up on a beach in the past, the past invades the present, and all stages of history coexist.

Not surprisingly, given the vivid fairy lore and troubled history of Ireland, a dose of magic realism seems to run through its writers' veins. Joyce certainly has it, as do James Stephens, and Samuel Beckett of course; but perhaps one of the most sublime pieces ever is Flann O'Brien's *The Third Policeman*, completed in 1940 but, in a scenario familiar from Bulgakov, not published for another twenty-seven years and then only after the writer's death. Quite unlike anything else, *The Third Policeman* is a comic nightmare set in a recognizable rural Ireland, in which such banal entities as bumbling village policemen are keepers of the secrets of infinity, watchers at the gates of a cosily familiar but skewed hell. O'Brien had already tampered with time in *At Swim-Two-Birds* (1939), in which a rag-bag of characters from Irish folklore, Hollywood, and the Dublin pub scene set off together on a hilarious ramble. This is the book in which the narrator's own characters turn upon him and demand autonomy.

O'Brien and others strike at the very foundations of fiction, the distinction between the creator and the creation; they assume the right of the created to fight back, the creator to appear as a character and participate in the action, much as the Word became flesh. Other writers who have played this game are John Fowles and Paul Auster, but the Italian writer Italo Calvino took a sideways step with the conceit in *If on a Winter's Night a Traveller* (1979). From the first line he involves the reader as a participant along with himself: 'You are about to begin reading Italo Calvino's new novel.' It is a book about You, the reader of books. Intrigued, you follow into a chilly possible spy story which dumps you abruptly, as the fictional You, the Reader, finds that his book is defective and returns it to the shop. There the Reader meets Ludmilla, who also has a defective copy of the book *If on a Winter's Night a Traveller* by Italo Calvino. The plot thickens as you follow the obviously attracted but circumspect pair on a quest through the repeatedly frustrated beginnings of ten separate novels, the first lines of which, when put together, make Zen-like sense.

Calvino's sophistication anticipates the short fictions of the Argentinian writer Jorge Luis Borges. Magic realism readily combines the scientific and the spiritual, and Borges is the prime example of this. He can appear dry at first, mathematically measured and academic in style, formidably intellectual in tone. Closer attention, however, reveals a liberated imagination, a gently ironic eye, and a profound spirituality. Borges is ideal for browsing. Dip in and come up with a delicate alchemical gem such as *The Rose of Paracelsus* (in *Shakespeare's Memory*, 1983), or a disorienting theological riddle like *Three Versions of Judas* (in *Labyrinths*, 1953). Borges presents life as a labyrinth, a fermentation of endless conundrums, unknowable but ineffably beautiful. If magic realism is story-telling freed to be as playful and profound as it likes, then Borges is its ultimate practitioner.

But it's a broad church and this is only a little of what's out there. Try also Luisa Valenzuela, Mario Vargas Llosa, Guillermo Cabrera Infante, Emma Tennant, Juan Rulfo, Peter Carey, Günter Grass . . . the list goes on.

See also CAROL BIRCH

Top Twelve

FRANZ KAFKA, *The Trial* (1925)

ALEJO CARPENTIER, *The Kingdom of This World* (1949)

JORGE LUIS BORGES, *Labyrinths* (1953), or his *Collected Fictions* (1998)

MIKHAIL BULGAKOV, *The Master and Margarita* (1966–7, in full in 1973)

GABRIEL GARCÍA MÁRQUEZ, *One Hundred Years of Solitude* (1967)

ANGELA CARTER, *The Magic Toyshop* (1967)

FLANN O'BRIEN, *The Third Policeman* (1967)

CARLOS FUENTES, *Terra Nostra* (1975)

ITALO CALVINO, *If on a Winter's Night a Traveller* (1979)

SALMAN RUSHDIE, *Midnight's Children* (1981)

ISABEL ALLENDE, *The House of the Spirits* (1982)

MILAN KUNDERA, *The Unbearable Lightness of Being* (1984)

Romance

Elizabeth Buchan

'Reader, I married him.'

In perhaps one of the most quoted (and misquoted) of fictional resolutions, Charlotte Brontë brings to a close a novel which an interested publisher had requested to be 'wild, wonderful and thrilling'. It is the finale of an emotional and physical journey brought to a conclusion by that most prosaic of rites of passage: marriage. Yet it is one which we perceive (and romantic fiction still tends heavily to this view) as a logical consequence of the erotic and spiritual experiences of passionate love for another human being—feelings which, incidentally, are absolutely democratic, for love is universal and available to all. 'For some of us, love will be the great creative triumph of our lives . . . and can lead the lover to transcending truths', suggests Ethel Spector Person in *Love and Fateful Encounters*. In this respect, romantic fiction could be seen as offering a template for personal resolution and a proponent of social order.

This is certainly true of Jane and her Mr Rochester. More than a century and a half later, *Jane Eyre* (1847) is still wild and wonderful—'one of the oddest novels ever written,' argues Angela Carter, 'a delirious romance replete with elements of pure fairy tale, given its extraordinary edge by the sheer emotional intelligence of the writer, the exceptional sophistication of her heart.'

A romance then, leavened by intelligence, intense emotion, psychological acuity, a passionate sense of natural justice, counterbalanced by Gothic thrills and a galloping narrative, it is a novel that educates the reader in the workings of the human heart and in the continuing battle between the individual's wishes and society's hypocritical and treacherous demands. Jane is abused by a so-called 'aunt', starved in the name of philanthropy at Lowood School, nearly led into the sin of bigamy by a man who professes to love her, and asked, in the name of religion, to sell herself in marriage to a zealot. Her struggle to find her place as a woman and a member of society is a profound and difficult one and nearly costs her her life and sanity. Despite the Gothic embellishments— the fire, the mad first Mrs Rochester, Jane's dramatic flight across the moors— the author has a shrewd grasp of social injustice. 'Do you think', cries Jane to Mr Rochester, 'because I am poor, plain and little, I am souless and heartless?' In one of the great affirmations in literature, she adds, 'You think wrong—I have as much soul as you—and full as much heart.'

Jane Eyre is the quintessential romantic novel with enduring appeal. Only a quick glance at the best-seller lists is necessary to reveal that romantic fiction dominates the market with novels such as Catherine Cookson's (who disliked being categorized as romantic in the narrow sense), *The Horse Whisperer* (1995) by Nicholas Evans, Rosamunde Pilcher's phenomenally selling *The Shell Seekers* (1987) or even, Sebastian Faulks' *Charlotte Gray* (1998), whose heroine contrives to have herself parachuted undercover into France in order to find her shot-down lover—a selfless/selfish gesture which underlines how intimately linked private concerns are to great historic events.

Romantic fiction has had an interesting, protean history, and not a few rough patches. In its early evolving form, a romance—usually written in verse —was an adventure. It was meant to entertain (and still does) and took as its subject courtly love and chivalry, often incorporating myth and fantasy. Those characteristics clung to it, via the story-cycles of King Arthur, the lays of French courtly love, and the early German poets. Chaucer paid it the compliment of satire in his *Tale of Sir Thopas* (in *The Canterbury Tales*, around 1387) and, during the English renaissance, both Spenser and Philip Sidney elaborated on the pastoral romance, but, with the development of the novel, the focus shifted and narrowed. In his dictionary, Samuel Johnson defined romantic as 'wild landscape'. This offers a clue to romantic fiction. For evident in the best novels is the wild landscape of mood, emotion, and psychology and the strange, and sometimes terrible, power of love—a heightened, altered consciousness which is not necessarily directed at another person but which always has the power to effect change.

Of course, authors pick and choose and borrow elements. Jane Austen gave us *Pride and Prejudice* (1813), arguably the best romantic comedy ever. Here we see the form developing but with an ironic style which is in direct contrast to the lively but preachy thrills of her contemporary, Maria Edgeworth. Boy meets girl, they encounter obstacles (in this case their own natures), overcome them and, thus, the way is open to the altar. But inserted into the bright and sparkling prose, there is a debate about the nature of love and marriage and also anger and terror. To be poor, unconnected, and female in this society was doom indeed. Later in the century Thomas Hardy observed much the same formula in *Far From the Madding Crowd* (1874)—the story of a young, headstrong girl and her relationship with three men. 'Romance', he tells us, taking leave of the chastened Bathsheba, 'grows up between the interstices of reality.' However, if we are to judge by the fatalistic, coincidence-strewn events and the haunting nostalgia and lyricism of his stories, he is not quite convinced.

The statement is better applied to F. M. Mayor's neglected classic, *The Rector's Daughter* (1924), a deceptively quiet novel of burning passion and renunciation. During the 1930s, in a dull East Anglian village, Mary, the rector's daughter, falls in love with Mr Herbert the curate. It goes wrong, and he marries another woman. But her love does not end and the one adulterous kiss she experiences irradiates the rest of her short life. This is an unforgettable and unerring portrait of duty observed at immense cost and of suffering.

Whether consciously or unconsciously, a natural justice—which can be interpreted as a kind of feminism—was creeping into the pages of these novels. The far better known *Rebecca* (1938) by Daphne du Maurier is tougher, showier, and heavier handed. A shy virgin marries an older man and he takes her to live in his beautiful house on the Cornish coast. Soon we are in dubious territory. Jealousy, sexual domination, cruelty, and murder, plus a gripping narrative with Gothic thrills, keep the reader glued to the page. But with whom does the power rest in the end? The answer lies in the overnight maturation of the shy virgin into the woman who chooses complicity for the sake of love. Quite properly, romantic fiction has its murky side.

'Women', wrote Stendhal, 'are hungry for emotion, anywhere and at any time.' During the twentieth century the market place fell over itself to feed this hunger. A huge industry for light, escapist fiction flourished, offering readers relief from the realities of living with Mr Right and the struggle to work the night shift. In *Friday's Child* (1944), the peerless Georgette Heyer gives us a template for stylish elegance, a lesson in the ridiculous, and a masterpiece of subversive satire on the literary form—not to mention the sheer pleasure of being made to laugh.

Today it is true that these novels, whose increasingly effective heroines can either dominate boardrooms or, *à la* Bridget Jones, battle to lose weight and find a boyfriend, are written and read by women. In this respect they provide a key to the female psyche. Here are dramatized the increasing conflict between biology and career, the desire for revenge on an unequal society, and, in direct counterpoint, the recognition of a female eroticism which responds to the freebooting, but ultimately tameable, male—the myth of Beauty and the Beast has not remained fresh without reason. In the age of equality, the phallic, plundering male is no longer acceptable and the challenge is to redefine those erotic truths within a rapidly changing context if only by presenting a contrast. Arthur Golden's *Memoirs of a Geisha* (1997) relies on a meticulously detailed pre-Second World War background of a sexual underworld whose entrapment was total. His story is of a female captivity, but it is also the one of the maiden immured in the cave, emerging with the help of love and self-knowledge—and the chivalric Chairman—into freedom.

As ever, the best writers are untrammelled by rules or formulas. Emily Brontë's *Wuthering Heights* (1847) envisages a transcendental love. In *Not That Sort of Girl* (1987), Mary Wesley slots a lifelong love-affair between Rose and Milo in between the social structures. Love, she seems to saying, is only possible when it is conducted illicitly. In contrast, Sue Gee's *The Hours of the Night* (1996), an intense and lyrical evocation of homosexual and heterosexual love set in a Welsh valley, mixes suffering and a non-sectarian spirituality to achieve reconciliation.

From the Gothic and swashbuckling, to the historical romance and the dramas of morality, feminism, and good old-fashioned man-meets-woman, this is a tradition that is hugely enjoyed. At its best it throws up the classic novels in our language: powerful, life-enhancing, revelatory, whose authors neither despise the power of the gripping narrative nor what Margaret Forster characterizes as 'the spirit of mystery, adventure and excitement'.

See also ELIZABETH BUCHAN

Top Twelve

JANE AUSTEN, *Pride and Prejudice* (1813)

CHARLOTTE BRONTË, *Jane Eyre* (1847)

EMILY BRONTË, *Wuthering Heights* (1847)

THOMAS HARDY, *Far From the Madding Crowd* (1874)

F. M. MAYOR, *The Rector's Daughter* (1924)

DAPHNE DU MAURIER, *Rebecca* (1938)

GEORGETTE HEYER, *Friday's Child* (1944)

MARY WESLEY, *Not That Sort of Girl* (1987)

NICHOLAS EVANS, *The Horse Whisperer* (1995)

SUE GEE, *The Hours of the Night* (1996)

ARTHUR GOLDEN, *Memoirs of a Geisha* (1997)

SEBASTIAN FAULKS, *Charlotte Gray* (1998)

Russia

Lesley Chamberlain

Russian literature mainly developed from the late eighteenth century as the country's social and political conscience. Repeatedly since then, writers have reworked key historical events and relived tragic political epochs. Their constant question is: how should we live? Any reader who works through the great novels chronologically will see this question echoing self-consciously down the generations. This is one of the world's most philosophical literatures, yet also one of the most straightforward. The burning desire for social reform, coupled with constant speculation about Russia's identity and future, tends to be expressed in lengthy, easy-to-read realism.

Alexander Pushkin, born on the cusp of the nineteenth century, is best known abroad for *Eugene Onegin* (1823–31), the lovelorn novel in verse which Tchaikovsky later set to wistful, enchanting music. Pushkin also loved historical subjects which he brought to life in limpid modern prose. The short novel *The Captain's Daughter* (1836) draws its colour from the 1770s, when a bandit pretender to the throne, Pugachev, terrorized provincial Russia in the name of social justice. It is a vivid and dramatic story of love and war and a young man's initiation into life, with more than a touch of swashbuckling Romantic adventure. Pushkin went on to die young in a duel.

Adventurousness is even more true of Pushkin's near-contemporary, Mikhail Lermontov. But Lermontov's short novel *A Hero of Our Times* (1840) suddenly moves Russian writing into the modern world. Its young anti-hero, a disaffected soldier in the Caucasus who feels himself most at home in nature, is preoccupied with the existential themes of will and identity, and that perennial Russian question 'how to live'. He kidnaps a woman and at last shoots a man in a bid to discover the limits of freedom.

The Ukrainian-born writer Nikolai Gogol, who finally burnt his manuscripts and starved himself to death, also reads like our contemporary, because of the way he approaches the big questions through laughter. His 1842 masterpiece *Dead Souls* is a crazy satire on the corruption and inertia of nineteenth-century provincial Russian life. Imagine Dickensian characters in a Russian setting, and an author fond of butting in on his own narrative, and you will have a sample of Gogol's unique world. His short stories have the stamp of the absurd, too, but with cruelty and hopelessness lurking behind the laughter. 'The Nose'

(1836) and 'The Overcoat' (1842) depict the little man who feels powerless in society and quite deserves his fate.

Fyodor Dostoevsky considers violence and powerlessness in *Crime and Punishment* (1866), a detective classic which is also a study of free will and guilt. In *Notes from Underground* (1864) Dostoevsky uses a rebellious anti-hero to explore the subjects of power and reason. His greatest religious and philosophical novel is *The Brothers Karamazov* (1880). A way into this powerful, difficult book is to read the famous extract called 'The Grand Inquisitor'. Christ and the Inquisitor meet in a legendary clash between compassion and worldly power.

Leo Tolstoy is often considered Dostoevsky's opposite in mood. Tolstoy probes the surface of conventional upper-class Russian life to expose the tragedies and insincerities lurking behind love and success. The characters he approves of tend to leave the city and lead simple lives close to the peasantry. But no thematic description can do justice to Tolstoy's magnificent long novels *War and Peace* (1863–9), set against Napoleon's 1812 invasion of Russia, and the classic story of adultery, *Anna Karenina* (1873–7). The characters are so vital they leap off the page. This is timeless, brilliant, endlessly enjoyable story-telling.

Ivan Turgenev is almost a miniaturist beside Tolstoy. While *First Love* (1860), the story of a young boy enchanted by his father's mistress, is a classic love-story, written with great delicacy, the novel *Fathers and Sons* (1862) has more to say about the fate of Russia. Young men who as students grow restless with static provincial life suggest how revolution will one day come upon Russia, helped on by a few obscure foreign philosophical ideas.

A uniquely tender and funny novel by Ivan Goncharov turns its back on politics. The eponymous hero of *Oblomov* (1859) is an aristocrat happy, against the strivings of ambitious men all around him, never to get out of his dressing-gown.

Revolution as a theme, also reflected in a transformation of writing style, bursts upon Russian literature as the twentieth century begins. It simmers away in Maxim Gorky's compellingly realistic evocations of harsh working life in the autobiographical trilogy *My Childhood* (1913), *My Apprenticeship* (1915), and *My Universities* (1921). By contrast Andrei Bely's *St Petersburg* (1922), a meditation on violence, has an experimental feel, close to the mood of symbolist poetry and avant-garde painting. Evgeny Zamyatin emigrated rather than toe the political line. His futuristic dystopian novel *We* (1920–1) has often been compared both to Huxley's *Brave New World* (1932), which it helped inspire, and Orwell's *Nineteen Eighty-Four* (1949). It turns on the theme that there can be no such thing as the final, perfect society.

For writing reflecting Russia's civil war after the Revolution the *Red Cavalry* stories (1923–5) of Isaac Babel are unsurpassed in their steely vividness and brutality. Mikhail Sholokov's authorship of *Quiet Flows the Don* (1928–40) has been questioned, but this panoramic novel of village life in southern Russia remains a superb, engrossing read, reflecting the fate of families and communities forced into fighting on different sides. The less-well-known writer Anatoly Mariengof balances 1920s gaiety with the increasing misery of wartime hunger in his cinematic novel *Cynics* (written 1928, published 1991). Boris Pasternak's *Dr Zhivago* (1957) is a great love-story and poetic meditation set in divided and famine-stricken Russia. In quite a different but equally striking modern style, Vladimir Nabokov, who emigrated at the start of the Revolution, created a nightmarish experience of totalitarian power in *Bend Sinister* (1947).

Mikhail Bulgakov stayed as a witness of the terror of the 1930s. His *The Master and Margarita* (1928–38) is probably the most loved fiction in Russia this century. This rich novel, finally published in full in 1973, over thirty years after Bulgakov's death, reflects by comic and fantastic means the corrupt life of 'official' writers, but its major subject is the tragedy of people either 'disappeared' by the secret police, or condemned as insane. *The Heart of a Dog* (1925), a novella about a transplant, chillingly reflects the attempt to create a post-revolutionary 'new' man.

In the Soviet period the dictates of official Socialist Realism forced novelists into a propagandizing mould. Viktor Nekrasov's *In the Trenches of Stalingrad* (1946) is nevertheless a vivid and realistic war novel. Much of Andrei Platonov's work went unpublished in his lifetime, but with the end of the Soviet Union has been rediscovered. *The Foundation Pit* is a short, unforgettable novel about how the enforced confiscation of private land and property in the 1920s turned confused and numbed human beings into brutes. But for the sheer extent and realism of his revelations, Alexander Solzhenitsyn towers over all others as a chronicler of his political times. *One Day in the Life of Ivan Denisovich* (1962) brought the taboo subject of Stalin's labour camps briefly into the Russians' own public domain before political repression returned. His later novels *Cancer Ward* and *The First Circle*, published outside Russia in 1968, continued his powerful reassessment of Soviet history. Vassily Grossman's *Life and Fate* (1980), another prose work centred on the battle of Stalingrad, is a fine indictment of the totalitarian age, though of such vast proportions that most readers will probably find Yury Dombrovsky's *The Keeper of Antiquities* (1966) more satisfying, with its well-drawn characters and mixture of comedy and menace. In Anatoly Rybakov's hands the novel of historical and political revelation has the engaging feel of a Tolstoyan saga. His two documentary novels, *Children of the Arbat* (1987) and *Fear* (1988), peppered with historical characters, vividly convey the darkest years of Soviet Russia.

For the most part it has been male prose writers who have unveiled the horrors of the public world this century. Women writers like Lyudmilla Petrushevskaya have rather depicted the effects of the Soviet system in the personal sphere. Petrushevskaya's *Time: The Night* (1992) shows us strained relationships and hopeless, burdened lives led in a cramped apartment: a harrowing read. Since the end of the Soviet Union writers have relished their ideological freedom and experimented with many styles. More women writers have emerged and older writers have been rediscovered. Viktor Pelevin stands out for his fantastic novellas *Omon Ra* and *The Yellow Arrow* (1994). But above all Venedikt Yerofeev's *Moscow Stations*, not available earlier in Russia, is a classic: a short, lovable monologue by an alcoholic which manages to evoke all the richness of the Russian tradition and the religious faith of the people, while showing the desperation the Soviet system inflicted. Yerofeev's drunken odyssey is literally a journey to the end of the line.

Top Twelve

NIKOLAI GOGOL, *Dead Souls* (1842)

IVAN GONCHAROV, *Oblomov* (1859)

IVAN TURGENEV, *Fathers and Sons* (1862)

FYODOR DOSTOEVSKY, *Crime and Punishment* (1867)

LEO TOLSTOY, *War and Peace* (1863–9)

MAXIM GORKY, *My Childhood* (1913), *My Apprenticeship* (1915), and *My Universities* (1921)

ANDREI BELY, *St Petersburg* (1922)

MIKHAIL SHOLOKHOV, *Quiet Flows the Don* (1928–40)

VLADIMIR NABOKOV, *Bend Sinister* (1947)

ALEXANDER SOLZHENITSYN, *Cancer Ward* (1968)

MIKHAIL BULGAKOV, *The Master and Margarita* (completed 1938, published 1973)

VENEDIKT YEROFEEV, *Moscow Stations* (written 1970 and first published in the West in 1977)

Science fiction

Livi Michael

Comic book adventure stories in which the unpronounceable meets the incomprehensible and battle ensues? Or a visionary blend of science and philosophy?

Both descriptions apply. Science fiction (sf) is a vast and accommodating genre; flexible enough to include the thriller, the romance, the adventure story, horror, and even the historical novel. The differences between the popular television series *Star Trek* and *The X-Files* should give you an idea of the scope, also of the effect time has had on both the style and the concerns of sf. To quote from a recent documentary: 'The future ain't what it used to be.'

This century the genre has been dominated by film. *Star Wars, Alien, ET*, have reached parts of the public who would never read sf. But the links between sf, comic books, and popular film have helped to undermine its respectability as a literary genre, though its roots are respectable enough. Think of Mary Shelley's *Frankenstein* (1818); a novel now considered a literary classic but which contains key elements of science fiction—a fascination with the possibilities of science and a concern for their social or moral implications. Echoes of the *Frankenstein* theme recur throughout sf; most notably in Philip K. Dick's *Do Androids Dream of Electric Sheep?* (1968) the novel from which the film *Bladerunner* was taken.

Many of the predictions of sf have come true this century, from moonlandings to satellites and black holes. Many sf writers come from a scientific background. Some are more famous for their literary output (Asimov, Clarke), others for their scientific status (Carl Sagan, Buzz Aldrin). Readers have found this kind of cross-fertilization a problem, citing narratives overloaded with technological information and unbelievable dialogue. But in the hands of the best writers, sf is a tool for reflecting contemporary society in much the same way that Swift's satires reflect to us all that is comic, grotesque, appalling about his world, and indeed our own.

H. G. Wells is one of the great originators of sf. His novels have inspired writers from Asimov, Heinlein, and Clarke, to, most recently, Ronald Wright, who in *A Scientific Romance* (1999) imagines the return of the time machine to London. Joseph Conrad called Wells a 'realist of the fantastic'. He is meticulous about the scientific background and this, together with his pithy, understated narration, makes his fantastic tales entirely convincing. Wells's mechanics may have dated since he wrote *The Time Machine* (1895), but the issue of time travel remains a central one for sf writers. And Wells's social analysis has been at least as influential as his scientific concepts. In *The Time Machine* his future world is divided into two classes, the subterranean workers, called Morlocks, and the decadent Eloi. Here, as elsewhere, his critique of sexual relationships is also highly provocative.

In *Nineteen Eighty-Four* (1949) George Orwell extends this social analysis into a devastating critique of the principles and processes of political rule. The world of *Nineteen Eighty-Four* is divided into the Inner Party, or 'Brain of the State', the Outer Party, 'its hands', and the Proles, who survive in a kind of squalid freedom. The plot centres around the attempts of one Outer Party Member, Winston Smith, to escape the totalitarian society in which he exists. His failure results not in execution, but, more chillingly, conversion, the surrender of his will. *Nineteen Eighty-Four* contains the famous sentence, 'If you want a picture of the future, imagine a boot stamping on a human face forever.' Not to be read as a pick-me-up, therefore, but for its searing analysis of the psychology of power, and its inexorable, unerring prose.

Isaac Asimov applies Wells's pragmatic, erudite style to the dazzling scope and surreal possibilities of twentieth-century science. His *Foundation* series (1951–93) has been called 'the most honoured epic in science fiction'. Two Foundations are set up at opposite ends of the galaxy. Between them they control both physical science and 'psychohistory'—the science of predicting human behaviour by mathematics. Inevitably conflict arises.

Contemporary social analysis combines with exploration of the possible in works that are both entertaining and profound; such as Robert Heinlein's *Stranger in a Strange Land* (1961) and Arthur C. Clarke's *Childhood's End* (1953), in which Clarke convincingly portrays an alien invasion of earth. Disconcertingly, the aliens are not hostile but supply us with everything we need. The great 'what if' of the novel is—what if the need for human effort and curiosity were removed? Clarke tells his tale with consummate skill, and the moment when the alien finally reveals himself to waiting humanity is classic sf.

Frank Herbert's *Dune* (1965) is the first of six novels set on the eponymous desert planet. The desert is inhabited by enormous sandworms that produce a mind-altering substance called melange. This and water are the most precious commodities. In the course of learning to control their environment and their own fateful vulnerability, the inhabitants develop not only technology but mysticism.

The first sf novel I ever read was Ursula Le Guin's *The Dispossessed* (1974). I was impressed enough by it to subsequently read all her others. Two worlds are contrasted—Anarres, on which an anarchist system prevails and resources are shared, and Urras, a violent, hierarchical world. Le Guin is a subtle writer and her story consists of far more than a contrast between utopia and dystopia. Her landscapes are compelling and her spare prose memorable and haunting.

Between 1979 and 1983 Doris Lessing produced five sf novels collectively titled *Canopus in Argos.* Each is self-contained, and my favourite is the first. *Shikasta* (1979) has its starting point in the Old Testament. Johor (Jehovah) is an emissary of the Canopeans. From his standpoint Lessing explores the religious and political heritage of humanity in a narrative which itself attains the status of myth.

The prospect of nuclear holocaust has loomed large in the imaginations of sf writers, but rarely has it been so powerfully or movingly portrayed as in Russell Hoban's *Riddley Walker* (1980). Do not be put off by the non-standard narration! Many sf writers touch on the problem of language—if your narrator speaks from some future world what will he/she sound like? As multiple stories are unfolded the whole fits together like a gigantic puzzle centred on language itself but reflecting the timelessness of man's predicament.

A significant number of sf classics have been produced by writers famous for non-genre fiction. In *The Handmaid's Tale* (1985) Margaret Atwood portrays a society dominated by religious fundamentalism, in which women are valued solely for their reproductive function. A major theme in this novel is censorship (cf. Orwell, *Nineteen Eighty-Four* and Ray Bradbury, *Fahrenheit 451,* 1953) and, like Suzette Elgin in *Native Tongue* (1984), Atwood explores the idea of women subverting a language that is controlled by men. If you enjoy futuristic portrayals of gender bias in society, try Joanna Russ, *The Female Man* (1975), or Marge Piercy's *Woman on the Edge of Time* (1976).

Iain M. Banks is one of the few authors who regularly produces both literary and generic works. *Consider Phlebas* (1987) was his first sf novel. It combines the galactic scope of Asimov's *Foundation* series with the pace and suspense of a thriller. Both the Culture and the Idirans are searching for Mind, an intelligence hidden on the Planet of the Dead, but it is Horza the Changer's quest to find it first. Presented with historical appendices, Banks's narration is clever, ironic, and unsettling.

Science fiction often takes itself very seriously but the lighter side should not be ignored. No other genre contains such potential for farce and satire, and no other writer has combined these quite so skilfully as Terry Pratchett. In the *Discworld* series Pratchett creates a carnivalesque planet pointedly reminiscent of our own and uses it as a device for poking fun at the conventions of sf itself. One of the best novels is *Reaperman* (1991), in which Death takes early retirement and chaos ensues. If this appeals to you, you should try Douglas Adams's

Hitchhiker (1979–92) series, or Michael Moorcock, whose prodigious output contains a similar blend of the ingenious and surreal.

Credited with having coined the term 'cyberspace', William Gibson is the acknowledged leader of a new branch of sf commonly known as 'cyberpunk' —an off-putting term for his elegant, immaculately structured work. Gibson has said that he doesn't see himself as a futurist; he uses the tools of sf in order to reflect the weirdness of contemporary reality. In 1984 his first novel, *Neuromancer*, won most of the major awards of sf and gained a cult status. *Idoru* (1996) is structured as a thriller; a quest through worlds virtual and real, both dominated by the concept of celebrity. A rock star announces his intention to marry an idoru, or virtual reality star. The machinery that constructs and feeds off celebrity is activated, and a mysteriously gifted 'netrunner' and a 14-year-old fan both attempt to find out more, but the quest takes a dangerous turn.

Finally, for those of you who view my list with a healthy scepticism, the Hugo, Nebula, and Tiptree award-winners are always worth reading (many of the writers on my list have won one or more of these). Enjoy exploring the field, it is well worth exploring. Sf can only gain in literary status in the coming century. That is my prediction.

See also LIVI MICHAEL

Top Twelve

H. G. WELLS, *The Time Machine* (1895)

GEORGE ORWELL, *Nineteen Eighty-Four* (1949)

ISAAC ASIMOV, *Foundation* series (1951–93)

ARTHUR C. CLARKE, *Childhood's End* (1953)

FRANK HERBERT, *Dune* (1965)

URSULA LE GUIN, *The Dispossessed* (1974)

DORIS LESSING, *Shikasta* (1979)

RUSSELL HOBAN, *Riddley Walker* (1980)

MARGARET ATWOOD, *The Handmaid's Tale* (1985)

IAIN M. BANKS, *Consider Phlebas* (1987)

TERRY PRATCHETT, *Reaperman* (1991)

WILLIAM GIBSON, *Idoru* (1996)

The sea

Tony Tanner

Joseph Conrad was without doubt the greatest writer of the sea. In an essay he wrote in 1898 called 'Tales of the Sea' he looked back fondly on the two sea novelists who had thrilled him as a boy, and who, in effect, initiated the genre of the sea novel. The novels of the Englishman Captain Marryat are 'the beginning and embodiment of an inspiring tradition'. But there is something primitive and 'unartistic' about his work. 'To this writer of the sea the sea was not an element. It was a stage, where was displayed an exhibition of valour, and of such achievements as the world had never seen before.' A good example is *Mr Midshipman Easy* (1836). More importantly for Conrad,

At the same time, on the other side of the Atlantic, another man wrote of the sea with true artistic instinct . . . James Fenimore Cooper loved the sea and looked at it with consummate understanding. In his sea tales the sea interpenetrates with life; it is in a subtle way a factor in the problem of existence, and, for all its greatness, it is always in touch with the men, who, bound on errands of war or gain, traverse its immense solitudes.

A good example is *The Pilot; a Tale of the Sea* (1824).

All the most interesting sea fictions explore and dramatize, in one way or another, how 'the sea interpenetrates with life'. At the start of one of his own sea stories, 'Youth' (1901), Conrad has his narrator, Marlow, state 'This could have occurred nowhere but in England, where man and sea interpenetrate, so to speak—the sea entering into the life of most men, and the men knowing something or everything about the sea, in the way of amusement, of travel, or of bread-winning.' This is no longer true in our air-borne age, and most people's experience of the sea is limited to bathing in it. But it *was* the case in Britain and America during the nineteenth century and up to the First World War, when German submarines finally put paid to the use of sailing ships for other than recreational purposes.

It is an interesting fact that, while Britannia may have been ruling the waves, she was not producing the stories about the waves. For those we have to look, for the most part, to the Americans, chiefly Herman Melville, whose masterpiece, *Moby Dick* (1851), was written during the golden age of sail—and a Pole, Joseph Conrad (albeit a Pole who served in the British Merchant Service from 1878 to 1894). Conrad personally experienced and witnessed both the gradual decadence of the sailing ship and the inevitable shift to steam—which he disliked intensely. 'The sea of the past was an incomparable beautiful mistress, with inscrutable face, with cruel and promising eyes. The sea of today is a used-up drudge, wrinkled and defaced by the churned-up wakes of brutal propellers.' Such feelings perhaps help to account for the elegiac strain in nearly all Conrad's writing about the sea. But it should be noted that he did serve on a number of steamships, and drew upon that experience for some of his finest voyage tales—*Lord Jim* (1900), *Typhoon* (1902), and 'The End of the Tether'.

Western literature begins with a difficult voyage home (known as a *nostos*) —Homer's *The Odyssey* (eighth century BC); and the novel conventionally regarded as the first modern example of that genre, Daniel Defoe's *Robinson Crusoe* (1719), is based on a voyage out and a shipwreck. Exploration, discovery, the quest, and perhaps the return—these generate very elemental narrative lines; and in one form or another, however thwarted or incomplete, these lines run through sea stories. There is one crucial feature which differentiates the genre— you leave the land behind, and along with it the stable structures of society and civilization. W. H. Auden outlined four principles of the literary attitude to sea voyages in the nineteenth century:

1. To leave the land and the city is the desire of every man of sensibility and honour. 2. The sea is the real situation and the voyage is the true condition of man. 3. The sea is where the decisive events, the moments of eternal choice, of temptation, fall, and redemption occur. The shore life is always trivial. 4. An abiding destination is unknown even if it may exist: a lasting relationship is not possible nor even to be desired.

Such an attitude, a desire for the physical and mental freedom of open ocean experience—what Melville's Ishmael calls 'landlessness'—animates many sea narratives.

When, in their restlessness, ambition, or curiosity, men do go 'down to the sea in ships', the narratives their voyages generate tend to centre on certain recurring themes or events. Men at sea find themselves alone with the primordial elements in a seemingly infinite vastness; at the same time, they are confined— imprisoned, it sometimes feels—with a number of other men (rarely women) in the constricted space of a ship. This produces stories in which the emphasis is on men's struggle with the elements, with each other, or with themselves (fear, self-doubt, loss of nerve, even madness). Of course, great sea stories contain all three, as, for example, Conrad's *The Nigger of the 'Narcissus'* (1897), a dazzling account of a perilous homeward voyage during which the men are in danger of being undermined both from without (bad weather) and within (cowardice, insubordination, threats to morale). The threats also produce heroism, endurance, and fidelity, which finally see the ship through. The two basic struggles with the elements are—the attempt to grapple with the destructive force of a great storm (as in Conrad's *Typhoon*); and the difficulties of coping with the poisonous stagnation of being becalmed (unforgettably described in Conrad's *The Shadow-Line*, 1917). We encounter men struggling with other men in Melville's *Billy Budd* (1924), and, set in the Second World War, Herman Wouk's *The Caine Mutiny* (1951). In such books, the shipboard inhabitants form a microcosm of society, and I should include here Katherine Anne Porter's *Ship of Fools* (1962), though her emphasis is more on the passengers. It is the story of a voyage from Vera Cruz, Mexico, to Bremerhaven, Germany, in 1931 with German, Swiss, Spanish, Swedish, Cuban, Mexican, and American passengers on board. Porter's real subject is a human community heading toward the horrors of the Second World War.

In the category of stories focusing on men struggling with themselves I would place those stories—we may call them a kind of sea *Bildungsroman*—which deal with the theme of initiation, in which naïve youth is tested by the extremities of life at sea, and wins through to mature adulthood. At its simplest, this can be a boy's adventure story, of which the best example is Rudyard Kipling's *Captains Courageous* (1897). More complex versions of the pattern include Richard Henry Dana's *Two Years Before the Mast* (1840); Herman Melville's *Redburn* (1849); and Jack London's *The Sea-Wolf* (1904), in which the young dilettante hero finds himself on a hell-ship with a ruthless skipper. There is also William Golding's remarkable trilogy *Rites of Passage* (1980), *Close Quarters* (1987), and *Fire Down Below* (1989), which chronicles a Royal Navy ship transporting passengers to Australia. This traces (among other things) the education in human nature of the young and pompous Edmund Talbot during an endless voyage on a slow and disintegrating vessel that should never have left port. It is set during the European wars between 1796 and 1815. This has proved to be a very fertile period for sea fiction, as may be seen from the enormously popular novels of C. S. Forester (featuring Captain Horatio Hornblower, hero of a series of novels starting with *The Happy Return*, 1937); and, more recently, the seemingly no less popular Aubrey/Maturin novels by Patrick O'Brian—up to eighteen volumes at the time of writing!

I have saved till last a specific form of the quest narrative—namely, the hunt for a great fish. Arguably the greatest of all sea novels is Herman Melville's *Moby Dick*, which follows Captain Ahab's monomaniacal pursuit of the great white whale, and ends with the foundering of him and his ship, leaving one survivor (Ishmael) to tell the tale. A sort of echo, or coda, to this work is Ernest Hemingway's *The Old Man and the Sea* (1952), which tells of the poor Cuban fisherman, Santiago, who ventures far out into the Gulf Stream and hooks and pursues a giant marlin. After an exhausting struggle, he finally harpoons his catch and lashes it to his small boat. By the time he reaches shore, the sharks have reduced his trophy to a skeleton. A short work, this book is really a parable of man's struggle with the natural world. *Moby Dick* is massive, mythic, encyclopaedic. Written when America was at the peak of its maritime powers, and when whaling was still vitally important (for oil = light = civilization), Melville's vast work pursues not only the whale, but everything else in creation. It is the epic of America and there has never been a sea novel like it.

Top Twelve

DANIEL DEFOE, *Robinson Crusoe* (1719)

JAMES FENIMORE COOPER, *The Pilot; a Tale of the Sea* (1824)

HERMAN MELVILLE, *Moby Dick* (1851)

JOSEPH CONRAD, *The Nigger of the 'Narcissus'* (1897) and *Lord Jim* (1900)

JACK LONDON, *The Sea-Wolf* (1904)

HERMAN WOUK, *The Caine Mutiny* (1951)

ERNEST HEMINGWAY, *The Old Man and the Sea* (1952)

KATHERINE ANNE PORTER, *Ship of Fools* (1962)

PATRICK O'BRIAN, *Master and Commander* (1970)

WILLIAM GOLDING, *Rites of Passage* (1980)

TONY TANNER (ed.), *The Oxford Book of Sea Stories* (1995)

Sexual politics

Maureen Freely

There are three things you notice when you look at the novels that have charted and changed our ideas on sexual politics. First, how fast they date. Second, most of the books that caused the greatest scandals in their day are now unreadable. Third, how rare it is for the protagonists in even the very best and most enduring books to know pleasure without punishment, sex without death.

Why is this? Most of the authors included here send their characters to cruel fates and have double-edged motives for doing so. The tragic endings both confirm the moral codes of the day while also suggesting that they are too harsh and need changing. But there are exceptions. Although *Anna Karenina* (1873–7) was written a century and a half ago, about a society that no longer exists, its portrayal of married life is complex and ultimately enigmatic. Tolstoy based it on a real story, about a love triangle that ended with the adulterous wife throwing herself in front of a train. When he sat down to write the novel, he disapproved of the Anna character. But as draft followed draft, she became increasingly noble, brilliant, tragic, while the two men in her life became less and less admirable. Her suicide is all the more disturbing for her having weighed up all the moral questions before throwing herself away.

In Kate Chopin's *The Awakening* (1899) Edna Pontellier is a disenchanted housewife who discovers sensuality—and younger men—while summering at a resort near New Orleans. By the end she knows the game is up—she is going to have to return to her duties or else. We leave her swimming into the night, almost too tired to continue, but still taking great joy from her every stroke. It was, I think, Edna's refusal to feel guilty about her love of pleasure that made the book so distasteful to most readers of the time. It got dreadful reviews. It was only in the post-feminist 1980s that Kate Chopin's books came back into vogue.

In the intervening years, she was entirely forgotten. The same cannot be said of Radclyffe Hall. *The Well of Loneliness* led to one of this century's most infamous obscenity trials, in 1928. For many lesbians of the time, this was the only book that affirmed them as human beings. Stephen Gordon, its hand-some, noble, 'invert' hero(ine) is now a *very* dated creature. The mood of the novel is high melodrama. But it describes with eloquent indignation wrongs that no one should have to endure, and so it still grabs the heart. As does

Stephen's final plea to her unfeeling critics: 'Acknowledge us, oh god, before the whole world. Give us the right to our existence!'

It would be another forty years before real people could make that demand in public. But it took even longer for E. M. Forster's *Maurice* (1971) to make it into print. In this case, it was the author himself who suppressed publication. He was perhaps very wise, because his aim was far more radical—to suggest that the open expression of homosexual love could be a good, and even a redeeming, thing. This is not, however, a lesson that comes easily to the eponymous hero. His first real love-affair, with the almost patrician, ultra-ambitious Clive, ends abruptly when Clive decides after an illness that he prefers women. Off Clive floats into marriage, politics, and the sombre beauties of convention, 'while beyond the barrier, Maurice wandered, the wrong words on his lips, and the wrong desires in his heart, and his arms full of air.' He has become such a bitter man by the time he meets a man who knows his worth that he comes very close to losing him.

The most remarkable thing about Virginia Woolf's *Orlando* (1928) is its refusal to admit even the slightest glint of bitterness. This is the story of a dashing Englishman who manages two great feats: to remain almost youthful even after staying alive for more than four hundred years, and to rise from his sickbed after a bout of fever to find that he has become a woman. However, the bending of her own gender does not stop her from taking great pleasure in the company of both men and women. Virginia Woolf was an exact contemporary of Radclyffe Hall. Although there are passages in *Orlando* that are far more radical than anything in *The Well*, it managed to get past the censors because of its clever use of disguises and distancing techniques. These ploys become less important as we move on to the second half of the twentieth century, but 'just deserts' continue to feature in all serious writing about the various types of love that continue to dare not say their name.

This is true even of the post-war he-men sexual liberationists like Henry Miller, Phillip Roth, Norman Mailer, and James Jones. If I were going to be fair, I would perhaps include at least one of them here. But the two books from this era that I like most stand well outside the then prevailing ideas about masculinity. One is James Baldwin's *Giovanni's Room* (1956), about an allegedly heterosexual American writer living in Paris in the 1950s. He has an intense affair with a beautiful young Italian man while his girlfriend is away. We know from the start that it all ends badly, with the girlfriend leaving him and the beautiful Giovanni sitting in a dungeon, waiting to be guillotined. The idea, I would say, was to make easy moral condemnation harder, and demand that the characters be seen and understood in their own terms. The book was extraordinarily open for its time in its evocation of homosexual love. It still has great power today as an indictment of emotional dishonesty.

And it's the same with my other choice from the post war era—Nabokov's *Lolita* (1955): the story of an ageing and urbane European gentleman's infatuation with a 12-year-old all-American girl. Possibly it is even more shocking today than it was when it first came out. I can't pick it up without marvelling at its high-wire stylistic brilliance, and its humility in the face of the passions that (sooner or later) make fools of us all.

The great feminist blockbusters are not big on ambiguity and humility. Their purpose was to get their readers so angry they had no choice but to 'wake up'. But now that we are all so *very* wide awake, they seem rather simplistic. Erica Jong's *Fear of Flying* (1973), once infamous for its zipless sex scenes, seems tame, and rather too personal. Marilyn French's *The Women's Room* (1977) has a bigger heart—but this heart is flooded with resentment. I prefer Margaret Atwood's cool, elegant feminist dystopia, *A Handmaid's Tale* (1985). Its description of a fascist gender-state is the purest picture you'll ever get of 'patriarchal society' as feminists of the time understood it. Could it ever come true? Visit Afghanistan and see for yourself.

The past two decades in this country have been a gentler place for sexual political fictional explorations. I've chosen books that (in my view) break most successfully with the gallows-and-tears conventions of their predecessors. None suggest that breaking with conventional morality is easy. The girl in Jeanette Winterson's *Oranges are Not the Only Fruit* (1985) has great difficulty coming out as a lesbian, most especially to her holy roller mother. The gay narrator of Joseph Olshan's *Night Swimmer* (1994) does not belong to the mainstream—he prefers the protection of a community of his own. But in both books, the overwhelming sense you have is that these characters are comfortable inside their own skins. The problems they have with their lovers are problems that all humans have with their lovers. In this greater security it is possible for Winterson to view her heroine's nutcase mother with generosity and humour. And even as Olshan evokes the pain of a community haunted by loss and death, he never forgets how to laugh.

Michèle Roberts' exquisite folding novel, *Flesh and Blood* (1994), begins with a story set in England in the present, which leads to another story, and then another that takes us over the Channel and deep into the past, eventually to meet the man whose name is shorthand for the mixing of pain with pleasure, and punishment with sex. Then the story retraces its steps until we are back at the beginning. Never once during the journey does anyone suggest that pleasure might be bad for you.

It's the same with my final offering—a Belgian novel that was written long before its time. Madeleine Bourdouxhe's *Marie* (1943) is about a married woman who is tired of her husband's casual infidelities, and dragged down by her suicidal sister's demands. She meets a younger man, and has an amazing affair with him. But nothing happens to her marriage. The only thing that changes is that she enjoys life more than ever. Imagine that!

Top Twelve

LEO TOLSTOY, *Anna Karenina* (1873–7)

KATE CHOPIN, *The Awakening* (1899)

RADCLYFFE HALL, *The Well of Loneliness* (1928)

VIRGINIA WOOLF, *Orlando* (1928)

MADELEINE BOURDOUXHE, *Marie* (1943; and 1997 in English for the first time)

VLADIMIR NABOKOV, *Lolita* (1955)

JAMES BALDWIN, *Giovanni's Room* (1956)

E. M. FORSTER, *Maurice* (written 1914, pub. 1971)

MARGARET ATWOOD, *The Handmaid's Tale* (1985)

JEANETTE WINTERSON, *Oranges are Not the Only Fruit* (1985)

JOSEPH OLSHAN, *Night Swimmer* (1994)

MICHÈLE ROBERTS, *Flesh and Blood* (1994)

Short stories

Lesley Glaister

To name even a fraction of the writers of short stories who deserve mention is impossible within the scope of this short essay and so my choice has had to be ruthless and even arbitrary. I have tried to stick to first thoughts: writers I return to, stories that have lingered in my mind.

Good novels tend to leave one feeling full and satisfied while good short stories whet the appetite for more. But the best way to read short stories is not to be greedy, to read one at a time and leave time for its effect to be absorbed. Because unlike novels, which are feats of extended creativity, short stories are distillations of the same. They differ from novels in more than length, they are a tighter form. Less is stated and sometimes more intuition and attention is required. V. S. Pritchett, himself a revered short-story writer, made a canny distinction between the reader's response to the two forms—one may lose oneself in a novel but turn to a good short story to find oneself. And Elizabeth Bowen, whose own stories provide a serene, delicately ironic take on middle-class life, described short stories as 'peaks of common experience' which move 'past an altitude line into poetry'.

However, Canadian writer Alice Munro's short stories are almost miraculous for the amount they contain. After reading a story of twenty or thirty pages, one emerges with the sensation of having read a novel's worth of insight. The stories in her collections are linked by place and character, which adds to the sense of continuity and layering, but within each separate story an astonishing amount happens. Take 'A Real Life' from *Open Secrets* (1994). It's ostensibly about the marriage of eccentric Dorrie, but evokes the sense of a community through the experiences of delivery man Dorrie's brother. It spans perhaps fifty years and tells almost the entire life histories of its three main female characters. Munro's stories have in common this richness and also a kind of tenderness. The characters live everyday lives yet their actions are crucial to each other and the slightest action seems imbued with grace. These stories don't really conform to the convention William Trevor has described as 'the art of the glimpse'. They would be a great introduction for a reader reluctant to stray from the novel to the short story form. Anyone who appreciates Alice Munro would certainly also enjoy the stories of Ellen Gilchrist, Carol Shields, and Margaret Atwood.

Raymond Carver's characters are also working people and the stories are undramatic, mysterious in that they work so brilliantly when in many of them almost nothing happens. His style has been called 'dirty realist', though it's not particularly dirty and it only seems realistic. There is so much invisible art at work, a hidden rhythm, a sort of secret poetry. Take 'Whoever was Using This Bed' from *Elephant* (1988). The story starts: 'The call comes in the middle of the night . . .', tilting one straight in. (Carver has especially delicious titles and first lines.) A couple are woken by a phone call which turns out to be a wrong number. All that transpires is that they can't get back to sleep and spend the rest of the night smoking and talking, worrying about their health, arguing about whether or not they would unplug each other from life support machines if they were ever in that predicament.

All the writers I've mentioned so far are American or Canadian—and there is something especially successful about the American approach to the form. This has partly to do with a certain laconic, colloquial style which lends a deceptive air of casualness, as if the stories have just happened. The title story of J. D. Salinger's collection, *For Esmé, With Love and Squalor* (1953)—about an American Serviceman's chance meeting with a 13-year old English girl during the war—has just such an informal feel, the narrator almost drawling through the page at you, that its emotional power is in the end quite devastating. The dialogue, particularly the girl's, at once dignified and quintessentially adolescent, is some of the best I've ever read. See also Lorrie Moore for stories that are immensely engaging and witty, spiked with word-play and peopled with a cast of characters who are idiosyncratic, fallible, and very recognizable.

But not all the best short story writers are American. Katherine Mansfield's short stories are cool, flawless gems. In the title story of *The Garden Party* (1922) an almost idyllic scene is evoked, filtered through the consciousness of young Laura. A thoughtlessly well-to-do family prepare for a garden party on a perfect summer morning. The greatest problem they have to contend with is where to erect the marquee—when the ugly news of the accidental death of a man from one of the local poor families intrudes. The story concerns the subtle battle of emotions within Laura between wanting the party cancelled out of respect and wanting it to go ahead so that she can look beautiful in her new hat. Mansfield's stories revolve like this about some delicate emotional point as they explore the elusive sources of grief and joy. Mansfield's stories have often been compared with those of Anton Chekhov, and anyone interested in reading some real classics of the genre might enjoy one of his collections, *The Kiss and Other Stories* (written 1887–1902), for instance.

As a reminder of the enormous scope of writing embraced by the term *short story*, Ian McEwan's collection, *First Love, Last Rites* (1975), could hardly provide a greater contrast to Katherine Mansfield's work. McEwan's stories are shocking, cold, and curiously gripping. 'Homemade' is about adolescence, the grim, grainy getting of experience told with a dreadfully convincing insouciance. McEwan's stories differ from Mansfield's not only in content but in manner and technique. While Mansfield's tend to balance on a single point, McEwan's—like Munro's—are more likely to evoke a stretch of time, a structural difference which gives a quite different emotional impact.

Most writers steer closer to one of these two tendencies, the single moment or the stretch of time, and in this sense Elizabeth Taylor's stories work in the way McEwan's do; although two writers could hardly be more different in their vision. Taylor's stories are miniature glimpses of provincial England and of the English abroad. She specializes in those who hover on the edges of drollness. 'Flesh' from *The Devastating Boys* (1972) tells the tale of a pub landlady convalescing after a hysterectomy and the gouty widower she meets on her package holiday. The two decide to have a fling which doesn't go quite according to plan. Taylor captures exactly the manner and speech of her characters—the absent-minded 'Go on!' of the half attentive Phyl, used to humouring her customers. Yet Taylor never patronizes her characters, absurd as they sometimes are.

It seems curious that James Kelman's tough contemporary Scottish stories are more closely wedded in structure and manner to Mansfield's than to McEwan's. They tend to be structured around a single moment and some are so brief—as short as a paragraph, absolutely *the glimpse*. In 'The Small Bird and the Young Person' from *The Burn* (1991) a boy and a bird collide—that is the story. Kelman employs an elastic variety of styles in his stories from manic stream of consciousness to lucid omniscience. He is linguistically exciting, exploring and exploiting the space between working-class Scots and literary English. (For other contemporary Scottish stories see Janice Galloway and A. L. Kennedy.)

James Joyce adopted the term 'epiphany' to describe the sudden 'revelation of the whatness of a thing' by which he meant the moment in which 'the soul of the commonest object seems to us radiant'. This seems perhaps a stronger manifestation of the moment, the point in time as a changing mechanism, seen to varying extents in some of the writers discussed above. In *Dubliners* (1914) the stories are linked by style and subject matter, and arranged by theme: childhood, adolescence, maturity, and public life, all reflecting the moral life of the Dublin of his day. The stories are muted as old sepia photographs yet there is a fascinating seething of life which makes these unforgettable. 'A Painful Case' is about Mr Duffy, a bank clerk, living a tidy, uneventful life who meets Mrs Sinico whose 'companionship was like a warm soil about an exotic'. His failure of nerve brings the relationship to an end with tragic consequences. It's a heart-breaking study in sterility.

Following Joyce are many, many fine Irish short story writers. William Trevor stands out for his prolific output of absorbing stories where widely differing characters come to terms with finding a place between illusion and reality. In 'The Piano Tuner's Wives' (from *After Rain*, 1996) a second wife, in her effort to compete with first, is reduced to destroying the pictures her predecessor had built up in her blind husband's mind, a small plausible cruelty that is resonant of human frailty. And it is this evocation of the larger human condition through a distillation of behaviour and experience that makes the best of short stories so richly rewarding to read, and causes them to linger in the mind.

See also LESLEY GLAISTER

Top Twelve

JAMES JOYCE, *Dubliners* (1914)

KATHERINE MANSFIELD, *The Garden Party* (1922)

J. D. SALINGER, *For Esmé, With Love and Squalor* (1953)

ELIZABETH TAYLOR, *The Devastating Boys* (1972)

IAN McEWAN, *First Love, Last Rites* (1975)

WILLIAM TREVOR, *Collected Stories* (1983)

RAYMOND CARVER, *Elephant* (1988)

JAMES KELMAN, *The Burn* (1991)

ALICE MUNRO, *Open Secrets* (1994)

T. CORAGHESSAN BOYLE, *The Collected Stories of T. Coraghessan Boyle* (1998)

LORRIE MOORE, *Birds of America* (1999)

ELIZABETH BOWEN, *Collected Stories* (1999)

Social issues

Valentine Cunningham

The novel has always demonstrated how the human subject intersects and interacts with the social, and one of the most important functions of the novel has been its acting as an instrument of social critique. Novelists have often been possessed by strong partisan political visions (frequently socialist) of how society should fare. Conservative and right-wing novels are far less usual.

For an archetypal fictional vision of humankind as necessarily social I turn to Daniel Defoe's *Robinson Crusoe* (1719). This magnetic tale of a marooned sailor planting and harvesting, keeping animals, building shelters, painfully learning how to make bread, pots, baskets, and clothes, kick-started the whole western capitalist myth of the individual who makes it economically by his own efforts (sanctioned, of course, by Protestantism's capitalist God: the baskets of provisions multiply wonderfully). But in fact, the novel powerfully celebrates the necessity of society. Crusoe would not manage without his Man Friday, effectively his slave. Crusoe needs social consolations. Isolation only spells anxiety. Fear of invasion and robbery keeps Crusoe neurotically reinforcing his shelter's barriers and walls. The misery of the self merely as owner, all on its own, could not be more starkly revealed. It was a foundational lesson about society that the novel genre, if not all the novel's readers, absorbed utterly.

The threat of social forces is what animates one of the best big novels by one of the greatest social-protest novelists, Charles Dickens's *Bleak House* (1852–3). This bursts at the seams with people variously oppressed by the slow grindings of Law and by religious, moral, and economic prejudice. One of England's first detective stories, and one of the most potent of our city fictions, *Bleak House* shows how human misery embraces every class and group from London's slum-kids to the poshest inhabitants of grand country houses. With garish, nightmarish detail, it rivetingly demonstrates the personal and civic ruin entailed when the old social divisions and moral prejudices get to run unchecked.

Even more convinced about the need for human goodness and sympathy in a world where the old cohesions of Christian belief have come unglued is George Eliot's *Middlemarch, a Study of Provincial Life* (1871–2). In the title's Midlands town—a place much like the Coventry George Eliot grew up in—connected lives (especially intellectually frustrated Dorothea Brooke, scientifically ambitious Dr Lydgate, and corrupt evangelical banker Bulstrode) converge in compelling stories of greed, bad marriages, failing ambitions, and of people learning to settle for less and to be truly human for the sake of true community.

George Eliot's aim was to win her public over to a religion of humanity by a steady inspection of the multiple human flaws in a large social scene. The social criticisms of Thomas Hardy—one of George Eliot's greatest admirers—are more narrowly focused and also more emotionally stressed-out in *Jude the Obscure* (1896), the marvellously grim story of a stonemason, Jude Fawley, beaten down and eventually done to death by social opposition. Anglican Christminster (i.e. Oxford) University won't admit him, despite his intelligence and great bookishness ('I have understanding as well as you; I am not inferior to you'). The marriage laws of Church and State and consequent ingrained popular prejudice make him and his common-law wife into moral and social outcasts. It's an utterly sad story, emotionally almost too much to bear. As is Upton Sinclair's *The Jungle* (1906), another classic protest about the dire fates of ordinary working-class people, this time the immigrant labourers in the meat industry of turn-of-the-century Chicago. The meat products big Jurgis Rudkus and his Polack neighbours have to produce are unhealthy muck, produced in filthy conditions for the great money profits of the bosses' tight cartels. The grossly ill-paid workers are forced into perpetual misery, ill-health, injury, early death. Communist Sinclair had done serious research among the foul abattoirs and the awful hovels of the Chicago poor. Scandal erupted when his novel came out. America's hearts and minds were greatly touched (as they'd been earlier by Harriet Beecher Stowe's anti-slavery novel, *Uncle Tom's Cabin*, 1851–2, and would be later by John Steinbeck's novel about midwestern agricultural depression, *The Grapes of Wrath*, 1939). Changes in pure food law followed. The novel's strong gusts of horror still turn one's stomach and stir one's social anger.

D. H. Lawrence is less simply wholehearted about the virtues of the Midlands working-class community he represents in *Sons and Lovers* (1913)—and, after all, this writer from the Nottingham–Derbyshire coalfield had long rejected his coal-mining father's life as a model for his own by the time he produced his great novel. None the less *Sons and Lovers* is the first major English novel to be written completely from the inside of a provincial labouring community, and it offers unrivalled access to the lives of working men and their fraught home-running wives—and what it means in particular for Paul Morel and his first girlfriend, Miriam, to grow up into life and art and love in the socially pinched but admirably thoughtful atmosphere of provincial chapel Christianity. Choppy and long-winded (much of the rambling original was cut out by Lawrence's anxious London editor), *Sons and Lovers* made one of the big breakthroughs in the progress of the English *Bildungsroman*—the novel about growing up.

A social world away from Lawrence, Virginia Woolf (middle-class, London, intellectual, bohemian) was eager for her own part to make the English novel-reader sit up with her particular less-than-conventional vision of social life. Her *Mrs Dalloway* (1925) is a still astonishing narrative of a day in the life of a group of Londoners, their memories packed with ghosts, especially the dead of the First World War, their paths and eyes crossing as they move about their city's centre, advancing towards evening, a party, a suicide. *Mrs Dalloway* does for our sense of the crowded modern city what James Joyce's *Ulysses* (1922) had earlier done for Dublin, and for that is one of the great classics of modernist urbanism.

D. H. Lawrence's friend the satirist Aldous Huxley aimed to examine twentieth-century society with the range and energy Dickens and George Eliot (and Dostoevsky) had brought to the nineteenth century. Pursuing the life of sociologist Anthony Beavis from its beginnings to the 1930s era of totalitarian dictators, his *Eyeless in Gaza* (1936) is hawkishly busy with a whole period's moral shifts and political shiftinesses. Beavis is even writing chapters of an *Elements of Sociology* in parallel with the chapters of the novel he's in. Huxley is particularly keen to advocate pacifism as a response to the threat of war, especially from the air, and there's no fiction I know offering a better allegory of war's violent horror than the moment when Beavis and a girlfriend sunbathing naked on a roof in the South of France are struck by a dead dog chucked from a passing aeroplane.

Even more troublingly war-preoccupied is the parable-like *Party Going* (1939) by Henry Green, one of modern English fiction's most attractively restless experimenters. In it a group of rich chums is holed up at a London railway terminus. Fog has stopped the boat trains leaving for France. Dissatisfied pro-letarians throng the station. The pals take fearful refuge in the management offices. We get a wonderfully tense revelation of how the privileged live in terror of the mob whose diminished lives essentially pay for their luxurious ones. Everyone lives in fear of bombing planes, but some groups do so more comfort-ably than others. The Old Etonian Green weighs into the moneyed with all the scathing dyspepsia of the socialist principles which drove him to leave Oxford early to work on the shop floor of his family's factory in Birmingham.

Money, the greed for it, the making of it, the failure to make it, are what animate the grippingly grisly transatlantic tradings of Martin Amis's *Money* (1984). John Self, a piece of bodily and moral junk seeking to make it in the New York porno movie scene, is on a kind of Pilgrim's Regress which calls into question every assumption of contemporary moral, cultural, and social value. The toughest prose around packs a compellingly old-fashioned critical punch.

Money's exact contemporary, Angela Carter's *Nights at the Circus* (1984), has more sheer relish for the grotesque behaviour its richly jammed paragraphs embrace, but it too shares the generally adversarial posture of the social-novel tradition. Carter's theme is the lives and treatment of women in a traditional patriarchal culture—the world of Victorian entertainment, brothels, freak-shows, circuses. Her main character is Fevvers, lovely, lively, motor-mouthed, vulgarian, magic woman (she can sprout wings and fly). Social panoramas—this one takes us from low-life London all the way to Tsarist Russia—never came more vividly cinematic, more naughtily exuberant, nor more demandingly critical.

Dickens remains a strong inspiration for contemporary social novelists of London. Iain Sinclair's typically comprehensive low-life *Downriver (or, the Vessels of Wrath), a Narrative in Twelve Tales* (1991) finely illustrates this. His London is a vast crowd of oddballs inhabiting places reeking with trouble, black memory, magic, crime, all fired by a sturdy political rage about the years of post-industrial Thatcherite depredations which these fictional encounters starkly reveal. The tradition of the utterly compelling angry social novel is safe in such hands.

Top Twelve

DANIEL DEFOE, *Robinson Crusoe* (1719)

CHARLES DICKENS, *Bleak House* (1852–3)

GEORGE ELIOT, *Middlemarch* (1871–2)

THOMAS HARDY, *Jude the Obscure* (1896)

UPTON SINCLAIR, *The Jungle* (1906)

D. H. LAWRENCE, *Sons and Lovers* (1913)

VIRGINIA WOOLF, *Mrs Dalloway* (1925)

ALDOUS HUXLEY, *Eyeless in Gaza* (1936)

HENRY GREEN, *Party Going* (1939)

MARTIN AMIS, *Money* (1984)

ANGELA CARTER, *Nights at the Circus* (1984)

IAIN SINCLAIR, *Downriver* (1991)

Spy

Michael Shea

There have been spies ever since there have been competing states. There have even been spies who were writers; for example William Wordsworth, in the late eighteenth century, was being paid by the Home Office when he travelled through northern Germany and France, to report back on what was going on in Europe in that turbulent revolutionary period. But it is only at the beginning of the twentieth century—a period of rampant xenophobia—that a distinct genre of spy story emerges: thrillers with an international setting, where the central element of the plot is usually a threat to the nation from spies sent into the country by a malignant enemy—usually Germany. Perhaps the most famous in this genre is *The Riddle of the Sands* (1903) by Erskine Childers. It is a story of two inexperienced young British yachtsmen sailing in the Baltic, who discover a dastardly German plot to invade Britain. Joseph Conrad's *The Secret Agent* (1907) gave the genre literary respectability: a foreign spy working out of a run-down shop in Soho is revealed as a double agent reporting to Scotland Yard.

Spy novels about earlier periods became popular in the general mood of national paranoia. The most outstanding were written by the Hungarian-born Baroness Orczy. She recorded the adventures of Sir Percy Blakeney, *The Scarlet Pimpernel* (1905), who, using many remarkable disguises, was pledged to rescue 'innocent' victims from the Revolutionary terror of Robespierre's France.

Until the Second World War, the nasty foreigners are invariably confronted by heroic amateurs, usually recruited in some gentleman's club in London. Such spies emerge in a variety of guises in the writings of John Buchan, for example *The Thirty-Nine Steps* (1915), and in the books of Sapper (pen-name of Herman McNeile), of which the best is perhaps *The Return of Bulldog Drummond* (1932). At a more demanding level, Compton Mackenzie's *Water on the Brain* (1933) reflects the workings, often comical, of the British Secret Service. Mackenzie became director of the Aegean Intelligence Service during the First World War. Somerset Maugham's *Ashenden* (1928), while it is episodic and somewhat dated, also captures the mood of gifted amateurism which was a feature of the actual (as well as fictional) intelligence services of the age. In Graham Greene's *Stamboul Train* (1932) spies and spycatchers chase each other along the rattling but gilded corridors of that famous train on its way to Constantinople. Eric Ambler was writing in a similar vein during the immediate pre-Second World War years, when Hitler and Nazism were threatening all of Western Europe. Two of Ambler's best-known works are *Epitaph for a Spy* (1938) and his famous *The Mask of Dimitrios* (1939), though he continued to write classic thrillers with an international setting long after the war as well. *Epitaph for a Spy*, in particular, continues to hold its allure, with its story of a very ordinary young man, a teacher, catapulted into the deadly world of international intrigue, accused of spying against the French. In a race against time, he has to find out who has framed him, and why.

The modern spy story comes from the Second World War and its cold war aftermath which finally professionalized the trade. The names which come to the fore include Ian Fleming, who brought James Bond, snobbery, sex, and new levels of violence into the gentlemanly club of spy fiction. Begin with *Casino Royale* (1953). Even today, largely through the popularity of the filmed versions, Fleming's books continue to maintain their fictional appeal. At a higher intellectual level (interestingly, spying has always attracted literary as well as popular authors) are John Le Carré's spy stories, in particular *The Spy Who Came in from the Cold* (1963), fêted by Graham Greene himself as the best spy story he had ever read. Le Carré brought moral ambiguity into the hitherto almost wholly patriotic spy novel, reflecting the doubts and divisions of the cold war period. In a similar mould came Len Deighton with *The Ipcress file* (1962) and *Funeral in Berlin* (1964), who contributed a ruthless working-class hero at a time when the country was rediscovering the lower classes in film as well as novels. Graham Greene returned to the genre in this period with his funny and clever *Our Man in Havana* (1958), telling the tale of a naïve Englishman gradually dragged into a web of double dealing when his designs for a vacuum cleaner are mistaken for secret weapon plans.

Spying and diplomacy go hand in hand and some of the best writers in the genre are also, often pseudonymously, diplomats. Douglas Hurd, a career diplomat turned politician, and latterly Secretary of State for Foreign and Commonwealth Affairs, wrote a number of books, usually with a diplomatic setting, but brimful of agents and counter agents. His near contemporary, Michael Sinclair, also produced a batch of well-received thrillers in the 1970s and 1980s, most of which had a strong diplomatic setting. East–West conflicts appear again and again over the decades up to the destruction of the Berlin Wall, with Checkpoint Charlie as a frequent location for the climax both in books and in the many films that were based on them. Several of Lionel Davidson's brilliant thrillers are, in essence, spy stories, often with a Middle Eastern setting. Start with *A Long Way to Shiloh* (1966). Moscow follows Berlin as a favourite setting for spy writers. Martin Cruz Smith's excellent *Gorky Park* (1981), while essentially a detective story with a Russian setting, has its East–West secrets and tensions embedded deep within it.

Many other contemporary writers of adventure fiction set occasional novels in espionage mode. Frederick Forsyth, Bryan Forbes, Jack Higgins, and Robert

Ludlum all draw on secret service backgrounds to paint vivid pictures of the constant undercurrent of tensions between nations as they battle for their own self-interests. Ted Allbeury, himself a former intelligence officer, Alan Judd, and Ken Follett, particularly his early *Eye of the Needle* (1992; previously published as *Storm Island*, 1978) and *The Man from St Petersburg* (1982) are other highly popular authors to look out for.

There is a commonly held belief that, with the end of the cold war, spying is no more, and that writers of spy stories have had to scrape desperately around looking for new villains to write about. Far from it. Espionage is still very active and is, by its very nature, a highly secret profession where truth and fiction run hand in hand. The new playing fields are now largely to do with industrial espionage, finding out about other companies' and other countries' economic and commercial secrets. The enemies too have changed, since we no longer have the Kremlin and the KGB to worry about. Or do we? Recently, the highly acclaimed *Archangel* (1998) by Robert Harris has to be seen against the real-life background of a continuing, inherited East–West conflict. A whole new wave of spy stories have Arabs or Chinese as the enemy, or stray into the general adventure story genre with Colombian drug barons as the villains. But given that the recently declared objectives of Britain's intelligence services—MI5, the Security Service, MI6, the Secret Intelligence Service, and GCHQ, the international eavesdropping service —are to defeat drug barons and the international money-laundering mafia, those professionals involved in the dubious art of spying still have a long career ahead of them, as do the writers of spy fiction who continue to feed from the reality.

See also ADVENTURE

Top Twelve

ERSKINE CHILDERS, *The Riddle of the Sands* (1903)

JOSEPH CONRAD, *The Secret Agent* (1907)

JOHN BUCHAN, *The Thirty-Nine Steps* (1915)

W. SOMERSET MAUGHAM, *Ashenden* (1928)

ERIC AMBLER, *The Mask of Dimitrios* (1939)

GRAHAM GREENE, *Our Man in Havana* (1958)

JOHN LE CARRÉ, *The Spy Who Came in from the Cold* (1963)

LEN DEIGHTON, *Funeral in Berlin* (1964)

LIONEL DAVIDSON, *A Long Way to Shiloh* (1966) and *Kolymsky Heights* (1994)

JOHN LE CARRÉ, *A Small Town in Germany* (1968)

KEN FOLLETT, *The Man from St Petersburg* (1982)

Supernatural

Michael Cox

The supernatural is one of the most difficult of all literary genres to define. It is less a genre in its own right than a mass of sub-genres that can include ghost stories and tales of terror; horror stories; macabre, grotesque, or weird fiction, and other sub-species of the fantastic in literature. For those who wish to begin exploring this vast and diverse region of fiction, the best approach is to focus on the indisputable landmarks and ignore categorization altogether.

The use of the supernatural in fiction signifies an imaginative response in the author to a fundamental and abiding strangeness interpenetrating the physical and moral universe; a recognition of some mysterious 'otherness' in our existence that is both beyond our grasp and, at times, fearfully present to our senses. How this is worked out in fiction depends on many factors, personal and cultural; but if we are looking for some unifying thread, then it is this willingness to suggest realities that transcend the ordinary course of nature, ranging from traditional ghosts to werewolves and vampires, with a host of terrors—seen and unseen—in between. For many writers there is also a more basic motive: to bring about what Edith Wharton called 'the fun of the shudder' —that curiously enjoyable sensation of feeling afraid when we are in no actual danger ourselves.

For those inclined to jump in at the historical deep end, the earliest supernatural fiction to constitute a major tradition in its own right was Gothic romance in the late eighteenth and early nineteenth centuries. Typically located in ancient castles or monasteries (the word 'Gothic' originally implied 'medieval') set in wild picturesque landscapes, these early narratives were a reaction against the rationalism of neoclassical culture. Supernatural incidents abound in Gothic fiction: spectral figures, eerie sounds, living statues, bleeding images, breathing portraits, magic mirrors. The tradition was set in train by Horace Walpole in *The Castle of Otranto* (1764) and reached its high point in *The Monk* (1796) by Matthew Lewis, a lurid and extravagant melodrama that irresistibly combined sex, violence, and the supernatural.

Gothic fiction—in its original form—is probably something of an acquired taste for most modern readers, but its influence has been far-reaching and still continues. Out of the early Gothic tradition sprang such literary landmarks as Mary Shelley's seminal *Frankenstein* (1818) and the tales of Edgar Allan Poe (e.g. 'The Fall of the House of Usher', included in his *Tales of the Grotesque and*

Arabesque, 1840), whilst its cultural impact not only infiltrated mainstream Victorian fiction (e.g. Emily Brontë's *Wuthering Heights*, 1847), it also prepared the literary ground for the development of two of supernatural fiction's most important sub-genres—the ghost story and the tale of terror.

Unlike their generally unconvincing Gothic predecessors, the fictional ghosts of the Victorian period typically lived in recognizable places. Victorian writers effectively domesticated the ghost story, making it reflect the landscapes and situations of their contemporary world. The Anglo-Irish writer J. S. Le Fanu (1814–73) transformed the Gothic inheritance, creating a new kind of tale in which formidable supernatural presences emerge from within the psyche of the human protagonists, as well as invade from without. Le Fanu displayed his gifts as a story-teller to the full in his first collection, *Ghost Stories and Tales of Mystery* (1851), which contains such classic stories as 'Schalken the Painter' (a powerful tale of supernatural abduction) and 'The Watcher' (later retitled 'The Familiar'). His other stories include the much-anthologized 'Green Tea' and his vampire classic 'Carmilla' (both reprinted in the 1872 collection *In a Glass Darkly*).

If your taste is for ghost stories of the traditional kind, then the half century from about 1860 to the outbreak of the First World War offers much to savour. Amongst the period's most famous individual stories are 'The Turn of the Screw' (1898) by Henry James; 'The Monkey's Paw' (1902) by W. W. Jacobs; and 'Oh, Whistle, and I'll Come to You, My Lad', a terrifying transformation of the traditional sheeted spook, from *Ghost Stories of an Antiquary* (1904) by M. R. James. This hugely influential volume, one of supernatural fiction's defining moments, set in train a vigorous sub-category of antiquarian ghost stories. James's sensitivity to place and to the living presence of the past, gives all his stories a distinctive resonance and edge. Above all, his supernatural presences are amongst the most convincing and disturbing in the literature—various in form, but always malevolent and fearfully palpable, like the moment in 'Casting the Runes' (from *More Ghost Stories of an Antiquary*, 1911), when the protagonist reaches under his pillow and touches 'a mouth, with teeth, and with hair about it'.

If ghost stories, strictly speaking, show us the doings of the returning human dead, in the wider category of the tale of terror we are presented with a more eclectic range of supernatural intrusions and, often, a more complex set of responses to the supernatural. Where many ghost stories observe a certain decorum in their effects, tales of terror are typically less restrained, though the emphasis remains placed on the arousal in the reader of an intense kind of fear. But again strict categorization is elusive: Le Fanu's 'ghosts' were a various lot (from a spectral monkey to a disembodied hand); whilst those of M. R. James include several that are terrifyingly non-human (such as the hideous demon in 'Canon Alberic's Scrap-book'). In Bram Stoker's *Dracula* (1897), the returning dead become the undead in a narrative that achieves much of its power by being set in the here and now. It also offers its own critique of contemporary values; and like that earlier iconic creation, *Frankenstein*, it has a wider purpose underlying the surface effects, expressed by Van Helsing's complaint that 'it is the fault of our science that it wants to explain all; and if it explain not, then it says there is nothing to explain'.

Dracula also exploits that heightening of terror in the face of something physically repulsive that is the distinctive feature of horror fiction. In the out-and-out horror story, physicality is vital: the fear induced is based on overt depictions of events and situations designed to arouse revulsion, rather than simple unease. Physical horror is often present in ghost stories as well. It is all a question of degree, and of the reader's individual reactions. Many pulp horror stories have no other aim but to shock, or even disgust readers (hence the contemporary term 'schlock'); but in the hands of the best writers—such as R. L. Stevenson in *The Strange Case of Dr Jekyll and Mr Hyde* (1886)—the horror that is aroused has an archetypal potency that speaks directly to our deepest and most primitive fears.

As the nineteenth century became the twentieth, supernatural fiction in all its forms continued to proliferate. For the authentic *fin de siècle* mood, try the tales and novels of Arthur Machen (1863–1947) such as *The Great God Pan* (1894) or *The Three Imposters* (1895), in which elemental forces of evil are portrayed with a kind of pagan intensity. More visionary depictions of sinister forces residing within the natural world itself can be found in the stories of the prolific Algernon Blackwood, whose particular forte was creating tales in which Nature itself provides a conduit between material and spiritual realities—as in his masterpiece 'The Willows' from *The Listener* (1907). More conventional fare is provided by H. R. Wakefield (1890–1964), a neglected writer whose impressive output includes several gems, including the short but hair-raisingly effective 'Blind Man's Buff' (from *Old Man's Beard*, 1929). Wakefield's near contemporary W. F. Harvey (1885–1937), best known for his terrifying story about a disembodied hand, 'The Beast with Five Fingers' (1928), is another underrated author of well crafted ghost stories—amongst them one that must rate as one of the scariest ever written, 'The Clock'. The ambiguous and densely written stories of Walter de la Mare—such as 'Seaton's Aunt', from *The Riddle* (1923) —are also worth seeking out.

In a different vein, the American H. P. Lovecraft, author of an influential essay on 'Supernatural Horror in Literature', created a powerful and consistent body of fiction with its own elaborate mythology; representative works include *The Dunwich Horror and Others* (1963) and *Dagon and Other Macabre Tales* (1965). Writing at much the same time, the work of the British author Robert Aickman, described by Aickman himself as 'strange stories', constitutes one of the most impressive bodies of supernatural fiction of the twentieth century. Aickman's subtle evocations of 'the experience behind the experience' can be sampled in collections such as *Dark Entries* (1964) and *Cold Hand in Mine* (1975). In the horror category, key modern works include W. P. Blatty's *The Exorcist* (1971), James Herbert's *The Rats* (1974), Peter Straub's *Ghost Story* (1979), and of course the novels of Stephen King—try *Carrie* (1974), King's first novel and one of his best, a dark study of a possessed adolescent. Finally, no supernatural fiction reading list should fail to include *The Haunting of Hill House* (1959), by the American writer Shirley Jackson, and Susan Hill's *The Woman in Black* (1983)—two of the best haunted house novels ever written.

Top Twelve

J. S. LE FANU, *Ghost Stories and Tales of Mystery* (1851)

BRAM STOKER, *Dracula* (1897)

M. R. JAMES, *Ghost Stories of an Antiquary* (1904)

ALGERNON BLACKWOOD, *The Listener* (1907)

H. R. WAKEFIELD, *They Return at Evening* (1928)

SHIRLEY JACKSON, *The Haunting of Hill House* (1959)

H. P. LOVECRAFT, *The Dunwich Horror and Others* (1963)

ROBERT AICKMAN, *Dark Entries* (1964)

STEPHEN KING, *Carrie* (1974)

PETER STRAUB, *Ghost Story* (1979)

SUSAN HILL, *The Woman in Black* (1983)

M. COX and R. A. GILBERT (eds.), *The Oxford Book of English Ghost Stories* (1986), contains W. Harvey's 'The Clock', W. W. Jacobs' 'The Monkey's Paw', and stories by R. Aickman, H. R. Wakefield, and others

Adèle Geras

Teenagers read everything. Some will be into Dostoevsky, others are fans of Point Horror. They can be enjoying *Trainspotting* (1993) by Irvine Welsh on a Monday and Agatha Christie on a Tuesday. They will veer between the good and the ghastly; the intellectually challenging and the frankly silly. Other categories in this volume, especially Supernatural, Humour, Crime, and Science Fiction, list books that young people will admire and enjoy. Publishers put books on the Young Adult list for many reasons. The text may be full of four-letter words. The subject may be controversial (drugs, abortion, homelessness, etc.) The language may be very literary and difficult for young children even though the story is not too shattering on its own. Every librarian and parent knows that it is mainly children of about 9 or 10 who read the books on the teenage lists. They are reading for information. They want to know what life will be like when they are older. What are they supposed to do about sex, clothes, school-friends, and so on? Of course, they could ask their parents, or elder siblings, but those relationships are often hedged around with embarrassment, and it's easier to discover such things as which bits go where (see Judy Blume, below) from a book. Teenagers are no different from anyone else. We all read to learn the truth about ourselves, and we read to escape from the world we know into someone else's universe. Sometimes we feel like one kind of book and some-times another. I've chosen books by writers whose work as a whole I admire, and in every case, the recommendation of a title is intended to steer the reader to other books by the same author.

A novel for adults, *The Catcher in the Rye* (1951) by J. D. Salinger, is the Daddy of all confessional-style teenage novels, and it has never been bettered. The Americans have in the main been more successful in the way they have followed Salinger than their British counterparts, and writers like Paul Zindel have adopted this style to great effect. They're written in the first person, and this has advantages and disadvantages. If you like the narrator and don't find one voice throughout the novel irritating, then it's easy to get into this kind of book. Young people like them, because they are chatty and direct, and it's easy to imagine that the writer is talking straight to you, as if you were being taken into the narrator's confidence.

Dodie Smith's *I Capture the Castle* (1949) was also published on the adult list but is a wonderful meaty family story, full of the kinds of things that teenage girls like reading about: love-affairs, ambitions, friendships. The setting in this work is important, and the house is almost a character in the book.

Judy Blume, who receives thousands of letters from young people to testify how well she understands their problems, has perfected the self-help manual kind of story, and her work tells pre-teens all about the traumas of growing up. She has covered everything from getting your first period to being too fat; from being bullied to being adopted; but *Forever* (1975) broke new ground by being the first young adult book not only to mention a penis, but to give it a name (Ralph). It describes first sex in clinical detail, and still sells very well.

A rather more literary account of young love, Ursula Le Guin's *A Very Long Way from Anywhere Else* (1976) is a tender, moving and beautifully written story, about two young classical musicians. Le Guin is better known as a science fiction writer, but in this short book she proved how well she understands modern young people.

S. E. Hinton was only 17 when her first novel *The Outsiders* (1970) was published. It tells the story of two rival gangs in a small Texas town and raises questions about loyalty, and love. The film adaptation starred Rob Lowe and Matt Dillon. It's a book with which teenagers identify. They also feel, because of the author's youth, that it must be an actuality report from a sort of teenage frontline.

Jane Gardam writes well about young people in her adult novels, as well as in her many children's books, and *Bilgewater* (1978) tells the story of a girl growing up as the daughter of a master at a boys' school. Gardam writes with a poet's intensity, and is very good at bringing landscape and place alive for the reader. This novel started life on the children's list and is now an adult paperback.

Pennington's Seventeenth Summer by K. M. Peyton (1970) is a romantic story about a moody young man: a musical genius who is rebellious, defiant, handsome: every girl's dream. Pennington falls into the Heathcliff category of hero. Every teenage girl imagines that she might be the one to reform such a character.

From the books I've mentioned so far, it might be thought that only girls read teenage books. It is true that boys at the same age are generally lost in the mists of Terry Pratchett or Stephen King, but they should not feel excluded from this list. Robert Cormier is a hard-hitting writer of plainly written but enormously exciting books which always deal honestly with sometimes very difficult issues. Cormier has written about rape, bullying, and violence of all kinds. From a very long bibliography, try *I am the Cheese* (1977) which is tense and intelligent. It tells the story of a boy in some kind of hospital recounting his story to an unseen interrogator. Why is he there? What has he done? The answers are not what one would expect.

Philip Pullman's *The Subtle Knife* (1997) is the second part of a trilogy—*His Dark Materials*—which is more than just a rip-roaring adventure, but which has enough thrills per chapter to satisfy lovers of action and conflict. It is a recasting of the story of *Paradise Lost*, and takes place in a universe that is and is not like our own.

The Haunting (1982) by the amazing Margaret Mahy shows what a really good writer can do with a supernatural story. This is light years away from the anodyne horrors children find in series books. In most novels of this kind, we know that the spooky stuff couldn't be true. In Mahy's work, however, there is a distinct possibility that some of what we are reading about could actually happen, and this makes her work more than a little unsettling.

They Do Things Differently There (1994) by Jan Mark is funny, surreal, and clever. Two girls living in a dull town ('like living inside a Fairisle jumper') invent an imaginary place which exists in the same locations but on a different level. They people it with weird characters and imagine strange happenings, and the way one level of reality overlaps the other makes for a hugely entertaining novel.

Young people are very preoccupied with their friends, and in *The Tulip Touch* (1996) Anne Fine deals with the relationship between two young girls. Each child would probably be perfectly normal on her own, but the book looks at what happens when they come together in a *folie à deux*. Fine was inspired by the James Bulger case to examine how far it is possible for a child actually to be evil. Her books are generally very funny and sharp about family life and its vicissitudes, but this one is all the stronger for being understatedly bleak. For example, Fine hints discreetly that there is a home-life of abuse in the background of one of the children, without ever stating it overtly.

Jean Ure, in *Play Nimrod for Him* (1989) tackles the difficult subject of friendship between young men. Is what they feel for one another legitimate? Could they be gay? Does it matter if they are? The novel tells of the close ties between two boys who feel themselves to be different from all their friends, and who form a sort of secret society with its own rules and invented games which puts an even greater distance between them and the rest of the world. They come from different backgrounds, and their intense relationship has effects not only on them, but on those around them. The ending is not the traditionally happy one, and leaves the young reader with something to think about and discuss.

If there is anything that links these books, any common denominator which makes them suitable for young adults, it is the emotional content of the works. They are all of them concerned with feelings and relationships; with how you fit in with other people in your world, and how you deal with rejection, disappointment, sorrow, loss, and pain. It doesn't matter if the setting is outer space or North Yorkshire. It doesn't matter if you're a girl or a boy, what these books are about is our common humanity; how we behave towards one another in all kinds of societies.

See also ADÈLE GERAS

Top Twelve

DODIE SMITH, *I Capture the Castle* (1949)

J. D. SALINGER, *The Catcher in the Rye* (1951)

S. E. HINTON, *The Outsiders* (1970)

K. M. PEYTON, *Pennington's Seventeenth Summer* (1970)

JUDY BLUME, *Forever* (1975)

ROBERT CORMIER, *I am the Cheese* (1977)

JANE GARDAM, *Bilgewater* (1978)

MARGARET MAHY, *The Haunting* (1982)

JEAN URE, *Play Nimrod for Him* (1989)

JAN MARK, *They Do Things Differently There* (1994)

PHILIP PULLMAN, *Northern Lights* (vol. 1 of *His Dark Materials*) (1995)

ANNE FINE, *The Tulip Touch* (1996)

Thrillers

Val McDermid

A thriller is the literary equivalent of the theme park white-knuckle ride. Stomach-churning suspense, heart-stopping fear, and the ever-present sense of jeopardy are all there, as well as that visceral uncertainty at the back of our reptile brains about whether we're all going to make it out of here alive. There are the dramatic highs, where everything seems held motionless at the point of no return, then the terrifying plunges into the depths, and finally the soaring sense of relief at the end. As well as that little niggle of nervousness at what might have been if things had just been slightly different.

The thriller encompasses such divergent books as the serial killer hunts of Patricia Cornwell, the action thrillers of Dick Francis, and the corkscrew twisting scams of Elmore Leonard. What they all share are those three elements of suspense, fear, and jeopardy. In a thriller, the suspense lies not in discovering whodunit but in how the protagonist will overcome the forces ranged against them. The central character of a thriller always faces jeopardy. Of course, a detective in a crime novel is habitually also under threat, but only because of his or her criminal investigation. The threat to thriller heroes often comes out of a clear blue sky and invariably turns their world upside down. Here, there is no closed group of suspects, and often the rest of the world of the book is turned remorselessly against our hero. And the price he will pay if he does not overcome what threatens him is usually the loss of all he holds dear.

This doesn't mean that the thriller is an endless sequence of dramatic set pieces. Often, the story involves a psychological investigation of threat, where the battle is as much a moral as a practical one. Often, too, that interior struggle is matched by violent confrontation. The father of the modern thriller is probably Robert Louis Stevenson. In *The Strange Case of Dr Jekyll and Mr Hyde* (1886) the chilling tale of obsession personifies the fight between good and evil and contains all the elements of suspense, jeopardy, and struggle that every good thriller needs. It's impossible not to be gripped by Jekyll's battle with his own dark side, released by the very potion he has himself created. It's a novel whose influence stretches down to the present day, continuing to inspire readers and writers alike.

Patricia Highsmith is clearly heir to Stevenson's fascinations, revealing penetrating insights into the minds of those who kill. She dazzles with her brilliant series of novels featuring the amoral con artist and killer Thomas Ripley, a bewildering charmer determined to let nothing and no one stand between him and his desires. Beginning with *The Talented Mr Ripley* (1955) she blazed a trail that has been followed with great success by, among others, Ruth Rendell, Thomas Harris, and Patricia Cornwell.

One of those who has developed the novel of psychological suspense in Highsmith's wake is Minette Walters. In *The Sculptress* (1993), she uses the device of a journalist deciding to write about a *cause célèbre* as a way to explore both the details of the crime and the mind of the woman serving life for the brutal murders of her mother and sister. Layer upon layer of deception is carefully constructed then stripped away, until at the end, the final shock of realization leaves as many questions as it answers.

Often, suspense comes from the battle of wits between the investigator and the killer. An extreme example of this is Thomas Harris's *The Silence of the Lambs* (1988), where fledgling FBI profiler Clarice Starling is thrown into a harrowing investigation into a serial killer who skins his victims. Can the FBI profilers manage to identify the killer before he strikes again? And will Clarice be both suitable and intelligent enough bait to persuade convicted killer Hannibal Lecter to give up his own insights? This is a classic example of a white-knuckle ride, leaving readers uncertain whether they'll be able to hold on to their lunch as the roller-coaster plunges vertiginously further into darkness.

Many central characters in thrillers are not connected to law enforce-ment but are merely bystanders inadvertently caught up in events. In Dick Francis's *Reflex* (1980), Philip Nore is a jockey and amateur photographer who acquires what appears to be a box of photographic rubbish belonging to a dead cameraman. But he gradually unravels the mystery behind each seemingly meaningless item and uncovers corruption, blackmail, only to find himself the next target of a ruthless killer. Interwoven with this is the mysterious story of Nore's own past and his quest to find a future.

Another example is Peter Høeg's dark chiller, *Miss Smilla's Feeling for Snow* (1992). Smilla Jaspersen, a resourceful, tenacious, and bloody-minded Greenlander refuses to accept that the death of a neighbour's 6-year-old son is an accident. What starts as an intellectual exercise soon becomes a psychological battle of wits, with a terrifying action climax on the Arctic ice-cap.

Such an exotic background is common in the thriller. Barbara Vine's evocat-ive and haunting *No Night is Too Long* (1994) alternates between Alaskan and East Anglian seascapes as the author unravels a dark tale of obsessive love and death, where the past casts a long and inevitable shadow over the present. Here, the sense of place contributes almost as much to the atmosphere as the story itself.

Lionel Davidson's *Kolymsky Heights* (1994) marries alien setting with the theme of the lone hero set against apparently insuperable odds. Mysterious messages from a secret laboratory in the deep permafrost of Siberia indicate to Professor George Lazenby that the Russians are exploring the murky depths of the gene pool. Science marries with breathtaking adventure to make this a page-turning thriller quite unlike any other.

Sometimes, the sense of being catapulted into a foreign world comes from a thriller's setting in time rather than place. Perhaps the most extreme example of this is Umberto Eco's striking novel, *The Name of the Rose* (1980), set in 1327 against the backdrop of a prosperous Italian abbey. English monk William of Baskerville—who owes more than a nod to Sherlock Holmes in his deductive powers—is on a mysterious mission which is sidetracked by a spate of bizarre murders. By day, William investigates murder, but by night, he attempts to penetrate the labyrinthine mysteries of the monastery library. *The Name of the Rose* is an intellectual challenge wrapped up in the guise of a complex detective thriller, showing how genre fiction can transcend its apparent limitations and stand comparison with any work of literature.

Another thriller absorbed with the effects of history on the present is Robert Wilson's *A Small Death in Lisbon* (1999). The roots of the novel lie in Berlin and Portugal during the the Second World War, where greed shapes the lives of a disparate group of people. Then the wheel turns, and in the late 1990s, a young girl is brutally murdered, drawing past and present together in an absorbing battle of wits. The weaving of past and present means we are never quite sure what is coming round the next curve of the track.

But it's not only the past that is a foreign country. In Philip Kerr's *A Philosophical Investigation* (1992) we are swept forward into a dystopic vision of London in 2013. The world is divided into information-rich and information-poor, and serial killing has become almost epidemic. To combat this, the authorities have devised a test that identifies potential killers. Then someone begins killing the men with the mark of Cain. Intelligent and imaginative, Kerr's thriller is one of the first truly successful examples of what amounts practically to a sub-genre, the serial killer thriller.

Along with Thomas Harris, the undoubted virtuoso of the American serial killer thriller is Patricia Cornwell. Although many crime writers in the United States have explored this corner of the thriller market, notably Michael Connelly, James Ellroy, Robert Crais, and Lynn S. Hightower, Cornwell has carved a niche uniquely hers. In *Post-Mortem* (1990), she introduced her protagonist Kay Scarpetta, a forensic pathologist with formidable skills and sufficient emotional problems of her own to provide a fertile source of subsidiary story-lines in this and future novels. In classic style, *Post-Mortem* pits Scarpetta against not only a brutal serial killer but also against those who desire her defeat for reasons of their own. The books are characterized by a high body count, a wealth of forensic detail, and an extraordinary build-up of tension that has readers turning pages well into the small hours.

The thriller is one of the most popular genres of fiction and continues to attract writers of great imagination and skill. Its range and variety continues to grow; every year, writers push the boundaries further and experiment with the form, providing readers with fresh treats. For as long as we love to be thrilled and excited in equal measure, the thriller will continue to satisfy.

See also VAL MCDERMID

See also CRIME

Top Twelve

ROBERT LOUIS STEVENSON, *The Strange Case of Dr Jekyll and Mr Hyde* (1886)

PATRICIA HIGHSMITH, *The Talented Mr Ripley* (1955)

DICK FRANCIS, *Reflex* (1980)

UMBERTO ECO, *The Name of the Rose* (1980)

THOMAS HARRIS, *The Silence of the Lambs* (1988)

PATRICIA CORNWELL, *Post-Mortem* (1990)

PHILIP KERR, *A Philosophical Investigation* (1992)

PETER HØEG, *Miss Smilla's Feeling for Snow* (1993)

MINETTE WALTERS, *The Sculptress* (1993)

BARBARA VINE, *No Night is Too Long* (1994)

LIONEL DAVIDSON, *Kolymsky Heights* (1994)

ROBERT WILSON, *A Small Death in Lisbon* (1999)

United States of America

Richard Francis

American fiction is not simply an off-shoot of English literature, but a separate tradition altogether, arising out of what was then a completely new experience: settling the wilderness and building up the institutions and social structure of a western country from scratch. The pilgrim fathers (and mothers) were English people, it is true, but they were refugees, disillusioned with the past, hopeful about the future. On his ship the *Arbella*, in 1630, John Winthrop looked towards the American coast and foresaw the building of a 'city on a hill', and the American dream was born.

The novel form began in Europe in the eighteenth century, a new kind of writing for the newly literate middle class which had grown in numbers and self-confidence as the commercial and manufacturing structure of the modern world came into being. The American colonies during that period were still agricultural and pioneering: in addition, the legacy of puritanism had produced a suspicion of any sort of artistic activity on the grounds that it was at best frivolous and at worst blasphemous (since it challenged God's role as the creator). But when the republic was established after the Revolution of 1776, a new society began to feel the need for a culture and literature to define itself by.

The paradox is that in this country of beginnings the earliest prose fiction tended to be nostalgic in tone, reaching back towards a pioneering way of life that was already in decline on the eastern side of the continent where the authors (and readers) lived. It is almost as if the early writers, like Washington Irving, James Fenimore Cooper, and Nathaniel Hawthorne, wanted to give voice to the two hundred years of white settlement that America had already experienced. More poignantly, they seem to have had a sense that in some fundamental way the dream had already been betrayed. Irving's famous character, Rip Van Winkle, sleeps his life away and misses the Revolution altogether; yet when he awakes, nothing has really changed. Cooper's hero, the explorer Natty Bumppo, sees his wilderness diminished and ultimately destroyed by settlement; Hawthorne dissects the psyche and explores the guilt of his puritan ancestors as they established their townships in the forests. Even Edgar Allan Poe, whose stories have a much more European flavour, uses the Gothic form to explore the lingering hold of the values of the past on the present.

Man and nature: the theme seems to imply man as male as well as man as representative human. Hawthorne places a female character, Hester Prynne, at the heart of *The Scarlet Letter* (1850), but on the whole female characters, and women writers, are thin on the ground for most of the American nineteenth century, apart from two who had immense popular success and influence: Harriet Beecher Stowe with her anti-slavery novel, *Uncle Tom's Cabin* (1851–2), and Louisa May Alcott and her celebration of American family life, *Little Women* (1868–9).

In the hands of the male authors, the relationship between the sexes seems to have been replaced by male bonding across the racial and cultural divide. Natty Bumppo has his Indian friend Chingachgook, the last of the Mohicans (over a century later the relationship would be echoed by Tonto and the Lone Ranger). Ishmael, narrator of the great *Moby Dick* (1851), has the south Pacific islander, Queequeg, as his opposite number (though it could be argued that the central relationship is that between Captain Ahab and the white whale itself— which shows in a nutshell how far we are from the world of Charles Dickens and George Eliot). Twenty years later, the hero of *Adventures of Huckleberry Finn* (1884), who loves and reveres his friend Tom Sawyer, shares a raft on the Mississippi with Jim, the runaway slave.

By the end of the nineteenth century Americans were beginning to live in large cities like New York and Chicago; department stores and skyscrapers were appearing; it was time for some fiction that dealt with an urban setting. Stephen Crane's *Maggie, a Girl of the Streets* (1893) revealed the depths of life in the Bowery slums; Theodore Dreiser's *Sister Carrie* (1900) also explored the ways in which money (or the lack of it) turned people into commodities. The move from nature (memorably chronicled in Willa Cather's *My Ántonia*, 1918) to a civilization that is equally red in tooth and claw allowed women, as authors and characters, to come to the fore. Kate Chopin's *The Awakening* (1899) dissected the frustration of a married woman coping with a stuffy husband and a fossilized social code in late-nineteenth-century Louisiana; Edith Wharton, in many novels, dealt with similar predicaments faced by women in New York and other American—and European—environments.

After a century of confronting American history and geography it was time for writers to look back to their origins. It was almost as if they had gone west, literally and imaginatively, as far as they could: lacking a promising horizon in that direction, the only thing for it was to turn round and look eastward. Henry James, like his friend Edith Wharton, was fascinated by what he felt was a European alternative to the materialistic values of America, a world free of the puritan and capitalist work ethic, valuing art and leisure. It was a rather selective perspective, of aristocratic privilege and refinement, but it enabled James to concentrate on psychological dilemmas without any distracting 'dailiness' (just as, ironically, Twain's raft, or Melville's whaling boat, or Cooper's wilderness, had permitted an equivalent focus and intensity).

A generation later, Ernest Hemingway and Scott Fitzgerald were seduced by Paris and Pamplona and the Riviera, where characters disillusioned by the First World War could spend time trying (and mostly failing) to find themselves, though Fitzgerald's most famous novel, *The Great Gatsby* (1925), was set on an American east coast that was as riven as Europe was with class warfare. Their great contemporary, William Faulkner, kept his imagination closer to home, exploring a disillusioned deep south of shabby gentility, impoverished white farmers, and black people who had swapped slavery for servanthood, but magically infusing this regional setting with modernist literary experiment.

The Wall Street crash brought the Jazz Age to an end and the 1930s was a grim and ominous decade, brilliantly satirized in Nathaniel West's novellas, and movingly documented in Steinbeck's *The Grapes of Wrath* (1939). The black writer Richard Wright produced an extraordinary combination of poetry and polemic in his story of the doomed Negro youth, Bigger Thomas, in his ground-breaking novel *Native Son* (1940).

After the Second World War the plot gets harder to follow, partly because we are nearer our own time, and partly because the literary scene has become richer and more diverse. Norman Mailer's development from the gritty wartime realism of *The Naked and the Dead* (1948), through existentialism and absurdism to the documentary novel, demonstrates that anything is possible, while Joseph Heller manages to combine all those elements at once in *Catch-22* (1961). Other Jewish writers like Saul Bellow and Bernard Malamud evoke the predicament of minority culture with a humanity that makes their preoccupations ring true to the wider reading public. Ralph Ellison grafted a hypnotic brand of surrealism on to the legacy of his one-time friend, Richard Wright. J. D. Salinger wrote his sad and funny account of teenage anxiety and rebellion, *The Catcher in the Rye* (1951), while Jack Kerouac helped to set the agenda for hippy culture with *On the Road* (1957). In the 1960s Thomas Pynchon began his investigation of American conspiracy (and paranoia) with *The Crying of Lot 49* (1966), issues which have been explored more recently in the novels of Don DeLillo.

American writing has often bridged the gap between popular and literary fiction, and in recent years Kurt Vonnegut has made science fiction into a mainstream genre with books like *Slaughterhouse-Five* (1969), a marvellous account both of the bombing of Dresden and the ennui of post-war suburban America. Anne Tyler has given a new lease of life to the theme of the family in *Dinner at the Homesick Restaurant* (1982), while a darker view of human relationships is apparent in the 'dirty realism' of Raymond Carver's sharply written tales of blue collar life and culture, or in E. Annie Proulx's poetic studies of modern-day cowboys, and girls, in her Wyoming short stories, *Close Range* (1999). Louise Erdrich has chronicled the interaction of whites and native Americans in South Dakota in *Love Medicine* (1984) and *Tracks* (1988). Black writing has flourished, with James Baldwin taking on the mantle of Wright and Ellison in the 1960s, to be followed by a new generation, including important women novelists like Alice Walker with *The Color Purple* (1982) and Toni Morrison with her great exploration of the trauma of slavery, *Beloved* (1987).

American writing is nowadays as diverse as it has ever been. In the late 1980s we have had Tom Wolfe's vast study of New York high (or at least rich) society, *The Bonfire of the Vanities* (1987), and a savage revisionist western by Cormac McCarthy, *Blood Meridian* (1985). Both these books reach back to earlier achievements, the works of Edith Wharton and Herman Melville respectively, and both relate to each other, in the way they show their central characters trying to find themselves and their place in the urban or natural wilderness. That was, after all, the American task when the first settlers landed, and it has been the American theme from the start of their fiction right up to the present.

See also RICHARD FRANCIS

Top Twelve

NATHANIEL HAWTHORNE, *The Scarlet Letter* (1850)

HERMAN MELVILLE, *Moby Dick* (1851)

HENRY JAMES, *The Portrait of a Lady* (1881)

MARK TWAIN, *Adventures of Huckleberry Finn* (1884)

F. SCOTT FITZGERALD, *The Great Gatsby* (1925)

ERNEST HEMINGWAY, *The Sun Also Rises* (1926)

WILLIAM FAULKNER, *The Sound and the Fury* (1929)

J. D. SALINGER, *The Catcher in the Rye* (1951)

RALPH ELLISON, *Invisible Man* (1952)

CORMAC MCCARTHY, *Blood Meridian* (1985)

TONI MORRISON, *Beloved* (1987)

E. ANNIE PROULX, *Close Range* (1999)

War

Mike Harris

It became a cliché of late-twentieth-century feminism that men needed to become more like women: getting in touch with their feelings, the better to empathize, understand, and support. But war fiction shows men doing precisely that, whilst at the same time committing acts of atrociously insensitive violence. Which is one reason why more women should read war fiction.

War is at least as old as recorded history. It provides the writer with the ultimate jeopardy plot in which character, ideas, hopes, and dreams can be tested to destruction. No surprise then that one of the oldest and most influential fictional texts in our tradition—*The Iliad* of Homer (around eighth century BC) —is a novel-length poem about a siege in which most of the conventions are already in place: panoramic battle scenes going into impressionistic close-up on terrifyingly confused hand-to-hand combat, horrific violence, homoerotic comradeship, men torn between battlefield and domestic loyalties, and a whole civilization—Troy—transformed and destroyed in the struggle.

So why is the war novel essentially a twentieth-century genre? Firstly, of course, the novel in English didn't exist until the early eighteenth century and for a hundred and fifty years after that most of our wars were localized conflicts, fought far away by small armies composed largely of lower-class illiterates, whose sufferings were of little account in a deeply undemocratic society. Jane Austen (1775–1817) more or less ignores the Napoleonic Wars, and even in the hindsight of Thackeray's *Vanity Fair* (1848) they appear only episodically, leaving the larger fictional world untouched. The American Civil War of 1861–5 began the transformation. It was a total war, fought on home territory by big armies whose ordinary soldiers were able to write down their experiences for a democratic public eager to read them.

Tolstoy's *War and Peace* (1863–9), written at the height of the American Civil War, is about Napoleon's invasion of Russia in 1812: an earlier total conflict that had to wait fifty years for history to provide the writer and the readership willing to imagine it. Tolstoy's epic describes the psychological effects of invasion on a whole society: no life is untouched by it; no idea or dream left unchallenged or unchanged. The battles are bloody and confused, their issue decided not by generals, but by ordinary soldiers torn between fight and flight.

Tolstoy has influenced all war novels written since, be they home-front dramas like Elizabeth Bowen's poignant *The Heat of the Day* (1949), or front-line combat books like Stephen Crane's *The Red Badge of Courage* (1895). Crane didn't fight in the American Civil War but he devoured the literature. His young hero runs from his first battle only to return next day and fight tenaciously. Both running and return seem equally random in a conflict without apparent direction or purpose. Like Homer, Crane is concerned with issues of bravery and honour, but his poetic, psychologically probing prose uncovers the shifting foundations of both.

With literate mass armies and a voracious novel-reading public securely in place, all the twentieth century had to do was provide a total war in the heart of Europe and the war novel couldn't help but become a full-blown genre. The century obliged.

It was poets who first drew the attention of a jingoistic public to the unique horrors of trench warfare. Two of the greatest—Wilfred Owen and Siegfried Sassoon—were homosexual, so when they extol male comradeship or cry out in pity and horror at the wanton destruction of young male bodies, their sexuality makes evident to us what had been more or less suppressed in both fiction and war since the Greeks. When the novels finally emerge in the 1920s and 1930s, even heterosexual writers make the point. Erich Maria Remarque's *All Quiet on the Western Front* (1929) movingly describes German soldiers enduring the unendurable, and fighting on not for patriotism but for the comrades who, in the absence of women, tend and sustain them. When those comrades die (as in V. M. Yeates' undeservedly neglected *Winged Victory*, 1934, which depicts with painful authenticity the drudgery, fear, and sheer mundanity of an allegedly more romantic air war), the hero grieves as for a wife or lover. When the hero of Ford Madox Ford's quirky, prolix masterpiece, *Parade's End* (1924–8), is visited at the front by his wayward wife, she is revealingly jealous of his relationship with his men, which she sees as clearly sexual: men are in some way *enjoying* this war; *all* of it—the comradely tenderness and mutual support; the destructiveness, absurd risk-taking, self-sacrifice and blood-lust.

As the teachings of Freud and his successors seeped into the century's consciousness, novelists made even more overt connections. In *The Thin Red Line* (1962), a gripping buddy-buddy, Second World War combat novel with philosophical pretensions, James Jones describes overt homosexuality at the front as well as the 'ball tingling' sexual thrill of being authorized by the state to break the ultimate taboo, and kill.

Interestingly, it took a woman, Pat Barker, at the very end of the century, to engage head-on with the troubling ambiguities of the male love–hate affair with war. Her Booker Prize winning *Regeneration* trilogy (1991–5), is about shell-shocked solders in the First World War. Barker is no stylist and her narrative is often perfunctory but her earnest exploration of new fictional material is compelling. Rivers, a humane military psychiatrist, attempts to cure soldiers suffering from a bizarre and horrific range of psychological injuries. In so doing he explores the nature of combat experience and the sexuality of both himself and his patients. The character of Billy Prior comes to dominate the trilogy. A chippy, bisexual, working-class officer who recognizes and fears the sadism that is part of his divided nature, he seemingly embodies all the conflicts and ambiguities of masculinity, and war itself. Barker is aware that Freud evolved his theories after observing the 'hysteria' of socially emasculated middle-class Victorian women. In these novels she makes the point that soldiers—caught between the prospect of death in combat, or ignobly abandoning their comrades and risking execution—are as trapped, and as impotent. Insanity is, therefore, a perfectly reasonable response to the inescapable madness of twentieth-century warfare.

Laughter is another. It would seem paradoxical that some of the greatest war novels are comedies. But comedy always operates when the gap between pretension and reality is widest. Politicians try to convince us that wars are not fought for money and power but to Make Things Better. Their warlords believe that order and discipline can control the battlefield and therefore the outcome of wars. But soldiers experience battle as a terrifying, brutal chaos, outside of the control of any individual and often see, at first hand, the dismal outcome of wars. When soldiers write novels it is therefore not surprising that they sometimes laugh darkly.

In one of the great books of the century, *The Good Soldier Švejk* (1921–3), Jaroslav Hašek's anti-hero is a 'certified idiot', conscripted to serve in the armies of Austria-Hungary during the First World War. He spends 800 episodic pages skilfully avoiding combat and, in the process, satirizes generals, doctors, priests, totalitarianism, and the very idea of war itself. Clearly indebted to Hašek is Joseph Heller's over-praised cult classic, *Catch-22* (1961). Its bomb-aimer hero, Yossarian, quite reasonably wants to get out of the war because the enemy is trying to kill him. Unfortunately he can only do so if Doc Daneeka declares him insane. But, explains, the doc, anyone who wants to get out of this war is clearly *not* insane, and therein lies the catch. Heller's book is full of outrageous comic characters such as the enterprising Milo Minderbender who contracts with the German army to bomb United States bases using American bombers. But there is little in it that moves or touches and Heller's delight in trivial verbal paradox is ultimately irritating. The book is an over-long, glorious cartoon that, unlike *Švejk*, has little to tell us about the period of history in which it is ostensibly set. It became a cult in the 1960s because it spoke to a generation who wanted to hear that their fathers' war was as absurdly pointless as Vietnam. Which it wasn't, quite.

By contrast Evelyn Waugh's *Sword of Honour* trilogy (1952–61) captures all the tragi-comic absurdity of the Second World War, without once losing sight of the obvious fact that real people are living, loving, and dying in it. It is also a deeply serious 'Condition of England' novel in which the ageing, impotent, Catholic hero, Guy Crouchback, joins up, falls in love with his regiment, and then feels his crusading zeal steadily dissolve as one absurd military disaster succeeds another and a shabbier, more morally squalid society emerges from the ashes. In life, Waugh became a risible, right-wing bigot. In these books his politics and theology are an essential framework for a profound and hilarious satire that never loses sight of the humanity of any of its characters, however laughable they may be. *Sword of Honour* is, arguably, not only a great war novel but one of the greatest English novels of the last fifty years.

Top Twelve

HOMER, *The Iliad* (around eighth century BC)

LEO TOLSTOY, *War and Peace* (1863–9)

STEPHEN CRANE, *The Red Badge of Courage* (1895)

JAROSLAV HAŠEK, *The Good Soldier Švejk* (1921–3)

FORD MADOX FORD, *Parade's End* (1924–8)

ERICH MARIA REMARQUE, *All Quiet on the Western Front* (1931)

V. M. YEATES, *Winged Victory* (1934)

ELIZABETH BOWEN, *The Heat of the Day* (1949)

EVELYN WAUGH, *Sword of Honour* trilogy (1952–61)

JOSEPH HELLER, *Catch-22* (1961)

JAMES JONES, *The Thin Red Line* (1963)

PAT BARKER, *Regeneration* trilogy (1991–5)

Western

Lee Clark Mitchell

Few other fictional genres can rival the Western in popularity, for reasons not altogether clear. True, the characters are simple and familiar, plots are rarely complicated, and the setting is so consistently spectacular that it has lent its name to the genre (unlike any other). Yet why should the image of a horseman packing a gun so have fascinated a post-industrial culture? Perhaps an answer lies in the question itself. For just when industrialism had triumphed over rural culture, nostalgia buffed up the allure of a vanishing wilderness and the stalwart virtues associated with it. Readers looked to the wide-open vistas of the American West to imagine alternatives to office and factory life—alternatives in which one acted alone with integrity, resorting to quick violence to resolve the unfair delays of the law.

Owen Wister first combined the ingredients—appealing gunman, sullen villain, pert schoolmarm, high plains setting—into a mix that established the Western as a popular genre with the regulation shoot-out as plot climax. *The Virginian* (1902) remains among the best of the genre in its celebration of quick-wittedness as well as quick-draws. The novel raises issues pursued in countless subsequent Westerns, including most centrally the question of how to comport oneself as a man. Wister's inability to capitalize on his success with a sequel opened the field to others, led by an Ohio dentist named Zane Grey. Like other prolific authors, Grey was guilty of churning out unimaginative, highly formulaic novels that flooded a new pulp fiction and slick magazine market. But perhaps his most engaging novel was also one of his earliest and most popular, *Riders of the Purple Sage* (1912). In it, Grey exaggerates a number of features borrowed from Wister, including the idea of open landscape that revivifies those who escape from the East. Grey also embellished two other features that quickly became staples of the genre (though hardly exclusively): sex and violence. The heightened erotic charge between leather-clad men and competent women parallels the quickening emotional tension between heroes and villains, manifested in the frequent gunplay that has since become a signature of the genre. And the morbid conspiracies that regularly drive plot in page-turning suspense are mirrored in the dazzling, labyrinthine terrain through which characters lose their way. The Utah landscape all but becomes a character in the novel, and rarely thereafter does the genre ever forget where it is set.

If neither Grey nor Wister could match their own early successes, nor could many of the others writing for a mass readership in the first three decades of the century. There were notable exceptions, of course, including Eugene Manlove Rhodes's short novel, *Pasó por Aquí* (1927): a brilliant account of a bank robber escaping from pursuers, who stumbles across a west Texan family suffering from diphtheria, and reveals a quietly steadfast heroism in nursing them back to health. Even earlier, Stephen Crane wrote perhaps the finest Western story ever—'The Bride Comes to Yellow Sky' (1898)—ironically, something of an anti-Western that appeared before Wister had consolidated the genre. Crane evokes the strong sense of nostalgia that permeates Westerns, and of resistance to civilization's clock-time. The story's absence of a final shoot-out nicely reveals the extent to which expectations themselves create the genre more than actual events.

Exceptions like these, however, only define a more common rule among pulp writers like Max Brand and Ernest Haycox. Fast-paced action occurs in frontier towns where black hats are worn by rapacious landowners, weak lawmen, and avaricious businessmen, and where white-hatted heroes appeal to higher laws to right wrongs. Heroines misunderstand these attempts, often actively resist them, before realizing the ennobling efforts that draw them to heroes in the closing pages. The most accomplished of these writers is Haycox, who despite the pressures of churning out fiction at enormous speed, brought a greater degree of verisimilitude to the genre with such novels as *Saddle and Ride* (1940) and *The Wild Bunch* (1943).

During this period two authors took a more reflective stance towards the genre, questioning some of its staple elements in revisionist Westerns that are at the same time powerfully engaging novels (made into important films). Walter Van Tilburg Clark's *The Ox-Bow Incident* (1940) focuses on the premiss of Wister's *The Virginian* that taking the law into one's own hands is unavoidable in the Far West. The novel describes a vigilante hunt leading to a mistaken lynching, narrated in the unenthusiastic but obliging tones of one of the mob. Southern chivalry, admired by Wister, has become a cover for simple brutality, with innocent men hung and no cowboy hero appearing to right the affair. Clark's narrative triumph is to evoke the actual feeling of mob hysteria, encouraging the reader to want to cut through the novel's talk and get on with extra-legal action, as the formula prescribes. Alan LeMay's *The Searchers* (1953) succeeds equally as a novel but takes a different tack; instead of simply embracing Wister's conservative view of race and culture, LeMay registers a sceptical vision underlined through the slow transformation of pursuing Texans into the brutes they imagine the Cheyenne captors of Debby to be. Moreover, the novel becomes an exercise as much for the reader in decoding contradictory signs as for the searchers themselves, offering an exhilarating analogy in reading a Western of what it would be like to act in one.

The 1950s were the heyday for Westerns in film, television, and novels. Louis L'Amour, the most widely read author of Westerns, began publishing with the advent of the paperback revolution. Part of his success lay in his devotion to an apparently authentic West, teaching the reader about frontier facts and arcane lore in the process of educating his characters. This trademark surfaces as early as *Hondo* (1953), which stresses the humanizing bonds of family life and the crucial knowledge fathers must instil in sons. This theme is also dominant in Jack Schaefer's *Shane* (1948), which offers a classic rendition of the Western from the point of view of a child, infusing renewed urgency into the mysteriousness of villainous gunmen, the heroism of buckskinned Shane, and the grandeur of Wyoming vistas. In this period, Frederick Manfred is one of the few whose Westerns warrant continuing attention thanks to his historical sweep and more complex characters. *Conquering Horse* (1959) is the first chronologically of five novels that comprise the *Buckskin Man Tales*, set in the 1830s West, when a Sioux chief's son must go through a series of strenuous trials to achieve manhood and leadership of his tribe. *Riders of Judgment* (1957) closes the series, set in Wyoming's 1890s Johnson County wars.

The end of the 1950s saw a self-conscious turn from a genre some felt was so repetitious that it could no longer reinvent itself. Yet imaginative writers like E. L. Doctorow exploited that flaw, opening *Welcome to Hard Times* (1960) with a grotesque version of the 'good man cleaning up the town' that then leads to a vicious cycle of deadly regeneration and destruction, the novel ending with the same scene it began with. Larry McMurtry is the Western's most successful modern practitioner. His *tour de force*, the 1985 novel *Lonesome Dove*, is an engagingly rambling narrative of a cattle drive from Texas to Montana, encompassing Indian torture, ranger pursuits, and frontier escapades along the way. An equally stunning achievement is McMurtry's early *Horseman, Pass By* (1961), which strips away conventional romantic pretensions. The narrator comes of age in a rural Texas that cherishes older frontier values but finds them ineffectual against the bitter economic realities of modern ranch life.

Among contemporary authors, Douglas C. Jones has the finest lyrical sense of the West. *Season of Yellow Leaf* (1980) offers a moving narrative of a woman taken by the Cheyenne in the 1840s, who gives birth to their future leader. *Gone the Dreams and Dancing* (1984) is a sequel set in the 1870s, with the Cheyenne leader now searching for his mother, long ago recaptured by Texas Rangers. *Roman* (1986) recounts the experiences of a young man making his way in post-Civil War Kansas, eager to see buffalo and Cheyenne before they disappear and able through quick wits and masculine strength to build a fortune. One of the few contemporary authors equal to Jones in celebrating the old West is Frank Bergon. *Shoshone Mike* (1987) narrates the eerie revival of just that older West in 1911, in the conflict between an itinerant band of Indians and their white pursuers, all of whom realize their own belatedness.

Critics have long chided the Western for its historical inaccuracy, or its narrative improbabilities, or its predictable stockpile of characters. Yet the most striking feature of the Western is that imaginative authors continue to be drawn to the genre. Perhaps the old West persists in fascinating us because it embodies the last period when individuals seemed to control their own destinies—when social problems had a local face and a voice, and one might aspire without a trace of embarrassment to such recognizable virtues as integrity, honour, steadfastness, loyalty. Westerns define a landscape imbued with the potential for self-transformation. That combined attention to both past and future continues to capture our imaginations, as Westerns play out our own more intractable problems in vistas far removed from the present, resolving conflicts in a rhythm of restraint and careful violence that is at once familiar and infinitely varied.

Top Twelve

STEPHEN CRANE, 'The Bride Comes to Yellow Sky' (1898)

OWEN WISTER, *The Virginian* (1902)

ZANE GREY, *Riders of the Purple Sage* (1912)

EUGENE MANLOVE RHODES, *Pasó por Aquí* (1927)

WALTER VAN TILBURG CLARK, *The Ox-Bow Incident* (1940)

JACK SCHAEFFER, *Shane* (1948)

ALAN LeMAY, *The Searchers* (1953)

FREDERICK MANFRED, *Riders of Judgment* (1957)

E. L. DOCTOROW, *Welcome to Hard Times* (1960)

DOUGLAS C. JONES, *Season of Yellow Leaf* (1980)

LARRY McMURTRY, *Lonesome Dove* (1985)

FRANK BERGON, *Shoshone Mike* (1987)

AUTHORS A–Z

A

Abbott, Edwin A. (British, 1838–1926) A leading theologian of the Victorian era and eminent Shakespearian scholar, Abbott published many learned works, yet is best remembered as the author of *Flatland* (1884), subtitled *A Romance of Many Dimensions*. This is an amusing and thought-provoking little book, part social satire, part speculation into the rarefied realms of theoretical science. The author—a Square, geometrically speaking—describes the arrival into his two-dimensional world of a being from the third dimension—a Sphere. Unable to perceive a solid body, the Flatlander would see only a circle intersecting his flat plane; extend this analogy to our world of three dimensions, and we become the Flatlanders, unaware of both past and future perpetually existing in fourth-dimensional spacetime. Remarkably, Abbott's artistic visualization came twenty years before Einstein formulated his Theory of Relativity, providing imagery which helps us grasp a mind-boggling concept.

📖 Jules Verne, Jonathan Swift, Olaf Stapledon   *TH*

Abish, Walter (US, 1931–) Born in Vienna, Abish lived in China and Israel before taking US citizenship in 1960. Formerly a city planner, he has been a full-time writer and holder of various visiting professorships since 1975. Begin with *How German is it?* (1979), which evokes tensions between contemporary appearances and historical realities in affluent post-war Germany. His first novel, the challengingly experimental *Alphabetical Africa* (1974), draws attention to the arbitrariness of language by restricting each chapter to words beginning solely with single, successive letters of the alphabet. Abish's other works include *Eclipse Fever* (1993), a complex narrative of defective relationships, which reflects the collision of modern materialism and traditional values in its Mexican setting.

📖 Robert Coover, Thomas Pynchon   *DH*

Achebe, Chinua (Nigerian, 1930–) Considered by many to be the finest Nigerian novelist, Achebe's writing career has won him international acclaim. Heavily indebted to the oral tradition, Achebe's novels are about colonial and postcolonial Nigeria. His first, *Things Fall Apart* (1958), is an elegantly written and informative depiction of Ibo society at the end of the nineteenth century. It follows the story of Okonkwo, a highly respected member of his village whose life is ruined because he cannot adapt to colonial rule.

The sequel to this novel, *No Longer at Ease* (1960), follows the life of Okonkwo's grandson, Obi, and the initial struggle by the Ibo people to keep their land away from the clutches of the colonizers. Unlike his grandfather, Obi has been brought up a Christian and has had a Western education. This creates an irreconcilable conflict between the traditions of his forefathers and his immersion into the western world. *Arrow of God* (1964) is set in the 1920s when the colonizers had established a firm grip on Nigeria. Again, the story centres around one man, Ezeulu, a chief priest who struggles to adapt to colonial rule and as a result, loses his grip on reality. *Anthills of the Savannah* (1987), a runner-up for the Booker Prize, is an impressive work about the insidious power of the Nigerian regime set against the backdrop of Third World politics.

📖 Amos Tutuola, Ben Okri, Wole Soyinka, Caryl Phillips. *See* AFRICA

EW

Acker, Kathy (US, 1947–98) A native New Yorker, Acker was initially seen as part of the punk movement; she came to prominence as a serious writer while living in London, and later moved to San Francisco. Her writing reflects an extreme response both to literary tradition and to the expectations of readers, often incorporating classic male texts, with graphic sexual language, and disrupting usual notions of authorship. This is brilliantly done in *Great Expectations* (1982), which takes off from Dickens's novel into far bleaker female autobiography, describing anguished personal relations; the narrative is constantly interrupted by other kinds of text. Similarly radical effects are at work in *Don Quixote* (1986), a nightmare journey through language and history to Nixon's America, and *Empire of the Senseless* (1988). A good way into Acker's difficult but fascinating work would be a collection of shorter pieces, *Eurydice in the Underworld* (1997).

📖 William Burroughs, Jean Genet

JS

Ackerley, J(oseph) R(andolph) (British, 1896–1967) Ackerley was the influential literary editor of the *Listener*

magazine, working for the BBC from 1928 to 1959. His books span autobiography and fiction, and were controversial for their portrayal of homosexual lifestyles and implicit advocacy of animal rights. They are highly engaging, cast as voyages of discovery in which the author's expectations are increasingly confounded. *Hindoo Holiday* (1932) depicts his time spent at the court of an extravagantly gay Indian Maharajah, observing sexual and social tensions among the servants and others. *We Think the World of You* (1960) comically develops the acquisition of an Alsatian bitch alongside the narrator's attachment to her previous owner, a working-class married man. Ackerley's best-known book was published posthumously, partly due to its sexual frankness. *My Father and Myself* (1968) is a minor classic, beginning as a family memoir but gradually revealing his father's secret life and his own.

📖 E. M. Forster, Jocelyn Brooke JS

Ackroyd, Peter (British, 1949–) Born in London, Ackroyd is well known as a biographer; his frequently amusing fiction habitually imagines the lives of diverse artistic figures, from Thomas Chatterton to Dan Leno, Nicholas Hawksmoor to John Milton. Such books link the past and present to great effect; complex but generally accessible, they often pastiche genres and period speech. *The Last Testament of Oscar Wilde* (1983) brilliantly evokes Wilde's manner. *Hawksmoor* (1985), which won the Whitbread and *Guardian* fiction prizes, uses the crime thriller to blend a multi-layered narrative in which a detective tries to solve cases of ritual murder in the eighteenth and twentieth centuries. *English Music* (1992) shifts between the world of dreams and visions and the story of a psychic small boy and his spiritualist father in 1925 London; they have to come to terms with their gifts, and each other. An alternative life for Milton, escaping to the New World to be the leader of a puritan settlement, is proposed by *Milton in America* (1996). The novel turns on experiences within an Indian camp by which the poet regains his sight.

Alasdair Gray, John Fowles, John Banville   *JS*

Adams, Douglas (British, 1952–) Adams came to prominence with the airing of his absurd and hilarious radio comedy, *The Hitchhiker's Guide to the Galaxy* (1978–80), the first half of which was converted to a television series and expanded as a novel (1979). It follows Arthur Dent, the last surviving human when Earth is demolished to make way for a hyperspace bypass, on a bewildered pilgrim's progress round various corners of space and time in the company of assorted, blasé humanoid aliens and Marvin, a depressed and paranoid android.

Adams was one of the first writers to realize science fiction's enormous comic potential and the second half of his radio series, expanded in print, took Dent and friends to the eponymous *Restaurant at the End of the Universe* (1980), an exclusive establishment where the universe's élite have booked places to witness the end of time. This was followed by three other *Hitchhiker* sequels. Just as extravagant and inventive are Adams's two Dirk Gently novels which satirize the hard-boiled detective genre. These elevate the detective's archetypal 'hunch' and the close-knitting of the traditional plot to the status of cosmic law, The Interconnectedness of All Things, which only Gently believes in. In

the second instalment, *The Long Dark Tea-Time of the Soul* (1988), Dirk is embroiled in a bizarre explosion at Heathrow airport that miraculously injures no one, and which we later learn was the temper-tantrum of the god Thor trying to buy a ticket.

Terry Pratchett, Rudy Rucker, Bob Shaw. *See* SCIENCE FICTION
                                             RP

Adams, Richard (George) (British, 1920–) Richard Adams was born in Berkshire, and served in the forces and the civil service before turning to fiction full-time. His first and most celebrated novel is *Watership Down* (1972), the story of a group of rabbits searching for a new home. The book, which draws on ancient myths and legends, began life as a children's story, but can also be seen as a novel about the need to live in harmony with the natural world. *The Plague Dogs* (1977) is the story of two dogs who escape from a laboratory, while myth and psychology are made the explicit subject of *The Girl on the Swing* (1980), in which an enigmatic woman acts as a link to the English pagan past. *Shardik* (1974) and *Maia* (1984) are ambitious fantasy novels set in the fictional world of the Belkan Empire.

Henry Willamson, Paul Gallico
                                             WB

Agee, James (US, 1909–55) Agee was an influential film critic for *Time* magazine and the *Nation*, as well as screenwriter on Huston's *The African Queen* and Laughton's *The Night of the Hunter*. He is equally known for *Let Us Now Praise Famous Men* (1941), with photographer Walker Evans, a richly poetic and engaged account of Alabama sharecropper families during the Depression. Agee put his awareness of film-making into his fiction, particularly *A Death in the Family* (1957), which uses flashbacks and emphasizes the visual. This intense and moving novel is in three parts; it follows a young boy's attachment to his father, the death of the father in a car crash, and the emotional impact on the whole family. Conflicts between a boy's religious feeling and growing self-awareness also feature in *The Morning Watch* (1951), during which he is awakened by a priest to stand his watch before the altar.

📖 John Steinbeck, Sherwood Anderson   JS

Aickman, Robert (British, 1914–81). *See* SUPERNATURAL

Aiken, Joan (British, 1924–) Joan Aiken, born in Rye, Sussex, writes children's books which can be read with equal pleasure by adults who still have an imagination. Her best known is probably *The Wolves of Willoughby Chase* (1962), in which she imagines a strange, dark Victorian England, like a Dickensian fairytale, where wolves prowl the countryside and it seems to be perpetual winter. Three children, Bonnie, Sylvia, and Simon, join forces in remote Willoughby Chase to oppose the unutterably evil governess, Miss Slighcarp. The illustrations by Pat Marriott are marvellous. See also the sequel, *Black Hearts in Battersea* (1964), in which the story continues, aided and abetted by hot-air balloons, and the eccentric old Duke of Battersea himself. Her writing for adults includes *Mansfield Revisited* (1984), a continuation of Jane Austen's *Mansfield Park*, and the savage stories in *The Windscreen Weepers* (1969).

📖 Mervyn Peake, Susan Hill, Charles Dickens   CH

Aird, Catherine (British, 1930–) A former chairman of the Crime Writers' Association, Aird is noted for her mastery of the traditional English 'whodunit'. Set in the fictional county of Calleshire, her books hinge on the investigative abilities of Detective Inspector Sloan and the ineptly enthusiastic Constable Crosby. Begin with *Harm's Way* (1992). When a crow drops a human finger in front of two walkers exploring a footpath, bizarre surprises await Sloan as he tracks down the rest of the body. *Injury Time* (1992) consists of linked stories in which civil servant Henry Tyler figures alongside Sloan when events in Calleshire have implications at high levels. Centred around a re-enactment of the Battle of Lewes, *The Body Politic* (1990) features a particularly ingenious murder. Foul play is not suspected when an industrialist dies, until something turns up in his ashes.

📖 Agatha Christie, Gladys Mitchell, P. D. James   DH

Alain-Fournier (French, 1886–1914) Alain-Fournier (real name Henri Alban Fournier) wrote his enduringly popular novel *Le Grand Meaulnes* when he was 26; he was killed in action in 1914. *Le Grand Meaulnes* is a magical, haunting novel about adolescence, narrated by François, the son of a schoolmaster. A charismatic older lad, Augustin Meaulnes, comes to board at the school and takes François under his wing. One day le Grand Meaulnes (as the other boys call him) gets lost in the countryside and discovers a mysterious domain full of happy children feasting and celebrating. There he meets a beautiful girl, who haunts him ever after. His and François's lives become dominated by the need to find Yvonne again. Mysterious events are intermingled with precise evocations of boyhood hopes and fears, rivalries and fights, and with the extraordinary glamour of significant teenage moments.

📖 George Eliot (*The Mill on the Floss*), Miles Franklin (*My Brilliant Career*). *See* CHILDHOOD   JR

Alcott, Louisa May (US, 1832–88) Although she is best known for her series of books about the March family, *Little Women* (1868) and its second part, *Good Wives* (1869), *Little Men* (1871), and *Jo's Boys* (1886), Louisa May Alcott wrote prolifically in most genres, from Gothic thrillers to first-hand accounts of working as a servant and a nurse. Alcott's father was an unsuccessful travelling salesman and rogue preacher, and initially she wrote to relieve the poverty of her family, only achieving international acclaim upon publication of *Little Women*. This is the book to begin with. Neither melodramatic nor sensational, it describes the daily trials and adventures of the March sisters, Meg, Amy, Beth, and Jo and the devotion of their mother, Marmee. Sentimental, but also an evocative portrayal of a tightly knit female household in which men are peripheral and the women are intensely supportive of one another. The central character Jo's struggle towards financial independence is compelling enough to have sparked off many imitations.

📖 L. M. Montgomery, Nathaniel Hawthorne, Jane Austen. *See* UNITED STATES OF AMERICA   LM

Aldiss, Brian (British, 1925–) Aldiss served during the war in Burma and the Far East, before becoming a bookseller and eventually starting to write in the mid-1950s. He is a prolific exponent and defender of science fiction. Many of his novels and short stories verge on pastiche whilst simultaneously pushing the limits of the genre. The short story 'Better Morphosis' (1967) is narrated by a cockroach who finds he's turned into Kafka, while *Frankenstein Unbound* (1974) and *The Eighty-Minute Hour* (1974) can be read as homage to Mary Shelley and Philip K. Dick, respectively.

Moreau's Other Island (1980), ostensibly a tribute to H. G. Wells's classic, tells of the sabotage of a space capsule on its return from the moon which kills one person on impact and leaves three to drift on a life raft in the middle of the Pacific. The only one to survive is the US Under-Secretary of State, Calvert Roberts, who is washed up on a strange island whose inhabitants are humans disfigured by bizarre forms of bestiality. These are the results of elaborate experiments conducted by Mortimer Dart, a thalidomide victim with a fascination for human deformity. The plasticity of the human form also inspired *Hothouse* (1962) which laces together exotic tales set in a far-distant future where the sun is dying, humans have regressed, and the Earth is covered by a single banyan tree.

📖 Mary Shelley, Isaac Asimov, Arthur C. Clarke, Kurt Vonnegut   RP

Aldrin, Buzz (US, 1930–). *See* SCIENCE FICTION

Alexander, Lynne (US, 1943–) Lynne Alexander is a novelist and poet. Born in New York, she has lived in Britain since 1970. She teaches creative writing at Sheffield Hallam University and Bolton Institute. Her works include *Safe Houses* (1985), *Resonating Bodies* (1988), and *Adolf's Revenge* (1994), in which two weird American sisters, Adolf and Pinball, in best fairy-tale tradition, curse and plot revenge for the capture of their niece. *Intimate Cartographies* (2000) tells the story of Magda Beard, a cartographer commissioned to map a famous avenue of beech trees—the scene of her small daughter's disappearance. The novel, structured round maps of different kinds, ingeniously and movingly charts Magda's progress back from overwhelming grief and despair to a kind of equilibrium.

📖 Angela Carter, Jenny Diski   *LG*

Algren, Nelson (US, 1909–81) Brought up in Chicago, Algren used his early experiences as a newspaperman and itinerant worker during the Depression to create powerful if rambling novels dealing with the seamy underbelly of American society. His most famous book, *The Man with the Golden Arm* (1949), was made into a controversial Frank Sinatra film. Back from the war, Frankie Machine makes good bucks as a poker dealer with his 'golden arm'; in return it demands a regular fix of cocaine, plunging him into junkie hell. Other novels include *Never Come Morning* (1942), set in the slums of Chicago, and *A Walk on the Wild Side* (1956) which follows naïve, handsome, well-hung Dove Linkhorn on his shambling adventures through the brothels of New Orleans. Algren's gallery of hustlers and fixers, gamblers, pimps, and prostitutes spring off the page, and he makes poetry of low-life street talk.

📖 John Steinbeck, Jim Thompson

TH

Allbeury, Ted (British, 1917–) An intelligence officer during the Second World War, Allbeury worked in advertising

before becoming a writer of spy thrillers in the 1970s. Begin with *All Our Tomorrows* (1982). Its depiction of Britain after a Soviet invasion draws on the preoccupation with the cold war which is evident in much of his fiction. *A Wilderness of Mirrors* (1988) deals with strategic exploitation of extra-sensory perception. MI6 and the CIA attempt to kidnap a young East German neurologist who has developed paranormal abilities while working on secret Soviet research into ESP. Germany in the period immediately after the cold war is the setting for much of *The Long Run* (1996). The secret services of Europe and America are confronted with threats of political upheaval as neo-Nazis and other extremists attempt to exploit the new situation.

📖 Len Deighton, John le Carré. *See* SPY   *DH*

Allende, Isabel (Chilean, 1942–) Isabel Allende was forced to leave Chile after the 1973 military coup that overthrew her uncle's government, and she began her first novel while in exile. *The House of the Spirits* (1985) traces the history of twentieth-century Chile through four generations of women of the Valle/Trueba family: Nivea, an early feminist; her daughter Clara, a clairvoyant; Clara's daughter Blanca, torn between family duty and her great love; and Blanca's daughter Alba, through whose eyes the military take-over is witnessed. Allende weaves myth and magic with realistic historical description. A strong theme in her writing is the capacity for human imagination to survive even the horrors of political violence, and she views story-telling as a means of 'bearing witness' to human experience.

The heroine of *Eva Luna* (1987) tells the story of her own life, alternating with chapters about Rolf Carle, a news journalist born in Austria. Eventually, the two meet through Huberto Naranjo, a guerrilla commander Eva befriended when they were homeless street children. Eva is a displaced person in an unnamed country which is clearly Venezuela, and must survive by her wits and through her skill in storytelling. At the end of the novel, she and Rolf become lovers and she finds success in writing her own television series in which she portrays the political injustices of her country. As in most of her novels, Allende mixes the colourful mythical imagery of South America with real political events.

📖 Gabriel García Márquez, Louise Erdrich, Jeanette Winterson. *See* FAMILY SAGA, MAGIC REALISM   *DJ*

Allingham, Margery (British, 1904–66) Allingham published the first of her Albert Campion detective novels at the age of 23. Campion has his roots in the tradition of gentlemen detectives—modest, frighteningly intelligent, and with impeccable aristocratic connections which are never fully revealed. However, he develops in stature, and there is a tone of ironic humour and a fondness for eccentricity in much of Allingham's work which distinguishes her from her contemporaries. Novels such as *Dancers in Mourning* (1937), *The Fashion in Shrouds* (1938), and *Police at the Funeral* (1931) can be enjoyed as much for their milieu as the plot. Campion likes to play his cards close to his chest, only revealing all at the end; the reader is thus often as much in the dark as the novels' characters. Allingham's later, and best, novels, such as *More Work for the Undertaker* (1948) and *Tiger in the Smoke* (1952), are as much psychological thriller as murder mystery.

📖 Agatha Christie, Ngaio Marsh, Dorothy L. Sayers. *See* CRIME   *KB*

Alther, Lisa (USA, 1944–) Widely known for her first novel, *Kinflicks* (1976), Lisa Alther was born and raised in Tennessee, and educated at Wellesley College. *Kinflicks* was an immediate success, being both a very funny and honest account of a girl growing up in Redneck country, at odds with her society and her family values. The novel switches between the present, when the heroine Ginny's mother is dying, and the past, when Ginny is a child. Feminist concerns preoccupy Lisa Alther in all of her novels. *Original Sins* (1981) looks at the lives of five childhood friends and *Other Women* (1984) concerns itself with therapy and lesbian relationships.

📖 Erica Jong, Marge Piercy, Toni Morrison   *SA*

Ambler, Eric (British, 1909–) Born in London and educated at the University of London, Ambler became a full-time thriller writer in 1937. His downbeat realism and emphasis on the amoral expediencies of power have won him acknowledgement as a major influence on the modern spy story. Begin with *The Mask of Dimitrios* (1939), considered his masterpiece, in which an academic visiting Istanbul investigates the death of a politically powerful spy, assassin, and drug-runner. *The Dark Frontier* (1936), his first book, sets the pattern for much of his fiction in its taut narrative of an Englishman's inadvertent entanglement in a web of European espionage. His other thrillers include *Dirty Story* (1967),

centring on conflicts of international interest over African mineral resources, and
The Intercom Conspiracy (1969), evoking
the 1960s as an era fraught with political
disenchantment caused by the nuclear
balance of terror.

📖 John le Carré, Lionel Davidson.
See SPY   *DH*

Ambrose, David (British, 1943–)
After working as a journalist, Ambrose
became a full-time writer, initially of plays
and film-scripts, in 1967. Begin with *The
Man who Turned into Himself* (1993). The
shock of his beloved wife's death in a road
accident thrusts the main character into a
parallel world where he appears insane.
As matters worsen, he begins to flip with
manic rapidity between his two realities.
Cyber-tensions mount in *Mother of God*
(1995) when an expert hacker turns serial
killer and uses the internet to select
his victims. *Superstition* (1997) concerns
a research project investigating the paranormal. A scientifically monitored seance
has surprisingly direct results, and disastrous consequences for those who participate in it.

📖 Christopher Priest, Iain Banks
                                            DH

Amis, Kingsley (British, 1922–95)
Kingsley Amis is one of the very few
novelists who can make you hoot out loud.
Long before the phrase was invented, he
was, and remained, politically incorrect; if
there was a balloon of pomposity or pre-
tentiousness around, Amis would puncture
it to wicked, gleeful effect. Born in London
and educated at Oxford, he spent several
years as a lecturer in English literature
at Swansea, which provided the backdrop
for his hugely successful and hilarious first

novel, *Lucky Jim* (1954). In Jim Dixon, Amis
created the archetypal comic anti-hero who
harbours a beady scepticism of the establishment, and the old farts who run it. *The
Old Devils* (1986), which deservedly won
the Booker Prize, about the return to
Wales after many years of a poet-cum-
television personality and the upset this
causes, pulls off the difficult trick of being
very funny and also a poignant account
of lifelong friendships, loyalties, and
betrayals. Jake Richardson in *Jake's Thing*
(1978) is a lecherous, middle-aged Oxford
don losing his libido, and here Amis seizes
the chance to poke fun at newfangled sex
therapies (and therapists) as well as the
loonier fringes of female liberation. *Stanley
and the Women* (1984) revisits a favourite
Amis battleground: the war between the
sexes. In addition to these satirical swipes
at contemporary life, Amis published four
volumes of poetry and tried his hand at
other genres: spy fiction, supernatural,
detective mystery, and a science fiction
novel, *The Alteration* (1976), in which the
Reformation never took place, and the
Pope proposes a drastic solution to ensure
boy soprano Hubert Anvil retains his
purity of tone. Martin Amis is Kingsley
Amis's son.

📖 John Wain, Simon Raven, Joyce
Cary   *TH*

Amis, Martin (British, 1949–) Amis
is one of those names that a lot of people
shy away from. The press dubbed him
'the Mick Jagger of fiction', accusing him
of arrogance and misogyny—which is
probably true, but he's still a great writer.
Don't read Amis for the plots, read him
for the riffs on contemporary culture. Start
with *Money* (1984), quintessential Amis;
John Self overdoses on pornography, drugs,

fast food, and fame; his descent into hell is hilarious and ultimately full of pathos. *London Fields* (1989) pushes the Amis formula into caricature as Nicola Six pursues her own death in a literary/sexual fulfilment. It's always hard to tell in Amis how much is satire and how much is confessional autobiography, the most famous example being *The Information* (1995), which chronicles the bitter envy of Richard Tull, failed novelist, for his friend, popular author Gwyn Barry. *Time's Arrow* (1992) takes the most emotive of subjects, the Holocaust, and treats it with dry, technical brilliance. Telling the story backwards is an extraordinary approach which cheats you into looking at the full horror of the concentration camps face on. Just when you think you've got Amis pinned down he hits you with something different. *Night Train* (1997) features his first ever female character to be more than a bust size and makes her vulnerable, sympathetic, and the good guy, in a take on the noir thriller.

Will Self, Ian McEwan, Saul Bellow, Vladimir Nabokov.
See SOCIAL ISSUES   *RV*

Anand, Mulk Raj (Indian, 1905–) Anand has had a very long writing career in Britain and India. He is a generously sympathetic writer of novels and short stories about Indian life. His early works explore the lives of some of the poorest people in Indian society before independence. Start with *Untouchable* (1935) or *The Coolie* (1936), moving novels about the struggles of poor workers. *Across the Black Waters* (1940) tells of the experience of Indian soldiers in the First World War; about a million Indians served Britain as soldiers or workers in that war, including Anand's father, and Anand is

one of the few to write about them in English.

Anita Desai, Salman Rushdie.
See INDIA   *TT*

Anderson, Poul (US, 1926–).
See FANTASY

Anderson, Sherwood (US, 1876–1941) Sherwood Anderson included the name of the state where he was born in the title of his most famous and influential book, *Winesburg, Ohio* (1919). This is a collection of linked short stories, in which the frustrations of life in a small mid-western town are graphically documented in simple, vivid prose that is perfectly suited to the ordinary people with which it deals. The inhabitants of Winesburg are described as 'grotesques' because the confines of the town have not allowed them to develop in the way they wanted to, and Anderson is unusually frank for his time in dealing with their sexual problems. He came to writing late and was not particularly accomplished as a novelist, but he produced other fine short stories, some of which are collected in *Death in the Woods and Other Stories* (1933).

Ernest Hemingway, William Faulkner   *RF*

Andrews, Lyn (British, 1943–) Born and brought up in Liverpool, Andrews has made Merseyside the setting of her very popular family stories. Begin with *The Leaving of Liverpool* (1992), in which a young lady's maid in 1919 dreams of having a grander life, through association with her mistress's shell-shocked brother, but then marries a drunken man her family despises. *Mist Over the Mersey* (1994) chronicles lives in a Liverpool slum street during the First World War, in particular for a rich family who have come down in the world. *When Tomorrow Dawns* (1998) is set at the end of the Second World War and follows the story of a young widowed mother and her son.

📖 Mary Jane Staples, Helen Forrester, Maisie Mosco   *JR*

Andrews, Virginia (US, 1923–86) The new-generation Gothic novelist Virginia Andrews was born in Portsmouth, Virginia, and is best known for her immensely popular domestic chiller *Flowers in the Attic* (1979). It is a florid, emotional, and somewhat tawdry story, recounting the traumas of the Dollanganger children who are locked in an attic by their selfish, evil mother for years on end. The novel is popular with teenagers and those who are not put off by over-written prose. *Petals in the Wind* (1980) and *If there be Thorns* (1981) continue the family saga. After Andrews's death the ghost-writer Andrew Neiderman has continued writing in her style from synopses of stories she left.

📖 Charlotte Brontë, Matthew Lewis
SA

Angelou, Maya (US, 1928–) Growing up as a black woman in America is the subject of Angelou's fascinating five-volume autobiography. Drawing on family, politics, and the arts, she has produced a moving narrative which is much more than a personal testimony. The first volume, *I Know Why the Caged Bird Sings* (1970) is about Angelou's early life in Arkansas and California. She tells how she was raped by her mother's boyfriend, of the ensuing trauma, and her five-year silence. A love of words is already playing a central role in her life. *Gather Together in My Name*

(1974) and *Singin' and Swingin' and Gettin' Merry like Christmas* (1976) follows Angelou to San Francisco where, after working as a waitress, she trains as a dancer and singer. Perhaps the most fascinating volume is *The Heart of a Woman* (1981) which charts Angelou's literary and political development as she becomes involved with the Harlem Writer's Guild and meets a host of eminent black actors, singers, writers, and politicians including Malcolm X and Billie Holliday. Invigorated, Angelou throws herself into the civil rights movement where she meets and marries the South African freedom fighter Vusumzi Make. In her final volume, *All God's Children Need Travelling Shoes* (1986) Angelou goes to Ghana and explores the complex and confused relationship of an African-American with her motherland. Angelou continues her commitment to issues of race and gender in her numerous poetry collections, including *Shaker, Why don't You Sing?* (1983). She is Professor of American Studies at the University of North Carolina.

📖 Zora Neale Hurston, Toni Morrison, Alice Walker   *EW*

Anthony, Evelyn (British, 1928–) Anthony was born in London and became a professional author in 1949. *Imperial Highness* (1953), an account of Catherine the Great, and *Victoria* (1959) are the best of her early historical novels, which have straightforwardly factual narratives. Her subsequent fictional adaptations of history include *Anne of Austria* (1968), recounting the marriage of a Hapsburg princess to France's homosexual Louis XIII. Her later works are chiefly contemporary thrillers. *The Poellenberg Inheritance* (1972) concerns the intrigues surrounding an art treasure in the hands of a former Nazi general. Two disaffected British women, one an embittered intelligence agent, the other close to the US President, pose security risks in *The Avenue of the Dead* (1981). *Exposure* (1993), set in the world of international publishing, is the story of a journalist who discovers blackmail and war crimes behind her boss's hatred of his arch-rival.

📖 Jean Plaidy (writing as Victoria Holt), Clare Francis, Len Deighton

DH

Anthony, Michael (Trinidadian, 1930–). *See* CARIBBEAN

Appelfeld, Aharon (Israeli, 1932–) Born in Chernovtsy in the Ukraine, as a boy Appelfeld escaped from a concentration camp and hid in woodlands for three years. He arrived in Palestine in 1947 and became a lecturer in Hebrew, the language in which he writes. Begin with *Badenheim 1939* (1981), set at the onset of the Holocaust. The book evokes the breakdown of identity among those awaiting the journey to the camps. *The Age of Wonders* (1987) opens with a child's account of life in a family of Austrian Jews in the 1930s. Thirty years later he seeks out his home, to encounter an awareness of terrible change. A woman and her son leave behind her marriage in Vienna in *To the Land of the Reeds* (1987). It is 1938, and they become lost and separated as they travel northwards through an increasingly vague world of confusion and understated menace.

📖 Primo Levi, Ivan Klima   DH

Archer, Jeffrey (British, 1940–) Jeffrey Archer was born in Weston-super-Mare. He entered the House of Commons in 1969, later becoming deputy chairman of the Conservative Party; he was obliged to stand down as Tory candidate for Mayor of London when charges of perjury were brought against him. His motivation for writing fiction came from the loss of his fortune through bad investment. His first novel, *Not a Penny More, Not a Penny Less* (1974), is loosely based on this. Archer's characterization is wooden, and his style clumsy; his novels are unapologetic mass-market narrative-driven thrillers, which often borrow real-life political figures for characters. *Shall We Tell the President?* (1977) is centred on Kennedy, and *The Fourth Estate* (1996) is about media moguls, based on Murdoch and Maxwell. *The Eleventh Commandment* (1998) concerns a CIA agent who is pitched against his female boss.

📖 Michael Dobbs, Robert Goddard, Arthur Hailey   SA

Arden, John (British, 1930–) Best known as a dramatist, his plays include *Serjeant Musgrave's Dance* (1959) and *Armstrong's Last Goodnight* (1964). In his early work, Arden refused to take sides on political problems, but after he and his wife and collaborator, writer Margaretta D'Arcy, fell out with the theatre establishment, their work became more polemical and overtly Marxist. *Silence among the Weapons* (1982), shortlisted for that year's Booker Prize, is Arden's first novel. It is set in the first century BC around the Mediterranean, and is told with startling immediacy by 'Ivory', a lame Greek theatrical agent and semi-retired transvestite comic actor, who becomes unwillingly involved in the struggle for power between two Roman generals, Mule-Driver and The Stain. The language is funny, vivid, and coarse, and the picaresque story brims with gangsters, pirates, confusion, and duplicity. Behind the humour is a fable of, in the author's words, 'comedy and tragedy . . . freedom and servitude.'

📖 Robert Graves, Anthony Burgess

FS

Armah, Ayi Kwei (Ghanaian, 1939–   ). *See* AFRICA

Ashford, Daisy (British, 1881–1972) Daisy Ashford dictated her first short story when she was 4 years old and wrote her last when she was 14. An avid reader of the novels of the period, and a keen observer of the curiosities of adult behaviour, she brings her penetrating child's-eye view to the world of Victorian High Society and Romance with unique comic effect (and eccentric spelling). Her masterpiece, *The Young Visiters* (1919), was written when she was 9, but first published thirty years later, with a preface by J. M. Barrie. In it she charts the successful attempt of Mr Alfred Salteena—'not quite a gentleman but you would hardly notice it'—to rise in Society, reaching the giddy heights of a position riding beside the Royal Carriage. He is less successful in romance, losing his beloved Ethel to the handsome and well-connected, if a little 'presumshious', Bernard Clark.

📖 Sue Townsend   KB

Ashworth, Sherry (British, 1953–   ) Currently living and teaching in Manchester, Ashworth writes novels that strive to liberate their female characters from specific anxieties and insecurities. Her witty, fast-moving dramas empower women to cast off self-made chains as well as man-made ones. Her first book, *A Matter of Fat* (1991) follows the fortunes of Stella,

the leader of a commercial slimming club, and its various dissatisfied housewives, obsessive over-eaters, and romantic English students. The arrival of a 'Fat Women's Support Group' nearby allows them to question the wider cultural obsession with thinness. In her fourth novel, *No Fear* (1997), the protagonist, Joy Freeman, is plagued by relentless, obsessive worrying, and operates in a permanent state of near-panic, constantly expecting the worst; just looking the mirror reminds her of Munch's *The Scream*. Ashworth's protagonists always brim with sufficient energy to keep you engrossed.

📖 Fay Weldon, Mary Wesley. *See* FAMILY SAGA   RP

Asimov, Isaac (US, 1920–92) Isaac Asimov was born in Russia, but his parents emigrated to America when he was 3 years old. He is the most prolific of the 'big three' of American science fiction, the others being Arthur C. Clarke and Robert Heinlein. Since the age of 19 he has published over 400 books dealing with a vast range of topics both religious and scientific. Start with *Foundation*, the first book of the *Foundation* series (1951–93), a sprawling tale of intergalactic empires and their wars which won him a special Hugo award. Asimov has also won most of the other awards of science fiction.

📖 Arthur C. Clarke, Frank Herbert. *See* SCIENCE FICTION   LM

Atkinson, Kate (British, 1951–   ) Kate Atkinson was born in York. Her writing career began with commercial magazine fiction. Her first novel, *Behind the Scenes at the Museum* (1995), enjoyed great literary and commercial success, and was Whitbread Book of the Year. The novel moves between the lives of the women of the Lennox family, spanning four generations, but is mostly concerned with Ruby, born in the 1950s and brought up above a pet-shop in York. Atkinson's writing is lushly detailed, and encompasses both humour and tragedy. Her second novel was *Human Croquet* (1997). It centres on Isobel Fairfax, whose mother vanished mysteriously when she was small. Again, Atkinson excavates layers of family history, this time with flights of magic realism and a somewhat grandiose time span. Her feel for 1950s English provincial life is unparalleled.

📖 Hilary Mantel, Jeanette Winterson, Lesley Glaister.

See FAMILY SAGA   SA

Atwood, Margaret (Canadian, 1939–) Margaret Atwood is Canada's most internationally celebrated contemporary novelist and poet. She has twice won the Governor General's award for poetry and her novels have been shortlisted several times for the Booker Prize. She is one of the sharpest political thinkers in fiction, and her books are both compulsively readable and elegantly written. In *The Handmaid's Tale* (1985) Atwood describes a society of the future which is dominated by fundamentalist religion and a male élite. Fertility has plummeted, and women are Handmaids, Marthas, Aunts, or wives to the élite. The book describes the attempts of one Handmaid, Offred, to construct an alternative history that undermines both the censorship and linguistic control of the élite. *Surfacing* (1972) was a landmark novel for the feminist movement and a Canadian classic, describing a journey into the wilderness that transforms the female narrator into a visionary. *Life before Man* (1979) tells the story of a sexual affair from

the utterly convincing points of view of all three protagonists, and is both humorous and very sad. *Cat's Eye* (1988) is a vivid exploration of bullying, through the character of a woman painter who is overwhelmed by memories of childhood cruelties and betrayals. Atwood is as unsparing of children here, as Golding is in *Lord of the Flies*. In *Alias Grace* (1996), Atwood takes the true story of Grace Marks who was sentenced to death for the murder of her employers, and uses it to explore the complex relationship between guilt and power. Atwood also writes short stories; the collection *Wilderness Tips* (1991) is highly recommended.

📖 Doris Lessing, Margaret Forster, Virginia Woolf, Nadine Gordimer.

See CANADA, SCIENCE FICTION, SEXUAL POLITICS, SHORT STORIES

                                                    LM

Austen, Jane (British, 1775–1817) Jane Austen is one of the greatest and most entertaining of English novelists. She was born in Steventon in rural Hampshire where her father was village rector. She lived there for most of her life, with occasional trips to Bath, Lyme Regis, and London, and died in Winchester at the age of 42. The settings for her novels are similar to her own life, reflecting the lifestyle and conventions of middle-class rural society of that time.

Austen's writing is not so much a direct criticism of genteel life, as an acute examination of the everyday, sometimes petty occupations of her world. Her observations of snobbery and vulgarity are humorous and subtle. Start with *Pride and Prejudice* (1813), where Mr and Mrs Bennet exert their energies to achieve suitable marriages for their five daughters.

At the centre is the romance between outspoken Elizabeth Bennet and Fitzwilliam Darcy, a wealthy aristocrat. The twin faults of the novel's title are corrected as Darcy moderates his snobbishness and recognizes individual worth in social ranks below his own; Elizabeth in turn recognizes her own limited judgements, particularly of Darcy whom she initially dismissed as an unfeeling aristocrat. The hero and heroine are surrounded by a host of finely drawn, often comic characters, most notably the rather vulgar Mrs Bennet. This is perhaps the most comic of Austen's novels.

In *Mansfield Park* (1814), Fanny Price is the poor relation brought up in a wealthy family's home. Fanny competes for the man she loves against a witty and beautiful rival. Her modesty and goodness eventually win the day. As in all of Austen's novels, true love between individual men and women is explored as a higher goal than marriage based purely on social and economic convention.

The heroine of *Emma* (1816) is brought up by a doting father and permissive governess. At the age of 21 she takes it upon herself to arrange the life and marriage of Harriet Smith, a pretty, dim 'natural daughter of somebody'. The novel charts Emma's gradual recognition of the arrogance of interfering in the lives of others, and ends with her marrying Mr Knightley, the only person who has the courage to criticize her. As in *Pride and Prejudice*, antagonism transforming into love creates a powerful romantic tension.

Anne Elliot, the heroine of *Persuasion* (1818), is initially persuaded that her lover Captain Wentworth is an unsuitable marriage partner. She mourns him for seven years. On meeting again, Wentworth apparently spurns Anne for the affections of another woman. Anne must search within herself in order to win his love back. The question of suitable romantic partnerships also features in *Sense and Sensibility* (1811). Elinor Dashwood embodies good sense and cool judgement, while her sister Marianne is highly imaginative and sensitive. These qualities are explored and challenged through the trials of love, but both sisters eventually find contentment through suitable marriage partners. All of Austen's heroines are faced with moral questions about courtship and matrimony, which are finally resolved by marriage based upon true love. All Austen's novels have been adapted for film and television.

📖 Anthony Trollope, Edith Wharton, Barbara Pym. *See* CHILDHOOD, CLASSICS, ROMANCE   *DJ*

Auster, Paul (US, 1947–) After graduating from Columbia University in New York, Auster spent several years in France working as a translator. His career as a novelist did not take off until the release of *City of Glass*, *Ghosts*, and *The Locked Room*, known together as *The New York Trilogy* (1987). These were written partly in the manner of the detective story, with a typical emphasis on narrative. But they also displayed a cartoonish instability— reflecting the author's own interest in the problems of identity. The playful styles on view in *The New York Trilogy* are also to be found in *Moon Palace* (1989), where penniless Columbia student Marco Stanley Fogg takes work as a paid companion to Thomas Effing, an old man whose life story he must transcribe. Effing's and Fogg's stories compete for our attention. Upon Effing's death Fogg must seek out his long-lost son and present him with the extensive obituary of his unknown father.

By the end of the book Fogg has crossed the continent, fallen in and out of love, and made touch with his own family roots. Fortunes are made and lost, and the fates conspire against the lives of each character we meet in a metropolitan allegory driven by outlandish, bizarre coincidence.

Auster has also written an autobiographical work, *The Invention of Solitude* (1982) and worked successfully on films such as *Smoke* and *Blue in the Face* (both 1995) with the director Wayne Wang.

📖 Jonathan Coe, Adam Thorpe, Thomas Pynchon   *AM*

B

Babel, Isaac (Emmanuilovich) (Soviet, 1894–1940) A short-story writer, born to assimilated, middle-class Jewish parents in Odessa, Babel wrote erotic fiction whilst translating for Lenin's secret police. His most famous work, *Red Cavalry* (1923–5), came from his experience as a war correspondent. It's a series of brief prose snapshots of the Russo-Polish conflict of 1920. Babel was attached to the notoriously anti-Semitic Red Cossacks and the ambiguous attitude of the narrator to the Jewish characters reflects Babel's own cultural divisions. The fascinating (and often brutal) subject matter is frequently obscured by an elliptical style that strains for poetic effect. Start with his later, sparer, and more traditionally narrative *Autobiographical Stories* (1925–37), about pogroms, childhood, and growing up in a richly imagined Tsarist Odessa. Babel was executed in one of Stalin's last purges, after years of circumspect literary silence.

📖 Mikhail Sholokhov, Stephen Crane. *See* RUSSIA   *MH*

Badami, Anita (Canadian, 1961–). *See* CANADA

Bagley, Desmond (British, 1923–83) Born in Kendal, Bagley began working in the printing industry at the age of 14. He was a journalist before becoming a prolific writer of thrillers in the early 1960s. Begin with a treasure quest through the Mexican rainforest in *The Vivero Letter* (1968), typical of much of his work in its tautly crafted

narrative of adventure in wild natural surroundings. *Bahama Crisis* (1980) is set amid the affluence of luxury hotels, whose business is threatened by violent sabotage. The hunt for a missing industrialist leads through the arctic forests of Scandinavia in *The Enemy* (1977), which centres on rivalries over genetic engineering secrets. *Juggernaut* (1985) follows the progress of a huge transporter-wagon as it bears its cargo of electrical equipment through an African state undergoing civil war.

📖 Jack Higgins, Hammond Innes   *DH*

Bagnold, Enid (Algerine) (British, 1889–1981) Enid Bagnold spent her early years in Jamaica before returning to England to attend Prior's Field, a progressive school. She worked as a nurse and ambulance-driver during the First World War, and married in 1920. Her best-known novel is *National Velvet* (1935), the story of a young girl whose dream of winning the Grand National is realized when she impersonates a man and enters the race. Filmed with Elizabeth Taylor in the leading role in 1944, the story has been enduringly popular since its first publication. Also notable is *The Squire* (1938), an account of a pregnant woman awaiting the return of the father of her child. Bagnold also wrote successful plays, including *The Chalk Garden* (1956), and two volumes of diaries and autobiography.

📖 Sylvia Townsend Warner   *WB*

Bail, Murray (Australian, 1941–) Bail has published three novels, of which *Eucalyptus* (1998), is the most interesting and rewarding. The plot is fairy-tale: a widower has a beautiful daughter, and sets a test for her suitors. The man to win her hand must be able to name the species of each of the hundreds of gum trees planted on the father's property. Suitors try and fail, until eventually a story-telling stranger appears. Attached to each species' name (the chapter titles) is a story. Inventive and dream-like, this is a beautifully written novel, although the characters —particularly the heroine, Ellen—are little more than cyphers. *Holden's Performance* (1987) is more comic, following the hero's epic progression from Adelaide to Sydney to Canberra, to become bodyguard to the Prime Minister. He encounters a number of larger-than-life characters along the way. Bail has also written short stories, and edited a collection of Australian stories.

📖 Angela Carter, Peter Carey   *JR*

Bailey, Hilary (British, 1936–) Hilary Bailey was born in Kent and educated at Cambridge. She has continued working as a literary journalist while producing her novels. Begin with *All the Days of My Life* (1984), which is set, like most of her fiction, in London. The novel evokes change in the 1950s and 1960s in following the fortunes of its *nouveaux riches* characters. In *The Cry from Street to Street* (1992) the heroine is a former brothel-keeper who moves through a Victorian underworld in which Jack the Ripper is at large. *Frankenstein's Bride* (1995) finds Mary Shelley's hero in London, pursued by nemesis after he has succumbed to his monster's demand for a female companion.

After the Cabaret (1998) is another inventive sequel, in which Christopher Isherwood's creation Sally Bowles returns to her native London in wartime.

📖 Emma Tennant, Penelope Mortimer   *DH*

Bailey, Paul (British, 1937–) Paul Bailey is a Londoner who is fascinated by his city and has edited an anthology about it. His novel *Kitty and Virgil* (1998) starts off with a meeting between two of its central characters in Green Park. One of them, though, Virgil Florescu, is actually in exile from his native Romania. What then follows is a cross-cultural romance. On the surface we have a comedy of manners, with witty dialogue and warm, enveloping humour. These qualities remain even as the relationship becomes more intense and potentially tragic. The book explores the dark absurdity of Ceauşescu's Romania, and the degree to which values, in particular literary ones (since Virgil is a poet), can transcend national divisions and be accessible on a European, or more simply a human, level (we have 'translations' of Virgil's poetry as an appendix). If Bailey's humanity and sharp intelligence appeal to you, read his earlier novels, like the Booker Prize-shortlisted *Peter Smart's Confessions* (1977) and *Gabriel's Lament* (1986).

📖 Graham Greene, Peter Ackroyd

RF

Bainbridge, Beryl (British, 1934–) Beryl Bainbridge was born in Liverpool, and began her career there as an actress in a repertory company. Her early novels are often set in the area. Bainbridge's characteristic vein is black comedy; she tells tales of dark deeds and the unexpected with economy and humour. She is a prolific novelist, held in high esteem by both critics and the reading public. Typical of her work is *The Bottle Factory Outing* (1974), the story of romantic skulduggery in an Italian-owned wine bottling factory, culminating in a works outing which ends in unpremeditated disaster. *Injury Time* (1977) won a Whitbread award, and combines the ordinariness of a dinner-party with an unexpected violent ending. *An Awfully Big Adventure* (1989) is related by 16-year-old Stella, an ASM in a Liverpool rep company, and treats of her relationship with an ageing actor, the youthful perspective giving an ironic detachment to the dark deeds that unfold. *The Birthday Boys* (1991) is a fictionalized account of Scott's expedition to the Antarctic, and *Every Man for Himself* (1996) describes the ill-fated maiden voyage of the *Titanic*. Both convey deep empathy for the male characters and are powerfully atmospheric. *Master Georgie* (1998, Booker shortlisted) is a vivid, concise, intense novella about a photographer/surgeon who goes to offer his services during the Crimean war, accompanied by his adoring adopted sister, his fire-eating photographer's assistant, and a lapsed geologist.

📖 Mavis Cheek, Alice Thomas Ellis, Bernice Rubens   SA

Baker, Nicholson (US, 1957–) Baker was originally from New York, but moved to northern California. His comedies of contemporary sexual manners may owe something to John Updike but are far more linguistically inventive and digressive. Baker published two novels, *The Mezzanine* (1988) and *Room Temperature* (1990), before the sexually explicit books which brought him widespread attention. *Vox* (1992), reputedly given by Monica Lewinsky to President Clinton, is concerned with phone sex; a long conversation between two people that is titillating and equivocal as to moral consequences. *The Fermata* (1994) is a brilliant parody of both pornography and science fiction, as temporary office worker Arno Strine enters 'The Fold', stopping time to examine the lives and bodies of those around him. The novel fully exploits the comically erotic possibilities of this conceit, and debates the moral issues involved.

📖 John Updike, Will Self   JS

Baldwin, James (US, 1924–87) Baldwin was born in Harlem, the eldest of a family of nine children. His stepfather was a Pentecostal preacher, and Baldwin himself served as junior minister at the Fireside Pentecostal Assembly as a teenager. After the death of his stepfather in 1943 Baldwin moved to Greenwich Village, determined to become a writer. Five years later he moved to Paris, in order to write more freely about the racial and sexual politics of America.

In a number of non-fiction books, Baldwin demanded revolution as the only solution to the despair and alienation of black Americans. In his fiction he also explores the theme of racial identity, but departed from the 'protest fiction' of writers such as Richard Wright, because of a need to explore the internal complexities of relationships within black society and the conflicting demands of sexuality, religion, and race. In *Go Tell It on the Mountain* (1953), a poor Harlem family is divided by born-again Christianity. Baldwin explores the mythic power of the victim, and its role in establishing cultural identity. Start with *Giovanni's Room* (1956), one of the first novels in

America openly to explore homosexuality; the central figure has to choose between his mistress and his male lover. *Tell Me How Long the Train's Been Gone* (1968) describes the attempts of two brothers to escape the ghetto.

📖 Toni Morrison, Alice Walker, Alan Hollinghurst, Ralph Ellison. *See* SEXUAL POLITICS, UNITED STATES OF AMERICA   *LM*

Ballard, J(ames) G(raham) (British, 1930–) As a schoolboy, Jim Ballard was interned with his family in a civilian prison camp when the Japanese invaded Shanghai, China, in 1942. Forty years later this formed the basis for his award-winning novel *Empire of the Sun* (1984), filmed by Steven Spielberg, which tells how 12-year-old Jim learns to survive the harsh conditions, and of his fascination with the kamikaze suicide pilots at the nearby airfield, which amounts to hero-worship of these fanatical young men. However, Ballard's main reputation is founded on a large output of science fiction novels and short stories. *The Drowned World* (1962) and *The Drought* (1965) are apocalyptic visions of our doomed planet as civilization crumbles and is reclaimed by nature in the raw. In later novels he brings a chill realism to his science fiction, creating modern fables of bleak, neon-lit landscapes in which frail humans are vulnerable and isolated. *Concrete Island* (1974) has a man marooned beneath a motorway flyover after crashing his car, ignored by the rushing traffic; this theme of alienation is taken to extremes and given an erotic charge in the cult novel *Crash* (1973), which the author describes in his introduction as the first pornographic novel based on technology.

Few British writers of his generation come near him in pushing their imaginative gifts to the furthest limit, and none has explored so relentlessly the collision of man and his man-made environment. *The Kindness of Women* (1991) returns to autobiographical material, including the early years in Shanghai.

📖 John Wyndham, Ray Bradbury, William Burroughs   *TH*

Balzac, Honoré de (French, 1799–1850) Balzac's great achievement was *La Comédie humaine*, the collective title of ninety-one novels intended to present a complete social history of the France he knew. Probably the most famous are *Eugénie Grandet* (1833), *Old Goriot* (1834), and *Cousin Bette* (1846). Start with *Old Goriot*, which studies the intersecting lives of characters in a Paris boarding-house. Goriot, doting father of two ungrateful daughters, reduces himself to poverty for their sake, finally 'dying like a dog' while they dance the night away at a grand ball. The corrupting effect of money is a major theme for Balzac. *Eugénie Grandet's* life is dominated by her father's obsession with gold, while *Cousin Bette* is the poor relation whose bitterness leads to the down-fall of a family. Balzac shows tremendous compassion for his larger-than-life characters, mixing realism with romance and melodrama.

📖 Gustave Flaubert, Stendhal   *CB*

Bambara, Toni Cade (US, 1931–95) A black feminist and civil rights activist, Bambara is a story-teller who believes that stories can save lives, snatching us back from the edge to hear what happens next. Her two main collections, with their gospel, blues, bebop, and jazz idioms, are deeply influenced by the musicians and orators she heard as a child in Harlem. Begin with *Gorilla My Love* (1972), which introduces Hazel, a bold and combative black girl, and her family and friends on the block, and then go on to *The Seabirds are Still Alive* (1977). Bambara's first novel, *The Salt Eaters* (1980), tells the stories past and present of the imaginary town of Claybourne, Georgia. The modern-day inhabitants are about to begin their spring festival when they witness an event which stuns them all. Thanks to their spiritual kinship and accumulated ancestral wisdom, they find the will to defy the menace which towers over them.

📖 Gloria Naylor, Ntozake Shange

JN

Banks, Iain (Menzies) (British, 1954–) Iain Banks writes both conventional literary novels and also genre science fiction under the name **Iain M. Banks**. He burst onto the contemporary scene with his first novel, *The Wasp Factory* (1984). The book soon gathered a reputation— and a cult following—for its Gothic, and graphic, scenes of horror. In a more recent novel, *Complicity* (1993), corrupt politicians are killed off in a variety of gruesome and very detailed ways. However, what raises Banks's work above the charge of simply being pornographically violent is his skill as a story-teller. Perhaps the best book to start with is *Whit* (1995), in which a fictional Luddite Luskentyrian religious community based near Stirling is seen through the eyes of 18-year-old Isis Whit, the community's 'Eyes of God'. Isis has healing powers and 'a way with animals' and is sent to London in pursuit of her errant cousin, Morag. There she comes to realize that all is not what it seems with either the cult or among the 'Unsaved' who live outside the community.

📖 Peter Ackroyd, Anthony Burgess, William Golding, Michael Moorcock. *See* SCIENCE FICTION *LM*

Banks, Lynne Reid (British, 1929–) Lynne Reid Banks was born in London, and educated in Canada and London. She is successful both as a children's author and a writer for adults, her most famous novel being *The L-Shaped Room* (1960). Unmarried Jane Graham discovers she is pregnant and chooses to live in a sordid bed-sit in Fulham. The people she meets in her lodging-house, and even the environment itself, have a transformational effect. The heroine is plucky and honest, and the book is an engaging read. Reid Banks wrote a sequel, *The Backward Shadow* (1970) in which Jane experiences motherhood in a country cottage not far from London. In 1962 Banks moved to Israel, and her most powerful novels for teenagers (such as *One More River*, 1973) are based on her first-hand understanding of the Arab–Israeli conflict.

📖 Monica Dickens, Nadine Gordimer, Margaret Drabble *SA*

Banks, Russell (US, 1940–) Banks's novels are searing examinations of American life; they are also pacey, well-plotted, and psychologically engaging. Begin with *Continental Drift* (1985), a devastating exploration of the American Dream gone wrong, which follows Bob Dubois, a central heating engineer who wants to be richer and more famous, into free fall when he takes his family to live in a trailer while he works for his wheeler-dealer brother. He ends up shooting a man; moves on to captaining a tourist fishing boat for a drug-running mate, and attempts to bring illegal immigrants into the United

States for cash. It's the story of an ordinary man, whose actions become unforgivable, and who knows it. Intercut is the story of two Haitians trying to get into the United States—imagining that in that ideal country, the horror and cruelty which is their daily fare will cease. *Affliction* (1989) explores the handing down of male violence from one generation to the next, again examining how a decent man can be twisted into something evil; and *Cloudsplitter* (1998) is a fictional exploration of the real abolitionist, John Brown, in pre-Civil War America.

📖 John Updike, Raymond Carver, Kazuo Ishiguro   JR

Banville, John (Irish, 1945–) Banville, who is literary editor of the *Irish Times*, writes fiction in which sensuous prose is infused with a deeply serious but playful imagination and a bracing intellect. His early novels, including *Doctor Copernicus* (1976) and *Kepler* (1981), had as central characters key figures in the history of European ideas. He found a wider audience with *The Book of Evidence* (1989), which was shortlisted for the Booker Prize and which presents the narrative of a cultivated drifter, Freddie Montgomery, who has committed the apparently motiveless abduction and murder of a young woman. Aspects of Freddie's guilt are explored further in *Ghosts* (1993) and *Athena* (1995). *The Untouchable* (1997), loosely modelled on the career of the spy Sir Anthony Blunt, is a highly readable portrait of the world of the Cambridge spies and of a fastidious, erudite, emotionally contained man.

📖 Vladimir Nabokov, John McGahern, Peter Ackroyd.
See IRELAND   NC

Barbusse, Henri (French, 1874–1935). *See* **Remarque, Erich Maria**

Barclay, Tessa (British, 1928–) Tessa Barclay, pseudonym of Jean Bowden, was born in Scotland and has worked in publishing and as a journalist. She is well known for her best-selling saga-style fiction. Typical of this is *The Millionaire's Woman* (1995), in which the heroine, Ruth Barnett, leaves her sheltered rural village for a more glamorous existence as secretary to a motor-racing driver. The novel is set in the 1920s and its dynamic is provided by a struggle between the hero's money-grabbing wife and the beleaguered heroine. In *The Saturday Girl* (1996), set in a Lancashire mill town in the 1930s, Libby, the heroine, is 'adopted' by a wealthy invalid who is also a renowned anthropologist.

📖 Catherine Cookson, Emma Blair, Pamela Oldfield   SA

Barfoot, Joan (Canadian, 1946–) Barfoot's remarkable first novel, *Gaining Ground* (1980) tells the story of a woman who leaves her perfectly ordinary husband and children to live alone in the wilderness, in an attempt to recover or discover her own identity. She is tracked down and called to account by her daughter. It is a feminist classic, a scrupulously, painfully honest exploration of female identity and motherhood, and provides a fascinating contrast to more recent novels about women leaving their families, such as Anne Tyler's *Ladder of Years*. All Barfoot's novels delve into women's lives; in *Charlotte and Claudia Keeping in Touch* (1994) two friends who have been respectively a mistress and a wife compare notes as they get older. In *Dancing in the dark* (1982, filmed 1986) a woman examines her reasons for murdering her husband.

📖 Doris Lessing, Margaret Atwood

JR

Barker, A(udrey) L(illian) (British, 1918–   )

Barker's novels and stories habitually strike a note of psychological unease, scepticism, and doubt, or concern the difficulties of interpretation; they are distinguished by a rare precision of language. Her collections are often organized thematically. Her debut was *Innocents: Variations on a Theme* (1947), in which most stories concern a child's perspective on experience or evil, and the others find adults disturbed by children. In *The Joy Ride and After* (1963) the same car accident is seen differently by the driver and a passenger, while another story explores the victim's loss of memory. A trilogy of her most sinister novels, including *The Gooseboy* (1987), was published in 1992. Barker's tone is well suited to the ghost story, where inanimate objects take revenge against the living and the uncanny enters the everyday world, sometimes humorously. Her finest are collected in *Element of Doubt* (1992), including 'Romney' in which a new tutor is forced to investigate his young pupil's conviction that he has killed his elder brother.

📖 Ivy Compton-Burnett, M. R. James

JS

Barker, Clive (British, 1952–   )

Clive Barker was born in Liverpool, and made an immediate impact with the stories collected in the six volumes of *The Books of Blood* (1984–5). Concentrating on the closely described details of anatomy and violence that he later translated to films like *Hellraiser* and *Candyman*, Barker's early work created a new kind of horror that owed as much to

a knowing sense of sexual danger as it did to the more conventional Gothic style of his near-contemporaries. *Weaveworld* (1987) is the most widely acclaimed of Barker's novels for its ingenious account of a world contained within a carpet where the rules of magical fantasy and horror combine to often startling effect. *The Great and Secret Show* (1989) is set in California and Hollywood and the story of magicians fighting for control of 'the art', a magical force of enormous power, is at least in part a satire on the entertainment industry. *The Damnation Game* (1985) is the tale of a gambler undone by a demonic opponent.

📖 Stephen King, James Herbert   *WB*

Barker, Elspeth (British, 1940–   )

Elspeth Barker is the author of the highly acclaimed *O Caledonia* (1991), a modern-day murder mystery centring on the emotional disintegration of Janet, an unloved and isolated teenager who moves with her family to the harsh, uncompromising society of Caledonia. The novel begins with the discovery of Janet's corpse underneath the stairs in her family's dilapidated castle, and ranges back over her childhood and adolescence, examining her life in an attempt to identify her killer. Barker's tone is grimly satirical. Her interest is in the relationship of the individual to society, and in the lasting psychological effects of childhood damage. *O Caledonia* won the David Higham award and was shortlisted for the Whitbread First Novel award.

📖 Muriel Spark, Hilary Mantel   *SR*

Barker, Pat (British, 1943–   )

Pat Barker's early novels, *Union Street* (1982) and *Blow Your House Down* (1984), earned her the reputation of being a searing commentator on the lives of women blighted by economic deprivation; yet she emphasizes the vitality and energy of her characters more than their oppression. But Barker gained fame, and the Booker Prize, for her trilogy about the First World War, *Regeneration* (1991), *The Eye in the Door* (1993), and *The Ghost Road* (1995). These books are dominated by working-class Billy Prior and his experiences in the trenches. Shell-shocked, Billy is sent to the Craiglock-hart hospital where he meets Dr Rivers. Rivers has treated the great war poets, Sassoon, Graves, and Owen, all of whom feature in the books. This unusual focus allows Barker to explore creativity, class, and sexuality. In *Another World* (1998) the focus is on a contemporary family in which the violence of the older child, Gareth, towards his younger brother is prefigured by the experience of his grandfather in the First World War. Barker's work characteristically retains a large scope while focusing on the minutiae of daily existence with unsentimental precision.

Erich Maria Remarque, Louis de Bernières, Nell Dunn. *See* HISTORICAL, WAR   *LM*

Barnes, Djuna (US, 1892–1982) Djuna Barnes was born into an extraordinary family which championed both free love and spiritualism. This may partly account for her characters' obsessions with sexuality and identity, explored in a writing style as remarkable for its poise and beauty as its eccentricity. Her major novel is *Nightwood* (1936) which was acclaimed on publication by T. S. Eliot, James Joyce, and William Faulkner among others. *Nightwood* concerns a group of bizarre characters and their sexual dilemmas: Dr O'Connor is a transvestite gynaecologist, Baron Felix Volkbein is a womanizer who thinks he

has found love with the novel's other main protagonist, Robin Vote. But Robin herself is in the middle of a search for redemption in a lesbian affair with Nora Flood. Other works, such as *Ladies' Almanack* (1928), also experiment with the transgression of sexual and artistic boundaries.

Gertrude Stein, Anais Nin, Colette *LM*

Barnes, Julian (British, 1946–) After graduating in modern languages from Oxford University, Barnes worked for three years as a lexicographer on the supplement to *The Oxford English Dictionary* before becoming a journalist and critic.

Metroland (1980) is a witty coming-of-age story charting the narrator's youth in west London and his experiences in Paris at the time of the student revolts in 1968. *Before She Met Me* (1982) is a story of obsessive jealousy. These are largely works of social observation, and offer few hints of the formal experimentation that marks Barnes's later works, including *Flaubert's Parrot* (1984) and *A History of the World in 10½ Chapters* (1989). The former follows a retired, widowed doctor, Geoffrey Braithwaite, on a tour to northern France to research a life of Flaubert; through his meditations on the French writer, Braithwaite reveals truths about the nature of biography and about his own life. The latter pushes the conventions of the novel even further: the chapters, through which common themes and images run, include a woodworm's view of life on Noah's ark, a critique of Géricault's painting *The Raft of the Medusa*, and the story of a heaven that provides an unlimited supply of comfortable and ultimately boring pleasures. The collection of stories *Cross Channel* (1996) deals with various aspects of the relationship between the British and the French. The novel *England, England* (1998), is a satire in which a tycoon is involved with a heritage centre devoted to Englishness.

Barnes's fiction continues to resist categorization. But all his writing displays an elegant, cool, sceptical intelligence. He has also written detective fiction under the name **Dan Kavanagh**.

📖 Jonathan Coe, Martin Amis, William Boyd, Gustave Flaubert.
See FRANCE   NC

Barnes, Linda (US, 1949–) Barnes writes the dry, witty Carlotta Carlyle stories, set in Boston, Massachusetts. Their heroine is an engaging, gutsy private investigator and part-time cab-driver. Although Carlotta is a strong and independent character she is no loner; she is close to her 'little sister' Paolina for whom she is a role model and she makes use of a circle of friends and acquaintances, including former partner Lieutenant Mooney, to help her with her cases. In *Coyote* (1991) Carlotta is drawn into the world of illegal immigration and onto the trail of a mass murderer. *Snapshot* (1993) involves Carlotta in a quest to find out whether a young girl's death was due to any medical malpractice. *Cold Case* (1997) sees her searching for the truth about Thea Janis, a brilliant author who was murdered over twenty years ago but has apparently produced a recently written manuscript.

📖 Sue Grafton, Val McDermid   CS

Barstow, Stan (British, 1928–) Barstow was working in the drawing office of a Yorkshire engineering firm when the critical acclaim and popular success of his first novel, *A Kind of Loving* (1960),

enabled him to become a full-time writer. The straightforward story—working-class Vic Brown gets his girlfriend pregnant and is forced into marriage—is given genuine warmth and immediacy through the depth of its characters. The film was equally memorable. The hero of *Ask me Tomorrow* (1962) is from a mining family (as was Barstow), struggling to make his way as a writer, and to escape the confines of the class system. The short novel *Joby* (1964) evocatively captures a young boy's last summer of innocence at the outbreak of the Second World War. An unshowy writer, Barstow is excellent at depicting the small dramas of ordinary lives and making us feel for them by the truth and honesty of his vision.

📖 Alan Sillitoe, Keith Waterhouse, John Wain   TH

Barth, John (US, 1930–) Barth's extravagant fiction has been much influenced by his career as a teacher of English and creative writing, mostly at Johns Hopkins University, and by oriental and medieval tale cycles. His works are usually lengthy and elaborate exercises in story-telling or pastiches of genres—the historical novel, science fiction, the novel in letters. Easily his best-known and most approachable novel is *The Sot-Weed Factor* (1960), a mock-picaresque tale of the seventeenth-century poet Ebenezer Cooke's journey to Maryland to claim his estate; amid language games, numerous bawdy characters and incidents occur. *Lost in the Funhouse* (1968), a classic of experimental writing, consists of games-playing stories, some hinting at autobiography, others with wildly various narrators. *Letters* (1980) takes the form of correspondence between characters in

Barth's previous books and the author himself.

📖 Laurence Sterne, Thomas Pynchon   JS

Bates, H(erbert) E(rnest) (British, 1905–74) Bates published novels, plays, short stories, critical essays, and auto-biographical works. He frequently writes about the misfortunes and fortunes of love. In Bates's first novel, *The Two Sisters* (1926), sisters Jenny and Tessa realize they are in love with the same man. Recently adapted for cinema, *The Feast of July* (1954) is set amid the countryside of nineteenth-century England, where Bella Ford, jilted by her unscrupulous lover, plans a revenge that ends in catastrophic violence. Much of Bates's fiction is set against the backdrop of the Second World War, exploring its effects upon ordinary lives. *Triple Echo* (1971) is the story of a poignant love-affair between a country woman and a young de-serter from the army. Bates was recruited to the RAF to write morale-boosting short stories (as in *How Sleep the Brave*, 1943) under the pseudonym of Flying Officer X. But his fiction rose above its propagandist purpose, and is amongst the best written about flying in the Second World War. *Fair Stood the Wind for France* (1944) tells of a British air crew brought down in occupied France.

In later life, Bates wrote a series of gentle comedies based on the Larkin family, and set in 1950s rural England. The first is *The Darling Buds of May* (1958), popularized through television. The Larkin novels reflect Bates's love of English country life and a humorous affection for his characters.

📖 Thomas Hardy, Tim Pears, Ivan Turgenev   DJ

Bawden, Nina (British, 1925–) Nina Bawden is a highly successful writer of both children's and adult fiction. She has stated that children are 'a kind of subject race; always at the mercy of the adults who mostly run their lives for them', and she is also an acute observer of the tension between wishes and fulfilment. A good example of this is *Carrie's War* (1973). Carrie and her brother Nick are evacuated to Wales where they are bullied by their landlord, Councillor Evans, and make their escape into the rather dream-like world of the characters who live nearby at Druid's Bottom. In her adult novel *Circles of Deceit* (1987), shortlisted for the Booker Prize, her narrator, an unnamed artist who makes a living out of copying Old Masters, de-scribes his misleading relations with his two wives, his aunt Maud, and his mother Maisie; each of whom has varying versions of the truth.

📖 Jane Gardam, Penelope Lively, Peter Dickinson   IP

Beattie, Ann (US, 1947–) Ann Beattie writes of her native New England, and of her own generation—idealists of the 1960s, like the characters in *Chilly Scenes of Winter* (1976), forced to face a harsher world in middle age. She presents their dilemmas with an unflinching eye, especially in *Picturing Will* (1990), where the collapse of a marriage is viewed through the eyes of a 5-year-old child. In *The Burning House* (1982), women are seen as alienated, mis-guidedly fragile creatures who 'need to learn how to fall'. *Another You* (1995) deals with the mid-life crisis of an English pro-fessor at a small New Hampshire college, and the attendant problems of those around him. *My Life, Starring Dara Falcon* (1997) is a study of obsession and its aftermath.

Ann Beattie also writes salty, sometimes bleak short stories.

📖 Sue Miller, Richard Ford, Alison Lurie   *AT*

Beauman, Sally (British, 1944–). *See* GLAMOUR

Beauvoir, Simone de (French, 1908–86) De Beauvoir read philosophy at the Sorbonne and was placed second to Jean-Paul Sartre, whose life-long partner she became. She wrote novels, plays, and essays, and is best known for her ground-breaking feminist study, *The Second Sex* (1949), and for her fascinating and detailed three-volume autobiography, opening with *Memoirs of a Dutiful Daughter* (1958). Her novels explore the philosophical and political ideas which were central to her life, in particular existentialism, which demands that the individual assume complete responsibility for all choices and actions he/she undertakes. This is clearly expounded in *The Blood of Others* (1948), set just before and during the Second World War, in which the hero, Blomart, leaves his wealthy bourgeois home to become a worker, then soldier, then a Resistance leader. The question of whether France should join the war after the annexation of Austria is debated and Blomart agonizes over whether he should try to persuade his countrymen to fight the Nazis and 'pay with the blood of others', or to 'shamefully' accept whatever happens in order to preserve peace. *She Came to Stay* (1943) is about a couple whose lives are disrupted by the man's affair with a beautiful younger woman, a friend of both. It fictionalizes aspects of de Beauvoir's relationship with Sartre. De Beauvoir's characters deliberate the motives for their actions with scrupulous honesty, and are at times in danger of becoming cyphers; her non-fiction, where real people are acutely observed, is much more rewarding to read.

📖 Doris Lessing, Jean-Paul Sartre, Albert Camus   *JR*

Beckett, Samuel (Irish, 1906–89) Born near Dublin, and educated at Trinity College, Beckett spent several years lecturing at Belfast, the École Normale Supérieure in Paris (1928–30), and Trinity, before permanently settling in Paris. Though his greatest achievements were in drama, it was through his early novels that Beckett was able to adapt the 'stream of consciousness' subjectivity of James Joyce's novels into his minimalist, monologue-like narration. The first instalment of his trilogy, *Molloy* (1951) is two first-person monologues: by the bed-ridden Molloy recalling his odyssey towards his mother, and by Moran, a private detective who is sent to find him. Similarly, *Malone Dies* (1951) depicts the decrepit Malone waiting for 'the throes' of death and filling his mind and his remaining time with memories and bitter commentary. The novel disintegrates as the protagonist does.

Beckett's goal was to create art out of increasingly simplified material, reducing his image of human existence to the sparest elements, both strikingly bleak and grotesquely comic. By the time he arrives at the third 'reworking' of the novel, *The Unnamable* (1953), though it seems to encompass its predecessors, the monologue is so opaque the narrator doesn't even know who he is, though he strives to find out, sitting nowhere, nowhen, 'like a great horned owl in an aviary'. Beckett was awarded the Nobel Prize for Literature in 1969.

📖 James Joyce, Albert Camus, Jorge Luis Borges, Mervyn Peake. *See* IRELAND   *RP*

Beerbohm, (Henry) Max(imilian) (British, 1872–1956) A cartoonist, essayist, and critic, the title 'man of letters' fits Max Beerbohm perfectly. He first made his name as a member of the 'decadent' group surrounding the magazine *The Yellow Book*, alongside writers like George Egerton and artists such as Aubrey Beardsley and James Abbott McNeill Whistler. *Zuleika Dobson* (1911) is Beerbohm's best-known novel, a whimsical and idealized portrayal of the disruption caused to life at Oxford University during the 1890s by the arrival of a beautiful woman. *Seven Men and Two Others* (1919) is more typical of Beerbohm's work, a collection of short stories, parodies, and 'pen portraits' of recognizable types from his age. In later years he became an entertaining and witty critic and broadcaster, and several collections of his essays, reviews, and caricatures were printed during his lifetime.

📖 Oscar Wilde, Evelyn Waugh, Ronald Firbank   *WB*

Bellow, Saul (US, 1915–   ) Saul Bellow, who was awarded the Nobel Prize for Literature in 1976, is one of the most important American writers of the twentieth century. His characters struggle with questions of meaning and self against a backdrop of moral and social unease. Many of his books are set in Chicago, and the theme of Jewish identity pervades. In *Herzog* (1964), we see the life of the eponymous anti-hero crumbling inexorably around him. Herzog writes letters compulsively, to the living and the dead, treading an existential trail as he pursues his identity to the edges of insanity.

The drama in Bellow often centres on sudden intense moments of realization. Move on from *Herzog* to his novella *Seize the Day* (1956), which follows middle-aged

Wilhelm through the course of one desperate day during which he confronts the failure of his life. The ending is typically Bellow: nothing more than a man weeping inexplicably at a stranger's funeral, yet a moment of passionate catharsis. Such epiphanies constantly redeem the bleakness of much of Bellow's vision. Turn now to *Humboldt's Gift* (1975), a complex novel full of humour and compassion, that interweaves the life of writer Charlie Citrine with memories of the friend and mentor of his youth, Humboldt, the archetypal self-destructive genius. Like the poet Delmore Schwartz, on whom he is based, Humboldt died young. Charlie has gone on to success on the back of a character based upon him. His spiritual odyssey brings him to an understanding of Humboldt's true worth and the debt he owes him.

📖 Kurt Vonnegut, Philip Roth, Bernard Malamud. *See* UNITED STATES OF AMERICA   *CB*

Bely, Andrei (Soviet/Russian, 1880–1934). *See* RUSSIA

Bennett, Arnold (British, 1867–1931) Born in the Potteries, son of a self-educated solicitor, Bennett began by working for his father, then escaped to a London firm. In London he began to write fiction, and when he was 35 he moved to Paris to write full-time. In his lifetime he wrote forty-two fiction books, plus plays, journalism, literary criticism, and a journal. By the time he died Bennett was one of the most popular and respected writers in London.

His three best-known novels are all set in the Potteries, and create a vivid picture of the Five Towns with their 'architecture of ovens and chimneys' and 'atmosphere as black as mud'; and of the cramped, often appalling lives of their denizens. Bennett was brought up a Wesleyan Methodist, and the effects of religion (good and bad) are an important theme in his work. He writes with loving detail; he will explain each step of an industrial process; he will delve into a boy's self-conscious silence at dinner; he will explain what the results of investments at certain percentages will be. Through this accumulation of detail he builds an intensely real world. Bennett is good on the degradations of poverty, which he often portrays with Dickensian humour—how dare the poor have the temerity to expect anything other than the worst! He is also exceptionally good on women, making them wholly convincing as central characters, moving easily into their thoughts and feelings.

Begin with *Anna of the Five Towns* (1902) the story of a young woman who keeps house for her tyrannical miser father. When Anna reaches 21 her father gives her deeds worth £50,000 that he has held in trust for her, but makes it impossible for her to obtain so much as £5 to spend. An industrialist falls in love with Anna, and escape from her father becomes possible; but in the mean time her father has forced her to tighten the screws on one of her tenants, Titus Price, who runs a business in a decrepit printshop. As Anna's personal fortunes rise, Price's plunge downwards—to a terrible end which will turn Anna's happiness to ashes in her mouth.

The domineering father surfaces again in the partly autobiographical *Clayhanger* (1910). Young Edwin Clayhanger longs to become an architect, but cannot escape the doom of joining his father (a self-made man) in the family business. Bennett's portrayal of the ways a father can subjugate

an intelligent child is marvellous, in both *Anna* and *Clayhanger*. And the psychological analysis of a miser is taken to even greater heights in the late novel, *Riceyman Steps* (1923). *The Old Wives' Tale* (1908) is a big, utterly absorbing novel about two sisters raised in the Potteries, one of whom escapes to a different life in Paris. The whole span of their lives is covered, the effects of the passage of time pitilessly explored. This is simply one of the best novels in the English language.

Margaret Drabble has written an excellent biography, *Arnold Bennett* (1974).

📖 Émile Zola, Charles Dickens, D. H. Lawrence   *JR*

Benson, E(dward) F(rederic) (British, 1867–1940)

E. F. Benson, born in Berkshire, was the son of the Archbishop of Canterbury. Cambridge-educated, he went on to become a prolific and varied novelist. Benson is most famous for his series of light social satires of 1920s' middle-class England. These centre around two queens of provincial society, Mapp and Lucia. The first novel, *Queen Lucia* (1920), introduces Lucia, who commands Riseholme, a 'sleepy' village in the Cotswolds. She is conjured to superb comic effect as Benson traces the battle for social supremacy between Lucia and Daisy Quantock. *Miss Mapp* (1922) deals with Lucia's social counterpart, in her South Coast realm, Tilling. Unlike Lucia, Mapp is single and this novel traces her ensnaring of the unsuspecting Major Flint. In *Lucia in London* (1927) Lucia descends on fashionable London society as the result of an inheritance. Benson also produced ghost stories such as *The Room in the Tower* (1926).

📖 Jerome K. Jerome, Evelyn Waugh, P. G. Wodehouse   *CJ*

Benson, Peter (British, 1956–) Benson was born in Kent; he became a full-time writer following the success of his first novel, *The Levels* (1987). Begin with this narrative of adolescent love in lyrically evoked rural Dorset, which combines subtlety and depth with poised simplicity of style. *Odo's Hanging* (1993) is an intricately constructed account of the making of the Bayeux tapestry. Bishop Odo struggles to oversee the work amid political intrigues and religious crises. Brighton forms the setting for *Private Moon* (1995), a tragi-comic treatment of middle-age. Its unsuccessful hero finds his world descending into chaos as he learns to live with a pregnant woman.

📖 Graham Swift, P. J. Kavanagh

DH

Bentley, E(dmund) C(lerihew) (British, 1875–1956) Bentley was for more than twenty years chief leader writer on the *Daily Telegraph*, and a regular contributor to the humorous magazine, *Punch*. He invented the clerihew, a bizarre biographical four-line nonsense verse. In 1910 he decided to write a detective story that would be an antidote to the high seriousness of Sherlock Holmes and his followers. *Trent's Last Case* was published in 1913. Philip Trent, investigative journalist, is called upon to solve the mystery of the murder of tycoon Sigsbee Manderson. In a series of brilliant deductive manœuvres he comes up with the logical solution, which proves to be entirely wrong. The plotting is ingenious, the tone by turns light and ironic. This was the first successful marriage of mirth and murder. Bentley wrote two further novels featuring Trent, neither of which matched his debut.

📖 Edmund Crispin, Colin Watson

VM

Bentley, Phyllis (British, 1894–1977) Bentley was born in Halifax and educated at the University of London. The landscapes, history, and inhabitants of her native West Riding of Yorkshire sustain much of her writing. Begin with *A Modern Tragedy* (1934), her vivid and occasionally harrowing treatment of Yorkshire manufacturing communities during the Depression of the 1930s. *Inheritance* (1932) opens a series of books following the Oldroyd family's rise over generations in the textile industry. Their story concludes with nineteenth-century affluence in *A Man of His Time* (1966). Her other historical novels include *Manhold* (1941), which is set in eighteenth-century Yorkshire. Bentley is also the author of several books on the Brontës and the autobiography *O Dreams, O Destinations* (1962), which reflects tellingly on the condition of single women in British society.

📖 Lettice Cooper, the Brontës DH

Berger, John (British, 1926–) Berger was born in London, where he was educated at the Central School of Art and Chelsea School of Art. Begin with *Corker's Freedom* (1964), describing a day in the life of an ageing man who attempts to escape from his stultifying suburban existence. Berger won the Booker Prize for *G* (1972), which traces the career of a doomed sensualist through its experimental blend of historical fact and poetic fiction. While the hero obsessively seeks fulfilment in sexual passion, Europe totters towards the First World War. *Into Their Labours*, a trilogy consisting of *Pig Earth* (1979), *Once in Europe* (1987), and *Lilac and Flag* (1990), forms his most celebrated work. The elegiac narrative is constructed from interlinking stories which use techniques of vivid montage and magic realism to evoke the destructive impact of modernity on a French peasant community.

⌨ Gabriel García Márquez, Émile Zola   *DH*

Berger, Thomas (US, 1924–) Berger was born in Cincinnati and educated at the universities of Cincinnati and Columbia. He worked as an editor before becoming a full-time writer in the 1950s. Begin with *Little Big Man* (1964), which, like most of his writing, offers an inventive critique of contemporary America. Narrated by the 111-year-old Jack Crabb, a white who has lived among the Cheyenne Indians, the book irreverently surveys a century of American history. A novel sequence beginning with *Crazy in Berlin* (1958) and ending with *Reinhart's Women* (1981) charts the career of Carlo Reinhart, an innocent vulnerably abroad in post-war America. Berger's other novels include *Robinson Crews* (1994), a recasting of the Robinson Crusoe story, in which an unhappy misfit survives a plane crash in the wilds and fulfils himself by rescuing a woman fleeing her abusive husband.

⌨ Philip Roth, Joseph Heller   *DH*

Bergon, Frank (US). *See* WESTERN

Beti, Mongo (Cameroonian, 1932–). *See* AFRICA

Binchy, Maeve (Irish, 1940–) Maeve Binchy was born and educated in Dublin, subsequently becoming a journalist. Her first attempts at fiction were in the form of short stories, but she became widely known for her first novel, *Light a Penny Candle* (1982). This deservedly popular romance tells the stories of the interwoven lives of two friends, Elizabeth and Aisling, who meet when Elizabeth is evacuated from London to a small Irish village during the Second World War. Binchy knows her territory well, and writes movingly and often humorously about the experience of Irish women both at home and abroad. She evokes the sense of community in rural Ireland, and is an astute observer of relationships between men and women. *Circle of Friends* (1990) is an engrossing account of the lives and loves of a group of students at University College, Dublin, and has been made into a film. *The Glass Lake* (1994) tells the poignant story of a woman who leaves her children to follow the love of her life to London. *Evening Class* (1996) is about a group of mature students learning Italian.

⌨ Clare Boylan, Molly Keane   *SA*

Bingham, Charlotte (British, 1942–) Charlotte Bingham, who has also written for television, writes big novels; they are often historical romances like *Debutantes* (1995), in which three young ladies from different backgrounds discover what it is to be part of a London 'season' in the 1890s, in the atmosphere of snobbery and ambition surrounding the Prince of Wales and his circle. Details of the required etiquette, the concerns about clothing and manners which trouble the girls' near relations, especially mothers and aunts, and some well-drawn characters, stop this being just another period romance. *Change of Heart* (1994) is a modern-day romance with a twist, in which an American composer rents a big house in the English countryside and falls in love at first sight with the strangely old-fashioned young girl he meets in the grounds. With elements of mystery and detective work, it's another big, romantic book.

📖 Georgette Heyer, Elizabeth Buchan, Daphne du Maurier   *FS*

Birch, Carol (British, 1951–   ) Birch, who was born in Manchester, writes novels which look back to the alternative life —drugs, squats, and communes—of the 1970s. Start with *Little Sister* (1998), about a lonely middle-aged woman in a northern town who is interrupted whilst contemplating suicide by a request to help trace her own younger sister after a ten-year absence. The quest leads her to other characters from her past, to an exploration of memory and the terrible rivalry between herself and her sister. *Come Back Paddy Riley* (1999) moves between the present (in which Anita betrays her safe husband by falling into a risky affair) and the past (when Anita, acting as go-between for her mother and her lover, committed another kind of betrayal). Birch's novels are good on place and feelings, and are shot through with black humour.

📖 Livi Michael, Lesley Glaister, Richard Francis   *JR*

Birdsell, Sandra (Canadian, 1942–   ). *See* CANADA

Birmingham, George (British, 1865– 1950) *See* IRELAND

Bishop, Elizabeth (US, 1911–79) Bishop is best known for her Pulitzer Prize-winning poetry, but she did write some short stories, which are available in her *Collected Prose* (1984). Her stories are often rooted in some event in her own life; memories of a drunken uncle, or of a childhood friend who died. They are beautifully and precisely narrated, with a complete lack of sentimentality, and yet without bleakness. The most striking, 'In the Village', describes a young girl whose mentally unstable mother has come to stay with the girl and her grandparents. Methodically, the girl runs through her days, with their specific pleasures—walking the cow to pasture past the village shoe-shop, listening to the clang of the blacksmith's anvil, taking a parcel to post—as if these routines can shield her from the horror of her mother's scream, her mother's disorder.

📖 Alice Munro, Katherine Mansfield
          JR

Bissoondath,   Neil (Trinidadian/ Canadian, 1955–   ) Bissoondath's books of short stories, *Digging Up the Mountains* (1985), and *On the Eve of Uncertain Tomorrows* (1990), display his ability to empathize with characters—for example, a young Japanese girl in Toronto trying to liberate herself from traditional cultural constraints—far from home. He is also able to enter imaginatively into the life of the Asian, both at home and abroad; but his African characters tend to be stereotypes. The 'Asian' stories form a link with those myths brought over from India by, among others, Seepersad Naipaul (a relative) in *Gurudeva and Other Indian Tales* (privately printed in Trinidad in 1943). Bissoondath's first novel, *A Casual Brutality* (1988) is about a doctor returning to his native Caribbean, but there encountering political upheaval and violence, which increase his sense of alienation. *The Innocence of Age* (1992) features a white Canadian hero, who identifies with the immigrant population against the violence and materialism of Toronto.

📖 V. S. Naipaul, Samuel Selvon. *See* CARIBBEAN   *EM*

Blackmore, R(ichard) D(odderidge) (British, 1825–1900) Blackmore's most famous novel is *Lorna Doone* (1869), a historical romance set in the 1680s on Exmoor. As a boy John Ridd is saved from death by the beautiful child Lorna Doone, and as an adult he is in love with her. But the Doones (who are a clan of aristocratic outlaws, terrorizing the neighbourhood) have murdered his farmer father, and he has to avenge this. Eventually Lorna is discovered to be not a Doone but the kidnapped heiress of a noble family, and the pair marry. But the drama does not end with wedding bells —in fact, Lorna is shot (but not fatally) at the altar. Monmouth's rebellion, and various historical characters including Judge Jeffries, play a part in the story, which, despite its dated language, is still a good and enduringly popular read. Blackmore was admired by writers as diverse as Thomas Hardy and R. L. Stevenson.

📖 Walter Scott, R. L. Stevenson, Alexandre Dumas   JR

Blackwood, Algernon (British, 1869–1951). *See* SUPERNATURAL

Blackwood, Caroline (Anglo-Irish, 1931–96) Born in Ulster into an aristocratic family, Blackwood worked as a journalist, producing notable studies of the Duchess of Windsor and the Greenham Common women's peace camp. Her fiction is characterized by her dark studies of women, often trapped by guilt, bitterness, and uncertainty; these are unsettling books but blackly humorous. Her first novel, *The Stepdaughter* (1976), is a monologue set in New York. The shortlisting of her second, *Great Granny Webster* (1977), for the Booker Prize, brought Blackwood wide acclaim. This short but compulsive novel gradually reveals the disturbed lives of several female generations in a landed Anglo-Irish family, a story set in train by a young girl's visit to the frigid household of her great-grandmother just after the war. *The Fate of Mary Rose* (1981) is a detached account of a girl's abduction and murder, and *Corrigan* (1984) concerns a widow's involvement with a possible conman.

📖 Rebecca West, A. L. Barker. *See* IRELAND   JS

Blair, Emma (British, 1942–) Iain Blair was born in Glasgow, Scotland, and educated there and in Milwaukee, Wisconsin. He spent twenty years as an actor and wrote four thrillers under his own name before becoming Emma Blair, writer of sagas and romantic fiction. Emma Blair's novels are characterized by vividly realized settings and believable, strong heroines who are forced to make difficult decisions. Typical is *The Daffodil Sea* (1994), in which Roxanne Hawkins runs away from her rural Devon home to join a music hall double act. A number of Emma Blair's novels are set in Scotland, such as *The Princess of Poor Street* (1986), where the hero, Ken Blacklaws, fights his way out of poverty, and *When Dreams Come True* (1987), a romance set in a Glasgow tenement.

📖 Tessa Barclay, Maeve Binchy   SA

Blatty, W(illiam) P(eter) (US, 1928–). *See* SUPERNATURAL

Bleeck, Oliver. *See* **Thomas, Ross**

Blincoe, Nicholas (British) Highly regarded among the younger British talents, Blincoe's fast-paced, blackly comic crime novels are noted for their bizarre narratives. Begin with *Jello Salad* (1997), in which the wife of a major criminal plans a restaurant after helping herself to his money. On opening night a corpse turns up on the premises, adding to the disorder prevailing among the highly irregular staff. In *Manchester Slingback* (1998; CWA Silver Dagger award) a London gambler returns to his old haunts in Manchester after the 1996 IRA bombing. A killing fifteen years earlier makes him the subject of attention from an unscrupulous police officer he knew in his drug-dealing past. Set chiefly in Jerusalem and Bethlehem, *The Dope Priest* (1999) follows the predicament of a hashish smuggler whose relations with Palestinian factions and Israeli officials become increasingly troublesome.

📖 Irvine Welsh, Iain Banks, Will Self

DH

Blish, James (US, 1921–75) Blish made good use of his specialism in biology in some of the earliest science fiction novels to deal with genetic engineering. In his classic short story, 'A Case of Conscience', a Jesuit priest, confronted with the discovery of an apparently sinless alien world, is forced to conclude that it has been created by the Devil to delude mankind into a loss of faith. This was expanded into a novel (1958) and became the centrepiece of a loose quartet whose other elements are a fictional biography of Roger Bacon, *Doctor Mirabilis* (1964), and a pair of novellas describing what happens to Earth when a black magician liberates Hell's imprisoned demons onto it. Four earlier novels which together make up a panoramic space opera, have been reissued as *Cities in Flight* (1999). Blish was one of the most rigorous and entertaining employers of science fiction as a medium for thought experiments.

📖 Arthur C. Clarke, Aldous Huxley

RP

Blixen, Karen (Danish, 1885–1962) Born into an upper-class family, Blixen's imagination was fired by the adventures of her father, a respected colonel, writer, and politician. Her famous autobiography, *Out of Africa* (1937), describes the years she spent in Kenya working as a coffee farmer. Blixen made her literary debut, however, with the publication of *Seven Gothic Tales* (1934), written under her pen-name **Isak Dinesen**. Using myth, the classics, and fantasy, Blixen explores a strange world inhabited by aristocrats, artists, romantics, and melancholics. One story, 'The Dreamers', follows the adventures of Lincoln Forsner, a wealthy Englishman, and a 'dreamer' who never takes charge of his own destiny, but lets the world glide by him. In this allegory of modern society, Blixen returns again and again to the damaging effects of civilization on individual instinct. A romanticist, Blixen believed that the artist is directly in touch with God and has, therefore, a unique vision: 'The Young Man with the Carnation' in *Winter's Tales* (1942) encapsulates this belief.

📖 D. H. Lawrence

EW

Block, Lawrence (US, 1938–) Lawrence Block is a prolific writer, creator of three very different crime series: the Matt Scudder novels whose hero is an ex-cop and struggling alcoholic stalking the mean streets of New York; the 'Burglar' Bernie Rhodenbarr books, witty with a much lighter touch, and the Evan Tanner series (the man who never sleeps). *Eight Million Ways to Die* (1983) shows us Scudder haunted by the crazy violence of the city and confronted by his own capacity for brutality as he works for a pimp to try and establish who is killing his prostitutes.

The characters are credible and complex, the city brilliantly evoked as is the relentless pull of addiction. Over the novels, Scudder's battle to stay sober develops as do his relationships with women, especially Elaine, a call-girl who eventually becomes his lover. The tensions of that relationship are depicted well in *The Devil Knows You're Dead* (1994).

📖 James Lee Burke, Walter Mosley

CS

Bloom, Amy (US, 1953–   ) Amy Bloom is a psychotherapist who lives in Connecticut and divides her time between writing and her practice. Her collection of stories *Come to Me* (1993) explores the experiences of bereavement, mental breakdown, and sexual non-conformity. Bloom's understated, almost minimalist style encourages the reader to understand rather than judge her characters. In 'Love is not a Pie', for example, Ellen tries to make sense of her dead mother's sexual relationship with a family friend and her father's collusion in it. In reaching an understanding of the generosity and love in this *ménage à trois*, Ellen decides not to marry the man who seems a 'sensible choice'. The passions, tragedies, and misdemeanours of human existence are also explored in Bloom's first novel, *Love Invents Us* (1997), through the life and loves of one woman, Elizabeth, from her youth into middle age.

📖 Alice Munro, Lorrie Moore, Colette

DJ

Blume, Judy (US, 1938–   ) At the height of her popularity Judy Blume was a publishing phenomenon, receiving over a thousand letters a week from teenagers who felt that she understood their prob-

lems, and that her books helped them to make sense of the world. She has written with humour and sensitivity for younger readers, too, as in *Tales of a Fourth Grade Nothing* (1972) but is at her best when addressing the preoccupations of young adults. The onset of menstruation—*Are You There, God? It's Me, Margaret* (1970)—and first sex—*Forever* (1975)—for example, are sensibly explored in her work, and *Forever* appeared at a time when frankness about sexual matters was much rarer in teenage literature than it is today. Her autobiographical novel, *Sally J. Friedman by Herself* (1977), and books such as *Deenie* (1973) are very readable. She has a lively and colloquial style, and even if what she writes is not deathless prose, she is an accomplished story-teller with a winning narrative voice.

📖 Anne Fine, Berlie Doherty.
See TEEN

AG

Bogarde, Dirk (British, 1921–99) Born in Hampstead, London, from the late 1940s Bogarde was one of the most distinguished film actors of his day. His novels often spring from events in his life. Begin with *A Gentle Occupation* (1980), which draws on his military experiences of political upheaval in South-east Asia at the end of the Second World War. The book displays his stylish accessibility, vivid descriptive qualities, and strengths of characterization and dialogue. His other work includes *Jericho* (1992), set amid a colony of English expatriates in the south of France. The book offers a detached treatment of the theme of homosexuality, which recurs in Bogarde's fiction. *Closing Ranks* (1997) deals with the decline of an aristocratic family facing revelations of treachery and injustice in its past. Bogarde is also well known for his autobiographies, among which are *An Orderly Man* (1983) and *A Short Walk from Harrods* (1993).

📖 Rumer Godden, Frederic Raphael, Francis King   DH

Bolger, Dermot (Irish, 1959–) One of Ireland's best-known poets and founder of the Raven Arts Press, Bolger is also a prize-winning novelist. His debut, *Night Shift* (1985), is the portrait of a young marriage in a fresh new country, set against the background of Dublin factory work. This is an abrupt comedy of manners, where memories are fresh and opportunites are true but few. It contrasts with *Emily's Shoes* (1992), which mixes elements of harrowing psychological portrait and hilarious pantomime, featuring cross-dressing and the troubles which afflict contemporary Irish Catholicism. Sympathetic and eloquent, *Emily's Shoes* is a brave and radical statement, a lyrical and sexy volume. Bolger is also a very successful playwright.

📖 John Banville, Roddy Doyle, Patrick McCabe   AM

Böll, Heinrich (German, 1917–85) Böll spent six years in the German army (1939–45). When Germany began to suffer outbreaks of urban terrorism in the early 1970s in protest against the return of the right, the government took emergency powers which alarmed Böll, among others. When Ulrike Meinhof was arrested in 1974 he wrote his most famous book, *The Lost Honour of Katharina Blum*. Arrested for harbouring her lover, Lutwig Götten, a suspected terrorist, Katharina Blum is hunted down by packs of police and reporters. Götten is in fact a deserter from the army who fled with his regiment's cashbox. A ruthless reporter confronts Blum at her mother's deathbed and when she meets him later he suggests they have sex. She shoots him dead. Katharina Blum is finally guilty of a serious crime.

Begin with *The Train was on Time* (1947), the story of a soldier convinced he is about to die. He meets the sympathetic prostitute Olina, who draws his emotions to the surface by playing Bach. Like him, Olina wished to be a pianist. Schubert also draws tears from him. The music hints at another, more creative side to German culture and also suggests the place of art in human life. This theme is developed in *The Clown* (1988), which also severely criticizes the Catholic Church. In 1992 Böll's first work, *The Silent Angel*, was finally published. Böll won the Nobel Prize for Literature in 1972.

📖 Günter Grass, Graham Greene, Marguerite Duras. *See* GERMANY   AT

Borges, Jorge Luis (Argentinian, 1899–1986) Born in Buenos Aires and educated in Geneva, Borges is often cited as the father of magic realism and his spectacularly idiosyncratic short stories, collected in *Fictions* (1945), *The Adelph and Other Stories* (1949), and *Labyrinths* (1953), explore, among other things, violence, the puzzles of detective fiction, the relationship between fiction, truth, and identity, and the cyclical nature of time. Many of his best stories are labyrinthine in form, metaphysical in speculation, and dreamlike in their presentation of life as an 'amber' of memories, perhaps being 'dreamt elsewhere'.

Start with 'Tlön, Uqbar, Orbis Tertius', a pseudo-essay purporting to refer to reality. It tells the discovery of archive fragments belonging to the meticulously catalogued history of an entire, fictional planet, named Tlön. This history was started by an eighteenth-century atheist determined to prove to a non-existent God that man can create his own world and, after generations of secret development, is released into the real with almost insane results.

Then try 'Funes the Memorious' which explores the existential predicament of a man with a perfect memory, and just relish the awesome imaginative reach of 'The Adelph', which speculates upon a point in space where all experiences are somehow focused and simultaneously available. These are tales of breathtaking inventiveness, and Borges is justly regarded as one of the most original writers of the twentieth century.

📖 Vladimir Nabokov, John Barth, Italo Calvino. *See* MAGIC REALISM

RP

Boulle, Pierre (French, 1912–94). *See* FILM ADAPTATIONS

Bourdouxhe, Madeleine (Belgian, 1906–). *See* SEXUAL POLITICS

Bowen, Elizabeth (Anglo-Irish, 1899–1973) Bowen's reputation as one of the greatest Anglo-Irish novelists and short-story writers has been growing hugely in recent years. She has always been admired for her treatment of women's lives and middle-class society, and for her evocative moody descriptions of houses and places, but more recently her diagnosis of the Anglo-Irish condition—semi-strangers in two countries—and her obsessively brilliant accounts of loss of innocence and emotional unease have been attracting increasing numbers of readers. Her mannered, elegant, edgy, sometimes difficult prose, her sharp-eyed characterizations, and her acerbic comedy are strangely mixed

with profound, violent passions, terrifying hauntings, and reckless love-affairs.

Her life story reflects the sense of displacement felt by many of her characters. She grew up in Anglo-Irish middle-class Dublin and Co. Cork (her family house, demolished in 1959, was Bowen's Court), but her childhood was traumatically interrupted by her father's breakdown and her mother's death when she was 13. Her marriage to an Englishman, her grand house in Regent's Park, her rich literary social life, were always unsettled—especially in wartime—by her links to Ireland and her private double life of long-term affairs.

Her greatest novels—*To the North* (1932), *The House in Paris* (1935), *The Death of the Heart* (1938), and *The Heat of the Day* (1945)—intensely act out these personal themes of childhood anxiety, internal exile, betrayal, and disillusion. Her own favourite was *The Last September* (1929), the story of a restless young girl in a Co. Cork Anglo-Irish house during the Troubles, a wonderfully evocative tragi-comedy of an isolated and malfunctioning class in a country at war. These novels, and her great stories of childhood, ghosts, love, and wartime London, are her finest work; but her troubling late novels, *The Little Girls* (1964) and *Eva Trout* (1969), are also interesting.

📖 Maria Edgeworth, Somerville and Ross, William Trevor, Rosamond Lehmann *See* IRELAND, SHORT STORIES, WAR HL

Bowering, George (Canadian, 1938–). *See* CANADA

Bowles, Paul (US, 1910–99) Born in New York, Bowles began his career as a successful composer, studying under Aaron

Copland. In 1947 he and his writer wife Jane settled in Tangiers where Bowles himself began writing. *The Sheltering Sky* (1949), an immediate best-seller later made into a film (Bertolucci, 1990), follows the hallucinatory journey of Kit and Port Moresby as they travel to North Africa seeking adventure and new experiences. Instead, they are forced to confront their own inner turmoil in the desolate landscape. In *Let it Come Down* (1952) Nelson Dyer gives up his banking job in the United States and travels to Tangiers where he finds himself catapulted into a grim world of drugs, murder, and psychological breakdown.

📖 Jack Kerouac, William Burroughs
EW

Bowling, Harry (British, 1931–) Harry Bowling was born in Bermondsey, London, and before turning to fiction worked as a lorry driver, milkman, and community worker. He writes popular Cockney sagas, brimming with atmospheric detail and a warm sense of humour. *Gaslight in Page Street* (1991) is set at the turn of the twentieth century and concerns the relationships between two families, the Tanners and the Galloways. George Galloway owns a successful carriage business, and William Tanner is his right-hand man. Carrie Tanner, his daughter, is the heroine, and her story continues in *The Girl from Cotton Lane* (1992), which includes many entertaining vignettes of London life. *The Glory and the Shame* (1997) is about the impact of the blitz on an area of Bermondsey.

📖 Maisie Mosco, Helen Forrester.
See FAMILY SAGA   SA

Boyd, William (British, 1952–) Boyd spent part of his childhood in Africa, which provided the setting for his first two novels, *A Good Man in Africa* (1981) and *An Ice Cream War* (1982). The former is a sprightly comedy about the misadventures of a cynical, overweight diplomat in an obscure West African state. The latter, shortlisted for the 1982 Booker Prize, is set during the First World War in East Africa, and mingles comedy with tragedy in the story of a group of Europeans engaged in a theatre of fighting that their countrymen back home seem to have forgotten about. Boyd is a story-teller, in a manner that is rare in contemporary literary fiction: his novels and short stories, even those with modernist elements, are written in unflashy prose, and move along at an energetic pace. They have, too, a strong element of farce, perhaps most successfully deployed in *Armadillo* (1998), in which Lorimer Black, a loss adjuster, finds his carefully ordered world shattered by a series of grotesque and sinister events. As well as novels, Boyd has written screenplays for television and film, and has directed a film, *The Trench* (1999).

📖 Kingsley Amis, Michael Frayn,
Julian Barnes   NC

Boylan, Clare (Irish, 1948–) Boylan was born in Dublin, and worked as a journalist and magazine editor before becoming a full-time novelist and short story writer. *Holy Pictures* (1983) is a good introduction to her work, evoking childhood in 1920s Dublin with her characteristic blend of moving seriousness, humour, and quirky imagination. Beginning in the 1890s, *Home Rule* (1992) is the story of a working-class family caught up in the struggle for Irish independence. The book contains a vivid account of the Easter Rising of 1916 and the subsequent extended conflict with the British. In *Room for a Single Lady* (1997) an impoverished

Dublin household begins admitting lodgers, becoming the scene of tensions between appearances of gentility and the harsh economic realities of the 1950s.

📕 Edna O'Brien, Julia O'Faolain. *See* IRELAND   DH

Boyle, T(homas) Coraghessan (US, 1948–) Boyle entered fiction through the short story, studying under Robert Coover at Iowa. *The Collected Stories* (1993) provides a clear guide to his sometimes zany, pun-fuelled prose. In 1988 he won the PEN/Faulkner Award for Fiction.

The Tortilla Curtain (1995) is a Californian tragedy sprung with characteristic comic detail, in which he handles liberal environmentalist Delaney Mossbacher's obsession with his Mexican counterpart—whom he accidentally runs down on a dark canyon road. The abrasive account strips away delusions about modern America, as it zeroes in on middle-class fads and angst. Elements of a modern western and a serious social drama emerge from the elegant writing and gripping narrative.

📕 John Barth, Robert Coover, Thomas Pynchon. *See* SHORT STORIES   AM

Boyt, Susie (British, 1969–) Boyt's second novel, *The Characters of Love* (1997), deals with themes of love and rejection, written with wry humour and great clarity of style. Abandoned by her psychiatrist father until she is 10, Nell responds warmly to his offer of weekly meetings in luxurious cafés and a re-acquaintance based on discussion of books and poetry. But then he disappears again, and Nell's longing for love focuses on another father-figure, her university tutor, with whom she enters into a wild and destructive relationship.

Boyt's first novel, *The Normal Man* (1995) demonstrated the same emotional perceptiveness alongside confident humour.

📕 Elizabeth North, Mary Wesley, Esther Freud   JR

Bradbury, Malcolm (British, 1932–2000) Bradbury has been one of the most influential teachers and critics of literature in Britain since the war. Start with his novel *The History Man* (1975), a witty and observant satire of university life; its hero is a charismatic firebrand whose radicalism is a cover for ferocious self-seeking.

The History Man is probably the best-known example of 'campus novel', of which Bradbury and his friend David Lodge have been the principal exponents. Bradbury's first novel, *Eating People is Wrong* (1959), was an engaging portrait of the floundering of a teacher at a provincial university. *Rates of Exchange* (1983), shortlisted for the Booker Prize, was about an academic's misadventures in an obscure state in eastern Europe. The international settings appeared to have imposed a strain on the author's comic invention by the time of *Doctor Criminale* (1992), set in the world of academic conferences.

📕 David Lodge, Kingsley Amis   NC

Bradbury, Ray (US, 1920–) Hailing from Waukegan, Illinois, Bradbury has been a full-time writer since 1943 when he began contributing horror and science stories to periodicals. There are numerous collections of these short stories, most famously in *Illustrated Man* (1951) in which they are described as being magically tattooed onto a traveller's body.

Bradbury's reputation as a leading science fiction author was secured with the publication of *The Martian Chronicles*

(1951). This describes attempts of Earthlings to conquer and colonize Mars during the years 1999–2026, the constant thwarting of such attempts by the gentle, telepathic Martians, the colonization, and ultimately the effect on the Martian settlers of a full-scale nuclear war back on Earth. As with much great science fiction, it stands as a work of displaced social criticism, reflecting many of the prevailing anxieties of liberal America in the early 1950s: the fear of nuclear war, Bradbury's contempt for racism and censorship, and the longing for a simpler life. Mars acts as a series of 'collective representations' of Nature, and the book culminates in a recognition by Earth's survivors of the Mars within themselves.

The fear of nuclear war also haunts Bradbury's most famous novel, *Fahrenheit 451* (1953), which depicts a totalitarian dystopia in which the written word is forbidden and 'firemen' are employed to burn books. While most of the citizens live oblivious, unemotional lives watching interactive television soap operas, a small band of outcasts determine to memorize entire works of literature and philosophy, for posterity.

📖 H. G. Wells, Kim Stanley Robinson, Roger Zelazny.
See SCIENCE FICTION   RP

Bradford, Barbara Taylor (British, 1933–) Barbara Taylor Bradford was born in Leeds and worked as a journalist before writing her first novel, *A Woman of Substance* (1979). It became an international best-seller and spawned a number of sequels and imitators. The novel tells the story of Emma Harte, servant girl at Fairley Hall in Edwardian Yorkshire, who, motivated by revenge, raises herself to multi-millionairess with a world-wide empire including oil companies, newspapers and department stores. On her way up she contends with seduction, attempted rape, and two world wars, and works her way through four men. Detailed descriptions of setting only partly compensate for lack of psychological realism. The story of Emma Harte's empire continues in *Hold the Dream* (1985) and *To Be the Best* (1988).

📖 Rosie Thomas. *See* GLAMOUR
                                   SA

Brady, Joan (US/British, 1939–) *Theory of War* (1993) established Joan Brady's corrosive and eloquent style. This fictionalized account of the true story of Brady's grandfather, sold into white slavery at the age of 4, won the Whitbread Book of the Year award. Brady's analysis of emotional violation and the repercussions felt by subsequent generations is fiercely convincing. In *Death Comes for Peter Pan* (1995), Brady's acid scrutiny is turned on the US Medicare system. Her most recent novel, *The Émigré* (1999), continues her major obsessions of power, art, and love, but the moral framework opens out and the tone is lighter as the reader is asked to decide whether con man Nikolas Strakhan, who steals money, sex, and talent, is supremely evil or supremely attractive.

📖 Fred D'Aguiar, A. L. Kennedy
                                   RV

Bragg, Melvyn (British, 1939–) Brought up in Cumbria, the setting of much of his work, Bragg was educated at Oxford, becoming a broadcaster, journalist, playwright, and prolific novelist. Start with *A Time to Dance* (1990), in which the obsessive love of a retired bank manager for a young woman turns to corroding jealousy. A cleverly written first-person narrative, told in flashback as a 'very long letter', and with an open ending, it is erotic and convincing. Move on to *The Maid of Buttermere* (1987), set in the Lake District of 1802, relating the legendary story of Mary Robinson, beautiful daughter of an innkeeper, duped into marrying a bigamist. Public reaction, manhunt, and execution follow. Read *Credo* (1996), an epic of Dark Age Britain, teeming with characters, factual and imaginary. Stories unfold in a rich narrative concerning the struggles of Bega, a banished Irish princess (worker of miracles), emotionally entwined with Padric, Prince of Rheged.

📖 Lettice Cooper, A. S. Byatt　　*GC*

Braine, John (British, 1922–86) A Bradford lad, a librarian and a Yorkshireman by profession, Braine wrote his first novel, *Room at the Top* (1957), while convalescing from tuberculosis in hospital. Nothing and nobody will stop Joe Lampton, its ruthless and calculating hero, from escaping his lowly origins and achieving success, even if it means marrying a rich man's daughter he doesn't love. *Life at the Top* (1962) continues Joe's saga to its predictable bitter finale. Although he was lumped with the Angry Young Men of the 1950s, Braine never really belonged there, and his own views became increasingly, and outspokenly, right wing. His later novels deal with the upset caused to middle-class morality when the sexual impulse rears its ugly head. In *The Jealous God* (1964) it's a reserved schoolmaster who defies his fiercely Catholic and possessive mother by having an affair with a divorced woman; *Stay with Me Till Morning* (1970) is about the break-up of a respectable couple's solid marriage through casual adultery.

📖 Stan Barstow, Alan Sillitoe,
David Storey　　*TH*

Brand, Dionne (Canadian, 1953–　).
See BLACK AND WHITE, CANADA

Brand,　Max　(US,　1892–1944).
See WESTERN

Brautigan,　Richard　(US, 1935–84) Born in the Pacific North-west, Brautigan moved to San Francisco and became one of the most distinctive writers of the Hippy era during the 1960s. His playful, easy-reading style of short chapters, simple deadpan language garnished with outlandish similes and casual irony, was quickly popular through early novels such as *A Confederate General From Big Sur* (1964) and especially *Trout Fishing in America* (1967). The latter novel follows a quest for ideal trout fishing with many digressions, becoming a metaphorical journey through America which ends in a wrecking-yard with Nature being sold by the foot. *Sombrero Fallout* (1976) is another jokey but ultimately pessimistic narrative, telling two stories in tandem. In one, a sombrero hat falls mysteriously from the sky and causes a chain of violent events in a small town; in the other, the author of that story, a heart-broken humorist, mourns the departure of his Japanese girlfriend.

📖 Kurt Vonnegut, Jack Kerouac　　*JS*

Brayfield,　Celia　(British, 1945–　).
See GLAMOUR

Brett,　Simon　(British, 1945–　) Brett joined the BBC as a producer straight from Oxford and is the author of popular radio shows like *After Henry* and *No Commitments*. He has written parodies, humorous factual books, books about coping with babies, and novels about Mrs Pargeter, the widow of a successful criminal, but Charles

Paris, the actor-detective, is his funniest creation. Charles is not terribly successful. He has problems with his wife, his agent, and the bottle, but still manages to land parts in all sorts of dramatic endeavours. Someone is done to death in whatever Charles is involved with, and he finds himself in everything from provincial rep to television sitcoms. From a long list of extremely funny, fast-moving stories try first *So Much Blood* (1976) and *Corporate Bodies* (1991). Brett has also written straight crime novels, the best of which is *A Shock to the System* (1984).

📖 Michael Dibdin, Edmund Crispin, Damon Runyon   *AG*

Breytenbach, Breyten (South African, 1939–) Born in the Western Cape, Breytenbach is an Afrikaner. A controversial and uncompromising figure, he has consistently spoken out against injustice in South African society. A painter, poet, and fiction writer, Breytenbach writes almost entirely in Afrikaans, his native tongue. Always experimental with language, Breytenbach's novels are dislocated and often stylized. *A Season in Paradise* (1973) is a moving philosophical novel which explores the predicament of the Afrikaner who has rejected his own people by speaking out against apartheid. *Return to Paradise* (1993) is a fascinating critique of post-apartheid South Africa where the new black government comes under as much scrutiny as the apartheid regime. In 1975 Breytenbach was imprisoned for entering South Africa illegally. His long and horrific experiences are recorded in *Mouroir: Mirrornotes of a Novel* (1983) and *The True Confessions of an Albino Terrorist* (1984).

📖 André Brink, Nadine Gordimer, Albert Camus   *EW*

Brindle, Jane. *See* **Cox, Josephine**

Brink, André (South African, 1935–) Born in the South African free state, Brink spent much of his youth in Paris, where he became actively involved in left-wing politics. Politicized by his travelling, he returned to South Africa and began a highly successful writing career. Brink was one of a new generation of Afrikaner writers who broke with tradition by openly criticizing the ruling Afrikaner Nationalist Party. In *A Dry White Season* (1979) Brink exposes the brutality of the South African police force towards its black citizens. Given that the leader of the black consciousness movement, Steve Biko, was murdered in 1977 under police detention, many people understandably believed that Brink based his novel on Biko's story. In 1989 *A Dry White Season* was made into a successful film starring Marlon Brando and Donald Sutherland.

One of Brink's more challenging but enjoyable novels is *An Act of Terror* (1991). Beginning with the attempted assassination of the South African president in 1989, Brink weaves a complex narrative saturated in mythology and South African politics. *Imaginings of Sand* (1996) pivots around the historic multi-racial elections of 1994. Through the central character, an Afrikaner expatriate who has returned to his country, Brink explores the fear, anger, anticipation, and political extremes displayed during the move towards democracy. Brink is currently Professor of English at the University of Cape Town.

📖 J. M. Coetzee, Alan Paton, Nadine Gordimer   *EW*

Brite, Poppy Z. (US, 1967–) Poppy Z. Brite is the mistress of contemporary

Gothic but her scope is much wider than

Gothic but her scope is much wider than that. If you've always tended to steer clear of horror, here is a seductive writer who might win you over. The writing is witty, lyrical, darkly erotic. The settings are atmospheric, whether the dead-end North Carolina town of Missing Mile, in *Lost Souls* (1994), or the vibrant, decadent French Quarter of New Orleans, where Brite now lives. Brite's empathy with gay male characters has resulted in two nominations for the Lambda Literary award for gay fiction. Unless you've got a very strong stomach don't start with her most recent novel, *Exquisite Corpse* (1996), which might take you further into cannibalism and necrophilia than you want to go! Try *Drawing Blood* (1994) first to convince you that there's more to this writer than repellent extremes.

📖 Dennis Cooper, Edgar Allan Poe, Anne Rice　　　　　　　　　　*RV*

Brodber, Erna (Jamaican, 1940–　). *See* CARIBBEAN

Brodkey, Harold (US, 1930–96) Born Harold Weintraub, Brodkey's troubled early life within his adoptive family in St Louis, Missouri, and his later bisexuality, formed the subject matter of his work. *The Runaway Soul* (1991), a massive novel, decades in the making, takes its form from the inner thoughts of its narrator Wiley, spanning the years 1930 to 1956, using flashbacks and interior monologues to capture the dynamics of memory and desire. Like Brodkey's other fiction, it is challenging, lyrical, and obsessionally detailed. His stories, many published in the *New Yorker*, were collected in *First Love and Other Sorrows* (1957) and *Stories in an Almost Classical Mode* (1988), often taking a child's-eye view. In the

fictions posthumously published as *The World is the Home of Love and Death* (1998), Brodkey returned to the emotional vindictiveness of the Silenowicz family ('Car Buying', 'Waking') and Wiley's Gentile girlfriend Ora, but also defiantly contemplated mortality.

📖 J. D. Salinger, William Faulkner
　　　　　　　　　　　　　　　JS

Brontë, Anne (British, 1820–49) Sister of Charlotte and Emily, Anne was educated largely at home where she grew particularly close to Emily, inventing with her the imaginary world of Gondal. Anne worked as a governess and this experience was vividly portrayed in *Agnes Grey* (1847) which charts the development of a young woman leaving her idyllic, close-knit home to receive harsh, disdainful treatment from her employers. Anne's hotheaded brother Branwell is often regarded as the inspiration for Arthur Huntingdon, the alcoholic husband of Helen Graham in Anne's more ambitious second novel, *The Tenant of Wildfell Hall* (1848). This tells of Helen's struggle to free herself from the excesses of her dying husband and her fears for the effect of Huntingdon's behaviour on their son. Though the latter novel proved particularly controversial at the time, both are powerful indictments of Victorian society.

📖 Charles Dickens, Elizabeth Gaskell, George Eliot　　　　　　*RP*

Brontë, Charlotte (British, 1816–55) Charlotte Brontë was born in Bradford, West Yorkshire but was brought up in the parsonage at Haworth where her father was perpetual curate. Charlotte was educated largely at home but the periods which she spent away were to prove fertile ground for her later novels. As a child she was sent to school at Cowan Bridge, the unhealthy situation of which led to the deaths of her two elder sisters. Later, she and her sister Emily travelled to Brussels to learn languages and teach. Here Charlotte met the charismatic but married M. Heger, with whom she enjoyed a brief, intense personal relationship. On her return to Haworth, he refused to answer her letters and their correspondence ceased. From 1844 Charlotte and her sisters wrote prolifically, and in 1846 their poetry was published under the pseudonyms of Currer, Ellis, and Acton Bell. *Jane Eyre*'s publication in the next year, and its immediate success, was overshadowed by illness in the family. When her remaining siblings died Charlotte was left to support her ailing and demanding father alone, until she married the Revd A. B. Nicholls. Within a few months she herself died.

In all of Charlotte Brontë's novels an unprepossessing heroine, socially deprived and very much alone in the world, struggles to find love and achieve fulfilment. Charlotte Brontë's first published novel was *Jane Eyre* (1847), appearing under the pseudonym of Currer Bell. Jane, an orphan, suffers torments as the poor relation in the Reed family, adult cruelty at Lowood School (a barely disguised Cowan Bridge), and the grinding monotony of life as a governess at Thornfield until she meets its master, the Byronic, enigmatic Mr Rochester. Her romance with him is central to the rest of the novel, although Christian duty presents itself in the form of the would-be missionary, St John Rivers. The novel has been filmed and televised many times, but no adaptation can do justice to its highly charged emotional prose and the intelligent analysis of the plight of the single Victorian woman.

Shirley (1849), Brontë's next novel, is more overtly political, set in Yorkshire in the time of the Luddite riots, and articulating the condition of women through two heroines, the assertive and independent Shirley, and the oppressed Caroline Helstone, whose impoverished circumstances threaten her relationship with the man she loves. Caroline's sufferings are examined minutely, as are those of Brontë's next heroine, Lucy Snowe, in *Villette* (1853). Villette is a Belgian town where Lucy goes to teach, and for much of the time she suffers from depression, described with an almost surreal intensity. Her relationship with the teacher M. Paul comes to dominate the last part of the novel. *The Professor* (1857) was published posthumously and was in fact Brontë's first novel, in which she relives her relationship with M. Heger through that of William Crimsworth and his female fellow pupil-teacher.

📖 Emily Brontë, Elizabeth Gaskell, George Eliot (*The Mill on the Floss*). *See* ROMANCE   SA

Brontë, Emily (British, 1818–48) Emily Brontë was born in Bradford, West Yorkshire, but soon moved to the parsonage at Haworth where her father was perpetual curate. Educated for the most part at home, she was a shy, introverted figure and during her brief lifetime was overshadowed by the figure of her sister Charlotte. Like her siblings, Charlotte, Anne, and Branwell, she wrote from childhood, inventing with Anne the imaginary kingdom of Gondal. Later, her poetry was published under the pseudonym of Ellis Bell, in a collection with poems by her sisters in 1846. However, Emily Brontë is best known for her only novel, *Wuthering Heights* (1847), which in its time was deemed by critics to be grotesque and uncivilized, the result of a febrile imagination. In fact it is one of the great love-stories of the nineteenth century. It concerns the vengeful and all-consuming passion of the Byronic hero Heathcliff for the equally unrestrained Cathy Earnshaw, and is set in the West Yorkshire moorland that Emily Brontë knew and loved so well. It traces the results of Cathy and Heathcliff's love through the subsequent generation, and most of the novel is narrated by a family servant. The achievement of the novel lies in its romantic intensity and wholly memorable characters. Emily died of consumption at the age of 30, unmarried.

📖 Charlotte Brontë, Anne Brontë.
See ROMANCE   SA

Brooke, Jocelyn (British, 1908–66) Born at Sandgate in Kent, Brooke served in the Royal Army Medical Corps during and after the war; army life, implicit homosexuality, and his own idiosyncratic childhood, are prominent in his books. Beautifully written but often with an elegiac air of desperate melancholy, his work should be seen as imaginative memoirs, observations of an upper-middle-class social scene in Oxford and London, intercut with the natural world and the military. His major achievement is *The Orchid Trilogy*: *The Military Orchid* (1948), *A Nest of Serpents* (1949), and *The Goose Cathedral* (1950), all of which were reprinted in 1992. *Private View* (1954) collects four character sketches, two of which brilliantly observe the passions and humiliations of a small boy. The central piece, 'Gerald Brockhurst', describes a friendship begun at Oxford in the 1920s and continued to a tragic climax during the war; the homosexual undercurrent is treated with

unexpected comedy. *The Image of a Drawn Sword* (1950) is a Kafkaesque fantasy.

📖 J. R. Ackerley, Simon Raven, Christopher Isherwood   JS

Brookner, Anita (British, 1928–) Anita Brookner was born and educated in London, and apart from being a highly successful and prolific novelist is also an art historian of some repute. Perhaps her best-known novel is *Hôtel du Lac* (1984), which won the Booker Prize. It is concerned with the plight of Edith Hope, a romantic novelist, who has been sent to a Swiss hotel by her friends, as a reprimand for declining a worthy but dull suitor. The novel is a study in romantic aspiration, and is not without humour. Brookner's territory is that of the solitary female who is cultured, middle class, and unlucky in love. Most of her novels explore this ground—try *Brief Lives* (1990) and *Altered States* (1996). She also writes about German-Jewish emigrant families, as in *Family and Friends* (1985).

📖 Barbara Pym, Mavis Cheek, A. L. Barker   SA

Brooks, Terry (US, 1944–). *See* FANTASY

Brophy, Brigid (British, 1929–95) Brigid Brophy is one of the wittiest of post-war British novelists and deserves to be much better known. Her books are usually simple to read, but her ideas are subtle and sometimes require the reader to fill in the gaps. Brophy was a great fan of Ronald Firbank, and wrote a book about him (1973). She also published a study of Mozart. Start with *The Snow Ball* (1964), her best novel, set at a costume ball on New Year's Eve. The main characters are disguised as people from

Mozart's opera, *Don Giovanni*. Move on to *Flesh* (1962), a funny and slightly grotesque book about sex. Less enjoyable, but interesting as an experiment is *In Transit* (1969), a fragmented short novel set in an airport lounge. Brophy makes ordinary life seem comical and unexpectedly bizarre. She is gently wicked about people's bodies, their sex lives, their egoistic desires.

📖 Angela Carter, Ronald Firbank, Muriel Spark   *TT*

Brown, George Mackay (British, 1921–96) Brown lived in the Orkney Islands, and although awarded a host of literary awards, and an OBE, he led a quiet, modest life, visiting England only once. He tells stories intimately bound up with the rhythms of Orkney—those of the sea and the seasons, the sun and moon, and the cycles of birth and death. In them we meet ordinary people who find their destiny through encounters with God and nature. His works are beautifully written, with a lyrical quality reflected in the fact that many have been set to music. They have a rare quality of simple yet compelling wisdom. *Magnus* (1973) tells the life story of the patron saint of Orkney. *Greenvoe* (1972) is the story of a small community from prehistory to modern times.

📖 Lewis Grassic Gibbon, Eric Linklater, Mary Webb   *EC*

Brown, Rita Mae (US, 1944–   ) Rita Mae Brown's first novel, *Rubyfruit Jungle* (1978), could be mistaken for just another in that genre of growing up gay, which you suspect is 95 per cent autobiography and 5 per cent fiction. But this powerful story of self-belief is now recognized as a classic of lesbian writing. The novel tracks Molly from her dirt-poor Southern childhood

to student life in the big city, tackling bigotry and sexism head-on. A satisfying story for any reader who loves a rebel. Brown's later ventures into genre writing, such as *Sudden Death* (1984), a thriller set on the tennis circuit, are best avoided, but don't let them put you off reading *Rubyfruit Jungle*, which is everything it's cracked up to be.

📖 Alice Walker, Charlotte Brontë
                                                         RV

Brunner, John (British, 1934–95) Born in Oxfordshire and educated at Cheltenham College, Brunner emerged in the 1960s as one of the most highly regarded science fiction authors of his day. Begin with *Stand on Zanzibar* (1968), which, like all his most memorable work, engages with contemporary social and political issues. The book offers a dystopian treatment of global overpopulation and the dangers of eugenics. In *The Shockwave Rider* (1975) he projects a civilization in which computer technology allows an oppressive government to manipulate all information. The only hopes for human progress lie in the sabotage attempts of a brilliant hacker. His other books include *The Sheep Look Up* (1972), a prescient and well-documented treatment of an industrially polluted future in which controlling commercial interests regard the threat of ecological disaster with indifference.

📖 John Wyndham, Iain M. Banks, Ian Watson   *DH*

Buchan, Elizabeth (British, 1948–   ) Elizabeth Buchan was born in Guildford, Surrey, and educated at the University of Kent. She worked in publishing before starting to write her own fiction. Her first novels were historical, *Consider the*

Lily (1993) being set between the two world wars. This novel, the winner of the Romantic Novel of the Year award, draws on the symbolism of the English garden and weaves a haunting tale of two cousins, rivals for the same man. *Perfect Love* (1995) is a contemporary novel, in which the central character, Prue, is researching the story of Joan of Arc. The happily married Prue begins an adulterous affair with her son-in-law. *Against her Nature* (1997) contrasts the world of London high finance with rural, village life. Elizabeth Buchan writes intelligent, atmospheric, psychologically astute romance.

📖 Elizabeth Jane Howard, Joanna Trollope, Angela Huth   SA

Buchan, James (British, 1954–)
Buchan, a former foreign correspondent for the *Financial Times*, is the author of six novels and two works of non-fiction. Rooted in the real world, with acute psychological portraits and thriller-like structures, his novels deal with individuals trapped by political circumstance. Issues of free will and determinism are a major theme as characters try to find personal resolution. Buchan tackles a wide range of situations: Iran in 1974 in *A Good Place to Die* (1999), as John Pitt, a young English teacher, falls in love with a pupil and is forced to escape; Germany during the cold war in *Heart's Journey in Winter* (1995, winner of the Guardian Fiction Prize); West Beirut in *A Parish of Rich Women* (1984, winner of the Whitbread First Novel award). Buchan writes beautifully and the backgrounds to his novels are as interesting and informative as the stories and characters are seductive.

📖 Sebastian Faulks, Nicholas Shakespeare   SR

Buchan, John (British, 1875–1940)
During the First World War, Buchan was Director of Information and later of Intelligence. He served as an MP then became Lord Tweedsmuir and ended his career as Governor-General of Canada. However, he is better remembered as the creator of Richard Hannay, hero of a series of adventure novels that blend Buchan's sense of duty, his love of country, and his own experiences at the heart of intelligence. While many of his attitudes may strike modern readers as racist and right wing, there is no denying the genuine excitement of the novels.

Begin with *The Thirty-Nine Steps* (1915), a rattling yarn of pursuit and politics. Hannay is given cryptic but crucial information by an informant who is murdered almost immediately afterwards. Suspected of the crime, Hannay goes on the run to protect his information and save his country from the German enemy. The book has been filmed more than once—a classic Hitchcock version featuring Robert Donat and one less exciting, though more faithful to the book, starring Robert Powell.

Hannay returns in *Greenmantle* (1916), where he attempts to stop the Germans mobilizing the Arabs into a Holy War against the British empire. In *The Three Hostages* (1924), Hannay is forced into a head-to-head struggle with the charismatic hypnotist Medina in his bid to rescue three young people held hostage by a criminal combine determined to cash in on post-war chaos. Also worth reading are *Mr Standfast* (1918) and the non-Hannay *John Macnab* (1925).

📖 Erskine Childers, Ian Fleming, Frederick Forsyth. *See* ADVENTURE, SPY   VM

Buck, Pearl S(ydenstricker) (US, 1892–1973) Pearl S. Buck was brought up in China where her parents were missionaries. Her books, many of which were best-sellers when first published, are based on her experience of China. Her most famous novel is *The Good Earth* (1931), for which she won the Pulitzer Prize, about the farmer Wang Lung. Wang exemplifies the virtues of hard work, self-sacrifice, and moral responsibility. Although this makes the book sound like a Christian tract, by focusing on the mundane details of daily life Buck evokes the sense of a culture that is both alien and ageless. In *Dragonseed* (1942), also a compelling read, Buck explores territory previously untouched by women writers; the brutality of war, mass killings, homosexual and gang rape, and the dramatic transformation of a Chinese way of life. She won the Nobel Prize for Literature in 1938.

📖 Lewis Grassic Gibbon, Willa Cather; also the non-fiction *Wild Swans* (1996) by Jung Chang   *LM*

Bukowski, Charles (US, 1920–94) Born in Germany, Bukowski was brought to Los Angeles as a small child. Equally prolific as a poet, he based his fiction on elaborating personal experience of the city's sleazy bars and rooming-houses, racetracks and blue-collar workplaces. Written for small magazines and underground newspapers, his anarchic tales were first collected as *Erections, Ejaculations, Exhibitions and General Tales of Ordinary Madness* (1972), capturing the underside of American urban life with misanthropic humour. Bukowski's novels use simple expressive language and an episodic format, and often feature Henry Chinaski; *Post Office* (1971) and *Factotum* (1975) satirize bosses, bureaucracy, and the working

process. *Ham on Rye* (1982) is possibly his best achievement, developing a clash of values between father and son during the Depression, as the surrounding society slides towards war. *Hollywood* (1989) fictionalizes Bukowski's experience as the screenwriter of the movie *Barfly*, and stands comparison with the funniest novels written about the movie industry.

📖 Henry Miller, Raymond Carver, Louis-Ferdinand Céline   *JS*

Bulgakov, Mikhail (Soviet, 1891–1940) Bulgakov trained as a doctor but devoted himself to writing after the Russian Revolution. Throughout his life he had trouble with the censors. Moving to Moscow from his native Kiev he concentrated on the theatre, especially science fiction satires, but without much success. *The White Guard* (1925), set in Kiev during the Russian Revolution, was his first major novel. It was published in Paris in 1928, the year he started *The Master and Margarita*, which was to occupy him for the rest of his life. *The Master and Margarita* is a fantastical and mesmeric mix; a grim comedy featuring the appearance of the Devil in contemporary Russia, interspersed with chapters inspired by the Bible, it loosens the bounds of Socialist Realism, satirizing Stalinism. Regarded now as a twentieth-century classic, a version was published in 1967, when copies appeared simultaneously in Russia, Germany, New York, and London, and it was finally published in full in 1973.

📖 Salman Rushdie, Italo Calvino. *See* MAGIC REALISM, RUSSIA   *AM*

Bunyan, John (British, 1628–88) Bunyan was a brazier's son, taking up his father's trade until he was drafted into the

Parliamentary army in the English Civil War. In 1660 he was arrested for preaching without a licence and many of his books were written in jail. *The Pilgrim's Progress* (1684) has remained a classic of popular Christianity for over three hundred years: phrases such as 'the slough of despond' have entered our language. In the book Bunyan transforms spiritual trials into an adventure story, where vices and virtues come alive as vivid characters, emotions as places. We identify with the hero, Christian, and root for him as he grapples with such foes as Giant Despair. The book turns theology into an action novel, and is still a great read.

📖 C. S. Lewis, Susan Howatch, Jonathan Swift *EC*

Burgess, Anthony (British, 1917–93) Burgess was born and brought up in Manchester, attended university there, and served in the medical corps during the war. A late-starter at fiction writing (nearly 40 when his first novel was published), he made up for it with relentless, prodigious industry—in one year alone writing five novels when he was wrongly diagnosed as having a brain tumour, in order to provide for his family's future.

He achieved fame with *A Clockwork Orange* (1962), made into a controversial film by Stanley Kubrick in 1971. A scary peep into the future, narrated by teenage thug Alex in the lingo of the delinquent underworld, it tells how an authoritarian society brainwashes him into docile compliance, and asks pertinent questions about individual freedom versus anti-social behaviour. All Burgess's fiction combines playful inventiveness in language with a satiric sidelong view of institutions. *Earthly Powers* (1980) is Burgess at full throttle: a massive novel being the reminiscences of 80-year old homosexual author Kenneth Toomey in which actual events and real people are woven into a sweeping narrative covering sixty years. After the war Burgess served in the colonial service in Malaya and Borneo. Out of this came his Malayan trilogy: *Time for a Tiger* (1956), *The Enemy in the Blanket* (1958), and *Beds in the East* (1959), which examine to comic, penetrating effect the clash of western and eastern cultures at the fag-end of colonial rule. He also wrote symphonies, a Broadway musical, many works of criticism, and an autobiography, *Little Wilson and Big God* (1987) —his actual name was Wilson, Burgess being his middle name.

📖 Vladimir Nabokov, J. G. Farrell, Paul Theroux.
See FILM ADAPTATIONS *TH*

Burke, James Lee (US, 1936–) James Lee Burke has carved a unique niche in American crime fiction with a clutch of evocative and atmospheric novels that blur the distinction between literary and genre fiction. He began his career with four non-crime novels, the last of which *The Lost Get-Back Boogie* (1986) won him a Pulitzer Prize nomination. In 1985 *The Neon Rain* introduced Louisiana detective Dave Robicheaux, a complex Cajun whose investigations lead him into every stratum of society. Burke is a master of intricate plots subtly handled, and his poetic prose manages to carry tremendously exciting narrative drive. His themes are redemption and grace, love and despair. *In the Electric Mist with the Confederate Dead* (1993) and *A Stained White Radiance* (1992) are among the best of the Robicheaux series. With *Cimarron Rose* (1997) he introduced a new character, lawyer Billy Bob

Holland, whose stories draw on Burke's own family history.

📖 James Ellroy, George V. Higgins
VM

Burroughs, Edgar Rice (US, 1875–1950) Born in Chicago, Edgar Rice Burroughs was educated at a military academy. He is best known as the creator of Tarzan, the English aristocrat raised by apes and subsequently discovered by explorers in Africa. *Tarzan of the Apes* (1912) was the first of over a dozen Tarzan adventures, and others in the series include *The Son of Tarzan* (1917) and *Tarzan Triumphant* (1932). Now better known through television and film adaptations, Burroughs's Tarzan books were immediate best-sellers, despite the fact that Burroughs himself is known never to have set foot in Africa. A series of novels set on Mars, including *The Princess of Mars* (1917), were less immediately successful, though they retain a following among science-fiction readers. Burroughs later became a journalist based in the Pacific during the Second World War.

📖 Henry Rider Haggard, Jules Verne, H. G. Wells
WB

Burroughs, William (Seward) (US, 1914–97). William Burroughs attributed his longevity to heroin, the subject of his autobiographical first novel, *Junky* (1953), originally published under the pseudonym William Lee. This is a plainly narrated account of how the central character became addicted to heroin and his various recoveries and relapses. Its distinctive black humour reappears in full force in the hallucinatory, episodic *Naked Lunch* (1959), which was released as a film in 1991, directed by David Cronenberg.

Naked Lunch is not easy reading, but is extremely inventive and playful—with, some have argued, a strong moral purpose. Burroughs's later novels such as *The Soft Machine* (1961)—a series of 'routines' on the theme of oppressive power—feature the 'cut up' and 'fold-in' techniques he developed. These involve literally cutting and folding different texts together, creating new, if not always very accessible, meaning.

📖 Jack Kerouac, Charles Bukowski, Irvine Welsh
SV

Butler, Octavia (US, 1947–) Butler uses science fiction to explore issues of race and cultural dominance. In *Kindred* (1979) a contemporary black woman is sent back in time to a pre-Civil War Southern plantation. Here she must save the owner's white son whenever he is in danger; because the white son is the woman's great-grandfather. In Butler's recent *Xenogenesis* trilogy (1987–9), an alien race, Oankali, wishes to absorb the human race into its own gene pool, by conquering and cross-breeding. The central figure, Lilith, has been bred with the Oankali, without her permission, but she chooses to keep the child, who becomes a key figure in the saving of the human race.

📖 Marge Piercy, Ursula Le Guin
LM

Butler, Robert (Olen) (US, 1945–) Butler served in Vietnam from 1969 to 1972 in military intelligence. He learned Vietnamese and became a translator and an expert in Vietnamese culture. His book of short stories, *A Good Scent from a Strange Mountain* (1992, Pulitzer Prize), provides a convincing voice for the Vietnamese attempting to adapt to American life after the war. Butler moves gracefully between the sexes and different age groups as they recollect their experiences in Vietnam and Louisiana. He has marvellous ability to create an atmosphere that is at once realistic and poetic. The title story and 'Fairy Tale' are simultaneously haunting and comic and show a writer in complete command of his craft. The image of Vietnam dominates Butler's fiction and this is clearly evident in *On Distant Ground* (1985), a novel of obsession and redemption.

📖 Amy Tan, Robert Stone, Norman Mailer   *GK*

Byatt, A(ntonia) S(usan) (British, 1936–) Born in Sheffield, A. S. Byatt is an academic as well as a popular literary novelist. Her work is often about the relationship between art and life, especially as both affect women. Her first novel, *Shadow of a Sun* (1964), describes a young woman's efforts to escape the influence of her novelist father. These themes are developed in a series of novels that begins with *The Virgin in the Garden* (1978). Set in Yorkshire in 1953, the book introduces Frederica Potter, a schoolgirl preparing to play the role of Elizabeth I in a Coronation pageant. The hopes of a second 'Elizabethan Age' are richly evoked, but shadowed by the disappointment of the late 1970s, when Byatt was writing. *Still Life* (1985) follows Frederica into a provincial marriage, while *Babel Tower* (1996) sets Frederica's turbulent divorce against the dangerous and heady background of the 1960s. The Booker Prize-winning *Possession* (1990) is Byatt's most ambitious novel to date. An academic studying the works of a neglected Victorian poet finds the tangled emotions of the past increasingly reflected in the present. A love-story on several levels, *Possession* is as much about the passions of the mind as the emotions. *Angels and Insects* (1992) returns to this Victorian setting to recount a love-affair between an enigmatic woman and a scientist making a study of butterflies.

📖 Marina Warner, Margaret Drabble, Elizabeth Jane Howard. *See* HISTORICAL   *WB*

C

Cabrera Infante, Guillermo (Cuban, 1929–) Cabrera Infante met Fidel Castro and Che Guevara in the years leading to the Cuban Revolution, but left Cuba permanently in 1965. His fiction since then has been much preoccupied with the recovery of the immediate Cuban past of Infante's own youth. His most celebrated novel is *Three Trapped Tigers* (1965), in which the memories of a Cuban exile cast a powerful shadow of nostalgia over an often irreverent human comedy, while *Infante's Inferno* (1984) is a semi-autobiographical account of Infante's own upbringing in the Havana of the 1950s. A self-confessed Marxist of the Groucho variety, Infante's style is characterized by densely layered puns and a relish for intellectual jokes. *Holy Smoke* (1985) is a non-fiction study of cigar-smoking that draws on the same themes of memory, exile, and pleasure as the fiction.

📖 Mario Vargas Llosa, Gabriel García Márquez, Isabel Allende.
See MAGIC REALISM   *WB*

Cain, James M(allahan) (US, 1892–1977) James M. Cain's career as crime novelist got off to a dazzling start with the bleak classic *The Postman Always Rings Twice* (1934). The book was filmed with enormous success, as was his famous tale of insurance fraud, *Double Indemnity* (1936). He wrote from the criminal's point of view, rather than the detective's ('the least interesting angle'). *Mildred Pierce* (1941) explores a mother's obsessive, self-destructive love of her child.

It is no coincidence that Cain's work regularly attracted the attention of film-makers; the explanation lies in the cinematic quality of his spare, yet vivid prose, as well as the box-office appeal of his frank (for the time) treatment of sex and violence. Cain's trademark plot centres around a man who falls for a beautiful woman but who is ultimately destroyed by his infatuation.

📖 Dashiell Hammett, Jim Thompson.
See CRIME   *ME*

Caldwell, Erskine (US, 1903–87) Born in Georgia, Caldwell enjoyed a long and prolific literary career, producing travel writing, social criticism, and fiction. Although he achieved the peak of his fame in the 1950s, his most enduring fiction was written in the 1930s. The central character of *Tobacco Road* (1934) is Jeeter Lester, a sharecropper struggling in the face of poor soil and depressed markets. But as in much of Caldwell's work, notably the later *Gulf Coast Stories* (1959), the documentation of acute poverty is bizarrely mixed with lurid attention to sexual escapades. Caldwell's finest book is perhaps *God's Little Acre* (1933) where the poor farmer, Ty Ty Walden, abandons growing crops in favour of digging up his fields in search of gold. Rural poverty is also contrasted with life in the cotton-mill towns, through the eyes of Rosamond and her militant husband Will.

📖 John Steinbeck, Carson McCullers, Truman Capote   *BH*

Calvino, Italo (Italian, 1923–85) Born in Cuba, Calvino grew up in Italy, settling in Turin, after working for the Resistance during the Second World War. His first novel, *The Path to the Nest of Spiders* (1947), was realistic. Thereafter he turned to allegory and experimentation. His status as one of Italy's greatest writers was confirmed by the acclaim which met the fantasy, *The Baron in the Trees* (1957), in which a nineteenth-century nobleman opts to pursue life without ever setting foot on the ground. The story examines the meeting-points of reality and imagination. The concertina of fictions which make up *If on a Winter's Night a Traveller* (1979) is a teasing and profound investigation of the experience of reading a faulty novel. Like *Cosmicomics* (1969), a surreal, scientific and metaphysical account of the world's creation in twelve chapters, Calvino's in-spired plot, mixing a variety of pastiches, is extraordinarily delicate and witty.

📖 Angela Carter, Milan Kundera, Jorge Luis Borges.
See MAGIC REALISM   AM

Camus, Albert (French, 1913–60) Camus was brought up in Algeria before moving to France and becoming a journalist. During the war he was active in the Resistance. In his first novel, *The Outsider* (1942), Meursault is a young French-Algerian clerk who leads a perfectly ordinary life until he is put on trial for shooting an Arab in self-defence. He refuses to feign any of the emotions that might gain the court's sympathy (it is revealed he slept with a woman on the evening of his mother's funeral, and that he did not cry). The court regards him as sub-human and condemns him to death; as death approaches, he realizes how much he values life. The flat, neutral, journalistic tone of the novel gives it extraordinary power. *The Plague* (1947), based on a real outbreak of typhoid in Algeria in 1941–2, is an allegory of the German occupation of France. Initially unable to believe the invasion of plague rats, the inhabitants of Oran are quarantined and assaulted by loss and grief. *The Fall* (1956) is a monologue whose narrator has been forced to recognize the complacent hypocrisy of his life. He has flung himself into debauchery and then into self-judgement, and now tells the story of his fall to an acquaintance in Amsterdam.

Camus's writing explores the irrational and contradictory nature of the human predicament—often through characters who rebel against conventional values. The world he explores is 'Absurd' (a term used to categorise the work of a number of his contemporaries, particularly playwrights): it is incomprehensible and purposeless. Camus was awarded the Nobel Prize for Literature in 1957.

📖 Samuel Beckett, Jean-Paul Sartre, Franz Kafka, Jean Genet   JR

Canetti, Elias (Swiss, 1905–94). Born in Bulgaria, Canetti was the son of a Spanish- and German-speaking Jewish family. He was educated in Zurich and Frankfurt and qualified as a chemist at the University of Vienna before coming to London in 1939, part of a mass emigration of Jewish intellectuals from Austria. His only novel is *Auto da Fé* (1935), the story of Peter Klein, a scholar who lives through books but ends up burning his own library. A parable about the nature of knowledge, politics and life, *Auto da Fé* was inspired by the 1927 burning of Vienna's Palace of Justice, and reflects on the book burnings of the Nazi regime. Canetti's other works include a study of mass behaviour, *Crowds and Power* (1962), three volumes of autobiography, and many collections of essays and philosophical speculations. Elias Canetti received the Nobel Prize for Literature in 1981.

📖 Primo Levi, Thomas Mann, Robert Musil   *WB*

Capote, Truman (US, 1924–84) Born in New Orleans and raised in Alabama, Capote's precocious talent won him many prizes in literary competitions. The publication of *In Cold Blood* (1966) aroused a good deal of controversy, dividing the critics because of its hybrid form—the fictionalizing of real events—thus coining the term 'faction'. It is a gripping and gruesome read, about two vicious criminals who murder a farmer and his family in the wilds of Kansas, and are then pursued, caught, and executed. Capote's other works might have been written by someone else. *Other Voices, Other Rooms* (1948) is a sensitive account of adolescence in the Deep South, while *Breakfast at Tiffany's* (1958) is a frothy story of fancy-free society girl Holly Golightly, made into a film with Audrey Hepburn. A writer of genuine talent, Capote never fulfilled his early promise, leaving behind at his death, instead of a major novel, the unfinished, inconsequential *Answered Prayers* (1986).

📖 Joan Didion, Raymond Carver, Christopher Isherwood. *See* CRIME
                                                          TH

Carew, Jan (Guyanese, 1925–) Carew's 1958 novel, *Black Midas*, set in the Guyana hinterland, tells the story of a pork-knocker (one of those early native pioneers prospecting for gold and diamonds in the interior). Something that wears well in the book is the love-interest across race and class lines—in this case African and Indian. These tensions still ring true in West Indian society. Carew is active in most branches of literature, including poetry and children's fiction; he is celebrated for his essays on the peoples of pre-Columbian America. Similarly, his book *Moscow is Not My Mecca* (1964, republished as *Green Winter*, 1965) is of special interest: Carew travelled in eastern Europe and studied in Czechoslovakia but it was a cousin's experiences in the Soviet Union that led him here to explode the myth of a non-racist, socialist brotherhood. Other novels include *The Wild Coast* (1958) and *The Last Barbarian* (1961)—this last being autobiographical, dramatizing his alienation as a student in America.

📖 Wilson Harris, V. S. Naipaul   *EM*

Carey, Peter (Australian, 1943–) Carey's books range from magic realism and fantasy to historical. He writes in beautifully simple language, with great clarity. Begin with his Booker Prize-winning *Oscar and Lucinda* (1988); the early sections of this huge book, describing Oscar's childhood, read like a nineteenth-century novel, but when Oscar—an Anglican clergyman who is addicted to gambling—goes to Australia in 1859 his story becomes stranger. There he meets the wealthy Lucinda who has just bought a glass factory. When he sees the model of an all-glass church which she has commissioned, they fall in love and share an obsession to build a glass church in the outback. Oscar and Lucinda are a prickly awkward pair of innocents whose thoughts and feelings keep you glued to the page. *The Unusual Life of Tristan Smith* (1994) is set in a world with its own culture and history (often explained in helpful footnotes) and its own politics—revealed through the hero's life in third world Efica and his travels in imperialistic Voorstand. Rarely has fantasy/allegory/satire (and this is a blend of all three) been used to such powerful effect. *Jack Maggs* (1997), set in London in 1837, concerns a deported convict who has returned from Australia before the end of his sentence, to meet his adoptive son. It tells a satisfyingly complicated, well-paced story from the interwoven viewpoints of a Dickensian range of characters.

📖 Tim Winton, Patrick White, Thomas Keneally. *See* AUSTRALIA, MAGIC REALISM   *JR*

Carpentier, Alejo (Cuban, 1904–   ). *See* MAGIC REALISM

Carr, Emily (Canadian, 1871–1945) Carr was born in Victoria, British Columbia. She studied art in San Francisco, London, and Paris and was recognized as Canada's leading woman painter from the 1930s on. She did not begin writing until 1937, when poor health interfered with her painting. *Klee Wyck* (1942) is the best of her books, drawing its richly episodic accounts of life among the native Canadian peoples from her expeditions to the wilds of Vancouver Island and elsewhere. 'Klee Wyck' is the name Carr was given by the Nootka Indians, in whose tongue it means 'laughing one'. *The Book of Small* (1942) vividly re-creates her childhood and early life in late-Victorian British Columbia. Her other works include *The House of All Sorts* (1944), which recounts with gentle humour her years as the proprietor of a boarding-house in Victoria.

📖 E. Annie Proulx. *See* CANADA
                                                   DH

Carr, J(ames) L(loyd) (British 1912–94) Carr, although well-travelled, chose to live away from metropolitan centres in a small town in the British midlands. His novels often evoke a rural, English world where tradition is on the verge of being overthrown. Begin with *A Month in the Country* (1980), which was Booker shortlisted and successfully filmed. Two survivors from the First World War, Tom Birkin, an art restorer, and Charles Moon, an archaeologist, meet in the Yorkshire Wolds. Their discoveries threaten to undermine the traditional assumptions of the village; Moon's, because the occupant of the grave he is working on may be a Muslim from the crusades; and Birkin's, because the mural he is uncovering is a masterpiece, news of which might threaten the nature of the village's life. *The Battle of Pollock's Crossing* (1985) is a comic novel which describes the visit of Bradford schoolteacher George Gidney to Palisades, South Dakota; small-town America at its most marginal.

📖 Graham Swift, Michael Frayn   *IP*

Carr, John (Dickson) (US, 1906–77) Carr was born in Uniontown, Pennsylvania, where he was educated at Haverford College. From 1932 to 1948 he lived in England, where the majority of his classic detective novels are set. Begin with *The Hollow Man* (1935), the best of some twenty stories featuring his lexicographer-detective, Dr Gideon Fell. The book is the most celebrated of Carr's 'locked room' mysteries, a genre in which no explanation seems possible for the murderer's unobserved entrance and exit. Henri Bencolin is the detective-hero in his earlier works, which are set in Paris. In *It Walks by Night* (1930) he arrives at the gruesome solution to a mysterious beheading. Carr also wrote as

Carter Dickson, his pseudonym for *The Plague Court Murders* (1934) and numerous other books hinging on the detective abilities of the eccentric Sir Henry Merrivale.

📖 G. K. Chesterton, Ellery Queen

DH

Carr, Philippa. *See* **Plaidy, Jean**

Carroll, Lewis (Charles Lutwidge Dodgson) (British, 1832–98). *See* HUMOUR

Carson, Michael (British, 1946–) Michael Carson's first impact on the reading public was his funny and touching account of the growing pains of Benson, a working-class ugly duckling, trying to reconcile his Catholic upbringing with his homosexuality—*Sucking Sherbet Lemons* (1988). *Yanking up the Yo-yo* (1992), the final part of the Benson trilogy, takes our hero to the United States as a counsellor on a children's summer camp—enjoyable for its large doses of 1960s' nostalgia. Carson uses his novels to take a swipe at institutions—church, empire, and, most recently, publishing in *Dying in Style* (1998), where the satire is packaged as a traditional whodunit. Carson has never lived up to the originality of his first novel but fans will still recognize his trademark of a sympathetic, gay central character in a lightly attacking farce.

📖 Evelyn Waugh, Jonathan Coe *RV*

Carter, Angela (British, 1940–92) Carter, often regarded as an exponent of magic realism, is known for Gothic, erotically charged tales derived from folklore and myth. But she was also a feminist critic interested in sexual politics; *The Sadeian Woman* (1979), for instance, reinterprets de Sade as potentially liberating, and there is a polemical undercurrent to almost all her fiction. *The Magic Toyshop* (1967) concerns orphaned children who go to live with their mysterious uncle, an inventor, and focuses on the awakening sexuality of an adolescent girl. Her fascination with the disturbing occupants and contents of the house leads to a destructive climax. Some of the stories in *Fireworks* (1974) are informed by Carter's two years in Japan, for instance 'The Loves of Lady Purple'; a prostitute turns into a stage puppet, then kills the puppet-master and regains human form. *The Bloody Chamber* (1979) formed the basis of Neil Jordan's 1984 film *The Company of Wolves*, showing Carter's rewriting of fairy tales as feminist fables. Her most widely acclaimed novel, *Nights at the Circus* (1984) is an exuberantly theatrical re-creation of turn-of-the-century London, featuring Fevvers, a larger-than-life trapeze artist with wings, and other exotic characters. The story follows Colonel Kearney's circus across Siberia to St Petersburg and contains numerous adventures and reversals.

📖 Jorge Luis Borges, Jeanette Winterson, Elizabeth Jolley. *See* MAGIC REALISM, SOCIAL ISSUES *JS*

Cartwright, Justin (South African, 1933–) Justin Cartwright was born in South Africa, and educated there, in the United States, and at Oxford. A documentary film-maker and travel writer, Cartwright is best known for his subtly comic and often satirical novels. *Look at It This Way* (1990), a story about a City broker eaten by an escaped lion in central London, is a good starting-point. *In Every Face I Meet* (1995) is a layered account of a single day in the life of Anthony Northleach, whose activities are counterpointed with the news of Nelson Mandela's release from prison. A portrait of a city, of a historic moment, and of an individual consciousness, the book was shortlisted for the Booker Prize in 1995. *Leading the Cheers* (1998), a comedy set at a school reunion in Michigan, is one of Cartwright's sharpest books, and shows his outsider's eye on social and political nuances at its most clearly focused. *Interior* (1988), set in 1959 in South and West Africa, tells the story of a journalist's search for the truth behind his father's disappearance.

📖 William Boyd, Christopher Hope
WB

Carver, Raymond (US, 1938–88) Carver was a short story writer and poet. The son of a lumber-mill worker and a waitress, he worked as a janitor, sawmill hand, delivery man, retail clerk, and editor before becoming a full-time writer and occasional teacher of writing. In 1956 Carver married Maryann Burkk, with whom he had two children. Just before his death in 1988 he married the poet Tess Gallagher. Carver suffered from alcoholism and came close to drinking himself to death several times. His drinking stopped in 1977—the year he met Gallagher. Carver's stories concern small-town characters struggling with the ordinary enormity of life, reaching moments of revelation which, typically, they note before carrying on as before, understanding that nothing has really changed. His narrative voice is informed by Hemingway's though his greatest influence was Anton Chekhov. His second collection *Will You Please Be Quiet, Please?* (1976) included the story 'Signals', a darkly comic account of a couple's argument over dinner in a posh restaurant. The dark side of marriage— the dis-ease of uncomfortable domesticity —was a fruitful subject for Carver.

The stories in *What We Talk About When We Talk About Love* (1981) represent his sparest, most minimal work but in his last decade his writing became increasingly expansive and affirmative. *Elephant* (1988) contains his seven final stories, including 'Errand'—a moving account of Chekhov's last days and the human business surrounding his death. Themes and characters from several of Carver's stories were woven together in Robert Altman's film *Shortcuts* (1993).

📖 Anton Chekhov, Lorrie Moore, John Cheever. *See* SHORT STORIES, UNITED STATES OF AMERICA   LG

Cary, (Arthur) Joyce (Lunel) (British, 1888–1957) Joyce Cary studied art in Edinburgh and Paris, fought in the Balkans before the First World War, and later travelled to Nigeria with the political service, serving in military campaigns in the Cameroons before returning to England in 1920. *Aissa Saved* (1932) is an account of the effect of missionaries on those they 'save', and *Mister Johnson* (1939) is a tragi-comic novel about an accommodating and ambitious black Nigerian who is betrayed by the British imperial service for which he works. Cary is best known for a trilogy telling the life stories of Gulley Jimson, a rakish English bohemian painter, Sara Monday, his model, and Mr Wilcher, a businessman. *Herself Surprised* (1941) and *To Be a Pilgrim* (1942) cover the early years, but it is *The Horse's Mouth* (1944), covering Jimson's final years in London, that remains one of the funniest and most astute fictional portrayals of a visual artist written in the twentieth century.

📖 Graham Greene, V. S. Pritchett, James Joyce   WB

Cather, Willa (US, 1873–1947) Willa Cather's family migrated from Virginia to Nebraska when Cather was 9 and her writing celebrates a time when women were central to the civilizing of the prairies. In *O Pioneers!* (1913), Cather describes the effect on Alexandra Bergson of the death of her father and the consequent need for her to become the 'head of the family'. As a result, Alexandra suppresses her own physical needs and desires in order to work the land. Although the message of strength through domesticity might seem a little old-fashioned, Cather's evocation of a spiritual attachment to the landscape of the prairies is haunting and her women unforgettable. In *My Ántonia* (1918), the central character survives both her father's suicide and an illegitimate pregnancy, eventually marrying and settling into the required role. Cather writes this novel from the point of view of Ántonia's neighbour and admirer, Jim Burden, and this allows her style to be both objective and erotic. Cather's style is one of the great joys of American literature; haunting and often heart-stoppingly tender, yet vast in scope. Her work is often concerned with the very contemporary issue of cultural conflict, either in the emerging society of the prairies, or, in one of her finest novels, *Death Comes for the Archbishop* (1927), in the contrast between the European values of two missionaries sent to New Mexico, and the world-view of the native New Mexicans. She won the Pulitzer Prize in 1922 for *One of Ours*.

📖 Ivan Turgenev, Thomas Hardy, Stephen Crane, Edith Wharton. *See* UNITED STATES OF AMERICA   *LM*

Céline, Louis-Ferdinand (French, 1894–1961) 'Céline' was the pseudonym of Henri-Louis Destouches, who served in the First World War, sustaining head injuries, and then worked as a doctor in the poorest areas of Paris. Though his works are usually written in the first person, and reflect his war service, travels, and knowledge of the Lower Depths, Céline is no realist. Both his best-known novels, *Journey to the End of the Night* (1932) and *Death on the Installment Plan* (1936), are hallucinatory, nightmare explorations of mankind's capacity for cruelty, triviality, and viciousness. Full of bitterly anti-humanist rhetoric, they mix street slang with despairing philosophical observations. *Journey* follows Bardamu's sufferings in the army, witnessing colonialism in Africa, and traversing New York and Detroit, dogged by his mysterious friend Robinson. *Death on the Installment Plan* is even more extreme, though also full of farcically funny episodes in the early Parisian life of its narrator, satirizing his family and social background. Céline's collaboration with the wartime Vichy regime led to his imprisonment, but he re-emerged as a dissident, cult figure.

📖 Samuel Beckett, Charles Bukowski   *JS*

Cervantes Saavedra, Miguel de (Spanish, 1547–1616) Cervantes wrote plays, short stories, and novels; it is for *Don Quixote de la Mancha* (Part I, 1605, Part II, 1615) that he is known today. Commonly praised as the first modern novel, and a comic masterpiece, *Don Quixote* is a lampoon on the chivalric romances of the sixteenth century; medieval soap operas ripe for Cervantes's ironic and philosophical eye. Born near Madrid to a middle-class family, Cervantes's ambitions were military, and in 1571 he served at the battle of Lepanto against Turkey. Badly wounded—he lost the use of his left hand—he was imprisoned for five years, and it was during this time that he first conceived of his tragical knight errant. Cervantes creates an opportunistic tale in which ridiculous and fantastical adventures arise with little regard to time or place. Minor characters abound as the vainglorious Quixote pursues his deluded wanderings on his nag Rosinante with the peasant Sancho Panza as his squire, in search of his true love, Dulcinea. Sancho's pragmatic presence provides a useful contrast to Quixote's madly romantic imagination. Where he famously sees proverbial giants, Sancho recognizes the reality of windmills gently turning. Underlying all is Quixote's belief in the world of the romance. The character's fantasy and the author's own commentary mix in a complex, uproarious entertainment.

📖 Laurence Sterne, James Joyce, Jorge Luis Borges. *See* CLASSICS   AM

Chamoiseau, Patrick (Martiniquan, 1953–   ). *See* FRANCE

Chandler, Raymond (US, 1888–1959)
For many readers, Chandler's creation Philip Marlowe is the archetypal private eye. It is hard to overestimate the influence on generations of hard-boiled crime writers of the man who wrote: 'Down these mean streets a man must go who is not himself mean, who is neither tarnished nor afraid.' The image of Marlowe, reinforced by many film adaptations starring the likes of Humphrey Bogart and Robert Mitchum, is that of the lone maverick driven by his own demons to take arms against the morally corrupt. That this

drives him to drink or into the arms of a beautiful woman merely adds to the romantic myth.

Chandler began writing short stories for pulp magazines when he lost his job as an oil executive. He went on to write seven classic novels, beginning with *The Big Sleep* (1939), a tortuous tale of the collision of family feuding and the world of mobsters. Chandler elevated the American detective story partly by his emphasis on atmospheric sense of place and character rather than plot, partly by his attraction to wider themes than mayhem and murder, but mostly by the elegance of his writing style, with its throwaway wisecracks and illuminating similes. In spite of his generally unsympathetic depiction of women, Chandler's novels are still the benchmark for private investigator writers. Among the best are *The Little Sister* (1949), which begins as a missing person case, and *The Long Goodbye* (1953), where friendship with a suspect drags Marlowe into a murder investigation.

📖 Dashiell Hammett, Sara Paretsky, Walter Mosley. *See* CRIME, FILM ADAPTATIONS   VM

Chandra, Vikram (Indian, 1961–   ) Born
in Bombay, Vikram Chandra was educated in California and studied film before turning to fiction. His debut novel, *Red Earth and Pouring Rain* (1995), was immediately acclaimed for its ambitious scale and inventive style. Set partly in nineteenth-century India among legendary poets and warriors, the larger-than-life Indian stories are interwoven with an account of a group of modern Indian characters driving across the American continent. Echoing the form of 'stories within stories' of traditional Hindu poetic dramas (like the *Mahabharata*), *Red*

Earth and Pouring Rain is a vivid account of the ways in which the past shapes the present. *Love and Longing in Bombay* (1997) is made up of five intricately linked stories set in present-day Bombay, and offers a revealing portrait of a rapidly changing city.

📖 Salman Rushdie, Arundhati Roy

WB

Charles, Will. *See* **Willeford, Charles**

Chatwin, Bruce (British, 1940–89) Chatwin worked at Sotheby's before studying archaeology and taking up travelling. He worked as a peripatetic correspondent for the *Sunday Times*, but gave this up to trek alone through the deserts of Argentina and Chile. His interest in place and in nomadic tribes is reflected in his strikingly original fiction. Start with *On the Black Hill* (1982), the story of two brothers on a farm in Wales. Chatwin creates the daily reality of their rooted lives and the land they work with a certainty that is reminiscent of Thomas Hardy. By way of contrast, read *The Songlines* (1987), whose narrator travels around Australian Aboriginal camps in search of the songlines, the invisible Dreaming tracks of the Ancestors which have given physical and spiritual guidance to the Aborigines. The central tenet of the novel is that being nomadic rather than being settled is the state most conducive to human happiness. Some of the explanations attributed to Aborigines here are fanciful, but as a bold novel of ideas this works well. *The Viceroy of Ouidah* (1986) tells the decadent story of a poor Brazilian who makes his fortune in the African kingdom of Dahomey in the early 1800s. *Utz* (Booker shortlisted, 1988) spans the middle years of the twentieth century in central Europe, in the life of the part-Jewish hero Utz, a collector of fine porcelains who is in hiding in Prague.

📖 John Fowles, Barry Unsworth, Julian Barnes   *JR*

Chaucer, Geoffrey (British, *c.*1343–1400). *See* ROMANCE

Chaudhuri, Amit (Indian, 1962–) Born in Calcutta, Amit Chaudhuri studied at the universities of London and Oxford. His debut novel, *A Strange and Sublime Address* (1991), received a number of awards, and established Chaudhuri among the best English-language writers from India in his generation. The deceptively simple tale of everyday life in a small Indian community, *A Strange and Sublime Address* is notable for its detailed and poetic prose style, where small events like a visit to the cinema or a family meal are pinned down with a clarity that belies their ordinariness. *Afternoon Raag* (1993) followed in a similar vein, and *Freedom Song* (1998) extended Chaudhuri's style to a more complex story, exploring emigration and politics. Chaudhuri's low-key style has perhaps allowed its qualities of subtlety and exactness to be underestimated.

📖 Arundhati Roy, Romesh Gunesekera, Salman Rushdie. *See* INDIA   *WB*

Cheek, Mavis (British, 1948–) Cheek's are sharply comic novels, usually set in London and satirizing contemporary social and sexual mores. Their persistently witty and ironic tone is apparent in debates about the merits of relationships, the exposure of the aspirations and self-deceptions of the characters. In *Janice Gentle Gets Sexy* (1993) the auth or of delicate romances has her placid life transformed, for good or ill, by the arrival of a pushy publishing executive from New York. *Sleeping Beauties* (1996) is a very amusing account of the makeovers of three middle-aged women in a suburban beauty parlour by ambitious assistant Chloe, with disastrous consequences. Another woman with a failing love-life, interior designer Pam, has to choose between her ex-husband and two ex-lovers in *Three Men on a Plane* (1998), when they each invite her to spend Christmas in Dublin.

📖 Shena Mackay, Candia McWilliam, Nigel Williams   *JS*

Cheever, John (US, 1912–82) Cheever published stories in the *New Yorker* from the mid-1930s onwards, gaining the reputation of a superb stylist chronicling the unease, depressions, and adulteries lurking in the lives of affluent suburban America. *The Stories of John Cheever* (1978) brings together five earlier collections and contains much of his best work, such as 'The Swimmer' and 'The Seaside Houses', haunting tales of loss. His novels work variations on the theme of lives shaken up by crises; *The Wapshot Chronicle* (1957) and its sequel *The Wapshot Scandal* (1964) tell of the rise and fall of a family in a small New England town. *Bullet Park* (1969) was commercially unsuccessful, but its evocation of moral disarray and darkness within the commuter classes is very powerful; the lives of two men, Hammer and Nailles, eventually clash. *Oh What a Paradise it Seems* (1982) is an elegiac short novel in which an ageing bisexual man tries to save his local skating pond from development.

📖 F. Scott Fitzgerald, John Updike
                                                    JS

Chekhov, Anton (Russian, 1860–1904) Chekhov began composing short, humor-

ous sketches for journals while studying medicine in Moscow. Although pressured to take up more 'serious literary work' Chekhov stayed loyal to the short story even after he began writing plays, for which he is perhaps better known. With his subtle blend of naturalism and symbolism, Chekhov revolutionized the short-story form, influencing writers as different as Kafka, Katherine Mansfield, Elizabeth Bowen, and Somerset Maugham. Start with 'The Kiss' (1887), the story of Ryabovich, an unprepossessing army officer whose brigade is invited to have supper with a retired general. Shy and withdrawn from the merriment, Ryabovich loses himself in the huge house, eventually finding himself in a dark room. There he is suddenly kissed by a young woman obviously awaiting a rendezvous with a lover. Although an accident, the incident transforms Ryabovich's outlook. In 'Gooseberries' (1898), Ivan Ivanovich tells how his brother, a minor official, aspires to enter the gentry, enduring decades of hardship and deceiving his wife for the dream of owning a country estate where he can grow gooseberries. Ivan meets his brother after he has finally achieved this goal and ends his tale with a strange, despairing diatribe on the nature of happiness, seeing it as a selfish, self-hypnotized state. Despite their brevity these stories are best read one at a sitting, and can be as thought-provoking as the strongest novels.

📖 Ivan Turgenev, Katherine Mansfield, Raymond Carver.

See SHORT STORIES   *RP*

Chesterton, G(ilbert) K(eith) (British, 1874–1936) Born in London, after studying art Chesterton embarked early on his career as a prolific journalist and author. Begin by meeting Father Brown, Chesterton's unassumingly philosophical Catholic priest-detective. Among the five collections of his exploits are *The Innocence of Father Brown* (1911) and *The Scandal of Father Brown* (1935). These vivid and charmingly witty stories have an understated seriousness reflecting Chesterton's abiding concern with good and evil. His technique of post-poning the culprit's identification until the concluding revelation was widely imitated in subsequent detective fiction. His novels include *The Napoleon of Notting Hill* (1904), a satirical fantasy envisioning London's future return to a feudal basis for society, and *The Man Who was Thursday* (1908), a high-spirited response to Edwardian fears of disorder that centres on a complex anarchist conspiracy.

📖 Agatha Christie, Dorothy L. Sayers
DH

Childers, (Robert) Erskine (Irish, 1870–1922) Born in London, Erskine Childers grew up in Ireland and studied law at Cambridge. He worked as a clerk in the House of Commons and served in the Boer War, publishing a non-fiction account of his experiences, *In the Ranks of the C.I.V.* (1900). He is chiefly remembered as the author of *The Riddle of the Sands* (1903), an adventure story that tells the tale of two amateur yachtsmen who stumble across a German plan to invade England while visiting the Baltic. The novel is often cited as one of the earliest spy thrillers. Childers moved to Ireland in 1920, and was made Director of Publicity for the Irish Republicans. Following the creation of the Irish Free State he fought with the IRA and was court martialled and executed by firing squad in Dublin in 1922.

📖 John Buchan. *See* ADVENTURE, SPY
WB

Chopin, Kate (US, 1851–1904). *See* SEXUAL POLITICS, UNITED STATES OF AMERICA

Christie, Agatha (British, 1890–1976) Dubbed the 'Queen of Crime', Christie is the most successful and widely read author of detective fiction of the twentieth century. With seventy-eight novels to her name, she has only been outsold by the Bible; her play *The Mousetrap* has played in London's West End since 1952. Her first novel, *The Mysterious Affair at Styles* (1920), introduced to the world the Belgian detective Hercule Poirot, with his egg-shaped head, luxuriant moustache, and faith in the ability of his 'little grey cells' to solve crime. Her inspiration came from Sherlock Holmes; in the early mysteries, Poirot has his own Watson in the form of Captain Hastings. Christie was a cunning creator of puzzle mysteries; no vital information is withheld from the reader, but it is well concealed within a variety of red herrings. Among Poirot's most intriguing cases are *The Murder of Roger Ackroyd* (1926), *The ABC Murders* (1936), and *Murder on the Orient Express* (1934). Miss Marple, the second of Christie's popular detectives, was a very different creation. Elderly and constantly knitting, she belongs in the seemingly timeless world of the English village. Using her experience of village life and the vagaries of human nature contained therein, together with her unassuming, listening presence, she is able to reach to the heart of the most devious of murder plots. Her successes include *A Murder is Announced* (1950) and *4.50 from Paddington* (1957).

📖 Patricia Wentworth, Ngaio Marsh, Dorothy L. Sayers. *See* CRIME
KB

Clancy, Tom (US, 1947–) Tom Clancy soared to fame in 1984 with the publication of his first novel, *The Hunt for Red October*. This introduced the charismatic Jack Ryan, a CIA analyst, and also paved the way for a new genre: the techno-thriller. Clancy's novels (three of which have been filmed) all reveal a threat to post-cold war civil liberty (terrorism, espionage, drugs) and the joint efforts of the CIA, the military, and individual heroism to set things to rights. Thus *Patriot Games* (1987) deals with the IRA, *Clear and Present Danger* (1989) with South American drug barons, and *The Sum of All Fears* (1991) with Middle Eastern fundamentalism. Although occasionally unwieldy in their technical detail, Clancy's novels are gripping, well researched, and skilfully avoid reducing the issues to Good versus Evil.

📖 John Le Carré, Ian Fleming, Robert Harris   *SB*

Clark, Mary Higgins (US, 1929–) Mary Higgins Clark writes gripping psychological suspense novels. *While My Pretty One Sleeps* (1989) is set in the glamorous New York fashion industry and involves Neeve Kearny, daughter of the former Police Commissioner, in trying to unravel the murder of gossip columnist Ethel Lambston. *All around the Town* (1992) finds student Laurie Kenyon accused of the murder of her professor and defended by her sister Sarah who believes that Laurie's childhood experience of kidnapping and abuse might lie behind the killing. In *Pretend You Don't See Her* (1997) Lacey Farrell is witness to a murder and recovers the diary that could lead back to the killer. Lacey assumes a new identity under the Witness Protection Program but eventually the murderer traces her and she begins a race against time to uncover the secrets of the diary before she too is killed. The stories bring tension and danger into everyday life and often include romance.

📖 Ruth Rendell (writing as Barbara Vine), Robin Cook   *CS*

Clark, Walter Van Tilburg (US, 1909–71). *See* WESTERN

Clarke, Arthur C(harles) (British, 1917–) Clarke is one of the most knowledgeable science fiction writers and was at one time president of the British Interplanetary Society. He has published scientific research on satellite communications and is credited with inventing the idea of the android. Clarke is probably most famous for a short story, 'The Sentinel', which was the basis for Stanley Kubrick's ground-breaking science fiction film, *2001*. This then developed into the *Space Odyssey* series, three novels published in 1968, 1982, and 1988. Clarke has specialized in writing about space travel and many of his non-fiction writings, on moon landings and the development of lasers, have accurately predicted scientific events, earning him prophetic status. Begin with the *Space Odyssey* series, and move on to *Childhood's End* (1953), an ingenious and thought-provoking tale about the transformation of humanity.

📖 Robert Heinlein, H. G. Wells. *See* SCIENCE FICTION   *LM*

Clarke, Lindsay (British, 1939–) Lindsay Clarke was born in Halifax and educated at King's College, Cambridge. His best-known novel is *The Chymical Wedding* (1989), the winner of that year's Whitbread Fiction award. Its subject matter is alchemy, and the narrative weaves between the present difficulties of the poet Alex Darken, who has retreated to East Anglia as his marriage is in ruins, and the attempts of the Victorian Sir Henry Agnew to penetrate the ultimate secrets of the alchemical art. The two stories are brought ever more closely together as the novel reaches its climax. The novel is rich in psychological insight, but is also particularly interesting for its treatment of alchemy.

📖 Peter Ackroyd, Umberto Eco　　*SA*

Claus, Hugo (Belgian, 1929–　) Born in Bruges, Claus held a variety of jobs before becoming a full-time writer in the 1950s. Among Belgium's most respected novelists, he is also a distinguished playwright and poet. Only two of his novels are available in English. Begin with *Sister of Earth* (1950), which captures the bleak mood of Belgium in the immediate post-war years in its story of incestuous love in a Flemish farming family. *The Sorrow of Belgium* (1983) is a compelling episodic account of a young man's growth to adolescence during the Nazi occupation. He joins the Hitler Youth, but becomes disaffected and views the hypocrisy of his collaborating neighbours with alienated detachment.

📖 Knut Hamsun, Jean-Paul Sartre
　　　　　　　　　　　　　　DH

Clavell, James (US, 1924–94) Born in Sydney, Australia, Clavell grew up in England and took American citizenship in 1963 after moving to the United States to work in the film industry. Begin with *King Rat* (1962), his first novel, in which his experiences as a prisoner of war in the notorious Changi jail, Singapore, underlie a story about extreme privation

and strategies for survival. *Tai Pan* (1966), his lavishly expansive treatment of the founding of Hong Kong in 1841, is the first of several fat historical novels set in the Far East. These include *Shogun* (1975), in which a seventeenth-century English seaman stranded in Japan rises to a position of high authority under the ruling warlord, and *Gai-Jin* (1993), set in Yokohama in the 1860s amid the conflict between various European interests over trading with Japan.

📖 Amin Maalouf, Alexander Cordell, Dorothy Dunnett　　　　　　　*DH*

Cleary, Jon (Australian, 1917–　) Cleary has published over forty novels, ranging from historical high adventure to the detective novels featuring Inspector Scobie Malone of the Sydney police. His stories are well crafted with a strong sense of place and history, and a pleasingly dry humour. *The Faraway Drums* (1981) is set in India in 1911 and concerns a plot to assassinate King George V at his coronation as Emperor of India. The hero, Major Farnol, intent on helping to preserve the Empire, falls in love with an American woman who is an anti-imperialist journalist. In *The Phoenix Tree* (1984) a navy lieutenant is spying for United States intelligence in Japan in early 1945, during the bombing of Tokyo and destruction of Hiroshima and Nagasaki. In *Endpeace* (1996) Inspector Malone has to solve the murder of a wealthy Sydney newspaper magnate, whilst in *Five Ring Circus* (1998) he has to find the source of vast sums of criminal money coming in from Hong Kong, in the run-up to the Sydney Olympics.

📖 Nevil Shute, John Buchan, Morris West　　　　　　　　　　*JR*

Cliffe, Michelle (Jamaican/US).
See CARIBBEAN

Cobbold, Marika (Swedish) Cobbold
was born and educated in Gothenberg,
Sweden, and she established her reputation as a novelist with *Guppies for Tea*
(1993). Begin with this serio-comic story
of a capable young woman's efforts to
survive her family and keep her beloved
grandmother out of a nursing home. The
main character in *A Rival Creation* (1994)
is learning to live with the fact that she
will never be a good writer. She becomes
caught up in a crisis of community as love
affairs and violent disagreements spread
through the village she lives in. A divorced
woman sets up home next door to an
alcoholic photographer in *The Purveyor
of Enchantment* (1996). Their relationship
deepens irresistibly as she comes to terms
with her new situation. *Frozen Music*
(1999) concerns the ill-starred love between
a British woman journalist and a Swedish
architect.

📖 Susan Hill, Mary Wesley, Shena
Mackay   *DH*

Cody, Liza (British, 1944–).
See CRIME

Coe, Jonathan (British, 1961–)
Cambridge-educated Coe has written
about Hollywood film star Jimmy Stewart
in *A Wonderful Life* (1994), and his passion
for film shows through in the loud characters and ingenious plotting of *What
a Carve Up* (1994). Like an English comic
horror film it tells the family history of
the Winshaws, starting with Mad Aunt
Tabitha, locked away in the family home
in Yorkshire since the war. Tabitha urges
the narrator, Michael Owen, to spill the
beans about the rich family's greedy
relatives; in the process accounting for
the years since 1942—especially the 1960s.
Coe followed this scathing political satire
with *The House of Sleep* (1997), in which
four students meet at a clinic for sleep dis-
orders. A thrilling and elegant romantic
mystery, *The House of Sleep* is a distinct
change from the anarchic humour of
What a Carve Up.

📖 Julian Barnes, John Irving, Nigel
Williams   *AM*

Coelho, Paulo (Brazilian 1947–)
Coelho, who has also written plays and
worked as a theatre director, is the author
of several best-selling novels. Tending to
be allegorical, and to be loosely structured
around a quest, these simple meditations
on spirituality have been translated world-
wide. Begin with *The Alchemist* (1988),
the story of Santiago, a young Brazilian
boy who decides to travel to Spain after
dreaming about treasure. He meets a
series of mentors on his journey, including an alchemist who helps him to adjust
his priorities, teaching him the true nature
of the riches he's looking for. Move onto
Veronika Decides to Die (1998), which
follows the spiritual journey of Veronika,
a young Slovenian woman who, having
survived a damaging suicide attempt, is
given less than a week to live.

📖 Jorge Luis Borges, François
Mauriac, Leo Tolstoy   *SR*

Coetzee, J(ohn) M(ichael) (South
African, 1940–) A prolific writer of both
fiction and criticism, Coetzee first won the
Booker Prize for his allegorical novel, the
Life and Times of Michael K (1983). A dispossessed and simple minded coloured
man, Michael K, aimlessly creeps round

the devastated political wasteland of 1980s South Africa. *Age of Iron* (1990) also focuses on the upheaval of the 1980s, this time through the eyes of the highly articulate and terminally ill Mrs Curran who grapples with her own mortality and the death throes of the apartheid regime. *Waiting for the Barbarians* (1980) is a deliberately disorientating and disturbing novel which explores the political complexities of life under a totalitarian regime. A quite different novel, *The Master of Petersburg* (1994) is an ambitious and fictionalized look at the year 1869 in the life of the great Russian writer, Dostoevsky. Coetzee became the first writer to win the Booker Prize twice, with *Disgrace* (1999) which explores life in post-apartheid South Africa. A professor's affair with his student is discovered to the university, and he refuses to apologize, resigning instead. He goes to live with his daughter on a remote farm where the black native people are increasingly antagonistic to the white settlers; and where his daughter is violently attacked and raped. As well as dealing with issues of race, this deals powerfully with relations between men and women.

Coetzee is Professor of Literature and Language at the University of Cape Town.

📖 Nadine Gordimer, Doris Lessing, Chinua Achebe. *See* AFRICA   *EW*

Cohen, Leonard (Canadian, 1934–). *See* CANADA

Cohn, Nik (British, 1946–) Born and educated in Derry, Cohn is best known as the author of a number of acclaimed books on rock 'n' roll and American popular culture, and these interests are the main subjects of his fiction. A good starting point is *Need* (1996), a story centred on four characters who seek sanctuary among the birds and snakes at a New York zoo during an intense heatwave as the city descends into chaos. *King Death* (1977) is a dark satire centred on a 'death artist' that reflects the nihilism of the punk rock movement. Cohn's theory that everything anyone ever needed to know about rock 'n' roll is contained in the chorus of Little Richard's 'Tutti Frutti' is expounded in *Awopbopaloobop Alopbamboom* (1969), a non-fiction study that is as informative as it is irreverent, and *Ball the Wall* (1989) is a comprehensive selection from his work.

📖 Thomas Pynchon, Roddy Doyle
    WB

Colegate, Isobel (British, 1931–) Isobel Colegate's novels offer a view of life that is often rather bleak, but richly ironic. Her best-known work is probably *The Shooting Party* (1980), a brilliant dissection of Edwardian manners and morals, with a country house weekend eerily treated as a dry run for the First World War. *Winter Journey* (1995) is about two very different siblings: the likeable but rather hopeless Alfred, who has done nothing very much with his life and has now settled down to a premature old age in a shabby house in the country, and his sister, Edith, a bustling proprietor of a language school, and a former MP to boot. Colegate has an exact eye for the significant minutiae of English conversations and behaviour, for the things left unsaid; and in this novel especially, she displays an acute sense of what it means to grow old.

📖 Barbara Pym, Penelope Lively
    CH

Colette, (Sidonie-Gabrielle) (French, 1873–1954) Colette wrote short stories and novellas, and adapted much of her work for the theatre and screen. It is often difficult to separate the autobiographical from the fictional in her writing; *My Mother's House* (1953) for instance, easily passes as fiction, yet is also a series of minutely observed sketches about Colette's own life, particularly of her mother. This gives her writing an immediacy and warmth. Her early short novels comprise the *Claudine* series, and are based on recollections of her schooldays and her development into adulthood, including *Claudine at School* (1900), *Claudine in Paris* (1901), and *Claudine and Annie* (1903). *The Vagabond* (1910) draws upon Colette's experiences as a music hall performer. Colette is an important figure in French feminism because it is felt that she gave female experience a voice, which was rare in her time. Thousands of women attended her state funeral in Paris.

Gigi (1944) is famous for its adaptation to cinema. Having reached adolescence, Gigi is being reared to follow in their professional footsteps by a grandmother and great-aunt who are both retired courtesans. Gigi is too honest and sceptical to be much affected by their instruction and outsmarts her teachers by marrying the bored and wealthy Gaston, for whom they had intended her only as a mistress. Colette does not invite the reader to judge her characters, but observes them with minute detail and gentle humour.

📖 Katherine Mansfield, Françoise Sagan, Miles Franklin. *See* FRANCE

DJ

Collier, John (British, 1901–80) Collier, first published as a poet, went on to write fantasy tales with moral and satirical subtexts. His first novel, *His Monkey Wife*

(1930), ostensibly the story of a pet chimpanzee's infatuation with and eventual seduction of Mr Fatigay, a schoolteacher based in Africa, is an allegory which undermines and questions a series of contemporary assumptions. Setting primitive instinct against superficial etiquette, old moral values against new, and the expectations of the male against those of the female, the story is a subtle exposure of social divisions and injustices. Move on to *Defy the Foul Fiend* (1934), the story of Willoughby, the illegitimate and neglected son of a nobleman, and his tumultuous marriage to Lucy. Also try *Fancies and Goodnights* (1951), for a selection of some of Collier's best short stories.

📖 Saki, Jonathan Swift, John Galsworthy *SR*

Collins, (William) Wilkie (British, 1824–89) The son of a landscape painter, Wilkie Collins worked as a tea-importer and qualified as a barrister before beginning his career as a writer. His first novel, *Antonina* (1850) was an account of the fall of Rome, but it was *Basil* (1852) that introduced the themes of mystery and suspense for which he is best known. *The Moonstone* (1868) is a brilliantly constructed and complex 'whodunit' about the theft of a jewel, and *The Woman in White* (1860) is the story of a woman's incarceration in an insane hospital that combines the trappings of the Gothic novel with the beginnings of the modern detective story. Later books are generally judged to have deteriorated in quality, dealing primarily with social issues, and it is as the creator of the 'novel of sensation' that Collins remains widely read and enjoyed.

📖 Charlotte Brontë, Edgar Allan Poe, Charles Dickens. *See* CRIME *WB*

Compton-Burnett, Ivy (British, 1884–1969) Compton-Burnett's life was disrupted and embittered by a succession of family tragedies, due to both combat and suicides, during the First World War. Though she published a novel as early as 1911, it was not until *Pastors and Masters* (1925) that she struck her authentic note of sharply observed family relations and astringent dialogue. The novel is set in a ghastly small private school, and dissects the mixed motives of staff and parents. The similarly titled works that followed usually have late-Victorian or Edwardian domestic settings and depict unsatisfactory relationships and family power struggles; outstanding are *A House and Its Head* (1935) and *Elders and Betters* (1944). The bitter conflict between a widower and his eldest daughter over his proposed remarriage in *The Mighty and Their Fall* (1955) draws on Compton-Burnett's younger self.

📖 Jane Austen, Evelyn Waugh   *JS*

Condé, Maryse (Guadeloupian, 1937–). *See* CARIBBEAN, FRANCE

Condon, Richard (US, 1915–96) Condon spent over twenty years as a publicist in the film industry before becoming a writer. This experience shows in novels that are tightly plotted and alive with vivid scenes, products of a fertile and febrile imagination. His best-known book, *The Manchurian Candidate* (1959), is a gripping political thriller, made into a brilliant Frank Sinatra film, in which the stepson of a US congressman is the brainwashed assassin of a presidential candidate. Condon's passion for authentic detail and setting, and his skill at character drawing, are used to chilling effect in *An Infinity of Mirrors* (1964), as the sordid depravity of Nazi anti-Semitism is seen through the eyes of a young French Jewess who falls in love with a German soldier. *Winter Kills* (1974) returns to the theme of political paranoia, with echoes of the Kennedy assassination. Late in his career Condon began a successful series of black comedy novels about the Mafia, starting with *Prizzi's Honor* (1982), for which he also wrote the Oscar-nominated screenplay.

📖 Thomas Pynchon, Terry Southern, Don DeLillo   *TH*

Connelly, Michael (US, 1956–). *See* THRILLERS

Conrad, Joseph (Polish/British, 1857–1924) Conrad had three lives: the first as a young Pole during a period in which Poland did not officially exist; the second as a sailor for twenty years; the third as a novelist in England. He started writing in his late thirties, in English, his third language after Polish and French. Once you adjust to Conrad's rhythms and his view of the world, he is mesmerizing. Like Ford Madox Ford, Conrad attempted a kind of literary impressionism. How things appear is often as important as how they actually are. And how can we tell the difference between the two? Conrad worries at these questions. He also worries how one can see anything at all; how one can tell a story; who is saying what to whom, and who is listening (or asleep).

His most famous work is *Heart of Darkness* (1899), a murky and disturbing story of one man's journey up the Congo river during a particularly vicious period of colonization in Africa. This is a powerful representation of the pitiless race for ivory in the Belgian Congo. Conrad himself travelled there a few years earlier, and felt he never really recovered from the horror of the journey. The book points towards the brutal treatment of the African people by the Belgian colonists, but it is especially interested in the ways in which greed and violence corrupt the oppressors. It has inspired many other works, including a strongly critical essay by Nigerian writer Chinua Achebe, and one of the best films about Vietnam, *Apocalypse Now* (1979). But this is a book to come to once you have acquired a bit of a feeling for reading Conrad.

Start with *The Shadow-Line* (1917), a moving story of a young man's first experiences as captain of a ship. This is partly based on Conrad's own first command, and was dedicated to his son and all the other young men then fighting in the First World War. In *The Secret Sharer* (1910) a young captain rescues a young man out of the water and hides him in his cabin. Here and in other works there is a subdued suggestion of tender love between men. *The Secret Agent* (1907) is a powerful domestic drama and spy novel, set in the brutal world of anarchist revolutionaries who plot to blow up Greenwich Observatory. Move on to some of the other great works: *Lord Jim* (1900), a story in which an idealistic young sailor commits an act of cowardice and tries to redeem himself; *Nostromo* (1904), a novel about political corruption set in the imaginary and exotic South American country of Costaguana during a period of turmoil and revolution; and *Under Western Eyes* (1911), a novel about a student caught up in Russian revolutionary activities against his will.
📖 Ford Madox Ford, Henry James, Virginia Woolf. *See* ADVENTURE, FILM ADAPTATIONS, THE SEA, SPY

TT

Conran, Shirley (British, 1932–). *See* GLAMOUR

Conroy, Pat (US, 1946–) Pat Conroy is well known as the author of *Prince of Tides* (1986), a chronicle covering forty years in the lives of the unhappy Wingo family in South Carolina, which was filmed in 1991, with Barbra Streisand and Nick Nolte in starring roles. Conroy also wrote *Beach Music* (1995), which tells the moving and intriguing story of Jack McCall, living in Rome with his young daughter after his wife's death. When his mother falls ill, he returns to Carolina, to learn the truth about his curious childhood and the histories of both his own and his wife Shyla's families, and the reason for her suicide. With its characters haunted by memories of nineteenth-century pogroms in Russia and the twentieth-century horrors of the Holocaust in eastern Europe, this huge novel exposes the closeness of patriotism and prejudice, and the political, social, and religious manifestations of both.
📖 Winston Graham (his contemporary novels), Nicholas Evans, Harper Lee   FS

Cook, David (British, 1940–) Cook left school at 15, and worked as an actor before turning to writing novels and television drama. Begin with *Walter* (1978) which follows the conception and life of a young mentally handicapped boy in a Lancashire town in the 1930s. Walter's mother's point of view is movingly (but never sentimentally) rendered, from the courage and determination it takes to coax her abused husband into making love with her, to her desperation at the hopelessness of the resulting child, and her wretched attempt to kill him. The book is very good on the narrow-minded hypocrisy of the time. *Sunrising* (1984) is set in the 1830s, in the rural Midlands where people are rioting against enclosures of common land, and in the teeming slums of London. *Second Best* (1991) brings together a single man who wants to adopt a son, and a boy who needs a father. Lighter and more humorous in tone, *Missing Persons* (1986) is the first of the Hetty Wainthropp books, about the doughty old-age pensioner who becomes a private investigator—televised with Patricia Routledge in the title role.

📖 Paul Bailey, Bernard MacLaverty, Paul Sayer   JR

Cook, Robin (US, 1940–) Dr Robin Cook is a graduate of the Columbia University medical school and is renowned for his best-selling medical thrillers. In *Vital Signs* (1991) two women desperate to have children explore the brave new world of reproductive technology and encounter unethical practices and dangerous forces. In *Terminal* (1993) a medical student at the Forbes Cancer Center finds that unsettling evidence of illegal activity lurks behind the clinic's excellent record in curing brain cancer. *Acceptable Risk* (1995) turns to the search for new wonder drugs and the devastating side-effects that can be unleashed; and in *Toxin* (1998) when a child dies of food-poisoning after visiting her favourite fast-food outlet her father tries to establish how it could have happened, and finds himself up against the corporate might and vested interests of the food industry. The books are well-paced and gripping with twists and cliffhangers a-plenty.

📖 Michael Crichton, John Grisham
                                                 CS

Cookson, Catherine (British, 1906–98) Catherine Cookson (real name Ann McMullen) was born in Jarrow in Northeast England, the illegitimate daughter of the woman she believed to be her sister. At the age of 14 she went into service, later moved south, and then began writing. She tells her life story in her first volume of autobiography, *Our Kate* (1969). Her novels have enjoyed immense popularity in Britain and regularly top best-seller lists. Most of them are set in Tyneside during the nineteenth century, and deal with working-class heroines, their hardships, and their attempts to overcome them. Her writing is unsentimental, energetic, and manages to skirt the clichés of popular romantic fiction. Her heroines tend to have several volumes devoted to them; typical is Tilly Trotter, who features in *Tilly Trotter* (1980), *Tilly Trotter Wed* (1981), and *Tilly Trotter Widowed* (1982). Tilly is an orphan brought up by her grandparents, poor but spirited, who is accused of witchcraft, works in the local coal-mines, rises to the position of mistress of the 'big house', emigrates to America and then returns. The *Mallen* trilogy (starting with *The Mallen Streak*, 1973) covers similar ground. A more recent single volume novel is *The Upstart* (1996) about the boot- and clog-maker Samuel Fairbrother, his uneasy relationship with his butler, and the adventures of his growing family.

📖 Helen Forrester, Josephine Cox, Elizabeth Gaskell. *See* ROMANCE   SA

Cooper, Dennis (US, 1953–) Cooper is one of the most controversial of contemporary gay writers, and his work is noted for its disturbing interweavings of sexuality and extreme forms of violence. *Frisk* (1992) concerns a gay serial killer who finds his victims among the lowest orders of drugged and degenerate youth. Necrophilia and physical mutilation are graphically handled as he pursues his erotic impulses into physical desecration. In *Closer* (1994) anarchic adolescent sexuality drives the fatally compliant George to a nasty end. Two gay men subject the child in their care to regular abuse in *Try* (1994). Involvement in pornography has fatal consequences when things go badly wrong during the making of a film. Pornography is a recurrent theme in the stories collected in *Wrong* (1994).

📖 William Burroughs, Hubert Selby, Jr.   *DH*

Cooper, James Fenimore (US, 1789–1851) Born in New Jersey, Cooper's early experiences at sea and on the family farm gave him contacts with Indians, settlers, and forest life along the Susquehanna river, which fed into his books. Initially he was under the influence of Sir Walter Scott's historical romances and his first successful novel, *The Spy* (1821), is set during the Revolutionary War period. Cooper's great achievement was in fictionalizing the American frontier in the five novels of the *Leather-Stocking* saga, each featuring the white woodsman Natty Bumppo, also known as Hawkeye or Pathfinder, alongside his Indian companion Chingachgook. It begins with *The Pioneers* (1823) and continues with the best known, *The Last of the Mohicans* (1826), whose central episode is the rescue of an abducted white woman. Each novel depicts a different stage in the westward settlement of America, and is an exciting adventure, encountering Indian tribes, often viewed sympathetically, and the enemy French. The later volumes such as *The Pathfinder* (1840), which returns to the

period of Natty's youth, are more sentimental and lyrically descriptive.

📖 Walter Scott, Jack London.
See THE SEA, UNITED STATES OF AMERICA   *JS*

Cooper, Jilly (British, 1937–) Jilly Cooper was born in Essex and brought up in Yorkshire. She established herself as a popular humorous columnist before turning to fiction. Her first novels were bawdy romances, such as *Emily* (1975). She achieved best-seller status with her first substantial novel, *Riders* (1985), a comic tale of sexual skulduggery set in the world of show-jumping. This has been followed by a number of other similar novels, all characterized by high comedy, sexual frankness, and blockbuster-style readability. Try *The Man Who Made Husbands Jealous* (1993) about the gorgeous Lysander Hawkley, let loose among the neglected wives of Rutshire, and *Appassionata* (1996) which examines the lives and, more particularly, the loves of the members of the Rutminster Symphony Orchestra.

📖 Erica Jong, Katie Fforde.
See GLAMOUR   *SA*

Cooper, Lettice (Ulpha) (British, 1897–1994) Cooper was born in Eccles, Lancashire, and educated at Oxford. She is best known for her novels set in Yorkshire, where she lived for many years. Begin with *National Provincial* (1938), widely considered her best work. Its unsentimental evocation of life in a northern manufacturing town captures the brooding pessimism that preceded the Second World War. *The New House* (1936) is a psychologically revealing treatment of the tensions produced in a middle-class Yorkshire family by a change of home. Like a number of her books, *Fenny* (1953) is set in Italy and concerns a forlorn romantic involvement in Florence, which is richly present in descriptive passages. Her other books include *Snow and Roses* (1976), based on the miners' strike of 1971, in which the socialist sympathies underlying much of her writing are clearly evident. She was awarded the OBE in 1980.

Phyllis Bentley, Pamela Hansford Johnson, Winifred Holtby   DH

Coover, Robert (US, 1932–) A resolutely experimental writer, Coover has abandoned the constraints of time and realism. None the less, his concerns remain those emotional and narrative truths which are central to the American novel. His first novel, *The Origin of the Brunists*, won the 1966 William Faulkner award. *Spanking the Maid* (1982) details the daily encounter between a maid and her master and the ritual of punishment which unites them. It is a far from simple story, made indeterminate by the author's wilful intellectual gymnastics. *Whatever Happened to Gloomy Gus of the Chicago Bears* (1987) is similarly complex. Taking 1930s Chicago, socialism, and American football for its material, it shapes an alternative biography of ex-President Nixon, from which he is of course utterly absent. Coover teaches at Brown University.

John Barth, Angela Carter   AM

Cordell, Alexander (British, 1914–97) Born in Colombo, Sri Lanka, Cordell became a civil surveyor in Wales in 1936 and wrote full-time from 1963 on. Begin with *Rape of the Fair Country* (1959), which opens his trilogy of historical novels flamboyantly depicting social and political struggle in nineteenth-century Wales. Set among the iron-workers of Monmouthshire, the book culminates in the Chartist riots. The trilogy continues with *The Hosts of Rebecca* (1960), dealing with the anarchic resistance in rural Wales in the 1840s to the encroachments of centralized political power. *Song of the Earth* (1960), the final part, concerns the changes wrought by Brunel's extensions of the railways into the mining valleys of South Wales. Cordell's other works include *The Bright Cantonese* (1967), a spy thriller set in China and America at a time of imminent nuclear conflict between the two nations.

R. F. Delderfield, Winston Graham, Richard Llewellyn   DH

Cormier, Robert (US, 1925–) Robert Cormier is a moralist. He is also a stylist, the master of pared-down, direct, and muscular prose, which packs a tremendous narrative punch. His protagonists often find themselves on the horns of extremely painful dilemmas, and the different ways they resolve these problems make for novels which are hard to put down. Start with *The Chocolate War* (1974) and *I am the Cheese* (1977) and go on to harrowing but elegant novellas such as *Fade* (1988) and *Heroes* (1998) People in Cormier's books are always pulled in two directions, but they are also often touched by deep feelings of love. He is never sentimental, even when (as in *Tunes for Bears to Dance to*, 1993) he is dealing—however indirectly—with a subject like the Holocaust. There is violence in some of his books, and he does not always provide his readers with a happy ending. He is without doubt one of the most important authors writing for young adult readers.

Raymond Carver, Margaret Mahy, Ernest Hemingway. *See* TEEN   AG

Cornwell, Bernard (British, 1944–)
Born in London, after a successful career in
television Cornwell moved to the United
States in 1980 and became a full-time
writer. Begin with *Sharpe's Eagle* (1981),
the first of his numerous treatments of
the Napoleonic wars, which takes place
in Spain during the Talavera Campaign of
1809. Richard Sharpe, Cornwell's pugnaci-
ously capable and courageous working-
class hero, having risen through the ranks
to lieutenant, overcomes disorder and
treachery to save his regiment's honour.
Sharpe's Waterloo (1990) finds him, by now
a lieutenant-colonel on the staff of the
inept Prince William of Orange, rising to
his finest hour in a compellingly detailed
account of the battle. Cornwell's other
works include *The Winter King* (1995), an
ambitious reworking of Arthurian legend,
which reflects radical historical change as
Christianity displaces paganism and the
Saxon invasions proceed.

George MacDonald Fraser,
Patrick O'Brian, C. S. Forester   *DH*

Cornwell, Patricia (US, 1957–)
Patricia Cornwell worked as a crime
reporter and morgue computer analyst
before introducing Dr Kay Scarpetta,
Chief Medical Examiner, in *Post-Mortem*
(1990). The series of psychological thrillers
has been extremely successful, not least
because of Scarpetta's well-drawn character; she is ambitious, dedicated, intelligent, but vulnerable as well. A cast of
supporting characters includes her young
and gifted niece Lucy and grouchy cop
Pete Marino. Cornwell gives us all the
gruesome details of post-mortems and
the painstaking work of the subsequent
forensic investigations. The stories are well
plotted and compelling, each building to

a tremendous climax. It is Christmas
time in *Cruel and Unusual* (1993) but no
holiday for Scarpetta; she has to do a post-
mortem on an executed convict then a
young boy is found mutilated. On top of
all this someone is sabotaging her work
and her precocious niece Lucy has landed
for the Christmas break.

Jonathan Kellerman, Lynda La
Plante. *See* CRIME, THRILLERS   *CS*

Coupland,   Douglas   (Canadian,
1961–) Born on a Canadian Nato base
in Germany, Coupland grew up and lives
in Vancouver. He has been described an
'anatomist of the sound-bite era, a taxo-
nomist of moods, icons, jargons and styles',
being the most style-conscious chronicler of
the 1990s. *Polaroids from the Dead* (1996)
offers a huddle of snapshots, literary and
literal (black and white reproductions),
exploring life in the early 1990s, showing it
as a period when the shadow of the approaching millennium made everyone acutely
time-conscious and immediately nostalgic,
even towards the very recent past. *Girlfriend
in a Coma* (1998) opens with a 17-year-old
girl losing her virginity on a ski-slope near
Vancouver and falling into a twenty-year
coma an hour later. Her eventual awakening is shortly followed by an apocalyptic
epidemic of fatal sleepiness to which only
Karen is immune. Though its mystical
elements are ambiguous (particularly the
narration of part-angel, part-incubus Jared),
its metaphoric diagnosis for cultural fatigue
is unequivocal.

William Gibson, Jeff Noon   *RP*

Cox,   Josephine   (British, 1938–)
Josephine Cox was born in Blackburn,
Lancashire. She worked as a teacher
before writing her first novel. Her fiction

is generally set in the north of England and concerns the struggles of women to find prosperity and happiness. She writes readable sagas that have sold well for a number of years. *Let Loose the Tigers* (1988) is about two women who, while starting up a guest house, uncover unsavoury secrets. In *Jessica's Girl* (1993), which is set in Blackburn, Phoebe, alone in the world, throws herself on the mercy of her cruel Uncle Edward. *Born to Serve* (1994) is about the rivalry of two women, Claudia and Jenny, her maid, for Jenny's lover, Frank. Josephine Cox also writes as **Jane Brindle**.

📖 Lyn Andrews, Iris Gower, Maisie Mosco   *SA*

Crace, Jim (British, 1946–) Jim Crace has worked in Sudan and Botswana, and wrote radio plays and journalism before moving on to fiction. His writing is distinguished by its wide-ranging and intellectually exciting subject matter. Begin with his first book, *Continent* (1986, winner of the Whitbread and *Guardian* Fiction prizes), seven linked stories about an imaginary Third World, a rich mixture of myth, fantasy, and cultural history. *Signals of Distress* (1994) is a straightforward historical novel, set in the 1830s in Cornwall. An American emigration ship runs aground near an isolated community, who offer such hospitality as they can to the crew. There is a vein of humour in the meetings and misunderstandings between natives and newcomers. *Arcadia* (1992) is less successful, a rather lifeless fantasy about city life. *Quarantine* (1997, Booker Prize-shortlisted) is a powerfully original novel about Christ's forty days in the wilderness. The story is revealed from several points of view, including Musa, a greedy merchant who is left for dead in the desert, his tough, abused little wife, Miri, and Christ himself, known here as Gally, an almost simple-minded innocent. Both the desert, and the extreme mental and physical states brought about by fasting, are vividly evoked, and we are led deftly into chance events which, given a little time and distance, and the offices of a good story-teller, are the stuff of miracles. In *Being Dead* (1999) Crace deals with the lives of a middle-aged couple, through charting the decomposition of their corpses.

📖 Peter Carey, William Boyd, Kazuo Ishiguro   *JR*

Craig, Amanda (British, 1959–) When copies of Amanda Craig's brilliant third novel, *A Vicious Circle* (1996), were first circulated in proof editions, it caused such a storm that parts of it had to be rewritten. This should not be taken as evidence that the book is cruel and vindictive; rather, that it rings so horribly true. An unsparing portrait of literary, political, and media London in the 1990s, it follows the fortunes of a group of friends from student days, as they each scale the ladder of success, sometimes falling off, sometimes nudging another off in their place. A satire with a conscience, Craig's novel is contemporary, and also old-fashioned, in the best sense: it subjects its characters to the most serious moral scrutiny, and never flinches.

📖 Martin Amis, William Makepeace Thackeray (*Vanity Fair*)   *CH*

Crais,   Robert   (US,   1953–). *See* THRILLERS

Crane, Stephen (US, 1871–1900) The son of a preacher, Stephen Crane quickly rejected middle-class life in favour of baseball, pool, poker, and 'unsuitable' relationships. After a turbulent spell at college he became a journalist, chronicling both the poverty-stricken underside of America's expanding cities and the Spanish-American and Graeco-Turkish wars. Poverty and war dominated his fiction. In his early novellas, *Maggie, a Girl of the Streets* (1893) and *George's Mother* (1896), he used highly charged language to explore the moral and psychological effects of life in a New York tenement block. His masterpiece, *The Red Badge of Courage* (1895), is set on the battlefields of the American Civil War, and re-creates the experiences of a young soldier, Henry Fleming. This remarkable book, which rewards careful reading, is both a powerful war story and a probing exploration of sensation and consciousness. Crane's story 'The Bride Comes to Yellow Sky' (1898) is an early classic of the Western genre.

📖 Upton Sinclair, Erich Maria Remarque, Joseph Conrad.
See UNITED STATES OF AMERICA, WAR, WESTERN   BH

Creasey, John (British, 1908–73) Creasey produced more books than any other twentieth-century writer, publishing over 600 under pseudonyms too numerous to list. Among many others, he wrote police procedurals as **J. J. Marric**, light adventures featuring The Baron as **Anthony Morton**, psychological crime stories as **Michael Halliday** and the thriller-style Inspector West novels as John Creasey. However, the writing is never a match for his clever ideas and exceptionally tight plotting. Perhaps the most enduring of his work is the J. J. Marric series, featuring Scotland Yard detective George Gideon.

With their multiple story-lines and the continuing soap opera of Gideon's family life, they paint a fascinating picture of London life in the 1950s and 1960s. *Gideon's Day* (1955) was filmed starring Jack Hawkins, and it's clear that books such as *Gideon's Fire* (1961) and *Gideon's Ride* (1963) influenced the style of television police series such as *Dixon of Dock Green* and *Z-Cars*.

📖 Evan Hunter (writing as Ed McBain), John Harvey, Colin Dexter
                    VM

Crews, Harry (US, 1935–) Born in Bacon County, Georgia, Harry Crews served with the US Marines in the 1950s and graduated from the University of Florida in 1960, though his career has also included spells working as a carnival barker and light heavyweight boxer. His novels are often set among the drifting communities of vagrants, carnival acts, and itinerant preachers of the American South, and *The Gospel Singer* (1968) is a good starting-point. Set during a religious revival, the book tells the story of a loss of faith and its effects on one of the revival's star attractions, an uncannily gifted singer. *Scar Lover* (1992) is a novel about the damage caused by abusive relationships, and *The Body* (1990) is a version of the Pygmalion story set in the world of competitive bodybuilding. Crews shares a fascination with rootlessness and the downbeat Americana of motelrooms and sideshows with the Beat writers, but combines this with balancing insights into American masculinity and obsession.

📖 Charles Bukowski, William Faulkner, Ernest Hemingway   WB

Crichton, Michael (US, 1942–) After training as a doctor, Crichton became a prolific writer of heavily researched yet thoroughly engaging science fiction thrillers. These are generally set in the near future and concentrate on single areas of technological advance. Crichton's first major success was *Westworld* (1974), which he himself adapted as a film starring Yul Brynner. This deals with a robot-manned theme park that simulates the dangers of the wild west without actually jeopardizing the visitors. Things go wrong when the robots start behaving like real wild west villains and the visitors have to fight for their lives. Nearly twenty years later *Jurassic Park* (1991) saw visitors endangered in another theme park, this time inhabited by genetically resurrected dinosaurs. Steven Spielberg's film may have broken all box-office records but the original novel is considerably more engaging for its scientific realism and closer attention to the ethical themes.

📖 James Blish, William Gibson, Richard Condon, Dean R. Koontz

RP

Crispin, Edmund (British, 1921–78) Crispin was the pseudonym of Bruce Montgomery, a composer of film and orchestral music. He wrote his first crime novel, featuring the eccentric Oxford don Gervase Fen, while still an undergraduate at the university. His books fizz with wit and energy, revealing Crispin's verbal flair and detestation of pomposity. Begin with *The Moving Toyshop* (1946), an excursion of high-spirited lunacy centring on the discovery of a strangled corpse in an unlocked toyshop at midnight. When poet Richard Cadogan takes his friend Gervase Fen, Oxford Professor of Poetry, back to the scene of the crime, the toyshop has disappeared. It's the starting-point for a remarkably well-plotted mystery.

Love Lies Bleeding (1948) draws on the works of Shakespeare to romp through the murders of two schoolmasters and the disappearance of a girl pupil from another nearby school. In *Buried for Pleasure* (1948), Fen becomes the unlikeliest of parliamentary candidates and finds himself embroiled in a poisoning case.

📖 Simon Brett, Colin Watson. *See* CRIME   *VM*

Cross, Amanda (US, 1926–   ) Amanda Cross is the pseudonym of Carolyn Heilbrun, a professor of humanities at Columbia University, and her books are rooted in the academic world. Her feminist heroine, Kate Fansler, is a professor of English literature, a lively, perceptive, and literate character whose enquiring mind leads her to play the amateur sleuth. In *The Theban Mysteries* (1990) Kate returns to her old school to conduct a seminar on Antigone, the defiant Greek heroine. Then a dead body is discovered in the school building and Kate is drawn into the investigation. *The Players Come Again* (1992) sees Kate commissioned to write the biography of recluse Gabrielle Foxx, wife of the famous writer. Was Gabrielle the handmaiden to Foxx or the creative talent that enabled him to write? Kate's research into the past points to a dark mystery.

📖 Joan Smith, Sarah Dunant   *CS*

Cunningham, Michael (US, 1952–   ) Brought up in California and living in New York, Cunningham is among the most highly regarded American gay novelists of his generation. Begin with *A Home at the End of the World* (1990), centring on a household of a woman and two men, one of whom is gay. Together they care for the baby that is born, and for the dying AIDS victim who moves in with them. AIDS is confronted again in *The Hours* (1999), the story of a writer who is sustained through his worsening condition by his relationship with a lesbian friend. The book's structure is modelled on that of Virginia Woolf's *Mrs Dalloway* (1925). *Flesh and Blood* (1995) presents three generations of the Greek-immigrant Stassos family, whose younger members break with tradition in opting for social and sexual alternatives.

📖 Armistead Maupin, Alan Hollinghurst, Adam Mars-Jones   *DH*

Cussler, Clive (US, 1931–) An advertising copywriter before becoming a full-time writer, Cussler has also made a career of marine exploration and is credited with locating over sixty shipwrecks. Begin with the cold war thriller *Deep Six* (1984). International tensions suddenly intensify after a ship is found off Alaska, all its crew having perished from a deadly cargo of nerve-agents. High-tech intelligence thwarts a Japanese conspiracy to take over the world by economic means in *Dragon* (1990). *Sahara* (1992) centres on the discovery of a secret scientific installation in the desert run by a ruthless French industrialist and a West African dictator. A Chinese gangster masterminds an illegal immigration racket in *Flood Tide* (1997). The investigation into his affairs involves searching for the ship that sank carrying Chiang Kai-shek's treasure when he fled China in 1949.

📖 Ted Allbeury, Desmond Bagley, Ken Follett   *DH*

D

Dabydeen, David (Guyanese, 1956–). *See* CARIBBEAN

D'Aguiar, Fred (Guyanese, 1960–) D'Aguiar won several awards with *The Longest Memory* (1994). Set on an eighteenth-century Virginia slave planta-tion, the brutality—as when the recaptured slave is beaten while others are ordered to watch—seems muted by the author's literary finesse: the many, very accom-plished narrative techniques almost giving an unnatural beauty to the barbarism. In *Dear Future* (1996) the main character is accidentally hit on the head (with the back of an axe) and this releases strange and telling visionary powers. Through a wide range of comic devices D'Aguiar builds a narrative full of warning. He returns to the slave past in *Feeding the Ghosts* (1998). A documented incident from the Middle Passage is re-imagined with great power and sensitivity: it is the practice of throwing sick slaves overboard with the dead. As buyers wanted healthy slaves, the insured value of such 'goods lost at sea' was likely to be higher than in the marketplace.

📖 Caryl Phillips, Barry Unsworth (*Sacred Hunger*). *See* CARIBBEAN   EM

Dahl, Roald (British, 1916–1990) Although Dahl wrote hugely successful children's fiction, his adult fiction and par-ticularly his stories are also well regarded. Some of those stories were translated to television as *Tales of the Unexpected*;

read them in *The Collected Stories of Roald Dahl* (1992). Dahl is a master of stories with unexpected twists at the end. 'The Visitor', from his collection *Switch Bitch* (1974), is a good example of his method. The narrator's Uncle Oswald, later to have a volume to himself, describes a visit to Abdul-Aziz and his beautiful wife and daughter, in the Sinai desert. Uncle Oswald believes that during the night one or other of them has visited his bed; the truth turns out to be somewhat different! Dahl's taste for the gruesome, so evident in his children's books, is often present in his adult writing.

📖 Edgar Allan Poe.
See CHILDHOOD   IP

Dana, Richard Henry (US, 1815–82). *See* THE SEA

Dangarembga, Tsitsi (Zimbabwean, 1959–). *See* AFRICA

Danticat, Edwidge (Haitian, 1969–). *See* BLACK AND WHITE

Darrieussecq, Marie (French, 1969–). *See* FRANCE

Davidson, Avram (US, 1923–93) Davidson is a prolific writer who has never settled on a central theme. Some of his writing must be classed as science fiction, the best examples being *Rogue Dragon* and *Rork!* (both 1965). In both we find future societies lapsed to medieval levels of technology, and threatened by alien creatures which resemble respectively dragons and giant spiders. These simple plots are animated, however, by Davidson's unique wit and linguistic inventiveness, qualities found also in his fantasies, especially *The Phoenix and the Mirror* (1969), a work whose hero is the poet-magician Vergil as created by medieval romancers; and *The Enquiries of Doctor Eszterhazy* (1975), which follows the adventures of a Holmes-like detective dealing with cases of magic in an imaginary and richly diversified Balkan state.

📖 Jack Vance, Fritz Leiber, Lyon Sprague de Camp. *See* FANTASY   TS

Davidson, Lionel (British, 1922–)
Born in Yorkshire, Davidson lived for many years in Israel before moving to London. Begin with *The Rose of Tibet* (1962), in which a schoolteacher searching for his missing brother falls in love with a young Buddhist abbess. Together they flee the Chinese invasion of 1950. In *A Long Way to Shiloh* (1966) newly discovered scrolls suggest the location of treasure from the Jerusalem temple destroyed in AD 70. Scholarship and Israeli intelligence work together to stay ahead of hostile interest. *The Sun Chemist* (1976) concerns attempts to reconstruct a formula discovered by former Israeli president and scientist Chaim Weizmann for harnessing solar power from vegetables. Soviet breeding experiments aimed at boosting human intelligence are being carried on in *Kolymsky Heights* (1994). A suicidal mission is launched to penetrate the top-secret Siberian laboratory.

📖 Desmond Bagley, Bryan Forbes, John Buchan. *See* SPY, THRILLERS
                                        DH

Davies, Robertson (Canadian, 1913–95)
Robertson Davies was born in Ontario, Canada, in 1913, and educated at Oxford. Back in Canada he worked in theatre, journalism, academia, and above all as a novelist. The rich, sprawling, extrovert novels of Robertson Davies can make other writers seem rather anaemic. He throws in everything—the occult, university life, sexual and financial shenanigans, astrology, humour, love—which, with a lesser writer, might produce only a mess. But everything is perfectly controlled and coherent, in the unique universe that he creates. He works on an epic scale, often in trilogies. *The Cornish Trilogy* is one such, of which the central novel, *What's Bred in the Bone* (1985), was shortlisted for the Booker Prize. It tells the life story of Francis Cornish, whose elusive father, known as the Wooden Soldier, is a spy, his mother a society beauty, and who himself grows up to be an art collector, his life spanning the Canadian twentieth century. It is a magnificent achievement, not least in the way that the story is actually told by Francis Cornish's personal guiding spirit, Maimas, to the Recording Angel, the Lesser Zadkiel. Such is Davies's exuberant confidence that one soon accepts this as a quite reasonable narrative method. *What's Bred in the Bone* really needs to be read as part of the trilogy—Davies is hugely addictive. You might also try *Murther and Walking Spirits* (1992), the fantastical, Gothic tale of Connor Gilmartin, a murdered journalist in search of vengeance. Always something of the showman, with his long white beard and glittering eye, Davies offers high entertainment that is uniquely humane and thought-provoking.

📖 John Cowper Powys, John Irving, Anthony Burgess. *See* CANADA   CH

Deane, Seamus (British, 1940–) The further you get into the book, the more you understand the title, *Reading in the Dark* (1996), because it applies to you, the reader, as much as it does to the boy narrator. It starts as a mystery story as you urge the boy on in his desire to understand the things he's not being told. Growing up in a large Catholic family in Derry in the 1950s, the boy's world is full of tales—family feuds, folk legends, religious parables. Deane mixes these with sharply realized snapshots of family life. The mounting pressure as you start to sift the truths from the fictions, to work out what really happened in the family's past, is unbearably gripping. A mature, unblenching first novel, eloquent and achingly sad. Deane is also known as a poet and a cultural historian.

📖 John McGahern, William Trevor, Tim Winton. *See* IRELAND   *RV*

de Bernières, Louis (British, 1954–) Born in London, de Bernières taught for a while in Columbia before turning his hand to fiction. After several moderately successful novels, *Captain Corelli's Mandolin* (1994) was published, and the reading public fell in love with it, ensuring it was rarely out of the best-seller charts. Set in the isle of Cephalonia during the Second World War, it tells the story of Pelagia, who falls reluctantly in love with a captain of the occupying Italian army. The relationships in the novel are brilliantly described, as is the contrast between the bucolic existence on Cephalonia and the atrocities of war. De Bernières's earlier novels are set in South America and include *The Troublesome Offspring of Cardinal Guzman* (1992), about a latter-day inquisition in a small South American country.

📖 Eric Linklater, Sebastian Faulks, Salman Rushdie. *See* HISTORICAL   *SA*

de Camp, Lyon Sprague (US, 1907–) Over a long career, Sprague de Camp has created some of the basic motifs and scenarios of modern fantasy and science fiction. In 1940, in collaboration with Fletcher Pratt, he began the *Incomplete Enchanter* series, in which modern scientists find themselves transported to the worlds of Norse, Irish, Finnish, or Renaissance myth, and have to survive by learning the underlying and quasi-scientific laws of magic: the stories were eventually collected as *The Intrepid Enchanter* (published in the USA as *The Complete Compleat Enchanter*, both 1989). In 1941 de Camp brought out *Lest Darkness Fall*, a work which resembles Mark Twain's *A Connecticut Yankee at King Arthur's Court* (1889) in sending a modern man back to the sixth century, but contradicts Twain by repeatedly demonstrating that modern knowledge does not confer automatic superiority. Another distinguished fantasy is his *Novaria* sequence begun in 1968 with *The Goblin Tower*, in which a 'king who must die' refuses to accept his fate, and escapes with the aid of an enchanter of limited competence.

📖 Avram Davidson, Fritz Leiber, Jack Vance. *See* FANTASY   *TS*

Defoe, Daniel (British, 1660–1731) Defoe, often considered to be the first English novelist, travelled extensively as a merchant, a secret agent and a journalist before turning to fiction. His ground-breaking first-person narratives merged popular genres such as travel journals, romances, picaresque tales, political writing, histories, and social reportage for what was probably the first time. Defoe was a liberal, optimistic writer, one of the earliest to portray the lives of the poor and uneducated. His novels implicitly challenge the moral and social assumptions of many of his contemporaries and are remarkable for their faith in the resilience of the human spirit.

Begin with *Moll Flanders* (1722), the lively, entertaining 'confession' of a woman who, having been born in a debtors' prison and separated early from her mother, is determined both to survive and to gain financial independence. As Moll relates the story of her early thieving and prostitution, detailing her concealed pregnancies, her marriages, her eventual conviction, and transportation, Defoe creates an entirely convincing sense of eighteenth-century London through realistic prose and detailed, carefully observed descriptions. Move on to *Robinson Crusoe* (1719), the classic story of a shipwrecked survivor and his attempts to civilize the desert island he is stranded on. *A Journal of the Plague Year* (1722) a semi-fictional account of the horrific devastation caused in London by the bubonic plague epidemic of 1665, is also highly recommended.

📖 Charles Dickens, Henry Fielding; for recent explorations of ideas in *Robinson Crusoe*, see Jane Gardam, *Crusoe's Daughter* (1985), and J. M. Coetzee, *Foe* (1986). *See* THE SEA, SOCIAL ISSUES   SR

Deighton, Len (British, 1929–   ) After doing his National Service, Deighton won a scholarship to the Royal College of Art and afterwards worked as an illustrator in advertising. His first novel, the outstanding spy thriller *The Ipcress File* (1962), brought a downbeat and brutal realism to the genre, with its truculent working-class secret agent, played by Michael Caine in the stylish film version. Deighton continued in this vein with *Funeral in Berlin* (1964) and *Billion-Dollar Brain* (1966), excellent spy yarns notable for their meticulous background research and terse, sardonic style. Other novels include *Bomber* (1970), a closely documented account of a bombing raid on Germany, and *SS-GB* (1978) about a Nazi-occupied Britain. He has returned to the labyrinthine world of cold war spying in three trilogies, the third of which is *Faith*, *Hope*, and *Charity* (1994–6).

📖 Graham Greene, Frederick Forsyth, Robert Harris. *See* SPY   TH

Delafield,   E(dmee)   M(onica) (Dashwood) (British, 1890–1943) E. M. Delafield wrote over thirty novels, of which the best known are the series beginning with *The Diary of a Provincial Lady* (1930). These wonderfully funny books are written as a journal, and describe the daily life of the narrator, her gloomily taciturn husband, her exuberant children and histrionic French governess, and a range of comically unsatisfactory servants. Delafield's humour arises from her narrator's diffident, bemused attitude to the small dramas (and lack of drama) in her life; and from her extremely sharp observations on social class. These novels are also an excellent source of social history, giving a precise picture of the life and attitudes of a particular type of middle-class, educated woman in the 1920s. All four Provincial Lady novels were reprinted together under the title *The Diary of a Provincial Lady* in 1984.

📖 Mary Wesley, Joanna Trollope, Sue Townsend   JR

Delderfield, R(onald) F(rederick) (British, 1912–72) R. F. Delderfield was born in Greenwich, London and eventually became editor of the *Exmouth Chronicle*. He is most famous for his romantic family sagas, many of which evoke an England of a bygone age, in a leisurely and skilful way. *God is an Englishman* (1970) is typical of these, being the tale of the life of Adam Swann who sets up a road haulage business in England in the 1850s and marries a younger but spirited wife. The novel is unashamedly middlebrow, and uses the whole of England as its canvas. The Swann family saga is continued in *Theirs was the Kingdom* (1971) and *Give Us This Day* (1973).

📖 H. E. Bates, John Galsworthy, J. B. Priestley. *See* FAMILY SAGA   SA

DeLillo, Don (US, 1936–   ) DeLillo grew up in the Bronx, the son of working-class Italian immigrants. After a spell on Madison Avenue as an advertising executive, he took to writing fiction. His debut novel, *Americana*, was published in 1971. Although highly acclaimed in literary circles, it was not until the mid-1980s that DeLillo's work reached a wider audience, when *White Noise* (1984) won the National Book Award. This darkly comic novel is narrated by academic Jack Gladney, inventor of 'Hitler Studies' and one of the discipline's prominent scholars. Gladney's matter-of-fact voice proves the ideal tool for DeLillo's relentless satire, which mines the bizarre, un-real quality of everyday life in a society overrun by rampant consumerism and the mass media. *Mao II* (1991) takes a broader view, surveying the turbulent international situation immediately after the cold war. The novel questions the role which the writer can play in a world of terrorism and mass hysteria.

Perhaps DeLillo's finest novels, *Libra* (1988) and *Underworld* (1997), reach back into America's own past. *Libra* tackles the Kennedy assassination, weaving fact and fiction into a taut thriller which challenges our ideas about both what we know and how we know it. *Underworld* is even more ambitious: it opens with a remarkable account of a 1951 baseball game, spins numerous story-lines from it, and develops into a profound but readable meditation on America during the cold war.

📖 E. L. Doctorow, Robert Coover, Thomas Pynchon. *See* UNITED STATES OF AMERICA   BH

de Lisser, Herbert G. (Jamaican, 1878–1944). *See* CARIBBEAN

Desai, Anita (Indian, 1937–   ) Desai was born in Mussorie, of German and Indian parentage, and has been shortlisted several times for the Booker Prize, most recently in 1999, with *Fasting, Feasting*. Like many of her novels this story inhabits the meeting-point between two traditions and explores Uma's efforts to carve out a psychic space between herself and her superficially westernized parents. Their attempts at marrying her off cause Uma deep humiliation and a sense of failure. Desai's style is richly descriptive and sharply conveys the city's character in *Baumgartner's Bombay* (1988). Hugo Baumgartner has lived in Bombay since leaving an internment camp after the war, being Jewish but regarded as German by the British. Always an observer, he survives, but the new Germany brutally catches up with him. *Fire on the Mountain* (1977) focuses on a character who is ultimately flawed.

Nanda Kaul has protected herself from her disappointment in her husband and children by her fierce solitariness. She allows her great-grandchild to come and stay, with shocking consequences. *Journey to Ithaca* (1995) follows the spiritual quest of two dissatisfied Europeans, Matteo and Sophie, each finding enlightenment according to their different natures.

📖 R. K. Narayan, Ruth Prawer Jhabvala. *See* INDIA   TO

Deshpande, Shashi (Indian, 1938–) Born in Dharwar, Shashi Deshpande has lived all her life in India, where she studied economics and law and brought up a family. One of the most important novelists writing in modern India, Deshpande has now published seven novels, four children's novels, and four collections of short stories. Deshpande's best novel is *That Long Silence* (1988) which tells the story of Jaya and her need to find a space for herself when the security of her domestic life collapses around her. It is a thoughtful, moving novel, rather than a page-turner, and will strike a chord with many women readers. Instead of being overtly political, it follows the tradition of novels by women established by Charlotte Brontë and Virginia Woolf, giving value to the private spaces of women that are so often dismissed in the public sphere.

📖 Anita Desai, Penelope Lively. *See* INDIA   SB

Dexter, Colin (British, 1930–) Colin Dexter taught classics before turning to writing. He is also a former crossword champion. His Inspector Morse novels have been adapted for television to great acclaim. Set in Oxford they involve Morse and his sergeant, Lewis, in homicide investigations. The clever, careful plots are laden with puzzles and clues which the reader can try to solve. A great appeal of the books is in the relationship between the two central characters; Morse is a bad-tempered, well-educated beer-drinker who enjoys the challenge of the puzzle and loves classical music while Lewis is a naïve but committed copper, much more in tune with contemporary culture. In *The Way Through the Woods* (1992) a Swedish tourist is missing and a poem with clues to her whereabouts is sent to the police and published in *The Times*. Soon after a body is found in Wytham Woods near Oxford and Morse gets to work.

📖 Reginald Hill, Frances Fyfield, John Harvey. *See* CRIME   CS

Diaz, Junot (US, 1968–) Diaz was born and raised in the Dominican Republic, moving with his family when he was 7 to rejoin his father, who was working in New York. He draws heavily on his own experiences in his short stories, *Drown* (1996). The narrators of the stories live in the barrios of Santo Domingo and the immigrant neighbourhoods of New Jersey, and speak with voices that are pungent and tough, but have a raw lyricism. 'Ysrael' is about two boys in Santo Domingo on the track of a contemporary, whose face has been mauled by a pig; 'No Face' is told from the point of view of the disfigured child. A teacher tells the narrator of the title story and his friends that most of them are like space-shuttles, due to burn out; the narrator comments: 'I could already see myself losing altitude, fading, the earth spread out beneath me, hard and bright.' The resigned eloquence of this is typical of the collection.

📖 Raymond Carver, Richard Ford   NC

Dibdin, Michael (British, 1947–)
Dibdin has not only written accomplished pastiches of classic detective fiction writers, notably of Conan Doyle and Agatha Christie, but has also developed the genre to include social and historical perspectives. *The Last Sherlock Holmes Story* (1978) takes the form of a discovered manuscript written by Dr Watson, telling of Holmes being brought in to solve the Jack the Ripper murders, and it has many satisfying plot twists. *A Rich Full Death* (1986) has another kind of Victorian setting, in Florence, with Robert Browning cast as an amateur detective. Dibdin is perhaps best known for his series of novels featuring Aurelio Zen, an Italian police commissioner facing the contemporary problems of civic corruption, terrorism, and kidnapping. In his investigations he also encounters the subtleties of traditional Italian society; *Ratking* (1988) is the first of the series, which also includes *A Long Finish* (1998), set in the wine-growing region of Piedmont.

📖 Arthur Conan Doyle, H. R. F. Keating, P. D. James.
See CRIME					*JS*

Dick, Philip K(indred) (US, 1928–82)
Dick has a huge following amongst science fiction fans. This is not only because he deals with many of the standard ingredients of the genre—robots, space travel, alternative worlds—but also because he writes in a witty, laconic style that is a model for many of his contemporaries in science fiction. His best-known book is *Do Androids Dream of Electric Sheep?* (1968), which was filmed as *Bladerunner*. This novel reworks the Frankenstein theme, blending it with the conventions of the detective novel. In *The Man in the High Castle* (1962), which won the Hugo science fiction award, Dick uses an old idea, that Hitler has won the Second World War, to explore the crisis of identity in a paranoid world.

📖 Kurt Vonnegut, Isaac Asimov, J. G. Ballard, William Gibson.
See SCIENCE FICTION				*LM*

Dickens, Charles (British, 1812–1870)
The impact of Dickens is such that the terms 'Dickensian' and 'Victorian' are sometimes used interchangeably. His works teem with characters who have entered the popular imagination—Fagin, Scrooge, Uriah Heep, Little Nell. High farce coexists with tragedy, exaggeration with stark realism, mawkishness with bitter sarcasm. To criticize Dickens as melodramatic and sentimental, as some do, is to miss the point. Unashamedly popular, Dickens was of his time but transcended it. *Oliver Twist* (1837–9), *A Christmas Carol* (1843), *The Old Curiosity Shop* (1840–1)—these are essentially fairy-tales, but they are also great stories, edged with profundity, in which the dark underside of life predominates.

David Copperfield (1849–50) is a wonderful introduction to Dickens. Packed with comedy and exaggeration, lyrically poetic, it is also moving and psychologically complex. David is a sensitive child whose world is shattered when his childlike young mother marries tyrannical Mr Murdstone. We accompany David through happiness with the Peggottys in their boathouse at Great Yarmouth, through misery at school, friendship, love, betrayal, and, eventually, success as a writer. There are numerous resonances with Dickens's own life. He was 10 when his father lost all his money and the entire family, apart from Charles, was incarcerated in the Marshalsea debtors' prison. Dickens went to work in a blacking warehouse, which he detested.

In *David Copperfield*, he placed the feck-less Mr Micawber in the Marshalsea, and would return there for *Little Dorrit*.

Great Expectations (1860–1) is another first-person narrative of a boy's progres-sion to manhood, but its hero is altogether different from David. Beginning with Pip's dreamlike encounter with the escaped con-vict, Magwitch, in a sinister marsh land-scape, the novel goes on to introduce us to one of literature's great grotesques: Miss Havisham, who, jilted on her wedding day, still lives with her cobwebbed bridal feast and wears the crumbling gown and one shoe in which she heard the news of her abandonment. Taken up by her, Pip is humiliated by her heartless, beautiful ward, Estella, and becomes ashamed of his lowly roots. His progress is assured, however, when a mystery benefactor bestows upon him the means to enter society. Humorous, disturbing, ironic, *Great Expectations* is an acute study in ambition, snobbery, and guilt.

Less well received in its day, *Our Mutual Friend* (1864–5) is now considered by many to be Dickens's greatest book. John Harmon's escape from drowning impels him to assume a false identity in order to test the character of the woman he loves. Meanwhile, as fashionable society prattles nastily in drawing-rooms, louche lawyer Eugene Wrayburn vies with pas-sionate but repressed schoolteacher Bradley Headstone for the love of river-girl Lizzie Hexam. The Thames in this powerful book is a fatal river, giving up its dead and drawing down others to retribution or rebirth. A study in avarice and corruption, love and obsession, *Our Mutual Friend* challenges accepted social barriers, depict-ing a London of extremes: the poor of the riverbanks and those who pick a living on

the dustheaps set against society with its old and new money.

📖 William Makepeace Thackeray, Fyodor Dostoevsky, George Eliot, Peter Carey. *See* CHILDHOOD, CLASSICS, FILM ADAPTATIONS, HISTORICAL, HUMOUR, MAGIC REALISM, SOCIAL ISSUES   *CB*

Dickens, Monica (British, 1915–1992) A great-granddaughter of Charles Dickens, Monica Dickens wrote her first novel at the age of 22 based on her experience as a cook: *One Pair of Hands* (1939) became a best-seller and was the first of more than thirty compellingly readable novels. Many of her novels deal with uncomfortable issues such as abuse in *Kate and Emma* (1964), adop-tion and identity in *Joy and Josephine* (1948), and love and violence in *The Angel in the Corner* (1956). Her novels can feel a little dated now, but they are still excellent reads, and given weight by the fact that they are all well researched: *The Listeners* (1970), for example, was based on her experience of working for the Samaritans. She has also written teenage children's books, and is best known for *Follyfoot* (1971).

📖 Lynne Reid Banks, Margaret Forster, Daphne du Maurier   *SB*

Dickinson, Peter (British, 1927–) Dickinson was for seventeen years assist-ant editor and a reviewer for *Punch*. His crime fiction is often set in claustrophobic and sometimes mysterious communities which he describes vividly. In *The Yellow Room Conspiracy* (1994) we meet the five aristocratic and rather dizzy Vereker sisters against the backdrop of the events of the 1950s. Their various lovers and hus-bands are an ill-assorted bunch ranging from a cabinet minister to businessmen and others on the fringes of violent crime. It all goes horribly wrong, of course. For Dickinson's children's fiction, begin with *Healer* (1986) in which Pinkie Proudfoot, a 10-year-old healer, is exploited by her father in the service of a cult he has formed. This too goes wrong but the positive ending has Pinkie helping the unhappy, 16-year-old narrator, Barry.

📖 Nina Bawden, Michael Dibdin, Patricia Highsmith   IP

Dickson, Carter. *See* **Carr, John (Dickson)**

Didion, Joan (US, 1934–) Born in California, Didion worked as an editor of and contributor to prestige magazines such as *Vogue* and *Esquire* before turning to fiction. Set in the glitzy, shallow world of Hollywood, *Play It as It Lays* (1971) is a lacerating examination of a woman's sense of herself, and of her own worth, in a rootless, fractured society. Didion's prose is taut and spare and keen as a scalpel, her insights into character just as incisive. *A Book of Common Prayer* (1977) tells the story of Charlotte Douglas, a naïve young woman seeking a new life in Central America, while *Democracy* (1984) traces the emotional seismograph of a passionate affair. As highly regarded for her journalism as for her fiction, Didion's collections of essays *Miami* (1987) and *The White Album* (1979) are penetrating dissections of the contemporary American scene.

📖 Tom Wolfe, Dorothy Parker, Nathanael West   TH

Dinesen, Isak. *See* **Blixen, Karen**

Disch, Thomas M(ichael) (US, 1940–) Born to the family of a travelling salesman, Thomas M. Disch encompasses poetry, criticism, and fiction in his work. He is a winner of two O. Henry Prizes for short stories, the W. Campbell Memorial award and the British Science Fiction award. He started his writing career with a short story, 'The Double Timer'—bought for $112 by the editor of *Fantastic Stories*, and he has continued to master the medium, maintaining a prolific output since *102 H-Bombs* (1966). Most of all he is known as a witty and clever science fiction entertainer. His speculative style is best displayed in novels such as the classic *Camp Concentration* (1968), in which American political prisoners are poisoned with experimental chemicals which boost brainpower to genius levels but bring on an awful early death. In *The Business Man* (1984), a jealous murder leads to a grimly fascinating haunting.

📖 Kurt Vonnegut, William Gibson   AM

Diski, Jenny (British, 1947–) Of Russian and Polish Jewish descent, Diski has published short stories and novels which explore the compulsions and neuroses of contemporary life, and the psychology of the outsider. In *Rainforest* (1987) Mo, a successful anthropologist, bases her life on predictability and order. A research trip to a rainforest in Borneo forces her to confront the illogical and unpredictable in herself, and disrupts her sense of identity. She returns to England, and becomes a house-cleaner in an attempt to restore order to her life. *Nothing Natural* (1986) explores the discovery of sexual pleasure for an ordinary single mother within a dangerous sadomasochistic relationship. *Like Mother* (1988) is a chilling examination of Frances, whose life of intense emptiness is narrated by her baby Nony, born without a brain. Through frank first-person narratives, Diski invites her readers to question accepted ideas of normality.

📖 Nina Bawden, Joyce Carol Oates, Doris Lessing   *DJ*

Dobbs, Michael (British, 1948–) Michael Dobbs is well-qualified to write political thrillers. In 1979 he was at Mrs Thatcher's side when she first stepped into No. 10 as Prime Minister, and in 1994 he was appointed Deputy Chairman of the Conservative Party. His greatest creation is the horribly captivating character of Francis Urquhart, immortalized by Ian Richardson in the BBC television series. *To Play the King* (1992) is the second in the *House of Cards* trilogy, in which Urquhart, now Prime Minister, faces his greatest challenge yet: opposition from the popular and idealistic young King, by the name of Charles. But, of course, Urquhart is not a man to let anyone stand in his way to absolute power. Not even an hereditary monarch of Britain.

📖 Gore Vidal, Tom Sharpe   *CH*

Döblin, Alfred (German, 1878–1957). *See* GERMANY

Dobyns, Stephen (US, 1941–) Dobyns began his writing life working for the *Detroit News*. Most of his novels feature the charismatic and amiable Charlie Bradshaw, a Saratoga Springs private eye. Dobyns brings a poet's imagination and deftness to his crime thrillers. In the gambling tale *Saratoga Bestiary*, the 50-year-old Bradshaw is faced with a bunch of hardened gamblers mixed up in the theft of an oil painting. More charming than violent, and with genuine narrative mystery, Dobyns's droll journalistic style shows his debts to American prose masters like Raymond Carver and Mark Twain. Other Dobyns titles include works of magic realism set in Latin America—*The Two Deaths of Senora Puccini* (1988) is a tense operatic mystery. And the American small-town horror novel *The Church of Dead Girls* (1997) was much praised by the master of that genre, Stephen King.

📖 Sara Paretsky, Michael Dibdin
AM

Doctorow, E(dgar) L(awrence) (US, 1931–) Doctorow has lived in New York for most of his life. Although he published two novels in the 1960s, it was *The Book of Daniel* (1971) which won him widespread critical acclaim. This difficult but rewarding novel retells the story of the Rosenbergs, who were executed in 1953 for allegedly passing information about nuclear weapons to the Russians. History needs to be rewritten, Doctorow once said, or it becomes mythology and then it can be used destructively. Like his distinctive take on the 1930s in *Loon Lake* (1980), or the 1870s in *The Waterworks* (1994), his second novel, *Ragtime* (1975), brings this principle into motion. Set largely in New York at the beginning of the twentieth century, this accessible and funny novel playfully imagines Freud, Houdini, Henry Ford, and the anarchist Emma Goldman rubbing shoulders.

📖 Robert Coover, Robert Stone, Don DeLillo. *See* HISTORICAL, WESTERN   *BH*

Doherty, Berlie (British, 1948–) Berlie Doherty is one of Britain's finest authors for young teen readers. She lives in the Peak District of England, a landscape which often features in her work. She has won the Carnegie Medal twice, first in 1986 for *Granny was a Buffer Girl*, a story based in the Sheffield steel industry. It tells the story of a number of girls whose fortunes, both economic and romantic, are caught up in the class divisions of industrial England. Doherty won the Carnegie again in 1991 for *Dear Nobody*, the fictional diary of Helen, a promising music student, who discovers that she is pregnant in the summer preceding her entry into university. Doherty's work is evocative and poignant and she has a talent for involving the reader in her characters' dilemmas.

📖 Nina Bawden, Anne Fine, Lynne Reid Banks   *LM*

Doherty, P(aul) C. (British) Doherty was born in Middlesbrough. He read medieval history at Oxford and combines his careers as a London headmaster and author of medieval murder mysteries. *The Assassin in the Greenwood* (1993) is a good introduction to Hugh Corbett, Edward I's chief clerk and investigator-protagonist of a growing number of Doherty's books. Corbett's hands are full, with espionage against the French and a visit to Nottingham to look into Robin Hood's reappearance. *The Demon Archer* (1999) finds him with a disconcertingly wide range of suspects after the detested Lord Henry Fitzalan is slain during a hunt. In *Satan's Fire* (1995) Corbett contends with the Knights Templar as he unravels a legacy of intrigue rooted in the last crusade. *A Tapestry of Murders* (1994) features Chaucer's Man of Law, whose off-record tale is of murder and treachery in London's medieval underworld.

📖 Ellis Peters, Umberto Eco, Robert Nye   *DH*

Dombrovsky, Yury (Soviet, 1909–78). *See* RUSSIA

Donaldson, Stephen (US, 1947–) Stephen Donaldson is the most original of the successors and emulators of Tolkien. His two trilogies, *The First* and *Second Chronicle of Thomas Covenant the Unbeliever*, are set in a magic land like Tolkien's Middle-earth, but their hero, Thomas Covenant, is both a modern American and a leper. His own health is intimately bound up with the health of the land to which he is transported; in the end he has to sacrifice himself for its healing. The sequence began with *Lord Foul's Bane* (1977). More recently Donaldson has switched to science fiction, with the *Gap* sequence of three novels begun by *The Gap into Conflict: The Real Story* (1990).

📖 Tim Powers, Michael Swanwick. *See* FANTASY   *TS*

Donleavy, J(ames) P(atrick) (US, 1926–) Donleavy was born in Brooklyn but educated at Trinity College, Dublin, and his writing reflects the dual influences of Irish and American literature. *The Ginger Man* (1955) was originally banned in the United States for obscenity and published first in an abridged version in Britain. *The Ginger Man* was instrumental in helping to change the censorship laws and is a raucous picaresque novel which follows the misadventures of Sebastian Dangerfield through Dublin and London. Donleavy creates an anarchic comedy of misrule, enlivened by moments of pure slapstick. Outrageous and melancholic in turn, *The Ginger Man* is an inventive novel which was deservedly listed as one of the hundred most important novels of the century by the Modern Library.

Donleavy's eye for the absurd can be seen in his play *Fairy Tales of New York* (1961) and the novel *The Saddest Summer of Samuel S* (1966).

📖 Flann O'Brien, Joseph Heller   *GK*

Dos Passos, John (US, 1896–1970)

U.S.A., first published as three books then in one volume in 1938, is on an epic scale. It includes contemporary newspaper extracts, and 'stream-of-consciousness' sections which reveal glimpses of the author's autobiography, interwoven with conventional narrative, making a collage of early twentieth-century America. The stories of hundreds of characters are set against vividly described cities and landscapes. Dos Passos' theme is hatred of capitalism and the 'elderly swag-bellied gentlemen' who control the working man's destiny. The use of interior monologue shows the influence of James Joyce and the characterizations have been compared with Dickens's, though some critics suggest that they are pawns in a technical experiment and lack depth. Dos Passos was accused by Edmund Wilson of damning 'the sufferers [from capitalism] along with the disease'.

Start with the shorter *Manhattan Transfer* (1925), a novel drawing impressionistic portraits of the inhabitants and the city. Again the theme is the dehumanizing effect of capitalism and of urban living. Sinclair Lewis said of it: '[Dos Passos] presents the panorama, the sense, the smell, the sound, the soul of New York, [in] the technique of the movie, flashes, cut-backs, speed.' The plot of this earlier book is more coherent, although the narrative is also fragmented and contains multiple perspectives. Jimmy Herf, working dispiritedly as a reporter, and Ellen Thatcher, an actress, are two of the many characters who live in the city; but Manhattan itself is the main character, revealed in all its grubby, soul-destroying, opportunistic glory.

📖 Theodore Dreiser, William Faulkner, Tom Wolfe, John Steinbeck

FS

Dostoevsky, Fyodor (Russian, 1821–81)

Dostoevsky published his first novel, *Poor Folk*, in 1846. Three years later he was sentenced to death for membership of a group planning to publish revolutionary pamphlets. He was told that his sentence had been commuted whilst facing the firing squad—an experience recounted in *The Idiot* (1868). He served ten years in Siberian labour camps, before returning to St Petersburg and a life of magazine publishing, writing, bouts of gambling, and constant indebtedness.

His novels, among the greatest ever written, explore characters whose behaviour, in extreme situations, is contradictory and paradoxical. They also tackle big ideas. In his lifetime some critics accused him of melodrama and even of 'metaphysical obscenity'. Start with *Crime and Punishment* (1866) in which poverty-stricken ex-student Raskolnikov decides to murder a greedy moneylender. Raskolnikov's motives are rational; the evil old woman's death will be no loss to mankind, and he can give her wealth to more deserving people. But his disturbed mind makes it difficult for him to cling to his own motives; even before the murder, he is tormented by doubt and self-loathing. After the murder his guilt, rage, and distress intensify; he is pursued with uncanny cleverness by a detective who seems able to read his mind, and encounters a range of characters who seem to embody the different attitudes he has to his own guilt, ranging from self-indulgent, amoral Svidrigailov to innocent, God-fearing, loving Sonya. This novel plunges the reader into an intense, nightmarish world where it is at times impossible to tell the characters' dreams from reality; as Dostoevsky later wrote of himself: 'I am a realist in a higher sense; that is, I depict all the depths of the human soul.'

Dostoevsky's handling of suspense is masterly; in *Crime and Punishment* every scene turns the screw and it is impossible to guess whether Raskolnikov will eventually be arrested, escape, give himself up, or kill himself. In Dostoevsky's masterpiece, *The Brothers Karamazov* (1880), suspense is created by the murder of an old man by one of his sons. There are three of them, and a bastard half-brother who works for his father as cook. Dmitri, the oldest, is passionate, violent, and desperate for money, and seems most likely to be guilty; Ivan is an intellectual and atheist, subject to terrible despair; while Alyosha, the youngest, has love and faith and compassion (without any kind of priggishness) for all. The structure of a murder mystery provides a framework inside which Dostoevsky explores the depths of the mind under extreme pressure, the selfish and destructive nature of romantic love, and argues for and against the existence of God. If this sounds daunting—and the first ninety pages *are* daunting, being largely concerned with the death of a monastic elder—persevering with this book is one of the most rewarding reading experiences ever.

Of Dostoevsky's other brilliant novels and stories, there is only space here to recommend one: *Notes From Underground* (1864), which opens with characteristic directness: 'I am a sick man . . . I am an angry man. I am an unattractive man. I think there is something wrong with my liver.'

📖 Franz Kafka, Charles Dickens, Leo Tolstoy. *See* RUSSIA   JR

Doyle, Arthur Conan (British, 1859–1930)

Although Arthur Conan Doyle himself thought his historical and adventure novels were his finest work, he will be remembered as the creator of two of the most famous characters in all fiction, the consulting detective Sherlock Holmes and his chronicler, Dr Watson. Modelled on Doyle's own mentor and teacher, Dr Joseph Bell, Holmes was a master of deduction and detection, applying the latest scientific methods to crime. Erudite, highly strung, and a master of disguise, the image of Holmes with pipe and deerstalker is recognized worldwide. When his creator, bored with Holmes, attempted to kill him off, the offices of the *Strand Magazine*, who published the short stories, were besieged by irate readers. Holmes first appeared in the novel *A Study in Scarlet* (1887), but it was only when Doyle began to publish his investigations in short story form that he captured the public imagination. First collected in *The Adventures of Sherlock Holmes* (1892), the Sherlock Holmes stories still grip today, as much for their portrait of Victorian London as the deductive leaps of their protagonist. Doyle is a riveting story-teller and a master of the short-story form. Begin with *The Adventures*, continue with *The Memoirs of Sherlock Holmes* (1894), and above all, *The Hound of the Baskervilles* (1902), a terrifying tale of family secrets set against the brooding background of Dartmoor.

📖 Wilkie Collins, Agatha Christie, Patricia Cornwell. *See* CRIME   VM

Doyle, Roddy (Irish, 1958–) Doyle worked as a teacher in the working-class areas of north Dublin that he depicts so successfully in his novels. His *Barrytown* trilogy, *The Commitments* (1988), *The Snapper* (1990), and *The Van* (1991) describes the attempts of the Rabbitte family to gain fame, fortune, and an escape from the poverty which surrounds them. In *The Commitments*, turned into a popular film by Alan Parker, Jimmy Rabbitte forms an American-influenced 'soul' band, which founders as the band members descend into violent antipathy. In *The Snapper*, Jimmy's sister gets pregnant and asserts a sense of self within the claustrophobic family atmosphere. In *The Van*, the Rabbitte men renovate a fish and chip van, a project doomed to failure when it runs into trouble with rival vendors. In 1993 *Paddy Clarke Ha Ha Ha* won the Booker Prize. This is an account of the life of a 10-year-old boy on a Dublin council estate, alternately hilarious and moving. *The Woman Who Walked into Doors* (1996) is different from Doyle's earlier books, a stark description of a woman who is the subject of continual physical abuse. Doyle's most recent project is a historical trilogy. *A Star Called Henry* (1999) is the first volume of this trilogy, in which the eponymous hero features in all the crucial events of Irish history this century. Doyle's style is fast-paced and colloquial, and is one of the reasons why so many people find his books so approachable.

📖 Patrick McCabe, James Kelman. *See* CHILDHOOD, FILM ADAPTATIONS, IRELAND   *LM*

Drabble, Margaret (British, 1939–) Born in Sheffield, Margaret Drabble was educated at Cambridge. She is best known as a novelist for her interest in questions of social responsibility. Early work like *The Millstone* (1966), in which an independent girl with a bright academic future finds herself pregnant, sealed Drabble's position as her generation's definitive chronicler of educated women's lives. *The Middle Ground* (1980) centres on a woman caught between the conflicting demands of parents and children, while *The Witch of Exmoor* (1996) portrays a tyrannical mother's hold over her family. *The Radiant Way* (1987) is an ambitious novel showing the changing relationships of a group of college friends against the political background of postwar England, and *The Gates of Ivory* (1991) describes the search for a missing novelist in Cambodia. Drabble is also an accomplished biographer and literary editor, and has published widely on a number of literary, social, and historical subjects.

📖 A. S. Byatt, Angus Wilson, Lynne Reid Banks   *WB*

Drakulić, Slavenka (Croatian, 1949–) Drakulic is a journalist of international reputation who lives chiefly in Zagreb. *Holograms of Fear* (1989), her first novel, forms a good introduction to her work's psychological intensities. Set in New York with flashbacks to Zagreb, it focuses on a woman's experience of major surgery. In *Marble Skin* (1989) an artist produces a sculpture of her mother, who reacts by attempting suicide. The subsequent dialogue between the two confronts a past of suffering and abuse they have formerly chosen to ignore. The war in Bosnia destroys the life of a young teacher in *As if I am not There* (1999) when a Serbian soldier walks into her home. Ordered to leave, she enters a nightmare of ethnic cleansing as her journey through the transit camps begins.

📖 Ivan Klima, Elaine Feinstein   *DH*

Dreiser, Theodore (US, 1871–1945) Dreiser grew up in a large immigrant German Catholic family and received no formal education. He began his writing career as a newspaperman, and wrote his first novel in his spare time. *Sister Carrie* (1900), which was highly controversial in its day, is seen by many as Dreiser's masterpiece. It follows the journey of Caroline Meeber to the bright lights of Chicago where she fulfils the American Dream, and emerges from poverty to become a wealthy actress. It is, however, the tragic downfall of Carrie's one-time lover, Hurstwood, from successful saloon manager to homeless vagabond, which becomes the dramatic focus of the novel. In the long but engrossing *An American Tragedy* (1925), Dreiser shows the American Dream turning into nightmare when the successful and unscrupulous social climber Clyde Griffiths finds himself accused of murder.

📖 Upton Sinclair, Frank Norris. *See* UNITED STATES OF AMERICA

EW

Drewe, Robert (Australian, 1943–) Drewe has worked as a journalist and travelled widely in the Pacific and Far East. His fiction explores Australian themes in a range of geographical and historical settings. Start with the short story collection *The Bodysurfers* (1983), depicting the hedonistic, materialistic lives of Australians whose culture revolves around the beach. The novel *The Drowner* (Australia, 1996) tells the story of Will Dance (skilled in the ancient Wiltshire art of drowning land) who becomes an engineer taking water to the Australian desert. The book is poetic and rich with watery images and tales, but this style is less successful for the love-story between Will and Angelina, which feels dreamily distant, and fails to compel the reader.

📖 Murray Bail, Peter Carey *JR*

Duffy, Maureen (British, 1933–) Duffy draws on her childhood for *That's How it Was* (1962), the semi-autobiographical story of the intense relationship between a working-class mother and her grammar-school-educated daughter. Duffy has spent most of her adult life in London, where she is active on behalf of fellow writers, and has successfully campaigned for public lending rights. Her strong, well-plotted novels often combine fantasy with a shrewd look at society. Begin with the prophetic *Gor Saga* (1982), televised in 1988. Half-human and half-gorilla, Gor is born into a bleak, futuristic Britain of genetic experimentation and mass unemployment. The novel combines the touching story of an outsider with a strong science fiction plot and a concern for animal rights. Duffy is known as a literary historian, and her London novel *The Microcosm* (1966) not only describes underground lesbian life, but also draws on the work of the fascinating eighteenth-century writer and performer, Charlotte Charke.

📖 Zoe Fairbairns, Marge Piercy *JN*

Dumas, Alexandre (French, 1802–70) After early success as a dramatist, Dumas turned to writing historical novels, the most famous of which is *The Three Musketeers* (1844). Although Athos, Porthos, and Aramis are the Musketeers of the title, the novel is really the story of the young D'Artagnan's ambition to join their ranks. The novel provides an exuberant display of swashbuckling heroism as the four men attempt to outwit the scheming Cardinal Richelieu and his accomplice Milady de

Winter. In Milady, Dumas creates a chilling villainess whose malignity is made more powerful by her ruthless use of her sexuality. The mythic dimensions of the Musketeers are enhanced in the sequels *Twenty Years After* (1845), *The Man in the Iron Mask* (1846), and *The Vicomte de Bragelonne* (1850). For Dumas, action and romance were the most important ingredients for a novel and these elements are seen to further effect in *The Count of Monte Cristo* (1844).

📖 Robert Louis Stevenson, Baroness Orczy, Patrick O'Brian   *GK*

du Maurier, Daphne (British, 1907–89)

Daphne du Maurier must be counted one of the best and most prolific Gothic novelists in the twentieth-century British tradition. The stock elements of nineteenth-century Gothic fiction—haunted mansions, brooding landscapes, and mad women—are used with huge success in her fiction. Her most famous novel is *Rebecca* (1938), in which the heroine marries the handsome, wealthy Maxim de Winter, and comes to live in his Cornish mansion, Manderley. But the new Mrs de Winter has to fight for her husband with the spirit of the first Mrs de Winter, Rebecca, and Rebecca's faithful servant, Mrs Danvers. The novel ends with the destruction by fire of Manderley, in a conscious imitation of *Jane Eyre*. This literariness, the sexual ambiguities, and the highly effective use of the unreliable narrator, as in *My Cousin Rachel* (1951), raise her novels above the generic, though perhaps the fact that so many of them have been made into films prevents them from being taken seriously as literature. Although famous for her depictions of Cornwall, one of her best-known stories (because filmed, starring Donald Sutherland and Julie Christie) is *Don't Look Now*

(1971), in which an architect working on the restoration of Venice is haunted by both the city and the death by drowning of his young child.

📖 Susan Hill, Susan Howatch, Mary Stewart. *See* HISTORICAL, ROMANCE   *LM*

Dunant, Sarah (British, 1950–)

Sarah Dunant has worked in radio, journalism, and as a television presenter. In addition to creating the Hannah Wolfe novels she has written a psychological thriller, *Transgressions* (1997), and has written for television. Hannah Wolfe is a private eye, cynical and independent with a shrewd view of the world and a witty turn of phrase. Hannah is based in London and works for Frank Comfort, owner of a security firm; her sister Kate and family appear in the stories. In *Fatlands* (1993) Frank sends Hannah to chaperone teenager Mattie Shepherd but Hannah isn't told that Mattie's father is being targeted by the Animal Liberation Front. Violent death leads Hannah to investigate the hidden side of livestock farming, big business, and terrorism. The novel is fast-paced with some excellent twists and turns along the way.

📖 Sara Paretsky, Gillian Slovo   *CS*

Dunmore, Helen (British, 1952–)

Helen Dunmore has published poetry, short stories, children's fiction, and novels. In *Burning Bright* (1994), a young runaway, Nadine, is unknowingly set up for sexual exploitation by her older Finnish lover, Kai, in a decaying Georgian house. Nadine's story is interwoven with that of Enid, an elderly sitting tenant in the house, whose own love-affair years before ended in violence. Dunmore uses poetic language to tell a gripping story about the ruthless exploitation of love and survival of its victims. In *A Spell of Winter* (1995, Orange Prize) siblings Catherine and Rob are abandoned by their parents and grow up in the house of their sinister grandfather just before the First World War. The atmosphere in this novel is intense, evoked through Dunmore's descriptions of winter on a decaying country estate. The darker elements of family relationships are explored in the context of social isolation.

📖 Alison Fell, Alice Thomas Ellis, Ian McEwan   *DJ*

Dunn, Nell (British, 1936–) Born in London, novelist and playwright Nell Dunn won immediate fame with *Up The Junction* (1963), a series of gritty short stories about working-class life in Battersea. *Poor Cow* (1967) follows heroine Joy down the spiral of deprivation into prostitution. Both were filmed by Ken Loach in semi-documentary style. Considered controversial at the time largely because of its frank treatment of female sexuality, Dunn's 1960s' work was a southern version of the mainly northern 'kitchen-sink' milieu. Other novels followed, including *I Want* (1972), with Adrian Henri. Dunn has also written for children, for television, and stage; *Steaming* (1981), a comedy with an all-female cast, reworked themes from *Up the Junction*. Her novel *My Silver Shoes* (1996) revisited *Poor Cow*'s Joy twenty years on.

📖 Pat Barker, Barry Hines   *CB*

Dunnett, Dorothy (British, 1932–) Dorothy Dunnett is a hugely popular historical novelist, as the number of websites dedicated to her show. *King Hereafter* (1982) is a dark and full-blooded re-creation of the life of the original Macbeth: Thorfinn II, King of Scotland in the eleventh century.

If, like many readers, you really fall in love with Dunnett's world, then you should certainly go on to the Lymond books, starting with *The Game of Kings* (1961), a series of six novels set in sixteenth-century Scotland, fabulously rich and romantic, and with one of modern fiction's most entrancing heroes: the darkly Byronic Lymond himself.

📖 Mary Renault, Mary Stewart, Walter Scott   *CH*

Duras, Marguerite (French, 1914–96) Marguerite Duras was born in Saigon. She returned to France in 1932, studied at the Sorbonne, joined the Resistance during the war, and was deported to Germany. She joined the Communist party but was expelled in 1950. Her novels are experimental, part of the French movement of the 1950s and early 1960s. They have a certain vagueness of plot, while atmosphere is all-important. Duras writes about passion of many kinds, often illicit. *Hiroshima Mon Amour* (1960), which became a film, recounts the love-affair between a man and a woman who use place-names instead of personal ones to identify themselves and their histories to one another. Her lovers tend to find themselves gripped by unexpected and inappropriate passions. *Blue Eyes, Black Hair* (1986) concentrates on love between an older woman and a younger man. An early work, *The Sailor from Gibraltar* (1952), one of her best known, is more conventionally structured, though still steeped in atmosphere and intensity.

📖 Ernest Hemingway, Simone de Beauvoir, Günter Grass   *AT*

Dürrenmatt, Friedrich (Swiss, 1921–). *See* GERMANY

Durrell, Gerald (British, 1925–95).
See CHILDHOOD

Durrell, Lawrence (British, 1912–90)
Durrell was born in India and spent the first
ten years of his life there before his family
returned to England. His prolific output
includes poetry, plays, and travel writing,
though he is best known for *The Alex-
andria Quartet*, comprising *Justine* (1957),
Balthazar and *Mountolive* (both 1958), and
Clea (1960) which combine literary experiment with lush, lyrical prose. Set in Egypt
before the Second World War, and with
an exotic, cosmopolitan cast of characters,
this highly popular sequence of novels
describes the same events from different
viewpoints, producing a kaleidoscopic effect
that reveals unexpected and contradictory
facets. Thereafter Durrell went out of fashion, and later novels such as *Tunc* (1968)
and *Nunquam* (1970) seem pretentious and
wilfully obscure. The *Quartet*, though, is
an absorbing read, and his travel books
Prospero's Cell (1945) and *Bitter Lemons*
(1957) are vividly evocative.

📖 Vladimir Nabokov, Thomas
Pynchon, Henry Miller   *TH*

E

Early, Jack. *See* **Scoppettone, Sandra**

Eco, Umberto (Italian, 1929–) Born in Alessandria, Italy, Eco was educated at the University of Turin and has held numerous distinguished appointments at universities in Europe and America. His academic expertise in semiotics, or the science of signs, strongly informs his fiction, in which systems of meaning and interpretation are central features. Begin with the best-selling *The Name of the Rose* (1980), made into a successful film, which vividly re-creates life in an ancient Franciscan monastery in 1327 during a turbulent period in papal history. The novel hinges on the detective skills of William of Baskerville, a visiting English monk. He penetrates the mystery surrounding a series of deaths within the monastic community through his skill in deciphering cryptic symbols. Rich in scholarly irony and esoteric digression, *Foucault's Pendulum* (1989) features a group of academics who stumble upon a Satanic conspiracy for global dominion while creating an elaborate computer program for their own amusement. The narrative shifts with entertaining informativeness through strata of culture and history from the Middle Ages onward. Set in the early seventeenth century, *The Island of the Day Before* (1995), Eco's third novel, evokes the mental and emotional experience of a young Italian nobleman stranded on a deserted ship in the South Pacific. His consciousness drifts through expanses of memory and philosophical reflection prompted by his dilemma.

📖 Jorge Luis Borges, Ellis Peters.
See THRILLERS   DH

Eddings, David (US, 1931–) Eddings was born in Spokane and educated at the University of Washington. He worked for Boeing Aircraft before becoming a full-time writer of fantasy novels. Enter his world of magical epics with *Pawn of Prophecy* (1983), which opens the *Belgariad* quintet. Garion is fated by legend to undertake a quest to save a realm imperilled by reawakening evil. *Enchanter's Endgame* (1984) concludes the sequence as Garion, now a sorcerer, returns through hazardous wilderness with the magical orb he has sought. The *Elenium* sequence begins with *The Diamond Throne* (1989), in which the knight Sparhawk returns from exile to find his queen encased in a block of crystal. A later tale, *The Hidden City* (1994), finds Sparhawk allying himself with the Troll gods to overcome the arch-enemy Klael.

📖 J. R. R. Tolkien, T. H. White.
See FANTASY   DH

Edgell, Zee (Belizean, 1940–). *See* BLACK AND WHITE

Edgeworth, Maria (Irish, 1768–1849) The eldest daughter of a Co. Longford landlord and estate owner, Maria Edgeworth was largely educated by her father. His eccentricities, political radicalism, and

233

interests in science and education were major influences on her writing, and he often 'edited' her work and acted as her literary manager throughout her life. Her best-known work is *Castle Rackrent* (1800), a novel with claims to being the earliest 'regional' and the first historical novel in English. A satirical portrait of a run-down estate, the novel draws heavily on Edgeworth's own Anglo-Irish background, and is notable for its wry comic tone and the freshness of its writing. Edgeworth's works are uneven in quality, though *Belinda* (1801) was very successful in its day. She also wrote a treatise arguing for the education of women, and stories for children.

📖 Jane Austen, Walter Scott.
See IRELAND, ROMANCE   WB

Elgin,   Suzette   (US,   1936–).
See SCIENCE FICTION

Eliot, George (British, 1819–80) George Eliot, whose real name was Marian Evans, broke with her conventional background, both by rejecting the Church and by living with a married man; and issues of morality and hypocrisy are central to her work. She is one of the greatest English novelists. Virginia Woolf described her masterpiece *Middlemarch* as 'one of the few English novels written for grown-up people'. Begin with *Silas Marner* (1861), the story of a lonely linen-weaver whose only pleasure is his hoard of silver and gold. His treasure is stolen, but soon after, a golden-haired little girl finds her way into his house after her mother has died in the snow. Marner adopts the child and comes to love her even more than his lost riches. This short, moving novel, about a man's isolation from humanity and his

reconnection through love, offers a vivid picture of village life, with all its superstitions and restrictions, at the beginning of the nineteenth century. Move on to *The Mill on the Floss* (1860), about the young life of Maggie Tulliver, bright, sharp, loving sister to her more stupid and self-satisfied brother, Tom. Maggie's childhood —as she runs away with the gypsies, incurs the displeasure of her dreadful aunts, and hungers rebelliously for school-learning —is unforgettable.

Middlemarch, a Study of Provincial Life (1871–2) has two central stories from which many others radiate. Dorothea Brooke is a young, idealistic, beautiful woman from an upper-class background. She hopes to find a useful role in marrying Casaubon, a man much older than herself, whom she imagines she can help in his scholarly researches. But Casaubon turns out to be a petty bully and his great studies a dead end. The second major story is that of Dr Lydgate, a newcomer to Middlemarch, ambitious to pursue scientific research which will benefit mankind. Lydgate marries Rosamund Vincy, a pretty spoilt child, whose social ambitions are the death of his youthful scientific hopes. The Vincy family in town, Lydgate's work as a doctor, and Dorothea's uncle's estate in the country, provide the links to vividly drawn characters of all classes, so that Eliot's portrait of English society in the early 1830s is wonderfully complete. At the heart of the book is the question about where those impulses—to do good, to break the stifling mould of social convention—can lead people, and whether characters who harbour such hopes must inevitably be crushed. Eliot has insight and sympathy for all her characters, but with a counterbalancing ironic humour.

No one escapes lightly. The interweaving of numerous narratives (a technique developed in response to the problem of serial publication in a magazine, where readers might forget characters unless they all appear in each instalment) gives the novel tremendous narrative drive.

All of Eliot's novels and stories repay reading, from the early *Adam Bede* (1859), a story of ill-fated love and betrayal, to the last, *Daniel Deronda* (1876), which is partly an exploration of dedication and commitment (to the artistic goal of music, and the political cause of Jewish nationalism).

📖 Leo Tolstoy, Elizabeth Gaskell, Arnold Bennett. *See* SOCIAL ISSUES

JR

Elliot, Janice (British, 1931–95) Elliot was born in Derbyshire, and educated at Oxford. After working on the *Sunday Times*, she became a full-time writer in 1962. Begin by sampling her acclaimed *England Trilogy*, comprising *A State of Peace* (1971), *Private Life* (1972), and *Heaven on Earth* (1975). This incisive depiction of conditions in England after the Second World War draws on her experiences of working in the East End of London in the late 1940s. A versatile and inventive author, Elliot's writing borders on science fiction in *The Summer People* (1980), a futuristic treatment of visitors who remain indefinitely at an isolated holiday resort to await the outcome of global catastrophe. *Figures in the Sand* (1994) is an imaginative historical novel, in which the governor of a Syrian outpost of the collapsing Roman Empire sets off across the desert in search of redemptive self-knowledge.

📖 Shena Mackay, Penelope Lively

DH

Ellis, Alice Thomas (British, 1932–)
Alice Thomas Ellis lived for many years in Wales, and has worked as a newspaper columnist. Her short novels tend to satirize contemporary family life and culture. *The Birds of the Air* (1980) is set over a Christmas holiday, when the Marsh family and friends gather following the death of Mary Marsh's son. Ellis sharply observes the comic elements of a family Christmas, yet also explores the inner workings of a mother's grief for her child. Although her novels are compact, Ellis's writing is often very lyrical: 'she could see the leaves of the sycamore dancing desultorily in the breeze against the night sky—like tired children driven on by an unkind but preoccupied master . . .' Her strong Roman Catholic faith and her feminism provide important themes in her work.

Ellis wittily observes the neuroses of contemporary city dwellers in *The Inn at the Edge of the World* (1990). Five guests at an inn on a remote Scottish island have at least one thing in common—they are all in flight from Christmas. Suggestions of the supernatural and mysterious disturb the surface of events. Family loss and grief are again at the centre of her first novel *The Sin Eater* (1977), set in contemporary Wales during a weekend when a troubled family gathers to await the death of the clan's patriarch.

📖 Muriel Spark, Fay Weldon, Beryl Bainbridge

DJ

Ellis, Bret Easton (US, 1964–) Ellis's debut novel, *Less than Zero* (1985) is written from the perspective of Clay, an 18-year-old student returning from college to spend the Christmas vacation at home in Los Angeles. Like the characters in Ellis's campus novel, *The Rules of Attraction* (1987),

Clay is both naïve and jaded: in spite of endless supplies of money, cocaine, and consumer goods, he feels emotionally empty and cut off from life. This mood is deepened in *American Psycho* (1991). Patrick Bateman is a Wall Street stockbroker, effortlessly earning more money than he can ever spend. Like Clay, Bateman is immune to shock, suffering, and pleasure, but unlike him, challenges his own deadened responses with stomach-churning violence. Bateman's story is a bizarre catalogue of designer clothes, casual affairs, and misogynistic mutilations, all recounted in the same deadpan tone. Although highly controversial and widely condemned as pornographic, *American Psycho*, like Jay McInerney's best books, attempts to probe the dark heart of America in the 1980s.

📖 David Leavitt, Jay McInerney

BH

Ellison, Ralph (US, 1914–94) Born in Oklahoma, Ellison travelled north to New York in 1936. Inspired by the communist writer Richard Wright and his contact with the black community of Harlem, Ellison set about writing his only novel. *Invisible Man* (1952) is about a nameless black character moved to political activism by the racism he encounters. Ellison draws upon radical African-American thought, existentialism, surrealism, and folklore to create a disturbing and often prophetic account of the black struggle for political and social equality. In 1953 Ellison became the first Afro-American to win the prestigious National Book Award. Ellison also wrote short stories, reviews, and criticism, published in anthologies and magazines. Some of his more inspiring essays on jazz, blues, and literature are collected in *Shadow and Act* (1967).

📖 Zora Neale Hurston, Richard Wright. *See* BLACK AND WHITE, UNITED STATES OF AMERICA   EW

Ellman, Lucy (US, 1956–   ) Lucy Ellman was born in Illinois, moving to England at the age of 13. She studied art before writing her first novel, *Sweet Desserts* (1988). The book is a very funny, angst-ridden cry from the narrator, Suzy Schwarz, about her relationship with her sister, her husband, her dying father, and food. The narrative is interrupted by extracts from her diary, radio advice shows, and the like. *Varying Degrees of Hopelessness* (1991) is also experimental. In this novel the heroine Isabel is studying art and enjoying a wholly imaginary love-life. As funny and spiky as the narrative is, it reveals the bleakness of the heroine's world. *Man or Mango?: A Lament* (1998) has as its heroine Eloise, also man-hungry, and concerns her relationship with an ex-lover, George, an Anglophobe.

📖 Sylvia Plath, Esther Freud   SA

Ellroy, James (US, 1948–   ) Perhaps no other crime writer suffered such a traumatic childhood as James Ellroy, and certainly none have explored the horrors of their past history in such an explicit and sometimes shocking manner. When Ellroy was 10 years old, his mother was brutally murdered; no one was ever charged with the crime. Elements deriving from this defining event in his life are to be found in novels such as *Clandestine* (1982) and *The Black Dahlia* (1987). The latter is the first book in *The L.A. Quartet*: this is a series of four dark and gripping novels set in Los Angeles of the 1940s and 1950s, the most renowned of which is *L.A. Confidential* (1990), which was made into an Oscar-winning film.

Ellroy's understandable obsession with his mother's death eventually led him to collaborate with veteran detective Bill Stoner in a belated attempt to resolve the mystery, which is recorded in *My Dark Places* (1996). *Crime Wave* (1999) comprises for the most part reportage previously published in the American edition of *GQ*, including a reprint of an article about his mother's death which preceded *My Dark Places*, together with the novella 'Hollywood Shakedown' and some shorter fiction. Ellroy's first novel was a private-eye story and his other books include three which feature Lloyd Hopkins of the Los Angeles Police Department. His writing is lurid, complex, and not for the faint-hearted.

📖 Dashiell Hammett, Jim Thompson. *See* CRIME, THRILLERS

ME

Elton, Ben (British, 1959–) Elton was one of the most prominent of a new wave of comedy writers who came to fame in the 1980s. He is known for his furiously energetic stand-up comedy routine, combining surreal outbursts about everyday life with scathing satire. His first three novels are like extensions of his stand-up act: compendia of hit-and-miss jokes and political outrage. But *Popcorn* (1996) is a huge advance on these efforts. It is the story of a director of amorally violent films held hostage by a disaffected young couple who might have stepped out of one of his screenplays, and is tightly plotted, funny, and thought-provoking. The author has also written a stage version. *Inconceivable* (1999) is a painful comedy about a couple stricken by their inability to conceive a child. Elton's many television writing credits include the hit series *Blackadder*.

📖 Tom Sharpe, Terry Pratchett   NC

Emecheta, Buchi (Nigerian, 1944–) Emecheta left Nigeria for London in 1962. After leaving her abusive husband she took a sociology degree and began writing. *In the Ditch* (1972) and *Second Class Citizen* (1974) are thinly veiled autobiographical novels which bluntly depict her early years in North London, focusing specifically on the political realities of being a single black mother in 1960s' Britain. Many of her subsequent novels concentrate on the status of the black woman in traditional Ibo society. Emecheta is particularly interested in the effects of colonialism on traditional society. Education is seen as a liberating force. One of her most compelling novels, *The Slave Girl* (1977), tells the tragic story of a young Ibo girl, sold into slavery by her brother. The girl, Ojebeta, is forced to grapple with traditional values, and the imposed values of capitalism and Christianity.

Ironically titled, *The Joys of Motherhood* (1979) traces the tragic life of Ibuza, born Nnu Ego, through two marriages and six children. Immersed in the disorientating values of the city and investing everything in her children, she dies alone on the roadside. *Double Yoke* (1982) concentrates on the new educational opportunities for women in 1980s' Nigeria through the central character who is both desperate to fulfil her role as devoted wife and eager to be an educated career woman.

📖 Jean Rhys, Maya Angelou, Wole Soyinka   EW

Endo, Shusaku (Japanese, 1923–) Among the foremost Japanese novelists of the twentieth century, Endo was an early convert to Catholicism. Begin with *The Girl I Left Behind* (1963), the story of a factory girl's enduring love for a young professional who ditches her after a one-night stand. *Silence* (1966) is based on the persecution of seventeenth-century European missionaries in Japan. Also set in the seventeenth century, *The Samurai* (1980) concerns a journey made from Japan to America and Europe by four Samurai and a Spanish missionary. The Japanese return home Catholic converts, but without the trading rights they have sought. *Foreign Studies* (1965) draws on Endo's experience of studying in France in the 1950s for its portrayal of a Japanese student baffled by an alien culture.

📖 Kazuo Ishiguro, Yukio Mishima, Graham Greene   *DH*

Engel, Marian (Canadian, 1933–85). *See* CANADA

Enright, Anne (Irish, 1962–). *See* IRELAND

Erdrich, Louise (US, 1954–) Louise Erdrich writes poetry, short stories, and novels and draws upon her Native American Chippewa and German-immigrant descent to create a vivid chronicle of American Indian and white experience in twentieth-century North Dakota. In *Love Medicine* (1984, revised and expanded, 1993), Erdrich utilizes Chippewa story-telling traditions, engaging in the spiritual world of the culture and its strong connection to the land. Fourteen interwoven short stories span the years 1934–84 through members of five Chippewa and mixed-blood families, all struggling to attain a sense of belonging through love, religion, home, and family. In *The Bingo Palace* (1994) Lipsha Morrissey answers his grandmother's summons to return to his birthplace. As he attempts to settle into his new job on the Indian Reservation, he falls in love with beautiful Shawnee Ray. Shawnee however, is deciding whether to marry Lipsha's boss who is planning to open a gambling complex on reservation land, threatening to destroy the community's links to the past.

The Beet Queen (1986) draws on the European-immigrant side of Erdrich's background. Deserted by her mother who runs away with an aeroplane stunt pilot, Mary Adare is raised by her Uncle Pete and Aunt Fritzie in the town of Argus. Mary rejects the dreaminess of her beautiful mother, and survives her life through a more plodding approach. The characters in Argus are driven by sometimes unwise obsessions, but retain a genuine love of life. All of Erdrich's novels powerfully evoke the vastness of the North Dakota landscape.

📖 E. Annie Proulx, Jane Smiley, William Faulkner. *See* UNITED STATES OF AMERICA   *DJ*

Ernaux, Annie (French, 1940–) Ernaux was born in Yvetot, Normandy, and lives near Paris. She combines her writing with her work as a teacher of literature. Begin with *Positions* (1983), which, like all her novels, has a firm basis in autobiography. Richly elegiac in its minute recollections, it concerns the gulf that opens between an unlettered father and his daughter in the course of her education. In *A Woman's Story* (1988) Ernaux pays homage to her mother's sacrifice of her individuality to the needs of her husband and daughter. In *Passion Perfect* (1991) the narrator is in her bedroom, awaiting a visit from her lover. She muses on desire and its various objects as she considers her circumstances and those of women in general. *Shame* (1998) focusses on a young girl who sees her father try to kill her mother.

📖 Simone de Beauvoir, Michèle Roberts, Marcel Pagnol   *DH*

Esquivel, Laura (Mexican, 1950–) *Like Water for Chocolate* (1989) is the first novel of screenwriter Esquivel, and is subtitled *A Novel in Monthly Instalments with Recipes, Romances and Home Remedies.* Set in turn-of-the-century Mexico, it is the magical tale of Pedro and Tita, the youngest of Mama Elena's three daughters. When Tita is forbidden to marry she pours her feelings into passionate, sumptuous cooking which affects everyone who eats it. This original and exciting love-story blends family saga, folklore, fairy-tale, and cookery book, with a surprise happy ending and a recipe for every chapter. *Like Water for Chocolate* has been made into the atmospheric and enjoyable film which inspired *An Appetite for Passion Cookbook* (1995), co-edited by Esquivel, in which celebrity entertainers such as Placido Domingo and Marla Trump present eighty inventive recipes.

📖 Isabel Allende, Gabriel García Márquez   *JN*

Evans, Caradoc (British, 1878–1945) Born in Llanfihangel-ar-Arth, Carmarthenshire, Evans left school at 14 to work as a draper's assistant and subsequently became a periodicals' editor in London. Begin with the stories in *My People* (1915), which gained him notoriety in Wales for their fiercely satirical treatments of the greed, hypocrisy, and religious oppression he saw behind the pieties of a chapel-dominated culture. The compelling originality of these pared-down tales is partly due to their surreally

eloquent blend of biblical pastiche and literally translated Welsh phrasings. Several further collections of similar material include *Capel Seion* (1916) and *Pilgrims in a Foreign Land* (1942). The best of Evans's novels is *Nothing to Pay* (1930), which draws on his experiences of the drapery trade in tracing its comically small-minded hero's career as a shop assistant in Carmarthen and London.

📖 Dylan Thomas, H. G. Wells *(Kipps)*   *DH*

Evans, Nicholas (British, 1950–) Nicholas Evans worked as a screenwriter and film producer for many years before turning to fiction. His debut novel, *The Horse Whisperer* (1995) is the story of a woman traumatized by a riding accident, and the effect on her of the gentle horse-trainer, Tom Booker, whose combination of rugged sensitivity and spiritual strength slowly changes her life. *The Loop* (1998) repeats this successful formula, and centres on a woman protecting a pack of wolves returning to its traditional terrain in Montana. As the superstitious fears of the local townsfolk grow, her efforts win over the son of her most formidable opponent and the fate of the wolves become linked to the book's central romance. Evans's writing is characterized by finely tuned observation of the natural and emotional worlds he creates.

📖 David Guterson, Cormac McCarthy, E. Annie Proulx.
See ROMANCE   *WB*

Everett, Peter (British, 1931–99) Everett was perhaps best known for his television and radio plays, but his most distinctive achievement lay in novels depicting the lives of artists, exploring their times and the nature of their creativity. His first, *Negatives* (1964), won the Somerset Maugham award and *Matisse's War* (1996) received critical acclaim. The novel is an account of Henri Matisse between 1939 and 1945 and is a wonderful evocation of occupied France. In *The Voyages of Alfred Wallis* (1999), a short but haunting work told through the consciousness of an elderly 'naïve' painter in St Ives, Cornwall, there are walk-on roles for admirers such as Ben Nicholson and Christopher Wood. Wallis's seafaring memories, religious mania, and visions of his dead wife are brilliantly woven together, and the book has a moving conclusion with Wallis overlooking the harbour, beyond his death. *Bellocq's Women* (2000) concerns the photographer E. J. Bellocq among his subjects, the prostitutes of New Orleans' Storyville district.

📖 John Fowles, D. M. Thomas   *JS*

F

Fairbairns, Zoe (British, 1948–) Zoe Fairbairns, born in Kent and educated at St Andrews University, Scotland, writes consistently from a feminist perspective, but in a number of different genres. *Here Today* (1984), winner of the 1985 Fawcett Book Prize, is a pacy, contemporary thriller about a temp secretary bent on discovering the fate of a missing office worker. Fairbairns' other novels are equally readable and thought-provoking, and include *Stand We At Last* (1983), a family saga highlighting the development of feminism in the twentieth century, and *Benefits* (1979), a futuristic political novel about the likely fate of a feminist revolution.

📖 Fay Weldon, Lisa Alther, Charlotte Perkins Gilman. *See* FAMILY SAGA

SA

Farah, Nuruddin (Somalian, 1945–) Farah is the author of eight novels, including two trilogies: *Variations on the Theme of an African Dictatorship* (1979–83), which deals with the personal effects of political injustice under the post-revolutionary Somalian regime, and the more recent *Blood in the Sun* (1986–98). Set during the Somalian civil war, this highly esteemed sequence begins with *Maps* (1986), the story of a young orphan wrestling with questions of identity and allegiance, and moves on to *Gifts* (1993), a love-story which also explores freedom and the ethics of giving. It finishes with *Secrets* (1998), as the reappearance of a childhood friend forces a young businessman to confront both his own past and his family's political history. Farah's novels are meditative, allegorical stories, which raise many disturbing questions about nationality and identity.

📖 Salman Rushdie, Ben Okri. *See* AFRICA

SR

Farrell, J(ames) G(ordon) (Anglo-Irish, 1935–79) Born in Liverpool, Farrell was educated at Brasenose College, Oxford, and travelled widely before becoming a writer in the early 1960s. Start with *The Lung* (1965), which draws on his experiences of polio in its blackly comic narrative of Martin Sands. Formerly a well-to-do hedonist, his confinement to an iron lung because of polio allows him to take stock of his life. Farrell is best known for a trilogy of novels based on critical episodes in the history of the British empire. The books combine moral and historical seriousness with pervasive irony and a comic emphasis on the bizarre and absurd. The first part, *Troubles* (1970), takes place in rural Ireland in 1919 amid the crumbling grandeur of the Majestic Hotel, which symbolizes the decay of Anglo-Irish rule. The building is finally destroyed by fire after fighting between British forces and Sinn Fein rebels. Based on events during the Indian Mutiny of 1857, *The Siege of Krishnapur* (1973, Booker Prize-winner) follows. The novel traces the shifts in values among a British garrison enduring the privations of a three-month siege. In *The Singapore Grip* (1979), considered his finest work, the trilogy concludes with the chaos of attempted defence and subsequent retreat as Singapore collapses to the Japanese assault in 1942. Major Brendan Archer, a bastion of chivalrous courtesy who looms large in *Troubles*, reappears in the novel to exemplify the outmoded dignities of empire.

📖 Evelyn Waugh, John Masters, Ruth Prawer Jhabvala   *DH*

Farrell, M. J. *See* **Keane, Molly**

Fast, Howard (US, 1914–) Fast was born in New York City. He began his career as a prolific novelist in 1933 after abandoning his study of art. Much of his fiction is set during the American Revolutionary War. A private soldier encamped with Washington at Valley Forge is the hero of *Conceived in Liberty* (1939), while *The Unvanquished* (1942) concentrates on the growth of Washington's character as a military leader and statesman. *Spartacus* (1951) deals with the rising of Roman slaves in 71 BC and reflects the Communist views for which Fast was ostracized during the McCarthy era. Notable among his later works is *The Confession of Joe Cullen* (1990), in which a Vietnam veteran working for the CIA in South America attempts to expose secret government deals in arms and drugs. Fast has also published crime fiction under the pseudonym **E. V. Cunningham**.

📖 Irving Stone, Leon Uris, Herman Wouk   *DH*

Faulkner, William (US, 1897–1962) Unarguably one of the greats of twentieth-century American literature, credited with writing no fewer than eighteen masterpieces. Faulkner briefly attended university and spent some time with writers and artists in Paris. However, he chose to write most often about the rural communities of Mississippi where he grew up and lived for most of his life, redefining this territory as the imaginary Yoknapatawpha County. He uses this imaginary county to mirror the whole of the Deep South, and writes about it with an archivist's obsessiveness. Faulkner's major theme is the decline of the South, the moral degeneration of white people, and the inability of black people to shake off the impact of slavery. His work is challenging, but supremely rewarding.

In *The Sound and the Fury* (1929), a novel with four narrative voices, we meet the Compson family who recur in several books. The dynasty has been traced from 1699 to 1945. In this novel the siblings Caddy and Quentin degenerate from a state of original innocence, succumbing to the family pattern of incest, erotomania, and suicide. One of their brothers, Benjy, is severely mentally handicapped; the first section, in his stream of consciousness voice, is extraordinary. Another brother, Jason, self-pitying and tyrannical, succeeds their father as head of the family. In the background, the Compson's negro servants watch and witness; in Faulkner's own words: 'They endured.'

As I Lay Dying (1930) is a shorter novel, and a good place for a reader to start. Written in six weeks, it charts the journey of a poor family to bury their mother Addie among her own people in Jefferson, Mississippi. The coffin is carried on their wagon, and at one point has to be rescued from the flooding Mississippi river. Again, the novel is told in the intercut voices of different family members—each with their own secrets—as they make their dramatic journey.

Critics have claimed *Light in August* (1932) and *Absalom, Absalom* (1936) as

Faulkner's finest novels. In them he returns to the same territory that features in *The Sound and the Fury*, writing about it with a 'feverish intensity and biblical grandeur'. Faulkner himself once claimed that the only books he read were the Bible and Greek tragedies, from which he derived his style. The compelling blend of epic, stream of consciousness, and Gothic has had a tremendous impact on writing from the South. Just as writers in Ireland have written in the shadow of Joyce, few writers from the South have escaped the visionary influence of Faulkner. Faulkner also worked in Hollywood, scripting films like *To Have and Have Not* and *The Big Sleep*. Faulkner was awarded the Nobel Prize for Literature in 1950.

📖 Carson McCullers, Flannery O'Connor, Ralph Ellison. *See* UNITED STATES OF AMERICA   *LM*

Faulks, Sebastian (British, 1953–) Much of Faulks's writing explores the impact of war upon relationships between individuals. *Birdsong* (1993) spans three generations from the First World War to the 1990s. A young Englishman, Stephen Wraysford, falls in love with Isabelle Azaire while serving in France. The descriptions of Stephen's experiences in the dark, surreal world of the trenches are vivid. Faulks's characterization of comradeship amongst the men struggling together in these horrific conditions is very moving. *Charlotte Gray* (1998) is set in England and France during the Second World War, and explores a love-affair which is shaped and thwarted by war. Charlotte has a brief but intense affair with an RAF pilot. When his plane is lost over France, she contrives to go there, work in the Resistance, and search for him. Faulks examines the ways in which hope can survive beyond reason in times of war.

📖 Nevil Shute, Pat Barker, Erich Maria Remarque. *See* ROMANCE   *DJ*

Feinstein, Elaine (British, 1930–) Elaine Feinstein is of Ukrainian-Jewish descent, and her novels deal with family histories which stretch across Europe. She also writes poetry and has translated the Russian poet Marina Tsvetayeva. Start with *The Border* (1984), a story of obsessive love and betrayal among characters trying to escape from Vienna after the Nazi occupation. *Mother's Girl* (1988) draws upon Feinstein's interest in psychoanalysis and feminism. It tells of two half-sisters who discover the secrets of their family's past. One sister loves their father; the other hates him; the novel unfolds the family history from pre-war Budapest to London in the 1980s. *Dreamers* (1994), less successful than the shorter works, traces a Jewish family's story across several generations.

📖 A. S. Byatt, Michèle Roberts   *TT*

Fell, Alison (British, 1944–) Born in Dumfries, Fell moved to London in 1970 and became active in feminist publishing, particularly with *Spare Rib*. Her fiction has evolved away from realism towards a style that incorporates theory, politics, desire, and dreams, within a poetic, sometimes fragmentary prose. *The Bad Box* (1987) signalled this change, with its use of myth and fantasy in its account of a young Scottish girl's maturing. Fell's most admired novel so far has been *Mer de Glace* (1991), a feminist romance, the story of an adulterous affair between a young American climber and an older woman, his college tutor. Much of the action takes place during a climbing holiday in the

Alps, climaxing in a dangerous ascent in which passion and endurance mix. Fell is also a skilled pasticheur. *The Pillow Book of the Lady Onogoro* (1994) is written in the form of a Japanese medieval chronicle, and *The Mistress of Lilliput* (1999) is a mock-eighteenth-century novel written from the viewpoint of Mrs Gulliver.

📖 Michèle Roberts, Marina Warner

JS

Ferguson, Helen. *See* **Kavan, Anna**

Ferrars, Elizabeth (British, 1907–95) Elizabeth Ferrars' crime-writing career spanned more than half a century. In that time she established herself as a reliable and prolific creator of mysteries in the classic British tradition. Five early books featured an amateur detective called Toby Dyke, but she later wrote many 'one-off' novels. Her regular characters included an estranged couple, Virginia and Felix Freer, who first appear in *Last Will and Testament* (1978), and Andrew Basnett, a retired professor of botany who keeps stumbling across murder. Even in her eighties Ferrars was producing enjoyable, crisply written stories such as *Answer Came There None* (1992). Her quality of output was so even that it is difficult to pick out particularly outstanding titles, but perhaps *The Small World of Murder* (1973) and *Skeleton in Search of a Cupboard* (1982) show this entertaining writer at her best.

📖 Agatha Christie, Ngaio Marsh

ME

Fforde, Katie (British, 1952–) Katie Fforde was born and educated in London, studying the arts, cookery, typing, and shorthand before setting up business on the canals with her husband. Her first novel,

Living Dangerously (1995), is a high-spirited contemporary romance set in Gloucestershire. Its heroine, who works in a health-food shop, might be faint-hearted, but finds true love nevertheless. *The Rose Revived* (1995) has three heroines who run a cleaning agency and live on a narrowboat. *Wild Designs* (1996) is another romantic comedy of manners with a heroine who loves gardening, and *Stately Pursuits* (1997) tells the story of disillusioned Hetty Longden who finds love in a decaying stately home. Katie Fforde writes unpretentious, entertaining romances in the Aga saga tradition.

📖 Joanna Trollope, Marika Cobbold, Jane Austen

SA

Fielding, Helen (British) Fielding has worked for the BBC producing documentaries in Africa for Comic Relief. Her first novel, *Cause Celeb* (1994), satirizes the juxtaposition between the image-obsessed western media and the struggling developing world. The immensely popular *Bridget Jones's Diary* (1996) began as a column in the *Independent* newspaper. A single woman in her thirties confides her hopes, dreams, her obsession with her weight ('Fat units 3457 (approx)—hideous in every way'), and her consumption of 5,277 cigarettes. Her New Year's resolution is the quest for the right man, leading her into a disastrous affair with her boss. Bridget's mother forces her into attending a party full of 'smug marrieds', where she meets Mark Darcy. Their mutual antagonism leads eventually to romance, which Fielding ironically bases on Elizabeth and Darcy's in Austen's *Pride and Prejudice*. She writes with sharp wit, revealing the lighter side of despair and self-doubt.

📖 Fay Weldon, Sue Townsend, Lucy Ellman. *See* ROMANCE

DJ

Fielding, Henry (British, 1707–54) Born in Somerset of aristocratic parents, Fielding was educated at Eton and moved to London in his late teens. There he wrote some twenty-five plays whose dense political allusions (with particular attacks on Robert Walpole's government) ensure they are rarely revived. After the Licensing Act of 1737 London theatre was politically censored and Fielding turned his attention to editing the thrice-weekly *Champion* (1739–41) before becoming a magistrate and co-founder of Britain's first organized detective police force, the Bow Street Runners. Fielding's first and perhaps funniest novel, *Joseph Andrews* (1741), is a parody of Samuel Richardson's highly popular *Pamela* (1740). Taking the brother of the famously moralistic Pamela as its hero, it follows the misfortunes of the innocent Joseph and his unworldly companion, Parson Adams, as they travel through the predatory world of Georgian England. The pair's naïve and disastrous longing to do right produces one of the most farcical duos in English literature. Just as scrupulous in design, if more ambitious in scale, is Fielding's masterpiece *Tom Jones* (1749). Its rapscallion hero is first introduced as a baby, discovered in the bed of an astonished Squire Allworthy, who adopts the boy despite the hostility of the rest of his family. A panoramic comic novel, it depicts Tom's picaresque adventures, the frustrations and coincidences he encounters, and his devotion to the beautiful, apparently unattainable heroine, Sophie Western. With its refreshingly un-idealized hero and a narrator who is almost a character in his own right, the book has become a sharp, sardonic classic.
📖 Charles Dickens, Laurence Sterne, Daniel Defoe, John Barth.
See HUMOUR   RP

Figes, Eva (German, 1932–   ) Figes' fiction is ambitious and original, tending to be built around impressions and fragmented observations rather than realistic plots. She has a strong interest in form and her prose is poetic, detailed, and minutely observed. Begin with *Ghosts* (1988), a meditative novel structured around four seasons of a year. Intense memories are interspersed with the thin reality of the present as the anonymous narrator looks back over her life and resolves her relationships with the people around her. Move on to *The Knot* (1996), which centres on Anna, following her from birth and considering her developing relationship with the world and with language through a series of isolated moments. Figes is also the author of the highly successful feminist study, *Patriarchal Attitudes* (1970), and of a number of critical works.
📖 Christa Wolf, Virginia Woolf, Franz Kafka   SR

Findley, Timothy (Canadian, 1930–   ). *See* CANADA

Fine, Anne (British, 1947–   ) Anne Fine was born in Leicester and educated at the University of Warwick. She is best known for her books for children and teenagers, which have enjoyed tremendous popularity. *Goggle-Eyes* (1989) tells how the schoolgirl Kitty tries to come to terms with her divorced mother's new boyfriend. Anne Fine handles this difficult subject with realism and humour. In *Madame Doubtfire* (1987) an estranged father attempts to re-enter his family by disguising himself as a nanny. The novel was filmed under the title *Mrs Doubtfire*, starring Robin Williams. *Flour Babies* (1992) concerns a boy's attempt to care for an artificial baby as a school project. Anne Fine also writes for adults; her novels tend to be black comedies of family life. Try *Telling Liddy* (1998), about the effect of family secrets.

📖 Berlie Doherty, Beryl Bainbridge. *See* TEEN   SA

Firbank, (Arthur Annesly) Ronald

(British, 1886–1926) Ronald Firbank inherited an income that allowed him to travel widely and to publish his own books. He was received into the Catholic Church while studying at Cambridge in 1907, and alongside his homosexuality, the theatrical and exotic elements of Catholicism helped to shape the sensibility of Firbank's novels. He is best known for *Valmouth* (1919), a comic novel set in a sauna dominated by a manipulative black masseuse. *Prancing Nigger* (1924, also known by Firbank's preferred title *Sorrow in Sunlight*) is the comic story of the social aspirations of a black family set in the Caribbean. The high artifice of Firbank's style is an acquired taste, and has been extremely influential despite the neglect he experienced in his own time. *Concerning the Eccentricities of Cardinal Pirelli* (1926) was Firbank's last completed work, and *The Artificial Princess* (1934), a novel which he had started in 1906 and completed in 1925, was published posthumously.

📖 Oscar Wilde, Evelyn Waugh, Brigid Brophy   WB

Fischer, Tibor (British, 1959–) Born in

Stockport to Hungarian parents, Fischer worked as a journalist before he began his first novel, *Under the Frog* (1993), which takes its title from the Hungarian expression for being at the lowest point in life—'under a frog's arse and down a coal-mine'. It is a sad but witty account of two young men surviving the chaos of communism as part of a travelling basketball team. Set in post-war Hungary in the years leading up to the revolution in October 1956, it follows the fortunes of the team in pursuit of sex and avoidance of work. Fischer's hilariously absurd third novel, *The Collector Collector* (1996), is narrated by an ancient, sentient bowl which has mentally catalogued a long history of extraordinary human behaviour and is now tired of the world, convinced that it will never be surprised again.

📖 David Flusfeder, Joseph O'Neill, Douglas Adams   RP

Fitzgerald, F(rancis) Scott (US, 1896–

1940) Fitzgerald was born in St Paul, Minnesota, and educated at Princeton. He worked briefly as an advertising copywriter, then fell in love with a Southern belle, Zelda Sayre, and the tremendous success of his first novel (*This Side of Paradise*, 1920) gave him the money and status he craved in order to marry her. The pair lived extravagantly, darlings of smart society in New York and the French Riviera, until Zelda's mental disintegration and Scott's alcoholism brought this high-flying fantasy crashing down in debt and despair. Fitzgerald ended his days a hack writer in Hollywood, churning out screenplays, few of which made it to the screen.

The hedonistic decade in which Fitzgerald achieved fame, the 1920s, became known as the Jazz Age, and Fitzgerald was its pre-eminent chronicler and brightest star. *The Great Gatsby* (1925), his most famous novel, shapes this material superbly. Jay Gatsby is a romantic figure around whom myths are woven; where he came from and how he acquired his fabulous wealth are shrouded in mystery. Gatsby's whole life is focused obsessively on winning the love of Daisy Buchanan, a frivolous, empty-headed young woman, already married, but Gatsby's self-delusion contains the seeds of its own tragic end. It is a supreme achievement that in this short novel Fitzgerald captured the dreams and heady aspirations of his age, and also the bitter dashed hopes of the 'lost generation'.

Fitzgerald was accused of possessing a fatal facility, that is, of squandering his beautiful talent and not taking pains with his writing. The exact opposite is the truth. Witness the blood, sweat, and tears he poured into *Tender is the Night* (1934) which ran to seventeen versions over nine years. Set in the south of France and elsewhere in Europe, this long novel follows the mental decline of Nicole, married to psychiatrist Dick Diver, and is closely based on Fitzgerald's own torment as Zelda's illness worsened. Despite its theme, the book is both poignant and lyrical, containing passages of great descriptive power, and shows how diligent Fitzgerald was in perfecting his simple yet elegant style, thoroughly meriting his reputation as one of the finest novelists of his generation.

A master of the short story, and always in need of money, he wrote prolifically for high-paying magazines. These are collected in *The Diamond as Big as the Ritz* (stories 1920–37) and several other volumes. Unlike the fictional Gatsby, Fitzgerald was clear-sighted and unflinchingly honest about himself. In *The Crack-up* (stories and autobiographical pieces, 1929–40) he recounts his slide into alcoholism without a trace of self-pity; indeed his fortitude in battling it is noble and inspiring. None of his books was in print when he died of a heart attack. At the time he was working on *The Last Tycoon* (1941), an incisive portrait of Hollywood as well as a tender love-story, which in the eyes of many critics had the potential to be Fitzgerald's crowning masterpiece. As J. B. Priestley wrote: 'I would rather have written this unfinished novel than the total works of some widely admired American novelists.'

📖 Ernest Hemingway, Nathanael West, Raymond Chandler.
See UNITED STATES OF AMERICA

TH

Fitzgerald, Penelope (British, 1916–2000) Fitzgerald started writing fiction in her sixties, and her first four novels are loosely based on experiences from her own life: of wartime journalism for the BBC; of teaching in a theatrical school; of working in a bookshop; and of living on a Thames barge. Her later novels have historical (and often foreign) settings. Her characters are depicted with a rare warmth and humour, so that although her short novels often deal with difficult subjects—love, death, loss—the reader is left with a vivid sense of human potential. Begin with *The Gate of Angels* (1990), set in Cambridge in 1921, about Freddy (impoverished fellow at an ancient and deeply eccentric college) and Daisy, determinedly independent sacked nurse from London, who fall in love after being knocked off their bikes together. Daisy's dirt-poor background is rendered without sentimentality. Move on to *The Blue Flower* (1995) set in late-eighteenth-century Germany and based on the life of the German poet and philosopher Novalis. It tells the story of the idealistic young man's love for a 13-year-old girl, who falls terribly ill. The style is elliptical and spare, but the novel covers a vast canvas—the country and times they live in, philosophy, medicine, domestic detail, and longings that go beyond words; in its concise brilliance, this is 220 pages that most writers would need 400 to cover. Booker Prize shortlisted four times, Fitzgerald won with *Offshore* (1979) about houseboat dwellers on the Thames in London in the 1960s; a book whose world is every bit as vivid as the historical settings, but which feels (fittingly, given the subject matter) rather more wandering in structure.

📖 Jane Austen, Elizabeth Jolley, Beryl Bainbridge   *JR*

Flanagan, Mary (US, 1943–) Flanagan moved to Britain in 1969 and her fiction uses both American and European settings. She is best known for her short stories; begin with *Bad Girls* (1984) which offers an array of mad, bored, unhappy women—mostly from wealthy backgrounds. Flanagan is particularly interested in bored middle-class wives and mothers seeking diversion. Sex is central to many of her stories, as it is to her 1997 novel *Adèle*, which describes the attempt of present day feminists to unearth the story of *Adèle*, sexually magnetic and physically extraordinary wild child, kept in 1930s Paris by a gynaecologist for sexual investigation, experimentation, and prostitution. The story is set in motion by the theft of mummified sexual organs from the British Museum. *The Blue Woman* (1994) is a second collection of whimsical and bizarre stories.

📖 Fay Weldon, Jane Gardam, Lesley Glaister   *JR*

Flaubert, Gustave (French, 1821–80) Born in Rouen, Flaubert abandoned his law studies at L'École de Droit, Paris,

in 1845 and returned to his birthplace to devote himself to writing. He had a major influence on nineteenth-century fiction through his rejection of romantic conventions in favour of a rigorous realism. The technical advances produced by his exacting concern with style and form were also widely influential. Begin with his masterpiece *Madame Bovary* (1857). The success of this harrowing account of marital discontent and infidelity was encouraged by an unsuccessful prosecution for moral offensiveness. The self-obsessed Emma Bovary, wife of a provincial doctor, inhabits a world of sterile middle-class respectability from which romantic delusion is her only escape. An agonizing suicide ends the increasingly hopeless descent into debt and adultery that results from her search for emotional fulfilment. Drawing on his own experiences of Paris during the politically unstable 1840s, *L'Éducation sentimentale* (1869) charts the intellectual and moral progress of provincial student Frédéric Moreau. After a succession of amours and transient political involvements, he achieves a detached individuality that reflects Flaubert's morally neutral attitude as a writer. *Salammbô* (1862), set during the siege of Carthage following the First Punic War, centres on the tragic love relationship between a Carthaginian priestess and a military leader. The novel is rich in carefully researched archaeological detail and possesses a mythological gravity unique in Flaubert's work.

📖 Victor Hugo, Guy de Maupassant, Stendhal, Julian Barnes. *See* CLASSICS, FRANCE, HISTORICAL   *DH*

Fleming, Ian (British, 1908–64) More than half the total population of the globe, so it is estimated, has seen a James Bond film. His fourteen adventures in print have sold over forty million copies. Yet Bond was created by Ian Fleming in a moment, he professed, of intense boredom. Educated at Eton and Sandhurst, Fleming served in naval intelligence during the war, and he was 42 when he wrote *Casino Royale* (1953). This is a cracking thriller with all the classic ingredients: a tense gambling scene, a beautiful Russian spy, a sadistic torture scene you won't forget—and of course the laconic, world-weary, devilishly handsome hero with his 007 licence to kill who actually does say 'My name is Bond. James Bond.' The early books are the best, before self-parody set in: *Live and Let Die* (1954), *Diamonds are Forever* (1956), and *Goldfinger* (1959). Even today these are gripping reads because, unlike most of his many imitators, Fleming was a stylish thoroughbred—just like his hero.

📖 John Buchan, Len Deighton.
See SPY   TH

Flusfeder, David (British, 1960–)
Flusfeder lives in London and has worked as a reviewer. He writes with black humour and great inventiveness. *Like Plastic* (1997), his second novel, is a tale of Jewish family life as you have never read it before; brothers Howard and Charlie jointly own the family firm (plastics). They hate each other, and Howard does a bunk from his responsibilities both at work and at home, where his self-contained wife and teenage children reinvent their lives without him. There is a surreal element to their behaviour (the son locks himself in his room and doesn't come out for three years, whilst other family members come and whisper their secrets under his door), yet the emotional truth and complexity of the characters is utterly convincing. *Man*

Kills Woman (1993) also deals humorously with devastating issues. *Morocco* (2000) is set in a fictional European city, and is based on events in the Warsaw Ghetto in 1941. It vividly creates the sense of the danger, fragility, horror, and surreal comedy of life in wartime.

📖 Genn Patterson, Jenny Diski, Martin Amis   JR

Follett, Ken (British, 1949–) Follett was born in Cardiff, educated at the University of London, and worked in publishing before becoming a full-time writer in 1977. Begin with *Eye of the Needle* (1992), originally issued as *Storm Island* in 1978. Stiletto-wielding German secret agent Henry Faber comes close to learning of plans for the D-Day landings, until he is thwarted by an encounter with a woman. Tobruk has fallen to the Nazis in *The Key to Rebecca* and the fate of North Africa is in the hands of allied agents attempting to penetrate German military intelligence. *Night over Water* (1991) is set aboard an airliner heading for the United States on the eve of the Second World War. The volatile mix of passengers includes some of the wealthiest people in Europe, a jewel-thief, and a murderer under FBI escort.

📖 Jack Higgins, Alistair MacLean, Desmond Bagley. *See* SPY   DH

Fontane, Theodor (German, 1819–98) Fontane was born in Neuruppin; he left his family's business to become a journalist in Berlin in 1849. His novels brought a new realism to German fiction and had a marked influence on Thomas Mann. Begin with *Effi Briest* (1895), in which the heroine's failure to come to terms with her social and emotional limitations leads to adultery and a fatal duel. *Before the*

Storm (1878) forms a compelling account of the Franco-Prussian War of 1812–13. Its nostalgia for Prussia's fading aristocratic order is echoed in much of his writing. In *Frau Jenny Treibel* (1892) the heroine rises socially through her marriage but is gradually diminished by the false values she acquires.

📖 Thomas Mann, Leo Tolstoy, Gustave Flaubert. *See* GERMANY   DH

Forbes, Bryan (British, 1926–   ) Since 1959 Forbes has combined a career as a novelist with his work as a film director and writer of screenplays. Begin with *A Song at Twilight* (1989), which opens during a period of critical instability in Britain. The socialist Prime Minister finds himself and his government threatened by an embittered MI5 officer armed with knowledge of links with Soviet Russia. In *The Endless Game* (1986) the murder of an old woman in residential care begins an investigation that leads British secret services into a web of treachery in high places. A man believed dead is sighted in Venice at the opening of *The Twisted Playground* (1993). The explanation opens onto the shadowy, brutal world of paedophile rings and child pornography.

📖 Gerald Seymour, Len Deighton, and John Le Carré. *See* SPY   DH

Forbes, Colin (British, 1929–   ) Forbes was born in Hampstead, London, and has been a full-time writer since 1971. Begin with *Deadlock* (1988), in which a senior figure in Soviet military intelligence disappears. Russian and British governments confer, as a connection with bullion robberies in Switzerland emerges. *By Stealth* (1992) opens with a kidnapping. The subsequent investigation develops into a counter-action against threats to Western interests from conspirators in the Far East. The Prime Minister's assassination throws Britain into chaos in *This United State* (1999). An unknown power begins a brilliantly planned attempt to take over the country. In *The Power* (1994) an explosion at a London intelligence office leads to the discovery of surprising and sinister American links.

📖 Frederick Forsyth, Ted Allbeury, Jon Cleary   DH

Ford, Ford Madox (British, 1873–1939) Ford was the grandson of the artist Ford Madox Brown and grew up among artists and musicians. His best books are difficult but very rewarding. Ford was a leading practitioner of modernist fiction and an influential editor who discovered, among others, D. H. Lawrence and Jean Rhys. As a young man he collaborated with Conrad, who recognized Ford as a marvellous stylist. Like Conrad, Ford has the capacity to generate subtle confusion in the mind of the reader—an experience which, once you get used to it, is quite exhilarating. He published more than seventy books, but only a handful do justice to his talent. Start with *The Good Soldier* (1915), one of the finest modernist novels in English. The narrator is a confused man who finds himself caught in a web of lust, betrayal, madness, and suicide among respectable middle-class people. Ford served in the British Army during the First World War and wrote about his experiences in *Parade's End* (1924–8). The book tells of Christopher Tietjens' tempestuous marriage to Sylvia and his affair with Valentine, a young suffragette. Tietjens goes to the war and endures the terror and suffering of the trenches. The book contains some of the most powerful descriptions of war to be found anywhere in English literature. Other interesting books by Ford include *A Call* (1910) and his autobiographies, *No Enemy* (1929) and *It was the Nightingale* (1933).

📖 Joseph Conrad, Jean Rhys, Dorothy Richardson. *See* WAR   *TT*

Ford, Richard (US, 1944–) Ford has won high praise for both his novels and short stories; begin with *The Sportswriter* (1986) in which suburban, middle-class sports journalist Frank Bascombe tells the story of his ordinary life, his failed marriage, the death of his son, his relationship with his girlfriend. What is endearing about Bascombe is his wistful uncertainty, his reflectiveness, and willingness to examine every aspect of his life—the sense that he has revealed himself utterly (and in so doing, revealed a good deal about what it is to be human). Move on to its sequel, *Independence Day* (1995, Pulitzer Prize), in which Bascombe is planning a 4th of July weekend with his son. *Rock Springs* (1988) collects short stories published over the preceding ten years; in many of them, the characters have the same sense of bewildered fatalism about their lives that Bascombe exhibits at greater length.

📖 Anne Tyler, John Updike, Garrison Keillor   *JR*

Forester, C(ecil) S(cott) (British, 1899–1966) Born in Cairo, C. S. Forester grew up in London and studied medicine before becoming a writer in the mid-1920s. Begin with *Mr Midshipman Hornblower* (1950), dealing with the start of Horatio Hornblower's naval career during the Napoleonic wars. In the course of eleven novels, the conscientious and resourceful Hornblower rises to the rank of Admiral. The books are notable for their historical accuracy, Forester having also published non-fiction studies of the Napoleonic era. In *The Happy Return* (1937) Hornblower distinguishes himself on the Spanish Main as captain of the *Lydia*, his finest fighting ship, before falling in love with his future bride. Forester's other novels include *The African Queen* (1935), about a dissolute engineer and a woman missionary forced to make a perilous river journey in Africa during the Second World War; it was made into a wonderful film starring Bogart and Hepburn.

📖 Bernard Cornwell, Patrick O'Brian, Nicholas Monsarrat. *See* FILM ADAPTATIONS, THE SEA
          DH

Forrester, Helen (British, 1919–) Helen Forrester was born in Hoylake, Cheshire, and lived for many years in Liverpool. She then emigrated to Canada and is now a Canadian citizen. She has written non-fiction as well as fiction, including a best-selling autobiography, *Twopence to Cross the Mersey* (1974), which continues in three further volumes. Many of her novels also describe working-class life in 1930s Liverpool. Typical is *Liverpool Daisy* (1979), the story of a good Catholic wife who is accidentally led into prostitution, and carries on in order to earn the money she so desperately needs. The novel is funny and dark in turn. Try also *Thursday's Child*, first published as *Alien there is None* (1959), about a Lancashire girl in love with an Indian student, and *The Moneylenders of Shahpur* (1987), a love-story set in India.

📖 Lyn Andrews, Harry Bowling, Nell Dunn   *SA*

Forster, E(dward) M(organ) (British, 1879–1970) Born in London, E. M. Forster was educated at King's College, Cambridge, of which he became an honorary fellow in 1946. Eminent for over fifty years among the liberal intellectuals of his day, he received the Order of Merit in 1966. Begin with his first novel, the tragi-comic *Where Angels Fear to Tread* (1905). Set largely in Tuscany, the book centres on tensions between the repressive codes of the English middle classes and the life-affirming spontaneity of Italian culture. Forster's characteristic tone of compassionate scepticism runs through the story of an Englishwoman's love-match with a young Italian and her family's fateful attempts to intervene. Italy is the source of regenerative possibilities in *A Room with a View* (1908), which contrasts the Surrey village of Summer Street with Florence and its surroundings. The story concerns Lucy Honeychurch's dilemma in choosing for a husband either the cultured but emotionally inert Cecil Vyse or the impulsively vital George Emerson. The comedy of fallibly refined English manners ends with Lucy and George released from the tedium of village life on their honeymoon in Florence. They are last seen happily staying at the pensione in which they met earlier in the novel.

The liberating effect of self-knowledge gained through emotional honesty in these novels remains an important theme in *Howards End* (1910). The book contains Forster's most ambitious treatment of conflicting class attitudes as a major English social ill. The differences between the intellectually cultivated Schlegels and the affluent, worldly Wilcoxes are eventually reconciled in a difficult but enduring marriage. The disastrous fate of the lower-class but culturally aspiring Leonard Bast, however, points the moral that cultivation and its part in human fulfilment are functions of social and economic privilege. Widely considered his masterpiece, *A Passage to India* (1924) drew on Forster's visits to India in 1912 and 1921 for its vivid descriptions of Chandrapore and memorable evocations of landscape. The novel attracted controversy for its portrayal of the prejudiced and exclusive society of British expatriates who turn against Aziz, a formerly respected Indian physician. He is groundlessly accused of abusing Miss Quested, a visiting Englishwoman, during an expedition to the Marabar caves which he has taken great pains to organize. Miss Quested's psychological instability becomes apparent when she withdraws her allegations at Aziz's trial. The affair forces him out of sympathy with the British and into a position of committed Indian nationalism. Years later Fielding, a former British official in Chandrapore, revisits India to find Aziz philosophically settled in his belief that the British must give up India. The posthumously published *Maurice* (1971), originally written in 1914, describes the hard-won emergence of its homosexual protagonist to a state of psychological health after he accepts his sexuality. Informed by Forster's own homosexuality, the novel is most directly autobiographical in the sections presenting Maurice as a young man at Cambridge.

📖 Henry James, D. H. Lawrence, Virginia Woolf. *See* SEXUAL POLITICS

DH

Forster, Margaret (British, 1938–) Born in Carlisle, Forster is an acclaimed and distinguished biographer, but it is as a writer of fiction that she deserves greater recognition. Her first novel, *Georgy Girl* (1965), was made into a successful film, but since *Mother, Can You Hear Me?* (1979) she has examined the complicated relationships within families, especially between mothers and daughters. *Have the Men Had Enough?* (1989) is an honest, moving and often very funny account of coping with Alzheimer's disease, and is based on the author's own experience. *Mother's Boys* (1994) looks at the consequences of violent crime from the point of view of the mothers of both victim and perpetrator who together try to understand what's happened. An unusual and brilliant off-shoot of her biography of Elizabeth Barrett Browning was *Lady's Maid* (1990) in which Forster imagines the unknown life of a real person. She has used her gifts for both biography and fiction recently on her own family, exploring her roots in such books as *Hidden Lives* (1997) and *Precious Lives* (1998).

📖 Deborah Moggach, Nina Bawden, Margaret Drabble. *See* ROMANCE

AG

Forsyth, Frederick (British, 1938–) Forsyth is one of the most successful thriller writers of the modern era. His first novel, *The Day of the Jackal* (1971), about an attempt to assassinate President de Gaulle, was initially rejected by publishers but went on to be an international best-seller and has been filmed twice (the 1973 version directed by Fred Zinnemann being by far the more accomplished). Forsyth's tales of international politics and crime hook readers less by conventional story-telling than by their authentic backgrounds, created by meticulous research. The more recent *Icon* (1996) is set in the near future in Russia, where a right-wing fanatic is threatening the stability of the world.

📖 John Buchan, Gerald Seymour. *See* SPY *NC*

Fowles, John (British, 1926–) Fowles has lived for many years in the English seaside resort of Lyme Regis, the location for *The French Lieutenant's Woman* (1969). In 1867 respectable and wealthy amateur palaeontologist Charles Smithson falls under the spell of a strange, 'fallen' woman, Sarah Woodruff. Smithson's pursuit of Sarah wrecks his engagement to a respectable young woman. While Fowles draws from the traditions of the nineteenth-century novel, he also experiments with the form, suggesting, for example, alternative endings to the novel. The natural environment of Lyme is described in rich detail. Place is also central to *The Magus* (1966), set on the Greek island of Phraxos, where the light, landscape, and lush vegetation are vividly described. A young schoolteacher, Nicholas, arrives on the island, ostensibly to do research. He is caught up in a series of mysterious events which seem to be part of a fantastic conspiracy designed to force him to confront his inner self. While this complex novel is written in a naturalistic style, it has a strongly surreal and mythological quality. Fowles's first novel, *The Collector* (1963), is a psychological thriller in which the narrator is a lonely repressed clerk who collects butterflies. Following a win on the football pools, he acquires a remote cottage, kidnaps a young art student, and imprisons her in the cellar. The novel ends in her death, and his plans for his next victim.

📖 Thomas Hardy, Bruce Chatwin, Graham Swift. *See* HISTORICAL *DJ*

Fox, Catherine (British, 1961–) Catherine Fox's novels reflect the tensions of trying to reconcile a religious nature with the demands of the flesh. In *Angels and Men* (1995), vicar's daughter Mara Johns negotiates her way through a stormy year of university. Damaged by involvement with a cult, she learns to trust people again and falls for unorthodox ordinand Johnny Whitaker, a former petty criminal who has turned to God. The characters reappear in minor roles in *The Benefits of Passion* (1997), in which Annie Brown, training for the priesthood, escapes the naggings of her hormones via the erotic novel she is secretly writing. Fox, who has a doctorate in theology and is married to a vicar, knows her territory. Her characters recoil instinctively from the prissiness and pomposity of church mores. However, though she delights in pulling back the veils of propriety, Fox never mocks belief.

📖 Katie Fforde, Barbara Trapido, Sara Maitland   *CB*

Frame, Janet (NZ, 1924–) Janet Frame's unhappy early life led to her repeated incarceration in mental hospitals from 1947 to 1955, and her writing is preoccupied with the themes of madness, sanity, and creativity. Start with *Faces in the Water* (1961), a harrowing and funny account of the narrator's stay in a mental hospital, with piercing insights into her own imagination, the lives of her fellow patients, and into the insanities of those who visit and care for them. Her later novels are more dense and difficult, with fragmented story-lines and multiple voices; *Living in the Maniototo* (1981) tells the story of a widowed writer who house-sits a Californian house and is invaded by friends of the house-owners. She has three personalities which operate at different levels of imagination. Frame, who has won many awards for her work, has also written short stories, poetry and a brilliant autobiography which was filmed by Jane Campion as *An Angel at My Table*.

📖 Sylvia Plath, Elizabeth Jolley, Jean Rhys. *See* AUSTRALIA AND NEW ZEALAND   *JR*

Frame, Ronald (British, 1953–) Frame was born in Glasgow, where he attended university before studying at Oxford. He became a full-time writer in 1981. Begin with the entertaining *Sandmouth People* (1987), which presents a day in the life of a genteel seaside town. Deft social comedy highlights behaviour ranging from the neurotic to the downright illegal beneath the rigid surfaces of 1950s respectability. *A Woman of Judah* (1987), which contains short stories in addition to the title novella, is an acute psychological study of a young lawyer's involvement with an unconventional couple and their haunting past. Each of the three novellas making up *The Sun on the Wall* (1994) hinges on disclosures that force radical reassessments of personal and familial identities. *Bluette* (1990) follows the extravagantly chequered career of its heroine from decadent youth in 1950s England through to self-knowledge and fulfilment in contemporary America.

📖 Paul Bailey, Allan Massie   *DH*

Francis, Clare (British, 1946–) Clare Francis, formerly a popular yachtswoman, has written three books about her voyages but is now better known for her best-selling novels of adventure and suspense. Begin with the strongly plotted *Wolf Winter* (1987), which opens in Norway in

1945, as the young Hal Starheim helps two young men fleeing from the Nazis. Fifteen years later his old friend Jan is one of two men shot dead on a secret cold war mission. Hal's investigations forge links between the past and present, gradually uncovering the extent to which Jan was betrayed. Move on to *Red Crystal* (1985), where Nick Ryder attempts to outwit a gang of international terrorists, and *Betrayal* (1995), as Hugh Wellesley's past is scrutinized and difficult questions raised during the police enquiry into the murder of his former lover, Sylvie.

📖 Frederick Forsyth, Michael Crichton, Evelyn Anthony   *SR*

Francis, Dick (British, 1920–   ) A former bomber pilot and champion steeplechase jockey, Francis became a racing journalist after retiring from the saddle in 1957. His first adventure thriller appeared in 1962. Francis has published a book a year since, winning lifetime achievement awards from his peers on both sides of the Atlantic. A typical Francis novel is set against a racing background and features a hero who must battle against personal adversity as well as external enemies to triumph—and usually get the girl. Sometimes violent, often ingenious, always page-turning, the books typify traditional values.

Begin with *Reflex* (1980), which features a double plot involving a jockey who is also an amateur photographer confronted with a mysterious collection of what appears to be meaningless photographic rubbish. Three books feature private eye Sid Halley —*Odds Against* (1965), *Whip Hand* (1979), and *Come to Grief* (1995). All are among Francis's most nail-biting work, placing his hero under tremendous personal

pressure. *To the Hilt* (1996) shows Francis is just as readable when he moves away from racing.

📖 Ian Fleming, Frederick Forsyth, John Buchan. *See* THRILLERS   *VM*

Francis, Richard (British, 1945–   ) Francis has lived in North Africa, the United States, and Manchester, where he worked as Professor of Creative Writing. Start with *Taking Apart the Poco Poco* (1995), which tells the story of one day in the life of an ordinary family, from the point of view of each family member including (very entertainingly) the dog. Each character meets dramas and traumas of which the others know nothing; as do the characters in *Fat Hen* (1999), another novel of family life, set in Stockport in 1948. This book is particularly good on the double life of Jack, who is away on holiday with his wife and family on the pre-arranged day when his mistress, Ruth, goes to Stockport registry office expecting to marry him. Francis makes the complicated double dealings and everyday betrayals of family life both comic and real, yet innocent of malice.

📖 David Flusfeder, Nigel Williams, Mark Twain   *JR*

Franklin, Miles (Australian, 1879–1954) Franklin's family were pioneers, mountain squatters in New South Wales, and she wrote her famous first novel, *My Brilliant Career* (1901), at the age of 16. This was inspired by Franklin's own frustration at the tedium and poverty of her family's life in the bush, and takes the heroine to her grandmother's beautiful farm where she is wooed by a rich landowner whom she makes up her mind to reject. Ignore the rather wordy opening and start at chapter 2, as the family moves to Possum Gully. The heroine's independence and passionate determination to make the most of her life are shot through with self-doubt, making her one of the most immediate and engaging of fictional voices; an Australian bush Jane Eyre. Franklin wrote many later novels including the *Bin-Bin* sequence (1928–56), a saga of Australian pioneering life, and, with the same subject matter, *All that Swagger* (1936).

📖 Charlotte Brontë, Christina Stead. *See* AUSTRALIA AND NEW ZEALAND

JR

Fraser, Antonia (British, 1932–) A popular biographer and historian, Fraser is also renowned for her strongly plotted and compelling mystery novels, which centre on Jemima Shore, a young television journalist whose research is often the starting-point for the complicated, dangerous investigations she is drawn into. Begin with *Quiet as a Nun* (1977), where Shore investigates the murder of Sister Miriam at a Sussex convent. Her death may have been connected with her money, and as the full complexity of the situation becomes apparent and the ghostly Black Nun begins to appear, Shore realizes she has to solve the mystery before the danger spreads. Move on to *Oxford Blood* (1985), where startling information and the murder of a student raise disturbing questions, deflecting Shore's attention from the programme she's making about Oxford undergraduates.

📖 Patricia Highsmith, Dorothy L. Sayers, P. D. James   *SR*

Fraser, Christine Marion (British, 1945–) Fraser was born in Glasgow, and

has been confined to a wheelchair since contracting a rare muscular disease at the age of 10. She now lives in Argyllshire. Her family stories are enormously popular; begin with *Rhanna* (1978), the first of five books evoking life on a Hebridean island. A young couple's love-affair sets them at odds with sections of the tight-knit community. *Kings Croft* (1986) begins a series of novels about an Aberdeenshire family. During the early 1900s they leave their croft for Glasgow, where they learn how to cope with city life. In *Noble Beginnings* (1994) a gifted young woman in a small Argyllshire town is held back by her father when opportunities for betterment present themselves. *Kinvara* (1998), set on the northern Scottish coast, tells of the unhappy love between a married lighthouse keeper and a single mother.

📖 Pamela Oldfield, Susan Howatch, Phyllis Bentley   *DH*

Fraser, George MacDonald (British, 1925–) A writer of meticulously researched historical adventure novels whose subjects range from piracy to a black American prize-fighter in nineteenth-century Britain and the adventures during the Second World War of Private McAuslin, 'The dirtiest soldier in the world'. But posterity will surely remember MacDonald Fraser for one glorious comic creation: Harry Flashman VC, the irresistibly likeable anti-hero of eleven (so far) rollicking tales set in every war, trouble spot, and boudoir the British empire, in its nineteenth-century heyday, has to offer. Flashman is a cad, a poltroon, a lecher, and a coward who cannot escape danger and intrigue no matter how fast he runs, but who always manages, inadvertently, to save the day which more noble souls put at risk in the first place. Written in a convincing pastiche of upper-class period slang, and stuffed with real characters and events (with copious and fascinating footnotes), the series offers serious insight into the Victorian character, sexuality, and empire whilst making you laugh out loud. Start with the first: *Flashman* (1969).

📖 Jaroslav Hašek, Joseph Heller, Evelyn Waugh. *See* ADVENTURE, HISTORICAL   *MH*

Frayn, Michael (British, 1933–) Born in London, Frayn was educated at Emmanuel College, Cambridge. He is a prolific playwright and journalist, and his fiction is notable for its witty treatments of contemporary social and cultural preoccupations. Begin with *The Tin Men* (1965), his first novel, which is set in a research institute dedicated to achieving automation of all everyday tasks. As a visit from the Queen approaches, Frayn inventively satirizes the scientists' dehumanizing technological obsessions. *The Russian Interpreter* (1966) is a cold war comedy featuring an English research student who is acting as interpreter for a Moscow businessman. The futuristic fantasy *A Very Private Life* (1968) imagines a civilization in which the isolation of the individual is complete. All domestic needs are supplied directly by advanced technology, all emotional experiences produced or relieved by universally available drugs. *Sweet Dreams* (1973) opens with the death of its trendy architect hero in a car accident. He finds himself in a brilliantly imagined afterlife that resembles a slickly celestial version of his former affluent existence. The main character in *Now You Know* (1992) is a charmer with a questionable past who heads an organization that campaigns for freedom of information.

Personal secrets and devious behaviour are typical of everyone involved in the movement. *Headllong* (1999, Booker shortlisted) is a comic novel revolving around an art historian who identifies a Bruegel and tries to separate it from its unwitting owner.

📖 Malcolm Bradbury, J. L. Carr, Kingsley Amis   *DH*

Frazier, Charles (US, 1950–) An academic, Frazier had published some travel writing and short stories before his bestselling Civil War novel, *Cold Mountain* (1997), about a wounded confederate veteran who discharges himself from hospital and takes a long walk home to the remote hills of North Carolina and the Woman He Left Behind. The style is self-consciously poetic. Inman's picaresque (if somewhat cinematically macho) adventures are gripping, but what really makes the book worth reading is the odd-couple relationship between his southern-belle lover, Ada, and Ruby, the abused hillbilly girl she takes in. Ada is pampered and impractical, Ruby is a survivor. Together they struggle to keep the farm going in the war-devastated South until Inman's return.

📖 Stephen Crane, Sebastian Faulks, Leo Tolstoy   *MH*

French, Marilyn (US, 1929–) Marilyn French, feminist philosopher and theorist, is best known as the author of *The Women's Room* (1977), a landmark in feminist writing which encapsulated the rise of the women's movement. Set in 1968 it tells the story of Mira Ward, suburban wife and mother, lonely and depressed, who returns to school and begins to re-examine her life. The novel depicts the reality of women's lives and examines gender divisions, the subordination of women, and the potential for change and liberation. *Bleeding Heart* (1980) tells the story of a relationship between Dolores and Victor, two Americans living in London who must return to their families at the end of the year. It is an intelligent love-story which explores issues of communication, guilt, expectations, and power. *Our Father* (1994) explores the stories of four women as they wait for their father to regain consciousness.

📖 Marge Piercy, Fay Weldon, Doris Lessing. *See* SEXUAL POLITICS

CS

Freud, Esther (British, 1963–) Esther Freud, the daughter of the painter Lucian Freud and a descendant of Sigmund Freud, grew up in Sussex and worked as an actor before turning to writing. Her first novel was *Hideous Kinky* (1992), a thoroughly engaging read, with a 5-year old narrator whose mother takes her on the hippy trail to Marrakesh. Partly autobiographical, this novel reveals family relationships and shows the child's ability to adapt to all sorts of surprising situations. *Peerless Flats* (1993) is an altogether darker novel, although still written with a characteristic light touch, in which the sane, 16-year-old Lisa struggles to keep her dysfunctional family together. *Gaglow* (1997) is set partly in the time of the First World War and concentrates on the rediscovery of family history.

📖 Lucy Ellman, Kate Atkinson. *See* CHILDHOOD   SA

Frisch,   Max   (Swiss,   1911–91). *See* GERMANY

Fry, Stephen (British, 1957–) Fry is a formidably clever writer, comedian, and actor. His favoured performing style plays elaborate variations on English man-

nerisms. *The Liar* (1991), his first novel, describes a young man's emotional journey through school, university, and after. One scene, describing a prep school cricket match, is a set piece in the tradition of mainstream comic fiction. *The Liar* is also outrageous and surreal, especially in those sections in which the hero finds employment as a rent boy in Piccadilly. In *Making History* (1996) the central character discovers that he can alter history to eliminate Hitler—only to see an even worse persecution of the Jews unfold.

📖 P. G. Wodehouse, Simon Raven

NC

Fuentes,   Carlos   (Mexican,   1928–) Educated at the University of Mexico and in Geneva, Fuentes worked for many years as a diplomat, before taking up a series of professorships around the world. Start with *The Crystal Frontier* (1998), a novel in nine interlacing stories which portray the lives of individuals both provided for and ruined by the Mexican-American border. A more daring novel, perhaps, is *Terra Nostra* (1975) with its enveloping fusion of fact and fiction centring on Philip II of Spain (Felipe, El Señor). In this account Felipe builds El Escorial, marries England's Elizabeth Tudor, and witnesses the discovery of the New World. Blending the miraculous and fantastic with the grim and the grotesque, it stands as a sustained allegory, encapsulating both the promise of the New World and the corrupt decline of Spanish glory.

📖 Mario Vargas Llosa, Gabriel García Márquez, Jorge Luis Borges. *See* MAGIC REALISM   RP

Fyfield, Frances (British, 1948–) Solicitor Frances Fyfield writes a series of books featuring Crown Prosecutor Helen West and Detective Superintendent Geoffrey Bailey. The novels are skilfully plotted, the characters complex and believable, and the central relationship between West and Bailey, which needs constant negotiation, is powerfully drawn. *Trial by Fire* (1990) sees the pair moving to the country and living together for the first time. A naked woman's body is found buried in the woods, a man is arrested; the lover of West's only village friend. In *Deep Sleep* (1991) a pharmacist's wife has died suddenly and inexplicably in her sleep and an unexploded bomb has been found in the area. Writing as **Frances Hegarty** Fyfield's novels focus on family relationships where individuals are pushed to psychological extremes with tragic results. *The Playroom* (1991) depicts a couple trapped in a disintegrating marriage; *Let's Dance* (1995) has a mother and daughter locked in a relationship of simmering violence.

📖 Joan Smith, Minette Walters   CS

G

Gaarder, Jostein (Norwegian, 1952–)
A high school teacher in philosophy in
the Norwegian town of Bergen, Gaarder
writes primarily for teenagers, and is a
firm believer in the importance for young
people of an understanding of religion and
philosophy. His breakthrough came with
Sophie's World (1991), an international
best-seller which has been translated into
over twenty languages and adapted into a
feature film. The novel follows 15-year-old
Sophie's mind-expanding journey after
she is introduced by a mystery mentor to
fundamental questions such as 'who am I?'
and 'where does the world come from?'
Through a skilful blend of philosophical
information and narrative she—and we—
are drawn into an exploration of the great
philosophies of the Western world, and
of the nature of philosophy itself.

📖 Iris Murdoch   *KB*

Gale, Patrick (British, 1962–) Patrick
Gale was born on the Isle of Wight and
educated at Winchester and Oxford. He is
a prolific writer, having written eight novels
since 1986, including *The Cat's Sanctuary*
(1990) about two warring sisters, set in
Cornwall. *The Facts of Life* (1995) owes something to family saga, telling the stories of
Edward Pepper, Holocaust refugee, and
his gay grandson who contracts AIDS. Yet
the novel is not gloomy; Gale has a lightness of touch and inveterate optimism. In
Tree Surgery for Beginners (1998), inspired
by Shakespeare's *The Winter's Tale*, the
same is true. The hero, Lawrence Frost,
is investigated for the murder of his wife,
then takes a comic but therapeutic journey
to northern California.

📖 Armistead Maupin, Alan
Hollinghurst, Edmund White   *SA*

Gallant, Mavis (Canadian, 1922–)
Born in Montreal, Gallant was educated
in Canada and the United States before
returning to her native city and finding work
as a journalist. In 1950 she left Canada for
Europe, eventually settling in Paris, where
she still lives. Although she has written
full-length novels, she is best known for
her short stories, which from the 1950s
have appeared regularly in the *New Yorker*
and other magazines. They are marked
by fine moral discrimination and ironic
sympathy; their blend of comedy with an
awareness of the tragedies of life has led
critics to liken them to the plays and stories
of Anton Chekhov. *The Selected Stories of
Mavis Gallant* (1997) is a 900-page representation of her best work. The volume
includes sequences about the Carette
family in Montreal, as well as the author's
own favourites, the semi-autobiographical
stories about Linnet Muir.

📖 Edith Wharton, Alice Munro.
See CANADA   *NC*

Gallico, Paul (British, 1897–1976) Born
in New York, Paul Gallico was a journalist before settling in England. His tiny
romance, *The Snow Goose* (1941), is a good
starting-point, depicting the unspoken
love between a young girl and lonely

hunchback, Philip Rhayader. United through the care of an injured goose, they are parted by war; Rhayader dies heroically rescuing soldiers from Dunkirk. This and *The Small Miracle* (1951) have a fable-like simplicity that only just saves them from the treacly sentimentality marring much of Gallico's prolific output, such as *Love of Seven Dolls* (1954), in which a brutal puppeteer is saved by the love of a waif girl in Paris. Gallico also wrote war adventures such as *The Poseidon Adventure* (1969), the *Mrs Harris* series about a comical Cockney landlady, and such fanciful tales as the hugely popular *Jennie* (1950), in which a small boy is turned into a stray cat.

📖 Richard Adams, Elizabeth Goudge, Ray Bradbury   *CB*

Galloway, Janice (British, 1956–) Although Janice Galloway's work has a Scottish dimension, it is concerned with gender rather than nation. Her first novel, *The Trick is to Keep Breathing* (1989), charts the descent of Joy into mental illness after the death of her married lover. Galloway's second novel, *Foreign Parts* (1994), is about a trip taken to the First World War graveyards in France by two Scottish women. Both novels represent, with irony and black humour, the everyday and existential aspects of women's lives, and experiment with narrative form. Galloway has also published two collections of short stories: *Blood* (1992) and *Where You Find It* (1996), which explore aspects of contemporary women's lives.

📖 A. L. Kennedy, Lorrie Moore, Anne Tyler. *See* SHORT STORIES   *SV*

Galsworthy, John (British, 1867–1933) Galsworthy studied law and travelled widely before beginning to write. He was prolific,

but his best-known work is *The Forsyte Saga* (1906–21). The sequence, made up of three semi-autobiographical novels linked by two shorter 'interludes', is a satirical exposure of the greed and hypocrisy of upper-middle-class London in the early years of the twentieth century. As a chronicle of changing times, the saga details the rivalries, loves, and failures of three generations of a family, beginning with *The Man of Property* (1906), an account of the materialistic, emotionally repressed Soames Forsyte's reaction to his unhappy wife's affair with an architect, and continuing in *In Chancery* (1920) with her later relationship with Soames's younger, more socially aware cousin, Jolyon.

Galsworthy's work often highlights injustice, sympathetically portraying the situation of those held back by poverty, class, gender, or by superficial moral codes. His plays were particularly didactic; *Justice* (1910) dealt with the unnecessarily harsh treatment of a minor convict, and was thought to have been instrumental in contemporary penal reforms. *The Silver Box* (1906) considered the different ways in which a poor and an affluent thief were treated. Galsworthy was the founder of the writers' organization, PEN. He turned down a knighthood, but was awarded the Nobel Prize for Literature in 1932.

📖 Anthony Trollope, George Gissing, John Collier. *See* FAMILY SAGA   *SR*

García Márquez, Gabriel (Colombian, 1928–) Gabriel García Márquez was born in Aracataca, a small town in Colombia, and educated at a Jesuit college in Bogotá. He became a journalist at the age of 18, writing for liberal papers in South America, and moved to Europe seven years later in order to work for the Liberal *El Espectador*. Here he rose to controversy and fame with the exposé of a Colombian naval disaster in 1955. Márquez had always written creatively, but it was the recognition that literature can—and in his opinion should—carry political and social comment that led to his greatest works. By 1982 he had won the Nobel Prize for Literature.

García Márquez occupies a crucial place in the history of twentieth-century literature. *One Hundred Years of Solitude* (1967) has been hailed as one of the most important examples of a mode of writing which has come to be known as magic realism. Seen as a way of compressing huge historical events into a single novel, magic realism has also made it possible to speak of forbidden issues, such as political oppression. Using comedy, pathos, and, most importantly, a narrative which requires a constant suspension of disbelief on the part of the reader, García Márquez wrote about his country's troubled history through the eyes of a single family, in a way that is accessible and enjoyable. It tells the story of the self-contained fictional village, Macondo, which had first appeared in 1955 in his novella, *Leaf Storm* (tr. 1972). *One Hundred Years* begins with the arrival at the village of a gypsy called Melquiades, who introduces new ideas and objects, such as a magnet, to the wide-eyed villagers. Prior to this, the villagers had been content with their lot, and oblivious to the world outside. Inevitably, the knowledge that there is something outside the confines of the village leads to corruption and change. José Arcadjo Buendía is the main character, in whose hands this knowledge both creates and destroys; his wife Ursula quietly, and ultimately in vain, trying to limit the trouble brewing in José's laboratory.

If *One Hundred Years* seems too long to start with, you could try his novella *Chronicle of a Death Foretold* (1981) in which innocence and experience are pitted against each other. It narrates the appearance in a small South American town of Bayardo San Roman, a wealthy businessman in search of a wife. You could also look at *The Autumn of the Patriarch* (1975), a brutal account of a military dictatorship, and the effect throughout society of political corruption; or *Of Love and Other Demons* (1994) which deals with superstition, madness, and decay. Do not be put off by the apparent seriousness of his subject matter: above all, his stories are lyrical, funny, and deeply moving.

📖 Isabel Allende, Günter Grass, Mario Vargas Llosa. *See* MAGIC REALISM   *SB*

Gardam, Jane (British, 1928–) Born and brought up in Yorkshire, Gardam has lived in the south since 1946. She writes particularly well about women's lives. Start with the beautifully crafted, linked short stories *Black Faces White Faces* (1975), set in Jamaica, where repressed English holidaymakers find themselves astonishingly liberated. Move on to *God on the Rocks* (1978, Booker shortlisted), set in the 1930s, about an adolescent girl's summer of awakening to the dark goings-on of the adults around her. *Queen of the Tambourine* (1991) (Whitbread Novel award winner) is narrated by elderly Eliza, and is a wonderfully funny and sad account of her life and delusions. *Faith Fox* (1996) centres on a baby whose mother has died, and reveals the intermingled and complex lives of some well-heeled southerners and an alternative religious community in Yorkshire, but the characters here feel more predictable than in the earlier novels, and the book is soft-centred in comparison to *Queen of the Tambourine*.

📖 Penelope Fitzgerald, Susan Hill, Mary Wesley. *See* TEEN   JR

Gardner, John Champlin (US, 1933–82) Gardner was a distinguished scholar in Old and Middle English, a Professor at New York State University, Binghamton, before his death in a motorcycle accident. The cult novel *Grendel* (1971) is a witty re-imagining of the Anglo-Saxon poem *Beowulf* from the monster's viewpoint; its reverse view of humankind invites readers to identify with the narrator, whose blood-thirsty visits to Hrothgar's mead hall are blackly humorous. Several of Gardner's other novels have a background of philosophy and academia, notably his last, *Mickelsson's Ghosts* (1982). It features a philosophy professor seeking to escape his students, the tax authorities, and a failed marriage by buying an old house in the country, only to encounter a series of paranormal events. *October Light* (1976) depicts an elderly brother and sister quarrelling over politics and ideas, while *Freddy's Book* (1980) is a fable about the Devil at large in sixteenth-century Scandinavia.

📖 Thomas Pynchon, Gerald Locklin
                                         JS

Garland, Alex (British, 1970–) The son of a newspaper cartoonist, Garland studied the history of art at Manchester University before travelling around Thailand and the Far East. His first novel, *The Beach* (1997), tapped into a ready-made subculture of student and graduate backpackers, describing an intriguing search for a mythically secluded and unspoiled beach. On reaching it, however, the heroes discover other paradise-hunters have already colonized it and before long hierarchical power-structures take hold. It was filmed starring Leonardo DiCaprio in 2000. Garland's stylized second novel, *The Tesseract* (1998), takes a more panoramic view of its environment, the modern city of Manila, including everything from westernized gangsters to anxious housewives and wily street kids.

📖 Jack Kerouac, Esther Freud   RP

Garner, Alan (British, 1934–) Garner is quoted as saying that his novels resemble onions. In other words, his work has many layers: a topmost narrative layer, which is the obviously visible story, to be enjoyed by young readers; within that, networks of imagery, and at the core a deep structure put together with meticulous intelligence. All of this should not put readers off. His early novels, such as *Elidor* (1965) and in particular the masterly *The Owl Service* (1967), which won the Carnegie Medal in 1968, are very exciting, and just as page-turning as many much easier books. *Red Shift* (1973) with its timeshifts and elliptical language, and *The Stone Book Quartet* (1976, 1977, 1978), with its poetic elegance and symbolic weight, are harder to dash through, but they amply reward the careful reader, particularly on a second reading. Garner is one of a handful of writers for young adults who assumes (quite rightly) that there are teenagers out there who are formidably intelligent and eager for books that stretch their minds and imaginations. His novel for adults, *Strandloper* (1997), moves from Cheshire to Australia and deals with myths and history.

📖 Russell Hoban, Philip Pullman, Ursula Le Guin. *See* FANTASY, TEEN
                                         AG

Garner, Helen (Australian, 1942–)
Garner has worked as a journalist and written non-fiction and scripts alongside her fiction. Begin with *The Children's Bach* (1984) a novel about a happy couple and their children living in Melbourne, whose lives are disrupted by the arrival of Elizabeth, a woman from the husband's past. Elizabeth has a daughter and an estranged partner; all three of them cause a fracturing of relationships and loyalties within the family. Garner writes with scrupulous honesty about love, jealousy, selfishness, and honour—a painful concept which is central to a number of her strong female characters. *Monkey Grip* (1977) shocked some readers with its descriptions of life with a heroin addict; 'A Vigil', a short story published with her novel *Cosmo Cosmolino* (1992), is also horribly disturbing, on the death of a drugged young woman; but *Cosmo Cosmolino* itself is full of the possibility of happiness. *My Hard Heart* (1998) brings together a number of fine stories from earlier collections.

📖 Elizabeth Jolley, Alice Munro, Doris Lessing. *See* AUSTRALIA AND NEW ZEALAND   *JR*

Garrett, Randall (US, 1927–87).
See FANTASY

Gaskell, Elizabeth (British, 1810–65)
Elizabeth Gaskell was brought up by her aunt in the Cheshire village of Knutsford, later marrying William Gaskell, a Unitarian minister like her father. Her life with her husband brought her into close contact with the poor of Manchester, and it is her sympathy for them that inspired her first novel, *Mary Barton* (1848). The heroine is the daughter of a trade union activist,

John Barton, who is chosen to kill Henry Carson, son of one the local employers, as a warning to the hard-hearted mill-owners. Henry Carson happens to be an admirer of Mary's. On one level, the novel is a page-turning romance; on another, it describes the plight of the workers in the industrial north graphically and movingly, based on Elizabeth Gaskell's first-hand observations and experiences. *North and South* (1855) similarly blends good story-telling with political insight, and concerns the clergyman's daughter, Margaret Hale, reluctantly falling in love with the stern, self-made, northern mill-owner, John Thornton. *Cranford* (1853) is a little different, being a series of affectionate, gentle stories about the inhabitants of a village (based on Knutsford). *Ruth* (1853), on the other hand, is a tragic story of a single mother. *Wives and Daughters* (1864–6) charts Molly Gibson's development from insecure girl to confident young woman, and takes in a wide range of classes and characters along the way. Few Victorian writers combine human interest with social issues so entertainingly, and fewer still demonstrate such a strong humanitarian desire for greater understanding between employers and employees. Gaskell also wrote a fine biography of her friend Charlotte Brontë.

📖 Charles Dickens (*Hard Times*), Charlotte Brontë, George Eliot   *SA*

Gee, Maggie (British, 1948–) Gee's first, vividly written experimental novel, *Dying in Other Words* (1981), made a strong impression. It combines elements of thriller (the heroine is discovered naked and murdered at the start) with blackly comic insights and hypnotically poetic language. Themes of family and romantic love loom large in her more conventional later novels, though these themes are often treated in the context of political ideas. *The Burning Book* (1983) deals with nuclear war, through the family saga of three generations, whereas *The Ice People* (1998) is set in the twenty-first century, during a swiftly encroaching ice age. Gee's analysis of the gulf between the sexes here, as fertility plummets and women become increasingly contemptuous of men (who turn to robots for comfort), is plausible and incisive; and the male narrator's quest to save his son is gripping. The combination of big ideas, together with concern for individuals' stories, makes this science fiction with a wide appeal.

📖 Doris Lessing (*Mara and Dann*), Jenny Diski   JR

Gee, Maurice (NZ, 1931–   )

Gee has worked as a teacher and librarian, and is one of New Zealand's best-known novelists. He also writes for children and for television. *Plumb* (1978, winner of the James Tait Black Prize) is the first in a trilogy about a New Zealand family, which covers five generations, and over 100 years of New Zealand history, dealing with the sharply differing perspectives of different individuals, and with wider historical and political developments. In *Going West* (1992) narrator Jack Skeat attempts to solve the mysteries in the life of his dead friend, a famous poet and ne'er-do-well, born in the same year as himself. In *Live Bodies* (1998) Joseph Mandl, an Austrian Jew now living in New Zealand, reviews his past, when he fought the Nazis in the streets of Vienna, and was later interned as an enemy alien in the New Zealand where he had sought refuge.

📖 Patrick White, Nadine Gordimer, Thomas Keneally   JR

Gee, Sue (British, 1947–   )

Gee spent her childhood on a Devon farm and in rural Leicestershire. She has worked in publishing, but now writes and teaches (writing, at Middlesex University) as a freelance. Begin with *The Hours of the Night* (1996), the romantic and moving story of mother (Phoebe, coldly undemonstrative, obsessed by her garden) and daughter (Gillian, poet, loner, suddenly discovering love) in a little village on the Welsh borders. The Welsh setting is vivid and integral to the story, and the uneasy relationship between the women is beautifully drawn. All Gee's characters here have to face up to loss of differing kinds. *Letters from Prague* (1994) follows another mother, Harriet, and her 10-year old daughter as they travel to Prague in search of Harriet's first love, lost in 1968 when the Russian tanks crossed the border.

📖 Elizabeth Buchan, Penelope Fitzgerald. *See* ROMANCE   JR

Gellhorn, Martha (US, 1908–98)

Martha Gellhorn, one of the first female war correspondents, reported from the Spanish Civil War in 1937 and covered many of the twentieth century's major stories, continuing to write and travel until 1996. Her second husband was Ernest Hemingway, who features in *Travels with Myself and Another* (1978) as U.C.—'unwilling companion'. Her detailed, evocative journalism is collected in three volumes, including *The Face of War* (1986). Gellhorn's early fiction centred on the American Depression, but her later novels are concerned with the effects of war as well as with issues of injustice and inequality. Begin with *Liana* (1944), set on a Caribbean island, which deals with the troubled marriage of a young local woman to an older Frenchman, depicting her affair with her tutor and its devastating resolution when war intrudes. Move on to *A Stricken Field* (1940), the story of Mary Douglas, an American journalist based in Czechoslovakia as the Nazis slowly approach.

📖 Mavis Gallant, Ernest Hemingway
SR

Genet, Jean (French, 1910–86) Jean Genet spent much of his early life in the criminal underworld and was sentenced to life-imprisonment until his sentence was commuted following campaigns for his release. His major achievements lie in the theatre, where plays like *The Maids* (1948) helped to create the 'Theatre of the Absurd' in the aftermath of the Second World War. His best-known prose work is *The Thief's Journal* (1954), an autobiographical account of his own life outside the norms of French society. *Querelle of Brest* (1953) follows a sailor who has left his ship, through various transient relationships, including one with a murderer, and *Funeral Rites* (1969) follows a 16-year-old boy's attempts to survive the Nazi occupation of France. *Our Lady of the Flowers* (1949) depicts the vicious underworld of Genet's own early experiences.

📖 Edmund White, Jean-Paul Sartre, William T. Vollmann
WB

Geras, Adèle (British, 1944–) Geras was born in Jerusalem and has lived in Manchester for over thirty years. She has written more than sixty books for children of all ages. Of her teenage fiction, start with *Voyage* (1983), set on a ship bearing emigrants (many of them Jewish) from Eastern Europe to America in 1904. The book explores the growing friendship and love between four young people, set against the harsh conditions of life at sea. The

Tower Room (1990, first book in the *Egerton Hall* trilogy) is a romantic story set in a girls' boarding-school in the late 1950s, which captures the mood of dreamy adolescence between girlhood and maturity. Narrator Megan falls in love with Simon, the new lab assistant—and then discovers that her own foster mother is her rival. *Troy* (2000) tells, with realism and humour, the story of two sisters inside the besieged city, who become the playthings of Aphrodite, goddess of love.

📖 Berlie Doherty, Lynne Reid Banks. *See* TEEN
JR

Germain, Sylvie (French, 1954–). *See* FRANCE

Ghosh, Amitav (Indian, 1956–) If you want an ambitious, imaginative, and thought-provoking read, Amitav Ghosh, not as well known as he deserves to be, will be a delight. More cleverly plotted and grounded in detail than Rushdie or García Márquez, not to mention easier to follow, *The Circle of Reason* (1986) has an extraordinary cast of characters and moves from Indian village politics to Calcutta and North Africa. *The Shadow Lines* (1988) reconstructs Indian and English history through childhood friends, linking private relationships with larger politics. Ghosh's writing is inventive and up-to-the-minute; *The Calcutta Chromosome* (1996), is a dazzling mix of cyberfiction, science, and history. Ghosh is also a travel writer and anthropologist.

📖 Lawrence Norfolk, Angela Carter. *See* INDIA
RV

Gibbon, Lewis Grassic (British, 1901–35) Lewis Grassic Gibbon was the pseudonym of **Leslie Mitchell**, a key figure in modern Scots writing alongside his friend Hugh

MacDiarmid. He came from a crofting background, and was largely self-educated. His masterpiece was *A Scots Quair*, set in his home territory of Kincardineshire, first published as a trilogy of novels in 1946. It follows the life of a woman, Chris, from childhood on a bleak farm to bitter maturity in the 1930s, using Scots rhythms and vocabulary; the rich Lawrentian narrative captures the feelings of characters oppressed by local prejudice, religion, and the war. The opening volume, *Sunset Song* (1932), is the most lyrical, in which Chris escapes from her family into marriage. Politics becomes the increasing subject of the other novels, and by *Grey Granite* (1934) Chris and her son are divided by his involvement with the Communist Party. Mitchell also wrote novels under his own name, the best of which is *Spartacus* (1932), a drama of the slave revolt in Rome during 73–71 BC.

📖 D. H. Lawrence, Naomi Mitchison, James Kelman   *JS*

Gibbons, Stella (British, 1902–89) Stella Gibbons was born and educated in London and is best known for her novel *Cold Comfort Farm* (1932). It is a delicious parody of those novels of rural life that take themselves too seriously, and is best enjoyed by those tired of D. H. Lawrence, Mary Webb, and Thomas Hardy. The common-sense heroine of *Cold Comfort Farm* is Flora Poste, who visits her brooding, moody country cousins, the Starkadders. Their names—Seth, Ezra, Urk, Caraway, and Aunt Ada Doom—speak for themselves. The novel provides high comedy and memorable satire.

📖 Mary Webb (*Precious Bane*), Jane Austen (*Northanger Abbey*).
See HUMOUR   *SA*

Gibson, William (US, 1948–) Born in the United States, though he now lives in Vancouver, Gibson became the leading explorer of the conceptual possibilities of contemporary technology. His first novel, *Neuromancer* (1984), pre-empted a whole raft of computer and business innovations, and single-handedly coined the concept of 'cyberspace'—the virtual landscape of computer-aided experience and communication technologies. The novel introduces readers to the Matrix, a world within a world, a graphically represented network of all databases, a consensual hallucination experienced daily by billions of users including the protagonist, Case, a former hacker coerced into hacking for a conglomerate. Since this book, Gibson's writing has been preoccupied by the implications of technological and cultural trends. He regards the present as 'a set of overlapping science fiction scenarios' and science fiction as a necessary naturalism. In *Idoru* (1996), Gibson looks at the power of media organizations to control our cultural interests. In particular he explores the way celebrity has become solely dependent on management and spin-control to the point that the celebrities themselves need not actually exist.

📖 Bruce Sterling, Neal Stephenson, Rudy Rucker. *See* SCIENCE FICTION
RP

Gide, André (French, 1869–1951) Born in Paris, the son of a Sorbonne law professor who died when he was 11, Gide had an irregular and lonely upbringing before entering into the coterie surrounding Oscar Wilde. Beginning as an essayist, Gide had emerged by 1917 as a prophet for French youth, an object of endless debate and attack. His first novel, *Strait is the Gate* (*La*

Porte étroite; 1909), tells of two cousins, Alissa and Jérôme, growing up together and falling in love. Alissa begins to believe, however, that Jérôme's love for her is imperilling his soul and so, for his salvation, sets about suppressing everything that's beautiful in herself—in both her mind and body. As well as broad metaphor for all forms of forbidden love, the novel is a powerful exploration of the destructive force lying within spirituality. *The Immoralist* (1902) is a more explicit parallel of Gide's own rebellion against social and sexual conformity. In 1947 Gide was awarded the Nobel Prize for Literature.

📖 Oscar Wilde, Albert Camus   *RP*

Gilchrist, Ellen (US, 1935–) Ellen Gilchrist grew up in Mississippi. Her first book of short stories, *In the Land of Dreamy Dreams* (1981), introduces Rhoda Manning and Nora Jane Whittington, two of her favourite heroines, both of whom have fraught, ambivalent relationships with the legacy of southern womanhood. They grow up and continue to struggle in their different ways with family, sex, ambition, and adventure— Nora Jane, the zanier of the two, once robbed a bar in New Orleans dressed as a nun—in several other collections including *Victory over Japan* (1984, winner of the American Book Award for fiction). In one story in *The Age of Miracles* (1994), Rhoda's children kidnap her to prevent her from having a facelift at 60. *Net of Jewels* (1992), a novel, deals with her turbulent, rebellious teenage years. The racial and social tensions of the South are the backdrop for most of Gilchrist's work.

📖 Barbara Kingsolver, Eudora Welty, E. Annie Proulx. *See* SHORT STORIES

AT

Gilman, Charlotte Perkins (US, 1860–1935) Gilman was known in her lifetime for her feminism and journalism, but it is mainly through one short story that she is remembered. 'The Yellow Wallpaper' (1891) is about a woman who suffers postnatal depression. Her doctor recommends that she avoid all mental stimulation (no reading, writing, or conversation). Her husband enforces the doctor's regime, so she is confined in an old nursery papered in a yellow pattern. She begins to see a shadowy figure of a woman creeping behind the patterns of the wallpaper. 'The faint figure seemed to shake the pattern, just as if she wanted to get out.' In the end her husband finds her crawling around the floor, crying: 'I've got out at last. And I've pulled off most of the paper, so you can't put me back!' This haunting story depicts the powerlessness of married middle-class women in the nineteenth century more effectively than a library full of history books. Gilman's utopian novel *Herland* (1979) is set in a country where there are only women; where there is no war, no competition, no slavery, no poverty; and also, interestingly, no sexual pleasure, which is seen as a decadent result of women's economic dependence on men. In this, as in her other novels, the ideas are fascinating, but plot and character are weak. Look for extracts of this and her other work in *The Charlotte Perkins Gilman Reader*, ed. A. Lane (1981).

📖 Sara Maitland, Michèle Roberts

JR

Gissing, George (Robert) (British, 1857–1903) George Gissing was born in Wakefield, Yorkshire, and educated at Owen's College, Manchester. He was imprisoned for stealing money to assist a prostitute whom he later married. Then he travelled to America, living in extreme poverty. His early novels, such as *Workers in the Dawn* (1880), reflect his experience of living on the breadline. *New Grub Street* (1891) exposes the creeping materialism in the late-Victorian literary world, through a series of characters with differing literary aspirations. *The Odd Women* (1893) is a remarkable book for its time, concerned as it is with the plight of single women in society. Three sisters are left penniless by their father's death; the difficulty of remaining respectable, if one does not marry, are vividly evoked. Rhoda Nunn, the book's feminist heroine, starts a typing school so that single women can earn their own keep.

📖 Robert Tressell, Upton Sinclair, George Orwell   *SA*

Glaister, Lesley (British, 1956–)
Glaister often writes about women whose experience has pushed them outside conventional life, towards horrific destinations. Begin with *Trick or Treat* (1991), which deals with three sets of neighbours, most memorably the aged couple Olive (too fat now to go out) and her skinny partner Arthur, still together and still socialist after fifty years. Move on to *Digging to Australia* (1992), which describes a young girl growing up, and veers between the innocence of her naturist parents' home and the evil lurking in the unholy church she visits. *Partial Eclipse* (1994) takes the same character on to commit arson. In *Sheer Blue Bliss* (1999) a disturbed youth takes hostage the elderly painter Connie, to try to force her to give him a magical elixir created by her dead partner. Connie is a wonderfully vivid, eccentric, sharply drawn character. There is a thread of dark humour running through all these books.

📖 Anne Fine, Hilary Mantel, Deborah Moggach   *JR*

Glasgow, Ellen (US, 1873–1945)
Glasgow's popular family saga novels were informed by the history, mentality, and social codes of the deep South of the United States, where she was brought up. They reflect especially on women's roles, and challenge the Southern romantic tradition; some are in the vein of social realism, others are comedies of manners. *Barren Ground* (1925) features a strong woman, Dorinda Oakley, who returns to the run-down family farm and sets about restoring it in the face of many adversities. *Vein of Iron* (1935) follows the Fincastle family, Scotch-Irish settlers in Virginia's Great Valley, from the turn of the century to the stock market crash of 1929 and beyond. Perhaps her most appealing book is *The Sheltered Life* (1932), a witty satire set amongst the decaying Virginian gentry. Eva Birdsong, a declining beauty, is depressed by her inattentive husband's involvement with a naïve young girl and takes drastic action.

📖 Willa Cather, Robert Penn Warren   *JS*

Glendinning, Victoria (British, 1937–)
Best known as the writer of acclaimed literary biographies including *Vita: The Life of Vita Sackville-West* (1983) and *Anthony Trollope* (1992), Glendinning has also written two novels. Begin with *Electricity* (1995) set in the 1880s, narrated by a young woman who marries a 'prophet of the new science of electricity'. While he wires a country mansion for electricity, she forms a liaison with its master. Written

in a beautiful limpid style, this is rich with historical detail, and the male characters particularly are powerfully drawn.

📖 Rose Tremain, Hilary Mantel   *JR*

Goddard, Robert (British, 1954–) After training as a teacher, Goddard worked in local government before becoming a full-time writer. His first novel, *Past Caring* (1986), contained the elements that have since won him many admirers: an intricate plot, a flawed protagonist, and the evil of a past crime infecting the present. Martin Radford, a historian *manqué*, is staying with an old friend on Madeira, where he reads the journal of Edwin Strafford, a member of the Cabinet in Asquith's government. Radford finds himself caught up in the mystery of Strafford's sudden resignation and doomed love-affair with a member of the suffragette movement. *Into the Blue* (1990), a contemporary mystery set on Rhodes and about a woman's sudden disappearance, won a 'Thumping Good Read' award given by bookseller W. H. Smith.

📖 Wilkie Collins, Daphne du Maurier, Ruth Rendell (writing as Barbara Vine)   *NC*

Godden, (Margaret) Rumer (British, 1907–98) Godden was a prolific writer of both adult and children's fiction; many of her novels reflect her time in India. She received the OBE in 1993. Godden came to wider public attention with *Black Narcissus* (1939), which was successfully filmed. Sister Clodagh takes a party of nuns to the harsh foothills of the Himalayas at Mopu to set up a new convent. In this psychologically taut novel, the privations of the beautiful but bleak landscape seem to force the women to struggle with their forgotten

desires and pasts. In *This House of Brede* (1969) Godden returns to the theme of monastic life. The crises in the community throw up issues of leadership, envy, and loss for the ex-civil servant heroine. *The River* (1946) and *The Greengage Summer* (1958) examine the experiences of young girls on the cusp of womanhood, and the changes and loss that involves.

📖 R. K. Narayan, Olivia Manning   *TO*

Goethe, Johann Wolfgang von (German, 1749–1832). *See* CLASSICS

Gogol, Nikolai (Russian, 1809–52) Born at Sorochintsy in the Ukraine, Gogol worked as a civil servant and lecturer in St Petersburg before devoting himself to writing. His work's ethical seriousness, together with its stark realism and imaginative power, made a major contribution to the nineteenth-century renaissance in Russian literature. Begin with *Evenings on a Farm near Dikanka* (2 vols., 1831–32), a collection of stories reflecting his deep familiarity with Ukrainian folklore. Fluctuating between comic and horrific effects, the narratives bizarrely blend the everyday and the supernatural. Ukrainian settings are retained in *Mirograd* (1935), which consists of four stories, each parodying a conventional literary genre. They emphasize the decay of the old rural order in their focus on moral decline and treachery. *Arabesques* (1835) contains the stories set in St Petersburg which are the most striking of his shorter works. Pieces like 'Nevsky Prospect' evoke the sterile respectability and grotesque social pretensions of the bureaucrats among whom Gogol had worked. Originally planned in three parts, *Dead Souls* (1842), his savage comic masterpiece, satirizes corruption and self-deception. The plot centres on the mysterious Chichikov's bartering for possession of dead peasants with provincial landowners. They are happy to do business with him, as taxes are levied on their dead serfs until the next census officially recognizes their non-existence. Gogol completed a second part, in which he wished to suggest possibilities of moral regeneration, but destroyed it during the spiritual crisis preceding his death.

📖 Fyodor Dostoevsky, Ivan Turgenev. *See* RUSSIA   DH

Golden, Arthur (US, 1957–). *See* ROMANCE

Golding, William (British, 1911–93) Golding served in the Navy during the Second World War, then worked as a schoolmaster for some years. He won the Nobel Prize for Literature in 1983. His novels have very diverse settings, but are often moral dramas depicting mankind's capacity for good or evil. This is certainly true of *Lord of the Flies* (1954), still his most widely read work. When a group of schoolboys are stranded on an island following a plane crash, their civilized values give way to superstition and savagery, leading to murder, before they are rescued. *The Inheritors* (1955), a beautiful and underrated novel, is written from the viewpoint of a Neanderthal family coming into contact and conflict with 'the new men'; visions and co-operative living give way before the scheming, ruthless new arrivals. Golding's largest fictional enterprise was a three-volume narrative of an early nineteenth-century voyage to Australia, starting with the Booker Prize-winning *Rites of Passage* (1980). Cast as the onboard

journal of young Edmond Talbot, the atmosphere and mentality of the times, and intrigues between passengers and crew, are superbly evoked; the opening volume turns upon Talbot gradually finding out the reasons for the death of a drunken clergyman. *Close Quarters* (1987) continues the voyage, as Talbot deals with various conflicts, falls in love, then discovers that the ship is slowly sinking. By complete contrast, Golding's comic novel, *The Paper Men* (1984), finds a famous novelist doggedly pursued by an American academic around the world, with many observations on the nature of biography and reversals of fortune between them.

📖 John Fowles, Patrick White, Barry Unsworth. *See* CHILDHOOD, THE SEA   JS

Goncharov, Ivan (Russian, 1812–91). *See* RUSSIA

Gordimer, Nadine (South African, 1923–) Gordimer's first stories were published in 1949 and, since then, she has written over 200 short stories and eleven novels. In 1991 she was awarded the Nobel Prize for Literature. She is a shrewd and elegant commentator on racial injustice, consistently and intelligently opposing the apartheid regime.

One of her earlier novels, *A World of Strangers* (1958), follows the initiation of an English publisher, Toby Hood, into the politics of 1950s' South Africa. Hood is straddled between the segregated white and black worlds. He finds the black townships with their illegal alcohol and jazz music 'exotic' while unavoidably benefiting from the privileges of being white. *The Conservationist* (1974), which was co-winner of the Booker Prize in that year, is a powerful story about a wealthy white South African farmer who, as the novel progresses, sees power slip away from him as first a black body is discovered on his farm and finally a flood destroys his crops. Set in the near future, *July's People* (1981) is one of many novels written during the 1980s which speculated on the end of apartheid and what future that would bring for the white oppressors.

Gordimer has many volumes of short stories, but a good place to start is her *Selected Stories* (1975), a judicious selection from her first five volumes. The stories are set in South Africa and all of them through different literary devices confront the effects of apartheid on individual lives.

📖 Alan Paton, Doris Lessing, André Brink   *EW*

Gordon, Mary (US, 1949–) From her writer-father Gordon learned the value of ideas and ambitions, while her mother taught her how to remember jokes and dinner-table conversations. Both thoughtful and domestic, Gordon's honest, inventive novels examine the demands of desire versus duty, and the pain of family loyalties that divide and bind its members across the generations. Begin with *Final Payments* (1978), about the obediently Catholic but passionate Isabel, who has spent eleven years caring for her exacting father. Supported by two old schoolfriends, she becomes involved with two very different men. But before she steps into the future, she must make her final payments to her father's former housekeeper, the sinister yet needy Margaret. *Men and Angels* (1985) is about the chilling, unlovable Laura Post, who starts work as the perfect babysitter, with alarming results. *The*

Other Side (1989) is an absorbing saga of Irish immigrants and their American descendants.

📖 Antonia White, Liza Alther   *JN*

Gorky, Maxim (Russian, 1868–1936). *See* RUSSIA

Goto, Hiromi (Japanese/Canadian, 1966–). *See* CANADA

Goudge, Elizabeth (British, 1900–84) Elizabeth Goudge lived in Wells, Ely, and Oxford as a child, and became a full-time writer in 1938. She wrote ten children's books, which were among her best work. *The Little White Horse* (1947) is a tale about Maria Merryweather's adventures at Moonacre Manor. Like many children's novels written after the Second World War, it believes in the restorative power of faith, particularly that of a child's. She has also written fourteen novels for adults, the best of which fuse religion with ideas about myth and magic. See *Green Dolphin Country* (1944), set in the Channel Islands and New Zealand in the nineteenth century, and telling of the love of two sisters for one man; *The White Witch* (1960), which pitches the Roundheads against the Cavaliers, in a pro-Royalist love-story; and *A Child from the Sea* (1970), which portrays the life of Lucy Walter, the wronged wife of Charles II. In later years she turned to religious non-fiction, and wrote her autobiography, *The Joy of Snow*, in 1974.

📖 Daphne du Maurier, Norah Lofts, Phyllis Bentley   *SB*

Gowdy, Barbara (Canadian, 1950–). *See* CANADA

Gower, Iris (British, 1939–) *Destiny's Child* (1999; previously published as *Bride of the Thirteenth Summer*, 1975), is set during the Wars of the Roses. Little Margaret Beaufort, sent to the court of Henry VI under the guardianship of the Duke of Suffolk, is married against her will to Suffolk's son. When the Duke is accused of treason the King declares her marriage null and void. At 13, Margaret marries the King's son, Edmund, whom she loves. In a static tale, Margaret works her tapestries and talks to her women, while occasional news is brought of the important events happening elsewhere. *Sea Mistress* (1995), fifth in the *Cordwainers* series, set in nineteenth-century Wales, includes much more action. It tells how Bridie Merchant, devastated at discovering that her beloved husband has married her for her fortune, joins forces with the newly widowed Ellie Hopkins to defeat the plans of the evil men who are plotting against them.

📖 Norah Lofts, Josephine Cox   *FS*

Goytisolo, Juan (Spanish, 1931–) A deeply serious writer, Juan Goytisolo's opposition to the Franco regime meant that he lived for many years in political exile in Paris. Since Franco's death, Goytisolo has been recognized as one of the most important Spanish novelists of the century. *Marks of Identity* (1966) is the first of a trilogy of novels about a Spanish exile in Morocco whose bitter criticisms of his homeland centre on the figure of Julian, a legendary traitor said to have opened the country to Moorish invasion during the Middle Ages. *Count Julian* (1970) and *Juan the Landless* (1975) complete Goytisolo's trilogy. *Virtues of the Solitary Bird* (1993) is an intense and lyrical novel based on the visions of St Teresa of Avila, while *Landscapes After the Battle* (1983) is a fragmentary account of the writer's own exile.

📖 Mario Vargas Llosa, Guillermo Cabrera Infante, Gabriel García Márquez   *WB*

Grafton, Sue (US, 1940–) Sue Grafton is author of the alphabet series which began with *A is for Alibi* (1986), charting the adventures of female private investigator Kinsey Millhone. Kinsey is a sassy, diligent, and independent character with a wry wit and a keen eye. Her home town of Santa Teresa in California is a fictional re-creation of Santa Monica where Grafton lives. Kinsey's neighbour, retired baker Henry Pitts, and other characters feature throughout the series. In *C is for Corpse* (1987) Bobby Callahan claims he was run off the road and his friend killed. He has suffered terrible injuries and memory loss but believes he is still in danger. Kinsey takes the case and three days later Callahan is found dead. Kinsey is determined to find out the truth. In *K is for Killer* (1994) Kinsey is hired to investigate the unsolved homicide of Lorna Kepler but first has to learn as much as she can about Kepler's life.

📖 Sandra Scoppettone, Sara Paretsky. *See* CRIME   *CS*

Graham, Laurie (British, 1947–) Graham writes journalism and non-fiction as well as novels. Her novels are funny and direct, dealing with ordinary lives. Begin with *The Ten O'Clock Horses* (1996), which is set in 1962 and describes the life crisis of housepainter Ronnie, as he realizes that the swinging sixties are dawning all around him, and that his wife (and life) are boring. He imagines becoming a real painter, and learning languages; he embarks on an affair with a sophisticated married woman. Graham's economical prose, and revealingly accurate dialogue, touch lightly on subjects which also have tragic potential. *The Dress Circle* (1998) is narrated matter-of-factly by Ba, married for twenty-nine years to Bobs. They have grandchildren, and a racehorse, but Ba suddenly discovers that Bobs also has women's clothes and lingerie bills in his wardrobe.

📖 Richard Francis, Anne Tyler, Sue Townsend   JR

Graham, Winston (British, 1910–) Graham was born in Manchester, left school at the age of 16, and began writing in the 1930s. Begin with one of his eleven novels portraying the Poldark family in Cornwall in the late eighteenth and early nineteenth centuries. In the first, *Ross Poldark* (1945), the hero returns from fighting in the American Revolutionary War and meets the abused girl he later marries. *The Twisted Sword* (1990), the last of the series, finds Ross's son on the field at Waterloo, where leadership is thrust upon him. *Marnie* (1961), filmed by Alfred Hitchcock, is the story of a wealthy man who marries a kleptomaniac and cures her, but cannot overcome her sexual frigidity. Graham's other books include *Tremor* (1995), which opens in a luxury hotel in Algeria and focuses on the guests' reactions to an earthquake.

📖 Bernard Cornwell, E. V. Thompson, Desmond Bagley   DH

Grant-Adamson, Lesley (British, 1942–) Grant-Adamson's early novels featured Rain Morgan, a gossip columnist with a taste for detective work. Rain is a likeable character and the books in which she appears are very varied. *Patterns in the Dust* (1985), Grant-Adamson's enjoyable debut, was an early example of her ability to evoke setting—in this case, rural Somerset—while *Curse the Darkness* (1990) is notable for its portrayal of homelessness in contemporary London. More recently Grant-Adamson has abandoned Rain, preferring to experiment with diverse central characters, although the amoral Jim Rush features in two books. *Flynn* (1991) introduces a female private eye, while in *Wish You Were Here* (1996) and *Evil Acts* (1996) the emphasis is on psychological suspense, a branch of the genre at which Grant-Adamson excels.

📖 Sarah Dunant, Ruth Rendell   ME

Grass, Günter (German, 1927–) Born in Danzig, Grass has published poetry, plays, and essays, and has been a popular and controversial public figure in Germany throughout the post-war period. *The Tin Drum* (1959) is Grass's masterpiece, the story of the dwarf, Oskar, whose refusal to grow is a response to the guilt of Germany after the Second World War. A dark and disturbing political fantasy, the book is a parable about individual and collective responsibility that retains its power to unsettle the reader. *Dog Years* (1963) is an account of German history starting in 1917, told from three distinct viewpoints, while *Cat and Mouse* (1961) describes an 'oversized' man who struggles to conform and is finally cut down to size by his neighbours. Grass's later work has retained this interest in German history and politics, but often in a more playful and satirical style. *Diary of a Snail* (1974) is a mordantly funny book that combines a history of the Jewish population of Danzig with an account of Grass's own campaigning on behalf of the German politician Willy Brandt. While serious in intent, the novel's creation of Grass himself as a comic character, struggling against all odds to do the right thing, keeps the book's politics on a firmly human footing. *The Flounder* (1978), a fantasy about a man called before a feminist tribunal to answer for his actions, is also a richly inventive and joyous book about the sensuous pleasures of food and sex, and is one of Grass's most celebratory works. Grass received the Nobel Prize for Literature in 1999.

📖 Heinrich Böll, Albert Camus, Elias Canetti. *See* GERMANY, MAGIC REALISM　　*WB*

Graves, Robert (British, 1895–1985) Graves was a widely published poet, historian, mythographer, critic, and translator of ancient languages. Most of his novels draw on his engagement with pre-Christian and early Christian history. *I, Claudius* (1934) is set in first-century AD Rome and written as an autobiographical memoir of the emperor Claudius. Physically weak and afflicted with stammering, Claudius is an embarrassment to his family and is shunted to the background of imperial affairs. He becomes a scholar and historian, and his apparent ineffectuality spares him the worst cruelties inflicted by the imperial family upon its own members during the reigns of Augustus, Tiberius, and Caligula. The first-person narration gives the reader a strong sense of witnessing, with Claudius, the endless greed and lust of the imperial family. The story ends with Claudius ascending to the imperial throne. *Claudius the God* (1934) covers Claudius' years as emperor, including his marriage to the treacherous Messalina. Graves's characterizations of real

historical figures offer the reader a vivid viewpoint on complex historical events. The two books have been adapted for both television and film. *King Jesus* (1946) is a fictional interpretation of the life of Jesus Christ, based on Graves's understanding of the history, politics, and beliefs of the time. *Count Belisarius* (1938) spans the period between the Roman Empire and the rise of Christianity. It centres on the power struggle between the Emperor Justinian and a commander of the Roman armies.

📖 Mary Renault, Allan Massie, Olivia Manning. *See* HISTORICAL　*DJ*

Gray, Alasdair (British, 1934–　) Gray has lived and worked in Glasgow, his complementary careers as an artist and a writer producing flamboyant-looking books. Visual imagination and authorial playfulness characterize his work, expressed through his own illustrations, mock reviews and blurbs, and unorthodox typography. Gray's stories and novels deal with politics, fantasy, Scottish social history, and polemic, while being great fun to read. Start with *Unlikely Stories, Mostly* (1984), a handsome collection of stories, some fantastical and humorous, others panoramic; 'Five Letters from an Eastern Empire' is a wonderful evocation of imperial China, an allegory of power and its human consequences. *Lanark: A Life in Four Books* (1981) is Gray's largest novel, interweaving the grim boyhood of Duncan Thaw in post-war Glasgow with his afterlife as Lanark in the fantasy city of Unthank. The narratives are further complicated by an 'index of diffuse and imbedded plagiarisms', in which the author comments on his sources and borrowings from world literature, a device that Gray uses in other novels. *1982, Janine* (1984) is a political satire, narrated by a security consultant drunkenly holed up in a hotel room. Both *Poor Things* (1992) and *A History Maker* (1994) are fantasy novels presented as discovered manuscripts, set respectively in the nineteenth and twenty-third centuries. *Poor Things* tells the Frankenstein-like tale of Godwin Baxter and his creation Bella, while the latter book, a kilted science fiction yarn, concerns border warfare and matriarchy versus militarism.

📖 Flann O'Brien, James Kelman, Salmon Rushdie, Will Self   *JS*

Green, Henry (British, 1905–73) Henry Green was rather deaf, and conversations often seemed rather surreal to him as he half-heard much of what people said. This delighted him, and he uses a similar effect in his writing. Things do not quite connect; his dialogue is full of near-misses as people misunderstand, mishear, or simply do not listen. Many of his novels are satires and they are full of small gaps in logic or sequence which the reader has to fill. Green is a master at telling stories in which nothing seems to happen, yet one is constantly intrigued and entertained. Start with *Party Going* (1939), set in a railway station in which a group of young people never quite sets off on a journey. This contains some of Green's finest comic writing. *Blindness* (1926) is an unsentimental story about a boy who is blinded and turns to writing. *Doting* (1952) is told almost entirely in dialogue and is a masterly and slightly nasty social comedy.

📖 Elizabeth Bowen, Ford Madox Ford, Evelyn Waugh. *See* SOCIAL ISSUES   *TT*

Green, Jane (British). *See* GLAMOUR

Greene, Graham (British, 1904–91) As a young man of 19 Greene took a revolver onto Berkhamsted Common and played Russian roulette, in order, he professed, to escape boredom. It was this same impulse, perhaps, that led him to scour the world restlessly in search of excitement and danger, and which provided material for over thirty novels and travel books.

He was educated at Berkhamsted School (where his father was headmaster) and Balliol College, Oxford. Soon after, he converted to Catholicism, and questions of faith and the dilemmas of personal morality came to play a central role in his writing. He himself stated that his theme was perfect evil walking the world where perfect good can never walk again—an apt summary of *Brighton Rock* (1938), set amongst the razor-slashing racetrack gangs of pre-war Brighton. Teenage gangster Pinkie Brown is like a cornered rat, unpredictable and extremely dangerous. A devout believer in hellfire and eternal damnation, he corrupts everything he touches; everything except Rose, the innocent young waitress whose purity of love for him is like an insult to Pinkie, and ultimately the cause of his downfall. The novel is stamped through like a stick of Brighton rock with what makes Greene such a distinctive and powerful writer, in particular its sleazy atmosphere of brooding menace.

Both *Brighton Rock* and *The Ministry of Fear* (1943) are examples of what Greene defensively called his 'entertainments' (as opposed to his more serious novels: he later dropped this label when it became recognized that his thrillers and murder stories were among his best work). *The Ministry of Fear* is set in the blitz and the black-out, and we follow Arthur Rowe, one of life's bystanders, as he is drawn slowly yet inexorably into a murky half-world where sinister organizations pursue their mysterious, murderous ends. The story, while realistically told, has the texture of a waking nightmare. The monstrous Mrs Bellairs, who conducts seances, is a chilling creation. *A Gun for Sale* (1936) is a revenge thriller about a hired killer, Raven, an embittered outcast of society in whose dark soul a young woman kindles alien sparks of decency, honour, even tenderness.

The term 'Greeneland' was coined by critics to describe both the physical and metaphorical terrain of his books. His view of human nature is bitter and sardonic, as of someone turning over a stone and poking at the life squirming beneath with fascinated disgust. Several of what he regarded as his serious novels are set in the heat and squalor of tropical locations: Vietnam in *The Quiet American* (1955), which relates how Pyle—the naïve young American of the title—with righteous zeal and the very best of intentions, blunders in and causes the deaths of innocent people. *The End of the Affair* (1951) is one of Greene's most personal novels. Told in the first person by a middle-aged writer, Bendrix, this is a brutally honest account of his affair with a married woman in London during the war, with a plot that turns grippingly on the terrible price of jealous revenge and a 'deal' made with God.

Greene achieved the rare distinction of being critically lauded, engaging important themes, and being also extremely popular. Many of his novels and short stories have been filmed, and he wrote original screenplays, notably *The Third Man* (1950), later published as a novella.

📖 Piers Paul Read, V. S. Naipaul, Patrick Hamilton, Brian Moore.
See ADVENTURE, SPY   TH

Greenwood, Walter (British, 1903–74)

Walter Greenwood was born in Salford, Lancashire, and experienced at first hand much of the hardship described in his most famous work, *Love on the Dole* (1933). This social documentary novel tells the story of the young members of the Hardcastle family, whose hopes and aspirations are destroyed by unemployment and poverty. It is one of the most vivid and moving fictional representations of the 1930s Depression in Great Britain. Greenwood himself co-adapted the novel into a play, and it was subsequently filmed in 1941. His next novel, *His Worship the Mayor* (1934), looks at corruption in local government. Greenwood spawned a generation of novelists who developed social deprivation as a theme.

📖 John Braine, Alan Sillitoe, Barry Hines   SA

Grey, (Pearl) Zane (US, 1872–1939)

Born in Zanesville, Ohio, a town named after his great-great-grandfather, Zane Grey won a basketball scholarship and qualified as a dentist, earning extra income by writing fiction for boys before becoming one of the most prolific and successful writers of Western novels of his time. His marriage to Lina Elise Roth in 1905 was a turning-point, since his wife funded his first trip to the West where he gathered material for his first fully fledged Western novel, *The Heritage of the Desert* (1910). She is also known to have corrected Grey's manuscripts and acted as his financial manager throughout his career. Grey published over seventy-seven titles, and among these *Riders of the Purple Sage* (1912) remains his single best-known work. *The U.P. Trail* (1918) and *The Vanishing American* (1925) also show

Grey's Arizona-set Western formula at its best.

📖 Larry McMurtry, Stephen Crane.
See WESTERN   WB

Griffin, W(illiam) E(dmund) B(utterworth) (US, 1929–) Griffin

was born in Newark, New Jersey, and writes war fiction based on modern American military history. Begin with *Semper Fi* (1986). The first of four parts of *The Corps*, an account of the US Marine Corps in the Second World War, it deals with mobilization following the shock of Pearl Harbor. *The Aviators* (1988) centres on the US Army Air Corps in the Vietnam War. New modes of combat must be learned to contend with an enemy unlike any in US military experience. In *Honor Bound* (1993) the Office of Strategic Services is on a mission to sabotage the refuelling of Nazi U-boats by South American sympathizers. Among the thrillers Griffin has also published is *The Assassin* (1993); Philadelphia provides the background to the story of a leading politician under threat from a contract-killer.

📖 Norman Mailer, James Jones, Ken Follett   DH

Grisham, John (US, 1955–) Grisham

studied law in Mississippi and practised as a lawyer for nine years; his phenomenally popular fiction owes a good deal to his legal knowledge. *The Rainmaker* (1995) is as good a place to start as any. The young, wet-behind-the-ears lawyer takes on the might of corporate America and, with the help of a seedy ambulance chaser, and a somewhat biased judge, wins the day. Grisham regularly fulfils the American need to believe that the small man can succeed

against the establishment. The lawyer isn't always a young male; *The Client* (1993) features a 50-year-old divorcee, recovering alcoholic Reggie Love. *The Firm* (1991) and *The Pelican Brief* (1992) both deal with central characters who are at risk because they have uncovered legal or political corruption. Read Grisham for the intricate plots, which cleverly draw on his legal knowledge, for example, jury vetting procedure in *The Runaway Jury* (1996). If you need something which will keep you hooked, Grisham always delivers the goods.

📖 Scott Turow, Tom Clancy   RV

Grossman, David (Israeli, 1954–)

Grossman's novels deal with the complicated social issues surrounding Israel's historical and political development. His work has been translated from Hebrew into sixteen different languages, and he is best-known for *See Under: Love* (1989), the unsettling account of a young Israeli boy whose great-uncle's moving stories stop him blocking out his parents' experiences of the Holocaust, and bring him closer to understanding both their suffering and the empowering strength of their love. Move on to *The Book of Intimate Grammar* (1991), where political tension impinges into the world of 12-year-old Ahron, who, as the Six Day War approaches and his friends turn towards Zionism, attempts to retreat from the violence of the adult world. *Sleeping on a Wire* (1992), a sensitive non-fiction account of the difficulties faced by Palestinians in Israel, is also recommended.

📖 Amos Oz, Primo Levi   SR

Grossman, Vassily (Soviet, 1905–64).
See RUSSIA

Grossmith, George (British, 1847–1912) and **Weedon** (British, 1854–1919) Both brothers were born in London, and eventually found their way onto the stage. George worked initially as a journalist, then later performed in many Gilbert and Sullivan operas; Weedon began his career as a painter, then joined a touring theatre company. *The Diary of a Nobody* (1892) was a collaboration, first appearing as a serial in *Punch* magazine. It concerns the affairs of Mr Charles Pooter and his wife, members of the genteel Victorian London lower-middle class, and tells in diary form of their mishaps and trials. It is tremendously funny, and its appeal has not diminished over the years. It was illustrated by Weedon, with excellent contemporary detail.

📖 Sue Townsend, Helen Fielding, Nigel Williams. *See* HUMOUR   *SA*

Gunesekera, Romesh (Sri Lankan, 1954–) Arriving in England in 1972, Gunesekera started publishing poetry and prose in newspapers and magazines. His lyrical debut, *Monkfish Moon* (1992), contained short stories handling the troubled lives of Sri Lankans amidst the political turmoil of their divided island paradise, or else surviving as exiles in London. His first novel, *Reef* (1994), was nominated for the Booker Prize (1994). Striking for its poetic prose and linguistic command, *Reef* is a historically charged and metaphorically radiant tale; especially in the use of the reef itself. Triton, a cook, narrates in single flashback a period from his life when he was a servant in Sri Lanka for Mr Salgado, a marine biologist working on an imperilled reef. The mutual dependency of master and servant, the colonial charade played out at Christmas, and the love they both bear towards Miss Nili before harmony is fractured by ethnic politics, are all story-lines superbly under Gunesekera's control.

📖 V. S. Naipaul, Salman Rushdie   *AM*

Gurnah, Abdulrazak (Tanzanian, 1948–) Gurnah was born in Zanzibar, which provides the setting for several of his novels, and he currently teaches literature at the University of Kent. Begin with *Paradise* (1994, Booker Prize-shortlisted) set in the Islamic world of early twentieth-century East Africa. It chronicles the rites of passage of the boy Yusif, sold by his father into the service of his rich, perfumed merchant uncle. Yusif's experiences range from a trading expedition into the African interior, to finding love in a paradisical garden. Gurnah draws on myth and traditional Arabian Nights story-telling, but never at the expense of Yusif's vividly real responses to his experience. *Admiring Silence* (1996), set in the present, describes a man's escape from his native Zanzibar to a new life in England, and his subsequent return home.

📖 Naguib Mahfouz, Tayeb Salih, Joseph Conrad (*Heart of Darkness*)   *JR*

Guterson, David (US, 1956–) Guterson wrote journalism and taught English on an island in Puget Sound off the north-west coast of America, before enjoying success in his late thirties with his first novel, *Snow Falling on Cedars* (1995). Set in Puget Sound in the 1950s, the novel tells the story of the trial of Kabuo Miyamoto, a Japanese-American accused of murdering a fellow fisherman. As the trial proceeds during the course of a snow-bound winter, a local newspaperman,

Ishmael Chambers, is torn between his embitterment at losing his childhood sweetheart to Kabuo and his belief that Kabuo is an innocent victim of prejudice. The novel is lyrical, atmospheric, and compellingly plotted. Guterson followed it with *East of the Mountains* (1999), similarly lyrical but with a more picaresque story, about a retired surgeon embarking on a final expedition to the mountains of Washington State.

📖 E. Annie Proulx, Cormac McCarthy   *NC*

Guy, Rosa (US, 1928–) Born in Trinidad, Guy grew up in Harlem, New York, and left school at 14 to work in a factory. The racism she encountered politicized her, and she later helped to found the Harlem Writers' Guild, to help black writers develop their skills. Her novels often centre on themes of racism and cruelty shown to outsiders. Her writing is direct and vivid. She is best known for her books for teenagers; begin with *The Friends* (1973), in which a new girl is bullied at school in the Harlem ghetto, but is reluctant to make friends with the girl who helps her. *And I Heard a Bird Sing* (1987) tells the story of a grocery delivery boy whose precarious life with his ex-alcoholic mother is disrupted when he is suspected of murder. *My Love My Love* or *The Peasant Girl* (1985) is a love-story, based on Hans Anderson's 'The Little Mermaid' and set on a beautiful Caribbean island.

📖 Alice Walker, Betty Smith, Joan Riley   *JR*

H

Haggard, Henry Rider (British, 1856–1925) Haggard's adventure romances are set in Iceland, Mexico, and Constantinople, but his best-known depict bellicose Victorians travelling to the heart of Africa, defeating evil witch doctors and 'heathen' sorcery. Christianity and scientific progress inevitably triumph. In *King Solomon's Mines* (1886) British men take an expedition to Africa where they initiate themselves into manhood by dabbling in traditional society, finally returning with 'native' treasure. Two years later Haggard wrote a Gothic romance, *She* (1887), considered his best work. Again, a group of male explorers set off to discover a remote African country, where a white queen presides over a lost empire. She, a mythical figure, simultaneously repulsive and seductive, falls in love with the central character. *She* is seen by many as an expression of Victorian anxieties about religious cynicism and the decline of imperial domination.

📖 Rudyard Kipling, Wilbur Smith.
See ADVENTURE   *EW*

Hailey, Arthur (Canadian, 1920–) Arthur Hailey was born in Luton, England, and served with the RAF before turning to fiction. His best-known book is *Airport* (1968), a tense story about a routine flight beset by bad weather and the threat of a terrorist bombing (later filmed to enormous popular success). *Hotel* (1965) is the story of the romantic and business entanglements of staff and residents at a luxurious California hotel, *The Moneychangers* (1975) deals with high finance, and *Overload* (1979) describes a threatened electricity shortage. *Detective* (1997) is set in a Miami homicide division. Hailey's formula of meticulous research and subjecting a disparate group of characters to high drama has been much copied, and remains hugely popular.

📖 Mario Puzo, Michael Crichton
     WB

Hall, Radclyffe (British, 1880–1943) Almost everything else Radclyffe Hall did is subsumed by the fact that she was the author of the first lesbian novel, *The Well of Loneliness*. Hall did write other novels, such as *The Unlit Lamp* (1924) and *Adam's Breed* (1926), and poetry, all of which were well received when first published. However, *The Well of Loneliness* was suppressed for obscenity when it was published in 1928 and has been famous ever since. The novel tells the story of Stephen Gordon, a woman who comes to terms with her sexual identity, eventually living the life of an English gentleman abroad. Although mild and restrained for us at the beginning of the twentieth-first century, it is a tender and touching portrait of suppressed love and emerging creativity.

📖 Djuna Barnes, Virginia Woolf, Gertrude Stein. *See* SEXUAL POLITICS
     LM

Halliday, Michael. *See* **Creasey, John**

Hamilton, Patrick (British, 1904–62) Fame came early to Hamilton, with the success of his stage play *Rope*, later filmed by Hitchcock. His real and lasting achievements, however, are his novels, which are wonderfully comic, sad, touching, and very readable. *Hangover Square* (1941) is his masterpiece. Set in the squalid bedsitland of Earls Court prior to the outbreak of war, it charts the hero's vain infatuation with beautiful Netta—one of the most excoriating portraits in modern fiction of a heartless bitch. His three novels *The Midnight Bell* (1929), *The Siege of Pleasure* (1932) and *The Plains of Cement* (1934), collectively known as *Twenty Thousand Streets under the Sky*, are about small, desperate lives lived out in gloomy pub parlours and seedy boarding-houses. At his creative peak, aged 28, Hamilton was badly injured when a car ran him down; this turned him into a moody depressive and self-destructive drinker. His later work duly suffered, though *The Slaves of Solitude* (1947), an achingly sad portrait of a lonely spinster in a wartime boarding-house, is Hamilton back at his best.

📖 Christopher Isherwood, Kingsley Amis, Paul Theroux, Brian Moore

TH

Hammett, Dashiell (US, 1894–1961) Hammett was a tough left-wing radical who left school at 13 for a string of unremarkable jobs that led to eight years as an operative for the Pinkerton detective agency, a career move that provided him with unrivalled knowledge of criminal investigation. Hammett, like Chandler, began writing pulp magazine stories, but his greatest achievement is his five novels. Stylistically, Hammett brought a dramatic starkness to the detective story, concentrating on telling his story and delineating his characters with telling detail rather than extravagant description. Begin with *Red Harvest* (1929), a blood-soaked narrative of rival gangs, crooked cops, and a detective who cleans up the town. Continue with the much-filmed *The Maltese Falcon* (1930), a intricate story of greed and double-cross, *The Glass Key* (1931), a novel as much about the complex demands of friendship as about crime, and *The Thin Man* (1934), a sparkling and charming read.

📖 Raymond Chandler, James M. Cain, Chester Himes. *See* CRIME   *VM*

Hammick, Georgina (British, 1939–) Hammick published a collection of poems in 1976, but her first major success was with her debut short story collection, *People for Lunch* (1987), which quickly became a best-seller. Disappointment, motherhood, family tension, injustice, and deception are major themes here, which continue into her next collection, *Spoilt* (1992), and are also resonant in her novel, *The Arizona Game* (1996), whose narrator, Hannah, looks back at a childhood fractured by the death of her younger brother, and tries to come to terms with the dysfunctional relationships of her adult life. Hammick's interest is in the messy chaos and secret unhappinesses of everyday life, but her tone is light and often witty, and her analyses of character are even-handed and exceptionally acute.

📖 Elizabeth Bowen, Jane Austen, Kazuo Ishiguro   *SR*

Hamsun, Knut (Norwegian, 1859–1952) For his seventieth birthday Hamsun received written tributes from, amongst many others, Thomas Mann, Maxim Gorky, André Gide, Arnold Schoenberg, and Albert Einstein. Writers as diverse as James Joyce, Ernest Hemingway, and Isaac Bashevis Singer have cited his work as hugely influential on their own. Yet Hamsun is comparatively unfamiliar to modern readers. The son of an impoverished farmer in northern Norway, he was sent away from home at the age of 9 to work for his uncle, in order to pay off a family debt. He published his first work at the age of 18, but it was not until twelve years later that he achieved critical recognition with his novel *Hunger* (1890), drawing on his own experience in this portrayal of an impoverished, starving writer's increasingly hallucinatory struggle to survive. In *Mysteries* (1892) Nagel, a stranger arriving in a north Norway town, mystifies himself and the local inhabitants, constantly reinventing himself in the stories he tells. In these novels, Hamsun broke radically with the narrative conventions of his time, putting consciousness itself at the centre of his work, with all its contradictions and inconsistencies, and using techniques of stream of consciousness and free association to explore the inner world of his heroes. *Pan* (1894), a dreamlike meditation on unconsummated love, and *Victoria* (1898), in which circumstances keep two lovers apart, gave him popular as well as critical success. These four remain the most widely known, and some would say the best, of his novels. In later works he drew closer to the tradition of the great European novel, without losing his emphasis on the subjective experience. *Under the Autumn Star* (1906) and *On Muted Strings* (1909; also published together as *The Wanderer*), and the *August* trilogy (of which only the first, *Wayfarers*, 1927, is currently available in English translation) stand out. In *Woman at the Pump* (1920)

he returned again to the more fragmented, shifting style, in a story of a crippled outcast. Increasingly, Hamsun became critical of the progressive urban development of the twentieth century, finding a deeper spiritual truth in man's relationship with nature, and in working the land; *The Growth of the Soil* (1917) expressed this view at its most deeply felt, and became a major success in Germany. It was Hamsun's public support for Hitler during the Second World War that fatally damaged his reputation. Though it is generally accepted that this support stemmed from the romantic, patriotic idealism of an old man rather than a true understanding of the destructive force of Nazi fascism, the stigma has remained with him. He was awarded the Nobel Prize for Literature in 1920.

📖 James Joyce, Ernest Hemingway, Thomas Mann, Isaac Bashevis Singer Fyodor Dostoevsky   *KB*

Hanley, James (Irish, 1901–85) Hanley was a neglected genius during his lifetime, and, shamefully, he remains so today. He wrote about the sea, about the lives of common sailors, and how their characters are shaped under the stress of elemental forces. He was born in Dublin, grew up in Liverpool, and ran away to sea when he was 13. His early novels, *Drift* (1930) and *Boy* (1931), deal so harshly and uncompromisingly with what he endured that *Boy* was prosecuted for obscene libel. Hanley went on to write forty-eight full-length works, including *The Closed Harbour* (1952) and *The Furys* (1935), a five-volume saga about a Catholic family in Liverpool during the General Strike. He also wrote some superb short stories, collected in *The Last Voyage* (1997). Hanley is not an easy read, but exceptionally rewarding. His stature is on a par with William Faulkner, an admirer of his work.

📖 Malcolm Lowry, B. Traven, William Faulkner   *TH*

Han Suyin (Chinese/naturalized British, 1917–   ) Han Suyin was born in China, to a Belgian mother and Chinese father. She qualified as a doctor in London, and, while living in Hong Kong, wrote the auto-biographical love-story which made her famous, *A Many-Splendoured Thing* (1952, filmed in 1955). The very different worlds of capitalist, cosmopolitan Hong Kong and newly revolutionary China are contrasted in this story of love across racial barriers. Han Suyin's novels, especially *The Moun-tain is Young* (1958) and *Winter Love* (1962) are highly regarded by feminists, the latter being about a lesbian affair in London in the 1940s. She is adventurous with her writing style, notably in *Cast But One Shadow* (1962). She has also written autobiography and a history of modern China, and has been regarded with suspicion by some, who see her as an apologist for Mao's regime.

📖 Jung Chang (*Wild Swans*), Timothy Mo   *FS*

Hardy, Thomas (British, 1840–1928) Most of Hardy's novels and stories are set in Wessex, a fictional county largely based upon Dorset where he was born. His descriptions of the landscape are detailed and vivid. These, and his dramatic plots, have inspired repeated screen adaptations of his novels. Many of Hardy's characters are driven by inner passions they cannot control, often leading them into unhappy fates.

Start with *Far From the Madding Crowd* (1874), where Bathsheba Everdene inherits a farm and must choose between three suitors. She rejects the selfless, devoted love of her shepherd, Gabriel Oak, for the dashing and unscrupulous Sergeant Troy, whom she marries. After Troy deserts her Bathsheba is relentlessly pursued by a neigh-bouring farmer, Boldwood. When Troy returns Boldwood shoots him and is pro-nounced insane. Only after these tragic events does Bathsheba recognize the value in Gabriel's steady devotion, and they marry. There are strong elements of humour and affection in the characterizations of rustic, uneducated people in Hardy's novels. The tragedy of unrequited love is power-fully drawn in *The Woodlanders* (1887). Set in Little Hintock, deep in the woods of Dorset, the novel vividly captures the rhythm of life and work for those who depend upon the land for their existence. Giles Winterbourne's heart is broken when his betrothed rejects him for a more wealthy suitor. Marty South, a village girl, is quietly devoted to Giles, and after he dies, spends her days tending his grave. There is a deeply moving section where the selfless Marty cuts off and sells her beautiful hair to enable herself and her father to live.

In *The Mayor of Casterbridge* (1886) Michael Henchard sells his wife and child at a fair for five guineas when he is drunk. Henchard solemnly vows never to touch alcohol again and as a result becomes pro-sperous, respected, and eventually Mayor of Casterbridge (Dorchester). While his remorse is clearly genuine, he loses every-thing when his wife returns eighteen years later. He dies alone in poverty and desola-tion. *The Return of the Native* (1887) is set on the haunting and vividly described Egdon Heath. Beautiful Eustacia Vye is desperate to leave the Heath, and sees her escape in

Clym Yeobright who has returned after training as a diamond merchant in Paris. Their marriage ends in tragedy because Clym wishes to stay on the Heath. Here, the brooding forces of nature symbolize those irrational forces that drive human beings. In *Tess of the D'Urbervilles* (1891), the genuinely innocent young Tess's marriage is wrecked through exploitation and by events over which she has no power. This novel, and the even darker *Jude the Obscure* (1896), were widely criticized for their pessimism, so much so that Hardy gave up novel writing to concentrate on his poetry.

📖 Emily Brontë, D. H. Lawrence, Tim Pears. *See* FILM, ROMANTIC, SOCIAL ISSUES   *DJ*

Hariharan, Githa (Indian, 1954–). *See* INDIA

Harris, Robert (British, 1957–) Harris was a television reporter for the BBC and a political journalist with the *Observer* and *Sunday Times* before his transformation into best-selling author. Taking a rather hackneyed plot (an alternative world history in which Hitler won the war), Harris turned it into a tense thriller, *Fatherland* (1992), which works because he employs his journalistic skills to create a plausible Nazi Berlin of 1964. Although *Enigma* (1995) is a more conventional espionage story about a brilliant young codebreaker at Bletchley Park (a real wartime location) trying to crack the German Enigma code, it gains from having more rounded characters and a touching love-story. *Archangel* (1998) deals with a historian's dangerous search for Stalin's hidden diaries.

📖 John Buchan, Eric Ambler, John le Carré. *See* SPY   *TH*

Harris, Thomas (US, 1940–). *See* THRILLERS

Harris, Wilson (Guyanese/British, 1921–) Wilson Harris and George Lamming vie for the title of most significant West Indian novelist; and Harris is the more innovative. He counsels against the 'narrative realist fallacy', and without himself being a magic realist, ignores the boundaries between genres. His first novel, *Palace of the Peacock* (1960), presents us with a crew making the journey up-river in the Guyanese heartland. The hallucinatory quality of the writing causes us to question what we're witnessing: has the journey already taken place? (For the crew are known to have died.) Or is this a fable to be enacted? Some characters have names, but the figures are mythic. The two women present (who have suffered/suffer violence) metamorphose into something either reassuring or prophetic. Harris's short novels (over twenty to date) demand the reader's concentration. Where to start? The first four, brought together by Faber as *The Guyana Quartet* (1985), flesh out, with recognizable characters and settings, Wilson Harris's unique poetic vision.

📖 Jorge Luis Borges, Italo Calvino, Pauline Melville. *See* CARIBBEAN
                                                        EM

Harrison, Harry (US, 1925–) Harrison was born in Stamford, Connecticut, and worked as an illustrator before emerging as a science fiction author in the 1950s. Begin with *Bill, the Galactic Hero* (1965), which inventively parodies the conventions of much science fiction. A series of novels continues the adventures of the unprepossessing Bill. 'Slippery Jim di Griz' is Harrison's anti-hero in *The Stainless*

Steel Rat's Revenge (1970) and numerous other stories. In this title, di Griz and his Amazon warriors take on a rebel planet. *Wheelworld* (1981), part of the *To the Stars* series about space exploration, is set on a remote planet where daylight lasts for four years and primitive tribes engage in ruthless conflict. *West of Eden* (1984) opens a trilogy of stories in an alternative world where humans and highly evolved saurians battle for survival.

📖 Larry Niven, Douglas Adams, Bob Shaw   *DH*

Harrison, Jim (US, 1937–) Born in Michigan, Harrison contrasts the serenity of the American landscape and natural world with the squalid antagonism of human relations. His fiction typically depicts a post-Vietnam America of drugs, guns, bluecollar bars, and potential violence. His style is, however, poetic and richly allusive; masculine concerns are sometimes viewed satirically. *A Good Day to Die* (1973), his second novel, takes shape as its narrator meets a speed-crazed Vietnam veteran in a bar and takes off across country to blow up a dam at the Grand Canyon as an ecological protest. The two men share a woman, and the book expertly charts the sexual tensions between them, leading to a despairing finale. Harrison is best known for his collections of three novellas: *Legends of the Fall* (1979), has a title story which evolves over fifty years in the life of William Ludlow, from his sons joining the Canadian army to battles with bootleggers. *The Woman Lit by Fireflies* (1990) shows a greater range, and even humour: in 'Sunset Limited' a group of former radicals return to spring a friend from jail.

📖 Richard Ford, William Faulkner, Ken Kesey   *JS*

Hartley, L(eslie) P(oles) (British, 1895–1972) Born in Cambridgeshire, educated at Harrow and Oxford, Hartley served in the First World War, after which he became a critic and writer, publishing short stories and a novella besides his novels. Begin with the trilogy, *The Shrimp and the Anemone* (1944), *The Sixth Heaven* (1946), and the title volume, *Eustace and Hilda* (1947), for which Hartley was awarded the James Tait Black Memorial Prize. These sensitively written novels chart the complicated relationship of the central character, Eustace, and his sister, Hilda, moving through the intensities of his childhood in Norfolk, undergraduate years at Oxford, and life on the Continent. Go on to read Hartley's highly acclaimed *The Go-Between* (1953). It is narrated by Leo who, in his sixties, discovers his boyhood diary of 1900, revealing how he was the innocent 'go-between' at his friend's Norfolk country house, carrying letters between his friend's sister and her lover, a farmer. A compelling story unfolds of a boy's sexual awareness, and how he is affected by what he learns during that hot summer, which changes his life, destroying his beliefs and hopes. Imbued with the atmosphere of Edwardian England and an undercurrent of class tensions, it captures a vanished age. 'The past is a foreign country: they do things differently there'—is the famous opening of this classic. Then read *The Hireling* (1957), in lighter vein but again concerning class taboos, the relationship of Lady Franklin and her chauffeur.

📖 Henry James, E. M. Forster, D. H. Lawrence   *GC*

Harvey, Jack. *See* **Rankin, Ian**

Harvey, John (British, 1938–   ) Poet, scriptwriter, and novelist John Harvey learned his craft writing pulp Westerns and young adult novels, but finally found the perfect vehicle for his talents with the ten detective novels featuring scruffy, jazz-loving, sandwich-munching Detective Inspector Charlie Resnick and his team. Set against the beautifully realized background of Nottingham, the series explores Britain in the 1990s with ruthless honesty and sensitive observation. Harvey's great strength lies in his ability to create a vivid and credible cast of characters, many of whom reappear in some or all of the books. For that reason, the books should be read in order. Begin with *Lonely Hearts* (1989) in which a series of attacks on women are linked by newspaper adverts. Other high points in the series are *Off Minor* (1992) which deals with child murder, *Wasted Years* (1993), where a series of armed robberies brings bad memories for Resnick, and *Easy Meat* (1996), which addresses male rape.

📖 Reginald Hill, Ian Rankin, Michael Dibdin. *See* CRIME   VM

Harvey, W. F. (British, 1885–1937). *See* SUPERNATURAL

Hašek, Jaroslav (Czech, 1883–1923) Born in Prague, Hašek gained a reputation as a satirist before being conscripted into the Austrian army in 1915. Captured by the Russians, he produced propaganda for the cause of Czechoslovakian independence from Austria. His sprawling comic masterpiece and only novel, *The Good Soldier Švejk* (four vols., 1921–3) draws on his wartime experiences in relentlessly satirizing the absurdities he saw in army life. Švejk hides his shrewdness beneath

an appearance of stupidity to avoid the dangers and personal inconveniences of military service. The anti-authoritarian attitude that enables him to survive the war represents the spirit of Czech resistance to Austrian rule. Collections of Hašek's stories include *The Red Commissar* (1981) and *Little Stories by a Great Master* (1984), which further illustrate the keenness of his sense of the absurd in their treatments of bureaucratic improbabilities and political deviousness.

📖 Joseph Heller, Eric Linklater, Franz Kafka. *See* WAR   DH

Hawthorne, Nathaniel (US, 1804–64) Born at Salem, Massachussetts, Hawthorne's imaginative preoccupation with New England's puritan past grew out of his own ancestry, and solitary apprenticeship as a writer. The result was a haunting body of work, full of characters oppressed by consciousness of sin, guilt, and retribution, but also full of symbols and the supernatural, which he called 'the Marvellous'. His stories were collected in *Twice-Told Tales* (1837, enlarged 1842), *Mosses from an Old Manse* (1842), and *The Snow Image* (1852). Among the best-known stories are 'Young Goodman Brown', in which a newly married man observes all the prominent citizens of a small town at a witches' sabbath in the woods, including his wife; and 'Wakefield', the story of a man's perverse self-banishment from home for twenty years. 'Rappaccini's Daughter', ostensibly an allegory of intellectual pride and evil, can now be read as a tale of voyeurism and repressed desire. Hawthorne's greatest work is *The Scarlet Letter* (1850), a dark moral fable revolving around the guilty secret linking the adulterous Hester Prynne with pious clergyman Arthur Dimmesdale, and her persecution by the community. Despite its deliberately archaic language, the novel's compelling characters and moments of supernatural intervention, most famously the letter 'A' appearing in the sky, have made it both memorable and influential. Hawthorne escaped the New England setting in *The Marble Faun* (1860), but characteristically dealt with repressed passion, leading to murder and guilt, among young Americans living in Rome.

Edgar Allan Poe, Henry James, Margaret Atwood. *See* HISTORICAL, UNITED STATES OF AMERICA   *JS*

Haycox, Ernest (US, 1899–1950). *See* FILM ADAPTATIONS, WESTERN

Head, Bessie (South African, 1937–86) In 1964, after training as a teacher and working in South Africa as a journalist, Head took a one-way exit permit to Botswana. All of Head's writing draws on her own traumatic life. *The Cardinals* (1993), a captivating novella published posthumously and thought to have been written around 1960–2, is an incestuous love story, between Mouse, an illegitimate coloured girl, and her white father. The story has stark parallels with the racist laws of South Africa which prohibited any contact between people of different colours (Head herself was of mixed race). Her most famous book, *A Question of Power* (1973), is a difficult but rewarding novel depicting the hallucinatory mental deterioration of a woman who is discriminated against because she is of mixed race. As well as writing novels, Head wrote many short stories. *The Collector of Treasures* (1977), Head's first collection, focuses on rural life in Botswana and particularly the status of women.

J. M. Coetzee, Buchi Emecheta, Nadine Gordimer, Boris Pasternak
          EW

Healy, Dermot (Irish, 1947–). *See* IRELAND

Heath, Roy (Guyanese/British, 1926–). *See* CARIBBEAN

Hegarty, Frances. *See* **Fyfield, Frances**

Heinlein, Robert (US, 1907–88) Heinlein was a graduate of the US Navy but had to retire, disabled, in 1934. He then read mathematics and physics at the University of California and began writing in 1939, becoming a pioneer of the 'future history' in science fiction. Heinlein's early novels tended to be rites of passage, typically depicting young men on some kind of frontier, undergoing ordeals which eventually produce adulthood and a poised narrative calm. In the futuristic *Starship Troopers* (1959) an army recruit is put through the toughest boot-camp known to man, before going into battle against a breed of giant cockroaches. When the book was adapted for the screen in 1997 by director Paul Verhoeven, its comparisons between Americanized gung-ho militarism and 1930s Nazi Youth caused a stir. But this was minor compared to the controversy surrounding *Stranger in a Strange Land* (1961) in which a Martian's perspective pokes a satirical finger at the materialism of human society—a tale said to have inspired the mass-murderer Charles Manson.

Arthur C. Clarke, John Wyndham, Brian Aldiss. *See* SCIENCE FICTION
          RP

Heller, Joseph (US, 1923–99) Heller was born and brought up during the Depression in Coney Island, New York. Aged 19, he enlisted and served as a bombardier, flying missions from Corsica, which provided the inspiration for *Catch-22* (1961), his first novel, which has attained, and deservedly so, the status of a cult classic. The title is based on the absurd logic that an aircrew can be relieved from duty by claiming insanity; but if they do, this proves they are sane and therefore fit to fly—Catch-22. Sensibly concluding that the US Air Force, as well as the enemy, is out to kill him, Captain Yossarian is driven to desperate measures, such as turning up on parade in the nude to receive a medal from General Dreedle. But in the madhouse of war such acts pale alongside the scams of Milo Minderbender, who replaces morphine in the first-aid kits with share certificates, or Colonel Cathcart who keeps raising the number of missions just before leave is due, or the unfortunately named Major Major Major, who becomes terribly depressed when promoted to Major. This exhilarating black comedy (originally titled *Catch-19*) is possibly the best—undeniably the funniest—novel of the Second World War.

The rest of Heller's output lives in its shadow. *Something Happened* (1974) dissects the hollow sham of corporate America and the farcical scramble up the greasy executive pole, while in *Good as Gold* (1979) he gives a surreal twist to New York Jewishness and the Washington political scene. *Closing Time* (1994), the sequel to *Catch-22*, picks up the lives of many of the characters as they approach old age, but lacks the original's satiric brilliance and proves what an impossible act it was to follow. He has also written a brief autobiography, *Now and Then* (1998).

📖 Richard Brautigan, Hunter S. Thompson, John Kennedy Toole. *See* HUMOUR, UNITED STATES OF AMERICA, WAR TH

Hemingway, Ernest (US, 1899–1961) Raised in the Chicago suburbs, Hemingway worked briefly as a reporter for the *Kansas City Star* before volunteering as an ambulanceman in the First World War. Badly wounded on the Italian front, he eventually moved to Paris where he associated with the experimental writers Ezra Pound and Gertrude Stein. These experiences informed Hemingway's finest work. His first book to appear in the United States was *In Our Time* (1925), a collection of stories which offers an ideal introduction to Hemingway's writing. 'The Big Two-Hearted River' stories follow the war-traumatized Nick Adams out into the natural world and reveal Hemingway's consummate style, where precise, simple language builds up a picture of external reality which reflects the character's inner feelings.

Hemingway's first novel, *The Sun Also Rises* (1926), is narrated by a war-wounded American writer living in European exile. The book chronicles the emigré life of the 1920s and develops Hemingway's broader concerns with suffering, survival, and the momentary but enduring clarity which ritualized confrontations with natural forces —like bullfighting and fishing—can bring. *A Farewell to Arms* (1929) raises the possibility of love providing a retreat from a harrowing war, whilst *For Whom the Bell Tolls* (1940), set behind Franco's battle-lines in the Spanish Civil War, reveals a new political commitment in Hemingway's writing. *The Old Man and the Sea* (1952) is about an old Cuban fisherman struggling to catch and land a huge marlin. Hemingway won the Nobel Prize for Literature in 1954.

📖 F. Scott Fitzgerald, Sherwood Anderson, Raymond Carver.
See THE SEA, UNITED STATES OF AMERICA   *BH*

Henry, O. (US, 1862–1910) 'O. Henry' was the pseudonym of William Sidney Porter, a former bank clerk and journalist who began writing stories while serving a prison sentence for embezzlement. On his release in 1901 he wrote at least a story a week for the *World* newspaper in New York, often drawing upon his colourful early life in the West, Texas, and New York. He produced a number of very popular collections, such as *The Heart of the West* (1907) and *The Gentle Grafter* (1908), and was known for the inventively plotted yarn, often humorous or sentimental, with trademark surprise endings. Covering some of the territory of Mark Twain, his stories feature lucky and luckless lovers, cowboys, shopgirls, confidence tricksters, and tramps. His best stories still make satisfying reading. A convenient modern edition is *The Collected Stories of O. Henry* (1979).

📖 Mark Twain, Damon Runyon   *JS*

Hensher, Philip (British, 1965–) Hensher has worked as a House of Commons clerk, and now reviews and writes novels and short stories. Begin with his stories collected in *The Bedroom of the Mister's Wife* (1999). These are written with beautiful simplicity, mostly narrated in the first person by a character who is bemused by his own situation. The most extreme example of this is 'God', where the narrator awakes in an unfamiliar room, with an unknown boy in his bed, and a briefcase full of money. ' "Where am I?" "Istanbul," he said. I took this in for a while. I live in Ealing.' 'To Feed the Night' is a delicious fable about a couple whose greed for property leads them to a sticky end. The novel *Kitchen Venom* (1996) features a hunchback who murders his gay lover. The characters' inner lives are beautifully observed, although the plotting is unconvincing.

📖 Raymond Carver, Adam Mars-Jones   *JR*

Henty, G(eorge) A(lfred) (British, 1832–1902). *See* ADVENTURE

Herbert, Frank (US, 1920–86) Best known for *The Dune Chronicles*, Frank Herbert has had a varied career, working as a journalist, photographer, lecturer, and consultant on social and ecological issues. He has written seventeen novels beside the six in the *Dune* series (including one, *Man of Two Worlds,* 1987, with his son, Brian), and several short stories, and has edited collections of fiction and non-fiction. The book to begin with is the famous *Dune* (1965), a book considered by many to be the most influential in its genre, and 'the most completely realized other world in the history of science fiction'. Set 2,500 years in the future, when the known universe is controlled by two powers, the Imperium and the Great Houses, *Dune* concerns the battle to control a desert planet, and its invaluable resource, 'melange'. There have been five sequels, a film, and many imitations.

📖 Isaac Asimov, Ursula Le Guin.
See SCIENCE FICTION   *IP*

Herbert, James (British, 1943–) Born in the East End of London, James Herbert worked as a rock 'n' roll singer and art director in advertising before turning to horror fiction. The graphic portrayals of dismemberment and sex in early novels like *The Rats* (1974), in which a plague of flesh-eating rats lays waste to London, were as controversial as they were popular. *The Fog* (1975), in which a mysterious mist isolates a Wiltshire village and subjects its citizens to the assault of dark supernatural forces, introduced a greater subtlety to Herbert's writing. *The Magic Cottage* (1986) took this further, with an almost whimsical tale of dark forces defeated by good, set among artists, musicians, and eccentrics in the English countryside. *Haunted* (1981) and *The Ghosts of Sleath* (1994) are updated, and often extremely effective, conventional ghost stories.

📖 Stephen King, Clive Barker.
See SUPERNATURAL   *WB*

Herriot, James (British, 1916–95) Think of Herriot and you immediately think of the Yorkshire Dales. And the qualities that draw thousands of visitors to Herriot Country are the same ones that draw thousands of readers to Herriot's stories of the life of a country vet—a glimpse of a purer, less complicated life before the days of factory farming, BSE, and genetically modified foods. *All Creatures Great and Small* (1975) introduced Herriot's characters, who stride around rugged landscapes in tweeds and wellies (middle/upper classes) or shabby raincoats held together with string and wellies (lower classes). The books are gently humorous and nostalgic. A tea-and-toast read for a cold November night.

📖 Compton Mackenzie, Miss Read
                              RV

Hesse, Hermann (German, 1877–1962) Hesse worked as a bookseller before he became a writer. He moved to Switzerland in protest against German militarism in the First World War, and remained there after his works were banned by the Nazis. In 1946 he was awarded the Nobel Prize for Literature. Throughout his books shines his belief in the value of the individual; readers speak of Hesse's novels awakening their own spiritual life. *The Glass Bead Game* (1943) is a complex vision of a society devoted to education and the intellect. *Narziss and Goldmund* (1930) tells the story of two friends, one devoted to the world and the flesh, the other to a monastic life of prayer and study. *Steppenwolf* (1927) is a surreal tale of how a disenchanted intellectual learns how to live, and love, at the hands of the hedonistic socialite Hermione.

📖 Heinrich Böll, Knut Hamsun.
See GERMANY   *EC*

Heyer, Georgette (British, 1902–74) A prolific and popular writer of historical romances set in the Regency period of the early nineteenth century. The background is carefully researched; the narrative lively and good humoured. It is a world of rakes, dandies, lace, and ruffles, in which life is a game and the making of a good marriage the biggest prize. However, her main protagonists are given more substance. The heroine may well be poor, and often the daughter of some feckless adventurer, but makes up for this with an abundance of spirit, wit, and beauty. The hero is tall, dark, handsome, and rich, but weary of the frivolity and artifice of society life and ladies, and thus readily amused and engaged by the escapades he will inevitably be drawn into by the headstrong girl who wins his heart. She in her turn can rest her head on his bosom after that heady kiss that will seal their fate, confident that marriage to such a man will never descend into the mundanity of washing his socks. Heyer also wrote contemporary detective stories with a similar lighthearted tone. Among her most popular romances are *The Masqueraders* (1928), *Cousin Kate* (1948), *The Grand Sophie* (1950), and *Frederica* (1965).

📖 Daphne du Maurier, Jean Plaidy, Charlotte Brontë. *See* HISTORICAL, ROMANCE   *KB*

Hiaasen, Carl (US, 1953–) Carl Hiaasen is a columnist for the Miami Herald who has single-handedly created a new school of modern crime writing that could be characterized as Florida comic noir. Passionately opposed to the destruction of the Florida ecology by tourism and building speculation, Hiaasen sides with the eco-terrorists and often bungling crooks who muddle their way through his novels to darkly comic effect. A satirist with a keen eye for sleaze, Hiaasen has attacked the greed of developers, bass-fishing competitions, theme parks, plastic surgery gone too far, insurance scams, and the strip-tease trade with much gusto in novels like *Tourist Season* (1986), *Double Whammy* (1987), *Skin Tight* (1989), and *Strip Tease* (1993). Many of his books feature an ex-governor of Florida, Skink, who has returned to nature and campaigns against the despoliation of his native state in most bizarre ways; he clearly attracts the author's sympathy.

📖 Charles Willeford, Sara Paretsky. *See* CRIME   *MJ*

Higgins, George V(incent) (US, 1939–99) Higgins, a journalist who became a lawyer, achieved international recognition

with his debut novel, *The Friends of Eddie Coyle* (1972), which was turned into a popular film starring Robert Mitchum. It established the pattern for many of his later books, being set in Boston, focused on criminal protagonists, and revealing Higgins's flair for dialogue. The way his characters talk seems to have a ring of authenticity, even if their motivations are sometimes only lightly sketched. His next two books, *The Digger's Game* (1973) and *Cogan's Trade* (1974), were equally effective. Making use of his knowledge of the legal world, Higgins wrote several novels featuring the attorney Jerry Kennedy, including *Kennedy for the Defense* (1980) and *Penance for Jerry Kennedy* (1985), but not all his later work lived up to the promise of the early books.

📖 Elmore Leonard, Charles Willeford. *See* CRIME   *ME*

Higgins, Jack (British, 1929–) Born in Newcastle-upon-Tyne, Higgins worked as a teacher and lecturer before becoming a best-selling thriller writer in the early 1970s. Begin with *The Eagle Has Landed* (1975), which typifies Higgins's dramatic fictionalizations of events in closely researched historical contexts. Set at the height of the Second World War, the book deals with a group of Nazi paratroopers who land in Norfolk in an attempt to kidnap Winston Churchill. *Exocet* (1983) reflects the commercial and political realities of the arms trade in describing a Russian plot to supply the Argentinians with sophisticated weaponry during the Falklands conflict. The topical emphasis in Higgins's work is sustained in *Angel of Death* (1995), set during a critical phase of the peace process in Northern Ireland. It centres on the efforts of British and Irish intelligence organizations to prevent further killings by a renegade terrorist faction.

📖 Tom Clancy, Eric Ambler.
See SPY   *DH*

Highsmith, Patricia (US, 1921–95)

Patricia Highsmith is the mother of the modern psychological suspense novel, once described by Graham Greene as 'a poet of apprehension'. In a series of often grim and always unflinching tales, she explored the psychology of guilt and the impact of love and crime on the individual. In spite of the darkness of her work, it is often shot through with shafts of dry wit. Her spare style heightens the chilling atmosphere of her novels. Often, she chooses a sensational jumping-off point for her novels. For example, her debut, *Strangers on a Train* (1950), notably filmed by Alfred Hitchcock, depicted two men who meet by chance and 'swap' murders, a set-up that escalates into a swirling drama of psychopathy and terror. Her second novel, *The Price of Salt* (1953), a lesbian love story, was first published under a pseudonym and reissued as *Carol* in 1991. Again, it is interesting for the depth of the psychological insight. She returned to crime with perhaps her most famous novel, *The Talented Mr Ripley* (1955), adapted most successfully for film by Anthony Minghella. Tom Ripley is a charming psychopath and con man who 'steals' other people's lives and somehow manages to extricate himself from the consequences of his murderous activities. Ripley features in four further novels. For a perfect demonstration of black humour, turn to her short story collection, *The Animal Lover's Book of Beastly Murder* (1975).

📖 Ruth Rendell (writing as Barbara Vine), Minette Walters, Josephine Tey.
See CRIME, THRILLERS   *VM*

Hightower, Lynn S. (US).

See THRILLERS

Highway, Tomson (Canadian, 1951–).

See CANADA

Hijuelos, Oscar (US, 1951–) Hijuelos

was the son of Cuban immigrants, and was born and brought up in New York. After working briefly in advertising, he began writing novels, and he won the Pulitzer Prize in 1990 for *The Mambo Kings Play Songs of Love* (1989). This is the story of two young 1950s' Cuban musicians who eventually find success in New York. The novel is remarkable for the detailed, sympathetic portrait of the brothers, Cesar and Nestor, and the authentic period background. All Hijuelos's novels concern themselves with the Latino experience, such as *The Fourteen Sisters of Emilio Montez O'Brien* (1993), which follows a huge Cuban-American family over a century, and the moving *Mr Ives' Christmas* (1995) about a devout Catholic whose faith is tested when his son is shot at Christmas.

📖 Gabriel García Márquez, Isabel Allende   *SA*

Hill, Reginald (British, 1936–)

Although Hill's roots are firmly in the traditional English detective novel, he brings to it an ambivalence and ambiguity that allows him to display the complexities of contemporary life, both moral and social. Among the most literate of writers in the field, he brings to life a cast of characters who change and develop in response to their experiences. He is best known for his Yorkshire-based series, featuring boorish but shrewd Superintendent Andy Dalziel and his sensitive but tenacious underling Peter Pascoe. Start with *A Clubbable*

Woman (1970) which introduces the detective duo. High points in the series include *Underworld* (1988), with the backdrop of a beleaguered mining community, *Bones and Silence* (1990), set against a contemporary production of a medieval mystery play, and the remarkable *On Beulah Height* (1998), an elegiac exploration of the deaths of children in a Yorkshire village, spanning twenty years. Hill has been awarded the Crime Writers' Association Diamond Dagger for his contribution to crime writing.

📖 Ruth Rendell, Ian Rankin, John Harvey. *See* CRIME   *VM*

Hill, Susan (British, 1942–) Susan Hill's work is characterized by a deeply serious, often bleak view of life. Expert at building tension and evoking atmosphere, she approaches her withdrawn, interior characters with insight and sensitivity, revealing them through quiet, measured prose and tense, sometimes almost stylized dialogue.

Air and Angels (1991) is a good starting-point. Containing some of her finest writing, its subject is a celibate Cambridge don who falls obsessively in love with a young girl. Tragedy and joy are two sides of the same coin in this book, something Hill captures with typical subtlety. It is partly set in the marshlands of East Anglia, an area she knows well and returns to again and again, notably in *The Woman in Black* (1983), which has been adapted for both stage and television. The tale of haunted Eel Marsh House successfully re-creates the feel of a classic Victorian ghost story, a genre she revisits in *The Mist in the Mirror* (1992). *In the Springtime of the Year* (1974) deals with bereavement, as does *I'm the King of the Castle* (1970), which won the Somerset Maugham Award. Too pessimistic for some,

this powerful book concentrates on childhood cruelty and suicide. Less successful is *Mrs de Winter* (1993), a somewhat contrived sequel to Daphne du Maurier's *Rebecca*. Susan Hill has also written short stories and radio plays, two volumes of autobiography, and children's books.

📖 Penelope Lively, William Trevor, Penelope Fitzgerald.
See SUPERNATURAL   *CB*

Hillerman, Tony (US, 1925–) Born in Oklahoma, Tony Hillerman was brought up on a farm and went to a school for Indian children. This initiated his fascination with American Indian culture and he tackles tribal culture with empathy and compassion in his popular whodunits featuring detective Joe Leaphorn of the Navajo Tribal Police and the younger detective, Jim Chee. *Dance Hall of the Dead* (1973) introduced Leaphorn and won the Edgar Award. Hillerman's novels are meticulously researched but the wealth of details about Indian practices and mores never overshadows tight plots with many twists. He first teamed Leaphorn and Chee in *Skinwalkers* (1987) and the contrast between the characters' education, attitudes to their cultural heritage, and sensibilities whenever they work an investigation together is both prickly and supportive. Despite the wealth of fascinating Indian lore, Hillerman's books are also perfect entertainments and he is a regular on the American best-seller lists.

📖 James Lee Burke, Evan Hunter (writing as Ed McBain)   *MJ*

Himes, Chester (US, 1909–84) Chester Himes was the first important African-American mystery novelist, and his books, in particular those forming the *Harlem* series, featuring 'Coffin' Ed Johnson and 'Grave Digger' Jones, occupy a singular place in the history of crime writing. The series begins with *A Rage in Harlem* (1957), about the violent consequences of a con job gone bad, and contains, among others, *Cotton Comes to Harlem* (1965) and *Blind Man with a Pistol* (1969), which ends with a full-blown race riot. First published in French, these detective novels dig deep into the heart of race relations and violence in America and evoke a strong sense of protest against the established social order, and against the disfranchisement of the black community. Violence and dark humour pepper Himes's pages to strong effect and he is not afraid to portray black villains as well as white. Himes, who spent some time in prison for armed robbery in his youth, also wrote many social novels in addition to mysteries, and volumes of memoirs about his own criminal identity.

📖 Walter Mosley, George V. Higgins
MJ

Hines, Barry (British, 1939–) Barry Hines was born in (and later played football for) Barnsley, before attending Loughborough College of Education. He is best known for his novel *A Kestrel for a Knave* (1968), retitled *Kes* in 1974 when it was reprinted and filmed by Ken Loach. It tells the story of Billy Casper, a boy from a deprived working-class background, whose relationship with his pet hawk gives his life meaning. Hines's earlier novel, *Blinder* (1966), is also about a working-class boy, but one who is given an opportunity to train as a professional footballer. *The Gamekeeper* (1975) has an older protagonist but also focuses on class issues. In *Elvis over England* (1998) Hines writes on a more comic note, in a novel which is warm-hearted,

readable, and in places very funny. He also writes original TV drama (including the award winning *Threads*) and has adapted his novels to film (*Looks and Smiles*, 1981).

📖 Alan Sillitoe, John Braine   *SA*

Hinton, S. E. (US, 1948–). *See* TEEN

Hoban, Russell (US, 1925–) Russell Hoban was born in Pennsylvania but has lived in London since 1965. He was an illustrator of children's books before turning to writing himself, and his output for children is huge. In *The Mouse and His Child* (1967) a clockwork mouse and his child are thrown out of the toy-shop. The book chronicles their attempts to regain their home, their happiness, and the power of 'self-winding'. Of Hoban's writing for adults try *Turtle Diary* (1975), in which a man and a woman separately decide to free the turtles from London Zoo. This was made into a film with Ben Kingsley and Glenda Jackson, and is one of Hoban's most accessible novels, though it shares with his more rarefied work a sense of the incurable alienation of humanity. Hoban's most important adult book, however, is *Riddley Walker* (1980), set either in the future or the distant past, in a world devastated by nuclear holocaust. Riddley and his companions live in a primitive, raw world where every day is a struggle for food, survival, and meaning. The book is written in an invented, post-holocaust language but don't let that put you off; the style is compelling after the strangeness of the first few paragraphs. And Riddley's struggle and vision make this one of the most poetic and moving masterpieces in contemporary literature.

📖 William Golding, J. G. Ballard. *See* SCIENCE FICTION   *LM*

Høeg, Peter (Danish, 1957–) Peter Hoeg was a dancer, actor, fencer, sailor, and mountaineer before turning to writing. *Miss Smilla's Feeling for Snow* (1992) catapulted him into the ranks of the best-sellers. It tells the story of Smilla Jaspersen, a Greenlander living in Copenhagen, who is moved to investigate the sudden death of her neighbour's 6-year-old son. Smilla is a compelling character, tenacious, angry, vulnerable, and brave. Her quest takes her from Denmark far into the Arctic Circle, into a world of icy fear. The book is a taut, elaborate thriller and whodunit which explores issues of power, politics, truth, and betrayal with a marvellous poetic style and memorable imagery. *Borderliners* (1995) is a remarkable study of damaged children and their fate in Danish institutions. *The Woman and the Ape* (1996) is a witty, fast-moving, cautionary fable which explores the relationship between humans and animals.

📖 Umberto Eco, Graham Swift, David Guterson. *See* THRILLERS   CS

Hoffman, Alice (US, 1952–) Hoffman's novels are usually set in ordinary American small towns where quiet respectability is playfully intermingled with the sinister and magical. In *Turtle Moon* (1992) Lucy moves to Verity, Florida, with her son Keith to start a new life after divorce. When Keith runs away with the baby of a murdered woman, and Lucy and Officer Julian Cash chase after him, respectable Verity becomes the location of a murder mystery. In *Second Nature* (1995) recently divorced Robin moves to a new town with her son. They secretly befriend Steven the 'Wolfman', raised by wolves and on the run from a psychiatric ward. Hoffman contrasts the sinister forces in the town with Steven's natural innocence. In *Practical Magic* (1995), recently adapted for a Hollywood film, two sisters are ostracized by a small Massachusetts community because their aunts are said to be witches.

📖 Anne Tyler, Carol Shields, Alison Lurie   *DJ*

Hollinghurst, Alan (British, 1954–) Born in Stroud and educated at Magdalen College, Oxford, Hollinghurst is among the best of gay male authors. His novels all deal with gay life, although the clarity, stylishness, and precision of his writing have universal appeal. *The Swimming Pool Library* (1988) looks at the relationship between a younger and older man, and casts a sombre look backwards at the effect of anti-homosexual legislation. *The Folding Star* (1994), set in Belgium, is a somewhat darker novel, its narrator as much consumed by lust as by love. *The Spell* (1998) deals with the pursuit of pleasure by some slightly older gay men, the writing being lighter in tone. *The Folding Star* was shortlisted for the 1994 Booker Prize.

📖 Adam Mars-Jones, Patrick Gale, Edmund White   *SA*

Holt, Victoria. *See* **Plaidy, Jean**

Holtby, Winifred (British, 1898–1935) Like Vera Brittain, whose close friend she was, Winifred Holtby's writing was much influenced by her time in the Women's Auxiliary Army Corps during the First World War and her political activism in England, Europe, and South Africa thereafter. Holtby's novels chronicle the ways in which changes in social structure affect the lives of women. Her masterpiece is

South Riding (1936) in which a panorama of Yorkshire life is unfolded and explored. At the centre of this novel is the relationship between the radical Sarah Burton, a passionate teacher at the local girls' school, and the Tory gentleman-farmer, Robert Carne. Although romanticized in parts, the book is also subtle, astute, and visionary.

📖 Muriel Spark, Phyllis Bentley, Lettice Cooper   *LM*

Homer. *See* THE SEA, WAR

Hope, Anthony (British, 1863–1933) Hope (full name, Anthony Hope Hawkins) wrote numerous novels, none of which have lasted except *The Prisoner of Zenda* (1894), a vastly entertaining, swashbuckling romance set in the invented central European kingdom of Ruritania. Its upper-class English hero, Rudolf Rassendyl, is a distant relative and exact double of the new king. When the latter is kidnapped before his coronation, Rudolf has to impersonate and then rescue him, foiling on the way the dastardly plots of the splendidly villainous Black Michael and his dashing henchman, Rupert of Hentzau, and falling hopelessly in love with the hapless King's prospective bride. The best of numerous film versions is the 1937 one with Ronald Colman and David Niven. Hope's sequel, *Rupert of Hentzau* (1898), is inferior but you'll want to read it if you liked the original.

📖 P. C. Wren, Henry Rider Haggard, Robert Louis Stevenson.
See ADVENTURE   *MH*

Hope, Christopher (South African, 1944–) Hope's early (and, some think, his best) novels were satirical, blisteringly powerful attacks on South African apartheid laws. Start with *A Separate Development* (1980), about the decline of a mixed-race boy, Harry Moto, who leaves his home in a privileged white community and begins to live as a black. Move on to *Kruger's Alp* (1984), an allegorical quest story which surveys the political and historical landscape of Afrikaner society, considering questions of corruption and deceit. Hope's concerns have shifted with political developments. *Serenity House* (1992) sets the corruption of a modern, mercenary society against that of Nazi Germany as Max, resident in an old people's home, faces a secret investigation into his past. Hope's prose is clear and economical, but his sensitive analyses of these complicated, politically sensitive situations always resist simplification.

📖 Alan Paton, Nadine Gordimer, J. M. Coetzee   *SR*

Hornby, Nick (British, 1957–) Hornby worked as a teacher before becoming a full-time writer. His first book, the autobiographical *Fever Pitch* (1992), about his obsession with football, was a best-seller; a funny, moving exploration of not just football but families, loyalty, masculinity, and identity. His first novel, *High Fidelity* (1995) also uses a first-person, male narrator, speaking in the present tense, with equal openness. Here the narrator is an obsessive record collector, but the story is about his relationships and sex; using humour and self-deprecating wit to reveal the weaknesses, delusions, and dishonesties of both men and women, and capturing with uncanny accuracy the mood of the mid-1990s. *About a Boy* (1998), Hornby's second novel, abandons the first-person voice and so feels less immediate, telling from the outside the story of Will Freeman, single and childless, who unintentionally becomes the friend and confidante of troubled 11-year old Marcus; the novel examines (again, with wry humour) the connections that people make to replace the conventional and increasingly non-existent ideal nuclear family.

📖 Roddy Doyle, Kingsley Amis, J. D. Salinger   *JR*

Horwood, William (British, 1944–)
William Horwood was brought up in the chalk downlands of Wessex, and his intimate knowledge of that ancient and dramatic landscape is what raises *Duncton Wood* (1980) far above most such animal sagas. The story follows the epic quest of Bracken, a rather solitary mole, to free all the moles of Duncton Wood from the terrifying tyranny of Mandrake, a kind of Stalin of the mole world. Such anthropomorphism can easily go wrong, but Horwood's control of his material is perfect and his imagination always triumphant. He has the same, precisely detailed knowledge of the English countryside, its flora and fauna, its seasons and weather, as Richard Adams, whose *Watership Down* is *Duncton Wood's* obvious precursor.

📖 Richard Adams, Henry Williamson   *CH*

Hosain, Attia (Indian, 1913–). *See* INDIA

Hospital, Janette Turner (Australian, 1942–) Hospital grew up in Brisbane and moved to the United States in 1965. She has also lived in Britain, India, and Canada. Her novels often explore multiple versions of stories. Start with *Borderline* (1985) which begins at the US/Canadian border when illegal immigrants in a butcher's van are arrested. Two onlookers, an insurance salesman and an art curator, end up helping to free (as they think) a woman who has been hidden in a beef carcass. The unreliable narrator is a piano tuner, poised between art and science, fiction and fact. *Charades* (1988) chronicles a girl's search for her father; but along the way she must tell and retell her past in all its possible permutations. *The Last Magician* (1992) is about four characters in Australia, bound together by a childhood trauma. The last magician is the Chinese-Australian photographer who records everything and allows the past to seep into the present.

📖 Elizabeth Jolley, Michèle Roberts, Toni Morrison   *JR*

Houellebecq, Michel (from Réunion, 1958–). *See* FRANCE

Howard, Audrey (British, 1929–)
Born in Liverpool, Howard turned to writing when her son left home, moving to Australia to work on her first novel. She now lives in Lancashire. She writes popular family stories, and *The Juniper Bush* (1988) won Romantic Novel of the Year award. Begin with her first novel, *The Skylark's Song* (1984), set in early twentieth-century Merseyside, and charting the life of beautiful slum-child Zoe who is adopted by the local schoolmistress but lives with the threat that she may have to return to the squalid poverty of the docks. *The Mallow Years* (1989) is a love-story set in 1830s' Oldham and on the Pennine moors, and detailing the lives of destitute weavers and cotton-spinning mill workers.

📖 Helen Forrester, Beverley Hughesden, Elizabeth Gaskell   *JR*

Howard, Elizabeth Jane (British, 1923–) Howard's meditative, atmospheric novels are acute studies of human need and of social interaction. She is sharply observant, allowing her characters difficult and complicated emotions which unfold gradually, in response to subtly changing situations and relationships. Begin with *Odd Girl Out* (1972), an account of a strong marriage slowly undermined by the arrival of the attractive, insecure Arabella, whose honesty leads everyone to question their own deepest moral beliefs. Move on to the best-selling *Cazalet Chronicle* (a quartet beginning with *The Light Years*, 1990), which follows three generations of an English family from 1937, through the Second World War, and into the slow economic recovery which followed. Howard is the author of eleven novels, and has also written scripts for film and television.

📖 Jane Austen, Monica Dickens, Angela Lambert. *See* FAMILY SAGA

SR

Howard, Robert E. (US, 1906–36). *See* FANTASY

Howatch, Susan (British, 1940–) Howatch worked in a solicitor's office, until, determined to become a novelist, she moved to New York, and while working as a secretary there wrote a series of successful stories. Her first best-seller was *Penmarric* (1971), the saga of two Cornish families from Victorian times until the Second World War. In 1979 this was made into a BBC television series. Howatch went on to live in Ireland and America, writing other hugely popular novels such as *Cashelmara* (1974). She caused media interest, and some contro-

versy, when she decided to spend some of the fortune earned from her books to endow an academic position in theology at Cambridge University. Her spiritual interests are evident, however, in one of her earliest books, *The Devil on Lammas Night* (1973), an occult thriller dealing with the arrival of the Devil among a community of women.

Her clerical series, set for the most part in and around the fictional West Country town of Starbridge, was written in her flat overlooking Salisbury Cathedral. These novels explore in a vivid and moving way the intense inner life and the crises— sexual, emotional, and psychological— which clergymen can undergo. *Mystical Paths* (1992) and *Glamorous Powers* (1988) tell the story of two generations of priests, Jon Darrow and his son Nicolas, who both must wrestle with the psychic gifts which can enhance or destroy their ministry. The novels bring spiritual experience to life in a compelling and accessible way.

📖 Anthony Trollope, Daphne du Maurier

EC

Hoyle, Fred (British, 1915–) Born in Bingley, Yorkshire, Hoyle was educated at Emmanuel College, Cambridge. A leading figure in twentieth-century astronomy, his science fiction gains credibility from his authoritative use of scientific speculation. Begin with *The Black Cloud* (1957), his first novel, in which an alien intelligence in the form of a cloud blots out the sun, threatening ecological disaster and social upheaval. *Ossian's Ride* (1959) resembles a conventional thriller when it opens with its main character on the run in rural Ireland. Science fiction takes over when he joins an extraterrestrial conspiracy to create a technologically advanced utopia. Hoyle's later novels are written jointly with his son Geoffrey. They include *Inferno* (1973), in which Earth is depopulated by the effects of a stellar explosion, leaving scattered groups of survivors to face their responsibility for the future of mankind.

📖 John Wyndham, Ray Bradbury

DH

Hoyle, Trevor (British, 1940–) Born and brought up in Lancashire, where he still lives, Hoyle's best work combines elements of science fiction and thriller into a dark, nightmarish vision. Start with *Blind Needle* (1994) whose hunted hero stumbles into a world of corruption and drugs in a Cumbrian town dominated by a nuclear plant. *Vail* (1984) is set in a future Britain where the rich south-east is fenced off from the savagery of the rest of the country, and where extremes of deprivation are pushed to queasily comic conclusions. *The Last Gasp* (1990) is an ecological thriller, while *Mirrorman* (1999) sees the Messengers offer eternal life to a convicted killer—if he can murder one more man.

📖 Graham Greene, J. G. Ballard, Lynda La Plante *JR*

Hrabal, Bohumil (Czech, 1914–) Hrabal was born in Brno and educated at Charles University, Prague. He worked in various occupations before becoming a full-time writer in the 1970s. Begin with *A Close Watch on the Trains* (1965), whose main character overcomes his sexual despair through a chance encounter and is inspired to action as an anti-Nazi saboteur in wartime Czechoslovakia. *Too Loud a Solitude* (1976) takes place chiefly in a cellar, where a solitary worker apocalyptically surveys modern history as he destroys waste paper and banned books. *I Served the King of England* (1971) exemplifies the bizarrely imaginative vein that runs through Hrabal's writing. It recounts the career of a diminutive waiter whose ambition sets him adrift in a blackly comic world of depravity and power. Hrabal's collections of stories include *The Death of Mr Baltisberger* (1966).

📖 Jaroslav Hašek, Josef Škvorecký, Günter Grass *DH*

Hughes, David (British, 1930–) Hughes was born in Alton, Hampshire, and attended Oxford and worked as a publishers' reader and magazine editor before becoming a full-time writer in 1961. Begin with *The Pork Butcher* (1984), in which a former German soldier, aware that he is dying of cancer, returns to the small French town where he committed war crimes forty years before. War and guilt are equally central to *The Major* (1964), the best of his earlier novels, which recounts the career of an army officer whose reliance on excessively harsh discipline leads him to crisis and suicide. The main character in *But for Bunter* (1985) is a man who claims to be the original for Billy Bunter in the stories by Frank Richards. Inventive and entertaining, the book wittily explores the relationship between fact and fiction.

📖 Piers Paul Read, Alan Judd *DH*

Hughes, Richard (British, 1900–76) Richard Hughes's first novel, *A High Wind in Jamaica* (1929, published in the USA as *The Innocent Voyage*), remains his best. The Thornton family live in Jamaica but put their children on a ship for England after a hurricane strikes. The ship gets captured by pirates, however. The situation is grim, but we come to realize that the children are even worse than their captors (children are mad, according to Hughes). The tone and plot of this novel are very disorientating: it's part children's adventure story, part adult psychological thriller. It's also very funny, and very cynical about human behaviour. It represents a kind of magic realism some decades before that term was invented. *In Hazard: A Sea Story* (1938) deals with men at sea who suffer a hurricane, then endure fears of a mutiny. A later book, *The Fox in the Attic* (1961), deals with English and German families as Hitler comes to power and war approaches, and is a fascinating but uneven read.

📖 William Golding.
See CHILDHOOD   *RF*

Hughes, Thomas (British, 1822–96). *See* CHILDHOOD

Hughesdon, Beverley (British, 1943–) Hughesdon was born in Surrey and studied history at Manchester University. After some years spent teaching she began to write historical romances, and her *Song of Songs* (1988) was published to critical and popular acclaim. The novel is set in the first quarter of the twentieth century, and tells the story of Helena who gives up her aristocratic life to nurse soldiers in France. The authentic background and emotional richness make the book a compelling read. Hughesdon's *Roses Have Thorns* (1992) and *Silver Fountains* (1994) are companion volumes, again set in and around the First World War, and are based on the myth of Beauty and the Beast.

📖 Margaret Mitchell, Winifred Holtby   *SA*

Hugo, Victor(-Marie) (French, 1802–85) One of the major writers of nineteenth-century France, Victor Hugo was the most prolific and influential figure of French Romanticism, writing poetry and verse-drama as well as his acclaimed novels. Hugo enjoyed an early success with *The Hunchback of Notre Dame*, a high romantic melodrama set in the year 1482. Frollo, the corrupt archdeacon, is foiled in his efforts to kidnap the gypsy Esmeralda by the hunchback, Quasimodo, whose love for the girl redeems the evil deeds he has performed in Frollo's service. An influential politician, Hugo was elected to the French Assembly in 1848, but was forced into exile in Guernsey three years later when his royalist and conservative sympathies clashed with the rise of Napoleon III. By the time of his return to Paris in 1870, his allegiances had changed, and he was appointed a deputy and later a senator under the Third Republic as a committed social democrat. *Les Misérables* (1862) reflects this change in its dense, realist style. The story of the pursuit of the reformed criminal, Valjean, through Revolutionary Paris by the police agent, Javert, is a vivid portrait of its period, and teems with memorable characters and scenes. Hugo's works, despite having become better-known in the adapted forms of musical theatre, film, and animation, remain widely read and enjoyed.

📖 Émile Zola, Honoré de Balzac, Leo Tolstoy. *See* HISTORICAL   *WB*

Hulme, Keri (NZ, 1947–) Hulme has Maori, Scottish, and English ancestry, and is known for her paintings and stories as well as for her Booker Prize-winning novel *The Bone People* (1984). This tells the story of Simon, a young autistic boy who is cared for by an isolated woman after he breaks into her home, a beautiful six-floored tower built near a beach. In Simon's wake follows his father, Joe. The heroine, Kerewin, is part-Maori, and Maori language and story are important in the novel, as are dreams and images from the characters' subconscious. But don't be put off. Kerewin is also exceedingly down-to-earth and offers the reader amusingly dry verdicts on events as they unfold. This compelling book is a wonderful exploration of the demands love makes.

📖 Marge Piercy, Margaret Atwood. *See* AUSTRALIA AND NEW ZEALAND

JR

Humphreys, Emyr (British, 1919–) Humphreys is a Welsh Nationalist, poet, and dramatist. His many novels are realistic, concerning moral questions, the nature of love, freedom, and conscience in post-Nonconformist Wales. Start with *A Toy Epic* (1958), following the development of three youths from contrasting social backgrounds in 1930s Wales. Seven novels centre on Amy Parry, beginning near her death when she is a titled lady, in *National Winner* (1971), then moving back to her poor beginnings as a working-class socialist. Then read *Open Secrets* (1988): during the Second World War Amy's husband Cilydd is a pacifist, while she pursues politics; her first child is not Cilydd's. Don't miss *Bonds of Attachment* (1991): Peredur, Amy's son by Cilydd, searching for the truth about his father's suicide, has an affair with Wenna, who is blown up in an Investiture protest. *The Anchortree* (1980) explores the importance of roots as Morgan seeks his Pennsylvanian ancestry.

📖 Jack Jones, James Hanley   GC

Hunter, Evan (US, 1926–) Since the publication of *Blackboard Jungle* (1954) Evan Hunter (who also writes as **Ed McBain**) has written over eighty works of fiction under several names and has won awards in the United States and Britain. *Privileged Conversation* (1996) depicts a heady sexual affair leading to inescapable tragedy. As Ed McBain he is renowned for his 87th precinct series, centred on a team of detectives, which established the police procedural genre and influenced developments in writing, film, and television. The routine details of the job, down to the actual reproduction of booking forms and memos in the novels, are interwoven with interaction between the cops, the tension and the humour, and with their personal and domestic lives. *Let's Hear It for the Deaf Man* (1973) pits the team against their old adversary, the Deaf Man, when they are already dealing with a series of cat burglaries, a shooting, and a horrific crucifixion. McBain also writes the *Matthew Hope* series which take their titles from fairy-tales.

📖 John Harvey, Tony Hillerman. *See* CRIME   CS

Hurd, Douglas (British, 1930–). *See* SPY

Hurston, Zora Neale (US, 1896–1960) Hurston was born in the self-governing black town of Eatonville, Florida, where her father was elected mayor. Much of the rest of her life was spent studying black folklore in the south and the Caribbean. However, the last ten years were spent in poverty and obscurity and she was buried in an unmarked grave. The book which rescued her reputation is *Their Eyes were Watching God* (1937). This is the controversial study of the life and loves of Janie Crawford, on the one hand the story of a strong and quick-witted woman's attempts to find self-fulfilment, and on the other this woman's search for romantic love. Hurston's innovative use of voice, at once lyrical, philosophical, and pithy, has been a major influence on later writers such as Alice Walker, and the novel contains some of the wittiest dialogue in twentieth-century literature.

📖 Maya Angelou   *LM*

Huth, Angela (British, 1938–) Huth is a journalist and has written for radio and television. Her stories and novels are sharp and entertaining, full of acute psychological insights. Begin with *The Land Girls* (1994), a compelling read about three girls in the Second World War working on a Dorset farm; Prue, fresh from her mother's hairdressing shop, determined on romance but also surprisingly hard-working; dreamy Angela, straight from Cambridge University; and beautiful, lovelorn Stella. Huth is excellent on the physical detail of farm life, and also in the way she dissects the feelings of each character, especially John Lawrence the farmer, at first reluctant to have his life invaded by the girls, and then struggling with an obsessive attraction to Stella. *Another Kind of Cinderella* (1996) is an engaging collection of stories, and *Easy Silence* (1999) takes the lives of a long-married musician and a painter, at a point at which each has secretly fallen for someone new; in the husband's case, so obsessively that he plans to murder his wife.

📖 Anne Tyler, Mary Wesley, Jane Austen   *JR*

Huxley, Aldous (British, 1894–1963) Aldous Huxley was born into a family of intellectuals; his grandfathers were Thomas Huxley, a colleague of Darwin, and Thomas Arnold, headmaster of Rugby school and father of the poet, Matthew Arnold. One of Aldous's aunts was the best-selling novelist, Mrs Humphry Ward, and his brother Julian was a scientist and writer. There is a combination of the intellectual and the moral at the heart of Huxley's novels. In 1928 he published *Point Counter Point*, perhaps his best book, in which a galaxy of characters across a range of times and places comment on morals, behaviour, and culture. However, the book to start with is *Brave New World* (1932). It is set seven centuries in the future where the dates are all AF (After Ford). Humans are divided into five castes, ruled by the Alphas and Betas at the top. Children are bred in bottles and sex is for recreation only; long-term relationships are frowned upon and people's rebellious urges are subdued by use of the drug soma. The central figure is Bernard Marx, a social isolate, who decides to visit one of the 'savage reservations' where 'Indians' preserve the old, 'dirty' ways. When he returns he brings back a young man; tragedy inevitably follows. Huxley's last novel, *Island* (1962), was on a similar theme. Here, however, pleasure and drugs among a community on a Pacific island bring personal freedom, and it is western capitalism which finally destroys them.

📖 George Orwell, Evelyn Waugh, Graham Greene. *See* SOCIAL ISSUES
                                      IP

Huysmans, Joris-Karl (French, 1848–1907) Set amongst the working class or the very poor, Huysmans's early novels were in the realist mode of Émile Zola. *Marthe* (1876) typically recounts the life of a young prostitute working in a licensed brothel. A better introduction is *Against Nature* (*A Rebours*; 1884), in which the aesthete Des Esseintes, probably the first openly bisexual hero in modern literature, retires from the world upon a quest into the sensual realm. Covering everything from sado-masochism to classical literature, taking in perfumery and circus acrobats on the way, the book is a meticulous catalogue of rarefied tastes and perverse appetites. In it, says Oscar Wilde in *The Picture of Dorian Gray*, 'the life of the senses was described in terms of mystical philosophy'. Huysmans later joined a monastery, cloistering himself away like Des Esseintes. *En Route* (1895), one of four autobiographical novels, recalls that period and recounts the progress of his spiritual development.

📖 Oscar Wilde, Émile Zola, Gustave Flaubert   *CB*

I

Iles, Francis (a.k.a. Anthony Berkeley) (British, 1893–1971). *See* CRIME

Ingalls, Rachel (US, 1940–) Rachel Ingalls is best known as the author of short stories and novellas where elements of fantasy and psychological horror erupt into everyday lives. *Mrs Caliban* (1982) is a good starting-point, a compelling short novel in which an ordinary woman finds herself involved with a mysterious sea-creature as her life slips into fantasy. *Theft* (1970) centres on two men held in a prison cell during a violent social disturbance. *Black Diamond* (1992) is a collection of five novellas linked by themes of kinship: in *Bud and Sis* adopted children seek revenge on their blood parents, while in *Be My Guest* a girl befriends a boy who claims to be an adult trapped in a child's body. Ingalls's themes are often focused on repressed emotions, and the damage they return to inflict, and her stories use updated versions of parables to dramatize them.

📖 Angela Carter, Patrick McGrath, Ian McEwan *WB*

Innes, Hammond (British, 1913–) Born in Horsham, Sussex, Innes worked as a journalist in the 1930s and became a full-time writer of adventure novels in 1946. Begin with *Attack Alarm* (1941), a compellingly vivid treatment of the London blitz, which draws on his wartime experiences as an anti-aircraft gunner. The novel's emphasis on action in extreme situations is typical of his subsequent fiction. *The*

Blue Ice (1948) deals with a mineral expert who becomes a fugitive in the mountains of Norway as commercial and political interests attempt to discover the whereabouts of valuable ore deposits. His numerous books with maritime settings include *The Wreck of the 'Mary Deare'* (1956), in which the dogged Captain Patch struggles against wild seas for survival after his old freighter runs aground on a reef south of the Channel Islands.

📖 Nevil Shute, Alistair MacLean *DH*

Innes, Michael (British, 1906–94) J. I. M. Stewart, who wrote under the name Michael Innes, was born in Edinburgh and educated at Oxford, where he taught English during his academic career. Begin with *Death at the President's Lodging* (1936), set in a traditional English university, in which Inspector John Appleby, the urbane detective who dominates Innes's crime fiction, first appears. Later stories include *The Long Farewell* (1958), which finds Appleby in Italy. Now knighted and retired, he investigates the apparent suicide of a visiting Shakespearian scholar. **J. I. M. Stewart** also published novels under his own name, the best five of which make up the series *A Staircase in Surrey*. This academic comedy of manners follows the life and loves of Duncan Patullo at his Oxford college through *The Gaudy* (1974) and *Young Patullo* (1975) to *Full Term* (1978).

📖 Dorothy L. Sayers, Malcolm Bradbury *DH*

Irish, William (a.k.a. **Cornell Woolrich**) (US, 1903–68). *See* CRIME

Irving, John (US, 1942–   ) John Irving was born in New Hampshire and educated in the United States and Vienna. His best-known novel is *The World According to Garp* (1978). In it he tells the story—or stories—of the life and times of T. S. Garp, illegitimate son of a feminist leader. The novel moves from unicycling bears through castration during oral sex to transsexual football players. Yet there is pattern and meaning in such bizarre motifs, and part of the fun of reading the novel is to work them out. The same is true of *The Cider House Rules* (1985), the story of Homer Wells from St Cloud's orphanage. In *A Prayer for Owen Meany* (1989), Irving's best novel, the eponymous hero hits a foul ball in a baseball game and kills his best friend's mother.

📖 John Barth, Thomas Pynchon   *SA*

Irving, Washington (US, 1783–1859). *See* UNITED STATES OF AMERICA

Isherwood, Christopher (British, 1904–87) Christopher Isherwood maintained that his works amounted to a fictionalized autobiography. They draw upon his life and times in pre-war Berlin and post-war America, and reflect his friendships, politics, adoption of Eastern religious beliefs and pacifism, as well as increasingly open depiction of gay lifestyles. His prose is witty and engaging, typically placing relationships in the context of current political upheavals, as in *Mr Norris Changes Trains* (1935) and his best-known book, *Goodbye to Berlin* (1939), both set in the last years of the Weimar Republic before the Nazi takeover. The

latter stories were freely adapted by John van Druten as *Cabaret*, the musical and film starring Liza Minnelli as Sally Bowles. In the Berlin stories many of the characters are homosexual, and either communist or Nazi sympathizers; the double-dealing Arthur Norris is presented as charmingly eccentric by the narrator. Several of the gay hustlers from the Berlin years reappear in a later book, *Down There on a Visit* (1962). The narrative is in four sections, linked by the narrator's younger self as it moves from 1928 to 1953, depicting the changing nature of memory and identity as well as Isherwood's experience in the film industry and as a conscientious objector. *A Single Man* (1964) describes in loving detail the last day in the life of an expatriate English professor in Los Angeles, reflecting upon his dead lover, friends, and students, with a quietly moving detachment.

📖 E. M. Forster, Adam Mars-Jones

JS

Ishiguro, Kazuo (British, 1954–   ) Ishiguro was born in Japan but moved to England at the age of 6. He writes beautifully understated, transparent prose which exposes every fluctuation of mood and feeling between his characters. The first two novels are set in Japan; begin with *An Artist of the Floating World* (1986) set in the aftermath of the Second World War, about an ageing painter whose best pictures now appear to have been propagandist; his daughters are critical of him; the past does not bear scrutiny by the present. These concerns are also central to the Booker Prize-winning *The Remains of the Day* (1989), where a butler in an English country house comes to understand that through devoting himself to his job serving Lord Darlington, now a discredited fascist sympathizer, he has betrayed himself and sacrificed his chance of personal happiness. The overlap between private and public life, and the issue of individual responsibility, are explored with formal precision. *The Unconsoled* (1995) marks a change of gear; set in a fictional central European city, and about a concert pianist who cannot discover any concrete information about his own imminent concert, this big novel is strongly reminiscent of Kafka. As if in a dream or nightmare, important characters from Ryder's life intrude at inappropriate moments, and terrible difficulties appear to block the most mundane tasks. Humorous but also full of pathos, this strange novel is as haunting as a recurrent dream. In *When We Were Orphans* (2000), set in the 1930s, the hero is a childishly innocent detective, looking for his parents, who vanished in Shanghai when he was a boy. His quest through the war-torn city is deeply disturbing.

📖 Ian McEwan, Henry James, Franz Kafka   *JR*

J

Jackson, Shirley (US, 1919–65). *See* SUPERNATURAL

Jacobs, W(illiam) W(ymark) (British, 1863–1943). *See* SUPERNATURAL

Jacobson, Dan (South African, 1929–) After completing his studies at the University of Witwatersrand, Jacobson left South Africa, eventually settling in London where he has become a prominent writer and critic. Most of his writing concerns itself with South Africa under the apartheid regime. In *A Dance in the Sun* (1956) characters range from the white boss, struggling to maintain his authority, to the recalcitrant black servant. The novel centres on two travelling students who are constantly forced, as they witness the complexities of race relations, to confront their liberal beliefs. Like *Her Story* (1987), a parable of the Virgin Mary, *A Dance in the Sun* gestures towards biblical stories. The two Africans, for example, are named Joseph and Mary. *The Evidence of Love* (1959) is an elegiac story of two young lovers, one coloured, one white, who, after meeting in London, return to South Africa. In a dramatic climax, they find themselves up against the draconian laws of the South African state.

📖 Nadine Gordimer, Alan Paton, J. M. Coetzee *EW*

Jacobson, Howard (British, 1942–) Born in Manchester and educated at Cambridge, Jacobson lectured for several years at Wolverhampton Polytechnic before publishing his first novel, *Coming from Behind* (1983). This tells of an English lecturer, Sefton Goldberg, marooned in the grim confines of Wrottesley Polytechnic, yearning for the warm sun of the South, and dreaming of achieving success as a novelist. The plot may imply autobiographical realism, yet it is a comedy of Rabelaisian proportions which displays moments of true comic mastery. *The Very Model of a Man* (1992) is perhaps more daring in its recreation of Cain, the world's first murderer. Condemned to permanent exile for killing his brother Abel, Jacobson's Cain challenges God's notions of love and creation in a characteristically irreverent display of philosophical fireworks.

📖 Tom Sharpe, William Boyd, Malcolm Bradbury *RP*

James, Clive (Australian, 1939–) Clive James first made his name as a critic, but is now best known to a wide public as the presenter of several long-running television shows. His early years are the subject of *Unreliable Memoirs* (1980), an hilarious account of growing up plump and bookish in the Australia of the 1950s. His adolescence is the subject of *Falling Towards England* (1985), while *May Week Was in June* (1990), an account of his arrival at Oxford, makes up the third volume of a comic trilogy. His first wholly fictional novel was *Brilliant*

Creatures (1983), the tale of a young executive making his way through the glamorous world of literary and media London. Like his television shows, James's books satirize the fashions and pretensions of the day through a cleverly constructed 'fish-out-of-water' character.

📖 Evelyn Waugh, Leslie Thomas, Howard Jacobson   *WB*

James, C(yril) L(ionel) R(obert)
(Trinidadian, 1901–89). *See* CARIBBEAN

James, Henry (US/British, 1843–1916)
James was born in New York, son of a prominent theologian and philosopher, who took his children to Europe repeatedly. In 1875 Henry James settled in Paris, then moved to London, living in England for the rest of his life, becoming a British citizen in 1915. Cultural differences between America and Europe are a central theme in many of his novels, with America representing openness and naïvety, and Europe standing for sophistication, culture, and deviousness. James makes dramatic use of point of view, taking the reader deep into individual characters' thoughts and feelings, and showing how little these inner thoughts are accessible to others. His novels reveal how often motives are misinterpreted; how innocence can be manipulated and betrayed.

Start with *Washington Square* (1880), set in New York. Rich, clever Dr Sloper regards his devoted daughter, Catherine, as plain and dull. Catherine falls in love with a handsome fortune-hunter, Maurice, and her father threatens to disinherit her. He takes her on a tour of Europe and regards her divided loyalties as an entertainment, finally revealing his contempt for her when she announces that she will marry Maurice.

Maurice, who has been much encouraged by Catherine's silly aunt, forsakes Catherine when he realizes she will be penniless. 'Maurice had trifled with Catherine's affection; her father had broken its spring.' Outwardly a very civilized story—no sex, no violence, nor even any raised voices—this is one of the most emotionally brutal and dramatic novels there is. Move on to *The Portrait of a Lady* (1881), which takes an American heroine to Europe; Isabel Archer is beautiful, rich, independent, high-spirited, and attracts several suitors but makes a bad choice, with disastrous consequences. James described the book as 'The conception of a certain young woman affronting her destiny'.

James wrote many short stories, of which the best known is *The Turn of the Screw* (1898), a powerful and ambiguous ghost story in which a governess becomes obsessed by the corruption of her young charges. James's later novels have been accused of being wordy. This is because he qualifies and modifies each statement so that it is precise; and the pleasures and revelations of these novels far outweigh any effort demanded of the reader. *The Wings of the Dove* (1902) echoes the story of Isabel Archer, but here the American heiress, Milly, is suffering from an incurable illness. In her search for happiness she makes friends with a dazzling woman who plans—through using Milly—to acquire the fortune and marriage she herself desires. This has been memorably filmed, starring Helena Bonham Carter. In *The Golden Bowl* (1904) innocence and betrayal are again central; a very rich American and his daughter both marry; but their new (European) spouses are each other's lovers, and their affair looks set to continue. In *The Ambassadors* (1903), James's own favourite, Strether is sent to Europe by wealthy widow Mrs Newsome, to track down her errant son. But Strether himself becomes romantically entangled in Paris. The use of point of view here to conceal information from the central character (and the reader) is brilliant.

📖 Edith Wharton, George Eliot, Patrick White. *See* CLASSICS, UNITED STATES OF AMERICA   *JR*

James, M(ontague) R(hodes) (British, 1862–1936) Born at Goodnestone, Kent, M. R. James was educated at King's College, Cambridge. He became Vice-Chancellor of Cambridge, then Provost of Eton College in 1918. Widely acknowledged as the master of the English ghost story, his concise tales are expertly crafted and imaginatively unsettling. Begin with his first collection, *Ghost Stories of an Antiquary* (1904), which, like much of his writing, is strongly coloured by his specialized knowledge of folklore and superstition. The gradual revelation of malign supernatural presences in his stories gains in effectiveness through his donnish restraint of tone and the fundamental ordinariness of his settings. Other collections include *A Thin Ghost and Other Stories* (1919), *The Five Jars* (1922), and *A Warning to the Curious* (1925). His *Collected Ghost Stories* appeared in 1931.

📖 J. Sheridan Le Fanu, H. P. Lovecraft   *DH*

James, P(hyllis) D(orothy) (British, 1920–) Although P. D. James left school at 16, she went on to work in the criminal policy department of the Home Office. This experience fuelled her detective fiction writing, which began in 1962 with *Cover Her Face*. Introducing her poetry-writing detective Adam Dalgleish, the novel is set in a backward-thinking village where Sally Jupp, from a home for unmarried mothers, meets an untimely death. Many of James's stories have been dramatized for television. Her later work plays with expectations of detective fiction, dealing with more serious themes than have been traditionally addressed in this genre. *Original Sin* (1994), for instance, is a mystery story set in a publishing house, and considers the decline of the 'gentleman publisher'. The Holocaust also appears as an important backdrop to this novel. Although this attracted praise from some quarters, it unbalanced the novel and added a worthiness that it could not quite carry.

The next Dalgleish novel, *A Shroud for a Nightingale* (1971), is a gripping story set in a nurses' training school, and begins with the inexplicable death of a young student nurse. Move on to one of James's best novels, *Devices and Desires* (1989), in which Dalgleish escapes to Norfolk for a much-needed holiday only to encounter the actions of a pyschopathic strangler of young women; the campaign against the local nuclear power station features as an interesting sub-plot.

You may also like to try her novels in which the feisty private detective Cordelia Gray leads the murder hunt. Start with *An Unsuitable Job for a Woman* (1981). *Children of Men* (1992) marked a new departure in James's writing. This futuristic novel is set in an authoritarian England where no children have been born for twenty-five years. The hero, an academic, attempts to change the course of history.

📖 Ruth Rendell (writing as Barbara Vine), Agatha Christie, Colin Dexter. *See* CRIME   *SB*

Jelinek, Elfriede (Austrian, 1946–).
See GERMANY

Jerome, Jerome K(lapka) (British, 1859–1927) Jerome K. Jerome left school at 14 and worked in a variety of jobs before publishing his first book, *On Stage and Off* (1885), a collection of humorous pieces about the theatre. He achieved lasting fame with *Three Men in a Boat* (1889), and there is no better introduction to his work than the story of narrator J.'s trip up the Thames with friends George, Harris, and the dog Montmorency. Full of wonderful set pieces, gentle irony, witty observation, and whimsical musings on life, it is one of the great comic novels of all time. The characters reappear in *Three Men on the Bummel* (1900), about a cycling tour in Germany, but the earlier magic is lacking. Jerome also founded the humorous magazine the *Idler*, and wrote plays and a volume of autobiography.

📖 P. G. Wodehouse, Saki.
See HUMOUR   CB

Jhabvala, Ruth Prawer (Polish/British, 1927–) Well-known for her collaboration with James Ivory on many of the scripts of the Merchant–Ivory films, Ruth Prawer Jhabvala is also a prolific novelist. She was the daughter of Polish-Jewish parents, born in Germany, brought up in Britain, lived in India for twenty-four years and moved to America in 1975. Her novels about India (which include *Esmond in India*, 1958, and *A New Dominion*, 1973) mainly deal with the themes of sexual, racial, and cultural identity. Her most famous novel, *Heat and Dust*, won the Booker Prize in 1975, and was turned into a film in 1983. This short but highly readable novel plots the story of two very different (British)

women, separated by over fifty years, and their experiences of India, during British Rule and after.

📖 Paul Scott, Anita Desai,
E. M. Forster   SB

Johnson, B(ryan) S(tanley) (British, 1933–73) Johnson was an experimentalist, most famously subverting fiction's conventions in *The Unfortunates* (1969), his novel-in-a-box which consists of looseleaf sections to be shuffled and read in any order. Another of his books features a hole in the page. His first novel, *Travelling People* (1963), disrupts narrative continuity by switching between styles. Prefigured by Sterne's *Tristram Shandy*, influenced by James Joyce, and to some extent anticipating Alasdair Gray's extravagance with narrative and typographical devices, Johnson's fiction is far less comic. Indeed, it is often enigmatic and pessimistic: the novel-in-a-box actually recounts the narrator's feelings about the death of a friend. The relatively accessible *House Mother Normal* (1971) is, however, subtitled *A Geriatric Comedy*. After a period of neglect, *A B. S. Johnson Omnibus* (2000) makes available again the work of this daring if sometimes frustrating author.

📖 Samuel Beckett, Alasdair Gray   JS

Johnson, James Weldon (US, 1871–1938). See BLACK AND WHITE

Johnson, Pamela Hansford (British, 1912–81) Born in south London, Johnson trained as a stenographer before the publication of her first novel, *This Bed Thy Centre* (1935). Begin with this story, which typifies much of her work in its focus on a love relationship in London settings with graphically evoked social conditions. Its attempt at sexual candour caused controversy. In a different vein, try the three books featuring her poet-heroine Dorothy Merlin. The first, *The Unspeakable Skipton* (1959), satirizes literary pretensions in its treatment of the eccentrically despicable Skipton. *Night and Silence! Who is Here?* (1963) followed, offering a richly comic view of American academic life. In the last of the Merlin books, *Cork Street, Next to the Hatter's* (1965), the vanity of the acting profession is her satirical target.

📖 Margaret Drabble, Ivy Compton-Burnett, Olivia Manning   *DH*

Johnson, Samuel (British, 1709–84). *See* CLASSICS, HUMOUR, ROMANCE

Johnson, Wayne (US, 1956–). *See* CANADA

Johnston, Jennifer (Anglo-Irish, 1930–) Johnston was born into the Anglo-Irish Protestant ascendancy in Dublin and the place of the Anglo-Irish in Irish society is a major theme of her work. Johnston often describes a relationship between an adult and an adolescent emerging into adulthood; a relationship which often ends in betrayal. In *Shadows on our Skin*, shortlisted for the Booker Prize in 1977 and set in Derry, the contact is between Joe Logan, a budding poet, and the teacher who encourages him, Kathleen Doherty. In *The Old Jest* (1979) the theme of safety versus change is embodied in Nancy Gulliver, an orphan living a cushioned life in a 'big house' beside the sea. Nancy discovers a republican revolutionary living in a hut on the beach. However, Nancy's longing for adventure inevitably leads to disaster.

📖 Elizabeth Bowen, Molly Keane, Edna O'Brien. *See* IRELAND   *IP*

Jolley, Elizabeth (British/Australian 1923–) Although she didn't move to Australia until she was 36, Jolley regards herself and is generally thought of as an Australian writer. She writes about women who are loners or outsiders, often with wicked humour and sharp (verging on painful) insight. Begin with *Miss Peabody's Inheritance* (1983), a beautifully constructed comic novel in which Miss Peabody, a lonely English spinster with a dreary office job and a demanding invalid mother, writes to the author of her favourite novel. The author replies, in hilarious cliché-ridden letters describing her idyllic life on her cattle station, and enclosing chapters of her novel-in-progress, about the lesbian headmistress of a girls' boarding-school. These three story-strands build to a surprising and satisfying climax as Miss Peabody gives up her job and goes to visit the author in Australia. *Foxybaby* (1984) describes Alma Porch's attempt to dramatize her unwritten novel at an appallingly run summer school creative drama class, where all the characters have conflicting agendas, and boundaries between real and imaginary blur. *The George's Wife* (1993) is darker, dealing with the memories of a young woman who is the secret lover of an older man—a man who is inseparable from his sister. Jolley's writing is so clear that you remember details of her novels as vividly as if they were your own life.

📖 Barbara Pym, Alice Munro, Katherine Mansfield. *See* AUSTRALIA AND NEW ZEALAND   *JR*

Jones, Diana Wynne (British, 1934–) Diana Wynne Jones is one of the foremost exponents of 'young adult' fantasy. Her works tend to bring characters of myth or fantasy into homely or domestic settings, as for instance in *Archer's Goon* (1984), in which an adolescent thug who appears in a middle-class kitchen turns out to be an emissary in a war of wizards and spaceships; or *Hexwood* (1993), in which an English copse becomes the focus of a struggle involving a galactic empire. Domestic and mythical themes are movingly mingled in *Fire and Hemlock* (1984), which on one level follows the fortunes of a teenager from a broken home, complete with inept father, neurotic mother, and hostile stepmother, and on the other re-enacts the traditional ballad of 'Tam Lin' and his rescue from the fairy queen.

📖 Ursula Le Guin, Alan Garner.
See FANTASY   *TS*

Jones, Douglas C. (US, 1924–).
See WESTERN

Jones, Jack (British, 1884–1970) Born
in Merthyr Tydfil, Glamorgan, Jack Jones became a miner at the age of 12 and was later a journalist. A notable left-wing speaker during the 1930s, his novels documenting conditions in industrial South Wales are coloured by his socialist convictions. Begin with *Rhondda Roundabout* (1934), which centres on the love between a chapel minister and a shop assistant. Jones depicts the Rhondda community retaining its identity in the face of growing economic hardship through its enthusiasm for religion, music, and sport. *Black Parade* (1935) chronicles the fortunes of a mining family from the beginnings of the coal boom in South Wales through to the aftermath of the General Strike. In *River out of Eden* (1951) the Regan family's rise to prosperity from their beginnings as Irish immigrants follows upon the growing prosperity of Cardiff as a major port.

📖 Richard Llewellyn   *DH*

Jones, James (US, 1921–77) Jones served
with distinction in the Second World War and the nature of military life was to be the major subject of his fiction. *From Here to Eternity* (1951) was the first book of a planned trilogy about soldiering, followed by *The Thin Red Line* (1962) and the unfinished *Whistle* (1978). *From Here to Eternity* dramatizes the brutal camaraderie of life in an army barracks in a direct naturalistic style. The struggles of Prewitt and Warden to overcome corruption in the institution they revere are powerfully handled. Less convincing, however, is the love-interest and Prewitt's romance is wickedly parodied in Joseph Heller's *Catch-22*. Jones portrays an authoritarian power structure, the army, which dehumanizes the individual and ironically leads to a crisis of masculinity in the most masculine of environments. The subject receives a more sensitive treatment in his novella *The Pistol* (1959).

📖 Norman Mailer, Robert Stone.
See WAR, SEXUAL POLITICS   *GK*

Jong, Erica (US, 1942–) Erica Jong
was born and educated in New York, and became both notorious and celebrated for her first novel, *Fear of Flying* (1973). In it the heroine, Isadora Wing, seeks sexual and personal fulfilment, moving seamlessly from relationship to relationship. The novel was ground-breaking in its openness and assumption that women want sexual happiness too. Jong wrote a number of sequels—*How to Save Your Own Life* (1977), *Parachutes and Kisses* (1984), and *Any Woman's Blues* (1990). The last is a darker novel, partly set in Venice, and deals in breakdown and recovery. Jong has also written historical pastiche,

many poems, and an autobiography, *Fear of Fifty* (1994). Her writing is feminist-inspired, and her main subject is her own life.

📖 Lisa Alther, Marilyn French. *See* SEXUAL POLITICS, UNITED STATES OF AMERICA   SA

Jordan, Neil (Irish, 1950–   ) Best known as a director of films like *The Crying Game* and *Angel*, Jordan began his career as a writer with an acclaimed collection of short stories, *Night in Tunisia* (1976), the title story of which describes a father and son reconciled by the music of jazz saxophonist Charlie Parker. Jordan's subsequent novels, starting with *The Past* (1980), introduced fantastic elements into his accounts of ordinary lives, and *The Dream of a Beast* (1983) creates a compelling dream landscape around an advertising copywriter trying to describe the scent of musk. *Sunrise with Sea Monster* (1995) is written from the viewpoint of an Irish volunteer imprisoned during the Spanish Civil War. Jordan's writing is marked by a visual clarity and emotional precision that makes his fiction as immediate and vivid as his cinema.

📖 Angela Carter, Patrick McCabe, Rachel Ingalls   WB

Jordan, Robert (US, 1948–   ). *See* FANTASY

Joyce, James (Irish, 1882–1941) James Joyce's reputation for inaccessibility is greatly exaggerated. Like Shakespeare, who could please royalty and *hoi polloi*, Joyce is a high intellectual for the erudite, a teller of filthy jokes to rival Chaucer, and simply a plain good story-teller. Granted, *Finnegans Wake* (1939) is formidable, but once you realize that it's permissible to browse, grazing playfully and expecting nothing more from it than diversion, even this opens up to an unexpected degree. But don't start here. Begin with *A Portrait of the Artist as a Young Man* (1914–15), Joyce's first published novel, in which he presents himself in the guise of its hero, Stephen Dedalus. Stephen, as the title implies, is a portrait rather than the complete Joyce, but the events of his life are essentially those of his creator. The book tells in vivid poetic prose of his earliest childhood memories, his Jesuit education, the family's move to Dublin, and Stephen's subsequent progression through adolescence, university, and finally self-imposed exile. Intense, full of brilliant set pieces and detailed observation, *Portrait* remains one of the classics of adolescence, along with *The Catcher in the Rye* (1951) and *The Sorrows of Young Werther* (1774).

Next read *Dubliners* (1914), a collection of stories about Dublin life. Along with Chekhov, Joyce perfected the art of capturing the essence of a seemingly trivial incident. He called these moments epiphanies, when a look, a movement, a passing encounter becomes charged with a kind of momentous significance. Often very little actually happens, but these are tremendously powerful stories, full of insight and sensitive observation. The collection culminates in 'The Dead', a wonderfully subtle piece in which a song overheard after a party leads to a revelation of lost love and youthful death.

Many of the characters in *Dubliners* reappear in *Ulysses* (1922), as does Stephen Dedalus, but the principal character is a Dublin Jew, Leopold Bloom. Following his wanderings around the city in the course of one single day, this vast book mirrors the journeyings of the Greek hero through the ordinary actions of an ordinary man. Reading *Ulysses* is an effort but an exhilarating one; it is a dazzling feat of creation performed in a variety of styles from the rompingly readable to the dense and impenetrable. Joyce perfected the stream-of-consciousness technique in the final soliloquy of Bloom's wife, Molly, and the influence of *Ulysses* on modern literature is so pervasive that it is now taken for granted. He wrote frankly and graphically about the sex act and bodily functions, delved into the wilder reaches of sexual fantasy, and imbued his fictional Everyman with an interior life so complete it mirrors the universal. It is perhaps hard now for the modern reader to comprehend the impact of this in 1922. Damned as obscene, banned for years in Ireland, *Ulysses* is now widely regarded as one of the most important books of the twentieth or any other century.

📖 Marcel Proust, Samuel Beckett, Flann O'Brien. *See* CHILDHOOD, CLASSICS, IRELAND, MAGIC REALISM, SHORT STORIES   *CB*

Judd, Alan (British, 1946–   ) 'Alan Judd' is the pseudonym of Alan Petty, who has worked for the Foreign Office and became Private Secretary to the Head of MI6. His satirical novels typically blend farce and tragedy in dealing with their subjects —the army, university life, the diplomatic service, and espionage—though they handle serious themes equally well. His first, *A Breed of Heroes* (1981), is an ironic treatment of modern soldiering, while *The Noonday Devil* (1987) is set at Oxford during the student political unrest of the early 1970s. In the latter, a student is directing a production of a Jacobean play while contemplating his final examinations; philosophical debates lead to an unexpected plot twist. *Short of Glory* (1984) is very much in the vein of Evelyn Waugh, a comedy centring around the British Embassy in South Africa. The figure of the Englishman floundering abroad reappears in *Tango* (1989): recruited by British intelligence, the manager of a bookshop becomes central to a coup involving a South American President and his mistress.

📖 Evelyn Waugh, William Boyd, Graham Greene. *See* SPY   *JS*

K

Kafka, Franz (Czech, 1883–1924) Kafka was born in Prague, into a wealthy German-speaking Jewish family. During his lifetime he published only a handful of short fragments and prose pieces, and left instructions to his friend from youth and literary executor, Max Brod, to destroy all his unpublished writings. After Kafka's death from tuberculosis, Brod disregarded this wish, and so the major works survived which place Kafka as one of the most original, influential, and disturbing writers of the twentieth century.

The fictional landscape he created, though naturalistic in detail, has the terrifying implacable logic of a never-ending dream from which there is no escape. Today we use the term 'Kafkaesque' to describe the sense of dislocation the individual feels when overwhelmed by a dizzyingly complex and threatening machine-society—memorably conveyed in one of the most famous opening lines in modern literature: 'Someone must have been telling lies about Joseph K., for without having done anything wrong he was arrested one fine morning' (from *The Trial*, 1925). Never openly accused of a specific crime, so unable to defend himself, Joseph K. is sucked into a labyrinthine bureaucracy of nameless officials, shadowy authority figures, and unfathomable procedures. The gloom is tempered by Kafka's sense of the absurd—even the most menacing situation teeters on the edge of farce—and the undercurrent of sensuality, which is all the more heated for being suggested, rather than explicit.

A good way into Kafka is through his shorter pieces, particularly *Metamorphosis* (1915), with another memorable opening line: 'As Gregor Samsa awoke one morning from uneasy dreams he found himself transformed in his bed into a gigantic insect.' And the absolutely harrowing *In the Penal Settlement* (1933) in which the accused prisoner is sentenced to die by having his crime imprinted on his flesh by needle points.

Amerika (so spelt in the original German edition, 1927) is lighter in tone and more playful, about 16-year-old Karl Rossman, a recently arrived immigrant from Europe, who is taken up and then rejected by a rich uncle. Kafka himself never visited America, and relied on guidebooks, which liberated his imagination to create a weirdly whimsical New World, and makes convincing the naïve charm and wide-eyed innocence of his hero.

Another full-length work, *The Castle* (1926), is an interminable tale about a land surveyor named K., who arrives in a peasant village and is forever balked from getting into the forbidding medieval castle and completing his job. Possibly Kafka's most profound statement, and most difficult book, it none the less repays the effort. The meaning in Kafka's books is notoriously elusive, but this is part of their attraction. Kafka's own explanation, in an extraordinary 50-page letter he wrote to his father, is interesting, but typically unhelpful: 'My writings are about you. I merely poured out in them what I could not pour out on your breast.'

Albert Camus, Kazuo Ishiguro, Günter Grass, Knut Hamsun.
See GERMANY, MAGIC REALISM

TH

Kavan, Anna (British, 1901–68) Anna Kavan published her first novel, *Let Me Alone* (1930), under her married name of **Helen Ferguson**. An account of a disastrous and abusive relationship, the novel featured a character, based on herself, called Anna Kavan. Following a period in a psychiatric clinic, Kavan changed her name by deed poll. Her best-known novel, *Sleep has His House* (1947), is an account of a mind on the borderline between dream and reality, and as in much of Kavan's writing the book blurs the distinction between fiction and autobiography. *Ice* (1967) is a novel set in a strange, symbolic, ice-bound country, narrated by a woman who is never named. Often considered a metaphor for the writer's lifelong heroin addiction, *Ice* uses the conventions of science fiction to explore an inner world. *I am Lazarus* (1945) and *Julia and the Bazooka* (1970) are collections of stories.

Franz Kafka, J. G. Ballard, Janet Frame
WB

Kavanagh, Patrick (Irish, 1904–67). *See* IRELAND

Kavanagh, P(atrick) J(oseph) (British, 1931–) Born in Worthing, Sussex, P. J. Kavanagh was educated at Oxford and writes poetry, journalism, and for television. Of his novels, begin with *A Song and Dance* (1968), which displays his characteristic gift for combining emotional seriousness with an optimistic lightness of tone. The heady atmosphere of the London media scene in the 1960s is evoked as a background to its heroine's doomed love-affair. A big win on the horses ends the main protagonist's uneventfully hedonistic routine in *A Happy Man* (1972). His philosophy of detached acceptance is tested while holidaying on a tropical island where his girlfriend deserts him and civil war breaks out. *Only by Mistake* (1986) moves rapidly between the home counties, Dublin, and the Scottish island of Hoy as a successful actor goes on the run after inadvertently angering the IRA.

John Wain, William Boyd
DH

Keane, Molly (Anglo-Irish, 1904–96) Molly Keane's novels are witty studies of Anglo-Irish upper-class society which centre on hunting, fashion, and romance, but also consider the hidden tensions and dangers of her characters' private lives. Those written up to 1952 are under the pen-name of **M. J. Farrell**. Begin with *Good Behaviour* (1981, Booker Prize-shortlisted), a black comedy narrated by Aroon, the unattractive and neglected daughter of the St Charles family. Used to concealing emotion under a veneer of socially acceptable conduct, Aroon discusses her mother's tyranny and her father's long illness, inadvertently shedding light on the secret desires and fantasies that pervade the house. Move on to *Devoted Ladies* (1934), which deals with the attempts of Jessica to stop her lover, Jane, from marrying George Playfair. Though superficially a society novel, it is also an absorbing dramatization of an increasingly sinister power struggle. Keane was also a successful dramatist.

Nancy Mitford, Edna O'Brien, Muriel Spark. *See* IRELAND
SR

Keating, H(enry) R(aymond) F(itzwalter) (British, 1926–) Keating was born in St Leonards and educated at Trinity College, Dublin. He was a journalist before becoming a full-time writer. Begin by meeting his best-known creation, the amiable Inspector Ganesh Ghote of the Bombay Police. The detective's many appearances include *Inspector Ghote Caught in the Meshes* (1967), in which the investigation of an American visitor's violent death finds Ghote caught up in intrigues between rival secret service organizations. *The Iciest Sin* (1990) thrusts Ghote into a web of illegality and corruption as he deals with the blackmailing of a government official. Keating has also written futuristic novels, notably *A Long Walk to Wimbledon* (1978), in which a man struggles to reach his wife after a catastrophe has wrecked London, and *The Strong Man* (1971), depicting a dystopia under a dictator whose removal has unforeseen results.

📖 Julian Symons, John Wain, John Carr *DH*

Keery, Sam (British, 1930–). *See* IRELAND

Keillor, Garrison (US, 1942–) Garrison Keillor was born in Minnesota and educated there. He started his career in radio in Minneapolis, both playing music and narrating stories about the inhabitants of a fictional town. These grew and developed into *Lake Wobegon Days* (1985), a series of loosely linked stories about some second-generation Scandinavian families. His easy narrative style and quiet, gentle humour ensured the book's success. He captures the atmosphere of Middle America to perfection. There are further stories about the same families in *Leaving Home* (1987)

and *We are Still Married* (1989). *Radio Romance* (1991) is a novel about a radio station in Minneapolis.

📖 Armistead Maupin, Elizabeth Gaskell (*Cranford*) *SA*

Kellerman, Jonathan (US, 1949–) Jonathan Kellerman is a former child psychologist. Dr Alex Delaware, the hero of his crime novels, is an academic and psychologist who assists the police, in particular his friend Milo Sturgis, with cases using his skills as a psychological profiler. Gripping and intelligent, the stories expose the disturbance and sickness of contemporary American society. *When the Bough Breaks* (or *Shrunken Heads*; 1985) has an emotionally burnt-out Delaware asked to help find out whether a young girl, who can't or won't talk to the police, has witnessed a double murder. *Self Defence* (1994) tells the story of a woman juror who has served at a harrowing trial and has since been tormented by a recurrent nightmare that might be a repressed memory of childhood horror. A different hero, Chief Inspector Daniel Shalom Sharavi, features in his serial-killer thriller *The Butcher's Theatre* (1988), set in Jerusalem.

📖 Patricia Cornwell, Robin Cook *CS*

Kelman, James (British, 1946–) Born in Glasgow, Kelman left school at 15 and after labouring jobs and a stint as a bus conductor, entered the University of Strathclyde at the age of 28. His writing derives from both a Scottish and a European tradition, and has been compared to that of Zola, Dostoevsky, and Kafka for its portrayal of people in socially alienated situations. His characters tend to be working class, but in *A Disaffection* (1989) the central character is Patrick, a teacher. Patrick wants to leave teaching because he no longer believes in conventional education. His life is further complicated by his unrequited love for a fellow teacher, Alison. *How Late It was, How Late*, which won the Booker Prize in 1994, depicts the attempts of Sammy to come to terms with the blindness which has overcome him as the result of a beating in a police cell. He has also lost his girlfriend and the work he was trying to fix up with a friend. From this unpromising material, Kelman makes a paean to the survival of the human spirit. Kelman is an uncompromising writer, whose work ranges between political rage and a tender lyricism, between social realism, surrealism, and a kind of dark burlesque. For virtuosity, try the short stories in *Greyhound for Breakfast* (1987).

📖 Samuel Beckett, Alasdair Gray, Franz Kafka. *See* SHORT STORIES

LM

Kempadoo, Oonya (Guyanese, 1966–). *See* BLACK AND WHITE

Keneally, Thomas (Australian, 1935–) Keneally is a prolific and versatile novelist who has fictionalized a number of key historical moments. Begin with his Booker Prize-winning *Schindler's Ark* (1982), which was filmed by Spielberg as *Schindler's List*. The real Oskar Schindler saved a number of Jews from the Nazi death camps by employing them in his Polish factory; Keneally researched the story and wrote it as a novel, exploring the nature of a man who has high-ranking Nazi friends and is making great profits from the war, yet who will do all in his power to protect his Jewish workforce. Move on to *The Playmaker* (1987). Set in the first year of the convict

settlement in Australia, and based on the real convict production of Farquhar's play *The Recruiting Officer*, this focuses on Lt. Ralph Clarke and his affair with a convict woman. Drawing on letters and diaries from 1788, Keneally brings the first settlement to life, particularly the criminal underworld and the difficult relations between officers. Among his other Australian novels, *The Chant of Jimmie Blacksmith* (1972, filmed 1978) stands out for its unflinching depiction of the white hypocrisy and cruelty meted out to an innocent hardworking Aboriginal boy in the years around 1900; and *Flying Hero Class* (1991) is interesting on the complexities of more recent white–Aboriginal relations, telling the story of the hijack of a plane bearing an internationally famous troupe of Aboriginal dancers.

📖 Barry Unsworth, William Boyd, Peter Carey, Brian Moore. *See* AUSTRALIA AND NEW ZEALAND, HISTORICAL

JR

Kennedy, A(lison) L(ouise) (British, 1965–) Kennedy writes with immediacy and power; begin with her short-story collection *Night Geometry and the Garscadden Trains* (1990) which offers vivid glimpses into the lives of apparently ordinary people. *So I am Glad* (1995, Encore award) is an extraordinary novel, narrated by a woman with a fine line in irony, who has been abused by her parents and whose relationship with her lover has become terrifyingly sadistic. The possibility of happiness enters her life in the form of the ghost of Cyrano de Bergerac, a physically real and present man, despite his tendency to glow silver-blue at times. *Everything You Need* (1999) is set on an island which is a writers' colony, and centres on the relationship between a writer father and his unknowing daughter Mary, who has been told he is dead. This long novel is peopled by characters in extreme emotional states.

📖 James Kellman, Ian McEwan. *See* SHORT STORIES   *JR*

Kent, Alexander. *See* **Reeman, Douglas**

Kerouac, Jack (US, 1922–69) Coming to prominence at the time of James Dean and Elvis Presley, it probably did Kerouac's literary career no harm that he possessed the dark rugged looks of a screen idol. He coined the term Beat Generation, whose creed Dig Everything! was an outright rejection of the Squares stuck in the rat race with their phoney American Dream and their decent moral values. The bible of the Beats was *On the Road* (1957), Kerouac's second novel, actually written in 1951. Narrated in the first person by Sal Paradise, it features Dean Moriarty as the wild-man hero, roaming across America in his restless quest for kicks, fuelled by booze, drugs, and sex. The book caught the mood of rebellious youth and inspired a thousand road-movies. Kerouac famously wrote his books very fast—in a few weeks, sometimes days, even —and out they poured: *The Dharma Bums* (1958), *The Subterraneans* (1958), *Desolation Angels* (1960). Together they constitute his search for intense experience as a means of self-exploration (the oldest American Dream of all), for which Buddhism seemed to provide some answers, filling the spiritual void of a materialistic society. Rambling and episodic, lacking plot and structure, these are slabs of raw experience which disregard literary ground rules, comparable in style

to free-form jazz improvisation. In his preface to *Big Sur* (1962), reflecting in the hazy aftermath of the Beat movement, Kerouac says that all his books are just chapters in the whole work . . . the whole thing forms one enormous comedy.

📖 William Burroughs, Henry Miller, Anais Nin. *See* UNITED STATES OF AMERICA   *TH*

Kerr, Philip (British, 1956–) Philip Kerr's early novels are exciting, unconventional thrillers which transpose the Deighton/Le Carré territory into new contexts. The *Berlin Noir* trilogy (1993) explores Nazi Germany from within, while Detective Grushko pursues the Mafia in the new Russia in *Dead Meat* (1993). These novels are fully researched and convincing in their detail as much as in their plots. Kerr's later novels seem to be pitching as Hollywood film-scripts, often set in the future with much less complex adventure plots. The best of them is *Gridiron* (1996) in which, although the characters are undeveloped, the building where everything is computer controlled is a brilliant and malevolent invention.

📖 John Grisham, Michael Crichton. *See* THRILLERS   *RV*

Kesey, Ken (US, 1935–) Kesey came to notoriety as a fugitive from drugs charges and leader of the anarchistic 'Merry Pranksters' during their bus trips of the mid-1960s, but he had already written two major novels. *One Flew Over the Cuckoo's Nest* (1962), an allegory of American society set in a mental hospital, tells a story of the clash between individualism and authority. As seen by inmate Chief Bromden, Randle P. McMurphy stimulates the patients into regaining their identities by introducing rebellious freedoms to the ward, but is eventually subdued by Big Nurse. *Sometimes a Great Notion* (1964) is rated even more highly by many critics; in a complex narrative, Hank and Lee Stamper fall out while running an Oregon logging operation and contending with a local union strike. By contrast, *Last Go Round* (1994) recreates the 1911 World Rodeo Championships in Pendleton, Oregon; this Old West romp features contending black, Indian, and Southern cowboys, cowgirls, and Buffalo Bill.

📖 Tom Wolfe, Robert Stone, Paul Sayer, Joseph Heller   JS

Keyes, Marian (Irish, 1963–) Keyes is a bestselling author of funny, romantic novels, aimed at women readers. Start with the first, *Watermelon* (1996), about a woman whose husband leaves her on the day she gives birth to her first child. *Rachel's Holiday* (1998) is set in a rehab clinic; the heroine is a lying, drug-addicted 27 year old who is in denial about her own state. *Sushi for Beginners* (2000) is set in the world of glossy magazines and deals with three women who are all looking (in the wrong places) for happiness. Believing that 'the best comedy is rooted in despair', Keyes examines the chaotic depths of her characters' unhappiness with lightness and black humour.

📖 Jane Green, Helen Fielding, Roddy Doyle   JR

Kiely, Benedict (Irish, 1919–). *See* IRELAND

Kincaid, Jamaica (Antiguan/US, 1949–) Kincaid was born in Antigua and emigrated to the United States in 1966. She is (with Erna Brodber) the most original

and controversial of the younger writers from the Caribbean. Her 1983 book of stories, *At the Bottom of the River*, excites with its mixture of apocalyptic imagery drawn from the Bible with snatches of folk-tale thrown in. The effect is often that of a prose-poem. The autobiographical novels, *Annie John* (1985), about a Caribbean girl growing to maturity, *Lucy* (1990), about a young Antiguan woman moving to New York as an au pair, and *The Autobiography of My Mother* (1996), all have that lyrical quality. Kincaid's narrative style and idiom have become increasingly classical, losing the inflections of Caribbean speech and not yet acquiring an American flavour. The transition is underlined in *My Brother* (1997) depicting her brother's dying from AIDS: here, the brother's (Antiguan) language is put in brackets; a translation.

📖 Jean Rhys. *See* BLACK AND WHITE, CARIBBEAN   EM

King, Francis (British, 1923–) King is a prolific writer, and his books vary widely in both subject matter and tone. Loosely speaking, however, his early novels can be categorized as studies of isolation and loss. Set in different countries and often told from multiple points of view, they tend to deal with outsiders: those seeking acceptance from an alien community, and those fighting to escape from their own. These themes acquire resonance in *A Domestic Animal* (1970), an openly gay novel and an eloquent, moving account of a one-sided love-affair. Move on to *Act of Darkness* (1983), a psychological thriller about the murder of a child in 1930s' India. Also try some of King's excellent short stories.

📖 Christopher Isherwood, E. M. Forster, Colm Toibin   SR

King, Stephen (US, 1947–) Born in Portland, Maine, Stephen King taught English before turning to writing full-time. The immediate success of *Carrie* (1974), a revenge drama about a disturbed girl who develops telekinetic powers at the onset of puberty, helped to create the template for much of King's writing. The idyllic small town invaded by inexplicable supernatural forces has been a persistent motif, as in *Salem's Lot* (1975) where two boys are terrorized by vampires when they move to a new town. The novel uses the fulfilment of childhood fears to create much of its effect. The writer as a character is another staple, used most effectively in *Misery* (1987), a suspense story in which, following a car accident, a best-selling author is kidnapped by his 'number one fan', whose alternating psychosis and sentimentality force him to resurrect his own fictional creation. *The Dark Half* (1989) features a writer haunted by the repressed side of his personality that produces his successful horror novels. *The Dead Zone* (1979) is a haunting tale about a man whose ability to see the future forces him into seclusion until he meets a corrupt minor politician who is destined to start a Third World War. Although King's later books lack some of the tautness of his earlier work, he remains one of the most inventive genre novelists of his generation. King has also written under the pseudonym **Richard Bachman**.

📖 Dean R. Koontz, Anne Rice, James Herbert. *See* SUPERNATURAL
WB

King, Thomas (US, 1943–). *See* CANADA

Kingsley, Charles (British, 1819–75). *See* CHILDHOOD

Kingsolver, Barbara (US, 1955–) Like her spirited heroine, Taylor Greer, Kingsolver grew up in Kentucky, and settled in Tucson, Arizona. A long-term human rights activist, Kingsolver has a keen ear for the speech of the poor whites, Mexicans, and Native Americans of the southern states. Begin with *The Bean Trees* (1988), in which the plucky Taylor has only two goals: to escape Kentucky and avoid getting pregnant. She sets out across country in a clapped-out car, but motherhood catches up with her in a service station when a traumatized Native American child is thrust into her care. Taylor's story is continued in *Pigs in Heaven* (1993), when a Cherokee lawyer challenges the adoption of the now 6-year-old child, and the reader is torn by two compelling arguments about the child's best interests. As in her memorable second novel, *Animal Dreams* (1990), Kingsolver finds the lives of her small-town characters both compelling and magical. *The Poisonwood Bible* (1999) is the story of an evangelical Baptist who takes his woefully unprepared family and mission to the Belgian Congo in 1959; Kingsolver is particularly good on his bullying character, and on Africa.

📖 Gloria Naylor, Ellen Gilchrist, Louise Erdrich
JN

Kingston, Maxine Hong (US/Chinese, 1940–) Hong Kingston's work bridges two cultures and *The Woman Warrior: Memoirs of a Girlhood among Ghosts* (1976) is her response to making sense of the two worlds. Her mother, once a respected doctor in China, told stories of strong Chinese woman through her native myths and fables but never spoke of the aunt who committed suicide. Hong Kingston writes passionately about the oppression

Chinese woman suffered. *China Men* (1980) does the same for the experience of her father and other male relatives in the United States. *Trip Master Monkey: His Fake Book* (1989) gives us a wonderful character in the form of Wittman Ah Sing, a Chinese-American hippie playwright and poet as he sets about writing and staging a play full of Chinese stories. Her writing pioneered the way for female writers' voices from other ethnic backgrounds, both stylistically and in content.

📖 Amy Tan, Toni Morrison   *TO*

Kipling, Rudyard (British, 1865–1936) Kipling, in his lifetime one of the best known and most popular writers in the world, was born in Bombay into an Anglo-Indian family. He was educated in England and spent most of his life in the west, but his work is generally associated with the assumptions of the British Raj. Some critics believe this association to be misleading, pointing out that he energetically and often respectfully supports Indian characters in his writing, and that he satirizes Anglo-Indian pomposity. None the less, the beliefs and established hierarchy of the Raj do form the background to much of his fiction.

Many of Kipling's early stories were autobiographical, influenced by his experiences in India and in Southsea, where he was sent at the age of 6. He began to write when he returned to India in 1882. His first publication was a collection of poems, and his second was *Plain Tales from the Hills* (1888), a wide-ranging depiction of everyday life in British India. He was a prolific short-story writer and some of his strongest work occurs in this genre; his stories are direct, economical, and realistic, with intensely visual, physical descriptions.

The short-story form allowed him to write with striking empathy about a variety of characters of differing racial and social status, often capturing them at moments of crisis or strong emotion. In particular, his portrayal of common soldiers is good. He wrote extensively about war and bereavement following the death of his teenage son John in the First World War.

Begin with stories originally published in *A Diversity of Creatures* (1917); 'Mary Postgate' is the disturbing story of a reticent and unbalanced middle-aged 'companion', who, brutalized by war and death, refuses to help a fatally wounded airman when he lands in her employer's garden. 'The Gardener' gives an account of Helen Turrell's grief at the death of her adopted son, Michael. Also try 'They' (1904), a story about the relationship of the living to the dead. All three, along with other well-known stories, have recently been collected in *Mrs Bathurst and Other Stories* (1991).

Kim (1901) is the more successful of Kipling's two novels. Centring on the picaresque adventures of Kim O'Hara, an orphaned Irish boy brought up by an opium-addict friend of his father's, the narrative depicts India in vivid detail, following the self-sufficient and attractive Kim as he befriends a Tibetan lama and guides him across the country. Kim passes through many different sections of society, unwittingly becoming embroiled in 'Government Service' as he searches for the destiny his father prophesied for him. There is a continual tension between the claims of Indian and Anglo-Indian societies on Kim, and his difficulties in resolving his ties to each when he is eventually forced to choose between them are intensely and persuasively portrayed in this accessible, often witty novel.

During his own lifetime, Kipling was known for his poetry as much as for his prose. He was also a popular children's writer (*The Jungle Book*, 1894), and was awarded the Nobel Prize for Literature in 1907.

📖 Saki, Joseph Conrad, E. M. Forster. *See* FILM ADAPTATIONS, THE SEA

SR

Klima, Ivan (Czech, 1931–) A popular playwright and novelist, active in the Prague Spring of 1968 during which his country challenged Soviet domination, Klima's works were published worldwide, but not in Czechoslovakia until Communism fell. In *Love and Garbage* (1986) a Kafka-obsessed writer wanders the streets of Prague as a binman, tormented by his adulterous love of Daria, helplessly musing on the body and soul. The narrator speculates on affairs of the heart and the nature of reality. Klima writes with intellect and imagination, sweeping a decaying regime into history's dustbin. In *Waiting for the Dark, Waiting for the Light* (1993) Klima returns to the internal monologue to explore dissatisfaction with the external world—this time after the collapse of Communism. *My Merry Mornings* (1989) is a collection of the smart, lyrical short stories for which Klima is renowned; a typical Czech mixture of the essayistic and fictional.

📖 Milan Kundera, Josef Škvorecký, Jaroslav Hašek, Franz Kafka   *AM*

Koestler, Arthur (British, 1905–83) Koestler, a Hungarian journalist who acquired British citizenship after fighting for Britain in the Second World War, was a political writer with a major interest in philosophy and psychiatry.

His first book, *Spanish Testament* (1937), was an autobiographical account of his imprisonment during the Spanish Civil War, when he narrowly escaped being shot as a spy. Begin with *Darkness at Noon* (1940), Koestler's best-known work and the middle section of his three-part study of revolution, its ethics and ideals. Set during the Moscow Trials of the 1930s, and partially based on the experiences of people Koestler knew, the novel begins with the arrest of N. S. Rubashov, an old Bolshevik accused of betraying the state he helped to create, and follows him until his execution several weeks later. The narrative details Rubashov's daily life, his memories, thoughts, and testimonies as he follows his own political logic to its furthest limits by agreeing to confess to fabricated crimes. Move on to *Arrival and Departure* (1943), the final part of the trilogy and the first novel Koestler wrote in English, which centres on Peter Slovak, a disillusioned revolutionary who arrives in Neutralia (an unspecified European country) and is taken in by Dr Sonia Bolgar, a family friend who, following his nervous breakdown, talks him through his previously suppressed memories, identifying a self-destructive urge issuing from the lasting guilt of a childhood accident.

📖 Franz Kafka, George Orwell, Alexander Solzhenitsyn   *SR*

Kogawa, Joy (Canadian, 1935–). *See* CANADA

Koontz, Dean R. (US, 1945–) Koontz paid his dues as a writer, graduating from pulp science fiction paperbacks to the hardback best-seller lists with a string of ingeniously plotted thrillers veering towards the supernatural. The hero of *Cold*

Fire (1991) is driven by his intuitive gift to rescue complete strangers from danger, but then has to confront the dark side of his own powers. *Mr Murder* (1993) is a Jekyll-and-Hyde tale of a happily married author haunted by an inner demon. This is a favourite plot device of Koontz's: a lurking malignant Presence which threatens the lives of ordinary people. In *Hideaway* (1992) a man is brought back from the dead by a brilliant physician—and brings something nasty back with him. *Intensity* (1995) eschews the supernatural for grisly realism, in which the young heroine has to pit her wits against a psychopath with a taste for fat black spiders. Creepy stuff, not for the squeamish.

📖 Stephen King, Clive Barker, H. P. Lovecraft   *TH*

Kosinski, Jerzy (US, 1933–91) Kosinski arrived in New York from Poland as a young man, and his semi-autobiographical novel *The Painted Bird* (1965) was an instant success. It concerns the fate of a boy on the run among East European peasantry during the Holocaust years; despite terrible traumas, told with compelling inventiveness, the boy survives. Kosinski's most successful other novel is *Being There* (1970), a fable about a gardener whose simple-minded sayings are taken as brilliant insights by the American social and political world; it was made into a film in 1979 by Hal Ashby.

📖 Kurt Vonnegut, Ken Kesey   *SV*

Krantz, Judith (US, 1928–) Judith Krantz made her name in the late 1970s with a series of novels centred on beautiful women in glamorous settings who compete and win in business and love. *Princess Daisy* (1980) is a modern-day fairy-tale about a Russian aristocrat stripped of her birthright. Following emigration to New York, she begins the climb to dazzling wealth, happiness, and success in the New World. *Mistral's Daughter* (1983), set in the Paris art world of the 1920s and the high-fashion world of the 1980s, is the story of three beautiful, red-haired women and their relationship with Julien Mistral, a tempestuous and romantic painter. *Dazzle* (1990) centres on a glamorous and successful photographer, Jazz Kilkullen, and the three men who love her, while *I'll Take Manhattan* (1986) is the story of magazine editor Maxi Amberville's fight to create the most successful glossy in New York.

📖 Danielle Steel, Mary Wesley.
See GLAMOUR   *WB*

Kroetsch, Robert (Canadian, 1927–).
See CANADA

Kundera, Milan (Czech, 1929–) Born in Brno, Kundera taught at the Institute for Advanced Cinematographic Studies in Prague, before losing the post and emigrating after the Russian invasion of 1968. *The Book of Laughter and Forgetting* (1979) is an evocation of the cultural, political, and sexual life of post-war Europe, seen partly through Kundera's own eyes, partly through those of his fictional inventions. His most famous novel, *The Unbearable Lightness of Being* (1984), is set in Czechoslovakia after the 1968 Soviet invasion and follows the incurable philandering of Tomas, a distinguished Prague surgeon, his struggle to settle down with Tereza, a bartender, and his conflict with the Party authorities. Among the novel's many themes are the desolate nature of life within a totalitarian state, the metaphysical conflict between body and soul, and the ultimate sense of weightlessness that afflicts us when we confront the meaninglessness of life. Motifs are interwoven like musical phrases in symphony, and though many of them were inevitably lost in Philip Kaufman's film adaptation (staring Daniel Day Lewis and Juliet Binoche), much of the book's tragic atmosphere remains.

📖 Robert M. Pirsig, Isabel Allende, Ben Okri. *See* MAGIC REALISM   *RP*

Kureishi, Hanif (British, 1954–) Kureishi writes plays, screenplays, short stories, and novels. *The Buddha of Suburbia* (1990) is set in 1970s Bromley, Kent, where Kureishi grew up. Karim is the son of an English mother and Indian father. When his father becomes a spiritual guru to white middle-class suburbanites, Karim embarks on a series of erotic teenage adventures. Kureishi explores the racial conflicts experienced by Karim's generation, and treats teenage sexuality with playful wit, strongly evoking the youth culture of 1970s Britain. The debates and culture of a particular place and time are also captured in *The Black Album* (1995), a thriller set in 1989 after the fall of the Berlin Wall, amidst the pulsating London rave scene. Shahid moves to London after his father's death to further his education and finds himself involved in talk of liberalism and fundamentalism. His relationship with Professor Dedee Osgood fundamentally changes his life. *Intimacy* (1998) is a novella narrated by a man who is leaving his wife and children, and is personal and confessional in tone.

📖 Roddy Doyle, Meera Syal, Timothy Mo   *DJ*

L

Laclos, Choderlos de (French, 1741–1803) Laclos served in the army for twenty years without seeing battle, entered politics in 1788, and was imprisoned, then served as a general under Napoleon. His writings range from light verse to a treatise on the education of women. His novel *Les Liaisons Dangereuses* (1782) is written in letters, and concerns a plot hatched by a couple of aristocrats to engineer the seduction and disgrace of an innocent, famously religious young married woman. The pair are ex-lovers and are both dedicated to conquering as many hearts as possible; each also feels a degree of jealousy at the thought that the other might actually enjoy happiness in love with someone else. The letters are vivid and direct, and the twists of the plot tighten like a noose. The novel is every bit as engaging as Christopher Hampton's stage version, and the excellent film based on it, *Dangerous Liaisons* (1988).

📖 Samuel Richardson (*Clarissa*).
See FILM ADAPTATIONS   JR

Laker, Rosalind (British, 1925–) Laker lives with her Norwegian husband in Sussex and became a full-time writer of historical fiction in the 1980s. Begin with *To Dance with Kings* (1988), set at Versailles during the French Revolution. It follows the lives and loves of four women who have risen to Marie Antoinette's private circle. An unsuccessful painter's daughter is apprenticed to Jan Vermeer in *The Golden Tulip* (1991). Her career as an artist draws her into the connected worlds of patronage and political intrigue. Seventeenth-century London is the background to *The Silver Touch* (1987). It tells the story of a young woman silversmith familiar with both abject poverty and extravagant affluence in an era when both are conspicuous. *Circle of Pearls* (1990) is set in the Cromwellian period. The daughter of a royalist family grows to womanhood and marries her childhood sweetheart, Christopher Wren.

📖 Norah Lofts, Mary Renault, Rosemary Sutcliff   *DH*

Lamb, Charlotte (British, 1937–) Having written over a hundred books for Mills and Boon, Charlotte Lamb is also the author of *In the Still of the Night* (1995), a romantic thriller in which the two men who were most important in the youth of television star Annie Lang are suspects in the hunt for her stalker. After several murders, the reader is unsure which of three or four people has done it. *Walking in Darkness* (1996) is about a US Senator with his eyes on the White House, and a young Czech journalist who is trying to ask an awkward question. What her question is, and why the Senator is so keen to stop her asking, is revealed early on—but behind this secret is another, far more shattering. *Deep and Silent Waters* (1998) is a story of murder and lust set in Venice, with another good and intricate plot.

📖 Daphne du Maurier, Mary Wesley, Sue Gee   *FS*

Lambert, Angela (British, 1940–)
Lambert worked as a journalist before beginning to write fiction. Her novels are entertaining and easy to read, but they also question the social assumptions of Middle England, setting emotion and desire against the deadening demands of responsibility and convention.

Kiss and Kin (1997), an irreverent account of marriage, follows the experiences of two generations of a family, offering a muted vision of optimism beyond the limits of social expectation as Jennifer's father and Roderick's mother embark on a secret love-affair. Lambert's other novels include *A Rather English Marriage* (1992), a searching study of bereavement and the story of two very different widowers' attempts to rebuild their lives.

📖 Joanna Trollope, Elizabeth Jane Howard, Emily Brontë   SR

Lamming, George (Barbadian, 1927–)
Lamming's *In the Castle of My Skin* (1953) united all strands of critical taste in pronouncing it the authentic novel about growing up in the West Indies. Set in the 1930s this accurately observed narrative transcends the 'realist' genre; stylish without being precious. Lamming's novels explore the grand themes—freedom, independence, nationalism; but in his best work the imagined world is not sacrificed to the big idea. In *Season of Adventure* (1960) what excites is the middle-class heroine's search for identity as she attempts to connect —through a closely-guarded 'ceremony of the souls'—with her forgotten and spurned African past. Of later novels *Water with Berries* (1971) explores the consequences for the artist devoid of a supporting community—a quirky reworking of Shakespeare's *The Tempest*. His 1972

novel *Natives of My Person* reconstructs a seventeenth-century voyage of colonization bearing out Lamming's belief that one has to 'return to bearings' to find a way forward.

📖 Chinua Achebe, Caryl Phillips.
See CARIBBEAN   EM

L'Amour, Louis (US, 1908–88).
See WESTERN

Lampedusa, Giuseppe di (Italian, 1896–1957) Giuseppe Tomasi, Prince of Lampedusa, was an erudite, cultured Sicilian who wrote just one novel which was published soon after his death—*The Leopard* (1958). Based on historical fact and on his own family's recent past, it is set at the time of the unification of Italy after the invasion of Garibaldi in 1860, and concerns the profound changes taking place in Sicilian social and class structures. Told from the point of view of Don Fabrizio, Prince of Salina, it is an elegant and elegiac story, with wonderful descriptions of the Sicilian countryside, its villages and grand houses. Widely regarded as an almost perfect novel, it contains the quote: 'If we want things to stay as they are, things will have to change.' In its widespread popularity, it was the *Captain Corelli's Mandolin* of its day.

📖 Morris West, Graham Greene, Italo Calvino. *See* HISTORICAL   FS

Lanchester, John (British, 1962–)
'This is not a conventional cookbook', is an appropriate opening to *The Debt to Pleasure* (1996) as you'll spend the first third of it thinking, 'What on earth's he up to?' Tarquin Winot, the narrator, is staggeringly pompous, opinionated, and won't use one word where five will do.

This makes for quite a challenging read but you won't be bored; Tarquin is genuinely knowledgeable about food and art. While he is engaged in describing four tempting dinner menus, one for each season, Tarquin's life story unfolds. The recipes are deliciously described and you will want to try them for yourself, but stay away from the wild mushroom omelette. And don't get attached to any of the other characters because they never last long. A very sophisticated first novel. His second, *Mr Phillips*, was published in 2000.

📖 A. S. Byatt, Angela Carter   *RV*

La Plante, Lynda (British, 1946–) La Plante trained as an actress and worked in cabaret, for the Royal Shakespeare Company, and in films, before turning to writing. She has written a number of award-winning television drama serials. The novels of these are a good read; *Prime Suspect* (1991), *Prime Suspect 2* (1992), and *The Governor* (1995) are strongly plotted, with powerful heroines who have to fight their battles in a man's world. (In *Prime Suspect*, the police force; in *The Governor*, rather less convincingly, as a prison governor.) La Plante's other thrillers include *Cold Shoulder* (1994) about an American policewoman who shoots an innocent boy whilst drunk; and *Entwined* (1992), a murder story featuring a pair of identical twins who were victims of experimentation in a Nazi concentration camp.

📖 Sara Paretsky   *JR*

Laurence, Margaret (Canadian, 1926–87). *See* CANADA

Lavin, Mary (Irish, 1912–) Mary Lavin moved in the opposite direction to most Irish emigrants, having been born in Mas-

sachusetts and moving back to Ireland with her parents when she was 9. She has lived in Ireland ever since. Her greatest achievement has been her short stories, which have won her the Katherine Mansfield Prize and the Gregory Medal, founded by W. B. Yeats as 'the supreme award of the Irish nation'. Her tales vividly conjure a world of rain-sodden rural Ireland, dark, repressive, and priest-ridden, in which nevertheless acts of spontaneous human kindness, generosity, or impulsive passion break out brightly and dramatically. In stories like 'The Will', or 'A Happy Death', for instance, she manages to evoke such powerful emotions in only a dozen pages that you can see why some have called her 'an Irish Chekhov'. But also Chekhovian is her light touch with humour, as in 'My Vocation'. A standard collection is *Selected Stories* (1959), published by Macmillan.

📖 William Trevor, James Joyce, Edna O'Brien   *CH*

Lawrence, D(avid) H(erbert) (British, 1885–1930) The son of a miner, Lawrence won a scholarship to Nottingham High School and his first novel was published while he was training for his teacher's certificate. He and his German wife Frieda travelled widely in Europe, Australia, and America, and towards the end of his life lived in New Mexico.

In his writing he sought to strip away convention and inhibition, and get to the elemental roots of human experience. Sexual desire and the ways that people behave in sexual encounters are therefore a centrally important strand in his novels. His explicit writing about sex caused several of his books to be banned, and *Lady Chatterley's Lover* (1928), read under school desks at the pages that fell open, became a byword for smut for a generation of schoolchildren. Today the sexual content of his novels is not shocking (and in places it is so poetic and abstract as to be almost incomprehensible) and some of his work can seem didactic and over-descriptive. But his best characters are utterly convincing, and his exploration of relationships between men and women, and of the differences between the sexes, is more radical and honest than almost anyone who has written since. He also writes with great clarity and vividness about nature.

Begin with *Sons and Lovers* (1913); springing closely out of Lawrence's own experience, the novel is about a mining family in Nottinghamshire. Mrs Morel, intelligent and refined, is married to a stubborn, inarticulate, and often drunken miner. Their second son, Paul, becomes his mother's favourite and on him she focuses all her own needs and hopes. The heart of the novel is this very close mother–son relationship and the painful movements Paul makes to break away from its stranglehold as he matures and becomes interested in other women.

The Rainbow (1915) describes the marriage of Tom Brangwen, a Nottinghamshire farmer, to a Polish widow; and the lives of two generations of their family. It analyses the emotional movements and shifts over years of marriage and of the growth of children, at a level below speech and action. Lawrence's supreme skill at revealing underlying emotions and desires, at exploring the contradictions in love, is never more effective than in this book. The section describing Tom's grand-daughter Ursula growing up and training to become a teacher is wonderfully vivid. *Women in Love* (1920) follows the characters of Ursula and Gudrun, her sister, as they fall in love with two very different men and move away from their home background into more self-consciously artistic and intellectual society.

Lawrence also wrote poetry, short stories, vivid accounts of his travels, and novellas of which *The Virgin and the Gypsy* (1930) is probably the best known. It describes a young girl's emotional awakening in the elemental presence of a gypsy, and feels schematic after *Sons and Lovers* and *The Rainbow*.

📖 James Joyce, Thomas Hardy, Christina Stead. *See* CLASSICS, FAMILY SAGA, SOCIAL ISSUES   JR

Laye, Camara, (Upper Guinean, 1928–) Born into a devout Muslim family deeply rooted in Malinke culture, Laye left his village to study engineering in France. This was the beginning of many exiles which become the subject of his three novels. Written in French, his first autobiographical novel, *The African Child* (1953; also translated as *The Dark Child*), broke new ground in the development of the novel in French-speaking Africa. Clearly and eloquently written, it is an idealistic celebration of rural life. *The Radiance of the King* (1956), is the story of a destitute white man in unnamed African territory. Desperately trying to embrace the values of the African people, he is constantly thwarted by his inability to cast off western civilization. His nightmarish third novel, *A Dream of Africa* (1966), finds the narrator, Fatoman, returning to Guinea after a six-year absence.

📖 Chinua Achebe, Ngugi wa Thiong'o, Abdulrazak Gurnah   EW

Leacock, Stephen (Canadian, 1869–1944) Born in Hampshire, Leacock went to

Ontario as a child and subsequently became Professor of Political Economy at McGill University. By retirement, he enjoyed the status of Canada's finest humorist, somewhat akin to Mark Twain and James Thurber, and his collections of sketches sold widely. His first success, *Literary Lapses* (1910), was actually self-published; the range of his writing developed in *Nonsense Novels* (1911), with its parodies of popular fiction. Perhaps its most enduring sketch, however, is the hilarious 'My Financial Career', about the perils of opening a bank account. Leacock's classic book is *Sunshine Sketches of a Little Town* (1912), set in the fictional town of Mariposa on Lake Wissanotti; its gently ironic tone, describing the misadventures of small-town characters, makes it wonderfully poised between affection and satire. Leacock's unfinished autobiography, *The Boy I Left behind Me* (1946), is also very well worth reading.

📖 James Thurber, Garrison Keillor

JS

Leasor, James (British, 1923–) Formerly a journalist, Leasor's best-known books hinge on the investigative talents of Dr Jason Love, whose collector's taste in motor cars provides a characteristic feature of the stories. Begin with *Frozen Assets* (1989), in which Love is pursued in an expensive vintage model by warring Afghani tribesmen. In *Host of Extras* (1973) he and his trusty mechanic nurse a 1930s Mercedes towards dangerous encounters in Sicily. The army officer who resigns his commission in *Ship of Gold* (1984) gets away from it all with a temporary job in Portugal. Violence and intrigue await, as he realizes he is involved in more than an attempt to raise sunken gold. *Who Killed*

Sir Harry Oakes? (1983) is a novelistic treatment of the murder of a member of the Duke of Windsor's circle in the Bahamas.

📖 Gladys Mitchell, Ian Fleming, Clive Cussler   DH

Leavitt, David (US, 1961–) Leavitt's subject matter is usually gay sexuality within the nuclear family in the AIDS era. His debut collection of short stories, *Family Dancing* (1985), gave a bitter account of the American middle classes. It was followed by the novel *The Lost Language of Cranes* (1986), a close observation of gay life and love using the social world of Manhattan, high and low, as its backdrop. Looking at gay love in the closet, and in a party mood, the novel has many layers. Leavitt has an effective metaphorical touch, in the stories and the novels. *While England Sleeps* (1995), unlike his earlier work, is set in the fascinating *demi-monde* of 1936 London, and takes Orwell for its mentor. While tracing hedonism's rapid transit from delight to guilt, it is also an interesting and unusual coming-out novel set against the Spanish Civil War.

📖 Edmund White, Christopher Isherwood   AM

Le Carré, John (British, 1931–) Le Carré (real name David Cornwell) was a master at Eton and a British diplomat before publishing his first novel in 1961. He is generally regarded as the finest living writer of the espionage novel and also as a significant literary figure. His themes are the pull of conflicting loyalties, the tension between the individual and the state, and the often corrupting struggle between idealism and pragmatism.

Begin with *The Spy Who Came in from the Cold* (1963). A British agent is sent to

East Germany, apparently to defect but actually to provide disinformation. After a typically complex series of twists, turns, and double-crosses, a very different picture emerges. This novel features George Smiley of the 'Circus' (British intelligence). Smiley is a pivotal character in many of the novels, in particular the *Quest for Karla* trilogy of *Tinker, Tailor, Soldier, Spy* (1974), *The Honourable Schoolboy* (1977), and *Smiley's People* (1980). These all centre around the continuing search for a mole within the Circus whose very existence undermines everything Smiley and his colleagues stand for. The terrible tension at the heart of the novels rises from the dilemma of protecting society without stepping outside what that society regards as acceptable and humane.

Even after the cold war, Le Carré has continued to produce successful novels such as *Our Game* (1995), because his work has always been rooted in character rather than situation. Five of his books have been made into films; the Karla novels were adapted for award-winning BBC television series starring Alec Guinness.

📖 Len Deighton, Gavin Lyall, Eric Ambler. *See* SPY   *VM*

Lee, Harper (US, 1926–) Harper Lee was born in Alabama, in the Deep South of the United States. Her first and only novel was *To Kill a Mockingbird* (1960), and it was sufficient to establish her literary reputation, winning her the Pulitzer Prize in 1961. Scout, the 9-year-old tomboy heroine of the novel, witnesses the trial of the black Tom Robinson, accused of raping a white woman. Her father, Atticus, is the defending lawyer. The trial is a device that lays bare the tensions and prejudice in Maycomb, a fictional town based on Monroeville, where the author grew up. The

novel is not only part of the anti-racism canon and a powerful plea for tolerance, but also a lyrical and humorous evocation of growing up in small-town America in the 1930s, with a memorable heroine coming to terms with the eccentricities and unfairnesses of adult society.

📖 Meera Syal (*Anita and Me*), Alice Walker, J. D. Salinger   *SA*

Lee, Laurie (British, 1914–96) Gloucestershire born, and educated locally, Lee is best known for his autobiographical writing, although he also wrote poetry, screenplays, and travel books. Start with *Cider with Rosie* (1959), his most popular work, a rich, lyrical evocation of his childhood after the First World War. In sensuous detail he conjures this secluded Cotswold valley and a lost world. Movingly, often with gentle humour, he tells of village life, local characters and legends, schooldays, madness, and violence. The memoir culminates in his sexual encounter with Rosie Burdock under the hay-wagon, drinking cider—that first 'secret drink of golden fire . . . Never to be forgotten, or ever tasted again'. Move on to *As I Walked Out One Midsummer Morning* (1969), Lee's experiences as a young man *en route* to London, Spain, the Mediterranean; and *A Moment of War* (1991), his recollections of the Spanish Civil War.

📖 Flora Thompson, J. D. Salinger   *GC*

Lee,   Sky (Canadian,   1952–). *See* CANADA

Le Fanu, J(oseph) Sheridan (Irish, 1814–1873) Le Fanu was a Dubliner of Huguenot descent, and a grandnephew of the dramatist, Sheridan. After the death of his beloved young wife he withdrew into a profoundly melancholy existence, spending much of his time reading mystical texts about life after death. The emotional intensity which Le Fanu invested in his ghost stories makes them uniquely memorable. One can never be sure whether the victims of the supernatural, such as the Revd Jennings in the eerie 'Green Tea', are really seeing the demons they imagine, or whether they are merely mentally disturbed. And which is more terrifying anyway? Added to that is a strong vein of gothic romanticism, in the perverse but heavily veiled sexuality of 'Carmilla', and 'Schalken the Painter'. Henry James called Le Fanu 'Ideal reading in a country house for the hours after midnight'. The best collection is *In a Glass Darkly* (1872).

📖 M. R. James, Henry James (*The Turn of the Screw*), Bram Stoker. *See* SUPERNATURAL   CH

Le Guin, Ursula (US, 1929–)

Born in Berkeley, California, the daughter of anthropologists, whose work clearly enriched her own vivid concepts of alien worlds, Le Guin is one of the few women to have made a lasting and honourable place for herself in science fiction. A prolific writer, Le Guin is famous for her books for children as well as for her adult novels. She published the *Earthsea* quartet for children starting in 1968 with *A Wizard of Earthsea*. This series concerns itself with the uses and abuses of magical power and contains some highly evocative scenes of the training of young wizards. In her adult work Le Guin raises some of the most interesting philosophical questions in science-fiction writing. In *The Left Hand of Darkness* (1969), for which she won a Hugo and Nebula award, she portrays a world called Winter, in which Arctic conditions prevail even through the warmest points of the year. It is also a world in which people change sex, complicating gender roles. The two worlds that feature in *The Dispossessed* (1974) are starkly contrasted models of consumer capitalism and a subsistence-level socialism. In her later work, such as *Always Coming Home* (1985) Le Guin's interest in linguistic and structural experimentation is evident.

📖 Joanna Russ, Doris Lessing, Robert Silverberg. *See* FANTASY, SCIENCE FICTION, TEEN   LM

Lehmann, Rosamond (Nina) (British, 1901–90)

Lehmann was born and brought up in Bourne End, Buckinghamshire. Her first novel, *Dusty Answer* (1927), was published just after she left Cambridge, and was hugely popular. The novel follows the developing relationship between a girl and her cousins next door. Her most famous work, *Invitation to the Waltz* (1932), concerns two sisters, Olivia and Kate Curtis. It opens on the morning of Olivia's seventeenth birthday and follows the events up to her momentous first dance, where we experience the night with her. The novel is not simply an acute observation of Edwardian middle-class life; Lehmann's understanding of the female journey into adulthood is powerful and immediate. The sequel, *The Weather in the Streets* (1936) follows the goings-on of the Curtis family, focusing on Olivia. It caused a public controversy when first published because it deals with topics such as unwanted pregnancy and abortion. Lehman's writing is poignant, atmospheric, vividly evocative of its period, and deeply romantic.

📖 Virginia Woolf. *See* SEXUAL POLITICS   CJ

Leiber, Fritz (US, 1910–92) Fritz Leiber is best known for his sequence of fantasy stories set on the world of 'Nehwon', and featuring the paired heroes Fafhrd and Gray Mouser. This began in 1939, but has now been extended to six volumes of collected stories, the latest being *The Knight and Knave of Swords* (1988), and one novel, *The Swords of Lankhmar* (1968): all volumes in the series have the word 'swords' in the title. The sequence is definitive of the 'sword and sorcery' genre (a phrase Leiber invented), but ideas which became clichés in other hands, like the barbarian adventurer entering the sophisticated but decadent metropolis, are handled by Leiber with ironic wit. Leiber's early occult story *Conjure Wife* (1943), about a university professor who discovers too late that his wife is not the only witch on campus, was filmed as *Burn Witch Burn* (1961). He has also written many works of science fiction, including *The Big Time* (1961), a story about two sides (the Spiders and the Snakes) who strive continually to alter history in their favour by changing the past.

📖 Lyon Sprague de Camp, Jack Vance. *See* FANTASY   TS

Leitch, Maurice (Irish, 1933–). *See* IRELAND

LeMay, Alan (US, 1899–1964). *See* WESTERN

Leonard, Elmore (US, 1925–) Elmore Leonard had already established himself as a notable writer of Westerns, including *Valdez is Coming* (1969), which was filmed with Burt Lancaster, before he decided to concentrate on crime fiction. His interest lies in the behaviour and personalities of the people who commit crimes, rather than in the unravelling of whodunit puzzles. His books feature a wide range of criminal activity: not just murder, but also robberies, swindles, and drug dealing. Leonard is concerned to give an impression of realism in his work and in recent years he has even hired researchers to assist him with background details which help to lend credibility to often bizarre and coolly ironic stories. His cinematic prose has attracted much interest in Hollywood and several of his thrillers have been adapted as films. *Mr Majestyk* (1974) was an exception: he wrote the screenplay first and then produced a novelization. Leonard has written many best-sellers, but one of the most enjoyable is *Get Shorty* (1990), which earned critical and commercial acclaim both as a novel and as a film starring John Travolta and Gene Hackman. Typical of his breezy style are *Gold Coast* (1980), in which Karen DiCilia's late husband leaves her $4 million and the instruction never to lay a finger on another man, and *Rum Punch* (1992), in which bail bondsman Max Cherry makes the mistake of falling for a client.

📖 James M. Cain, Carl Hiassen. *See* CRIME, THRILLERS   ME

Lermontov, Mikhail (Russian, 1814–41). *See* RUSSIA

Lessing, Doris (British, 1919–) Lessing was brought up in Rhodesia (Zimbabwe) and her first novel, *The Grass is Singing* (1950), is a brilliant depiction of the way racial segregation poisoned the lives of both black and white people. Her politics and beliefs fire her writing but never cause her to toe a line—whatever comfortable beliefs you hold, Lessing asks the questions that make you squirm. She writes about big ideas in a straightforward and accessible way. Begin with *The Good Terrorist* (1985), a book about self-deception: a naïve group of would-be terrorists squat in a derelict London house and are mothered by Alice, who makes the house comfortable for them by sponging off her own mother whilst reviling her for her pathetic bourgeois lifestyle. Move on to the semi-autobiographical *Children of Violence* sequence, starting with *Martha Quest* (1952). These five novels chart the heroine's progress from adolescence towards her own old age and the end of the world, taking in Africa, communism, marriage, and its breakdown, motherhood, 1960s' London, feminism, mysticism, and an unceasing need to make sense of the world. *The Golden Notebook* (1962), which is made up of the story of Anna Wulf intercut with stories from her four notebooks, explores the fragmentation of human experience, and examines female identity. *Mara and Dann* (1999) is set in Africa in a future where much of the continent has been destroyed by drought, and traces the journey northwards of a brother and sister. There are rich echoes here of her earlier books; the fascination with exile and the open-mindedness and courage that come from being an outsider; the horror of stifling, claustrophobic, petty-minded communities.

Lessing also writes space fiction, and powerful evocative short stories. Her autobiography (first vol., *Under My Skin*, 1995) is highly recommended.

📖 Nadine Gordimer, Simone de Beauvoir, Margaret Atwood.
See AFRICA, SCIENCE FICTION   *JR*

Lette, Kathy (Australian, 1958–) Kathy Lette first made her name with a novel about puberty published while still in her teens, and she has since worked as a newspaper columnist, television and radio presenter, and scriptwriter. *Girls' Night Out* (1991) follows seven friends on a night on the town where the alcohol flows, the girls' tongues loosen, and their secrets and thoughts about the men in their lives are revealed. *Foetal Attraction* (1993) tells the story of a woman made pregnant by her self-regarding television executive lover, and *Mad Cows* (1996) opens as a woman takes her baby out for the first time and gets arrested for shoplifting at Harrods. *Altar Ego* (1998) is the story of a bride who runs out on her own wedding. Lette's fiction is lightweight and upbeat, and her gift for packing each page with quotable one-liners and sparky dialogue has ensured her widespread popularity.

📖 Helen Fielding, Fay Weldon, Helen Simpson   *WB*

Levi, Primo (Italian, 1919–87) Levi worked as an industrial chemist before and after the war. In 1943 he joined a partisan group in northern Italy, was arrested and deported to Auschwitz. Of the 650 Jews who entered the camp with him, 525 went to the gas chamber. In his novel *If Not Now, When* (1982) Levi describes a group of Russian and Polish Jews stranded in occupied territory and offering resistance to the German army. The novel is based on truth and explores the complex relationships within the refugee band, as well as the hardships they endure.

His autobiographical writing includes *If This is a Man* (1958) and *The Truce* (1963), which describe his experience in the death camp. He writes simply and precisely, without sensation. In his preface he describes the need to tell the story of the period of incarceration as 'violent, competing with other elementary needs', and says that writing the book was an interior liberation. It works in the same way for the reader, by calmly presenting the worst that man can do, and revealing that the best cannot be destroyed by it. *The Truce* describes his tortuous journey home to Italy via Russia, Romania, Hungary, and Austria. *The Periodic Table* (1975) is more widely autobiographical, ranging from Levi's childhood to his later working life. Each chapter title is the name of a chemical element which is connected sometimes literally, sometimes metaphorically with the chapter's events, people and memories.

📖 David Grossman, Isaac Bashevis Singer, Alexander Solzhenitsyn   *JR*

Levy, Andrea (Jamaican/British, 1956–). *See* CARIBBEAN

Lewis, C(live) S(taples) (British, 1898–1963) The best known of C. S. Lewis's fiction is his seven-volume sequence for children, *The Chronicles of Narnia*, begun with *The Lion, the Witch and the Wardrobe* (1950). These are (with one exception) 'gateway' stories in which modern children find themselves in a fantasy world of talking animals, ruled by the divine lion, Aslan. Lewis is surprisingly successful in blending overt morality with romantic or fairy-tale adventure. Lewis also wrote an adult trilogy, which began as science fiction, with travels to Mars and Venus, but ended as fantasy, with the revival of Merlin to thwart a plan of world domination in *That Hideous Strength* (1945). The sequence is held together by Lewis's attempt to reconcile traditional Christian teaching about the Fall and the Devil with modern scientific knowledge. Lewis's last work of fiction

was *Till We Have Faces* (1956), a retelling of the myth of Cupid and Psyche.

📖 Alan Garner, Diana Wynne Jones. *See* FANTASY   *TS*

Lewis, Matthew (British, 1775–1818) Matthew Lewis was 19 when he wrote his first and most successful novel, *The Monk* (1796). It is an enthusiastic attempt at the Gothic, and all the ingredients are there— murder, torture, the supernatural, sex, and religion. Lewis's central character is Ambrosio, a saintly Capuchin monk, whose very perfection lays him open to temptation by the Devil. The novel is unashamedly sensational. *The Monk* clearly owes a great deal to the fashion for Gothic novels, such as Horace Walpole's *The Castle of Otranto* (1764), also set in Italy, and the more ladylike Ann Radcliffe's *The Mysteries of Udolpho* (1794), where yet another maiden is pursued by a malevolent Italian. Lewis wrote two later novels, as well as plays, verse, and a journal about managing a Jamaican sugar plantation.

📖 Mary Shelley. *See* SUPERNATURAL   *SA*

Lewis, Sinclair (US, 1885–1951) Lewis, a best-selling satirist of Middle American values between the wars, was the first American to receive the Nobel Prize for Literature, in 1930. In a series of novels, the best known of which are *Main Street* (1920) and *Babbitt* (1922), he portrayed the split in America between idealism and materialism, criticizing small-town narrow-mindedness, the business and medical professions, and Americans abroad. *In Main Street*, Carol Milford's attempt to escape the confines of life in Gopher Prairie ends in her return to her husband, and in *Babbitt*, George F. Babbitt's rebellion against his family and business colleagues ultimately succumbs to their pressure. Lewis's cynical comedy is well realized in *Elmer Gantry* (1927), the ever-topical story of an unscrupulous and philandering evangelist whose eloquence turns each threatened exposure to his own advantage.

📖 Sherwood Anderson, F. Scott Fitzgerald, Ford Madox Ford   *JS*

Lewis, (Percy) Wyndham (US, 1882–1957) Lewis was born in the United States but spent most of his life in Britain. He was a brilliant polymath and founder of the Vorticist art movement, who deliberately stoked up dissent and controversy between the wars in London artistic and literary circles. Always a prickly character and never an easy writer, his most accessible novel is *The Revenge for Love* (1937), about an artistic group with communist sympathies, and how their political naïvety leaves them open to cynical exploitation and betrayal. Lewis aimed for jagged prose in his satirical first novel, *Tarr* (1918), set in the bohemian art world of Paris, in which the characters are mouthpieces for Lewis's élitist views of society. *The Childermass* (1928) is a fantastical presentation of philosophical ideas; *The Apes of God* (1930) a savage satire on arty poseurs and intellectual frauds as were exemplified for him by the Bloomsbury group. An extremist in everything, his right-wing views had Lewis labelled the most hated writer in Britain.

📖 Aldous Huxley, Ford Madox Ford, Iris Murdoch   *TH*

Lingard, Joan (British, 1932–) Lingard writes both adult and teenage fiction. She was born in Edinburgh and lived in Ulster until she was 18. Out of this experience she wrote what are probably her best-known novels, the *Kevin and Sadie* series. *Across the Barricades* (1972) has been read and loved by many schoolchildren. It explores the growing relationship between Kevin McCoy, a Catholic, and Sadie Jackson, a Protestant. It is a sophisticated treatment of the complex situation in Northern Ireland and still has resonance even in these changing times. *Into Exile* (1973) follows Kevin and Sadie to England as they flee to avoid the bigotry they face as a mixed partnership. Lingard returns to similar themes in *Dark Shadows* (1998)

📖 Anne Fine, Jennifer Johnston   *TO*

Linklater, Eric (British, 1899–1974) Linklater wrote over twenty novels, plus histories, poetry, radio plays, autobiography, and journalism. His fiction is entertaining, serious, and difficult to categorize; inevitably therefore he is underrated critically. Born in Wales but brought up in the Orkneys (where a number of his novels are set), Linklater read medicine at Aberdeen before serving as a sniper in the First World War. *Juan in America* (1931), the picaresque and satirical adventures of an innocent abroad, brought him fame, but his critical reputation is probably best defended with *Private Angelo* (1946), based on his experiences as a war correspondent in Italy during the Second World War. Angelo is a deserter from the Italian Army, whose struggle to avoid battle only embroils him further in it. As a good-natured satire on the brutal absurdities of war *Private Angelo* is strongly reminiscent of Hašek's *The Good Soldier Švejk* but Linklater's writing is more lyrical and sentimental, losing in satirical edge what it gains in humanity.

📖 Jaroslav Hašek, Evelyn Waugh, H. E. Bates   *MH*

Lively, Penelope (British, 1933–)
Penelope Lively was born in Egypt, married
a don, and lives in a sixteenth-century farm-
house. In those three details one has something of an insight into her writing concerns
as a whole: a sense of other cultures and
other places, an academic setting for several
of her novels, and her intense consciousness
of the presence of the past. Her Booker
Prize-winning *Moon Tiger* (1988) is the life
story of the ebullient Claudia Hampton,
intertwined with an entire history of the
world, an admirably bold idea. *Perfect Happiness* (1983) is a brief, powerful, emotionally exact novel about love and loss,
following the life of the gentle Frances after
the death of her husband, the dominating,
charismatic Steven. Her recovery is partly
aided by her wonderfully feisty friend,
Zoe, and, with rich irony, by the injury
of her son, Harry, by a terrorist bomb at
Venice airport. Finally, after those lonely
months she spent 'trudging that level grey
plain of sorrow', she finds herself 'hitched,
again, to time and to the world'. Lively's
prose is lyrical but precise, and always hints
at the richness of human life, that cannot
be predicted or controlled. Though 'perfect
happiness' may be a chimera, happiness of
some sort is always possible. Lively's concerns surface again in her marvellous books
for children, such as *The House in Norham
Gardens* (1974) and *The Ghost of Thomas
Kempe* (1973). She is one of those rare
writers whose writing for both adults and
children forms a seamless whole.

📖 Susan Hill, Alice Thomas Ellis,
Nina Bawden   *CH*

Llewellyn, Richard (British, 1906–83)
Born in St David's, Llewellyn wrote film-
scripts and stage-plays after army service
and working in film studios. A Welsh

environment in childhood, and his research,
including several months as a collier, contributed to the authenticity of his best-
selling novel *How Green was My Valley*
(1939), made into a popular film. Llewellyn
depicts, with lyricism, realism, and humour,
a Welsh mining community and the gradual disintegration of its unity and ideals.
There are strong emotional resonances in
the narrative told by the central character
who, with those left of his family (like
many others before them), eventually has
to leave their valley. A massive tip hangs
over the community, symbolic of economic greed. Realism and romanticism
are fused, with a power Llewellyn never
achieved again. He wrote twenty-three
novels, including *None But the Lonely
Heart* (1943), set in 1930s' London, and
Bride of Israel, My Love (1974), a vivid
story of love, danger, and idealism in
modern Israel.

📖 Dylan Thomas, Alexander Cordell
                                      GC

Locklin, Gerald (US, 1941–) Born at
Rochester in New York, Locklin moved
to the West Coast during the mid-1960s,
becoming Professor of English at Long
Beach. His stories and novellas mix social
satire with literary joking, autobiography
with fabulatory elements; they are usually
Bacchanalian, politically incorrect, and
often really funny. *The Case of the Missing
Blue Volkswagen* (1984) is a spoof detective
fiction crossing Hammett with Brautigan,
an exercise in surreal story-telling. *The
Gold Rush* (1989) has stories that highlight
the zaniness of West Coast life, though
'The English Girl' reflects upon cultural
and emotional differences between Britain
and America. Jimmy Abbey, a libidinous
college teacher, features as the protagonist

of many Locklin fictions, notably *The First Time He Saw Paris* (1997) and *Down and Out* (1999). The latter is a full-length novel set in the London of the early 1970s and is full of comically absurd details.

📖 Charles Bukowski, Richard Brautigan   *JS*

Lodge, David (British, 1935–   ) Born in London and educated at the universities of London and Birmingham, David Lodge was for many years Professor of Modern English Literature at Birmingham University. His early novels, *Changing Places* (1975) and *Small World* (1984), are set in a fictional university, and are high-spirited comedies of campus life. They work by contrasting the life of British provincial universities with their more glamorous American counterparts. *Nice Work* (1989) is also partly set on a campus, but here Dr Robyn Penrose, feminist academic, shadows the manager of an engineering firm, Vic Wilcox. The contrast and interactions of their worlds, academic–industrial and male–female, gives rise to effective social comedy. Lodge's novels are always thoughtful, deliberately structured and never without humour. He is an acute observer of lower-middle-class life and manners. Themes that have absorbed him more recently include religion, in particular, Catholicism, and growing older, as in his *Paradise News* (1991), a comic novel about an agnostic theologian's visit to Hawaii. In *Therapy* (1995), a writer of television sitcoms suffers a mid-life crisis. Lodge is also an eminent literary critic.

📖 Howard Jacobson, Kingsley Amis, Malcolm Bradbury   *SA*

Lofts, Norah (British, 1904–83) The books of Norah Lofts are scarce now and mostly out of print. This is a pity. Generally filed under historical/romance, there is a seriousness about her work that sets it slightly apart. If you can get it, begin with *Jassy* (1944), a dark, very moving tale about an ugly girl, the perpetual outcast, who loves unrequitedly and is eventually unjustly hanged. The plain unsentimental prose and the force of the fractured narrative lift this far above the mawkish. Lofts' numerous books deal with everyone from royalty to the very poor. *How Far to Bethlehem?* (1965) tells the story of Christ's birth realistically from the point of view of Mary and Joseph, portrayed as ordinary people. *The Town House* (1959), first in a trilogy, launches the complex story of several generations from the fourteenth century onwards in one house, showing in a tragi-comic way how the present evolves out of what is, for the living, the unknown past.

📖 Jean Plaidy, Edna O'Brien   *CB*

London, Jack (US, 1876–1916) Born in San Francisco, London's tough early experiences as an oyster pirate, seal-hunter, hobo, and gold prospector gave him a wealth of material for his fiction. He was an overtly commercial and prolific writer, becoming one of America's first celebrity authors. *The Son of the Wolf* (1900), with its stories of men and animals in Alaska and the Yukon, lyrical descriptions of frozen landscapes and life-or-death situations, proved popular. But he was made famous by *The Call of the Wild* (1903), which has become an enduring children's classic; a placid St Bernard dog is abducted from his California home and taken to work in Alaska, where he is forced to rediscover his natural savage instincts in order to survive. *White Fang* (1906) reverses the process, following a wolf-cub into its maturity as a fighting dog and into domestication, and is more sentimental, though still powerful in its criticism of human cruelty. London's later works can be seen as philosophical adventure novels, often rather wordy but always highly enjoyable. *The Sea-Wolf* (1904), for instance, superbly sustains its survival-of-the-fittest theme; the sadistic captain of a seal-hunting boat, Wolf Larsen, is a great villain, defeated in the end by co-operation not individual action. *Martin Eden* (1909), often regarded as his best novel, is based on his own struggle from poverty to become a successful but despairing author. The main character is alienated from his own class, and finds romantic ideals and worldly success to be ultimately meaningless.

📖 Robert Louis Stevenson, Rudyard Kipling, Ernest Hemingway.
See THE SEA   JS

Loos, Anita (US, 1888–1981) Loos was something of a prodigy, working as a screenwriter in Hollywood in her teens. She numbered D. W. Griffith and the iconic Louise Brooks amongst her friends. Her novel *Gentlemen Prefer Blondes* (1925) is the fictitious diary of Lorelei Lee, a not-so-dumb blonde who certainly believes that diamonds are a girl's best friend. In a thinly veiled satire of the Lost Generation, the novel recounts Lorelei's experiences in Europe before she returns to America to marry her millionaire. Lorelei's social and artistic pretensions are betrayed by a series of misspellings and malapropisms. *But Gentlemen Marry Brunettes* (1928) features Lorelei's attempts to embrace the world of literature whilst recounting the misadventures of her friend Dorothy. The novels are comic exposés of the world of the flapper with a subtle subtext of

hypocrisy and violence. Loos's autobiography, *A Girl Like I* (1966), is characterized by a cynical, knowing wit.

📖 Dorothy Parker, Damon Runyon
GK

Lovecraft, H(oward) P(hillips) (US, 1890–1937) H. P. Lovecraft is a cult writer, whose influence on others has in the end been more remarkable than his own relatively small corpus, which consists almost entirely of short stories and novellas. These are continually reprinted under varying titles, such as *The Haunter of the Dark* (1951) or *The Colour Out of Space* (1964). Lovecraft's major invention was 'the Cthulhu Mythos', which alludes continually if inconsistently in many stories to an elder race of supernatural beings, self-destroyed by sorcery but still capable of being awoken once more. Lovecraft's allusions to lost works such as the 'Necronomicon' and the archives of Miskatonic University have inspired many fictional attempts to expand his hints and fill in the gaps.

📖 Fritz Leiber, Michael Shea.
See SUPERNATURAL   TS

Lovelace, Earl (Trinidadian, 1935–   ) In his novels, plays, and stories, Lovelace's subject matter is often the after-effects of colonialism, and the quest for regeneration. *The Dragon Can't Dance* (1979), his widely popular masterpiece, dramatizes through carnival—music, dance, colour; a magnificent portrait of the Calypsonian—the confusions of a folk community in transition. From *The Schoolmaster* (1968) to *A Brief Conversion and Other Stories* (1998) the rural community is evoked with intimacy and without sentimentality. The richly textured, beautifully written title story of *A Brief Conversion* is a minor master-piece. Lovelace's prize-winning fifth novel, *Salt* (1996)—an epic ranging over three generations—explores the themes of iden-tity and personal integrity. Didactic in parts, it contains some of Lovelace's best writing, in a rich variety of Caribbean registers.

📖 Samuel Selvon, Lawrence Scott, Fred D'Aguiar. *See* CARIBBEAN   *EM*

Lowry, Malcolm (British, 1909–57) Lowry came from a well-to-do family in New Brighton, Cheshire, and before going to university signed on as deckhand on a voyage to the Far East, an experience he used in his first novel, *Ultramarine* (1933). Thereafter he lived in the United States, Mexico, and for several years in a squatter's beach shack in Dollarton, Canada.

During his lifetime he published only one other novel, hailed as a work of genius, and on which his reputation rests. The action of *Under the Volcano* (1947) takes place on a single day in a small Mexican town, during the annual festival of the Day of the Dead. Geoffrey Firmin, the dis-graced ex-consul, is drinking himself to death, while his ex-wife and brother look on helplessly; he ends up shot in a ravine with a dead pariah dog for company. The book is dense and complex, interweaving past and present, charting Firmin's urge to self-destruction with lacerating and unsparing honesty. For Firmin, read Lowry. A chronic drunk for most of his life, driven by demons of guilt and self-disgust, he worked manically for recognition as a writer, and when it came it killed him. His posthumous works were compiled from a disordered mountain of unfinished drafts. *Lunar Caustic* (1968) tells of his three weeks of hallucinatory hell in Bellevue psychiatric hospital; *Dark as the Grave*

Wherein My Friend is Laid (1968), set in Mexico, is about the break-up of his first marriage. There was also a short volume of *Selected Poems* (1962), a fragment from which might serve as Lowry's epitaph: 'Success is like some horrible disaster Worse than your house burning.'

📖 B. Traven, Joseph Conrad, Hermann Hesse   *TH*

Ludlum, Robert (US, 1927–) Author of a best-selling series of taut action thrillers, Ludlum is a master of the conspiracy theory, pitting his heroes against complex and murderous webs of corrupt vested interests. No institution, be it church, state, or corporate, is immune from infiltration; the fight for decency and justice is left to the individual who can trust no one except, perhaps, the woman who wins his heart. Traditional enemies feature strongly—settings include the Second World War (*The Rheinman Exchange*, 1975, *The Bourne Identity*, 1980); the cold war (*The Matarese Circle*, 1979), and the fight against interna-tional terrorism (*The Scorpio Illusion*, 1993) —but in Ludlum's world, corruption has deeper roots than the obvious. Even Ivy League universities are not immune (*The Matlock Papers*, 1973).

📖 Tom Clancy, Frederick Forsyth, Colin Forbes. *See* SPY   *KB*

Lurie, Alison (US, 1926–) Lurie's subject matter, portrayed with humane irony, is the ways in which people fool themselves and each other. The amused detachment with which she writes about her deluded characters has led to her being likened to Jane Austen. An academic herself, she has set most of her novels in academic communities. Possibly her best-known work is *The War Between the Tates*

(1974), which charts, from both the husband and the wife's viewpoints, a crisis in a couple's marriage. The Tates have spent their young adulthood thinking of themselves as attractive, successful, enviable people; Lurie shows the chastening process by which they learn their frailties. Lurie won the Pulitzer Prize with *Foreign Affairs* (1985), another story of emotional education. Two American academics are in London; one, Fred Turner, has an unhappy affair with a well-heeled and selfish young Englishwoman; the other, Vinnie Miner, finds unexpected happiness with an unintellectual tourist.

📖 Mary McCarthy, Carol Shields, Anne Tyler   NC

Lyall, Gavin (British, 1932–) A former RAF pilot and journalist on aviation matters, Lyall began his fiction-writing career with adventure-thrillers, drawing extensively on his flying experience and characterized by sharp, wisecracking dialogue, dramatic set pieces, and a wide range of exotic locales, from Arctic Finland to tropical Jamaica. *The Most Dangerous Game* (1964) and *Judas Country* (1975) are among the best of these. The creation of Major Harry Maxim, former SAS man transformed into Whitehall trouble-shooter, signalled a change in direction. Begin with *The Secret Servant* (1980), where Lyall's gift for dialogue finally finds a marriage with tight and cohesive plotting to produce a taut thriller. Continue with *The Conduct of Major Maxim* (1982), where Maxim investigates a murder in a German garrison town, and *The Crocus List* (1985), probably the best of the Maxim books, which begins with an assassination attempt on the American president in London.

📖 Dick Francis, Len Deighton, John Le Carré   VM

M

Maalouf, Amin (Lebanese, 1949–)
Maalouf was born in Beirut, and has lived
in Paris since 1976. Begin with *Leo the
African* (1986). Maalouf characteristically
fuses history and a richly exotic imagination in this expansive account of Leo
Africanus, the sixteenth-century chronicler of Africa. *Samarkand* (1988) follows
the fortunes of the manuscript of Omar
Khayyám's *rubáiyát*, which is ultimately
lost aboard the *Titanic*. *The First Century
after Beatrice* (1992) ends with the aged
narrator in Switzerland in retreat from
the consequences of what he has foreseen
—a world facing a gender crisis resulting
from the availability of a drug that ensures
male children. Set in the Middle East during nineteenth-century power-struggles
within the Ottoman Empire, *The Rock of
Tanios* (1993) follows the wanderings of
a sheik's illegitimate son. Afflicted by his
family's guilt and the alienating political
climate, he disappears mysteriously in
Cyprus.
James Clavel, Umberto Eco,
Lawrence Norfolk   *DH*

Macaulay, Rose (British, 1881–1958)
Macaulay was a popular author of travel
books, biographies, and satirical novels
with a liberal social ethos and ironic tone.
Potterism (1920), for instance, deals with
the excesses of newspaper journalists, and
Crewe Train (1926) takes a flippant view of
London literati and society life. Her most
interesting works tend to fall outside these
categories, notably *They Were Defeated*

(1932), a historical novel set in the English
Civil War. *Non-Combatants and Others*
(1916) is an absorbing narrative about
the First World War at home; the main
character, Alix, comes to question the
war's purpose following the suicide of
her brother at the Front, and throws
herself into organizing pacifist activities.
Macaulay's post-war novels are her most
famous. *My Wilderness* (1950) is about an
alienated youngster in bomb-damaged
London, and in *The Towers of Trebizond*
(1956) a journey round Turkey by camel
occasions many pointed observations of
cultural difference and the consolations
of Anglicanism.
Winifred Holtby   *JS*

McAuley, Paul J. (British, 1955–)
McAuley is a research biologist by profession; his science fiction began appearing
in 1984. Begin with *Four Hundred Billion
Stars* (1988), in which a telepathic astro-
nomer investigating an uninhabited planet
becomes aware of the presence of a powerful intelligence. *Eternal Light* (1991) finds
Earth ruled by a religious cult called the
Witnesses in the aftermath of an interstel-
lar war. Resources are exhausted and further attacks loom. Elysium is an unspoiled
planet colonized by humanity in *Secret
Harmonies* (1989) until conflict breaks out
between the inhabitants and an oppressive
administration. An alternative version of
sixteenth-century Florence is the setting for
the entertaining *Pasquale's Angel* (1994).
Warfare, transport, and industry have all

been transformed by developing Leonardo da Vinci's inventions, while Machiavelli is an unscrupulous journalist investigating a murder conspiracy.

📖 Ian Watson, Larry Niven, Bob Shaw   DH

McBain, Ed. *See* **Hunter, Evan**

McCabe, Patrick (Irish, 1955–) Patrick McCabe's characters are irrepressible, they make you laugh and sympathize no matter what horrible acts they commit. His first-person voices pull the reader in and make it impossible to distance yourself when the violence erupts (and it will!). There is a huge pleasure for the reader in the exuberance and easy rhythms of McCabe's language. His books are a brilliant depiction of the different faces of Ireland; rural village life in *The Butcher Boy* (1992), two generations of schoolmasters in *The Dead School* (1995), and an unexpected take on the Troubles seen from the perspective of a transvestite prostitute in the 1970s, in *Breakfast on Pluto* (1998). McCabe is deliciously nasty but the black comedy conceals a serious purpose, analysing the religious, social, and sexual pressures which have shaped Irish history.

📖 Poppy Z. Brite, Roddy Doyle, Flann O'Brien   RV

McCaffrey, Anne (US, 1926–) Anne McCaffrey was the first woman winner of the Hugo award for science fiction for *Weyr Search* (1967), the first volume in the highly successful and ongoing *Dragonriders of Pern* series of novels. McCaffrey has reacted against the stereotypical depictions of women in science fiction writing, creating active and volatile heroines. With Ursula Le Guin she is one of the most established and respected women writing in science fiction today. Start with *Dragonrider* (1968).

📖 Michael Moorcock, Stephen Donaldson   LM

McCarthy, Cormac (US, 1933–) Cormac McCarthy did not achieve fame until the publication of his sixth novel, *All the Pretty Horses* (1992), but when it came attention turned to its predecessor, *Blood Meridian, or the Evening Redness in the West* (1985). This book is set in the south-west borderland between the United States and Mexico, and follows the experiences of the (unnamed) kid, as he gets involved with a gang of mercenaries called the Glantons, and meets one of the most menacing figures in modern literature, Judge Holden, a huge, pale, manic individual who seems to know every aspect of human culture and to conduct a single-handed and satanic campaign to destroy it all. This is a savage book, full of rape and pillage, with more scalpings described in more detail—the Indians are just as savage as the whites—than (surely) in any other book. It is also beautifully written, a great poetic exploration of nature and the myth of the West.

📖 Ken Kesey, Flannery O'Connor. *See* UNITED STATES OF AMERICA

RF

McCarthy, Mary (US, 1912–89) McCarthy was a critic and an intellectual, and there is a satirical objectivity in her fiction, which revealed women's perspectives on previously taboo subjects. Her best-known novel, *The Group* (1963), observes eight women graduates seeking careers or husbands, taking lovers and (rather graphically) discovering birth control. The characters struggle to make sense of a world organized by men; one is certified insane by her abusive husband. The book predated the 'new' feminist writing of the 1960s, and some feminist critics complain that the women are either vacuous or apologetic and that McCarthy merely accepts male standards and women's experiences. However, she allows each woman to tell her own story, and readers to make up their own minds. McCarthy caused a sensation with *The Company She Keeps* (1942), especially with the unsentimental female viewpoint on a casual sexual encounter, in the episode 'The Man in the Brooks Brothers Shirt'.

📖 Alison Lurie, Flannery O'Connor

FS

McClure, James (British, 1939–). *See* CRIME

McCrum, Robert (British, 1953–) McCrum was born in Cambridge, where he was educated at the University, before becoming an editor and writer. *In the Secret State* (1980), his first novel, is a good introduction to the unsettling world of political corruption and psychological isolation featured in much of his writing. As traditional values decay, the book's disenchanted bureaucrats cynically manipulate the political system in order to preserve their hold on power. Vividly depicting events during the Prague Spring of 1968, *The Fabulous Englishman* (1984) deals with a once-successful English author whose journey to Prague involves him in painful confrontations with his past. McCrum's other novels include *The Psychological Moment* (1993), dealing with a presidential speech-writer in retreat at Cape Cod who is beset by treacheries and

painful personal choices when he learns of a British political conspiracy.

📖 Piers Paul Read, Frederic Raphael, James Buchan. *See* ADVENTURE *DH*

McCullers, Carson (US, 1917–67) Born in Columbus, Georgia, McCullers suffered from an extraordinary range of illnesses throughout her life, which finally caused her to relinquish the idea of a musical career. She writes almost obsessively about outsiders. Often, as in *The Heart is a Lonely Hunter* (1940), the outsider is a young girl nearing puberty. Mick Kelly wants to become a famous pianist, but sees that accepting womanhood will mean staying in socially acceptable roles and stifling her ambition. As a result, she comes to identify with others on the margins of society, including a deaf mute—memorably played by Alan Arkin in the film version—and a black doctor trying to raise the standards of his community. In *The Ballad of the Sad Café* (1951) the heroine is Amelia Evans. Immense, introverted, and mannish, Amelia falls in love with Cousin Lymon, a sexually impotent and malevolent dwarf. The theme of the unacceptable female, and the female who is unacceptably creative, recurs repeatedly in McCullers' work, more conventionally in *The Member of the Wedding* (1946), in which another tomboy, Frankie Adams, dreams of becoming a great poet. When she is not allowed to go on her brother's honeymoon, Frankie is faced by the facts of adult sexuality, finally accepting the role of 'southern belle'. McCullers writes in a clear, beguiling style that makes her freakish world absolutely compelling.

📖 Flannery O'Connor, Karen Blixen (writing as Isak Dinesen), Eudora Welty

LM

McDermid, Val (British, 1955–) Val McDermid grew up in a Scottish mining community and read English at Oxford before working as a journalist. She has written two crime series which feature female protagonists; the Kate Brannigan novels, set in Manchester, are characterized by a witty and engaging style and the Lindsay Gordon novels feature the first 'out' British lesbian detective. McDermid has also published chilling, graphic, psychological thrillers pitting the policeman Tony Hill and his team against serial killers. In the award-winning *The Mermaids Singing* (1995) someone is killing gay men, and in *Wire in the Blood* (1997) Hill's National Profiling Task Force is asked to identify any sinister link between the disappearances of young girls. His colleague Shaz Bowman has a hunch as to the killer's identity but it seems so far-fetched that she is ridiculed, at great cost to herself and the success of the investigation.

📖 Patricia Cornwell, Sandra Scoppettone, Linda Barnes. *See* CRIME

CS

MacDonald, Ann-Marie (Canadian, 1959–) Ann-Marie MacDonald was already well known as an actress and scriptwriter in Canada before the publication of her first novel, *Fall on Your Knees* (1996, winner of the Commonwealth First Novel Prize). This beautifully written novel—in some ways a family saga—tells the story of the four Piper sisters, all of whom are unconventional, weighed down by poverty and religious uncertainty, yet determined to make their mark on a rapidly changing twentieth century. It is music that gives them hope, and ultimately takes it away, and the novel is haunted by a strangely compelling lyricism. It is difficult in places because of its breadth (it moves from turn-of-the-century Canada to New York in the 1950s), various plot-lines, and unusual narrative voice, but it is nevertheless both deeply moving and, in places, very entertaining.

📖 Kate Atkinson, Margaret Atwood, Salman Rushdie

SB

McEwan, Ian (British, 1948–) Ian McEwan has been at the forefront of English fiction since the mid-1970s. Known mainly as a novelist, he also writes short stories and screenplays. His pared-down style and even delivery maintain a sense of distance, and a McEwan book is typically a novel of ideas, engaging the intellect rather more than the feelings. Often he is concerned with the split between material and spiritual perceptions of life. *Enduring Love* (1997) tells the story of a happily married and determinedly rationalistic science writer, who falls prey to an obsessive stalker with a mission to bring him to God. The book has tremendous narrative drive and keeps the reader guessing throughout. McEwan is a master of the slow build and leans towards the macabre, a talent used to great effect in his psychological thriller, *The Innocent* (1990). Leonard Marnham, the innocent abroad in post-war Berlin, is part of a surveillance team involved in the making of the Berlin Tunnel. Falling in love with the enigmatic Maria, he becomes entangled in a chain of events that culminates nightmarishly in the disposal of a body.

At this point backtrack to McEwan's first novel, *The Cement Garden* (1978), in which four children decide to tell no one and fend for themselves when their reclusive parents die. Less thoughtful than his later books, this is nevertheless powerfully claustrophobic, zooming in on the fine detail of greasy adolescence and the urban wasteland in which the incestuous, fantasy-fuelled roles are played out. McEwan's *Amsterdam* (1998) won the Booker Prize; *The Child in Time* (1987), a more likeable and haunting book, about a couple's reaction to the abduction of their child, won the Whitbread award.

📖 Jim Crace, Julian Barnes,
Iain Banks. *See* SHORT STORIES   *CB*

McGahern, John (Irish, 1934–)
McGahern's novels are evocative, slow-paced stories which portray the political and social development of rural Ireland in simple, often poetic prose. Begin with *Amongst Women* (1990), where the three Moran sisters attempt to re-create the festive Monaghan Day, anxiously evoking, for their father's sake, an idyllic past that never actually existed. As the narrative begins to detail the reality of that past, it develops into a close analysis of family life, centring on the tensions surrounding Moran, a complicated, unhappy man hardened by his experiences as a Republican fighter, and unable to accept responsibility for his difficult relationship with his sons. McGahern is also a prolific writer of short stories. Move on to *Getting Through* (1978), a diverse, observant collection, and a tolerant consideration of human frailty and love. His very fine *Collected Short Stories* (1992) is also available.

📖 William Trevor, Bernard
MacLaverty, James Joyce.
See IRELAND   *SR*

McGrath, Patrick (British, 1950–)
The son of a former head psychiatrist at an asylum, Patrick McGrath made his name with *Grotesque* (1989), a blend of the traditional country house mystery and contemporary horror. Centred on the unsettling events that surround the arrival of a new butler at a run-down manor, where the head of the house is busy reconstructing a dinosaur skeleton, the book was quickly labelled 'New Gothic'. *Dr Haggard's Disease* (1993) recounts a passionate love-affair whose end appears to have physically poisoned the narrator, and *Asylum* (1996) is set in the 1950s, at a bleak mental hospital where dark secrets and strange forces seem to be at work. McGrath's fiction is exquisitely crafted, and his novels present a veneer of civilized traditional story-telling beneath which chaotic and disturbing forces quickly make themselves felt. *Blood and Water* (1988) is a collection of stories, and a good introduction to his work.

📖 Ian McEwan; Rachel Ingalls   *WB*

Machen, Arthur (British, 1863–1947).
See SUPERNATURAL

McIlvanney, William (British, 1936–)
A Scottish teacher and poet, William McIlvanney's first crime novel, *Laidlaw* (1977), won the Crime Writers' Association Silver Dagger. He had already achieved a strong reputation in mainstream writing, winning the Whitbread award in 1975 for *Docherty*, a son's view of his father's courage and endurance during the depression. *Laidlaw* is a dark and realistic yarn set in Glasgow, about a private eye whose rough exterior belies his own inner moral certitude and who toils in a world of grey uncertainties. Jack Laidlaw reappeared in *The Papers of Tony Veitch* (1983) and *Strange Loyalties* (1991). Both novels display powerful portraits of machismo undone and vivid descriptions of the Scottish underworld. *The Big Man* (1985) mines a similar social realist vein in its portrayal of a directionless man hired as a fighter by an

underworld boss and the ensuing moral dilemmas and crumbling of his marriage. Some minor characters from the Laidlaw novels appear in *The Big Man*.

📖 Ian Rankin, John Harvey, James Kelman   *MJ*

McInerney, Jay (US, 1955–) McInerney's first novel, *Bright Lights, Big City* (1984), became the talk of New York and an immediate best-seller. Written in a slick, fast-moving style, the book deals with a Manhattan magazine writer struggling in a whirlpool of plentiful cocaine and endless parties. The grim but funny *Story of My Life* (1988) stays on the same terrain and tells the story of Alison Poole, a privileged, hedonistic, and directionless New Yorker who speaks in cutting one-liners. The more substantial *Brightness Falls* (1992) addresses the stock market crash of 1987, but unlike its predecessors, pans beyond the 'beautiful people' of the yuppie set to include those who never benefited from the Reagan boom.

📖 Bret Easton Ellis, David Leavitt
                                                         BH

Mackay, Shena (British, 1944–) Some of Mackay's novels and stories are domestic comedies, with sharp observations of the British class system, in which women typically battle the odds. Others have an elegiac dimension in which the past is viewed critically, expressed in richly evocative prose. *Redhill Rococo* (1986) is of the first type: a woman struggles to keep her family together while her husband is in prison, and takes on a middle-class young lodger. *Dunedin* (1992) has a much larger canvas, its two narratives divided between 1909 New Zealand and contemporary London, contrasting the lives of a Presbyterian minister with his female descendant. Mackay's best and most acclaimed novel so far is *The Orchard on Fire* (1995), a dark idyll of childhood set in the Kent village of 'Stonebridge' during 1953. It is a haunting re-creation of childhood's fears and fantasies as seen by a returning adult, and avoids nostalgia. Her stories are frequently hilarious and poignant by turns. 'Death by Art Deco', in *The World's Smallest Unicorn and Other Stories* (1999), concerns a successful woman author who employs an aspiring writer as a disastrous domestic.

📖 Mavis Cheek, Candia McWilliam, Ronald Firbank   *JS*

McKay, Claude (Jamaican/US, 1890–1948). *See* CARIBBEAN

Mackenzie, (Edward Montague) Compton (British, 1883–1972) Born in West Hartlepool, Mackenzie became a professional writer after graduating from Oxford. Begin with *Whisky Galore* (1947), his entertaining comedy about a shipload of whisky falling into the hands of Scottish islanders. Capri, where he lived in the 1920s, is the setting for *Extraordinary Women* (1928), remarkable in its day for its light handling of homosexuality. *The Vanity Girl* (1920) tells of a chorus girl's prudent course to fame and subsequent marriage into the aristocracy. For literary depth, Mackenzie's most impressive work is the two-volume *Sinister Street* (1913, 1914), which charts a young man's corruption after leaving Oxford. The book vividly evokes the atmosphere among Mackenzie's generation on the eve of the First World War, his own experiences of which are recounted in *Gallipoli Memories* (1929).

📖 Hugh Walpole, Eric Linklater. *See* SPY   *DH*

MacLaverty, Bernard (British, 1942–) MacLaverty was born and brought up in Belfast. He worked as a lab technician for ten years before reading English at university and becoming a teacher. He moved to Glasgow after graduation. In his novel *Lamb* (1980) he deals with the consequences of Ulster's sectarian violence. Brother Sebastian, né Michael Lamb, runs away from a reformatory with a 12-year-old boy, which the press and police regard as kidnap. Lamb sees it as rescuing an abused child, however, and the pressures on Lamb drive the situation to a terrible crisis. Again, in *Cal* (1983) MacLaverty deals with terrorist violence in the province. Cal, a young man living with his father, is attacked as a member of the only Catholic family on their estate. The novel traces the protagonist's tragic love-affair and the ways in which he becomes embroiled in terrorist activities whilst trying to avoid it at all costs. *Cal* is a brilliant account of the ways in which the complex political and religious situation in Northern Ireland inevitably enmeshes all its citizens. MacLaverty was short-listed for the Booker Prize for his novel *Grace Notes* (1997). This is about a young composer, Catherine McKenna, and her relationships with her parents back in Northern Ireland and her daughter in Glasgow as she struggles with depression and the ability to compose.

📖 Glenn Patterson, Ian McEwan, Seamus Deane   *CJ*

McLaverty, Michael (Irish, 1904–92). *See* IRELAND

MacLean, Alistair (British, 1922–87) MacLean was born in Glasgow, where he was educated at the University before becoming a schoolteacher. Begin with *HMS Ulysses* (1955), his best-selling first novel. Based on his experiences during the Second World War, the book's account of the shipping convoys to Russia vividly evokes voyages through Arctic winters under constant danger of U-boat attack. *The Guns of Navarone* (1957) is typical of his work in featuring a group of courageous commandos on a mission of urgent importance. The story of the destruction of a crucial Nazi gun installation on an island off Turkey was, like a number of his novels, successful as a film. In *Ice Station Zebra* (1963) the atomic submarine *Dolphin* is imperilled under the Arctic ice cap in an attempt to rescue survivors of a weather-station adrift on the pack ice.

📖 Hammond Innes, Nicholas Monsarrat, Gavin Lyall   *DH*

McLennan, Hugh (Canadian, 1907–90). *See* CANADA

McMurtry, Larry (US, 1936–) McMurtry has lived the majority of his life in Texas. He was born in Wichita Falls, and went on to study at Rice University, where he now teaches. It is this Texan location which McMurtry features in his novels. His most famous novel, *Lonesome Dove* (1985)—awarded the Pulitzer Prize for literature (1986)—has been described as a 'novel of the mythic west'. Set in the town of Lonesome Dove, it features the antics of two rangers turned horse rustlers, Augustus McCrae and Woodrow F. The main characters feature in a series of novels including *Deadman's Walk* (1995), which is the *Lonesome Dove* prequel. Here the two are arrogant young 19-year-olds. They attempt to seize Santa Fe from the Mexicans and in the ensuing action they encounter everything from natural disasters to romance.

📖 John Steinbeck, Ken Kesey.
See WESTERN   *CJ*

McNab, Andy (1960–   ) Andy McNab was an SAS commander during the Gulf War, and his first book, *Bravo Two Zero* (1994), was a detailed autobiographical account of a risky top-secret mission to penetrate Iraqi defences, during which he was caught and tortured. Following the book's outstanding success, McNab went on to write *Immediate Action* (1996), the story of his difficult childhood and early days in the Army, and of his subsequent entry into the Special Forces. McNab has also written two best-selling thrillers, both of which centre on Nick Stone, a fictional ex-soldier who served in the SAS and is now a special agent. Begin with *Remote Control* (1997), as Stone is forced to go underground following the murder of a close friend. Move on to *Crisis Four*, the fast-moving story of Stone's entanglement with Sarah, an enigmatic colleague with a dangerous secret past.

📖 Stephen Crane, Frederick Forsyth, Alan Judd, Len Deighton   *SR*

McWilliam, Candia (British, 1955–   ) Born in Edinburgh, McWilliam is known for her unsettling yet witty novels, which have an assured grasp of narrative pace and great precision of language. Her work is typically sardonic about her characters' pretensions and foibles, and about Scottish history and identity. Her first novel, *A Case of Knives* (1988), revolves around an odd triangular relationship involving a heart surgeon; *A Little Stranger* (1989) develops its black comedy from an employer's increasing suspicion of her new nanny.

The increasing closeness of the nanny to her employer's husband and son leads to a violent climax. In *Debatable Land* (1994), which won the *Guardian* Fiction Prize, the crew of the yacht *Ardent Spirit* sail from Tahiti to New Zealand. Mostly Scots, some burdened by the past, their conflicts and attractions absorb them, and they then encounter a storm.

📖 Shena Mackay, Elizabeth Bowen, A. S. Byatt   *JS*

Madden, Deirdre (British, 1960–   ) Madden's novels are set in her native Northern Ireland, and deal with friendship, family, creativity, and loss, through the lives of her women characters. Her writing is elegantly simple and muted; begin with *One by One in the Darkness* (1996) which traces a week in the lives of three sisters just before the start of the 1994 IRA ceasefire, intercut with episodes from their childhood. It offers an honest, angry and affectionate account of life in Northern Ireland over the past thirty years. *Nothing is Black* (1994) focuses on three women at a defining moment in their lives, meeting at the Donegal house of solitary painter Claire. *Remembering Light and Stone* (1992) is set in Italy and Ireland, and deals with the heroine's attempts to come to terms with her past.

📖 John McGahern, Glenn Patterson, Jennifer Johnston. *See* IRELAND   *JR*

Mahfouz, Naguib (Egyptian, 1912–   ) Naguib Mahfouz is one of the giants of world literature, both in status and output. He was born in Cairo, the youngest of seven children, and graduated in philosophy from the University of Cairo, choosing to spend his working career as a civil servant. He was awarded the Nobel

Prize for Literature in 1988, the Swedish academy writing that 'through works rich in nuance—now clear-sightedly realistic, now evocatively ambiguous—[he] has formed an Arabic narrative art that applies to all mankind'. Mahfouz has written some forty novels and fourteen volumes of short stories. Begin with the Cairo trilogy: *Palace Walk* (1956), *Palace of Desire* (1957), and *Sugar Street* (1958). In these novels, Mahfouz traces the evolution of Egyptian society from the First to the Second World War, by focusing on three generations of the Abd al-Jawwad family, who begin the saga living a life of moral and social claustrophobia under the yoke of a traditional patriarchy. Yet, even by the end of the first book, the family structure has been undermined as one of the brothers of the second generation is killed in a riot against British rule. In *Palace of Desire*, the new generation discovers sexual freedoms and responsibilities the older generation did not have. In the final book, *Sugar Street*, one of the new generation is a communist and another a fundamentalist, yet another is a homosexual who is trying to use his charms to promote himself and his family in the civil service. Mahfouz's style is leisurely and yet at one with the narrative tradition which has produced the Egyptian soap operas so popular all over the Arabic-speaking world; he is a masterly story-teller.

📖 Tayeb Salih, Nawal El Saadawi, Doris Lessing   IP

Mahy, Margaret (NZ, 1936–) Margaret Mahy, who spent many years working as a librarian, has won the Carnegie Medal twice: in 1982 for *The Haunting* and in 1985 for *The Catalogue of the Universe*. She is an original and somewhat eccentric writer

whose work could never be mistaken for anyone else's. She has been writing for many years and for all age groups, and her work for younger children, like *The Man Whose Mother Was a Pirate* (1972), is characterized by a gloriously zany and surreal humour. When she writes for young adults one of her qualities is the fierce intelligence she brings to a genre (the supernatural) in which it is all too easy to be silly and unconvincing. While you are reading a Mahy book, you believe in everything. Her novel *Memory* (1987) is a wonderfully sensitive and gripping exploration of old age, and in particular of Alzheimer's disease and its effects. A more recent novel, *The Other Side of Silence* (1995), touches on fairy-tale themes: an old lady in a house in the forest is hiding a terrible secret in a locked room.

📖 Iain Banks, Elizabeth Jolley.
See TEEN   AG

Mailer, Norman (US, 1923–) Mailer became a celebrity author with his first book, and a public personality shortly afterwards; he has since been vastly prolific, with several landmark achievements in nonfiction. The ambitious scope of Mailer's cultural reportage has tended to overshadow his novels, but they remain fascinating. Some are huge panoramas, such as *Harlot's Ghost* (1991), a grand speculation about the CIA and the nature of power in America. Others are much shorter entertainments: *Tough Guys Don't Dance* (1984) is a pastiche crime thriller in the manner of Dashiell Hammett. The reception of Mailer's fiction has varied wildly, but the reputation of *The Naked and the Dead* (1948) seems secure. A realist study of conflict, both within the army and against the Japanese, the novel draws upon Mailer's war service in the Pacific. *An American Dream* (1965) was published in serial form, and initially greeted with derision for its luridly sensational plot involving wife-murderer Stephen Rojack and his existential speculations about sex, violence, and corruption. But it is a compelling book and has become a modern classic; the rich texture of Mailer's prose, placed alongside hardbitten dialogue, carries the murder thriller into the sphere of the philosophical novel. A good introduction to the range of Mailer's work would be a recent omnibus selection, *The Time of Our Time* (1998).

📖 Don DeLillo, Tom Wolfe, Ernest Hemingway, James Jones. *See* UNITED STATES OF AMERICA   JS

Mais, Roger (Jamaican, 1905–55). *See* CARIBBEAN

Maitland, Sara (British, 1950–) Maitland grew up in a large family in south-west Scotland, then read English at Oxford, where she discovered socialism and Christianity. A feminist theologian, she explores maternity, spirituality, and female friendship in her fiction and non-fiction alike. Begin with *Virgin Territory* (1984), a powerful novel exploring sex and violence. Its heroine is Sister Anna, a troubled, unorthodox nun who has come from a South American mission house to London, where life forces her to reassess her vow of chastity. Less turbulent but equally poignant, *Daughter of Jerusalem* (1978) is about Elizabeth and Ian, a married couple who want a child but cannot conceive. *Three Times Table* (1991) is a multi-layered story of one night in the life of three generations of women. As is shown in *Telling Tales* (1983,) Maitland is an inventive, exuberant short-story writer, who often reworks fairy-tales and archetypes to celebrate her favourite themes.

📖 Michèle Roberts, Zoe Fairbairns   JN

Malamud, Bernard (US, 1914–86) Born in Brooklyn to a Russian immigrant family who kept a shop, Malamud spent most of his writing life as a teacher. Influenced by the Yiddish tradition, his stories and novels tend to be moral fables, combining realism with fabulous or allegorical characters and events. His first novel, *The Natural* (1952), however, concerns the fall, rise, and subsequent failure of Roy Hobbs, a star baseball hitter, whose career succumbs to corruption. *The Assistant* (1957) is a more subtle and morally serious work, telling how a petty thief becomes attached to an impoverished Jewish grocer's life, taking on responsibility for the shop and eventually embracing Judaism's values. Malamud's several volumes of stories, notably *The Magic Barrel* (1958) and *Rembrandt's Hat* (1973), are lighter in tone and often ruefully comic. Jewishness is seen in conflict with other cultures and races: a black angel comes to the assistance of a disbelieving Jewish tailor; there are miracles and marriage brokers, while 'The Jewbird' and 'Talking Horse' are symbolic tales of conscience and humanity. *Dubin's Lives* (1979) is a richly meditative novel about biography, the writer, and middle-aged sexual obsessions. It follows the disruptive entry of a young woman, Fanny, into the comfortable life of a successful biographer who is writing on D. H. Lawrence. As is characteristic of Malamud, the characters are matured by experience and personal suffering.

📖 Isaac Bashevis Singer, Saul Bellow. *See* UNITED STATES OF AMERICA   JS

Malouf, David (Australian, 1934–)
Malouf often writes on Australian subjects, although his powerful second novel,
An Imaginary Life (1978), is about the
poet Ovid in exile on the Black Sea.
Begin with the award-winning *Remembering Babylon* (1993). Set in the 1850s, in
a remote settlement in Queensland, the
story centres on a creature ('hopping and
flapping towards them out of a world
over there, that was the abode of everything savage and fearsome') who turns
out to be a white man, Gemmy. Gemmy
was thrown overboard as a cabin boy,
and has lived with Aborigines for sixteen
years. The novel moves effortlessly between
Gemmy's struggle to ingratiate himself and
cling to his own identity, his memories
of life with the Aborigines, and the nightmare cruelties of his childhood, and the
rivalries between various members of the
settlement, who are haunted by a sense of
their own futility.

Harland's Half Acre (1984), a family
saga set in rural Australia about a hundred
years later, interweaves the stories of
Frank Harland, a visionary painter who
lives the life of a tramp, and the boy
who becomes Frank's protector. The
half acre of the title is the amount of
canvas Frank covers with his paintings.
'It wasn't much, no more than a glimpse.
But as much as one man might catch
sight of.' This novel remains episodic,
lacking the synthesis Malouf achieved
in *Remembering Babylon*. In *The Great
War* (1990) Malouf depicts Australian
life through differing reactions to war.
Malouf is also known as a poet, librettist,
and critic.
📖 Thomas Keneally, Patrick White,
Elizabeth Jolley. *See* AUSTRALIA AND
NEW ZEALAND   JR

Malraux, André (French, 1901–76)
Malraux was a prominent anti-fascist during the 1930s, and active in the wartime
Resistance. As a close ally of de Gaulle, he
later became a Government minister. His
novels combine action with philosophy,
and are usually set in political hot spots
like Shanghai, Germany, or Civil War
Spain. They also anticipated existentialism, with figures finding authenticity
through political action and solidarity. *La
Condition Humaine* (1933; *Man's Estate*,
1948) was an influential work, dramatizing
the human cost of political necessity; its
heroes are communists, slaughtered by
Chinese nationalist forces under Chiang
Kai-shek. *Days of Hope* (1938) is a large
documentary novel written during the
early stages of the Spanish Civil War,
ending on an uplifting note of solidarity,
and is regarded as Malraux's best work.
The Walnut Trees of Altenburg (1943),
written when Malraux had been captured
in the early stages of the war, is interesting
mainly for its central section concerning
the narrator's father, who is shown fighting for the Germans during the First World
War. *Anti-Memoirs* (1968) puts accounts
of de Gaulle, Nehru, and Mao alongside
fictional elements.
📖 Albert Camus, Norman Mailer,
Jean-Paul Sartre   JS

Manfred, Frederick (US, 1912–).
See WESTERN

Mann, Thomas (German, 1875–1955)
Born in Lübeck, Mann achieved renown
with *Buddenbrooks* (1901), his first novel.
Its lengthy treatment of the decline of a
merchant family, which draws on his own
privileged background, is not, however, a
good introduction. Begin with *Death in*

Venice (1912), a masterpiece of the novella form, in which an exhausted writer is spiritually rejuvenated through his obsession with a Polish boy. After the boy's departure he remains in Venice to die of cholera. *The Magic Mountain* (1924) is set in a Swiss sanatorium, where its main character, the young engineer Hans Castorp, arrives a visitor but remains for seven years. A major novel of ideas, the energetic conversation among the patients sets forth the political and cultural state of Europe on the eve of the First World War. In the sanatorium's exclusive society of individuals whom illness relieves of responsibility, Castorp slowly matures as he absorbs a range of intense intellectual and emotional experiences. He finally returns to the world of action, to be glimpsed in wartime Flanders at the close. In *Doctor Faustus* (1947) Mann subtly allegorizes Germany's descent into the evil of Nazism in his creation of the menacingly charismatic composer, Adrian Leverkuhn. Leverkuhn believes he has struck a deal with the Devil for the brilliant but dehumanized musical system he has discovered. Thought mad when he informs his friends of his approaching damnation, he is reduced to imbecility by a stroke upon completing his greatest work.

📖 Leo Tolstoy, Hermann Hesse, Albert Camus. *See* FILM ADAPTATIONS, GERMANY   DH

Manning, Olivia (British, 1908–80) Manning led a precarious existence in 1930s London, writing romantic magazine fiction, before publishing her first novel in 1937. She married a British Council lecturer in 1939 who whirled her off to Bucharest. Her experiences there, and subsequent wartime wanderings, form the basis of her six most famous novels. *The Balkan*

Trilogy (1960–5) is a portrait of her own marriage, set amongst expatriates in a Romania struggling to maintain independence as Nazism encroaches. It's long and largely uneventful, with a curiously inactive heroine, but Manning's readable prose, the gallery of eccentric characters, and unusual historical context maintain constant interest. *The Levant Trilogy* (1977–80) follows Harriet and Guy Pringle to the Middle East and vividly describes the desert war from the point of view of a young subaltern. Manning wrote seven other novels and two volumes of short stories.

📖 Herman Wouk, Evelyn Waugh, Elizabeth Bowen. *See* HISTORICAL

          MH

Mansfield, Katherine (NZ, 1888–1932) Mansfield (whose full name was Kathleen Mansfield Beauchamp) moved to Europe from New Zealand when she was 20, and after living in England and Germany was diagnosed with tuberculosis while still in her twenties, and spent her last few years travelling in search of a cure. Her short stories are among the most perfect in English; typically, she will take one incident in the life of a character, and reveal through that the hopes and fears and inner sense of a whole lifetime. In 'The Daughters of the Late Colonel' (*The Garden Party*, 1922) two spinster sisters are left bewildered and aimless by the death of their tyrannical father, whose personality still dominates his room to the extent that they are terrified to touch his possessions. Their lives have been 'looking after father, and at the same time keeping out of father's way. But now?' The fearful confinement of their lives is reflected in their anxious attempts to placate the bullying maid. In 'The Life of Ma Parker' an old woman cleans for a literary gentleman, on the day after her beloved grandson's funeral; the man's callous snobbery—'these people set such store by funerals'—is unfelt by Ma Parker, who finds herself at the bitter pass of needing to cry and having nowhere in the world to do it. 'The Woman at the Store' (*Something Childish and Other Stories*, 1924) is set in New Zealand, and in the desolate country store conjures up a nightmare world of isolation, ruined hopes, and terrible revenge.

📖 Anton Chekhov, Raymond Carver, Christina Stead. *See* AUSTRALIA AND NEW ZEALAND, SHORT STORIES   *JR*

Mantel, Hilary (British 1952–) One of the most versatile of British novelists, Hilary Mantel was born in the north of England, but has lived in London, Africa, and Saudi Arabia. *Eight Months on Ghazzah Street* (1988) gives in exquisite and painful detail the reactions of one woman to living in a Middle Eastern country with all the cultural alienation and darkness that lie beneath the surface of expatriate life. Mantel has also written about the French Revolution in *A Place of Greater Safety* (1992), about the underworld of eighteenth-century society in *The Giant, O'Brien* (1998), and about the profound effects of trauma and loss on the lives of an English family who have lived in Africa in *A Change of Climate* (1994). Her work sets the internal, psychological worlds of her characters against the broad landscape of cultural revolution in a way that allows her to combine the minutely detailed with the panoramic. The book to start with is *Fludd* (1989), which describes, to darkly comic effect, the effect of an ambiguous yet charismatic priest on a village in Derbyshire. Mantel's sense of place is sharply and powerfully realized,

and the satirical moments coexist, or even depend upon, her acknowledgement of the inherent mystery of human life. Mantel has said that she is influenced by Muriel Spark, and works such as *Memento Mori* contain a similar dark wit.

📖 Lesley Glaister, Jane Rogers, Deborah Moggach   *LM*

Mare, Walter de la (British, 1873–1956). *See* SUPERNATURAL

Mariengof, Anatoly (Russian, 1897–1962). *See* RUSSIA

Mark, Jan (British, 1943–) Jan Mark has won the Carnegie Medal twice: in 1977 for her first book *Thunder and Lightnings* (1976) and in 1984 for *Handles* (1983). The first is a moving novel with an unusual friendship between two boys at its heart, and the second is more picaresque, but is basically about families. Mark is good at families. She is good at a great many things: animals, science fiction, schools (and in particular conversations between young people), planes, and love. Her short stories, especially her ghost stories, are brilliant. Try *In Black and White* (1991). Her work is characterized by intelligence and originality, and she assumes intelligence in her readers. She can turn her hand to anything from an epic to a picture book. Her work is often very funny, and *They do Things Differently There* (1994) is a hilarious masterpiece of the surreal, in which two girls discover a more interesting place lurking beneath their dull home town. Her novel for adults, *Zeno was Here* (1987), is one of the most moving love-stories of recent years, while being also extremely funny.

📖 J. D. Salinger, Russell Hoban. *See* TEEN   *AG*

Markandaya, Kamala (Indian, 1924–). *See* INDIA

Markham, E(dward) A(rchibald) (British, born Monserrat 1939–). *See* CARIBBEAN

Marric, J. J. *See* **Creasey, John**

Marryat, Captain (Frederick) (British, 1792–1848). *See* THE SEA

Marsh, Ngaio (NZ, 1899–1982) Marsh went to art school and became an actress before turning to detective fiction in the 1930s. She was created a Dame for her contribution to the theatre, and her knowledge of that world informs several of her novels, such as *Opening Night* (1951) or *Enter a Murderer* (1935), in which theatrical intrigue plays as great a part as the murder mystery. Her detective Roderick Alleyn is a policeman with an aristocratic background, constantly surprising his potential suspects by his good breeding, erudition, and sensitivity (matched by the ability of his faithful sidekick, Inspector Fox, to charm the servants below stairs). Alleyn likes to share his deductive process with his cohorts, and thus with the reader. His romancing of and marriage to the painter Agatha Troy, which begins in *Artists in Crime* (1938), provides the opportunity for Marsh to use her artistic background. Several of her books, such as *Colour Scheme* (1943), are set in New Zealand.

📖 Agatha Christie, Margery Allingham, Josephine Tey. *See* CRIME
KB

Mars-Jones, Adam (British, 1954–) Born in London, son of a High Court judge, Mars-Jones has worked as an arts journalist and established a reputation for subtly satirical, carefully nuanced fiction. His first collection of stories, *Lantern Lecture* (1981), was acclaimed for its witty observation and coolly descriptive prose, recreating the life of an eccentric aristocrat, and, more seriously, the criminal career and trial of Donald Neilson, the so-called 'Black Panther'. In 'Hoosh-Mi', the Queen catches rabies from a corgi. With *The Darker Proof: Stories from a Crisis* (1988, with Edmund White), Mars-Jones's subjects became much darker, but comic details sometimes impinge upon the death and dying of AIDS patients. In 'An Executor', for instance, a 'buddy' has difficulty disposing of leather fetish gear following the death of a friend. *Monopolies of Loss* (1992) is a further collection of beautifully crafted, moving stories about HIV and AIDS. In *The Waters of Thirst* (1993), Mars-Jones's belated first novel, kidney disease rather than AIDS is the subject, but amusing observations of affluent gay lifestyles prevent the story from being too grim.

📖 Armistead Maupin, Christopher Isherwood, Edmund White
JS

Martin, George R. R. (US, 1948–) George R. R. Martin's work was, to begin with, entirely within the science fiction genre, notable successes including the story collection *Sandkings* (1981), and *Tuf Voyaging* (1986), a set of linked stories about a wandering ecological engineer on a giant if half-derelict starship. Martin began to diverge into the area of fantasy, however, with *Fevre Dream* (1982), a vampire story set on a nineteenth-century Mississippi paddleboat, and has begun an extensive heroic fantasy sequence with *A Game of Thrones* (1996). He has also worked as a scriptwriter for the television series *The New Twilight*

Zone and *Beauty and the Beast*. Martin has not been innovative in terms of plots or scenarios, but his stories are fast-paced, and often act as defining examples of the sub-genre they have adopted, whether this is within fantasy or science fiction.

📖 Tim Powers, Michael Swanwick. *See* FANTASY   TS

Mason, Anita (British, 1942–) Mason is a novelist who deserves more recognition. Her books combine great intelligence with readability and she has explored new territory with each work, even though she returns to such themes as power, and the way we are manipulated both personally and politically. Her first novel, *Bethany* (1981), is about an experiment in communal living, told in the first person by a young woman who loves the house's female owner. Mason captures brilliantly all the cross-currents and fluctuating tensions and emotions of the group. Her Booker Prize-shortlisted novel *The Illusionist* (1983) tells the story of Simon Magus, and makes Judaea and Samaria as close and real as the West Country was in *Bethany*. She takes us straight to the past without striking a single mock-biblical note, and the narrative is dazzling, as befits a tale about a magician. *Angel* (1994) is about a female German flyer in the 1930s and gives a completely original perspective on a period about which we thought we knew a great deal. It is wonderfully poetic about flying and aircraft, and tells a moving story of love between two women.

📖 Richard Hughes, Marguerite Yourcenar, Susan Hill   AG

Mason, Bobbie Ann (US, 1940–) After writing critical books about Vladimir Nabokov and detective fiction, Mason turned to fiction. Her award-winning debut, *Shiloh and Other Stories* (1983), chronicles the everyday lives of people trying to make sense of a rapidly changing world. Like *Shiloh*, Mason's first novel, *In Country* (1987), is set in Kentucky. It movingly depicts a young woman's quest to find out about her father, who was killed in the Vietnam war. *Feather Crowns* (1994) charts the life of Christianna Wheeler, a tobacco farmer's wife who gives birth to America's first known quintuplets in 1900. Through Christianna's struggle to prevent the world from exploiting her babies, the book explores the growth of American consumerism and the difficulties of resisting it.

📖 Jayne Anne Phillips, E. Annie Proulx   BH

Massie, Allan (British, 1938–) Born in Singapore and educated at Trinity College, Cambridge, Massie was a schoolteacher before becoming a full-time writer in 1976. Begin with *The Death of Men* (1981), a sophisticated treatment of political ethics with the pace of a good thriller. Based on the kidnapping of Aldo Moro in Italy in 1978, it concerns a fundamentally decent politician abandoned to terrorists by an unscrupulous government. In *One Night in Winter* (1984) an antiques dealer confronts his past involvement in extreme Scottish nationalism as he plunges into a disastrous love-affair. Massie's historical novels set in ancient Rome include *Tiberius: The Memoirs of the Emperor* (1991), in which the aged emperor reviews his past with weary honesty. *Caesar* (1993) is narrated by Brutus, who vividly recounts their former comradeship-in-arms and explains his betrayal of Caesar.

📖 Frederic Raphael, Robert Graves. *See* HISTORICAL   DH

Masters, John (British/US, 1914–83) Masters was born in India, where his family had lived for five generations; he was educated at Wellington and Sandhurst. Having served in the Indian Army until India gained independence, he became a full-time writer in 1950. His best-known novels trace the history of the Savage family in India from the seventeenth century onward. Begin with *Bhowani Junction* (1954), which tells of Colonel Savage's love for an Anglo-Indian woman during the widespread disturbances preceding India's independence. In *The Deceivers* (1952), set in the early nineteenth century, William Savage struggles against the Thugs, a sect of murderous Hindu fanatics. His other works include the *Loss of Eden* trilogy, starting with *Now, God be Thanked* (1979) which follows the lives of several inter-connected families throughout the First World War.

📖 R. K. Narayan, Amit Chaudhuri, J. G. Farrell   *DH*

Maugham, W(illiam) Somerset (British, 1874–1965) A very prolific writer over a career that spanned fifty years, Maugham achieved prominence as a play-wright, novelist, short-story writer, and critic. His simple aim was to tell a good story in a straightforward manner and uncluttered style. He liked a beginning, a middle, and an end. His short stories (collected in four volumes) are the best introduction. Maugham travelled widely, reflected in his stories' wide-ranging locations, from the boulevards of Paris to the South Seas to a Scottish sanatorium. His gallery of characters, from titled toffs to prostitutes, are drawn vividly and with economy. Too often, though, there is a peevish strain of condescension towards them that at times comes uneasily close to sneering.

The Razor's Edge (1944) tells of a young American's rejection of material values and his search for spiritual fulfilment; an ambitious novel, and remarkably modern for a man of 70 to produce. *Cakes and Ale* (1930), about a self-important man of letters and his ex-barmaid wife, is satire disguised as comedy. Maugham squeezed every drop of his varied life experience into his fiction. In *Ashenden* (1928) he recounts his adventures as a secret agent in the First World War, while his early training as a doctor was the basis for *Of Human Bondage* (1915), in which the young hero, handicapped with a club-foot (Maugham himself had a terrible stammer), suffers pangs of unrequited love for a callous waitress. Maugham's gift for story-telling meant that his novels and stories were snapped up for the big and little screen.

📖 O. Henry, V. S. Pritchett, Barbara Pym. *See* SPY   *TH*

Maupassant, Guy de (French, 1850–93) During his brief life Maupassant, a pupil of Flaubert, produced novels, plays, and journalism, but it is for his short stories that he is remembered. 'Boule-de-Suif' (1880) was his first success, about a patriotic prostitute betrayed by snobbery and hypocrisy during the Franco-Prussian war. Prostitution was a favourite subject, but he also wrote about aristocrats, civil servants, Norman peasant life, and the war in which he had served. His style was simple and concise, the tone detached and ironic yet sympathetic. The grimly comic 'Family Life' (1881), about the stultifying existence of a civil servant, reflects his own early employment; 'Mouche' (1890), about a group of male friends spending summer days on the river with a charming girl, recalls the simple fun of his boating days. Though he could write movingly about the beauties of nature, his ultimate vision was deeply pessimistic. In 'The Necklace' (1884), a woman works for years paying off debts incurred replacing a diamond necklace she borrowed and lost, only to find the original was a worthless fake. In 'Bed 29' (1884), prostitute Irma contracts syphilis during the war, sacrificing herself by refusing treatment in order to infect as many of the enemy as she can. Maupassant himself contracted syphilis, which led to insanity, the first signs of which appeared the year he published his terrifying story of possession, 'Le Horla' (1887). He became reclusive and fearful, suffering delusions and attempting suicide before his death at the age of 42.

📖 Gustave Flaubert, Émile Zola.
See FRANCE   CB

Maupin, Armistead (USA, 1944–   )
Armistead Maupin was born in Washington and educated at the University of North Carolina, but is best known for being the chronicler of the burgeoning gay culture of San Francisco in the 1970s. His first novel, *Tales of the City* (1978), began life as a series of sketches for the *San Francisco Examiner* concerning the *ingénue* Mary Ann Singleton; Mouse, the love-hungry gay protagonist; and the enigmatic landlady, Mrs Madrigal. Maupin's writing is dialogue-based, warm, and witty. There are five more novels in the *Tales of the City* series, including *More Tales of the City* (1980) and *Further Tales of the City* (1982). The later novels are written under shadow cast by the AIDS epidemic and are darker in tone. *Maybe the Moon* (1993) concerns a

midget actress and the prejudices she encounters.

📖 Alan Hollinghurst, Evelyn Waugh, Hanif Kureishi   SA

Mauriac, François (French, 1885–1970)
Mauriac, first published as a poet, was a devout Catholic whose elegantly written novels are acute psychological studies of human morality and need. Tending to centre on crises in which worldly and emotional impulses are set against spiritual and religious demands, they are powerful, observant portraits of internal conflict. Begin with *Thérèse Desqueyroux* (1927), which deals with a young woman's murderous attempts to liberate herself from her husband, and her subsequent struggle with her own spirituality. Move on to *The Unknown Sea* (*Les Chemins de la mer*; 1939), the story of the upper-middle-class Revolou family and their various responses to sudden poverty and loss of social standing after their father's financial ruin and suicide. Mauriac's work has been widely translated. He was elected to the French Academy in 1933, and received the Nobel Prize for Literature in 1952.

📖 Graham Greene, André Gide, William Golding   SR

Mayor, F(lora) M(acdonald) (British, 1872–1932). *See* ROMANCE

Mayr, Suzette (Canadian, 1967–   ). *See* CANADA

Mehta, Gita (Indian, 1943–   ) Mehta was brought up in India and educated at Cambridge. She now divides her time between London, India, and New York, where her husband is a leading publisher.

She made her name with a non-fiction work, *Karma Cola*, a scathingly satirical examination of the invasion of India by consumer culture. Of her two novels, by far the more notable is *A River Sutra* (1993), a jewel-like fable, drawing on traditions of Indian story-telling, about a bureaucrat who retires to live by the Ganges in search of tranquillity. Each chapter tells a story stemming from his encounters: he meets a Jain monk, who describes how he has withdrawn from the world; he hears of a poor music teacher's discovery of a young boy with an exquisite singing voice; he reads the diary of a man whose psychological equilibrium is shattered when he is put in charge of an isolated tea estate. Mehta's writing is restrained, delicate, and touching.

📖 R. K. Narayan, Anita Desai   *NC*

Melville, Herman (US, 1819–91) At the age of 20, Herman Melville shipped on board a packet ship bound for Liverpool. Though traumatic, his experience as a deck hand instilled in him the love of the sea that was to take him on further voyages and inspire much of his work, including the magnificent whaling epic, *Moby Dick* (1851). Though massive and endlessly digressive, there is no better introduction to Melville's work; this was the book into which he poured his soul, encompassing both his genius for telling a stirring adventure story and his ambition to use the novel as a vehicle for presenting spiritual truth. Ranging far and wide through the great beliefs and philosophies of the world, in one sense it is a fable about the human quest for meaning. But it is also, quite simply, a great yarn, the tale of young Ishmael's gruelling voyage aboard the *Pequod* under the command of the obsessive Captain

Ahab. Ahab's insane pursuit of the great white whale, Moby Dick, a creature symbolizing the sea itself, is a classic seafaring drama and a dazzling feat of invention.

The factual detail of *Moby Dick* was based on Melville's own experiences as a whalerman in the South Seas, as was *Typee* (1846). Those who find the sheer scale of *Moby Dick* intimidating might prefer to try this first. It is a simpler adventure story, fast-paced, full of cliffhanging suspense and South Sea romance: 'naked houris—cannibal banquets—groves of cocoa-nuts—coral reefs—tattooed chiefs —and bamboo temples.' Sailors Tommo and Toby jump ship in the Polynesian islands and live with the cannibal Nukuheva society. As lively and humorous as all of Melville's work, *Typee* is also typically reflective, presenting two flawed worlds. The cannibalism of Tommo's hosts reflects the devouring of Polynesia by the civilized world, the pernicious effects of the missionary influence, and European colonization apparent in the loss of tribal culture and the devastating introduction of malaria and syphilis. But there are no paradises. The Polynesian world is gorgeous and innocent, but dangerous: Eden with a nightmare shadow of totemic ritual and cannibalism. *Typee* is a book of contrasts. Unable to speak the language, lamed and obliged to be carried by his 'servant', Kory-Kory, Tommo is infantilized, while the Nukuheva 'savages' come to represent authority.

Melville produced many other works during his life, but it was not until long after his death that his final book, *Billy Budd* (written 1888–91), was published (1924). Again both a drama of life at sea and an allegory (this time of innocence and wickedness) it is set on a British man-of-war against the background of the British fleet's Great Mutiny and naval uprisings at Spithead and the Nore. Blue-eyed Billy, the handsome sailor with a nervous stammer, childlike, peaceable, and charming, falls foul of the malignant master-at-arms, Claggart, is falsely accused of fomenting mutiny, and ultimately sacrificed to the implacable martial law of the navy. Short and simple, it was a fitting swansong.

📖 Nathaniel Hawthorne, Mark Twain. *See* THE SEA, UNITED STATES OF AMERICA   CB

Melville, Pauline (Guyanese, 1941–) Melville's collection of stories, *Shape-Shifter* (1990), picked up major literary awards. The characters, lively and odd and often malevolent, stay in the mind. 'You Left the Door Open', about an abuser summoned by the imagination of the victim, is terrifying. The settings, whether in Guyana or London, are sharply observed, the language so full of colour that you have the sense of encountering a visual artist. *The Migration of Ghosts* (1998) is just as imaginatively daring—for example, an Orinoco parrot encounters Descartes—but with an intellectual rigour which saves the conceits drifting off into cloudy magic realism. Melville's *The Ventriloquist's Tale* (1997, Whitbread First Novel Award) is a rich, expansive, sensuous depiction of Amerindian life, which is about (among other things) belonging. Characteristically, the ventriloquist-narrator embodies the search for the right voice to tell the story, and the right story to tell.

📖 Lawrence Scott, Earl Lovelace. *See* CARIBBEAN   EM

Mendes, Alfred (Caribbean, 1897–). *See* CARIBBEAN

Michael, Livi (British, 1960–) Michael writes about the lives of northern working-class women with compassion and accuracy, exploring the impoverishments and tragedies of their lives but never descending into grimness, sentiment, or political posturing. Her heroines are vividly real. Start with *All the Dark Air* (1996) which traces the pregnancy of Julie, living in a rubble-strewn wreck of a terrace with *Big Issue*-seller Mick, his junkie mate Darren, and damaged, not-quite-there Uncle Si. Julie seeks escape through her weekly meditation group meetings, and gradually learns the stories of the friends she makes there. Her journey towards understanding—of herself and others—is profoundly satisfying. *Under a Thin Moon* (1992) charts the lives of four young women on a council estate, while *Their Angel Reach* (1994), the most violent and disturbing of the three, traces the lives of women in a Lancashire village.

📖 Carol Birch, Pat Barker, Raymond Carver   JR

Michaels, Anne (Canadian, 1958–) Anne Michaels had published two collections of poetry in her native Canada before she became an international celebrity for her first novel, *Fugitive Pieces* (1997), which won the Orange Prize. It is written in a highly poetic style, and its first half concerns the rescue of a young Polish boy, Jakob Beer, during the Holocaust by a Greek archaeologist. The second half tells the story of Ben, Jakob's son, a second-generation Holocaust survivor, and his efforts to come to terms with his parents' trauma.

📖 Virginia Woolf, Caryl Phillips, Michèle Roberts   SV

Michener, James A(lbert) (US, 1907–98) Michener was a Lieutenant Commander in the US Navy Pacific fleet during the Second World War, and afterwards worked in publishing and lecturing. His first work, *Tales of the South Pacific* (1947), won a Pulitzer Prize and was the inspiration for the Rodgers and Hammerstein musical *South Pacific*. His fiction is based on fact, and is on an epic scale: many of his books, for example, *Mexico* (1992) and *Alaska* (1988), are histories of whole countries or states told through the fortunes of several families: the plot passing like a relay race from generation to generation. To read Michener's books is not just to be entertained by his characters but to be educated —in subjects ranging from archaeology to shipbuilding and cookery.

📖 Leon Uris, Herman Wouk   *EC*

Middleton, Stanley (British, 1919–)
Middleton sets all his fiction in his native Nottingham, and it is concerned with relationships and family life. Start with *Holiday* (1974, Booker Prize), the story of a teacher whose marriage collapses after the death of his son. He runs away to the seaside resort where he holidayed as a child, to take stock and, through meeting other holidaymakers, to work out his next move. In *Against the Dark* (1998) a couple who have both been hurt in previous relationships, make a new start together, with all the complex moral and practical decisions that involves.

📖 Melvyn Bragg, Alan Sillitoe, Barry Hines   *JR*

Miller, Henry (US, 1891–1980) Aged 40, Miller left America and settled in Paris, determined to become a serious writer; he certainly became a notorious one. His first novel, *Tropic of Cancer* (1934), was published in Paris and banned everywhere else until the early 1960s, as was its successor, *Tropic of Capricorn* (1939). Written in a confessional, exuberant, pell-mell style, the books chronicle Miller's early life in New York and his days (and nights) amongst the low life of bohemian Paris, recounting his sexual adventures in frank detail and explicit language. Other works include the trilogy, *Sexus*, *Plexus*, and *Nexus* (1949–59), which are autobiography thinly disguised as fiction. With the unbanning of his novels, Miller, then in his seventies, was transformed from underground writer of 'dirty' books to champion of sexual liberation and freedom of literary expression.

📖 William Burroughs, Lawrence Durrell, Anais Nin. *See* SEXUAL POLITICS   *TH*

Miller, Sue (US, 1943–) Miller's first novel, *The Good Mother* (1986), is the story of a child-custody battle lost by the mother due to a brief but, in the eyes of the court, damning incident between her child and her partner. Miller's later novels tend to revolve around similar unexpected but inevitable events and their consequences, like the tragic death of the young au pair in *For Love* (1993), which tells the story of a woman who leaves her husband because she misses the romantic love she no longer feels for him. In *While I was Gone* (1998) Jo Becker, a successful, happily married vet with three children reviews her past when Eli Mayhew appears out of it. Eli attracts her, but he is connected with the brutal murder which quashed her hippie illusions. In *The Distinguished Guest* (1995) an elderly writer with Parkinson's disease must look at her life again as she goes to live with her son and his wife.

📖 Ellen Gilchrist, Alison Lurie   *AT*

Milligan, Spike (British, 1918–) The Goons shaped British comedy for half a century and Milligan's unique brand of zany, surreal humour was the essence of Goonery. Milligan's output is prolific; novels, poems, scripts, memoirs, spoofs on classic texts, and he is also a performer and broadcaster. The original Milligan is best displayed in *The Goon Show* (available in several volumes of *Goon Show Scripts* and on audio). *Puckoon* (1969) is a hilariously anarchic comic novel set in the fictional Irish town of Puckoon. In six volumes of war memoirs, starting with *Adolf Hitler: My Part in His Downfall* (1971), Milligan's crazy insights into the life of a soldier in combat are powerfully expressive of the unbelievable insanity of war. The humour doesn't numb the pain of the experience. Milligan's memoirs can now be seen as among the most poignant of the Second World War.

📖 Joseph Heller, Howard Jacobson
RV

Mishima, Yukio (Japanese, 1925–70) Mishima's autobiographical *Confessions of a Mask* (1949) describes his own sexual confusion as well as the chaos of post-war Japan. Bitterly ashamed of Japan's renunciation of her imperial past, Mishima founded a paramilitary society called the (Emperor's) Shield Society in the late 1960s. In ritual manner, precisely described in his short story 'Patriotism' from *Death in Midsummer* (1966), Mishima committed suicide by *seppuku* or disembowelment in 1970. *The Temple of the Golden Pavilion* (1959) works back from the trial of an arsonist who has destroyed a centuries-old Buddhist shrine, to trace the motives for the crime. *The Sailor Who Fell from Grace with the Sea* (1964) is Mishima's most famous work, and not for the squeamish. A young boy sees his mother's lover offend against the code of honour he holds sacred, with horrific consequences. Mishima began his tetralogy *The Sea of Fertility* in 1965, and finished it the night before he died.

📖 Albert Camus, Fyodor Dostoevsky, Oe Kenzaburo   *AT*

Mistry, Rohinton (Indian, 1952–) Mistry has lived in Canada since 1975. He writes big books, the size and scope of classic nineteenth-century novels. But if you want to get a flavour of his writing, the short story collection *Tales from Firozsha Baag* (1987) is a good place to start. All the stories revolve round life in one apartment building in Bombay and establish Mistry's hallmarks of finely differentiated characters, detailed observation of the habits of everyday life, and clear, graceful language. Then settle in for a long, easy, deeply satisfying read with *Such a Long Journey* (1991), which tells the story of Gustad Noble, bank-worker and family man, or *A Fine Balance* (1996) which brings a lively widow, two Untouchable tailors, and a student of refrigeration to share accommodation during Mrs Gandhi's Emergency.

📖 Vikram Seth, Graham Swift, V. S. Naipaul. *See* CANADA   *RV*

Mitchell, Gladys (British, 1901–83) Mitchell was born in Cowley, Oxfordshire. She worked until 1961 as a schoolteacher in the suburbs of west London where much of her idiosyncratic crime fiction is set. Begin with *Dead Men's Morris* (1936), in which Mrs Beatrice Lestrange Bradley, psychiatric advisor to the Home Office and quirky detective-heroine of some seventy books, investigates a series of apparently accidental deaths in rural Oxfordshire. In *Three Quick and Five Dead* (1968), Mrs Bradley's esoteric learning enables her to track down a mass-murderer who pins a cryptic note to each of his victims. The impersonation of a man who has been dead for five years is discovered in *Late, Late in the Evening* (1976), providing Bradley, now in retirement and elevated to Dame, with the key to a double murder.

📖 Agatha Christie, Margery Allingham, John Carr   *DH*

Mitchell, Leslie. *See* **Gibbon, Lewis Grassic**

Mitchell, Margaret (US, 1900–49) Margaret Mitchell was born in Atlanta and educated at Smith College. Her only novel is the much-loved romantic-historical saga *Gone With the Wind* (1936). In this compulsively readable best-seller the heroine, Scarlett O'Hara, a spoilt Southern belle, is challenged by the cataclysm of the American Civil War and the loss of her family's land and wealth. As she struggles almost single-handedly to re-establish her home, Tara, she becomes involved in a tempestuous relationship with the Byronic hero, Rhett Butler. The sweep of history together with Scarlett's strength of character have ensured *Gone With the Wind* a permanent place among the classics of popular fiction, and a successful transfer to the Hollywood screen.

📖 Louis de Bernières, Beverley Hughesdon, Sebastian Faulks   *SA*

Mitchell, W(illiam) O(rmond) (Canadian, 1914–   ). *See* CANADA

Mitchison, Naomi (British, 1897–1999) A pioneering feminist and political campaigner, Mitchison maintained a prolific output of journalism, travel writing, autobiography, and especially historical novels. Her reputation in fiction is largely as a highly imaginative re-creator of the ancient world, sometimes with contemporary politics in mind. *The Conquered* (1923) is set in Gaul at the time of the Roman conquest, while her best-known book, *The Corn King and the Spring Queen* (1931), is a 700-page epic quest narrative. It follows the young Erif Der's travels from her home village on the Black Sea to Sparta and Egypt around 228 BC, and has an underpinning of myth and magic; yet it is also a convincing human story of divided loyalties. By contrast, *Memoirs of a Spacewoman* (1962) depicts extraterrestrial life. *Cleopatra's People* (1972) partly returns to her earlier works.

📖 Allan Massie, Alison Fell   *JS*

Mitford, Nancy (British, 1904–73) Nancy Mitford was born into the family of the famously eccentric 2nd Lord Redesdale, and she chronicled the early years of her life in her first successful novel, *The Pursuit of Love* (1945). But a more mature novel, *The Blessing* (1951), has much to recommend it: a portrait of a marriage between a very proper English girl and a charming, arrogant French Marquis with several mistresses. A further obstacle to a happy marriage is the 'Blessing' of the title, their young son, Sigismond, who realizes that, as long as his mother and father are estranged, he gets twice as many presents and treats as usual. *The Blessing* is witty and amusingly perceptive on the differences between the English and French character. Mitford's sister **Jessica** has written a hilarious autobiography, *Hons and Rebels* (1960) which is recommended.

📖 Evelyn Waugh   CH

Mittelholzer, Edgar (Guyanese/British, 1909–65). *See* BLACK AND WHITE, CARIBBEAN

Mo, Timothy (British, 1950–) Son of a Cantonese father and English mother, Timothy Mo was born in Hong Kong and came to England when he was 10. He was at Oxford, and worked as a journalist before writing novels. The best introduction to his work is *Sour Sweet* (1982). Funny, touching, and absorbing, it introduces us to the Chen family, immigrants from Hong Kong who run a Chinese takeaway. Follow this with *The Redundancy of Courage* (1991), an epic dealing with a bloody coup on a fictional south-east Asian island. Mo's work, however serious the subject, is always shot through with humour and irony, qualities also found in *An Insular Possession* (1986). Blending history and fiction and using a diversity of techniques including letters, diary extracts, and newspaper articles, it tells the complex story of two young Americans in China who get caught up in the Opium Wars.

📖 Salman Rushdie, Caryl Phillips, Julian Barnes. *See* HISTORICAL   CB

Moggach, Deborah (British, 1948–) Moggach writes short stories and novels, some of which have been transferred to television. She chronicles all aspects of contemporary British life. In *Seesaw* (1997)

the Prices' comfortable family life slowly unravels when their eldest daughter is kidnapped by a couple who believe them to be wealthy. This is further complicated by the relationship that is formed between the daughter and her male kidnapper. Moggach's stories often explore a time when an unexpected event forces a character to reassess his or her life. In *Driving Through the Night* (1988) Desmond is thrown out by his tempestuous wife and journeys in a stolen coach up and down England, in a quest for his lost son. *Porky* (1993) examines an incestuous father–daughter relationship.

📖 Penelope Lively, Margaret Forster
                                  TO

Monsarrat, Nicholas (British, 1910–79) Born in Liverpool, after graduating from Cambridge Nicholas Monsarrat worked in a solicitor's office before becoming a full-time writer in 1934. Begin with his best-seller, *The Cruel Sea* (1951), which is vividly based on his wartime experiences as a corvette commander. The force and directness of his writing are maintained throughout a succession of episodes in the war against the U-boats. *The Nylon Pirates* (1966) is an entertaining crime story about a gang of stylish confidence tricksters who exploit the gullible rich on ocean cruises. *The Kappillan of Malta* (1973) is set during the siege of Malta in the Second World War. Richly evoking the island and its history, the story concerns Father Salvatore and his heroic endeavours during the continual bombings. Much of the novel is set in catacombs where the priest cares for those made homeless.

📖 Alistair MacLean, Patrick O'Brian, C. S. Forester   DH

Montague, John (Irish, 1929–).
See IRELAND

Montgomery, L(ucy) M(aud)
(Canadian, 1874–1942) Born on Prince
Edward Island, Montgomery was raised
mostly by her maternal grandparents and
began writing while looking after her
grandmother. Her heroines have enduring appeal, particularly Anne, the orphan
sent by mistake to Matthew and Marilla
Cuthbert, whose gift is an ability to imaginatively transform her world. Although
Montgomery's prose style is sometimes
flowery, it never ignores harsh realities,
and her view of adolescence is never
simple-minded. Start with *Anne of Green
Gables* (1908); this is the first of the
Anne series which follows the heroine's
career from childhood to marriage and
motherhood. There is also the *Emily*
series beginning with *Emily of New Moon*
(1923).

📖 Louisa May Alcott. *See* CANADA

IP

Moorcock, Michael (British, 1939–)
Moorcock is a hugely prolific and popular author of science fiction novels. He
first came to prominence in the 1960s
as the editor of the *New Worlds* magazine
whose work was much influenced by
the psychedelic drug-oriented culture of
the period, and which published, among
others, Brian Aldiss and J. G. Ballard.
Moorcock wrote a number of books in
which Jerry Cornelius is the anti-hero, a
free-wheeling, often scatological character
who lives a highly coloured life. This
series began with *The Final Programme*
in 1968. Moorcock's later work is slightly
less over-heated but characterized by

richly comic writing which satirizes contemporary society through time travel into
versions of Britain in the past and future.
He has often written about London in
various decades and under various kinds
of threat, most successfully in *Mother
London* (1988).

📖 Terry Pratchett, Ray Bradbury,
Christopher Priest. *See* SCIENCE
FICTION   LM

Moore, Brian (British/Canadian, 1921–
99) Born in Belfast, Moore served in North
Africa and Europe in the Second World
War, then worked for the United Nations
before emigrating to Canada in 1948. He
adopted Canadian citizenship and lived
in California until his death. His work is
wide-ranging and intensely involving: begin
with *The Lonely Passion of Judith Hearne*
(1955). The heroine is a lonely, religious,
alcoholic spinster in Belfast, who falls in
love with a man whom she thinks has had
important work in New York. *Black Robe*
(1985) is set in the seventeenth century,
and concerns the attempt by two Jesuit
monks to relieve a mission in the northern
wilds of Canada. The Indians find the
Catholic Blackrobes greedy and evil, the
older priest thinks the Indians repulsive
savages, but the younger, Daniel, finds them
beautiful and mysterious, and abandons
his vows for an Indian girl. This is compelling, and Moore engages sympathy for
the differing viewpoints of all his characters. Equally fast-paced is *The Colour
of Blood* (1987, Booker Prize-shortlisted,
Sunday Express Book of the Year), a
thriller about a cardinal in a communist
state, whose personal faith is tested to
the limit. *No Other Life* (1993) is set on a
fictional Caribbean island and concerns a

young black boy, Jeannot, who has been rescued from poverty and educated by a Canadian missionary. Jeannot urges his compatriots to rise against their oppressors, thus making enemies of the island's ruling military junta, the church, and the rich. As in Graham Greene, Moore's heroes are often finally in conflict with their own consciences.

📖 Graham Greene, William Trevor, John McGahern. *See* IRELAND   *JR*

Moore, George (Anglo-Irish, 1852–1933) In his day, George Moore was regarded as a writer every bit as scandalous as Bret Easton Ellis in our own. Born into a wealthy Anglo-Irish family, he studied painting in Paris as a young man, where he discovered the uncompromising, naturalistic, anti-romantic novels of French writers such as Zola. He introduced their techniques into his own novels, beginning with *A Modern Lover* (1883), set in a louche artistic world far removed from conventional Victorian morality. *Esther Waters*, Moore's most successful novel, describes the life of a young woman who is seduced then deserted and endures a humiliating struggle to bring up her son; the boy's father eventually marries her, but her troubles are still not over. *A Drama in Muslin* (1886; later retitled simply *Muslin* by the author) is similarly outspoken and candid: an examination of female sexuality and desire in repressive bourgeois society, based upon the proposition, in Moore's own words, that 'every married woman today will admit she could manage two men better than her husband could manage two wives' (discuss!).

📖 Emile Zola, Arnold Bennett. *See* IRELAND   *CH*

Moore, Lorrie (US, 1957–) In her short-story collection *Self Help* (1985), Moore emphasizes her characters' self-obsessions by playfully using the language of popular self-help philosophies in contemporary America. 'First, try to be something, anything, else,' begins the story 'How to Become a Writer'. 'Fail miserably. It is best if you fail at an early age—say, fourteen. Early, critical disillusionment is necessary so that at fifteen you can write long haiku sequences about thwarted desire.' Alongside the irony, Moore also inspires sympathy for her characters' inner dilemmas. The typical protagonist in the collection *Birds of America* (1999) is a woman in her thirties or forties who has come to terms with life's compromises. In the novel *Who Will Run the Frog Hospital* (1994), Berie recalls the summer of 1972, when she and her best friend, Sils, were 15. Driven by restlessness, they embarked on a summer that shattered the bond between them.

📖 Amy Bloom, Alice Munro, Anne Tyler. *See* SHORT STORIES   *DJ*

Moravia, Alberto (Italian, 1907–90) Born Alberto Pincherle in Rome, Moravia was also a journalist and noted cultural commentator. His novels and stories concern politics, psychology, and especially the erotic, and are filled with amoral, macho characters generally alienated from the teeming Roman world around them. They are written in a cool and detached prose. *The Woman of Rome* (1947), his first commercial success, is the autobiography of a young prostitute involved simultaneously with a radical student and a Fascist bureaucrat, but it is more convincing as a portrait of life in a police state. *The*

Conformist (1951), brilliantly filmed by Bertolucci in 1969, again links sex and politics. Marcello, haunted by an attempted seduction in his boyhood by a chauffeur, represses his homosexuality in marriage and by becoming an assassin for the Fascist state. Moravia's stories are collected in volumes such as *The Voice of the Sea* (1976), enigmatic short episodes often involving power struggles between the sexes, and *Erotic Tales* (1983).

Albert Camus, Milan Kundera   *JS*

Morrison, Toni (US, 1931–) Toni Morrison was born in Ohio of working-class parents. Her novels are set in African-American communities, and she has explored both their sustaining and their self-destructive qualities. In her first novel, *The Bluest Eye* (1970), we see the impact of cultural icons (a blonde doll, Shirley Temple) from a black child's perspective, and explore the close correlation between images of beauty and power. *Sula* (1973) describes the friendship of two black women growing up in Ohio in the 1920s. Taken as a whole, Morrison's work redefines the history of black women in America, and her literary style is the perfect vehicle for this. Vernacular and lyrical, interweaving folk memory and community life, it combines an awareness of the minutiae of daily life with the broad span of history. The best novel to start with is *Beloved* (1987; Pulitzer Prize 1988). Set in Ohio in the post-Civil War period, this focuses on Sethe, a slave who kills her baby to save her from slavery. At first the baby haunts the house and then comes back as the young woman, Beloved, who wants stories and love. Morrison delivers this Gothic history in a blend of poetry and horror that slowly reveals the traumatic processes by which memory is recovered. *Beloved* is the first of a trilogy that includes *Jazz* (1991) and *Paradise* (1998). Morrison was awarded the Nobel Prize for Literature in 1993.

Alice Walker, Pat Barker, William Faulkner, James Baldwin. *See* BLACK AND WHITE, HISTORICAL, UNITED STATES OF AMERICA   *LM*

Mortimer, John (British, 1923–) Born in London and educated at Brasenose College, Oxford, Mortimer has combined his career as a barrister with his success as a novelist and playwright. Begin with some of the stories featuring his best-known creation, the irascible barrister Horace Rumpole. Eccentrically on the side of the angels, his shrewd triumphs in many curious cases are recorded in such collections as *Rumpole of the Bailey* (1978) and *Rumpole and the Age of Miracles* (1985). The early novel, *Like Men Betrayed* (1953), concerning a solicitor whose son misuses a client's money, is an atmospheric treatment of middle-class values colliding with criminal degeneracy in post-war London. *Paradise Postponed* (1985) takes stock of English village life in the post-war era in its comic treatment of events in Rapstone. Following the death of the Revd Simcox, his estate is left unexpectedly to the unscrupulous MP, Leslie Titmuss. The reasons are revealed as secrets of Titmuss's working-class background emerge. In the sequel, *Titmuss Regained* (1990), Titmuss, having risen to a cabinet post, buys up the mansion where his mother once worked and lets the village fall into the hands of the heritage industry. Politicians, conservationists, and property developers are targets of Mortimer's satire in the ensuing confusion of incompetence and greed.

📖 David Lodge, Keith Waterhouse, Evelyn Waugh   *DH*

Mortimer, Penelope (British, 1918–99) A journalist, short-story writer, and novelist, Penelope Mortimer wrote *Joanna*, her first novel, in 1947. She is, however, best known for *The Pumpkin Eater* (1962), which was made into a successful film scripted by Harold Pinter. This short but compelling novel was a frank account of an emotional breakdown, and begins with the protagonist, Mrs Armitage, telling her story to a therapist. This, and her later work, including *The Home* (1971), *My Friend Says it's Bullet Proof* (1967), and *Long Distance* (1974), are simply constructed, moving novels, placing ordinary women at the centre of the story. As such they were important contributions to the new movement of women's writing which emerged in the 1960s.

📖 Margaret Drabble, Muriel Spark
                                 SB

Morton, Anthony. *See* **Creasey, John**

Mosco, Maisie (British) Maisie Mosco was born in Manchester and has worked as a journalist. She has written a number of radio plays as well as many best-selling sagas and romances. However, it was her family saga set in the Manchester Jewish community, *Almonds and Raisins* (1979), that established her reputation. This novel follows a typical immigrant Jewish family from its arrival in Manchester, penniless and seeking accommodation, through its problems with earning a living and assimilation over three generations. The saga is continued in *Scattered Seed* (1980) and *Children's Children* (1981). The

characters are warm and believable, the background is authentic and the books are true page-turners.

📖 Jessica Stirling, Zoe Fairbairns, Sherry Ashworth. *See* FAMILY SAGA
                                 SA

Mosley, Nicholas (British, 1923–) Mosley's complex novels are serious and morally questioning, sometimes told in narrative fragments; their subjects are politics, science, and religion. This daunting combination is rendered palatable, however, by the relationships and human emotions with which his books also deal. The change from the realism of his early work to a more experimental style was signalled by *Accident* (1965); narrated by a philosophy don in an elliptical fashion, it concerns a triangular affair and was made into a film by Joseph Losey. Mosley's major novel is *Hopeful Monsters* (1990, Whitbread award), part of a project attempting to deal with the history of twentieth-century politics and experience. Spanning the period from 1919 to 1939, with a post-war epilogue, this is cast in the form of exchanges between a German-Jewish woman and a British scientist, ending with a moving reconciliation in old age. *Children of Darkness and Light* (1996) is a thriller with spiritual and political elements, featuring a previously cynical journalist investigating strange events involving children in Cumbria and war-ravaged Bosnia.

📖 Iris Murdoch, William Golding
                                 JS

Mosley, Walter (US, 1952–) Nominated by US President Bill Clinton as his favourite mystery writer, Walter Mosley has used the traditional format of the private-eye novel to produce a revealing picture of the black experience in America. Spanning three decades, his series featuring Easy Rawlins and his psychopathic friend Mouse explores the racial and political tensions of Los Angeles, while remaining firmly in touch with the need to tell a good story. *Devil in a Blue Dress* (1990) is set in 1948. War-veteran Rawlins becomes embroiled in the search for a woman who has gone missing with someone else's cash. By *A Red Death* (1991) it's 1952 and Rawlins' new-found prosperity comes under threat, forcing him to carry out an unwilling undercover investigation that puts him in the murder suspect's chair. In *Black Betty* (1994) it's 1961 and civil rights are in the air. But for Rawlins, it's mayhem and murder as usual.

📖 Chester Himes, Raymond Chandler, Sara Paretsky. *See* CRIME

VM

Mukherjee, Bharati (Indian/US, 1940–). *See* INDIA

Muller, Marcia (US, 1944–). *See* CRIME

Mungoshi, Charles (Zimbabwean, 1947–). *See* AFRICA

Munro, Alice (Canadian, 1931–) Munro writes short stories set in rural and semi-rural southern Ontario, where she grew up and now lives. She has been compared to Chekhov and Proust, but the brilliance of her stories is unique. They are set in a small, intimately known world (just as Jane Austen's novels have restricted settings) and they explore lives and characters with piercing insight. Their structure is fluid and complex, moving easily through time; a story by Munro often contains as much as a full novel by another

writer. Begin with *The Beggar Maid* (1980, Booker Prize-shortlisted; (published in the USA as *Who do You Think You Are?*, 1979). This presents linked stories of stepmother Flo and daughter Rose, living with Rose's father behind a store in Hanratty, until Rose grows up and moves on, through marriage and divorce. Rose's acute embarrassment at Flo, and her intense teenage curiosity and dread of appearing foolish, are captured beautifully in the sordid train ride of 'Wild Swans'. In *The Progress of Love* (1986) the story 'Miles City Montana' moves with typical circularity from the narrator's childhood memory of a drowned boy, to a family holiday twenty years later, and on to many years after that, when the marriage is over, then back to the holiday, where one of the daughters is saved from drowning by her mother's sudden intuition—a sense which she herself knows cannot be trusted. In the course of its twenty wonderful pages this explores the ways adults betray children, a failing marriage, memory, and parental love. *Open Secrets* (1994) is also highly recommended.

📖 Anton Chekhov, Raymond Carver, Elizabeth Bishop. *See* CANADA, SHORT STORIES

JR

Murdoch, Iris (Irish, 1919–99) Few post-war novelists have divided critics as sharply as has Iris Murdoch. Admirers point to the imaginative generosity, the playfulness allied to fundamental seriousness, and the seductive readability in her work. Detractors accuse her of whimsy, artificiality, and affected melodrama. She was one of the few modern writers to have constantly measured herself—even though she was aware of coming up short—against the great novelists of the past. Her occasional lapses may be seen as the price of such ambition.

Murdoch was born in Dublin and educated in England. After the war, when she had done relief work for the United Nations, she studied philosophy, going on to teach it at Oxford. Her first novel, *Under the Net* (1954), showed the influence of Jean-Paul Sartre in following the picaresque adventures of an existential hero and his friends in London, and had a high-spirited humorousness. The comedy became more ethereal, and sometimes darker, in Murdoch's middle period. In *The Nice and the Good* (1968), a civil servant, John Ducane, fits the description 'nice', but when severely tested is revealed to lack the faculty for goodness. His moral compromises and their destructive consequences are grippingly portrayed. Murdoch's long, intricate later novels explore, often with the help of mystical and mythological elements, the theme of good and evil. There is usually at the centre of them a charismatic, quasi-shamanic figure, such as Professor Rozanov in *The Philosopher's Pupil* (1983), whose reappearance in an English spa town sets off a complex series of intrigues, jealousies, and betrayals.

📖 A. S. Byatt, Angela Carter, John Fowles   *NC*

Musil, Robert (Austrian, 1880–1942) Born in Klagenfurt, Austria, Robert Musil trained as a military officer, a scientist, and a philosopher before coming to his vocation as a novelist. He wrote stories, fables, and two plays, but is best known as the author of *The Man without Qualities* (1930–43), a lifelong work regarded as one of the masterpieces of European literature, despite remaining unfinished at Musil's death. A sprawling, tragi-comic portrait of the last days of the Austro-Hungarian empire, *The Man without Qualities* (published in Britain 1953–60) begins on the eve of the First World War. Ulrich, a man determined to keep his distance from the idiocies he sees in the world around him, is contrasted with the figure of Moosbrugger, a charming murderer who represents the forces of chaos lurking beneath the civilized surfaces of society. An earlier novel, *Young Torless* (1906), is a fictional account of Musil's experience at military school.

📖 Henry James, Thomas Mann, Franz Kafka. *See* GERMANY   *WB*

Myles, na Gapalean. *See* **O'Brien, Flann**

Nabokov, Vladimir (Russian US, 1899–1977) Born in St Petersburg to an aristocratic family with estates (grandfather Minister of Justice to the Tsar, grandmother a baroness), Nabokov's privileged future was curtailed by the 1917 Revolution; after studying at Cambridge he lived a migrant life in Berlin and Paris, before fleeing the Nazis in 1940 to settle in the United States. His early novels were written in Russian; in 1941 he began writing in English, but it wasn't until the publication of Lolita (1955) that Nabokov gained wide public recognition—and notoriety. The novel purports to be the confession of a middle-aged professor, Humbert Humbert, about his obsessive infatuation with, pursuit and seduction of, a 12-year old nymphet. Naturally it caused a storm of protest, and narrowly escaped being banned, but has survived to become regarded as a classic work of lyrical fiction, beautifully and tenderly written and not in the least smutty or salacious. *Lolita* is also quite clearly Nabokov's European sensibility getting to grips with the myth of America: its slick consumer culture, teenage slang, freeways, and fast-food joints, and in which he pokes malicious fun at a society awash with plenty of everything except good taste.

Nabokov is a conjuror, delighting in fanciful wordplay, literary pyrotechnics, and puns (some dreadful); you can almost see him lurking in the wings of his books with a wickedly amused gleam in his eye, often rather too beguiled by his own erudition and wit. Never more so than in *Pale Fire* (1962), which is fiction dressed up as a learned critique of 'A Poem in Four Cantos' by the deceased John Francis Shade, including the 40-page poem itself with all the academic apparatus. While bubbling with Nabokovian high spirits, this is perhaps his most extreme, and supreme, literary jest.

Less tricksy and hugely enjoyable is one of the early Russian novels, *Laughter in the Dark* (1933; original title *Kamera Obskura*). Albert Albinus, a prosperous and respectable married man in Berlin, becomes hopelessly infatuated with a pretty 16-year old cinema usherette, Margot Peters, who fancies herself as a film star. She in turn falls for the odious and sadistic Axel Rex, a cartoonist, and together they manipulate poor Albinus (the final scenes in which the pair taunt the recently blinded Albinus are mesmeric and horrible) and bring about his downfall. *Bend Sinister* (1947) is the story of Adam Krug, a dreamy philosopher, caught up in a fascist regime of the self-styled Average Man. Situated in a strange Slavic/German fantasy land, it veers, not always successfully, between whimsical fantasy and surrealistic nightmare, the hero finally rescued from oblivion by a sleight of the pen. Closely shadowing the author's own English education and wanderings in Europe, *Glory* (1932) evokes the intoxicating rapture of youth, the discovery of passion, and heart-wrenching loss—the thrill and the glamour in the most ordinary pleasures as well as in the seemingly meaningless adventures of a lonely life, to quote

Nabokov. In addition to some seventeen novels he also wrote short stories, translations, literary criticism, and the autobiography *Speak, Memory* (1967).

📖 James Joyce, Marcel Proust, Thomas Pynchon. *See* RUSSIA   TH

Naipaul, Shiva (Trinidadian, 1943–85) The younger brother of V. S. Naipaul, Shiva's first two novels are *Fireflies* (1970), and *The Chip Chip Gatherers* (1973), which won the Whitbread Novel award; both focus on wealthy Indian fmilies whose Hindu culture is withering and fading in the face of life in contemporary Trinidad. A collection of short prose pieces, *Beyond the Dragon's Mouth*, appeared in 1984. Naipaul gives us a privileged glimpse of the East Indian family at home in Trinidad, and if the language doesn't have the power and sharpness of V. S. Naipaul, the insights are nevertheless perceptive. *Black and White* (1980), his investigation into the Jonestown affair (the settlement in Guyana where, in 1978, the unbalanced American Revd Warren Jones persuaded his entire community of 900 to commit suicide) earned Naipaul great praise.

📖 Samuel Selvon. *See* CARIBBEAN
EM

Naipaul, V(idiadhar) S(urajprasad) (Trinidadian, 1932–) V. S. Naipaul was born in Trinidad, into an Indian Brahmin family. He is much admired abroad and much criticized in the Anglophone Caribbean where his characterization of Caribbean people is seen to be one-dimensional. But few deny that he is a major writer. His masterpiece, *A House for Mr Biswas* (1961), is the fullest portrait we have of a East Indian family in the process of creolization. This is sometimes contrasted with his portraits of African characters who are generally seen from the outside and made figures of fun. *A Bend in the River* (1979), set in a Conrad-like Africa, bears this out. But then again when, in an early book, Naipaul trained his sharp eye for comic detail on the residents of a Port of Spain yard, the resulting *Miguel Street* (1959) was exemplary.

Naipaul has won many awards for his writing (including the Booker Prize for *In a Free State*, 1971), and the elegance of his 'phrase-making' is universally acknowledged—a quality also evident in his extensive non-fiction. This includes history, autobiography, travel (three books on India), and literary journalism. In *The Enigma of Arrival* (1987), a semi-autobiographical novel, Naipaul deals with a charge levelled against him that he is a professional outsider—in Trinidad, in England, in India—and that, whatever the personal cost, this grants him sharper insights than might be afforded the insider. *Among the Believers: An Islamic Journey* (1981) and *A Turn in the South* (1989) constitute some telling insights into social discontents, East and West.

📖 Joseph Conrad, Shiva Naipaul, Neil Bissoondath. *See* CARIBBEAN
EM

Narayan, R(asipuram) K(rishnaswami) (Indian, 1906–) Narayan, one of the first internationally successful Indian novelists to write in English, is renowned for his creation of Malgudi, the remote, self-enclosed fictional town where most of his novels and short stories are set. Taken to be representative of rural southern India, Malgudi is relatively sheltered from political disturbance and social change, and there is a timeless quality to Narayan's accounts of the small concerns and everyday routines of his entirely convincing characters. The books are often slow-paced, but are written with an elegant simplicity. They provide a close, sharply defined portrait of Indian culture over the twentieth century, subtly addressing a range of specific social issues, such as the effects of poverty and the position of women in the community, while simultaneously exploring universal themes of jealousy, ambition, mortality, and love.

Begin with *Malgudi Landscapes* (1992), a collection of Narayan's best short stories, and move on to *The Grandmother's Tale* (1993), a sequence of three novellas about family life, money, women, and writing. The title story depicts four generations of social change as the present-day narrator-novelist questions and cajoles his grandmother into telling the story of her mother's child-marriage to the 10-year-old Viswa, his subsequent disappearance, and her journey to retrieve him. *The English Teacher* (1945), the story of Krishna's attempts to rebuild his corporeal and spiritual worlds after his wife's death, is among the most absorbing of the earlier novels.

📖 V. S. Naipaul, Amit Chaudhuri, Anita Desai. *See* INDIA   SR

Nawal El Saadawi (Egyptian, 1931–). *See* AFRICA

Naylor, Gloria (US, 1950–) Naylor was born into a black working-class family from the rural South, and became a sort of street preacher before enrolling at Brooklyn College aged 25. The characters in her novels live out their lives in troubled but distinctive black communities of both rich and poor. Begin with *Mama Day* (1988),

an unusual love-story which moves from New York to the imaginary offshore island of Willow Springs. The astonishing tale of Cocoa and her husband George unfolds in this ancestral setting with its legends, witchcraft, and belief in the future. Equally rich in character and atmosphere is *The Women of Brewster Place* (1983), a novel made up of seven stories about poor but courageous black women who defy and sometimes transcend the circumstances of their ghetto. *Linden Hills* (1985) deals not with the poor but with middle-class black aspirants on a rich estate with cruel and inverted values.

📖 Toni Cade Bambara, Ntokaze Shange, Barbara Kingsolver   JN

Nekrasov, Viktor Soviet/Russian, 1911–). *See* RUSSIA

Ngugi wa Thiong'o (Kenyan, 1938–) Ngugi's writing concerns itself with the struggle for Kenyan independence. The political message of his play, *I Will Marry When I Want* (1977) led to his arrest and detention without trial in 1977. In the same year he renounced the use of the colonizer's language (English) and committed himself to writing only in his native tongue (Kikuyu). *Weep Not, Child* (1964), a beautifully written novel, re-creates the Mau Mau's fight against the oppressive white state. Ngugi focuses on the effects of political turmoil on the lives, and particularly the education of two young boys. The Mau Mau rebellion is also the binding theme in *Petals of Blood* (1977). *A Grain of Wheat* (1967) is arguably his most impressive work. Through flashbacks and multiple narratives, Ngugi weaves the compelling story of a village anxiously awaiting independence at the end of 1963. In 1982 Ngugi left Kenya to live in self-imposed exile in London.

📖 Wole Soyinka, Chinua Achebe, Amos Tutuola. *See* AFRICA   *EW*

Nin, Anais (US, 1903–77) Anais Nin lived in Paris between the wars, and trained as a psychoanalyst. Her writing was eclipsed for many years by her better-known contemporaries, but has recently been reprinted and widely read. The best introduction to her poetic style is *Under a Glass Bell* (1944), a collection of stories characterized by striking imagery and an unsettling clarity. *A Spy in the House of Love* (1954) is an atmospheric novel about a woman and her relationships with several men, and *Collages* (1964) is a more experimental patchwork of moods and stories that shows Nin at her most inventive. She is perhaps best known for the collection of erotica *Delta of Venus* (1977), which gathered pornographic stories originally written for a private collector during her years in Paris, and for the many volumes of her published diaries.

📖 Henry Miller, Lawrence Durrell, Elizabeth Smart   *WB*

Niven, Larry (US, 1938–) Niven was born in Los Angeles and educated at Washburn University, Kansas. He began his career as a prolific author of technologically inventive science fiction in 1962. Begin with *Ring World* (1970), the central work in his celebrated *Tales of Known Space* series, in which aliens and humans unite in exploration of a gigantic artificial world built around a distant star. The book continues from *World of Ptavus* (1966), featuring the escape from an imprisoning 'stasis field' of a hostile survivor of an extinct civilization. *A Gift from Earth* (1968) recounts a revolt over economic conditions on a planet colonized by humans. The descendants of a terrestrial space-crew inhabit a gaseous envelope around a neutron star in *The Smoke Ring* (1987), which describes their attempt to discover their origins from the computer program on their ancestors' spacecraft.

📖 Frederick Pohl, Isaac Asimov, Kim Stanley Robinson   *DH*

Noon, Jeff (British, 1958–) Noon is sometimes cited as Britain's answer to American cyberpunk author, William Gibson, and the similarities in style—staccato and often jagged—and subject matter—highly coloured, often drug influenced, free-wheeling narratives—are close. But Noon sets his narratives in Manchester, exploiting both its musical legacy and atmospheric, post-industrial decline. His first two books, *Vurt* (1993) and *Pollen* (1995), are essentially futuristic quest novels. Perhaps the easiest Noon novel to start with is *Automated Alice* (1996), Noon's self-proclaimed 'trequel' to Lewis Carroll's *Alice* books. Although Alice steps into futuristic Mancunian nightmare, the style is less convoluted and Noon's abundant gifts as a story-teller are more readily accessible.

📖 Philip K. Dick, William Gibson   *LM*

Nordhoff and Hall (Charles Nordhoff, US, 1887–1947, and James Norman Hall, US, 1887–1951) Captain Nordhoff and Lieutenant Hall met while they were flying French planes in the First World War. After the war they formed a writing partnership and took one of the most celebrated shipboard mutinies ever for their subject matter. *Mutiny on the Bounty* (1932) is a well-researched, gripping adventure story, describing the voyage of HMS *Bounty* to Tahiti in 1787 to pick up a cargo of breadfruit trees. A portion of the crew, led by Lieutenant Fletcher Christian, mutiny against the harsh and vicious regime of Captain William Bligh, and put Bligh and his supporters off the ship. Narrated by young Byam, on board to make a dictionary of Tahitian languages, the book charts the lives of its characters beyond the mutiny and back to trial in England. It has been memorably filmed, and never better than in the 1935 version starring Charles Laughton and Clark Gable.

📖 Robert Louis Stevenson,
C. S. Forrester, Patrick O'Brian *JR*

Norfolk, Lawrence (British, 1963–)

Lawrence Norfolk made an immediate impact with his debut novel, *Lemprière's Dictionary* (1991), an enormously inventive tale that draws together the founding of the Dutch East India Company in 1600, a massacre of children, and the compilation of the great *Classical Dictionary* of the title during the turmoil of the French Revolution. Norfolk's wayward approach to neglected corners of European history manages to remain both accessible and entertaining throughout, and *The Pope's Rhinoceros* (1996) uses a similar technique to weave a complex tale involving a repressive monastic order, African tribes, and the Vatican. Norfolk's books are entertaining historical fantasies, rooted in fact, but playfully aware of history itself as a story that we tell about the past.

📖 Umberto Eco, Vikram Chandra
WB

Norris, Frank (US, 1870–1902)

Born to well-off and supportive parents, Frank Norris made a huge contribution to American literature with his journalism (he covered the Boer War and the Spanish-American war), with the novels he wrote and with the theories he developed to describe them. After a spell in Paris studying painting, he wrote his first and perhaps most powerful novel, *McTeague: A Story of San Francisco* (1899), which traces the spectacular downfall of a brutish young dentist. His other two important novels, *The Octopus* (1901) and *The Pit* (1902), were planned as part of an unfinished trilogy dealing with wheat production in modern America, and dramatize the conflict between the small farmer and relentless, profit-hungry business symbolized by the new railroads. Norris died of peritonitis before he was able to complete the third volume.

📖 Stephen Crane, Theodor Dreiser, John Steinbeck *BH*

North, Elizabeth (British, 1936–)

North, who was born in Hampshire, did not begin writing until she had been married and had four children. Her novels deal with family, relationships, and the larger groupings which bind and divide us. Start with *Worldly Goods* (1987) set in the late 1950s, about the wedding between a southerner and a northerner. With sly humour North explores the snobberies, hypocrisies, and desires which operate between the various members of the wedding-party. *Ancient Enemies* (1984) is narrated by teenager Petra, about her life and the joys and horrors of growing up. *Enough Blue Sky* (1977) is a funny, moving, and dramatic account of an admiral's wife travelling to Gibraltar with her children at the outbreak of war, a story based on North's own childhood.

📖 Jane Gardam, Penelope Fitzgerald

JR

Nye, Robert (British, 1939–) Nye left school at 16, at which age he had already published poems, and he has lived by his writing ever since. Nye has been described as a Literary Time Lord: he tells stories of characters from history and fiction, bringing them to vibrant and colourful life, often making them tell the stories of their own lives, making us feel as if we were inside their heads. His portrayal of character is compassionate and sensitive, his style full of wit and humour. *Merlin* (1979) combines Arthurian magic and legend with graphic eroticism to tell the story of the famous wizard and his father the Devil, his seduction, and eventual fate of imprisonment within an oak-tree. *Falstaff* (1976) allows its famous hero to indulge in bawdy wit and humour, while revealing the humanity within him.

📖 A. S. Byatt, John Gardner, Barry Unsworth

EC

O

Oates, Joyce Carol (US, 1938–) Oates is fascinated by violence of all kinds. In *Them* (1969), which won the 1970 National Book Award, the main character, Maureen Wendall, whom Oates states is based on a student she taught at the University of Detroit, faces conflicts and challenges as she struggles to cut free of her grim, poverty-stricken roots. *Wonderland* (1971) traces the fate of a boy, Jesse, lone survivor of a family killed in cold blood by its father, while *Because It is Bitter and Because It is My Heart* (1990) charts the careers of two teenagers, a white woman and a black man, who commit a murder and, in the obvious sense at least, get away with it. *Bellefleur* (1980), is a Gothic, complex, and symbolic family epic complete with ghosts, a departure from Oates's usual realism. In 1992 Oates published a short novel, *Black Water*, which attempts to re-create the events of Chappaquiddick, 1988, from the point of view of the young woman drowned in the car of Senator Edward Kennedy.

📖 Raymond Carver, Grace Paley, Edith Wharton   *AT*

O'Brian, Patrick (British, 1914–2000) Patrick O'Brian is a writer of sea-going Napoleonic war novels in the tradition of C. S. Forester's Hornblower. His heroes are Jack Aubrey, the bluff English navy captain, and Steven Maturin, his Irish ship's surgeon; a more complicated character who struggles with an addiction to laudanum whilst pursuing interests that range from natural history to spying. Like Forester, the plots usually involve undertaking some bold mission culminating in an exciting sea-battle. O'Brian's publishers, and some serious critics, claim him as 'one of our greatest contemporary novelists', and he does have a greater interest in character than other writers of Napoleonic sea fiction. The language is subtler, the historical research more meticulous, idiosyncratic, and better integrated, and O'Brian allows himself greater liberties with the genre. He spends half of one book describing Maturin's exploration of the flora and fauna of a tropical island. In another he focuses almost entirely on an Austen-esque exploration of Aubrey's home-life. But the sea-battles always come in the end, we know that Aubrey and Maturin will win through, and the detailed descriptions of exactly how you sail a Napoleonic man-of-war are mind-numbing (and skippable). Which is why he is only a great writer of genre fiction. Start with *Master and Commander* (1970) and work through the twenty books in order.

📖 J. G. Farrell, C. S. Forester, Joseph Conrad, George MacDonald Fraser. *See* HISTORICAL, THE SEA   *MH*

O'Brien, Edna (Irish, 1932–) O'Brien was born in a small village in Co. Clare. After marriage and the birth of two sons she moved to her current home of London, where she began writing and got divorced. Begin with *The Country Girls* (1960), for the film of which O'Brien later wrote the screenplay. Though drawing on the poverty and narrowness of her Catholic upbringing, it is a witty and exuberant read. The story of its contrasting heroines is continued in *The Lonely Girl* (1962), which changed its title to *The Girl with Green Eyes* for the film version. The third novel in this famous trilogy is the ironically entitled *Girls in Their Married Bliss* (1964), which deals with the typical O'Brien subject of problems, passions, and infidelities between the sexes. O'Brien is an accomplished short-story writer, and her volume *Lantern Slides* (1990), like later novels such as *The High Road* (1988), is stylish, experimental, and keen-eyed.

📖 Clare Boylan, Shena Mackay, Jennifer Johnston. *See* IRELAND JN

O'Brien, Flann (Irish, 1911–66) 'Flann O'Brien' was one of several pseudonyms adopted by Brian O'Nolan while working as a senior civil servant in Dublin; as **Myles na Gopaleen** he contributed a long-running humorous column to the *Irish Times*. *At Swim-Two-Birds* (1939) was recognized as a modern classic only on its reissue in 1960, belatedly hailed for its comic boldness and sophisticated blend of fantasy, parody, and Irish myth. Influenced by Sterne and Joyce, it is a comic anti-novel that plays with novelistic conventions; the author Dermot Trellis is put on trial by his characters, Irish folklore is sent-up, and student life in contemporary Dublin provides a framework for the whole extravaganza. *The Third Policeman* (1967), written in 1940, took even longer to find an audience but is O'Brien's masterpiece. Again, the book operates on several levels. Events surrounding the murder of a farmer by the narrator and his accomplice become part of a circular plot involving a comically ominous vision of damnation and eternity; the narrative is accompanied by hilarious mock-scholarship in the form of notes on the eccentric philosophy of De Selby. O'Brien's other significant work, *The Poor Mouth* (1941), was written in Gaelic and is a satire on 'Oirishry' in the far west of Ireland, full of comedy about poverty, rain, and potatoes. In *The Dalkey Archive* (1964) James Joyce is discovered working as a barman and joining the Jesuits.

📖 James Joyce, J. P. Donleavy, Spike Milligan. *See* HUMOUR, IRELAND, MAGIC REALISM JS

O'Brien, Kate (Irish, 1897–1974) O'Brien was born and brought up in Limerick, Co. Cork, Ireland. After attending University College, Dublin she left Ireland and lived in both England and Spain. She was originally known as a playwright, but novels such as *The Ante Room* (1975) brought her fame. It deals beautifully with the precarious position of an Irish middle-class family in politically turbulent times. The action centres around an unusually unromantic love-story. *That Lady* (1946) is a fabulous historical novel with an unconventionally beautiful heroine, Ana, who has lost an eye in a childhood accident. The novel is set in Spain at the time of Philip II (Mary I of England's ex-husband). The development of the love triangle involving the king himself, his old friend Ana, and one of his closest advisors, Antonio Perez, is gripping.

📖 Elizabeth Bowen, Rose Tremain CJ

O'Connor, Flannery (US, 1925–64) O'Connor was born in Savannah, Georgia, and it is the sense of the South at its most grotesque and violent which characterizes her writing. She was a deeply religious Catholic and her small group of works— she died of congenital lupus at the age of

39—focus on prophetic figures who are corrupted by pride and hypocrisy. Religious in the sense of visionary, her work is characterized by a macabre humour and deadly powers of observation. The easiest way into it is through the short stories, particularly *A Good Man is Hard to Find* (1955). In her most important book, *Wise Blood* (1952), the central figure, Hazel Motes, is a religious fanatic driven by the need to escape his own fanaticism. While the subject matter may not seem appealing, O'Connor's economical style and devastating wit are to be relished.

📖 Graham Greene, William Faulkner, Carson McCullers   *LM*

O'Connor, Frank (Irish, 1903–66) Frank O'Connor was the pseudonym of Michael O'Donovan, born in Cork and largely self-educated. Although best known as a writer of short stories, O'Connor was a highly successful translator into English from the Gaelic. He was also a playwright who was closely involved with the Abbey Theatre in Dublin. His stories, in collections including *My Oedipus Complex and Other Stories* (1963), are quiet, usually comic, beautifully written masterpieces which were highly successful in their day and often published in the *New Yorker*. They dramatize the trivial incidents of Irish life in such a way that the characters are at the same time sympathetic yet ironically distanced. O'Connor also writes wonderful dialogue.

📖 William Trevor, Sean O'Faolain.
See IRELAND   *IP*

O'Connor, John (Irish, 1920–66).
See IRELAND

O'Connor, Joseph (Irish, 1963–) As well as being a novelist and short-story writer O'Connor is an astute commentator on the Irish male at home and abroad. He worked for the British Nicaraguan Solidarity Campaign, the setting for *Desperadoes* (1994) where Johnny Little goes missing and his divorced parents try to find out more about his disappearance. O'Connor's writing deftly balances the serious and darkly humorous. *The Salesman* (1998), set in Dublin, is imbued with the same painful humour. Bill Sweeney's life is falling apart around him. His daughter Maeve lies in a coma after a robbery, providing the focus for revenge for all the things that have gone wrong in his life. Then fate intervenes.

📖 Brian Moore, Glenn Patterson
          TO

O'Donnell, Peadar (Irish, 1893–1986).
See IRELAND

Oe, Kenzaburo (Japanese, 1935–) Now well known in the West, Oe is one of Japan's leading contemporary novelists. His novels are subtle, closely evoked explorations of personal crises, family relationships, and the enduring, relentless strength of human nature. Begin with *A Personal Matter* (1964), a moving account of the emotional development of Bird as he struggles to come to terms with having a mentally handicapped son. Move on to *Nip the Buds, Shoot the Kids* (1958), which deals with a group of troubled boys left alone in an isolated Japanese village during the Second World War after a plague develops among them. Oe was awarded the Nobel Prize for Literature in 1994.

📖 Kazuo Ishiguro, Tim Parks, Shusaku Endo   *SR*

O'Faolain, Julia (Irish, 1932–) O'Faolain was born in London, and grew up in Dublin, where she was educated at University College. Begin with the high-spirited *Godded and Codded* (1970), which satirizes repressive Irish attitudes to sexuality through the adventures of a young woman in Paris. Set in sixth-century Gaul, *Women in the Wall* (1975) concerns the quest for sainthood of Radegund, wife of the King of Gaul, who founds a convent where religious hysteria breaks out. The oppressive conditioning of women by Church and State in modern Ireland is a central theme in *No Country for Young Men* (1980), in which a distinguished family conceal a dangerous secret from the early days of Irish independence. Her other books include *The Judas Cloth* (1992), which traces the Vatican's decline under Pius IX as political power becomes increasingly secularized in nineteenth-century Italy.

  📖 Clare Boylan, Edna O'Brien.
See IRELAND   *DH*

O'Faolain, Sean (Irish, 1900–91) 'Sean O'Faolain' was the pseudonym of John Whelan, a one-time director of Republican publicity who later became a distinguished editor and biographer, and was widely regarded as one of Ireland's finest short-story writers. His works are both lyrical and realistic, portraying the clash between Catholic and secular values in Irish society, often with wry humour. *Midsummer Night Madness* (1932) shows his early phase of romantic nationalism; a story such as 'Fugue' sympathetically portrays an IRA man on the run who finds temporary respite in a remote cottage. His first novel, *A Nest of Simple Folk* (1933), concludes with an explosive quarrel between a father and son over politics. From *A Purse of Coppers* (1937), 'A Broken World' is one of O'Faolain's classic stories, symbolizing post-Civil War tensions in its train conversation between a garrulous priest, an old farmer and the vehement narrator. *The Collected Stories* (3 vols., 1980–3) demonstrates his great range, from humour to elegiac grace, satire, and fantasy.

  📖 William Trevor, Julia O'Faolain, Anton Chekhov. *See* IRELAND   *JS*

O'Flaherty, Liam (Irish, 1897–1984) O'Flaherty was born on the Aran Islands, fought in the First World War and then for the Republican cause. His first successful novel, *The Informer* (1925), powerfully conveys the Dublin slums and the dynamics of Republican circles; its protagonist is the powerful but limited Gypo, who betrays an IRA man for the £20 reward and is then pursued himself. O'Flaherty's fiction is passionate, melodramatic, and sometimes sensual; his stories in particular cast an ironic eye on the brutalities of Irish rural and working-class lives. The title story in *The Mountain Tavern* (1929) has wounded IRA men seeking assistance from a woman bombed out of her own home; 'The Fairy Goose' and 'Red Barbara' satirize peasant piety and superstition. His most important novel is *Famine* (1937), concerning family conflicts and emigration during the Great Hunger of the 1840s. By contrast, *Two Years* (1930) is an engaging bottom-dog view of his world travels.

  📖 Sean O'Faolain, Neil Jordan.
See IRELAND   *JS*

O'Hara, John (US, 1905–70) After doing numerous unskilled jobs, O'Hara became a journalist in New York. His varied experiences coupled with his proficiency as a writer produced novels and short stories about the country-club set in suburban Pennsylvania as well as urban tales of petty gangsters and call-girls. Start with *Butterfield 8* (1935), which is based on a real murder. It is the sad story of Gloria Wandrous and her lovers, set in the speakeasies of the Prohibition era. With some original, stylish writing, O'Hara draws a sympathetic portrait of a neglected child who becomes a debauched young girl. *Appointment in Samarra* (1934) is about bourgeois socialites in a Pennsylvanian city, and concerns the disagreements and dirty dealings of a collection of unattractive, ambitious characters. The books contain surprisingly explicit sexual descriptions for the period. *Pal Joey* (1940), another New York story, was turned into a musical.

📖 John Cheever, Ford Madox Ford

FS

Okri, Ben (Nigerian, 1959–) Most of Okri's fiction explores the unscrupulous politics of contemporary Nigeria and the resilience of the African people. In 1991 Okri was awarded the Booker Prize for *The Famished Road* (1991), a magical novel about the spirit child, Azaro, who glides between the real and imagined world. Set against a crisis of Nigerian democracy, the novel was widely celebrated for its fusion of literary styles and cultural influences. Azaro is also the narrator of *Songs of Enchantment* (1993), a novel set in a nameless African village in the midst of civil war. In this trance-like novel with a panoramic vision, Azaro can see giants, unicorns, spirits, and at one point unwittingly enters his father's dream to encounter a talking white horse. Okri's recent novel, *Infinite*

Riches (1998), returns once more to the life of Azaro. *Astonishing the Gods* (1995) is a fragmentary and mesmerizing narrative. The immortal and invisible story-teller leaves home to search for the secret of invisibility. Discovering an enchanted island, he must carry out a series of endurance tests, including battling with demons, before he can acquire self-knowledge. Okri is also an accomplished short-story writer. His compelling collection, *Incidents at the Shrine* (1986), rehearses some of Okri's principal concerns.

📖 Amos Tutuola, Gabriel García Márquez, Angela Carter *EW*

Oldfield, Pamela (British, 1931–) Oldfield was a schoolteacher before becoming a full-time writer. Her family stories often evoke the late Victorian and early Edwardian eras. Begin with *Green Harvest* (1983), which is set in the hop-gardens of Kent. The orphaned heroine from the London slums is adopted by a country family. In *The Turn of the Tide* (1988) conflict breaks out between a tyrannical Victorian nanny and a nursery maid. The latter is aboard the *Titanic* when the mother of the children in her care elopes with an American. *String of Blue Beads* (1994) centres on a love-affair between a young music hall artiste and a wealthy but aimless man. A doctor's wife endures an unsatisfactory marriage in *A Dutiful Wife* (1989), until an irresistible lover appears. Her husband's unorthodox lusts lead him to the East End backstreets where Jack the Ripper lurks.

📖 Sarah Woodhouse, Tessa Barclay, Jean Plaidy *DH*

Olsen, Tillie (US, 1913–) Tillie Olsen is one of the commanding voices of

American radical writing. She was born in Nebraska and brought up in the Jewish-Socialist community in Omaha. Her early success was in the field of the short story with *Tell Me a Riddle*, a collection from 1961 winning numerous awards including the O. Henry. The best way into Olsen's fiction is her novel *Yonnondio: From the Thirties* (1974), begun at the age of 19 but abandoned for thirty years because of domestic and political commitments. The novel describes the effects of economic hardship on the Holbrook family in powerful, experimental prose. But it is for a non-fiction book, *Silences* (1978), that she is most widely known. *Silences* is in the tradition of Virginia Woolf's *A Room of One's Own*, discussing the relationship between creativity and economics, class, race, and gender, and is a groundbreaking study.

📖 D. H. Lawrence, John Steinbeck

LM

Olshan, Joseph (US). *See* SEXUAL POLITICS

Ondaatje, Michael (Canadian, 1943–)
Born in Sri Lanka, Ondaatje moved to Britain in 1953, and now lives in Canada. He is well known as a poet, and his fictional prose is intensely poetic. *The English Patient* (1992, joint Booker Prize winner) tells the story of the entanglement of four damaged lives in a crumbling Italian monastery as the Second World War comes to an end—the exhausted nurse, Hana; the maimed thief and spy, Caravaggio; the wary Sikh sapper, Kip. Each is haunted by the riddle of the English patient, the nameless burn victim who lies dying in an upstairs room and whose memories of passion, betrayal, and rescue gradually

unfold. Most of these memories are of Egypt just before the start of the war. Ondaatje captures the atmosphere of both the Egyptian desert and the bombed Italian monastery with great vividness. *Coming Through Slaughter* (1976) is based on the life of cornet player Buddy Bolden, legendary jazz pioneer of early twentieth-century New Orleans. The novel takes the form of a documentary re-creation of Bolden's life, expressed through a collage of fragmented memoirs. *In the Skin of a Lion* (1987) is the story of Patrick Lewis who arrives in Toronto in the 1920s and earns a living searching for a vanished millionaire and tunnelling beneath Lake Ontario. Patrick's life intersects with the lives of characters who reappear in *The English Patient*. The novel vividly captures the Canadian wilderness, and explores the boundaries between myth and fact.

📖 Gita Mehta, J. G. Farrell, Kazuo Ishiguro. *See* CANADA, HISTORICAL

DJ

O'Neill, Joseph (Irish, 1964–)
O'Neill was born in Cork and educated in the Netherlands and England. He works as a barrister. *The Breezes* (1995) is a tragicomic novel about the desperate bad luck of the Breeze family (which embraces not only the mother being killed by lightning, but also redundancy, car accident, death of a friend, burglary) and their inadequate mechanisms for coping with it (insurance, security systems, lucky underpants, shaky religious beliefs, management maxims). The ear for dialogue is exact, the comic timing good, and the ludicrous triumph of hope against all the odds makes this a very satisfying read.

📖 Nigel Williams, David Flusfeder

JR

Orczy, Baroness (Hungarian/British, 1865–1947) After spending her childhood chiefly in Paris and Brussels, at the age of 15 Orczy (real name, Mrs Montague Barstow) came to London, where she studied art. Her hugely successful *The Scarlet Pimpernel* (1905) has as its central character Sir Percy Blakeney, leader of a small group of Englishmen dedicated to rescuing victims of the Reign of Terror in revolutionary France. Sir Percy, who conceals his heroism beneath a foppish and indolent exterior, appears in various sequels, which include *The Elusive Pimpernel* (1908) and *Child of the Revolution* (1932). *The Case of Miss Elliott* (1905) and *Unravelled Knots* (1909) are among her numerous detective stories featuring 'The Old Man in the Corner', who conducts investigations from his habitual seat in a London teashop.

📖 Anthony Hope, Georgette Heyer, Alexandre Dumas. *See* HISTORICAL, SPY   *DH*

Orwell, George (British, 1903–50) Orwell was one of the most influential English writers of the twentieth century. His real name was Eric Blair, which he dropped when he started writing seriously. His first book, *Down and Out in Paris and London* (1933), was a social documentary about his true-life experiences doing menial jobs for a pittance. The change of name is significant. It signalled the shedding of his previous persona— comfortable upper-middle-class family, father a civil servant in India, himself educated at Eton—and with it a rejection of the élitist values and blatant snobbery of the ruling classes. As 'George Orwell' he quite literally reinvented himself. Orwell insisted that all writing was political in the broadest sense, and in his last and finest novel, *Nineteen Eighty-Four* (1949), written while he was dying of tuberculosis, he produced a nightmare vision of a future society crushed into submission by a totalitarian regime, ruled and watched over by Big Brother and fed on spin-doctored Newspeak. The spectre of this book lay like a shadow of grim prophecy over the latter half of the twentieth century. His fears were more concentrated in the modern fable, *Animal Farm* (1945). When the animals take over from the tyranny of humans, there is the prospect of a fairer farmyard society, with due respect for the dignity of each species. Then the pigs, once installed as leaders, take on the worst traits of their former oppressors, while mouthing such slogans as 'All animals are equal but some animals are more equal than others.'

With these two books Orwell lost a lot of friends on the left, who accused him of betraying the cause of socialism. But he had come to distrust any political creed that cynically manipulates the truth to suit itself. Shining bright and clear through all Orwell's writing is the voice, honest and compassionate, of a decent man who rejects intellectual humbug and exposes injustice wherever he finds it; and does so in simple transparent prose that is stripped of literary pretension.

Keep the Aspidistra Flying (1936) is closely autobiographical, seething with the frustration Orwell himself had endured, as penniless, struggling poet Gordon Comstock, working in a bookshop, desperately seeks some small measure of success, and does in the end find happiness with a new, pregnant wife. *Coming Up for Air* (1939) has sad, middle-aged George Bowling seeking to escape a joyless marriage and death-in-life existence by revisiting the golden past of his childhood; alas, it has vanished for ever, and war darkens the horizon.

The importance and enduring value of Orwell's legacy to us rests as much on his essays, social commentary, and non-fiction books as with the novels. *The Road to Wigan Pier* (1937) is a passionate, factual document of the Depression in the North of England; *Homage to Catalonia* (1938) recounts his own experiences during the Spanish Civil War, in which he fought and was wounded.

📖 James Hanley, Aldous Huxley, Arthur Koestler. *See* HUMOUR, RUSSIA, SCIENCE FICTION   *TH*

Ousmane, Sembene (Senegalese, 1923–   ). *See* AFRICA

Oz, Amos (Israeli, 1939–   ) Amos Oz writes gripping novels about modern Israeli life, interweaving a shrewd analysis of Israel's politics and history with intimate stories about love, sex, and betrayal. Start with *Fima* (1991), the story of a man who works as a receptionist in a gynaecologist's clinic and spends much of his life fantasizing about solving his nation's political problems while undertaking a series of sexual adventures. *Black Box* (1987) traces the break-up of a marriage through letters exchanged between a husband and wife seven years after their divorce. *Panther in the Basement* (1995) is a short, entertaining book set in Jerusalem in 1947, at the end of the British occupation of Palestine. The narrator is a 12-year-old boy who yearns to become a hero, but finds himself accused of treachery.

📖 Saul Bellow, Mordecai Richler, Iris Murdoch   *TT*

P

Pagnol, Marcel (French, 1895–1974)
Pagnol was born in the Provençal town
of Aubagne, and worked as a schoolteacher after serving in the First World
War. Following the success of his plays, he
became a full-time writer in 1928 and later,
a noted film-maker. Begin with *The Water
of the Hills* (1962), a nostalgic depiction of
life in the Provence of his youth. The story
concerns a long-standing feud among
farmers over rights to a water supply. It is
in two parts, *Jean de Florette* and *Manon
des Sources*, which were filmed by Claude
Berri in 1986. His other major work as
a prose writer is the *Souvenirs d'Enfance*
trilogy, a richly lyrical recollection of childhood. The first two parts are published
in English as *My Father's Glory* and *My
Mother's Castle* (formerly titled *The Days
Were Too Short*, 1957).

📖 Laurie Lee, Alain-Fournier,
George Mackay Brown   *DH*

Paley, Grace (US, 1922–) Paley has
lived and worked in New York, the city and
its multi-ethnic character being integral to
her stories, which reflect her Russian-Jewish
heritage as well as urban realities. Her collections are vivid and entertaining, showing
her fine ear for dialogue, and often concern
women trying to survive and raise children,
with or without men. *The Little Disturbances
of Man* (1959) established her reputation
for sardonic observations of family life. In
'An Interest in Life', for instance, a deserted
wife makes a list of her troubles, hoping
to appear on a television show; instead,

she gains a new lover, but remains haunted
by her husband. The fictions in *Enormous
Changes at the Last Minute* (1968) are generally open-ended slices of life, some informed
by Paley's campaigning community politics.
Others, such as 'A Conversation with
My Father', are pure story-telling. *Later
the Same Day* (1985) is another fine, more
recent collection.

📖 Dorothy Parker, Philip Roth   *JS*

Paretsky, Sara (US, 1947–) V. I.
Warshawski (Vic) is the private eye
heroine of Paretsky's novels and was one
of the female sleuths who helped redefine
the genre. Tough, streetwise, intelligent, and
fiercely independent, she tackles the cases
that come her way with gusto, often to the
dismay of her close friends Lotty and Max
and her neighbour Mr Contreras, co-owner
of Vic's dog, Peppy. Warshawski has a
smart mouth and quick wit, and she is
physically skilful too, using her martial arts
expertise to escape from violent situations.
Paretsky's Chicago is sharply observed, the
gritty industrial heritage of the city, the graft
and corruption that developed with it are
there in all their seedy reality. Warshawski
is hired by Mr Thayer in *Indemnity Only*
(1982) to find his son's missing girlfriend.
When she goes to interview the boy she
finds his corpse and her client is revealed
to be an imposter. *Bitter Medicine* (1987)
tells the story of Consuelo, a pregnant
teenager and her young husband, Fabiano.
Warshawski takes her to hospital when
she becomes ill but tragedy follows and

Warshawski is determined to find out exactly what happened. In *Guardian Angel* (1992) Warshawski is outraged when Hattie Frissell, who has the messiest house in the street and a menagerie of dogs, is taken to hospital and neighbours get granted guardianship over Hattie and have the dogs put to sleep.

📖 Sue Grafton, Sarah Dunant.
See CRIME   *CS*

Park, Ruth (NZ, 1922–) Park worked in Australia as a journalist and in a range of jobs in the outback; she has written prolifically for adults and children, and won a number of Australian prizes for her work. *Poor Man's Orange* (1949) is set in the post-war slums of Sydney, and deals with the family life of a young girl growing to adulthood. From the rats that bite the babies, to the death of a beloved sister, and falling in love with her grief-stricken husband, Park chronicles the tragedies and joys of a crowded, working-class life with humanity and compassion.

📖 Miles Franklin, Betty Smith,
Maisie Mosco   *JR*

Parker, Dorothy (US, 1893–1967) At 23 Dorothy Parker was hired by the fashion magazine *Vogue* as a caption writer. Very quickly her bright talent as a penetrating observer and wickedly comic satirist put her at the centre of New York intellectual society. She became as famous for her acerbic wit, often quoted, at the Algonquin Hotel Round Table ('With my crown of thorns, why do I need a prick like you?') as for her literary output. Her first volume of poetry, *Enough Rope* (1926), was a best-seller, and she wrote some superb short stories. 'The Lovely Leave', 'A Telephone Call', and 'Big Blonde' (collected in *The Penguin Dorothy Parker*) lay bare with lacerating honesty how women suffer and (sometimes) survive in relationships, from the bittersweet yearning of young love to the anguish of the spurned older woman. And her wit and wisecracks still have a diamond sparkle—even such trifles as 'Men seldom make passes | At girls who wear glasses'. It's that 'seldom' that makes her a poet.

📖 Anita Loos, F. Scott Fitzgerald,
Nathanael West   *TH*

Parks, Tim (British, 1954–) Born in Manchester, Parks has lived in Italy since 1981, and his more recent novels range satisfyingly across cultural and geographical divides. Start with *Europa* (1997, Booker Prize-shortlisted) which charts the coach-journey from Milan to Strasbourg of Jerry Marlow, one of a group of lecturers taking a petition to the European Parliament. As he travels Marlow reflects on his life, his failed marriage, his ex-mistress, and his dreadful relationship with his daughter. Narrating in the first person, Marlow maintains the story of the present journey (which is very funny) at the same time as delving into painful memories, so that there are farcical conjunctions and explosions of insight, for the reader. This technique is taken a stage further in *Destiny* (1999), again narrated in the first person by a middle-aged English man married to an Italian, here struggling through the days after his son's suicide. His voice encompasses both the present and numerous layers of memory within single sentences—a technique which conveys all the complexity and comic contradictions of experience, and renders Parks's self-centred hero enormously sympathetic. This novel's exploration of a long marriage is one of the best in contemporary fiction. Earlier novels include *Goodness* (1991), about a couple's conflicting attitudes to their handicapped child. Parks has also translated Italian fiction.

📖 John Updike, Hilary Mantel   *JR*

Pasternak, Boris (Soviet, 1890–1960) Born in Moscow into a cultured Jewish-Russian family, Pasternak studied philosophy before becoming a highly regarded lyric poet. His epic novel *Dr Zhivago* (1957) was banned in Russia for its implicit criticism of the Revolution, but published to huge acclaim in the West. A vast, teeming novel set against the background of the First World War and Russian Revolution, *Dr Zhivago* follows the fortunes of a good man through desperate times. Doctor and poet, Zhivago's comfortable, happily married life is shattered by war. He becomes a doctor to the troops, returning to a home transformed by revolution. Attempts to live in simple obscurity are doomed to failure as politics intrude. Through horrors and sorrows he clings to human dignity and love, embodied in the character of his mistress, Lara, who is married to the revolutionary Strelnikov. Her story is entwined with his throughout. The book is pervaded by a sense of chaos, of people being washed about like flotsam and suddenly ripped apart. Zhivago is a particularly Russian hero, the traditional holy fool, his task to celebrate life through poetry. Restlessly seeking after truth, his rebellion is one of peace through the example of his own life and work. He embodies the life force as opposed to blind ideology and the life-denying powers of the monolithic state. As Pasternak said: 'There can be no Party line about life.'

📖 Leo Tolstoy, Mikhail Sholokhov. *See* RUSSIA   *CB*

Paton, Alan (South African, 1903–88) Paton began his career teaching at Diepkloof reformatory for young black offenders before joining the South African Liberal Party of which he subsequently became chairman. Even after the party was disbanded in 1968 he dedicated his life to the principles of liberal politics. He is primarily known through his best-selling novel *Cry, the Beloved Country* (1948), published the same year as the Nationalist government came to power and later made into a successful film. An African priest from the rural reserves travels to Johannesburg in search of his son, Absalom, and is catapulted into a world of racial hatred, abject poverty, crime, and a corrupt judicial system that have subsequently come to characterize apartheid South Africa. He is finally reconciled with his son, but Paton's liberalism will not allow him to envisage any real alternatives to the oppressive regime; a change of heart for his characters is the most we can expect.

In *Too Late the Phalarope* (1953) a young male Afrikaner has illicit sex with a black woman, and his father disowns him. This moving story exposes the horror of the Immorality Act imposed by the Nationalist Government in 1950 which legislated against people with different coloured skins having sexual relationships. Paton also wrote short stories, biography, two volumes of autobiography, and numerous political and religious pamphlets.

📖 Nadine Gordimer, Bessie Head, Christopher Hope   *EW*

Paton Walsh, Jill (British, 1937–) Jill Paton Walsh, initially established as a highly successful children's writer, has also published eight books for adults. *Knowledge* *of Angels* (1994), a moving meditation on spirituality, was shortlisted for the Booker Prize. Set in medieval times (the exact date is deliberately unspecified) on Grandinsula, an island housing a self-enclosed Christian community, the novel raises uncomfortable questions about religion as it tells the interconnected stories of a child found amongst wolves and misused in an attempt to prove the innate nature of God, and of a foreigner tried as a heretic by the Inquisition. Move on to *The Serpentine Cave* (1997), the account of a middle-aged woman's attempt to find out more about her father and about her own past following her mother's death.

📖 Fay Weldon, Marina Warner   SR

Patterson, Glenn (British, 1961–) Patterson was born and brought up in Belfast, and taken together his novels present a fascinating and detailed picture of life there over the past forty years. Begin with *Fat Lad* (1992), which follows the life of a Belfast man returning to work there after ten years in England, moving between glimpses of his parents' and grandparents' lives, to his own matter-of-fact memories of childhood, of violence on the streets, of his father's abuse (itself a response to the violence outside) and his haphazard present-day life, with sexual and emotional entanglements which seem beyond his control. The way in which a life is shaped by its past is brilliantly revealed, and the language is witty and utterly engaging. Move on to *Burning Your Own* (1988), Patterson's first novel, an account of a Belfast boyhood; and then to *The International* (1999), set in a Belfast hotel on the eve of the troubles in 1967, and describing a day in the life of an apolitical, non-religious young barman there,

embracing that historical moment in the city with humour and irony.

📖 Bernard MacLaverty, Roddy Doyle, Deirdre Madden. *See* IRELAND   JR

Peacock, Thomas Love (British, 1785–1866) Peacock, a friend of Shelley, wrote seven novels. He satirized the contemporary political and cultural scene in *Nightmare Abbey* (1818), a book all the more enjoyable if the works and ideas of the Romantic poets are familiar to the reader. Lord Byron, Coleridge, and Shelley himself are among the noted literary figures to be lampooned in this short, witty examination of the change in contemporary literary tastes. *Headlong Hall* (1816) is also a satire on romantic idealism. The story takes place over Christmas at the eponymous country house, and is largely composed of the philosophical conversations about the merits of 'modern society' between a pessimist, an optimist, a character happy with the status quo, and the Revd Dr Gaster, who has won over his host with a learned dissertation on the art of stuffing a turkey.

📖 Jonathan Swift, Laurence Sterne

FS

Peake, Mervyn (Laurence) (British, 1911–68) Peake was born in China to missionary parents. A brilliant artist and illustrator, he was among those who liberated Belsen, the concentration camp. What he saw there never left him, and he died in London after struggling with mental disturbance and Parkinson's disease. The *Gormenghast* trilogy has elements of the Gothic, the fantastic, and the Kafka-esque. *Titus Groan* (1946), set in a world resembling our own, is the first book and concerns the birth of Titus. It introduces us to extraordinary characters like Swelter, the hideous palace cook, Barquentine, and Flay. The rise and fall of the dreadful scullion, Steerpike, is the main plot of the trilogy, and Peake creates an arcane society where atmosphere and landscape are as important as events. *Gormenghast* (1950) examines the world of the castle, whose landscape has much in common with Sark, where Peake lived for some years. *Titus Alone* (1959) describes the hero's exile from Gormenghast and the author's deteriorating state of mind is evident in this surreal dystopia. These remarkable books are unlike anything else in literature.

📖 Karen Blixen (writing as Isak Dinesen), Edgar Allan Poe, Franz Kafka   *AG*

Pears, Tim (British, 1956–) Pears' first novel, *In the Place of Fallen Leaves* (1993), vividly and hypnotically captures the landscape of rural Devon, seen through the eyes of 13-year-old Alison during the long hot summer of 1984. Alison describes the hardships of life on a farm, the bitterness and rivalry between her two older brothers, her own first experience of death in the loss of her grandmother. There is also a strong sense of place in *In a Land of Plenty* (1997), set in a small industrial town in middle England. Following the Second World War, ambitious Charles Freeman successfully expands a small metal manufacturing company, marries young, artistic Mary, buys a grand house, and becomes the father of three sons and a daughter. The family encounter tragedy and conflict in their relationships as the children grow to adulthood, against the backdrop of a changing town. This novel has been adapted as a television drama series.

📖 Jane Gardam, Sebastian Faulks, Thomas Hardy   *DJ*

Pelevin, Viktor (Russian). *See* RUSSIA

Perec, Georges (French, 1936–82) Georges Perec was born in Paris to a family of Polish Jews, and both his parents were killed during the Second World War, his father on active service in 1940, his mother in a concentration camp in 1943. These experiences were the subject of *W, or the Memory of Childhood* (1975), but Perec's most celebrated work is *Life: A User's Manual* (1978), an ingeniously linked series of stories set in a Paris apartment-block. The extreme forms taken by Perec's novels are almost legendary, as in *A Void* (*La Disparition*, 1969), a novel written entirely without the use of the letter 'e'. Unlike many experimental novels, Perec's books remain highly accessible and readable, and his vivid descriptions of ordinary lives are full of humour and warmth. *Species of Spaces* (1997) brings together shorter pieces from Perec's whole career.

📖 Italo Calvino, Michel Tournier   *WB*

Perriam, Wendy (British, 1940–) Wendy Perriam was expelled from a strict convent school, read history at St Anne's College, Oxford, and worked in a variety of jobs including advertising before becoming a writer. Her novels are erotic, irreverent, very funny, and frequently outrageous. Certainly not for the prudish or the puritanical. *After Purple* (1992) explores the story of Thea Morton, desperate for sex, love, and eternal salvation. Her quest takes her from a violent relationship to pursuing a Franciscan priest to Lourdes hoping to seduce him and save her soul. In *Sin City* (1987) Carole Joseph and Norah Toomey meet in a psychiatric hospital.

Carole wins a holiday in Las Vegas and takes along Norah who has spent her life in institutions. The pair are thrown into the sleazy world of brothels and casinos in a funny and poignant adventure.

📖 Clare Boylan, Erica Jong, Fay Weldon   *CS*

Peters, Ellis (British, 1913–95) Ellis Peters (pseudonym of Edith Pargeter) was a prolific novelist who spent her life in Shropshire except for war service in the WRNS. *She Goes to War* (1942), a semi-autobiography, and her war trilogy *The Eighth Champion of Christendom* (1947), following Jim Benison in action from Dunkirk to Singapore, deserve to be better known. Like all her novels, these are strong in plot, realism, and characterization. In crime fiction, Peters's thirteen Inspector Felse books precede *The Chronicles of Brother Cadfael* (1977–94), twenty novels fusing history and mystery. Her sleuth Cadfael, a Welshman and herbalist, is a Benedictine monk of Shrewsbury Abbey. Peters uses twelfth-century history and Shropshire's topography to create complex plots of intrigue, treachery, revenge, and love. Questions of morality, faith and redemption underlie the rich tapestry.

Start with the first, *A Morbid Taste for Bones* (1977), establishing Cadfael's character, the close community of the abbey, and its personalities. The plot hinges on the transit of St Winefred's bones from Wales to Shrewsbury, two murders, and a romance. In *The Virgin in the Ice* (1982) Cadfael investigates the disappearance of two children and the murder of a nun, found frozen. He also discovers he has a son. Don't miss *The Summer of the Danes* (1991): Cadfael is in North Wales when a Danish fleet approaches and a corpse

is discovered. Move on to Peters's fine historical novels, The *Brothers of Gwynedd* quartet (1974–77), based on the last Welsh princes. She also translated Czech literature and published three collections of short stories.

📖 Umberto Eco, P. C. Doherty   *GC*

Petrushevskaya, Lyudmilla (Soviet/ Russian, 1938–). *See* RUSSIA

Peyton, K. M. (British, 1929–). *See* TEEN

Phillips, Caryl (British, 1958–) Phillips was born in St Kitts and grew up in England, producing his earliest writing for the theatre. In his 1987 travel book, *The European Tribe*, he casts an outsider's eye, somewhat like V. S. Naipaul, at well-known bits of Europe, including two intriguing chapters set in Venice, making us look at the familiar differently. His first novel, *The Final Passage* (1985), takes up the theme of migration to England, in a much less jazzy way than did Selvon in the 1950s, the sombre tone signalling a shift in psychology between the migrant and someone trying to make a new home.

Two novels dealing with the theme of slavery stand out. *Cambridge* (1991) features an absentee plantation-owner, and an unfathomable overseer whose relationship with the highly educated Christian slave Cambridge and the black obeah-woman puzzles the innocent daughter of the estate, newly out from England. *Crossing the River* (1993) spans centuries and continents showing how members of an enslaved family surmount their fate. The voice of the guilt-ridden father 200 years on, and the diary of the slave-purchaser, are brought richly into play. These are imaginatively sophisticated novels, not tracts of indictment, but they do indict. In *The Nature of Blood* (1997) Phillips develops the parallel drawn in *The European Tribe*, between the historical experience of Jews and of black people. The *Othello* story is retold. Fifteenth-century persecution of Jews in Vienna (the background to *The Merchant of Venice*) and much more, come alive in the narrative. Here, Phillips makes us alert to just how precarious are notions of 'security', say, or 'home'.

📖 George Lamming, Ben Okri, Hanif Kureishi. *See* CARIBBEAN   EM

Phillips, Jayne Anne (US, 1952–)
Phillips began her writing career with short stories, and *Black Tickets* (1979) remains the best book to start with; the stories are powerful and vivid, shocking in their intensity, and simultaneously lush, the language luxuriant and sensual. Usually narrated in the first person, many of them deal with drifters and loners and offer a poetically condensed glimpse— sometimes only a page or two long—of a life. *Machine Dreams* (1984) follows an American family from the 1950s to the 1970s and the horror of Vietnam, through a succession of voices, letters, and dreams. *Shelter* (1994) is a haunting exploration of young adolescence and evil, set in a West Virginia girls' summer camp in 1963. The language, capturing the rhythms of characters' thoughts and fears, is hypnotically powerful.

📖 Eudora Welty, Raymond Carver, William Faulkner   JR

Piercy, Marge (US, 1936–) Piercy's writing originates in the women's movement and the anti-war movements of the 1960s. Her early works were often naturalistic depictions of life for women in that period. However, the book for which she is most famous, *Woman on the Edge of Time* (1976) is set in two worlds: present-day America and the future. Connie Ramos, the central character, has been separated from her daughter and locked up in a mental hospital. Here she becomes part of an experiment, the side-effects of which allow her to contact a future where the world has achieved a kind of social equality and ecological balance. However, the future world is also engaged in a war and in other visions Connie sees the dystopic potential of the future.

📖 Ursula Le Guin, Marilyn French, Jane Smiley. *See* SCIENCE FICTION
    LM

Pilcher, Rosamunde (British, 1924–).
See FAMILY SAGA, ROMANCE

Pinckney, Darryl (US, 1953–)
Pinckney, born and brought up in Indianapolis, is an essayist and critic as well as a novelist. His only novel to date, *High Cotton* (1992), follows the maturation of its unnamed narrator who, like Pinckney, attends Columbia University, and is probably a novelist. It is a deeply ambivalent portrait of a privileged middle-class black culture, known as 'the talented tenth', or as Pinckney calls them 'the also chosen'. The novel deals with the protagonist's confusion and alienation in comprehending his 'blackness'. This is most clearly shown through his relation to his grandfather, Eustace, who embodies the young man's relationship with his African-American past. The novel itself is elliptical, and has been described rather as

a collection of essays. However, Pinckney's engagement with debates about ethnicity and rootedness is superb.

📖 James Baldwin, Richard Wright, Toni Morrison   *CJ*

Pirsig, Robert M(aynard) (US, 1928–) Born in Minneapolis and educated at the University of Minnesota, Pirsig worked as a technical writer before the appearance of his best-selling *Zen and the Art of Motorcycle Maintenance* (1974). Its main narrative of a motorcycle journey to the Pacific coast drifts continually into absorbing flashbacks and digressions. The result is a powerful record of psychological crisis and recovery out of which Pirsig develops his philosophy that value resides in the quality of human effort. *Lila: An Inquiry into Morals* (1991) is set on a sailing boat going down the Hudson river. The narrator, having picked up Lila in a bar, finds her a volatile opposite to his own reflective nature. As their relationship deteriorates, he disenchantedly surveys contemporary American life and begins a painful re-evaluation of beliefs central to his identity.

📖 Kurt Vonnegut, Herman Melville
                                                                 DH

Plaidy, Jean (British, 1906–93) Jean Plaidy was one of seventeen pseudonyms of Eleanor Hibbert, who produced over 200 books. As Plaidy she attempted 'authentic history in the form of the novel', from the Normans to the Victorians. Spanish, French, and Italian history are also covered. Steeped in intrigue and romance, the Catherine de' Medici trilogy gives the full flavour. *Madame Serpent* (1951) deals with Catherine's marriage at the age of 14 to Henry II of France; *The Italian Woman* (1952), with her growing twistedness; and *Queen Jezebel* (1953) shows her murderously wielding power. From the Tudor series, try *Murder Most Royal* (1949), about the executions of Henry VIII's wives Anne Boleyn and Catharine Howard, then dip into the Plantagenet saga for *The Plantagenet Prelude* (1976) about Eleanor of Aquitaine's stormy union with Henry Plantagenet, and the story of Thomas à Becket. Or simply choose the period that interests you and take it from there. Hibbert also wrote Gothic romance under the name **Victoria Holt**.

📖 Rosalind Laker, Norah Lofts.
See HISTORICAL   *CB*

Plath, Sylvia (US, 1932–63) Although Sylvia Plath was born and brought up in America, she spent the last few years of her life living in England, married to the poet Ted Hughes. Known foremost as an exceptionally talented poet herself, she is also the author of *The Bell Jar* (1963), one of the most haunting and powerful twentieth-century novels about mental breakdown. Set in America, it traces the story of Esther's illness, but in its acute satirical portrait of the values of 1950s' New York society, it makes the reader question where the true disease lies.

📖 Antonia White (*The Lost Traveller*), J. D. Salinger, Ken Kesey, Virginia Woolf (*Mrs Dalloway*)   *SA*

Platonov, Andrei (Soviet, 1899–1951). *See* RUSSIA

Poe, Edgar Allan (US, 1809–49) Poe had a short and tragic life. His macabre vision was fed by the death of his first wife and continuing poverty. He died after one of his notorious drinking binges. A poet, short-story writer, and respected journalist, Poe is best known for his tightly focused Gothic horror tales. 'The Pit and the Pendulum' (1843) features Nicholas Medina, grieving husband living in a castle replete with a complex chamber of horrors built during the Spanish Inquisition. Convinced that he has buried his wife alive, Medina becomes increasingly tormented. In 1961 the story became one of many Roger Corman films starring Vincent Price. In 1964 Corman also adapted 'The Masque of the Red Death' (1842). To avoid death from a plague, Prince Prospero shuts himself and a thousand chosen people in his castle. Here, he cultivates the perfection of Beauty through a series of special effects until the arrival of a chilling masked intruder brings evil and inevitable death. Apart from Gothic horror tales, Poe wrote more light-hearted fiction and detective stories. 'The Man that was Used Up' (1839), shows the bellicose General Smith reduced to a small, ungainly bundle when he has removed all his finery. 'The Murders in the Rue Morgue' (1841) is widely regarded as the first detective story. Poe's influence on later writers has been enormous.

📖 Arthur Conan Doyle, Jules Verne.
See CRIME, SUPERNATURAL,
UNITED STATES OF AMERICA   *EW*

Pohl, Frederick (US, 1919–) Pohl was born in New York. He began editing science fiction magazines in 1940 and became a full-time writer in 1953 following the success of *The Space Merchants* (1953), which was written in collaboration with C. M. Kornbluth. Like much of Pohl's best work, the story, which tells of space exploration dominated by commercial interests, functions as a futuristic satire on American values. *Gateway* (1977) begins a series of novels concerning mankind's exploration of the galaxy by making use of installations abandoned by aliens known as the Heechee. Succeeding stories include *Heechee Rendezvous* (1984) and *The Annals of the Heechee* (1987). Among Pohl's many other books is *The Cool War* (1980), envisioning a world in which conventional warfare is obsolete and hostility between ostensibly peaceable nations is conducted by means of drugs and disease.

📖 Ian Watson, Bob Shaw   *DH*

Porter, Katherine Anne (US, 1890–1980) Porter was a Southerner by inheritance, her fiction informed by her early life in rural Louisiana and Texas, and by experiences as a journalist during the Mexican Revolution. Her stories and novellas were greatly admired for their conscious use of symbol and allegory; some are reminiscent of early Joyce. 'Maria Concepcion' is a characteristic early story, depicting murderous jealousy among Mexican peasant women; the title story of her first collection, *Flowering Judas* (1930, enlarged 1935), also has a Mexican setting. But it is an altogether more sinister tale of revenge, with a famous ending. The central novella in *Pale Horse, Pale Rider* (1939) tells of a love-affair between a soldier and a woman journalist at the time of the 1919 influenza outbreak. It drew upon Porter's own personal background, as did *The Old Order: Stories of the Old South* (1944). Her only novel, written over two decades, is highly regarded. *Ship of Fools* (1962) is a large, crowded, and inevitably symbolic story set on a German passenger boat during the 1930s, and features characters of various nationalities struggling together. She was awarded the Pulitzer Prize in 1965 for her *Collected Stories*.

📖 Katherine Mansfield, Carson McCullers, Robert Penn Warren.
See THE SEA   JS

Potok, Chaim (US, 1929–) Chaim Potok was born and raised in the Bronx, New York, in a traditional Orthodox Jewish family. He was ordained as a rabbi in 1954, then turned to writing fiction. His first novel, *The Chosen* (1967), tells the story of the friendship between two boys, Reuven Malter, son of a Jewish scholar, and Danny Saunders, son of a Chassidic rabbi, revered as the divinely inspired leader of his community. As well as giving a fascinating insight into the lives and customs of American Orthodox Jews in the 1940s, the novel offers a tender, sensitive examination of the relationships between fathers and sons. Potok has an abiding interest in the influence of the twentieth century on traditional Judaism, and this theme is continued in *The Promise*, a sequel to *The Chosen* (1970), and *In the Beginning* (1975), about another young Jewish boy, David Lurie, a gifted yeshiva student whose passion for truth awakens controversy.

📖 Amos Oz, David Grossman, Saul Bellow   SA

Powell, Anthony (British, 1905–2000) Powell worked in publishing, literary journalism, and the film industry and was awarded an OBE. His first novel, *Afternoon Men*, a satirical account of the empty lives of a group of London socialites, was published in 1931, but he is best-known for his 12-volume sequence *A Dance to the Music of Time* (1951–75, televised as a serial in 1997). *Dance* is narrated by Nicholas Jenkins, a scholarly, detached figure (and,

some think, Powell's alter ego) whom we first encounter in *A Question of Upbringing* (1951). The novels follow Jenkins's effortless progress through public school and university, into art publishing (*A Buyer's Market*, 1952), the Great Depression (*The Acceptance World*, 1955), the war, and the literary world.

The main characters are almost entirely upper class, and Powell has been criticized for cataloguing the twentieth century in a limited, élitist way. There is some truth in this, but his novels are marked by an unusually tolerant, easy-going tone, and he manages a huge and realistic cast, delicately handling a wide range of social and political issues from the 1920s to the 1960s. Begin with *A Question of Upbringing*, but then pick and choose; there is a chronological order, but each novel is self-contained. Move on to the recent *Journals* (published from 1995) for witty recollections and revelations about writers and contemporaries.

📖 Evelyn Waugh, E. M. Forster, Marcel Proust   SR

Powers, Tim (US, 1952–) Tim Powers is one of the most original of modern fantasy authors. His early work, *The Drawing of the Dark* (1979), is one of many stories of King Arthur's return, but unlike all the others it is set in sixteenth-century Austria, while the 'dark' of its title is dark beer, brewed once a century to bring life back to the Fisher King. *The Anubis Gates* (1983) is also in part a historical novel, set in nineteenth-century London; it is one of the defining works of 'steampunk' (science fiction crossed with Victorian Gothic). Powers uses his knowledge of romantic poets also in *The Stress of Her Regard* (1989), in which Byron, Shelley, and Keats appear as characters haunted by vampiric beings who provide them with their inspiration. Powers's later works, *Last Call* (1992) and *Expiration Date* (1995), are set in modern America, but continue the themes of demonic possession, identity exchange, and quasi-Arthurian return to heal the waste lands of Las Vegas or Los Angeles.

George R. R. Martin, Michael Swanwick. *See* FANTASY   *TS*

Powys, John Cowper (British, 1872–1963) The influence of Powys's West Country boyhood is seen in his fiction. After Cambridge and lecturing, he lived in the United States before settling in Wales. His prolific writings range from poetry, essays, philosophy, and autobiography to the epic novels on which his reputation rests. Start with *A Glastonbury Romance* (1932), set in the modern town and its ancient ruins. The inhabitants are influenced in their lives and loves by Glastonbury's legends, pagan and Christian. Complex in plot and characters, rich in sense of place, mythic and supernatural elements, this novel is Powys at his best. Read *Wolf Solent* (1929), an interplay of opposites, centred on Wolf and Gerda; *Weymouth Sands* (1934), the psychologically interesting story of Jobber Skald; and *Maiden Castle* (1936), interconnecting several pairs of lovers. *Owen Glendower* (1940) is based on the Welsh rebel leader and his cousin, Rhisiart.

Thomas Hardy, Emily Brontë   *GC*

Powys, T(heodore) F(rancis) (British, 1875–1953) T. F. Powys was one of eleven children born to a clergyman in Dorset. (An older brother was the novelist John Cowper Powys.) After running his own farm in Suffolk, T. F. Powys retired to Dorset where he lived an extremely secluded life. He writes in a simple, biblical style, and his novels and short stories are allegories for the twentieth century. His best-known book is *Mr Weston's Good Wine* (1927) about the inhabitants of the small rural community of Maidenbridge. The town is presided over by Mr Weston who is not only a commercial traveller but also, it seems, God, who dispenses the light wine of joy and the dark wine of tragic acceptance. Mr Weston's efforts are aided by the Archangel Michael. If you can get past the 'Mummerset' language and attitudes, T. F. Powys offers a visionary literature about rural Britain which was unique in the twentieth century.

Flannery O'Connor, D. H. Lawrence, H. E. Bates   *LM*

Pratchett, Terry (British, 1948–) In terms of sales Terry Pratchett is the most successful British author writing today; it has been calculated that 1 per cent of all fiction titles sold in Britain are of his writing. Yet, although he has a multitude of devoted readers, his work has attracted very little attention from critics. It is not hard to see why. Although he has written other kinds of fiction, notably books for children, his chosen genre is one not usually regarded as 'serious' in literary circles. His best-selling works are novels of fantasy: his *mise-en-scène* being Discworld, a plate-shaped planet which sails through the universe supported by four elephants, who in turn stand on the back of a great turtle. Magic is essential to keep such a world in being and figures largely in the *Discworld* novels, of which there are now over twenty. The first of them, *The Colour of Magic* (1983), which makes an excellent introduction to the series, has as hero the incompetent magician Rincewind, who appears in several novels. So do the witches Granny Weatherwax and Nanny Ogg, down-to-earth country-women who stoutly defend traditional ways of life against destructive powers such as cruel fairies (*Lords and Ladies*, 1992— one of the best stories) and sophisticated vampires (*Carpe Jugulum*, 1998). Given their magical background the novels are remarkably matter-of-fact, and they are also saved from the romantic artiness of the 'swords and sorcery' fantasies by Pratchett's acute sense of humour. He even humor-ously portrays Death, who appears as a character in *Mort* (1987)—perhaps the best Discworld novel of all—and in several others, accompanied by his white horse 'Binky'. Establishing his own world has given Pratchett unlimited scope to create new scenes and characters, and his vein of invention shows no signs of petering out.

📖 Ursula Le Guin, Charles Dickens, Philip K. Dick. *See* FANTASY, SCIENCE FICTION   *KB*

Pratt, Fletcher (US, 1897–1956). *See* FANTASY

Priest, Christopher (British, 1943–) Priest was born in Manchester, and was an accountant before becoming a full-time writer. His earlier science fiction writings include *Fugue for a Darkening Island* (1972). Begin with this futuristic view of political tensions in England as African refugees arrive from a homeland devastated by nuclear war. In *A Dream of Wessex* (1977) a group of experimenters link their minds through a computer network and lose contact with reality in the cyber-world they inhabit. *The Affirmation* (1981) marks Priest's move away from science fiction into

more realist modes marked by psychological tensions. The story concerns the victim of a breakdown whose attempt to write a therapeutic account of his difficulties leads ultimately to madness. In *The Prestige* (1995) an investigative journalist becomes embroiled in the legacy of evil surviving from the conflict between two nineteenth-century stage magicians.

📖 Iain M. Banks, J. G. Ballard, Michael Moorcock   *DH*

Priestley, J(ohn) B(oynton) (British, 1894–1984) Priestley's literary career spanned fifty years. He survived long enough to be among the last in the line of what used to be called 'a man of letters' —producing a vast output ranging from journalism, essays, and critical works to novels, stage plays, and film-scripts. He renamed his home town of Bradford 'Bruddersford' in his most popular novel, *The Good Companions* (1929), a rumbus-tious, wryly humorous tale of a touring concert-party, the Dinky Doos, which owes a debt to Dickens in its profusion of character and incident. *Angel Pavement* (1930), set in London, is another sprawl-ing novel but bleaker in tone and finer in execution, revolving around a small city firm and the threadbare, treadmill existence of its clerks and typists. The seedy glamour of the theatre obviously appealed to Priestley; he returned to it in *Lost Empires* (1965), which lovingly re-creates the music-hall of 1914. *Bright Day* (1946) is perhaps his most interesting novel, in which a middle-aged screen-writer (Priestley not even thinly disguised) looks back with unsentimental nostalgia at his younger self in the promising 'bright day' before the outbreak of the First World War.

Much of Priestley's fiction can be described as a rollicking good read, in that his characters are slapped on with a broad brush and the plot rushes on regardless; yet there is always exuberance and vitality. He himself felt unjustly dismissed by the critics, and he is best remembered for his so-called Time plays, such as *An Inspector Calls* and *Dangerous Corner*. To catch Priestley's distinctive voice—that of the bluff, down-to-earth Yorkshireman dispensing common sense—read *English Journey* (1934), a trenchant and highly enjoyable account of his travels.

📖 Arnold Bennett, H. G. Wells   *TH*

Pritchett, V(ictor) S(awdon) (British, 1900–97) Best known as a short-story writer and literary journalist, V. S. Pritchett was born in Ipswich, the son of a travelling salesman. He spent his childhood in the English regions and left school in 1915 to take up an apprenticeship in the leather trade. He travelled to Paris in 1921, working as a photographer, then became a journalist in Ireland and Spain. Pritchett published the first of many story collections in 1930, and *The Camberwell Beauty* (1974), with its title story's wryly observed account of the rivalry in love and trade of a group of small-time antique dealers, is typical of Pritchett's style. *The Collected Stories* (1982) is a good selection from Pritchett's many collections up to that date, and *More Collected Stories* (1983) appeared the following year. Pritchett's two acclaimed volumes of autobiography, *A Cab at the Door* (1968) and *Midnight Oil* (1971), vividly evoke the textures of a past which the author knew at first hand, but which even as he wrote was coming to seem remote and inaccessible. Pritchett also published biographies of Turgenev

and Balzac, travel writing, and several collections of literary essays and criticism. He is widely regarded as one of the finest writers of short fiction to emerge in England in the twentieth century, and his style is marked by humour, compassion, and an eye for telling detail.

📖 Elizabeth Bowen; D. H. Lawrence; Anton Chekhov   *WB*

Proulx, E(dna) Annie (US, 1935–) *The Shipping News* (1993) is that most unusual thing in contemporary fiction, a novel with a convincing happy ending. When we meet the hapless Quoyle, his life is falling apart; bratty kids, failed marriage, no career, no-hoper. He moves to the Atlantic coast of Newfoundland, and within that harsh landscape finds fulfilment. Proulx's quirky, original style made *The Shipping News* a prizewinner. Its combination of grittiness and tenderness seduced millions of readers. Proulx's writing is grounded in accurate knowledge of everything she's describing, whether it's boat-building, upholstery, or small-town journalism. The short stories in *Heart Songs* (US, 1988, UK, 1995) are much bleaker. Proulx has been compared to Hemingway and Faulkner, but the power and simplicity of these stories is better compared to the master of the American short story, Raymond Carver. The descriptions of the harsh rural New England landscape are brilliantly done. The lives of the people in the stories are equally bleak. The themes of revenge, regret, isolation are condensed but big in scale. *Accordion Crimes* (1996) is a grim exposé of the American Dream through generations of immigrants who are linked by ownership of the same green button accordion. It's an astonishing *tour de force* but doesn't quite bring off what it's trying to do. It's not that you're not convinced by Proulx's characters or research, but the catalogue of disasters becomes so unremitting you begin not to care any more. Women writers this ambitious are few and far between, however, and the stories in *Close Range* (1999) are beautifully crafted.

📖 Margaret Atwood, Ernest Hemingway, David Guterson.
See UNITED STATES OF AMERICA

RV

Proust, Marcel (French, 1871–1922) Marcel Proust was born into a wealthy French-Jewish family, and lived for some years as a young man-about-town, moving among the most fashionable echelons of Parisian society. Ill-health, the death of his beloved mother, and perhaps boredom, drove him in later years to retire to the seclusion of his cork-lined bedroom, to work on his masterpiece, *A La Recherche Du Temps Perdu* (1913–27), best translated as *In Search of Lost Time*, also sometimes known by its older title of *Remembrance of Things Past*. It is one of the best and one of the longest novels of the century, extending to over 3,000 pages. In the first part, 'Combray', we are introduced to the world of the narrator, well-heeled bourgeois provincial France—not TOO far from Paris— during the *belle époque*: the years leading up to the First World War. Early on in 'Combray' there is that celebrated moment when he dips his 'petite madeleine' into his tea, and the aroma instantly recalls whole vistas of his forgotten past. From here on the narrator makes it his task to redeem his own, limited time, by remembering and recapturing it in exact and beautiful detail. 'Swann in Love' turns its attention to a neighbour in Combray, Charles Swann, a fashionable dandy very

much at home in Parisian society, and a kind of 'superfluous man', deeply infected with irony. 'Sometimes he would go so far as to express an opinion, but he would cloak his words in a tone of irony, as though he did not altogether associate himself with what he was saying.' The subsequent course of Swann's love-affair with the vulgar but sensual Odette is one of the finest, most truthful depictions of romantic infatuation, its onset, and its inevitable demise, in all literature.

I recommend Alain de Botton's *How Proust Can Change Your Life* (1997), a quirky, original, and devoted study, half biographical sketch, half literary criticism. One of the most reassuring pieces of advice that de Botton offers is that you should say to yourself, not 'I am going to read all of Proust this year', but 'I am going to read all of Proust some time over the rest of my life'. Reading Proust should not be rushed, or you will certainly miss something important, or perceptive, or just very, very funny. For, as with that other great and supposedly 'difficult' modernist, James Joyce, it is a delight to discover how amusing Proust can be. He can be sly, satirical, gently mocking human beings and their often ludicrous opinions and behaviour. He can be charmingly dry, as when he refers to that 'most intoxicating romance in the lover's library, the railway timetable'. Above all, it is his characterization that makes one laugh with recognition, whether it is the 'little clique' of the Verdurins, or the preposterous M. Legrandin. Translating Proust has always posed difficulties, but the edition by Scott Moncreiff and Terence Kilmartin, revised by D. J. Enright, does justice to the original.

📖 Henry James, Virginia Woolf, Alain-Fournier, Robert Musil   CH

Pullman, Philip (British, 1946–)
Pullman has been a teacher and lecturer, but has for many years been writing lively and enjoyable children's novels, like *Ruby in the Smoke* (1985) and *Broken Bridge* (1988). The first part of a trilogy, *His Dark Materials*, appeared in 1995. Called *Northern Lights*, it won awards including the Carnegie Medal. In the United States it was called *The Golden Compass* and reached a wide adult readership too. The second part, *The Subtle Knife*, came out in 1997 and together they show how exciting children's literature can be: enormous in scope, original in detail, and full of thrilling special effects. A version of *Paradise Lost*, these books tell of the struggle between good and evil in worlds which are like and not like our own. Pullman also writes for younger children and *Clockwork* (1995) is a fable with the poetic simplicity of the fairy-tale which carries the traditional fairy-tale's freight of meaning.

📖 Russell Hoban, Jan Mark, Alan Garner. *See* TEEN   AG

Pushkin, Alexander (Russian, 1799–1837). *See* RUSSIA

Puzo, Mario (US, 1920–99) Puzo was born to illiterate Italian immigrants in the notorious 'Hell's Kitchen' neighbourhood of Manhattan, and this provided the backdrop to most of his novels. *The Godfather* (1969) is a detailed depiction of the world of the Mafia centred on the life of Vito Corleone. Corleone cultivates an image of respectable family values whilst being the most ruthless of criminals. Puzo skilfully uses the ritualized world of the Mafia to reflect and parody the brutal world of American business. *The Fortunate Pilgrim* (1965) dramatizes the conflict between traditional Italian values and looser American morals. The novel is significant for its powerful portrait of Lucia Santa (based on Puzo's mother) as she struggles to keep her family together. *The Sicilian* (1984) and *Omertà* (2000) are further examples of Puzo's fascination with the violent and clannish nature of the criminal world. Puzo also worked as a screenwriter providing the scripts or stories for *The Godfather* and *The Godfather II* as well as *Superman* and *The Cotton Club*.

📖 Richard Condon, Elmore Leonard
                                          GK

Pym, Barbara (British, 1913–80) After graduating from Oxford, Pym spent most of her working life in London, then retired to live with her sister in an Oxfordshire village where, like many of the characters in her novels, she devoted herself to church, gardening, local history, and country walks. She is a subtle and engaging chronicler of middle-class manners whose fiction went out of print during the 1960s despite its readability and wit. In 1977 she made a comeback as the author of splendid English social comedies. Begin with *A Glass of Blessings* (1958), which is about the married but bored Wilmet Forsyth, an endearingly respectable but reckless woman who is drawn to the three unmarried priests in her Anglo-Catholic church, then on to the enigmatic Piers, with nearly disastrous results. Although it had been written earlier, *The Sweet Dove Died* (1978) was published after Pym's rediscovery. Its heroine is the glamorous but rash Leonora, who is entangled with the antique dealer, Humphrey, and his nephew, James, whom she tries to captivate against the odds. The ninth of Pym's eleven published novels, *Quartet in Autumn* (1977), was shortlisted for the Booker Prize. More sombre in tone than the others, it is a poignant yet sparkling account of two men and two women in their sixties who are all facing retirement. Completed shortly before Pym died, *A Few Green Leaves* (1980) is an affectionate account of the changes in contemporary village life, as seen through the eyes of the anthropologist heroine.

📖 Jane Austen, Elizabeth Taylor, Ivy-Compton Burnett   *JN*

Pynchon, Thomas (US, 1937–) Pynchon is a mysterious figure who never communicates with the press. He worked in aircraft design for a while, and his works relate scientific ideas, big business organization, American society and popular culture to each other. *The Crying of Lot 49* (1966), the second of his five novels, is the shortest and most approachable—in fact it is very funny, with lots of brilliant set piece scenes (including a reverse strip-tease). The heroine has been made executrix of the will of her late lover, and sets out to discover the full extent of his affairs. She stumbles upon a mysterious underground organization which communicates by means of an international, alternative postal system that has been going for centuries. The suggestion is that mainstream society needs, and maybe even creates, the very forces that appear to challenge and undermine it, because the interaction thus created allows it to survive. And it's all related to Newton's second law of thermodynamics!

If you enjoy this, go back to Pynchon's much longer first novel, *V* (1963), which takes us on a dizzying journey from nineteenth-century colonialism to the Second World War bombing of Malta, to the alligator-infested sewers of New York. If you can cope with that you are probably ready for the hugely demanding third, *Gravity's Rainbow* (1973, Pulitzer Prize), which covers the V2 bombing of London, the birth of bebop and even *The Wizard of Oz*. His more recent novels, *Vineland* (1990) and *Mason & Dixon* (1997), are just as inventive but some people find them less energetic and compulsive than the earlier work.

📖 Don DeLillo, Norman Mailer, Neal Stephenson, John Barth. *See* UNITED STATES OF AMERICA   *RF*

Queen, Ellery (Frederic Dannay, US, 1905–82, and Manfred Bennington Lee, US, 1905–71) Dannay and Lee, cousins, began writing in the 1920s as Ellery Queen, pseudonymous author and, as Inspector Queen, protagonist of their many stories. Begin with *The American Gun Mystery* (1933), set in the world of modern rodeos, which typifies their work in setting a puzzle which an astute reader may solve from information provided. In *The King is Dead* (1952) Queen has a dangerous brush with the secret services during a murder investigation. *Double Double* (1950) finds Inspector Queen in a small New England town after he receives a press cutting concerning the death of an eldery eccentric. In 1941 Dannay and Lee founded *Ellery Queen's Mystery Magazine*, which became the major forum for shorter crime fiction until it ceased publication in 1982.

Dashiell Hammett, Raymond Chandler   *DH*

R

Rabelais, François (French, c.1494–c.1553). *See* CLASSICS

Rampling, Anne. *See* **Rice, Anne**

Rand, Ayn (US, 1905–82) Born in Russia, Rand moved to America at the age of 21 where she founded a right-wing political philosophy she called 'objectivism' and which has much in common with contemporary libertarian movements, and capitalist liberalism generally. Her first truly science fiction novel was the short anti-communist polemic, *Anthem* (1938), which owes a great deal to several existing science fiction dystopias. It describes the loss of identity within a totalitarian collective, using a manipulation of language even more extreme than Orwell's 'newspeak', namely, the removal of singular pronouns. The considerably longer, near-future novel *Atlas Shrugged* (1957) tells of individualist entrepreneurs who withdraw their labour from an America which has succumbed to 'creeping socialism'. However you orientate yourself to the political implications of Rand's work, its moral verve and vivid sense of heroism demand admiration.

📖 Yevgeny Zamyatin, George Orwell, Aldous Huxley   *RP*

Rankin, Ian (British, 1960–) Ian Rankin has written non-series books and thrillers under the pseudonym of Jack Harvey, but his fast-growing reputation rests on the books featuring the maverick Scottish detective, Inspector John Rebus.

Rankin's laconic, often witty style was evident in the first Rebus book, *Knots and Crosses* (1987), but the author experimented with other characters and themes before returning to Rebus four years later. Since then, the series has gone from strength to strength and the complex and compelling *Black and Blue* (1997) won the CWA Macallan Gold Dagger. *The Hanging Garden* (1998) and *Dead Souls* (1999) were worthy successors and the series has been adapted for television. Rankin is also an accomplished writer of short stories and *A Good Hanging* (1992) is a crisp and entertaining collection of Rebus investigations.

📖 Reginald Hill, John Harvey.
See CRIME   *ME*

Rao, Raja (Indian, 1908–). *See* INDIA

Raphael, Frederic (US, 1931–) Born in Chicago, Frederic Raphael grew up in England and was educated at St John's College, Cambridge. Begin with *The Glittering Prizes* (1976), his acclaimed treatment of the lives of a group of Cambridge students in the years after graduation. The main protagonist's comically inept attempt to pursue a dynamic media career provides much of the entertainment. Raphael's versatility is suggested by the very different *Lindmann* (1963). Its experimental narrative deals movingly with a British civil servant's efforts to atone for his part in the sinking of a ship carrying Jewish refugees to Palestine in 1942. He goes about doing so by adopting the identity of one of the passengers on the voyage. Much of the action in *Like Men Betrayed* (1970) is set in Greece during the Second World War. It follows the career of military commander Artemis Theodoros, whose great abilities are wasted in Greece's confused political opportunism after the war. *Coast to Coast* (1998) follows an apparently contented middle-class couple on their drive across America to their son's wedding in Los Angeles. At every stop on their journey memories are triggered which force them to confront unresolved aspects of their pasts. The early novel, *The Limits of Love* (1960), deals with the psychological alienation of a disaffected Jew. As his isolation grows increasingly intolerable, he begins to renew his connections with the community of his upbringing.

📖 Howard Jacobson, Allan Massie, Saul Bellow   DH

Rathbone, Julian (British, 1935–). *See* HISTORICAL

Raven, Simon (British, 1927–) Raven was educated at Charterhouse school and Cambridge, and subsequently served in the army; these institutions have formed his fictional territory, in which the upper classes collide with bohemia, foreigners, and especially each other. Raven's fiction is organized into two novel sequences, *Alms for Oblivion* (10 novels, 1964–76) and *The First Born of Egypt* (7 novels, 1984–92), featuring a vast range of interconnected characters. Variously good, evil, weak, or merely unfortunate, they all revolve around the bisexual author, Fielding Gray, and the friends and acquaintances made at school and in the army. The first series begins with *The Rich Pay Late* (1964), centring

on political and business corruption, and ends in Venice with *The Survivors* (1976) and the impending marriage of scheming Lord Canteloupe to the psychic, sexually precocious Baby Llewellyn. The second series opens with *Morning Star* (1984) and concludes destructively in *The Troubadour* (1992), essentially working through the horrendous, though often comical consequences of their union. Raven's novels are crowded, addictive, and very entertaining, full of scandal, blackmail, murder, and sexual activity. The first series moves backwards and forwards in time, while the second is more sequential. Their appeal also lies in their architecture, their air of erudition, snobbery, and high camp, the pleasures of reading about the utterly immoral. Raven has also written two mock-Gothic works outside the sequences but featuring some of the same characters. The best is *September Castle* (1983).

📖 Anthony Powell, Evelyn Waugh, Hugh Walpole   JS

Rayner, Claire (British, 1931–) Claire Rayner was born and educated in London, then trained and worked as a nurse before starting her writing career. She is also well-known as a television agony aunt. Her fiction includes historical sagas and medical thrillers. Her style is straightforward, pacy, and narrative-driven and her books include much authentic background detail. Try *Jubilee* (1987), the first volume of *The Poppy Chronicles*, a family saga spanning the twentieth century. In *London Lodgings* (1994) the heroine opens a lodging-house in Victorian London, and her story continues in *Paying Guests* (1995). *Second Opinion* (1995) is typical of Claire Rayner's medical murder mysteries, in which a resident pathologist, the female Dr George Barnabas, acts as sleuth when there is a series of murders in her hospital.

📖 Patricia Cornwell, Harry Bowling, Maisie Mosco   *SA*

Read, Miss (British, 1913–) 'Miss Read' is the pseudonym of Dora Jessie Saint whose writing-career started with *Village School* (1955), since when she has written more than forty books, many of which have been collected into omnibus editions. Her novels and collections of short stories about the inhabitants of Thrush Green and Fairacre, are character studies of village people, their concerns and lives. Begin with *Encounters at Thrush Green* (1998), an omnibus edition of two Thrush Green books, and where we meet the village schoolmistress and her assistant on the verge of retirement, the village curmudgeon, Albert Piggott, and his long suffering wife, Molly, the village doctor, and assorted other characters.

📖 E. M. Delafield, Elizabeth Goudge
                                        IP

Read, Piers Paul (British, 1941–) Born in Beaconsfield, Buckinghamshire, Read was educated at Cambridge. Begin with *The Junkers* (1969) in which middle-class refinement and state-sanctioned brutality are chillingly compatible aspects of Germany during the Nazi era. *The Free Frenchman* (1986) is a treatment of divided loyalties within the French Resistance during the Second World War. Love is ultimately the greatest obstacle to the main character's pursuit of his ideals. *The Professor's Daughter* (1971) is set at the height of 1960s' student radicalism. It charts the breakdown of relationships in a family whose outward respectability is undermined by sexual promiscuity and psychological disorder. The main protagonist of *Monk Dawson* (1970), finding it impossible to maintain his values in a morally degenerate society, is driven by despair to enter a monastery.

📖 Graham Greene, Robert Goddard, Paul Theroux   *DH*

Reed, Ishmael (US, 1938–) Ishmael Reed emerged in the 1960s as one of black America's sharpest satirical voices, and has won awards for his poetry and cultural criticism as well as his wilfully subversive fiction. *Mumbo Jumbo* (1972) is Reed's most ambitious single novel, an account of the history of Black America in the form of a bizarre journey across the continent that takes in everything from voodoo and jazz to a critique of Black Muslim thought. *Flight to Canada* (1976) is a witty subversion of the traditional 'slave narrative' set during the American Civil War, and *Yellow Back Radio Broke Down* (1968) is an exuberantly surreal comic Western about a travelling circus centred on 'the Loop Garoo Kid', a hip black gunslinger in a town where the water supply is spiked with mind-altering drugs.

📖 Toni Morrison, Russell Banks, Caryl Phillips   *WB*

Reeman, Douglas (British, 1925–) Reeman was in the Royal Navy during the Second World War, first on a destroyer doing Atlantic convoy duty and later in motor torpedo boats. He then worked as a detective in London before becoming a full-time writer. He has used both experiences to produce thirty (to date) meticulously researched sea-going novels of the Second World War under his own name, and another twenty-one (recounting the adventures of Captain Richard Bolitho in the Napoleonic period) under the pseudonym **Alexander Kent**. Reeman has neither the flair of a C. S. Forester nor the psychological insight and style of a Patrick O'Brian but his books are exciting and, for the addict, what they arguably lack in literary quality they make up for in sheer quantity.

📖 C. S. Forester, Patrick O'Brian, Nicholas Monsarrat   *MH*

Reid, V. S. (Jamaican, 1913–87). *See* CARIBBEAN

Remarque, Erich Maria (German, 1898–1970) Remarque served as a soldier in the German army in the First World War. The war disgusted him, and he wrote *All Quiet on the Western Front* (1929), one of the great anti-war books of all time. The writing is simple and completely gripping. It tells the story of Paul Bäumer and his friends, young German men who are encouraged by their teachers and parents to fight in the war. They very quickly become disillusioned, and the novel describes the real conditions of trench warfare in graphic and horrible detail. Although the story is told in the first person, it is not an autobiography. Remarque based the book on the experiences of people he knew. He also drew some of his material from the very first novel to criticize the war, *Under Fire (Le Feu)*, published by **Henri Barbusse** in 1916. The original translation of *All Quiet* by A. W. Wheen is still the best. When the Nazis came to power in Germany in 1933, *All Quiet* was one of the books they burned. It is a brilliant novel and still a great read.

📖 Robert Graves, Siegfried Sassoon, Pat Barker. *See* GERMANY, WAR   *TT*

Renault, Mary (British, 1905–83) Born in West Ham, London, and educated at St Hugh's College, Oxford, Mary Renault is best known for her historical novels vividly evoking life in ancient Greece. Begin with *The Last of the Wine* (1956), the story of the lovers Alexias and Lysis and their roles in the Peloponnesian war. Socrates and Plato are among the characters encountered in the headily democratic atmosphere of Athens following the defeat of Sparta. *The King Must Die* (1958) and *The Bull from the Sea* (1962) retell the legend of Theseus. *The Mask of Apollo* (1966) is based on the life of Dion of Syracuse (408–354 BC). Told by the actor Nikeratos, it provides a detailed account of theatrical life in the period. Alexander the Great is the subject of her impressive trilogy chronicling his life from boyhood to death. It consists of *Fire from Heaven* (1969), *The Persian Boy* (1972), and *Funeral Games* (1981).

📖 Robert Graves, Naomi Mitchison, Allan Massie. *See* HISTORICAL   *DH*

Rendell, Ruth (British, 1930–) Ruth Rendell is unique among British crime writers. No one can equal her range or her accomplishment; she has won every major award, at home and abroad. Since she published the first Inspector Wexford novel, *From Doom with Death* in 1964, she has demonstrated that the genre can continually reinvent itself, assuming new concerns and exploring new ways of telling stories. Her work falls into three broad strands—the Wexford novels, the psychological Ruth Rendell novels, and the psychological suspense novels written as **Barbara Vine**. The Wexfords are mostly set in fictional Kingsmarkham, and reflect the changes wrought on a small Home

Counties town over the passage of time, painting a picture of British society since the mid-1960s that is far from neutral. The non-Wexford Rendells demonstrate a keen interest in the collision between society and the individual. What interests her is the reality behind surfaces and what happens when outside events trigger internal seismic changes. She has a keen understanding of the power of sexuality and how it can be perverted. With the Barbara Vines, she demonstrates a fascination for the long shadows that the past casts over the present. All three series show a keen sense of place and how environment can shape events. Her best work includes the Wexford novel *A Sleeping Life* (1978), the non-Wexford *A Demon in My View* (1976), and the Barbara Vine novels *A Dark-Adapted Eye* (1986) and *No Night is Too Long* (1994).

📖 Minette Walters, Reginald Hill, Patricia Highsmith. *See* CRIME, THRILLERS   *VM*

Rhinehart, Luke (US, 1932–)

Rhinehart, who trained as a psychologist, is best known for his comic novel *The Dice Man* (1972), which quickly established a cult following and has been reprinted twenty-seven times. The novel, which begins with the tone and detail of a realist narrative but becomes more fantasy-driven as it goes on, is a satirical account of trends in American psychiatry. Told from the point of view of 'Luke Rhinehart', a bored psychoanalyst, it describes how, acting on a drunken impulse, he begins to make decisions on the throw of a die. Pleased by the moral, sexual, and social liberation these random choices give him, 'Rhinehart' continues to consult the dice, basing a new therapy on the idea as his own

life disintegrates. Rhinehart has written several other novels, including *The Search for the Dice Man* (1993). He is a teacher of Zen.

📖 Bret Easton Ellis, Jay McInerney
                                                         SR

Rhodes, Eugene Manlove (US, 1869– 1934). *See* WESTERN

Rhys, Jean (Caribbean/British, 1890– 1979)

Jean Rhys was born to a Creole mother and a Welsh-born doctor on the island of Dominica. This inheritance gave her the sense of being a permanent outsider and led her to partially identify with the internally divided, black community of her childhood. Her early novel, and perhaps the best work to start with, is *Quartet* (1928) which describes how Marya Zelli, attractive and vulnerable, meets and marries an older Polish man. When he is arrested, Marya drifts around Paris to be taken up by an English couple. Marya is a jazz-age flapper poisoned by the exigencies of life itself. Rhys once said 'I only ever write about myself', and two other novels of this period, *Good Morning, Midnight* (1939), and *Voyage in the Dark* (1934), both deal with disorientation and dispossession of women. In the first, the heroine reviews her life from the safety of retreating to Paris. In the latter, the 19-year-old Anna Morgan leaves Dominica and tries to come to terms with her life in England. Rhys's most famous novel is *Wide Sargasso Sea* (1966), a retelling of Charlotte Brontë's *Jane Eyre* from the perspective of Rochester's first wife, Bertha. Rhys's Bertha becomes the focus of unbearable cultural tensions and the book is therefore a critique of the way colonialism devastates the values and traditions of the cultures it invades. *Wide Sargasso Sea* is compelling and deeply moving.

📖 Jamaica Kincaid, Anita Desai.
See CARIBBEAN   LM

Rice, Anne (US, 1941–) Born in New Orleans, Rice is best known for her enormously successful *Vampire Chronicles*. The first, *Interview with the Vampire* (1976), is the story of a guilt-ridden vampire's 300-year history focused on his time with Lestat, an undead libertine whose thirst for sensation is matched only by his thirst for blood. The novel was followed by six further instalments, including *The Vampire Lestat* (1985) and *The Queen of the Damned* (1988). Lushly descriptive, and often incorporating events from Rice's own life, such as fears of alcoholism and the deaths of her mother and daughter, Rice's *Chronicles* are authentic Gothic novels reinvented in a popular form. Rice has also written a series known as the *Lives of the Mayfair Witches*, which includes *The Witching Hour* (1990), and under the pseudonyms **Anne Rampling** and **A. N. Roquelaure**.

📖 Bram Stoker, Stephen King   WB

Rice, Elmer (US, 1892–1967) Rice is best known for his plays. He trained as a lawyer and used his legal expertise in his first dramatic success, *On Trial* (1914), which made original use of a flashback technique. He used expressionism again in his best play, *The Adding Machine* (1923), in which the symbolically named Mr Zero is driven to madness and murder by the mechanized conditioning of society. In 1935 he joined the radical Federal Theatre Project and his plays of this period show the dramatist struggling to come to terms with the social nightmare of the Great Depression. Rice's first novel *A Voyage to*

Purilia (1930), on the subject of his experiences in Hollywood, reveals his gift for satire, while *The Show Must Go on* (1949) draws on his life in the theatre.

📖 John Dos Passos, Upton Sinclair
                                   GK

Richards, David Adams (Canadian, 1950–). *See* CANADA

Richardson, Dorothy (British, 1873–1957) Dorothy Richardson wrote one of the longest novels in English. *Pilgrimage* (1915–38) is an autobiographical account of a young woman whose wealthy family loses all its money. At the age of 17 she sets off to make her own living, first as a teacher in Germany, then as a dental secretary in London. The novel celebrates the freedom of city life in the 1890s as Miriam Henderson learns about politics, work, and love. Eventually she leaves London to spend time with a Quaker community and prepares herself to write the novel that will become *Pilgrimage*. The novel is atmospheric, and was the first book ever to be described as 'stream of consciousness'. It tells Miriam's thoughts and perceptions as well as her actions and can be slow-moving in parts. It was written as thirteen separate books (collected in four volumes). Most readers prefer the first four or five books and a later book, *Oberland* (1927), which has a marvellous account of living in a small Swiss village in winter. For an easy introduction to Richardson, try her short stories and autobiographical sketches, collected as *Journey to Paradise* (1989).

📖 Djuna Barnes, Jean Rhys, Virginia Woolf   TT

Richardson, Samuel (British, 1689–1761) Samuel Richardson received little formal education, though by the age of 13 is reputed to have gained employment writing letters on behalf of young lovers. He was apprenticed to the print trade, and later successfully set up his own printing business. A manual of 'correct-style' in letter-writing served as the blueprint for his first and most popular novel, *Pamela* (1739–40), the story, told entirely through letters sent between the various characters, of a serving-girl whose refusal of her master's advances result in her eventual reward through marriage. *Clarissa* (1747–8) is a complex psychological study centred on a young woman's rape, and although at first considered 'indecent' in England, achieved great influence in Europe. *Sir Charles Grandison* (1753–4) portrays a 'good man' choosing between two women, though its extreme length has meant that it is now little read.

📖 Henry Fielding   *WB*

Richler, Mordecai (Canadian, 1931–) Born in Montreal, Richler is often regarded as a black humorist, but his novels have a far greater range and depth of social commentary than that term implies. He both celebrates and satirizes the Jewish experience in Canada, and his work is full of pungently funny dialogue and politically incorrect observations. *The Apprenticeship of Duddy Kravitz* (1959), described by its author as the adventures of a teenage, working-class Jewish kid on the make in Montreal around 1949, is a modern classic. Duddy's rise and fall in business, as he schemes to buy land and exploits everyone around him, is rendered with both comedy and pathos; he encounters anti-Semitism and Jewish chauvinism. Richler lived in London during the 1960s, producing *The Incomparable Atuk* (1963), in which an Eskimo poet becomes a short-lived media celebrity, and *Cocksure* (1968), featuring a mysterious, surgically enhanced tycoon. Both are short novels with a gallery of outlandish types and numerous satirical targets. Richler's fascination with Jewish-Canadian entrepreneurs resulted eventually in larger-scale works; *Solomon Gursky was Here* (1989) tells the story of the Gurskys from the 1850s onward against the background of Canada's development as a nation. His later novel, *Barney's Version* (1997), is structured around the three marriages of Barney Panofsky, a television producer with Alzheimer's disease. It manages to be both poignant and —as when Barney leaves his own wedding reception to pursue another woman— wildly funny.

📖 Philip Roth, Joseph Heller   *JS*

Ridpath, Michael (British, 1961–) Ridpath was born in Devon, and educated at Oxford before becoming a bond trader on the London stock exchange. He has been a full-time writer since 1995. Begin with *Free to Trade* (1995), in which a young man in a high profile firm of stockbrokers penetrates a web of corruption after the death of a female colleague. In *Trading Reality* (1996) an advance in virtual reality technology threatens to put big firms out of business. Its discoverer is murdered and his stockbroker brother begins piecing together an explanation. A disillusioned academic turns to bond trading in *The Marketmaker* (1998). He comes up against the power of the one man who seems to control the entire South American market.

📖 John Grisham, Ross Thomas   *DH*

Riley, Joan (British, 1958–) Riley was born in St Mary, Jamaica, educated at the universities of Sussex and London, and began working for welfare agencies in London in 1983. Begin with *The Unbelonging* (1985), characteristic of her work in its treatment of a woman's experiences after emigrating to England from the Caribbean. The book's 11-year-old heroine takes refuge from racism and her father's violent abuse by immersing herself in her education. *Waiting in the Twilight* (1987) tells the story of Adela, who leaves her home and her children in Jamaica to join her husband in Britain after the Second World War. Desiree and Verona, the sisters at the centre of *Romance* (1988), find their complacency challenged when visitors from Jamaica renew the sisters' contact with their origins. Set in Jamaica, *A Kindness to the Children* (1992) finds the lives of three women fatefully converging as each is forced into a confrontation with her past.

📖 Rosa Guy, Ntokaze Shange, Olive Senior   *DH*

Robbins, Harold (US, 1912–97) Harold Robbins made his name in the 1950s as the author of a string of best-sellers about the seamy side of American life, and *A Stone for Danny Fisher* (1955), the story of the descent into crime of a promising championship boxer, later adapted for film as the Elvis Presley vehicle *King Creole*, remains widely regarded as Robbins's single best novel. More typical is *79 Park Avenue* (1955), a story about a high-class call girl in New York. *The Carpetbaggers* (1961), a tale about the decadent lifestyles of the rich, marks a change of focus from pulp to high gloss in Robbins's books, and *The Betsy* (1971), a glamorous, big-business story about an inventor's fight to put his dream car into commercial production, and *Memories of Another Day*

(1979), the rags-to-riches tale of a poor Midwesterner making it as a powerful union boss, are both representative of Robbins's later work.

📖 Arthur Hailey, Mario Puzo   *WB*

Robbins, Tom (US, 1936–) Born in North Carolina, Tom Robbins studied art, drama, and music before turning his hand to surreal comic fiction. His most celebrated book is *Even Cowgirls Get the Blues* (1976), an irreverent Western about Sissy Hankshaw, a woman whose oversized thumb grants her Zen-like hitch-hiking powers, and her involvement with a cosmetics manufacturer and a gang of rebellious cowgirls. *Another Roadside Attraction* (1971) is set at a combination burger-bar, zoo, and flea-circus where a drummer and an ex-clairvoyant meet against a background of motorcycles, soft drugs, and whimsical philosophy to discover their fates. *Jitterbug Perfume* (1984) is a tale about a janitor in possession of a leaky bottle rumoured to contain the elixir of life. Robbins's cult combination of folksy wisdom and psychedelic story-telling has appealed to wide audiences in recent years.

📖 Ishmael Reed, Richard Brautigan, Robert M. Pirsig   *WB*

Roberts, Michèle (British/French, 1949–) Roberts's novels and stories are distinctive for the poetic sensuous quality of her writing, and for her feminist exploration of women's lives, particularly the mother–daughter relationship. Religion is also an important theme. She is always inventive with structure, using multiple narrative voices and telling stories within stories. Begin with *In the Red Kitchen* (1990), a powerful, immediate novel about four women in three different times, ancient

Egypt, Victorian England, and present-day London, linked via a woman claiming to be a medium. In *Daughters of the House* (1992), which was Booker Prize-shortlisted, two cousins, Léonie and Thérèse, are together again in Léonie's house in France where Thérèse (now a nun) grew up. The house is alive with family memories and secrets and a scandal dating back to wartime Nazi occupation. The past is unravelled little by little, and along the way there are lovingly vivid descriptions of household objects, and particularly (as often in Roberts's work) of mouth-watering food. *Flesh and Blood* (1994) tells stories within stories, like a set of Russian dolls, as its narrator (on the run after murdering his mother) changes sex and identity and moves back through time. In *Fair Exchange* (1999) two women who are peripheral to the lives of Mary Wollstonecraft and Wordsworth are centre stage, waiting together in an old French convent for their babies to be born. Roberts also writes poetry.

📖 Angela Carter, Sara Maitland, Virginia Woolf. *See* SEXUAL POLITICS   *JR*

Robinson, Derek (British, 1932–) Robinson writes authentically about air wars in which he was too young to have fought. His best work occupies the intellectual no man's land between genre fiction and serious literature, which is probably why he has not had the recognition he deserves, although *Goshawk Squadron* (1971), the second novel in a trilogy about a brutal RFC squadron leader bullying callow pilots into survival, was shortlisted for the Booker Prize. His masterpiece, though, is *Piece of Cake* (1983), a revisionist take on that great British myth, the Battle of Britain. He describes death, wounding, and burning in brutal anatomical detail, shows his class-ridden, public-school 'knights of the air' deliberately shooting down their own (incompetent) squadron leader, killing parachuting German pilots, and pissing in their cockpits in sheer terror, but never loses sight of their bravery or humanity.

📖 Joseph Heller, H. E. Bates. *See* WAR   *MH*

Robinson, Kim Stanley (US, 1952–) The *Mars* trilogy, *Red Mars* (1992), *Green Mars* (1994), and *Blue Mars* (1997), re-established the credibility of science fiction set in space. In dealing with the colonization of another planet, Robinson raises major issues of our time—politics, economics, and the impact of technological decisions on human welfare. The three novels can be read independently but are more satisfying read in sequence. The scale of Robinson's achievement in imagining a whole history of a planet has been recognized by all the major science fiction prizes. Enjoyable for their lyrical descriptions of Martian landscapes and understanding of the way political factions manœuvre, the books will appeal to those who like topical thrillers as well as to traditional science fiction readers. *Antarctica* (1997) brings political debate closer to home, in an adventure story which explores green issues in the last wilderness on earth.

📖 Ray Bradbury, Philip K. Dick, Arthur C. Clarke   *RV*

Roche, Mazo de la (Canadian, 1885–1961) Mazo de la Roche is best known for her Whiteoaks family saga. Dominated by a fierce matriarch with a parrot, the family, while coming in for its share of romantic drama, is often shown as comic and ridiculous. *Jalna* (1927) is the best place to start. Introducing the six Whiteoak siblings, it chronicles their romantic entanglements and ends with Grandmother Adeline's hundredth birthday party. After that, it's a matter of working forward through the sixteen books. *Finch's Fortune* (1931) is about the melancholy, musical fourth brother. *The Building of Jalna* (1944) recalls the first Whiteoak coming to Ontario. *Mary Wakefield* (1949) is about the 'poor pretty flibbertigibbet mother' of the four youngest brothers; and in *Return to Jalna* (1949) a younger generation embarks upon adventures of its own. With all its intrigues and reversals, the rambling chronicle of a communal dynasty on a great country estate foreshadowed modern American soap opera.

📖 Catherine Cookson, Rosamunde Pilcher, Vikram Seth. *See* FAMILY SAGA   CB

Rodi, Robert (US) Rodi is notable for the humorous lightness of touch and occasional farcicality with which he handles gay themes. Begin with *Closet Case* (1993), in which an advertising executive is leading a double life. Cowed into pretences of convention by homophobia in his workplace, he indulges in wild gay socializing by night. In *Drag Queen* (1995), the revelation that he has a twin brother throws a discreetly gay professional's life into chaos. His embarrassment that the twin is a drag artist fades as his perspectives broaden. *Kept Boy* (1997) is the story of a man in his thirties who has long been the companion of a Chicago theatrical impresario. Anxieties over age and identity beset the hero as he begins to suspect he is losing his charms.

📖 Alan Hollinghurst, Michael Cunningham   DH

Rogers, Jane (British, 1952–) Start with *Mr Wroe's Virgins* (1991), the remarkable, true story of a nineteenth-century prophet who announces to his congregation that they should give him seven virgins for his 'comfort and succour'. The story is told by four of the virgins, including the brutalized, inarticulate Martha, and allows the question of whether Mr Wroe is a visionary or a charlatan to remain mysterious. While Rogers never tackles the same territory twice, the character who is deprived and/or inarticulate features repeatedly in her work, as does the visionary. In *Promised Lands* (1995, Writers' Guild best novel award) the sense of vision connects two very different narratives, one in Australia in 1788 and the other in the present. In *Island* (1999) a young woman's plot to murder her mother leads her to a surprisingly magical place.

📖 Margaret Atwood, Hilary Mantel
                                    LM

Rohan, Michael Scott (British, 1951–). *See* FANTASY

Roquelaure, A. N. *See* **Rice, Anne**

Rossner, Judith (US, 1935–) Rossner has lived in New York all her life. Perhaps her most renowned novel, *Looking for Mr Goodbar* (1975), is about Theresa Dunn, a teacher by day, and Terry, her alter ego, who cruises bars at night. Mr Goodbar's is one of her haunts. Rossner's novel is both a pithy exploration of failing relationships and a study of 'women's fluctuating roles across generations'. Different generations of women also feature in *Perfidia* (1997), in which Rossner examines a smotheringly close mother–daughter relationship. It is set in 1974. Anita Stein leaves her husband

and moves to Santa Fe with her 5-year-old daughter. Anita's relationship to her daughter is complicated by the arrival of her second child, a son.

📖 Vladimir Nabokov, Anne Tyler, Colette   CJ

Roth, Henry (US, 1906–95) Apart from a collection of short stories, Roth's only published work for sixty years was his autobiographical novel *Call It Sleep* (1934). This remarkable work tells the story of David, the son of Jewish immigrants in the Lower East Side of New York. The novel is linguistically rich; although on the one hand it is an often comic depiction of a vanished world, it is also the story of a young man growing up among family mysteries and feuds. In 1944 Roth published the first two volumes of a sequence of autobiographical novels; a posthumous novel, *From Bondage*, which also drew on his own experiences, appeared in 1995.

📖 James Joyce, Isaac Bashevis Singer, Mark Twain   SV

Roth, Joseph (Austrian, 1894–1939). *See* GERMANY

Roth, Philip (US, 1933–) Roth was born in Newark, New Jersey. His work has developed from satirical outrages and Kafka-like fantasies to the fictionalizing of post-war American history. He is both a popular and serious novelist, whose consistent themes are Jewishness and masculinity. Roth's debut collection of stories, *Goodbye, Columbus* (1959), proved controversial, portraying conflicts around traditional values within Jewish families, as in 'Eli, the Fanatic', and their accommodation to mainstream America. *Portnoy's Complaint* (1969) was an international best-seller, and it remains one of the funniest books of its era. It takes the form of Alex Portnoy's fantasies, jokes, and confessions to a psychiatrist about compulsive masturbation and later sexual addictions, originating in his Jewish family life. The comic energy of the satire is still fresh even though its explicitness now seems rather tame. *The Professor of Desire* (1977) signalled a greater seriousness, as Professor David Kepesh travels to Prague in search of Kafka's grave, meets writers living under Communism, and contemplates his Jewish roots. Roth has also written a series of novels featuring a successful author, Nathan Zuckerman, at various stages of his life. In *The Ghost Writer* (1979), he stays the night at the home of his mentor E. I. Lonoff, and fantasizes that the student he meets there is the surviving Anne Frank. *I Married a Communist* (1998) is an absorbing novel about personal and political betrayal, set in the McCarthyite era of blacklisting. It finds Zuckerman as a 65-year-old, listening to his former teacher tell the full story of activist Ira Ringold's life and death. The Pulitzer Prize-winning *American Pastoral* (1997), one of Roth's most brilliant and gripping novels, goes back to the 1960s and places its well-meaning Jewish hero, 'Swede' Lvov, at the very centre of everything that was most violent, berserk, and alarming in the politics and society of the time.

📖 Saul Bellow, Mordecai Richler, Milan Kundera   JS

Rouand, Jean (French, 1953–). *See* FRANCE

Roy, Arundhati (Indian, 1961–) Arundhati Roy broke through from nowhere to win the Booker Prize in 1997 with her first novel, *The God of Small Things*. Its rich and pungent descriptions will take you to an India off the tourist track, rural Kerala in 1969. The story explores the complex intricacies of a family collapse. You know something terrible has happened almost from the first page but the flashback structure means you have to read to the end to find out what. The sense of foreboding travels with you throughout the book and lingers after you've fitted the pieces together. Roy's style is fresh and unexpected—lyrical one moment, barbed digs at hypocrisy the next, with a wide frame of cultural reference—Karl Marx, *The Sound of Music*, and the Bible Society.

📖 Kate Atkinson, Roddy Doyle, R. K. Narayan. *See* INDIA   RV

Rubens, Bernice (British, 1928–   ) Born in Cardiff and educated at the University of Wales, Rubens's other career was in film-making. Psychologically interesting, her novels often deal with loneliness, rejection, bleak private worlds, and she is adept at mixing tragedy and comedy. She often writes about Jewish characters. Begin with *The Elected Member* (1969). Norman, a barrister, is also a drug addict. His mind and relationships are gradually destroyed and he is committed to a mental hospital, seeing himself as the family scapegoat. This compassionate novel won the Booker Prize. Move to *Go Tell the Lemming* (1973), in which Angela Morrow experiences two reversals—her husband's betrayal, and then his change of heart when, bored with his mistress, he invites her to work on his new film on location in Rome. Love and hate are mingled; social politeness is a veneer.

Next read *Mr Wakefield's Crusade* (1985), a first-person narrative, beginning with a dead man's letter opened by Luke Wakefield, leading him into hilarious amateur detective work and obsession with a murdered wife. Go on to *Our Father* (1987): Veronica Smiles, an explorer, returning to the family home in Surbiton, is drawn to search her own background; different kinds of revelation arise from peeling off the layers. Humour and grief are in perfect balance. Highly recommended, *The Waiting Game* (1997) deals with old age, a home, and its residents. Funny and poignant, its underlying theme is survival.

📖 Beryl Bainbridge, Alice Thomas Ellis, Philip Roth   GC

Rucker, Rudy (US, 1946–   ) Rucker is a professor of mathematics and a founding father, with William Gibson and Neal Stephenson, of 'Cyber-punk' science fiction. He has published eight novels (and several works of non-fiction that operate in that imaginatively fertile area in which higher mathematics, particle physics, and relativity part company with common sense). He won the Philip K. Dick award for both *Software* (1982) and *Wetware* (1988), the first two parts of a wonderfully insane comic novel sequence in which sentient robots (Boppers) blend with humans (Meat-Bops) to create all manner of crazy miscegenated hybrids with attendant sexual, political, and philosophical problems. Rucker is no respecter of taboos, or proprieties (fictional or otherwise), and pushes science fiction into areas H. G. Wells could only have imagined in his most Freudian nightmares. You will either love him or loathe him.

📖 William Gibson, Neal Stephenson, Philip K. Dick   MH

Rulfo,   Juan (Mexican, 1918–86). *See* MAGIC REALISM

Runyon, Damon (US, 1884–1946) Runyon was born in Kansas but is indelibly linked with the *demi-monde* of gangsters and performers who worked on Broadway. Indeed, Runyon's ashes were scattered over Broadway from a plane piloted by the famous air ace, Eddie Rickenbacker. In both his syndicated journalism and his fiction, Runyon captured his era's fascination with celebrity and display. His stories *Guys and Dolls* (1932) and *More Than Somewhat* (1937) were instant best-sellers. The stories centre around the narrator's wary involvement with such luminaries as Harry the Horse, Dave the Dude, and Izzy the Cheesecake. Runyon created an idiosyncratic slang remarkable for its immediacy and its use of extravagant metaphor. His narratives are controlled by a precise and comic use of the historical present. The darker side of Runyon's world can be seen in 'The Informal Execution of Soupbone Pew' in *Runyon First and Last* (1949).

📖 Anita Loos, P. G. Wodehouse
GK

Rushdie, Salman (British, 1947–) Rushdie was born into a Muslim family in Bombay, and educated in England; his family joined the Muslim exodus to Pakistan in 1964. He is a richly inventive writer who straddles cultures and draws on the traditions of both East and West. Start with *Midnight's Children* (1981, Booker Prize), which established him as the voice of post-colonial India. Saleem Sinai, one of the children born with India's independence at midnight on 15 August 1947, tells stories to his bride-to-be. Panoramic and chaotic, *Midnight's Children* demonstrates how history evolves through the telling of countless stories, none of which

is infallible. *Shame* (1983) has a similar sense of the unreliability of fixed versions. Omar Khayyam, another bi-cultural narrator, recounts events in a fictional Pakistan where the central characters echo Bhutto and General Zia. Set 'at a slight angle to reality', *Shame*'s exaggerations convey the preposterousness of life in this problematic nation.

After this, try *The Satanic Verses* (1988), the book which earned the author a death sentence from the Ayatollah Khomeini, on the grounds of blasphemy against Islam. Rushdie's magic realism reaches full flower in this huge erudite novel. Two men, Gibreel Farishta and Saladin Chamcha, fall from the sky over the British Channel after their plane explodes. On the way down they begin to transform, Farishta developing a halo, Chamcha hooves and horns. A series of metamorphoses and visions ensue, which are comic and witty, exploring faith and deception, appearance and reality, fame, migration, and colonialism in a modern multicultural whirlpool that twists and turns on itself.

📖 Gabriel García Márquez, Günter Grass, V. S. Naipaul, Mikhail Bulgakov. *See* INDIA, MAGIC REALISM
CB

Russ, Joanna (US, 1937–) Joanna Russ has written science fiction and non-fiction on feminist issues. In her science fiction her female characters liberate themselves through acts of dramatic courage. Marriage is an institution Russ has frequently chosen to attack. She won a Nebula award for *When It Changed* (1972) and a Hugo award for *Souls* (1983). In her novel *The Female Man* (1975) Russ creates five concurrent realities; in one, women lose their fight for equality, but gain by becoming female men. In another world, women exist through men, and gain their freedom from social constraint through fantasizing. In one future world, women wage biological war on men, and in another, men are dismissed as simply aliens and women's needs are met with few constraints. Russ envisages a range of possibilities for women, where they can all be heroines.

📖 Marge Piercy, Ursula Le Guin, Ian Watson. *See* SCIENCE FICTION

LM

Rybakov, Anatoly (Soviet/Russian, 1911–). *See* RUSSIA

S

Sagan, Carl (US, 1934–96).
See SCIENCE FICTION

Sagan, Françoise (French, 1935–)
Sagan has written a number of plays as well
as several novels. Her first novel, *Bonjour
Tristesse* (1954), published when Sagan
was just 19, explores the inner world of a
teenage girl as she begins to experience
sexual desire. Sagan's style is minimalist,
using everyday speech, and may appear
to be simple. Yet it enables the reader to
recognize the deep-seated emotions and
desires that lie behind everyday actions
and conventions. Many of her novels are
concerned with the ways in which middle-
class life constrains the expression of love,
particularly for women. In *Aimez-vous
Brahms* (1966) for example, the heroine is
torn between a stable yet unfulfilling and
a passionate yet unstable relationship. In
Wonderful Clouds (1961), Sagan explores
the powerful use of emotional blackmail
by a young American who is obsessively
jealous of his Parisian wife.

📖 Colette, Amy Bloom,
Marguerite Duras   DJ

Sahgal, Nayantara (Indian, 1927–).
See INDIA

St Aubin de Teran, Lisa (British,
1953–) St Aubin de Teran's life has provided the material for much of her fiction;
at 16 she left school to marry an exiled
Venezuelan landowner; after two years in
Italy they returned to his family estates in
the Andes, where she managed his sugar
plantation and avocado farm for seven
years, while his mental health deteriorated. She escaped to Norfolk, and now
lives in Italy. Start with her first novel,
Keepers of the House (1982), which is based
on the South American experience. In
Nocturne (1992), set in 1930s Italy, village
boy Mezzanotte falls in love with a girl
from a travelling fair; then comes the war;
and in the 1990s a young soldier becomes
the confidant of the horribly wounded
old soldier Mezzanotte, and learns the
rest of his haunting story. Time and place
are beautifully conjured here. *Southpaw*
(1999) is a collection of stories, many of
them spiced with South American magic
realism.

📖 Louis de Bernières, Isabel Allende
                                    JR

Saint-Exupéry, Antoine de (French,
1900–44) Saint-Exupéry led a life crammed
with more romantic adventure than most
fictional heroes. A pioneer aviator in the
days when flying depended as much on
guts and instinct as on instruments, he
was among the first to depict not only the
perils of flight but also its ethereal poetry.
Night Flight (1932) tells of carrying the
mails over the Andes peaks and jungles of
Brazil, while *Wind, Sand and Stars* (1929)
deals with his experiences as a courier in
remote desert regions. In *Flight to Arras*
(1942), the hero undertakes a near-suicidal
mission during the fall of France, May
1940. Exciting action apart, the books are

meditations on the nature of courage. Saint-Exupéry also wrote a very popular children's story, *The Little Prince* (1943), about a crashed pilot's encounter with a boy from another planet. The author himself disappeared on a flight in the final months of the war.

📖 Albert Camus, André Malraux, Elias Canetti   *TH*

St Omer, Garth (Caribbean, 1931–   ). *See* CARIBBEAN

Saki (British, 1870–1916) Although Hector Hugh Munro, better known as Saki, wrote two novels, *The Unbearable Bassington* (1912) and *When William Came* (1913), his reputation stems from his mastery of the short story. Witty and erudite, Saki's stories expose the absurdities of the English Edwardian upper classes. Many of his stories originally appeared in newspapers like the *Daily Express* and the *Westminster Gazette*. His first collection, *Reginald* (1904), reveals the satirical musings of the irreverent Reginald as he reluctantly attends a garden party with a pompous colonel, and in another story the theatre with a vague, superficial duchess. One of Saki's most poignant stories, 'Sredni Vashtar', included in his third collection, *The Chronicles of Clovis* (1911) demonstrates his quite extraordinary empathy for children who are bullied by domineering adults. Saki was killed by a sniper while serving in the 22nd Royal Fusiliers in the First World War.

📖 Anton Chekhov, O. Henry   *EW*

Saleh, Tayeb (alternative spelling: **Salih, al-Tayyib**) (Sudanese, 1929–   ) Born in the north of Sudan, Tayeb Saleh studied at London University and later became Head of Drama in the Arabic Service of the BBC. His novel *Season of Migration to the North* (1971) has been described as one of 'the six finest novels in modern Arabic literature' and as 'an Arabian Nights in reverse'. In it an unnamed narrator recounts his meeting with Mustafa Saeed who has been a brilliant student and lecturer in Britain. But Mustafa Saeed has been imprisoned for killing his female lovers; killing them at climax of sex. Put like this, *Season of Migration to the North* seems like an exotic penny dreadful. In fact, it is a masterpiece about the contradictions of colonialism and post-colonialism written in a supple and hypnotic prose, brilliantly translated by Denys Johnson-Davies.

📖 Naguib Mahfouz, Abdulrazak Gurnah   *IP*

Salinger, J(erome) D(avid) (US, 1919–   ) J. D. Salinger was born in New York and educated at New York University and Columbia University. He has written both short stories and novels, but is best known for his first novel, *The Catcher in the Rye* (1951), which has achieved huge success. The novel's narrator, Holden Caulfield, leaves his prep school three days early, wanting to put off the moment when his parents discover he's been kicked out again. Alone, he survives in New York, moving from hotel to theatre, from Radio City Music Hall to Central Park. The novel is trenchantly satirical, extremely funny, and Holden's teenage slang is a remarkably effective tool for laying bare the hypocrisies of New York society. Salinger's other writing is chiefly concerned with the Glass family, and we meet them in *Franny and Zooey* (1961). Also set in New York, these stories again focus on young people at crisis point, who are starting to question the superficiality of the world they live in. The stories are narrated by Buddy Glass, the writer's self-confessed alter ego. Glass also narrates *Raise High the Roof Beam, Carpenters*, and *Seymour* (1963), stories about his brother Seymour's wedding, which results in a jilting and elopement, and then his suicide. Salinger now lives the life of a recluse, avoiding all publicity.

📖 Sylvia Plath, Mark Twain.
See CHILDHOOD, SHORT STORIES, TEEN, UNITED STATES OF AMERICA
SA

Salter, James (US, 1926–) Salter was born and raised in New York. As a young man he trained at West Point Military Academy then went on to become a fighter pilot. His first two novels, *The Hunters* (1956) and *Arms of Flesh* (1961), both deal with his experiences as a fighter pilot flying combat missions during the Korean War. Perhaps Salter's most renowned work, however, is *A Sport and a Pastime* (1967). The novel, which has been described as an 'erotic tour de force', features an American, Philip Dean—a Yale drop-out—and his stay in France where he seduces or 'educates' a local waitress, Anne-Marie Costallat. The story is told by a third character, a young student, who is in France for 'the season' and shares a house with Dean. This highly charged erotic novel traces the relationships in vibrant detail.

📖 Anais Nin, Henry Miller   *CJ*

Sand, George (French, 1804–76).
See FRANCE

Sapper (pen-name of Herman McNeile) (British 1888–1937). *See* SPY

Saramago, José (Portuguese, 1922–) Saramago's wide-ranging, meditative novels are powerful, often philosophical explorations of human nature and of society. Begin with *Blindness* (1995) which, opening with a description of a man abruptly losing his sight as a traffic light changes from red, is an allegorical portrait of a city struck by a growing epidemic. Chaos, distrust, and violence also spread as civilization gradually disintegrates. Move on to *The History of the Siege of Lisbon* (1989), where Raimundo Silva, a proofreader, challenges the veracity of a written account of the siege, illicitly altering the text. The novel raises questions about truth, history, and facts as the new interpretation Silva goes on to write is juxtaposed with his own story when he embarks upon a relationship with his editor. Saramago was awarded the Nobel Prize for Literature in 1998.

📖 Italo Calvino, Jorge Luis Borges, William Golding   *SR*

Saro-Wiwa, Ken (Nigerian, 1941–95) Saro-Wiwa was primarily a political writer, publicizing his tribe's battle with the Nigerian government over environmental and humanitarian issues through his poems, plays, stories, children's books, novels, and essays, believing that his work would 'enable the Ogoni people to confront their tormentors'. The author of over twenty books, an ex-teacher and businessman, he was also the writer and producer of the popular Nigerian sitcom, *Basi and Company*, a social satire banned in 1992. Begin with *A Month and a Day: A Detention Diary* (1995), a personal story posthumously published after he was hanged by the Nigerian administration. Move on to *A Forest of Flowers* (1986), stories which, systematically portraying individuals defeated by a range of social mechanisms, make a wider point about distrust, betrayal, and corruption in a community.

📖 Ben Okri, Wole Soyinka, William Boyd   SR

Sarton, May (US, 1912–95) Born in Belgium, Sarton was a novelist, poet, and teacher. She is also known for her autobiographical writings, particularly *Journal of a Solitude* (1973), written as a year's diary reflecting on depression and creativity. Her novels usually concern friendships between women, the discovery of their sexuality, and the importance of human dignity. In *The Magnificent Spinster* (1985), a writer re-creates the life of her recently deceased friend and former teacher. *The Education of Harriet Hatfield* (1989) addresses the issue of homophobia more directly in its story of a bereaved woman who opens a feminist bookstore, encountering local prejudice as well as support. *Mrs Stevens Hears the Mermaids Singing* (1965) depicts an elderly woman poet forced to review the sources of her creativity in her early marriage and subsequent lesbian relationships.

📖 Virginia Woolf, Elizabeth Bowen
                                          JS

Sartre, Jean-Paul (French, 1905–80) Sartre was a central figure in the French philosophical movement known as existentialism. A professor and writer of philosophy, he also used plays and novels to explore his philosophical ideas, arguing that existence is meaningless and that our concern should be what human beings can do in the face of the absurdity of their condition. In his first novel, *Nausea* (1938), the main character, Roquentin, confronts the purposelessness of his life and is stricken by nausea and a sense of alienation from his bourgeois world. He is forced to question his identity. For Sartre, this experience is the point at which human beings can see true freedom and make sincere choices about how to live an individual life. Yet Roquentin chooses the safe bourgeois world of convention and chooses (according to Sartre) 'inauthentically'. Sartre was a committed socialist and worked for the French Resistance. In *The Age of Reason* (1945), a professor of philosophy is obsessed with the idea of personal freedom. Individual lives are explored in the setting of Paris in 1938, with its nightclubs, galleries, students, café society, and the looming threat of war. This is the first in Sartre's *Roads to Freedom* trilogy, followed by *The Reprieve* (1945) and *Troubled Sleep* (1949) which depicts the fall of France in 1940 and the anguished response of individual French people to the German occupation.

📖 Albert Camus, Ian McEwan, Simone de Beauvoir. *See* FILM ADAPTATIONS   DJ

Sassoon, Siegfried (British, 1886–1967) Brought up in a Kent country house, educated at Marlborough and Cambridge, Sassoon volunteered in 1914. An officer at the Western Front, he was wounded, won an MC (which he threw away), and publicly protested against the conduct of the war, also publishing compassionate, ironic anti-war poetry. Instead of court-martial, he was sent for shell-shock treatment. After the war he wrote a semi-autobiographical trilogy in which, as 'George Sherston', he charts in detail his early life as a country gentleman, loving cricket, hunting, and golf, and his development during intensive war experience in

Memoirs of a Fox-Hunting Man (1928), *Memoirs of an Infantry Officer* (1930), and *Sherston's Progress* (1936). Three later volumes of autobiography, notably *The Old Century* (1938), relate his idyllic childhood and youth. Sassoon also wrote a biography of George Meredith, but is chiefly remembered for his war poetry.

📖 Henry Williamson, Robert Graves. *See* WAR   GC

Sayer, Paul (British, 1955–) Sayer worked as a nurse in a psychiatric hospital, and his first novel, *The Comforts of Madness* (1988, Whitbread Book of the Year), draws vividly on that experience. It is the interior monologue of a 33-year-old catatonic man in hospital, reflecting on his treatment, his memories, and the world around him, without sentiment. If you only read one Sayer novel, this should be it. Amongst his other novels dealing with social issues and mental instability is *The Absolution Game* (1992) about a social worker isolated by his own do-gooding, who attempts a relationship with a woman client, and finds a hostel place for a murderous boy. The novel charts the hero's mental disintegration in the grim town he has chosen for his work. *Men in Rage* (1999) traces a week in the life of an angry and murderous young man.

📖 Janet Frame, David Cook, Paul Bailey   JR

Sayers, Dorothy L(eigh) (British, 1893–1957) One of the first women to be granted a degree from Oxford, Sayers was a medieval scholar who completed a notable translation of Dante's *Divine Comedy* as well as establishing herself as second only to Agatha Christie in the Golden Age of the classic English mystery

novel in the 1920s and 1930s. Few writers provoke such extreme responses. In a recent poll of crime writers, Sayers' *The Nine Tailors* (1934) was voted the best Golden Age mystery; yet the critic Edmund Wilson called the same book 'one of the dullest . . . I have ever encountered in any field'. Admirers praise her erudition in the genre, craftsmanship, care with detail, and ability to expose failings in her society. Above all, they love her detective, the upper-class polymath Lord Peter Wimsey. Detractors find Sayers' work snobbish, long-winded and pretentious.

Begin with *Strong Poison* (1930); Wimsey is called on to exonerate mystery writer Harriet Vane who stands accused of poisoning her lover. Social attitudes in this novel are radical for their time and Sayers shows strong sympathy for Vane, whose main crime seems to be unconventional behaviour. Continue with *Murder Must Advertise* (1933) where Sayers' own experience in advertising provides the background for an undercover investigation by Wimsey; *The Nine Tailors*, with its English village background and carefully researched theme of church bell-ringing; and *Gaudy Night* (1935), a curiosity in the crime-writing field—a mystery without a murder.

📖 Agatha Christie, Margery Allingham, P. D. James. *See* CRIME   VM

Schaefer, Jack (US, 1907–91). *See* WESTERN

Schreiner, Olive (South African, 1855–1920) Born to white parents on a mission station, Schreiner spent the early years of her life working as a governess on remote karoo farms. Her most acclaimed work,

The Story of an African Farm (1883), is ground-breaking. Through the two main characters, Lyndall, desperate to be an independent woman, and Waldo, who searches for eternal truths, Schreiner challenges the status quo of late-nineteenth-century South Africa. She questions the tenets of colonialism, the institution of marriage, and the disintegration of religious faith. After a trip to England Schreiner became involved with the socialist and feminist movement. *Undine* (1929) and *From Man to Man* (1926) were published posthumously and continued to question the role of women in her society.

📖 Doris Lessing, Nadine Gordimer

EW

Scoppettone, Sandra (US, 1936–)

Sandra Scoppettone is the author of the crime series featuring lesbian private eye Lauren Laurano, an immensely likeable character whose life with her psychotherapist lover Kip concerns the reader as much as does her investigative work. Scoppettone writes fluently with witty dialogue and touching humour and creates an affectionate portrayal of life in the Greenwich Village area of New York. Friends Jenny and Jill and cop Peter Cecchi reappear in the books. In *I'll be Leaving You Always* (1994) Lauren's oldest friend Megan is found brutally murdered behind the counter of her jewellery store and as Lauren investigates she finds out how little she really knew about Megan. *Let's Face the Music and Die* (1997) has Lauren's friend Elissa as chief suspect for her aunt's murder and the relationship between Lauren and Kip in deep trouble. Sandra Scoppettone also uses the pseudonym **Jack Early** for mysteries she has written.

📖 Sara Paretsky, Val McDermid   *CS*

Scott, Lawrence (Trinidadian, 1943–   )

Scott trained as a Benedictine monk and then turned to writing fiction. His first novel, *Witchbroom* (1993) was shortlisted for the Commonwealth Writers' Prize. That, and the collection, *Ballad for the New World & Other Stories* (1994), show him creating a comic world; rhythmic, full of colour, vibrancy, and imaginative daring. Scott's depiction of the antics of the Great House is as original as any in Caribbean fiction. *Aelred's Sin*, his 1998 novel, is a revelation: its themes are religion, race, history, and homoeroticism. He takes us behind the monastery walls (in England) where faith, passion, and sexuality are depicted in a way new to West Indian fiction (except, perhaps, for Edgar Mittelholtzer).

📖 Gabriel García Márquez, Jean Rhys. *See* CARIBBEAN   *EM*

Scott, Paul (British, 1920–78)

Paul Scott was born and brought up in north London, and initially began training as an accountant. His service in the Second World War took him to India, and his experiences and observations there were to prove an undying source of inspiration in his writing career. Scott is best known for his novel sequence *The Raj Quartet*, which was successfully televised in 1984. The quartet consists of *The Jewel in the Crown* (1966), *The Day of the Scorpion* (1968), *The Towers of Silence* (1971), and *A Division of the Spoils* (1975). The novels look at the last days of the British occupation of India, chiefly from the British point of view, although there is much sympathy for the native Indians. The setting is powerfully evoked, and the characters are strong and memorable. Scott's last novel, *Staying On* (1977), a Booker Prize-winner, is a humorous but poignant account of British life in India after 1947.

📖 Salman Rushdie, Ruth Prawer Jhabvala, John Masters, E. M. Forster

SA

Scott, Walter (British, 1771–1832) Scott was born in Edinburgh, where he studied law at the University and became a barrister in 1792. From his early years he acquired the deep familiarity with the ballad and folk-tale traditions of the border regions which strongly informs his work in both verse and prose. Initially famous for his narrative poems, after 1814 Scott devoted himself to the historical novel, a form he effectively invented. The social realism of his fiction and its balance between rational and romantic elements had a marked influence on the course of nineteenth-century writing. His vast scope in the creation of character and his work's vivid richness of detail are qualities that make his novels enduringly readable. The leisurely pace with which his narratives unfold their plots and multiple sub-plots is underpinned by frequent passages of high drama and emotional intensity. Begin with *The Heart of Midlothian* (1818). At the opening, its heroine Effie Deans awaits trial for infanticide in Edinburgh's Tolbooth Prison while the Porteous riot of 1736 rages outside. Reprieved from execution by Queen Caroline, Effie marries to become Lady Staunton and enters London society. *Ivanhoe* (1819) is set in the reign of Richard I, whom Wilfred of Ivanhoe serves on the Crusade in Palestine. Having returned to England in disguise, Richard and Ivanhoe triumph over the enemies of the crown in the great tournament at Ashby de la Zouch. The epic narrative of swashbuckling chivalry ends with

the King intervening to reunite Ivanhoe and his beloved Rowena. Set in turbulent eighteenth-century Scotland, *Redgauntlet* (1824) concerns an attempt to put Bonnie Prince Charlie on the throne in 1765. Herries of Birrenswork, a die-hard Jacobite fanatic, kidnaps his nephew Darsie Latimer, the head of the House of Redgauntlet, in his efforts to gain support for the planned rebellion. Darsie rejects his uncle's sense of historical destiny, which is buried with the last Jacobite hopes when the rising fails. *Woodstock* (1826) deals with events following Charles II's defeat at the battle of Worcester in 1651. Disguised as a page, he seeks refuge at Woodstock lodge, where he is helped to escape by Sir Henry Lee and his family following the arrival of Cromwell and his troops. The novel ends with the reconciliation of Sir Henry and his honourable but misguided Roundhead nephew, Colonel Everard, who, having assisted in the King's escape, marries Alice, Sir Henry's daughter. *Rob Roy* (1817) opens with Francis Osbaldistone's arrival at his uncle's home in the Cheviot hills. Threatened with the destruction of his family's fortunes by his cousin Rashleigh, Francis travels north to enlist the help of the outlaw Rob Roy Macgregor. Rob Roy ultimately kills Rashleigh for betraying Jacobite plans for the rising of 1715, leaving Francis to enjoy his malevolent cousin's inheritance.

📖 Victor Hugo, Charles Dickens, James Fenimore Cooper.

See HISTORICAL   *DH*

Sebald, W. G. (German, 1944–) Sebald has lived and worked in Britain for more than thirty years, but writes in German and is published in his adopted homeland in translation. His writing interweaves bizarre and moving incidents from Sebald's life with even stranger stories from the lives of the famous, and the histories of places in Germany, Britain, Italy, and elsewhere. Start with *Vertigo* (1990) which tells four related stories about melancholia, obsession, and vertigo, and manages to be weirdly funny as well as disturbing. *The Rings of Saturn* (1995) describes a long walk down the Suffolk coast and meditates upon the violence as well as the pleasures of our shared past. *The Emigrants* (1993) is a poignant account of four Jewish exiles living in Britain. The English translations by Michael Hulse are as lyrical and exhilarating as Sebald's own prose.

📖 Günter Grass, Joseph Conrad.
See GERMANY   TT

Selby, Hubert, Jr. (US, 1928–) Born in Brooklyn, Selby saw war service with the Merchant Marine and was hospitalized with tuberculosis, during which time he became addicted to morphine. His fiction is both extreme and morally serious, and includes detailed descriptions of drug dependency, paranoid states of mind, rape, and sado-masochistic sexual fantasies. Though his intention is to put readers through a wrenching experience, Selby also brings compassion to his visions of modern urban hell, often combining street language with biblical echoes. His best-known book is *Last Exit to Brooklyn* (1964), the subject of a landmark obscenity trial at the Old Bailey. *The Room* (1971) explores the mind of a prisoner, switching between first- and third-person narration as it describes his fears, fantasies of revenge against the police and the legal system, and sexual obsessions. *The Demon* (1976) and *Requiem for a Dream* (1978) are equally not for the

squeamish, dealing respectively with sex and narcotics.

📖 Samuel Beckett, James Kelman, Bret Easton Ellis   JS

Self, Will (British, 1961–) Controversial newspaper columnist, Self is at the jagged cutting edge of contemporary fiction. His witty and highly articulate style presents a gritty and detailed vision of contemporary society and language. His realism includes violence and sexuality—the content of his books is correspondingly strong and explicit, embracing torture, rape, mutilation, necrophilia, paedophilia, and bestiality, and dwelling in intimate detail on sexual and bodily functions. *Great Apes* (1997), a biting satire of a man who wakes in a world dominated by chimpanzees and is studied by an ape scientist, abounds in startling reversals which question our preconceptions of humanity. *Tough Tough Toys for Tough Tough Boys* (1998) is a collection of short stories connected by the twin themes—frequent in Self's writing—of drug use and the confusion, or subversion, of identity.

📖 Bret Easton Ellis, Irvine Welsh, Martin Amis   EC

Selvon, Samuel (Trinidadian, 1923–94) Samuel Selvon is a master story-teller and the one most associated with the Caribbean folk tradition. He emigrated to Britain in 1950 and to Canada around 1980. His 1957 collection of stories, *Ways of Sunlight*, contains not just nostalgia but his classic 'hymn to London', 'My Girl and the City'. Of his eleven novels, those set in London have had the widest appeal. *The Lonely Londoners* (1956), narrated in what is now called 'nation language', shows how migrants to England in the 1950s coped with the alien conditions—humour and guile usually saw them through. In *The Housing Lark* (1965), though, these migrants are subject to rackrenting landlords. The lesson—to club together (or strike it lucky) and buy a house—informs a couple of other Selvon novels.

📖 V. S. Naipaul. *See* BLACK AND WHITE, CARIBBEAN   *EM*

Senior, Olive (Jamaican, 1941–) Senior's *Summer Lightning and Other Stories* (1986) won the Commonwealth Writers' Prize. Here she re-creates the life of rural Jamaica in all its colour- and class-conscious complexity, employing the full range of West Indian idiom and humour. One memorable aspect of the stories is the portrait of the child trying to make sense of the adult world. Not that the child always loses out, as evidenced in the much-anthologized piece 'Do Angels Wear Brassieres?'—a question put by a knowing little girl to the rather complacent visiting Archdeacon. Senior's other two collections, *Arrival of the Snake-Woman and Other Stories* (1989) and *Discerner of Hearts* (1995), extend her story-telling techniques and confirm the humour and wit. This is the card of the character who informs the 1995 collection: 'Father Burnham, M.H.C., G.M.M.W., D.D., K.R.G.D., Bringer of Light, Professor of Peace, Restorer of Confidence, Discerner of Hearts, Consultation and Advice. The Man. Our Man.'

📖 Pauline Melville, Lawrence Scott. *See* CARIBBEAN   *EM*

Seth, Vikram (Indian, 1952–) Vikram Seth was born in Calcutta and educated in India and the universities of Oxford and Stanford. He established himself as a poet, and author of a verse novel, *The Golden Gate* (1986), before writing the novel that has brought him mass readership, *A Suitable Boy* (1993). It is a long, sprawling, fascinating family saga set in post-independence India. It concerns four families, both Hindu and Muslim, and their interlocking stories. The central character, Lata, and her mother have different ideas on what constitutes a suitable boy for Lata to marry. There is gentle social comedy, detailed political analysis, and romance, all set against the vividly realized backdrop of India in the 1950s. *An Equal Music* (1999) is set in Europe and is a love-story about a violinist who pursues the woman he loved and lost in his youth; she is now married, and —terrible fate for a musician—increasingly deaf. Seth explores the hothouse world of a professional quartet, and writes brilliantly about music.

📖 Isabel Allende, John Galsworthy, Arundhati Roy, Paul Scott. *See* FAMILY SAGA, INDIA   *SA*

Seymour, Gerald (British, 1941–) Formerly a television news reporter, Seymour became a full-time writer in 1978. Begin with *Harry's Game* (1975), in which an undercover agent in Ireland is both hunter and hunted in tracking down an IRA assassin. An Englishman working with the African National Congress awaits execution in South Africa in *A Song in the Morning* (1986). His estranged son is galvanized into attempting a rescue. A young Englishwoman working as a nanny in Sicily in *Killing Ground* (1997) is central to plans for the arrest of the Mafia drugs boss who employs her. In *The Heart of Danger* (1995) a cynical private detective is hired by a couple seeking information about their daughter's death in a Croatian village. What he learns makes him committed to ensuring the conviction of a Serbian war criminal.

📖 Colin Forbes, Jack Higgins, Robert Harris   DH

Shadbolt, Maurice (NZ, 1932–) Shadbolt's novels and stories typically engage with relations between whites and the native Maori culture in New Zealand, and depict the natural world in vivid, painterly prose. In his first collection of stories, *The New Zealanders* (1959), young people travelling abroad redefine their feelings about home and discover themselves. *Among the Cinders* (1965) is an engaging novel in which a disturbed young boy escapes into the bush with his irascible grandfather, following the trauma of the death of a Maori friend, and heals wounds while living off the land. In *This Summer's Dolphin* (1969), the arrival of a tame dolphin has a magical effect on a rundown island community; it is a fable about innocence and corruption, written during the Vietnam war. *Season of the Jew* (1980) is perhaps Shadbolt's most acclaimed work, the first in a series of historical novels set during the Maori wars of the 1860s.

📖 Patrick White, Thomas Keneally, Maurice Gee   JS

Shakespeare, Nicholas (British, 1957–) Shakespeare was named as one of Granta's Best Young British Novelists in 1993, and has won several literary prizes. His first novel, *The Vision of Elena Silves* (1989) is an evocative exploration of Peru's culture and complex political history. Centring on a semi-fictional guerrilla organization based on the Shining Path Movement, the story focuses on the search of escaped terrorist Gabriel Rondon Lung

for his former lover, Elena Silves. Move on to *The Dancer Upstairs* (1995), effectively a sequel, which begins with the investigations of Dyer, a journalist, into captured guerrilla leader Ezequiel and develops into the story of Ezequiel's entangled relationship with his mistress. *Bruce Chatwin* (1999), Shakespeare's biography of the charismatic writer and traveller, is also highly recommended.

📖 James Buchan, Graham Greene
                                                        SR

Shange, Ntokaze (US, 1948–) Born in Trenton, New Jersey, Shange was educated at the University of Southern California. Begin with *Betsey Brown* (1985), which draws on her experience as a black teenager during the turmoil surrounding the ending of segregation in 1960's America. The novel graphically depicts the struggles of the civil rights movement in the South as its young heroine is thrust into heightened awareness of her racial and cultural identity. *Sassafrass, Cypress and Indigo* (1982) deals with the experience of three sisters, each with a different attitude to personal relationships. The novel shifts experimentally between conventional narrative, letters, poems, and journal entries. In *Liliane: Resurrection of the Daughter* (1995) Shange (who is also a well-known playwright) includes extended passages of dialogue. The novel traces the divisions in the New York black community as internal class differences emerge after the civil rights victories.

📖 Alice Walker, Toni Morrison   DH

Sharpe, Tom (British, 1928–) Tom Sharpe studied at Cambridge University and did National Service with the Marines, later emigrating to South Africa, where he was employed as a social worker and teacher before setting up his own photographic studio. He was deported in 1961, and took up a post as a lecturer in history on his return to Britain. Early novels like *Riotous Assembly* (1971) were set in South Africa, and satirize the sexual, racial, and political assumptions of the apartheid regime. This satirical bent was later turned onto the traditional English establishment and its institutions. *Porterhouse Blue* (1974) is set in a fossilized Oxbridge college where the fellows eat roast swan and the students learn about sex from their cleaners ('bedders'). *Blott on the Landscape* (1975) describes the struggle between developers, aristocrats, and environmentalists surrounding a road-building proposal that threatens a mediocre country house. Sharpe's novels typically combine sexual embarrassment, comic violence, and grotesque, larger-than-life characters, and they quickly took their place among the most popular satires of the 1970s. *Wilt* (1976), the story of a timid provincial college lecturer whose attempts to discard an inflatable sex-toy lead to his arrest for murder, generated a successful film. Its sequel, *The Wilt Alternative* (1979), embroils the hapless lecturer with terrorists.

📖 J. P. Donleavy, Howard Jacobson
WB

Shaw, Bob (British, 1931–) Shaw was born in Northern Ireland, and worked in engineering, aircraft design, and public relations before becoming a full-time science fiction writer in 1975. Begin with *Orbitsville* (1975), typical of his work in its technological ingenuity, in which Vance Garamond discovers a habitable alien structure in deep space while fleeing a predatory commercial organization. *The*

Wooden Spaceships (1988), part of Shaw's saga about neighbouring worlds called Land and Overland, finds Land blighted by a deadly disease, while Overland prepares to defend itself from refugee-invaders by constructing a fleet of wooden spacecraft. In *The Peace Machine* (1976) a scientist discovers a device capable of detonating simultaneously all the nuclear weapons on Earth. He attempts to force governments to disarm as a serious international crisis threatens destruction.

📖 Ian Watson, John Brunner   DH

Shaw, Irwin (US, 1913–84) Born in New York and educated at Brooklyn College, Shaw was 23 when his play *Bury the Dead* was produced on Broadway. Begin with the impressive *The Young Lions* (1948), which follows three soldiers, two American and one German, through the Second World War. When they meet amid the desolation of a concentration camp, only one survives. *The Troubled Air* (1951) deals with anti-Communist hysteria in the post-war United States. A radio station is plunged into crisis when broadcasters are accused of being Communist sympathizers. The expansive evocation of American life from the 1940s to the 1960s in *Rich Man, Poor Man* (1970) is based on the contrasting careers of two brothers. The success of one and the rootlessness of the other result from differences of personality that symbolize diverging attitudes in American society.

📖 Herman Wouk, James Agee, John Irving   DH

Shea, Michael (US, 1946–) Shea's career began with *A Quest for Simbilis* (1974), a work which was set (with Vance's permission) in the fantasy world of Jack

Vance's 'Dying Earth', and which acted as a sequel to one of Vance's works seemingly left incomplete. Though this novel was a pastiche, Shea showed that he was one of few authors able to match his model in inventiveness. In this, as in his later works *Nifft the Lean* (1982) and *In Yana, the Touch of Undying* (1985), Shea shows his liking for taking his characters down into fantasy infernos or underworlds. Shea has also written sequels to or pastiches of H. P. Lovecraft's works in *The Color out of Time* (1984) and *Fat Face* (1987).

📖 Jack Vance, Fritz Leiber.
See FANTASY   TS

Sheldon, Sidney (US, 1917–) Sheldon worked as a television producer and scriptwriter, and began publishing fiction in 1963. Begin with *A Stranger in the Mirror* (1976), the story of an emotionally scarred superstar comedian who falls in love with a disastrously ambitious woman. The 90-year-old woman in *Master of the Game* (1983) has inherited a legacy of corruption along with her fortune. She reviews the past as America's social élite gather at her birthday celebrations. *If Tomorrow Comes* (1985) concerns a career woman jailed after accidentally shooting her assailant during a rape attempt. Struggling to clear her name, she comes up against dangerous criminals. In *Morning, Noon and Night* (1995) a wealthy man drowns while sailing his yacht off Corsica. The young woman who appears claiming a share in his fortune brings with her revelations of blackmail, drug deals, and murder.

📖 Michael Crichton, Richard Condon, Wilbur Smith   DH

Shelley, Mary (British, 1797–1851) Daughter of political philosopher William Godwin and feminist Mary Wollstonecraft, and second wife of poet Percy Bysshe Shelley, Mary Shelley is regarded by many as the founder of science fiction. Inspired by a late-night session of ghost-story telling with her husband-to-be and Lord Byron, *Frankenstein* (1818) tells of a young surgeon's successful re-creation of life from the dismembered dead. The doctor's dream descends into a Gothic horror when, terrified by the results, he rejects his creation and then has to suffer its merciless, protracted revenge. While continental Utopianists were projecting the Enlightenment into later centuries, this young girl was introducing the unexpected and irrational into the future, an innovation that has haunted science fiction ever since. Shelley's later novel, *The Last Man* (1826), portrays the collapse of civilization until there is only one man left—yet another theme to have been widely imitated since.

📖 Robert Louis Stevenson, Edgar Allan Poe, Bram Stoker. *See* SCIENCE FICTION, SUPERNATURAL   RP

Shields, Carol (US, 1935–) Carol Shields has lived in Canada since 1957. Her work looks mainly at the lives of women, and reveals them in fascinating detail. Two early novels tell of one weekend in the life of a married couple, first from the husband's point of view and then from the wife's. These appeared together as *Happenstance* (1991) and readers can begin the book at either end. The husband is left to look after home and children while his wife is at a quilting conference, and he sees what a woman's daily existence is like from the inside. *The Stone Diaries* (1993), the fictional biography of an ordinary woman, was shortlisted for the Booker Prize and broke new ground by including family photographs in the text, thus making the point Shields makes often: that every individual is extraordinary. The art of writing about other lives is also at the heart of *Mary Swann* (1990), which satirizes the phenomenon of literary fame. *Larry's Party* (1996) won the Orange Prize for Fiction in 1997 and examines the life of a man who designs mazes. The novel is skilfully structured and takes the maze as a guiding metaphor. *The Republic of Love* (1992) is about the possibility of happiness, not through wealth or glory, but through a shared humanity. Shields's short stories in volumes such as *Various Miracles* (1989) look closely at small incidents with the loving attention to detail, quiet humour, and love of language and what it can achieve, that are characteristic of this author. She chooses words with the elegance and precision of a poet.

📖 Margaret Atwood, Alice Munro, Jane Smiley. *See* CANADA, SHORT STORIES   AG

Sholokhov, Mikhail (Soviet, 1905–84) Sholokhov fought for the Reds during the Russian Civil War and *Quiet Flows the Don* (1928–40) was written out of that experience. It's a massive, compelling epic of the Don Cossack uprising against Bolshevik power, but at heart it's a love triangle between the peasant-warrior Gregory Melekhov, his devoted wife Natalya, and his village mistress Aksinya. Melekhov is as torn between the warring armies and ideologies of Red and White as he is between women, shifting allegiances until he is left alone, fighting on bravely but without hope, against historical forces he can neither understand nor master. Sholokhov was much influenced by *War and Peace* but lacks Tolstoy's range and psychological penetration. Many of Sholokhov's characters are ciphers but his portrayals of the Melekhov family and Cossack peasant life are as vivid and sexually earthy as Zola, his evocation of the Don country is magnificent, and his depiction of the Civil War brutally honest and politically unbiased. It's clearly Gregory Melekhov the 'reactionary' rebel with whom we sympathize, not the pitiless 'progressive' Bolshevik, Koshevoi. Which is why he had to justify the book personally to Stalin who, astonishingly, gave it his blessing. In later life Sholokhov's powers waned—*Virgin Soil Upturned* (1932–60), is a dull apologia for Stalin's brutal land collectivization. He became a scourge of Soviet dissidents, and his post-Soviet reputation has suffered accordingly (to the extent of being—wrongly—accused of plagiarizing his greatest book), but *Quiet Flows the Don* remains one of the great books of the century. Sholokhov won the Nobel Prize for Literature in 1965.

📖 Leo Tolstoy, Émile Zola, Fyodor Dostoevsky, Charles Dickens. *See* RUSSIA   MH

Shreve, Anita (US) Shreve's fiction is dramatic and involving, dealing with contemporary characters in crisis. Start with the US bestseller, *The Pilot's Wife* (1998), about the loving wife of an airline pilot whose plane crashes, killing all on board. As investigations into the cause of the crash get underway, it begins to emerge that the pilot led a double life which included another wife and children. Shreve deals here with emotions of loss, betrayal, and rage, with great precision and a complete absence of sentimentality or melodrama. Equally, *Strange Fits of Passion* (1991) deals with the difficult subject of a battered wife, conjuring powerful sympathies and insights, without ever resorting to cliché. *The Weight of Water* (1997), beautifully written, and with a gripping narrative, was shortlisted for the 1998 Orange Prize.

📖 Anne Tyler, Jane Smiley, Carol Shields   *JR*

Shute, Nevil (British, 1899–1960) A highly skilled aeronautical engineer, Shute was co-opted onto the team working on the famous airship R101 in the 1930s, an aspect of his life which is related in his fascinating autobiography, *Slide Rule* (1954). He was an imaginative and naturally gifted story-teller. Some of Shute's most interesting fiction, such as *No Highway* (1948) and *Trustee from the Toolroom* (1960), is set in the technological and business world.

In 1949 Shute moved to Australia, the setting for *On the Beach* (1957), one of his most popular works. A shocking anti-war story, it tells of the survivors of nuclear war, awaiting the arrival of a deadly post-war radiation cloud from the northern hemisphere. It is a gripping, realistic, cold war horror story: a classic of the 1950s. Shute's plain, precise style and affectionate character portraits are well represented in the romantic post-war classic, *A Town Like Alice* (1950). In this affecting adventure, Jean Paget and Joe Harmon are fated to meet in the worst circumstances on a 'death march' at the hands of Japanese captors in occupied Malaya during the war. He thinks she is married: she comes to believe he has been killed by the enemy. But after the war they seek each other out in a tale which is an intriguing narrative conducted at more than one level.

📖 Larry Niven, Ernest Hemingway
AM

Sillitoe, Alan (British, 1928–   ) Born in a Nottingham council house, Sillitoe left school at 14, and after various factory jobs joined the RAF as a wireless operator. While living in Majorca and struggling to be published, it was the poet Robert Graves who suggested he write something set in Nottingham, as the place he knew best. The result was *Saturday Night and Sunday Morning* (1958), which dropped like a bombshell into the staid and snooty post-war literary scene. Here was real working-class life, written from the inside, in language of raw energy that was direct and down-to-earth. It tells the story of hard-drinking, womanizing Arthur Seaton, a worker at the Raleigh bicycle factory, whose creed is 'Don't let the bastards grind you down'. Played by Albert Finney in the hugely successful film, the bolshie anti-hero caught exactly the emerging spirit of the age. Mining the same rich seam, the stories in *The Loneliness of the Long Distance Runner* (1959) focus on loners and misfits who won't knuckle under and do what society demands. Like his creation Arthur, Sillitoe's an awkward customer, with his own dogged vision and stubborn honesty, never more so than in the semi-autobiographical *Raw Material* (1972) with its unflinching picture of a poor family in the Depression. As well as many novels, he has published several volumes of poetry, and particularly recommended are his *Collected Stories* (1996) containing a selection from five volumes over four decades, and his fascinating autobiography, *Life Without Armour* (1995).

📖 John Braine, Stan Barstow, John Wain   *TH*

Silverberg, Robert (US, 1935–   ) Silverberg was born in New York, published his first novel while a student at Columbia University, and has since written over 300 science fiction and fantasy books, both under his own name and using pseudonyms. Begin with *Hawksbill Station* (1968), set in a bleakly imagined future. Time travel is used to banish political prisoners to a camp located in the Cambrian era where much of the action occurs. *Hot Sky at Midnight* (1994) envisions attempts to genetically redesign human beings to make possible survival in a terminally polluted world. Ruthless commercial interests struggle for control of habitable territory in space. Planet Earth has been destroyed in a catastrophe in *The Face of the Waters* (1991). Among the survivors is a group who sail ceaselessly over a sea-covered planet searching for a rumoured island. Silverberg's best known fantasy novels make up the *Majipoor* trilogy, which begins with *Lord Valentine's Castle* (1980). Following his dethronement, Valentine, cursed with loss of memory, wanders through Majipoor seeking his identity. The stories contained in *The Majipoor Chronicles* (1980) survey the culture and ecology of a world where humans coexist with alien species. Their uneasy peace is shattered in *Valentine Pontifex* (1983) when the Metamorphs make a bid for domination. Power is thrust upon Valentine, and Majipoor's fate is in his hands.

Arthur C. Clarke, Ursula Le Guin, David Eddings   *DH*

Simenon, Georges (Belgian, 1903–89) Born in Liège, Simenon lived in Paris from 1923 to 1939, working initially as a journalist before becoming a prodigious writer of crime fiction. Far more than a pulp author, he invested the genre with psychological, even existential depths,

conveyed in his trademark unemotional prose. Simenon's great fictional detective is Maigret, hero of seventy-six short novels written between 1931 and 1972. The first is *The Death of Monsieur Gallet* (1931). Maigret is a patient observer of the ordinary lives of criminals and their victims; he typically plays cat-and-mouse with suspects. *Maigret's Pipe* (1947) is a characteristic collection of stories in which details are more important than plot twists; the title story is resolved by a young boy's theft of Maigret's favourite pipe, while 'Storm in the Channel' finds the inspector assisting provincial police while on holiday. Simenon's numerous other crime novels have a much darker edge, often with erotic undercurrents, as with *In Case of Emergency* (1956): a successful lawyer becomes obsessed with a young prostitute who is then found murdered.

Ruth Rendell, H. R. F. Keating.
See CRIME   *JS*

Simpson, Dorothy (British, 1933–) Although Dorothy Simpson's first book, *Harbingers of Fear* (1977), was an accomplished novel of suspense, four years passed before it had a successor. *The Night She Died* (1981) marked a change of direction, introducing Detective Inspector Luke Thanet and starting a series which has attracted many readers who enjoy the traditional British police story. The books are set in an imaginary town in Kent and derive much of their appeal from the way they follow the lives of Thanet and his sergeant, Mike Lineham, and of their families. Simpson is conscientious and skilled at characterization, and, although they do not break new ground, her books are consistently enjoyable. Perhaps the most successful of all are

Last Seen Alive (1985), which won a CWA Silver Dagger, and *Close her Eyes* (1984).

📖 Ruth Rendell, Elizabeth Ferrars

ME

Simpson, Helen (British, 1957–) Simpson is a former fashion journalist. In her first collection of short stories, *Four Bare Legs in a Bed* (1990), a number of women reveal the inadequacies of their relationships with men. Ranging from the fourth century to the present, Simpson's women are patronized (like the student treated like a pet by her professor in 'Zoe and the Pedagogues'), despairing (like the seventeenth-century woman made pregnant by her lover in 'Good Friday 1633'), or simply dissatisfied (like the secretary trying to relieve the tedium of her relationship in 'The Bed'). Simpson's often bleak view of the relationships between men and women is tempered by a witty delivery, and at their best her stories are entertaining and full of insights. *Dear George and Other Stories* (1995) follows in the same vein.

📖 Helen Fielding, Fay Weldon   *WB*

Sinclair, Andrew (British, 1935–) Sinclair was born in Oxford and educated at Harvard and Cambridge. He was a lecturer during the 1960s and subsequently worked in publishing. Begin with the serio-comic view of army life in *The Breaking of Bumbo* (1959), based on his experiences of National Service at the time of the Suez crisis. *The Albion Triptych* projects its fantasy and satire across English history from the Druidic era to post-war Britain. It is made up of *Gog* (1967), presenting Labour's victory in the 1945 elections in a vast historical context, *Magog* (1972), dealing with the decline of post-war

Britain, and *King Ludd* (1988), which moves between modern Cambridge and the Luddite Riots of 1811–16. His other novels include *The Project* (1960), concerning the development of the ultimate nuclear weapon, which is about to destroy the world as the book ends.

📖 Janice Elliot, William Golding

DH

Sinclair, Iain (British, 1943–) Sinclair was born in Cardiff and educated at Trinity College, Dublin. From the 1960s onwards he has lived in London, the legends, history, and topography of which pervade much of his writing. Sinclair describes his work as 'baroque realism' for its complex and suggestive interplay between the past and the present. *Lud Heat* (1975) explores the history of the eight east London churches of the architect Nicholas Hawksmoor and how they seem to be connected by a network of ley lines. *Radon Daughters* (1994) portrays a one-legged author of a single novel eking out a sordid existence in an abandoned building in Wapping, and taking his only pleasures from his fantastical relationship with a television weather-girl and his addictive fixes of radiation bought from an engineer in a London hospital. *White Chapel, Scarlet Tracings* (1997) combines a sort of spiritual inquest or seance into the Whitechapel Ripper murders with the pursuit by seedy book-dealers of rarities of that period.

📖 Peter Ackroyd, Charles Dickens.
See SOCIAL ISSUES   *RP*

Sinclair, Michael (British, 1938–). *See* SPY

Sinclair, Upton (Beall) (US, 1878–1968) Throughout his life, Sinclair wrote at least ninety novels. His series of socialist pamphlets discussing aspects of American political society contributed to the genre of journalism known as 'muckraking'. Seen by many as a prophet of social justice, Sinclair is best known for his novel *The Jungle* (1906), an exposé of the meatpacking industry. Dealing with corruption, exploitation, and horrific working conditions, *The Jungle* shocked many of its readers and influenced the implementation of the Pure Food Law. *World's End* (1940) is the first of eleven novels following the fortune of Lanny Budd as he travels around the Western world. The series is an epic portrayal of Western history from 1913 to 1949. The series ends with *The Return of Lanny Budd* (1953), and the third volume, *Dragon's Teeth* (1942), was awarded the Pulitzer Prize in 1943.

📖 Émile Zola, Theodor Dreiser, George Gissing. *See* SOCIAL ISSUES

EW

Singer, Isaac Bashevis (Polish/US, 1904–91) Educated at a rabbinical seminary in Warsaw, Singer emigrated to the United States in 1935 and joined the staff of New York's *Jewish Daily Forward*, which published his fiction in its original Yiddish. In 1978 he received the Nobel Prize for Literature. Begin with some of the short stories, often considered to be his finest work. These entertaining tales of the vanished Jewish ghettos of Poland colourfully combine historical fact, Yiddish folklore, and the supernatural. Collections include *Gimpel the Fool* (1957) and *The Death of Methuselah* (1988). Set in seventeenth-century Poland, *Satan in Goray* (1955), his first novel, deals with the rise of the false messiah Sabbatai Levi. Amid violence and religious hysteria, Rabbi Benish struggles

to restore order. The novel concludes with his dramatic exorcism of the epileptic prophetess Rechele. *Enemies* (1972) is the story of a survivor of the Nazi Holocaust. He remakes his life in New York, where destiny and irresponsibility result in his being married simultaneously to three women. His attempts to sustain a situation in which he loves all three while each loves him prove unendurable. Singer's numerous other novels include *Scum* (1991), which tells of Max Barabander's return to his native Warsaw from Buenos Aires. Formerly an impoverished petty criminal, he has prospered in South America, but becomes very lonely following his homecoming. He reacts by desperately reaching out for sexual contact which ultimately results in violence.

📖 Primo Levi, Isaac Babel, Leon Uris

DH

Singh, Khushwant (Indian, 1915–). *See* INDIA

Škvorecký, Josef (Canadian, 1924–) Born in the former Czechoslovakia, Josef Škvorecký is a highly respected novelist, translator, and screenplay writer. His work covers several genres ranging from crime/thriller fiction to novels about jazz and classical music. His writing reveals a refined political consciousness. His Danny Smiricky cycle parallels much of his own life. This includes *The Engineer of Human Souls* (1984)—a reference to Stalin's definition of a writer—in which novelist Danny moves to Canada. Set in an academic environment, it casts a despairing satirical look at contemporary politics but its subtitle—*An Entertainment on the Old Themes of Life, Women, Fate, Dreams, the Working Class, Secret Agents, Love and*

Death—suggests its true range. *The Miracle Game* (1990) takes place in 1968 in Prague, examining the impact of Soviet invasion on the Czech psyche; the reader gets a sense of Škvorecký's abiding but clear-eyed love of his birthplace through these novels.

📖 Milan Kundera, Ivan Klima   *TO*

Slovo, Gillian (South African, 1952–) Slovo was born in South Africa, daughter of anti-apartheid activists Ruth First and Joe Slovo. She has written a painfully honest and illuminating autobiographical memoir of her childhood with her journalist mother (later assassinated for her political beliefs) and her Communist Party leader father, *Every Secret Thing: My Family, My Country* (1997). A family saga, *Ties of Blood* (1989), also draws on her own experience. Her series of feminist crime novels featuring journalist and detective Kate Baeier has been hailed as one of the best depictions of the collision between radical and establishment worlds in contemporary British fiction. Begin with Kate's debut in *Morbid Symptoms* (1984) where the sudden death of a left-wing playboy pushes Kate into investigating the radical circles that have formerly nourished her. Four further novels, culminating in *Close Call* (1996) which deals with the politics of policing, continue Kate's progress in a series of well-plotted investigations that allow this engaging protagonist to develop in consistently interesting directions.

📖 Sara Paretsky, Val McDermid
    VM

Smart, Elizabeth (Canadian, 1913–86) Born into a wealthy Ottawa family, Elizabeth Smart was educated at private schools and King's College, London, before she met the poet George Barker and began a complex affair that produced four children. Smart's most celebrated work is the short, highly condensed novella *By Grand Central Station I Sat Down and Wept* (1945). Half-way between poetry and prose, the book is a passionate and intense account of the breakdown of a relationship, and has almost no exact equivalent in English. *The Assumption of the Rogues and Rascals* (1978) adopts a similar poetic style to satirize and celebrate the bohemian lifestyle of the artists and writers Smart knew, but the book lacks some of the force of its predecessor. Smart also wrote poetry, and her journals were published as *Necessary Secrets* (1986).

📖 Anais Nin, Anna Kavan   *WB*

Smiley, Jane (US, 1951–) After *A Thousand Acres* won the Pulitzer Prize in 1992 Smiley came rather belatedly to the attention of British readers. This inspired recasting of the *King Lear* story is set in the farmlands of Iowa, and adds an extra and very modern dimension to the tale, explaining why the Goneril and Regan characters feel as they do towards their father. It has recently been made into a film. Smiley writes brilliantly about rural life. She is a keen rider (she now owns horses herself), and she describes them and their world particularly well. In her early volume of short stories, *The Age of Grief* (1988), she deals with painful human relationships in a careful and sensitive way. *At Paradise Gate* (1981) is very perceptive about old age, and the novella *Ordinary Love* (1990) is a short and poignant masterpiece about family breakdown and heartache. The happiness of a mother, father, and small child living in an idyllic setting unravels before our very eyes. By contrast, in her campus novel *Moo* (1995), set in an agricultural college, Smiley manages to keep several narrative balls flying through the air with the skill of a juggler. The college, set in the Mid-West, is anxious to develop a perpetually-lactating cow. Smiley manages to see things from everyone's point of view. She gets into the minds of faculty, students, and even a prize pig, and the results are frequently hilarious. Her historical epic *The All-True Travels and Adventures of Lidie Newton* (1998) gives a woman's perspective on American frontier sagas, and has been compared with Mark Twain's *Huckleberry Finn*.

📖 E. Annie Proulx, Carol Shields, Richard Ford   *AG*

Smith, Betty (US, 1896–1972) Betty Smith's famous novel about a Brooklyn childhood, *A Tree Grows in Brooklyn* (1943), is closely drawn from her own life. Young Francie is brought up by her singing-waiter father (rather too fond of the bottle) and her energetic, determined mother, who works as a caretaker and reads Shakespeare and the Bible to her children at night. It evokes life in the teeming poverty-stricken Brooklyn tenements in photographic detail, and traces Francie's growing understanding of the world, and her struggle for education. The book was a best-seller when first published, and has been frequently reprinted; it is warm and engaging, thanks to Francie's innocent optimism, and it vividly re-creates the racial mixture that was early twentieth-century Brooklyn.

📖 Willa Cather (*My Ántonia*), J. D. Salinger   *JR*

Smith, Dodie (British, 1896–1990) 'Shopgirl Writes Play' ran the headline.

A one-time actress (trained at RADA), at 35 Dodie Smith was hardly a girl when her first play was staged, and in fact was in charge of a department at Heal's, the fashionable furniture store. Exiled in America during the war, desperately homesick for England, she wrote *I Capture the Castle* (1949). From its memorable opening line, 'I write this sitting in the kitchen sink', the 17-year-old narrator, Cassandra Mortmain, captivates the reader as she describes a life of penury in a gloomy Gothic castle with her odd-ball family. Wise beyond her years, romantic and lyrical, yet beadily perceptive ('A thoroughly dangerous girl', someone observes), Cassandra is wonderfully engaging and believable. The book has become a classic with both adults and teenagers. Late in her career Smith produced another classic, *The Hundred and one Dalmatians* (1956), made into a Disney film—and created another immortal female character in Cruella de Vil.

📖 Daisy Ashford, Laurie Lee, Saki.
See TEEN   *TH*

Smith, Joan (British, 1953–) Joan Smith began her writing career as a journalist working in Manchester and Blackpool. As part of that work she covered the Yorkshire Ripper case which she writes about in her non-fiction book *Misogynies* (1989). In Smith's crime fiction her detective, Loretta Lawson, nervy yet persistent, is a London University teacher of literature. However, the settings of the books range between Oxford, Paris, and the New York of *Full Stop* (1995). The book to begin with is the first in the Lawson series, *A Masculine Ending* (1987), in which Lawson stumbles on a murder victim in a Paris flat. Lawson, her ex-husband, journalist John

Tracey, and her amiable sidekick, Bridget, investigate and uncover sexual indiscretion in the academy. In *Full Stop* Lawson, staying in a friend's flat, receives mysterious phone calls which become salacious and ultimately threatening.

📖 Val McDermid, Amanda Cross, Sarah Dunant   *IP*

Smith, Martin Cruz (US, 1942–) Smith has worked as a reporter, and his novels are meticulously researched, supporting complicated and compelling plots with sharp social observation. He has written a number of crime and suspense novels under a variety of pseudonyms, but is best known for *Gorky Park* (1981), which is set in cold war Russia and follows the investigation of Soviet detective Arkady Renko into a triple murder after bodies are discovered frozen in Gorky Park. Renko's enquiries unveil many levels of corruption, as he follows leads through a cross-section of society. Renko's popularity led Smith to reuse the character, but unrelated novels such as *Nightwing* (1977), a nightmarish story about a plague of vampire bats and their link to deaths within a Hopi Indian community, are also well worth reading.

📖 Stephen King, Evan Hunter (writing as Ed McBain), Raymond Chandler. *See* SPY   *SR*

Smith, Stevie (British, 1902–71) Stevie Smith grew up in Palmers Green, London, and lived there with her beloved aunt for most of her life. She worked as a secretary and freelance writer and broadcaster, and is known for her poetry, of which she published eight volumes, many illustrated by her own drawings. Her novels are all autobiographical, and the first, *Novel on Yellow Paper* (1936) is by far the best

known. It's narrated in the first person by Pompey Casmilus, who lives with her darling Auntie Lion, and is an outpouring of her thoughts and feelings about the world around her—about fear, love, death, marriage, religion, sex, anti-Semitism; about her friends and lovers and her childhood. To list the topics cannot begin to capture the delicious flavour, which is whimsical, poetic, self-deprecatingly (or at times, mercilessly) humorous, and often absurd: 'How richly compostly loamishly sad were those Victorian days, with a sadness not nerve-irritating like we have today . . . These childhood impressions make a difference as the psychoanalysts charge a pound an hour for saying.' Or: 'When I was eight years old I went away from my parents to a convalescent home, where I was so proud and so furious to be separated from my mother I would not eat, and I would not stop crying, I thought: If I go on crying long enough I shall die. But after crying days and days I was still alive, so then I at once became rather cynical.'

📖 Dorothy Parker, James Thurber, E. M. Delafield   *JR*

Smith, Wilbur (South African, 1933–) Wilbur Smith was born in Central Africa in 1933, educated at Michaelhouse and Rhodes University, and has a deep commitment to the African continent as a whole. He is that increasingly rare figure, a writer who is also a man of action: explorer, naturalist, deep sea fisherman. His novels are unique: they are not thrillers, but pure adventure stories of the kind that few write any more. *When the Lion Feeds* (1964) is the first in the magnificent *Courtney* sequence, beginning in the wilds of Natal in the 1870s with the birth of twin brothers, Sean and Garrick, who could not be more different. Smith's world is so physically vivid that you are immediately transported to the epic landscapes of Africa. He offers pure escapism, which is why he is one of the world's best-selling authors.

📖 Henry Rider Haggard, Arthur Hailey, Jon Cleary   CH

Smollett, Tobias (British, 1721–71) Born near Dunbarton, Smollett studied medicine in Glasgow before moving to London, where he practised as a surgeon. He is among the great novelists of the eighteenth century. *The Adventures of Roderick Random* (1748) is a good introduction to his fiction; the novel's energetic action sees the young Scot winning his beloved's hand after trials at sea, in the French army, and in London, where he falls victim to trickery and dissipation. *The Adventures of Peregrine Pickle* (1751), a robust satire on manners and morals, narrates its aimless hero's career of debauchery and wild practical jokes, which ends when he comes to his senses in jail. Smollett's masterpiece *The Expedition of Humphry Clinker* (1771) consists of letters from five members of Matthew Bramble's party travelling from Wales to Scotland. The upright Humphry, their postilion, is revealed as Matthew Bramble's son, and the novel ends with the celebration of four marriages.

📖 Henry Fielding, Charles Dickens
DH

Solzhenitsyn, Alexander (Soviet/ Russian, 1918–) Born in Kislovodsk in the Caucasus and educated at the University of Rostov, in 1945 Solzhenitsyn began eleven years as a political prisoner. He received the Nobel Prize for Literature in 1970 and was expelled from the Soviet Union in 1974. After living in the United States, he was invited back to Russia in 1994. Begin with *A Day in the Life of Ivan Denisovich* (1962), his stark novella of life in a Soviet penal colony. Rich in inventive prison slang, the book shows the unheroic peasant Denisovich surviving inhuman conditions through a fundamental toughness of spirit. *Cancer Ward* (1968) and *The First Circle* (1968) are major novels of ideas, dramatizing arguments about the human condition. In the former, Oleg Kostoglotov arrives from a labour camp to be treated for cancer. *The First Circle* is set among a group of highly educated political prisoners. Of the three main characters, one is released, one is sent to a tougher camp, and the third remains where he is. Focusing chiefly on the Battle of Tannenberg and using a range of experimental techniques, *August 1914* (1971) is the first part of *The Red Wheel*, an unfinished cycle of novels based on the Russian Revolution. It continues with *October 1916* (1985), a treatment of wartime conditions among the people of Moscow, and *March 1917* (1986), a monumental re-creation of social and political life in Petrograd in the months before the Revolution.

📖 Thomas Mann, Arthur Koestler, Vladimir Nabokov. *See* RUSSIA   DH

Somerville and Ross (Edith Oenone Somerville, Irish, 1858–1949, and Violet Florence Martin, Irish, 1852–1915)

Somerville and Ross were second cousins; Edith was actually born in Corfu, moving with her parents to Ireland as a young child. The two met in Co. Cork, where they formed a lifelong writing partnership. Probably their most famous works are *Some Experiences of an Irish RM* (1899), short stories which deal with the bumbling new English Resident Magistrate, Major

Yeates, and his goings-on with the local Munster community. The romping hilarity is created by the antics he is embroiled in by his landlord/'Man Friday', Flurry Knox. Their other novels deal with Anglo-Irish relations in rural Ireland, but tackle the same subject in very different ways. *The Real Charlotte* (1894) features a magnificent female protagonist, Charlotte, who, while detestable, is a joy to follow as she manipulates and ruins everyone who gets in the way of her fin-ancial or marriage schemes.

📖 Jennifer Johnston, Anthony Trollope, Jane Austen. *See* IRELAND

CJ

Sontag, Susan (US, 1933–) Born in New York, Susan Sontag is best known for her essays on subjects as diverse as photography, illness, and pornography, and she has also worked as a writer and director in theatre. Her novels and stories are often extensions of the ideas explored in her essays, but Sontag at her best writes accessibly on intellectual themes. A good starting-point is *The Volcano Lover* (1992), a richly detailed historical romance based on the lives of the renowned eighteenth-century beauty, Emma Hamilton, and her husband William. *The Benefactor* (1963) explores the same period, following a young man named Hippolytus whose dream- and waking lives begin to merge and become confused during a Grand Tour of Europe. *Death Kit* (1967) is an imaginative reworking of themes and ideas drawn from the writings of Franz Kafka, and *I, Etcetera* (1978) is a collection of short stories.

📖 John Berger, Franz Kafka, Simone de Beauvoir WB

Southern, Terry (US, 1924–97) Southern was the screenwriter of films such as *Dr Strangelove, Easy Rider,* and *Barbarella,* but he also wrote a number of outlandishly funny novels full of sex and drugs. The best known of these weirdly plotted social satires are *Candy* (1958) and *The Magic Christian* (1960). In *Flash and Filigree* (1958), an underrated and very funny book, the targets are the medical profession, the courts, and the media; a typical scene involves a stoned dermatologist and a private detective stumbling into a live television show called *What's My Disease.* Southern's short stories, collected in *Red-Dirt Marijuana* (1967, reissued 1990), are more conventional, sometimes reflecting upon his Texas background and time spent in Paris.

📖 William Burroughs, John Barth, Thomas Pynchon. *See* HUMOUR JS

Soyinka, Wole (Nigerian, 1934–) Soyinka has been imprisoned repeatedly and exiled in his fight for Nigerian democracy; he is fiercely intelligent and energetic. He studied at Leeds University and directed for the Royal Court Theatre. Primarily known as a playwright, he is also a poet, actor, critic, and novelist. In his first novel, *The Interpreters* (1965), a group of disenchanted yet enthusiastic intellectuals pontificate on the unscrupulous and cynical society around them. Soyinka's second novel, *Season of Anomy* (1973), is set against the background of the Nigerian Civil War. His writing is a beautiful blend of English, Yoruba, and Pidgin English, and in 1986 he became the first African to win the Nobel Prize for Literature. A critic of the former Nigerian leader, General Sani Abacha, the politically outspoken Soyinka returned to Nigeria in October 1998 after four years in exile.

📖 Chinua Achebe, Buchi Emecheta, Ben Okri EW

Spark, Muriel (British, 1918–) Spark was born in Edinburgh and her best-known book, *The Prime of Miss Jean Brodie* (1961), is drawn from memories of her schooldays there in the 1930s. This is a good place to start; a charismatic teacher encourages her girls to high achievements, but her charisma is dangerous as well as inspiring. An excellent film of the book starred Maggie Smith as Miss Brodie. Spark is fascinated by the ways in which people try to outsmart one another, and how we often betray the people we love. Her most extreme study of power is *The Driver's Seat* (1970), a rather horrible book about a woman who seeks—and finds—someone to murder her. Spark is particularly good at dialogue; like Iris Murdoch, she conveys a good deal through what is not said. She is also a brilliant and subtle satirist. *The Abbess of Crewe* (1974) parodies the Watergate scandal; it is set in a convent with a powerful and paranoiac Mother Superior who spies on the nuns. *A Far Cry from Kensington* (1988) is a gentle satire on the world of publishing, narrated by a serene young woman who likes being fat and who dispenses sage advice to the reader as well as the characters. She advises all aspiring authors to acquire a cat, but warns that, unfortunately, the cat will not write the book for you. Spark's first volume of autobiography, *Curriculum Vitae*, appeared in 1992. She lives in Italy.

📖 Brigid Brophy, Iris Murdoch, Evelyn Waugh   *TT*

Staincliffe, Cath (British, 1956–) Cath Staincliffe's first novel, *Looking for Trouble* (1994), features Sal Kilkenny, perhaps the only single-parent detective in crime fiction, who solves a young

man's disappearance; this leads her into the underbelly of Manchester, the murky waters of child abuse, and high level corruption. In Staincliffe's second novel, *Go not Gently* (1997), Kilkenny investigates the sudden descent into Alzheimer's of a resident in a nursing home. This takes her into the world of medical malpractice. Staincliffe writes with a realism which is forceful but never cloying.

📖 Val McDermid, Sara Paretsky   *IP*

Stapledon, Olaf (British, 1886–1950) Stapledon was born on the Wirral and educated at Oxford and Liverpool universities, lived on a private income, and worked as a part-time tutor in philosophy. Begin with *Last and First Men* (1930), a majestically imagined survey of two billion years of human history. Its twentieth-century narrator is a channel for an advanced human intelligence in the remote future, who foretells planetary migration. In *Odd John: A Story of Jest and Earnest* (1935) an evolutionary leap gives rise to a race of supermen whose superiority to ordinary humans is spiritual and intellectual. They are forced to destroy themselves when invasion threatens their colony. The disembodied narrator of *Starmaker* (1937) conducts a vast survey of the future and outlines a philosophical system of belief before facing the impassive deity at the powerful conclusion.

📖 Isaac Asimov, Arthur C. Clarke, H. G. Wells   *DH*

Staples, Mary Jane (British, 1911–) Staples is a very popular writer of family stories. There are sixteen books in *The Adams Family of Walworth* series, a readable saga of Cockney life set in the 1930s and 1940s, many of them reflecting wartime experience. Begin with the first, *Down Lambeth Way* (1988). Staples has also written novels outside this series, still with a London setting—such as *The Pearly Queen* (1992), set in the Depression, in which a woman leaves her family to join a fanatical religious sect, and her role as mother is taken up by warm, generous Aunt Edie.

📖 Harry Bowling, Maisie Mosco, R. F. Delderfield   JR

Stead, Christina (Australian, 1902–83) Stead led a wandering life, moving from Australia to London, to Paris, to various places in the United States, back to different homes in Europe, and then to Australia again. She worked as a teacher and secretary before writing full-time (including a stint in Hollywood, which she disliked). Left-wing politics were central in her own life and that of her partner, William Blake.

As a writer she is strikingly original, plunging the reader into the complex and extraordinary lives of her characters, very much as if one has been dropped into a roomful of unknown extroverts who simply carry on around one. Start with *The Man Who Loved Children* (1940), her masterpiece; the hero shapes his family's life with a naïve kind of tyranny which leads to tragedy so inexorably that it feels normal. *For Love Alone* (1944) charts the life of a young woman determined to break away from her ramshackle Australian family, discovering in England that what she thought was love was simply obsession —and eventually discovering a different kind of love. *Cotter's England* (1966) has another emotional tyrant at its centre: Nellie, who is from a northern working-class background, and makes outrageous

demands on her friends and family, weaving them into her web of self-serving lies and fantasies, with her crooning hypnotic monologues. The privations of post-war England are described with unflinching accuracy. Stead's depictions of selfishness and the twisted dynamics of family relationships at times ring searingly true, at others almost as grotesque parody. Her ear for dialogue, and her sure grasp of social class, are a constant pleasure.

📖 D. H. Lawrence, Patrick White, Helen Garner, Virginia Woolf.
See AUSTRALIA   JR

Steel, Danielle (US, 1947–) Steel is mother of nine, and a bride four times over. Her lifestyle is reflected in her novels which are glamorous and feature women who juggle many different roles. Steel appeals to massive audiences and often covers more than one generation, following the lives of her strong female characters. *Full Circle* (1985) follows Tana Roberts on her travels from New York to the South through the 'turbulent' civil rights struggles of the 1960s as she strives to become a successful career woman. In *Accident* (1995) Page Clarke's 'perfect' world is thrown into turmoil when her daughter sneaks out on a date and is involved in a car crash. The tragedy forces Page to question her comfortable life. In *Granny Dan* (1999) the discovery of a box of keepsakes reveals a rollerblading grandmother's secret past as a prima ballerina in turn-of-the-century Russia.

📖 Penny Vincenzi, Barbara Taylor Bradford, Mary Wesley   CJ

Steffler, John (Canadian, 1947–). *See* CANADA

Stein, Gertrude (US, 1874–1946) For most of her adult life Stein lived in Paris, where she was friends with avant-garde writers and painters, including Picasso and Matisse. Stein wrote poetry, short stories, essays, novels, plays, and auto-biographies. Her experimental writing is difficult and has been compared to Cubist painting, as if Stein were rearranging the very building-blocks of language. How-ever, she also wrote a number of witty and entertaining books. Start with *Three Lives* (1909), three relatively accessible stories of working-class women in Baltimore. *The Autobiography of Alice B. Toklas* (1933) is actually Stein's autobiography, told from the point of view of her lesbian lover. It was a best-seller in its day, and is full of mischievous gossip about Stein's famous friends. *Brewsie and Willie* (1946) is also a good read. This is the story of two young American soldiers in Paris during the Second World War. A more challenging work is *Wars I Have Seen* (1945), a fascin-ating meditation on Stein's experience of living in France through two world wars.

📖 Brigid Brophy, James Joyce   *TT*

Steinbeck, John (US, 1902–68) Born in Salinas, California, Steinbeck worked at various jobs while studying at Stanford University, and saw at first hand the often appalling conditions endured by migrant workers and their families during the Depression. His fiction, from early realist novels to later parables, always observes working-people with great sympathy, using spare and simple language. He won the Nobel Prize for Literature in 1962. *Of Mice and Men* (1937) is a short but powerful study of farm labourers in California, focus-ing on the friendship between George and simple-minded Lennie; the arrival of the boss's wife arouses passions that lead to tragedy. Steinbeck's masterpiece is *The Grapes of Wrath* (1939), whose human drama and documentary elements had a huge social impact at the time; it was quickly made into a film by John Ford, with Steinbeck's friend Henry Fonda as the dignified Tom Joad. The Joad family are dispossessed 'Okies', looking for a better life in California but finding their aspirations bitterly checked by nature, exploitative bosses, and by their own weak-nesses. *East of Eden* (1952) is a saga of family conflict with an epic sweep from the Civil War to the First World War, and it too became a famous film starring James Dean. Some of Steinbeck's books are more light-hearted, even sentimental; *Cannery Row* (1945), for example, and its sequel *Sweet Thursday* (1954). They depict down-and-outs, cannery workers, and prostitutes, a multi-ethnic community on the California coast held together by hard-drinking marine biologist Doc.

📖 Harper Lee, William Faulkner, Ernest Hemingway, Russell Banks. *See* SOCIAL ISSUES, UNITED STATES OF AMERICA   *JS*

Stendhal (French, 1783–1842) Stendhal, the pseudonym of Henri Beyle, is known for two long novels, the first of which is *Scarlet and Black* (1830). This is set during the Restoration in France, when suspicion and intrigue were widespread and people were seeking a satisfactory replacement for the monarchy. The narrative follows the fortunes of Julien Sorel, a carpenter's son who becomes tutor to the local mayor's children. He becomes entangled in a banal affair with the mayor's wife. Stendhal's tone is satirical, disgusted with 'polite' society. He explores minutely the contradictions making up human nature. Julien sets his will above his natural feeling, but his mistress allows her emotions to rule her behaviour. Julien suffers from inverted snobbery: ever suspecting that those with money despise him, he is keen to prove himself cleverer than they. When he is sent away to the seminary to train as a priest, his cleverness becomes a handicap and he envies the peasants. Julien frequently asks himself, even after love-making, 'Have I played my part well?' and the author comments: 'our hero fell short of daring to be sincere.' A new job takes him to Paris, fashionable society, and a new mistress, Mathilde, but his past misdeeds will not be buried. Typical of Stendhal's perception is that characters often experience two opposing emotions at once. Mathilde feels both anger and attraction towards Julien, for instance.

The other great book is *The Charterhouse of Parma* (1839), set in Italy, beginning at the time of Napoleon, in whose army Stendhal had fought and who, along with Lord Byron, was the writer's hero. His protagonist at the provincial court is the son of a soldier at the battle of Waterloo, Fabrizio, who becomes both priest and lover.

📖 Honoré de Balzac, Émile Zola. *See* ROMANCE   FS

Stephens, James (Irish, 1882–1950) Born in Dublin, James Stephens became a clerk at the age of 14 and was active in Irish cultural nationalism from 1910 onward. Begin with *The Charwoman's Daughter* (1912), which draws on Stephens's impoverished Dublin background. The book's lyrical treatment of transformation through make-believe has a starkly realistic setting of backstreet squalor. *The Crock of Gold* (1912) makes rich use of the fantasy and folklore found in much of Stephens's writing. The story takes place in a forest, where two philosophers are visited by a succession of transient presences, including leprechauns, police constables, and the god Pan. The group of tinkers at the opening of *The Demi-Gods* (1914) are caught up in a supernatural struggle for power. Vividly evoking occult dimensions, the book's moral is that men and gods are alike motivated by love and desire.

📖 Flann O'Brien. *See* IRELAND   DH

Stephenson, Neal (US, 1959–) Stephenson injects old-fashioned 'sci-fi' with mind-expanding drugs, magic realism, dodgy sex, paranoia, cutting-edge technologies, and turns it into 'cy-fi'. Start with *Snowcrash* (1992). In Reality Hiro Protagonist delivers pizzas for the Mafia but in the (virtual) Metaverse, he's a hack-'em-up warrior prince fighting a virus from ancient Sumeria which is destroying All Known Data. Move on to *The Diamond Age* (1995), Nano-Technology and a future ruled by a retro-Victorian élite. Then try *Cryptonomicon* (1999), whose 900-page paranoid narrative cuts between code-breaking in the Second World War and future attempts to set up an encrypted info-haven free from government and commercial spies. Its literary model is clearly Thomas Pynchon's *Gravity's Rainbow* (1973), whose historical grasp, outrageous imagination, posturing style, fondness for conspiracy theories, and inadequacies of characterization Stephenson shares.

📖 William Gibson, Bruce Sterling, Rudy Rucker   MH

Sterling, Bruce (US, 1954–) Born in Brownsville, Texas, Sterling was educated at the University of Texas and, with William

Gibson, is regarded as an originator of 'cy-fi'. Begin with *Islands in the Net* (1988), the story of a world free of ecological or political crises in which computer tele-communications generate a global sense of community. Data piracy takes the heroine into remote corners of the world where obsolete capitalist economies still exist. *Involution Ocean* (1978) is an extravagant fantasy in which a young man finds himself on a whaling-ship crossing a dust ocean on a planet without water. Global warming has finally wrecked the atmosphere in *Heavy Weather* (1994). A group of hedonistic scientists styling themselves 'The Storm Troupers' travel in search of extreme mete-orological events. A tornado of unpreced-ented power gives more than they bargain for as it tears across North America.

📖 Christopher Priest, William Gibson, Brian Aldiss   *DH*

Sterne, Laurence (Irish, 1713–68) Born at Clonmel, Ireland, Sterne spent most of his life as a minor clergyman in North Yorkshire, writing only sermons and journalism. The suppression by church authorities of his Swiftian satire *A Polit-ical Romance* (1759) provided the impetus for Sterne's masterpiece, *The Life and Opinions of Tristram Shandy, Gentleman* (1760–7), which greatly expanded the pos-sibilities of fiction. Published serially in nine volumes, the novel was immediately both acclaimed and derided for its narrat-ive eccentricities and scurrilous humour, and it made Sterne into a celebrity. *Tristram Shandy* can be read as an end-lessly digressive and entertaining cock-and-bull story, but it is much more, playing games with narrative and the experience of reading. Tristram's life story from conception onwards is constantly

interrupted, particularly by the author. A gallery of delightful characters are encountered: benevolent Uncle Toby, his servant Trim, blustering Dr Slop, the amorous Widow Wadman. Comical and sentimental episodes are interspersed with learned puns, mock scholarship, comments on time and mortality. The book's self-consciousness as fiction made it especially influential with twentieth-century writers, and it remains fun to read, albeit with now essential footnotes. Parson Yorick, whose death causes an entirely black page in *Tristram Shandy*, reappears as the narrator of *A Sentimental Journey* (1768), which is based on Sterne's own travels in France. In a burlesque of the Grand Tour, Yorick encounters squalor, pathos over the death of an ass, and sexual temptation.

📖 Jonathan Swift, Flann O'Brien, Jaroslav Hašek, James Joyce   *JS*

Stevenson, Robert Louis (British, 1850–94) Stevenson was brought up in Edinburgh, son of a lighthouse engineer. Unsuited to the Scottish climate because of poor health, he travelled widely, fin-ally settling in Samoa. His finest book was *Weir of Hermiston* (1896), on which he was working at the time of his death. It was, he said, 'an attempt at a real his-torical novel, to present a whole field of time'. The story of Archie Weir, arrested for murder and sentenced to death by his own father, is the most psycho-logically complex of Stevenson's books. Move on to *Treasure Island* (1883), in which young Jim Hawkins's discovery of a treasure map leads him on a peril-ous voyage, along with a crew consisting largely of buccaneers led by the infam-ous Long John Silver. *Kidnapped* (1886), set during the aftermath of the Jacobite rebellion, tells how David Balfour is deprived of his inheritance, kidnapped, and bundled onto a slave-ship bound for the Carolinas. He is helped to escape by rebel Highlander, Alan Breck Stewart, and the two flee across Scotland. Illustrating the darker side of Stevenson's imagination is *The Master of Ballantrae* (1888). Here the lifelong feud between two brothers ends in the death of both. *Dr Jekyll and Mr Hyde* (1886) explores the double life led by a respectable doctor and his evil alter ego. Stevenson also wrote some excellent fables and short stories, including the horrific 'Thrawn Janet' (1881) about diabolic possession, and 'The Song of the Morrow' (1885), a sinister little fairy-tale about circular time.

📖 Walter Scott, James Fenimore Cooper. *See* ADVENTURE, HISTORICAL, SUPERNATURAL, THRILLERS   *CB*

Stewart, J(ohn) I(nnes) M(acintosh). *See* **Innes, Michael**

Stewart, Mary (British, 1916–)

Stewart was born in Sunderland, and educated at Durham University, where she lectured until 1945. Begin with *My Brother Michael* (1960), which typifies her fiction's blend of mystery, adventure, and colourful foreign locations. Set in Delphi, it tells of the search for the truth about the death of an Englishman working with the Greek resistance during the Second World War. In *Airs above Ground* (1965), an Englishwoman in post-war Vienna becomes involved with the international security forces. The book includes scenes in Vienna's Spanish Riding School and reaches a dramatic climax high in the Austrian Alps. Her earlier novel, *Nine Coaches Waiting* (1958), concerns an English girl who becomes a governess in France. Tension mounts when she learns of a plot to kill the boy in her charge and implicate her as the murderer.

📖 Evelyn Anthony, Daphne du Maurier, Dorothy Dunnett   *DH*

Stirling, Jessica (British, 1935–) Hugh

Crawford Rae has written under several names, but as Jessica Stirling he writes very popular historical family stories. Begin with the Stalker trilogy, of which the first is *The Spoiled Earth* (1974), set in a Lanarkshire pit village in 1875. An underground explosion kills a shift of 118 men, and the story traces the subsequent lives of their families (in particular, the Stalkers), and of the wealthy mine-owner. The physical detail of the period is conjured vividly and accurately. Other sequences include a trilogy about the Beckman family; the first novel, *The Deep Well at Noon* (1979) is set in London in 1918 and follows Holly Beckman's life after she has been bequeathed a share in the antique shop where she works—to the rage of her employer's children. *Prized Possessions* (1998) is the story of an indomitable family of women in Glasgow in the Depression.

📖 Susan Howatch, Beverley Hughesden, Norah Lofts   *JR*

Stoker, Bram (Irish, 1847–1912) Born in

Dublin to middle-class Protestant parents, Stoker went to London in 1876 to become manager for the actor Henry Irving. Although he wrote short stories and several novels including *The Lair of the White Worm* (1911; idiosyncratically reinterpreted by Ken Russell in a recent film, 1988), he is best known as the author of the vampire classic, *Dracula* (1897). This blood-curdling and engrossing story revolves around Jonathan Harker's journey to the dark, dilapidated castle in Transylvania where he battles with the evil forces of Count Dracula who can only be stopped from sucking the blood from his living victims by the power of the crucifix, garlic, and wood. In 1931 *Dracula* was adapted for the screen igniting the 1930s horror-film boom and inspiring many more *Dracula* films including Francis Ford Coppola's 1992 box office hit, starring Gary Oldman.

📖 Mary Shelley.
See SUPERNATURAL   *EW*

Stone, Irving (US, 1903–89) Stone was born in San Francisco, and educated at the University of California, Berkeley. He worked as a teacher and hack writer before the sensational success of *Lust for Life* (1934) launched his career as a prolific biographical novelist. Begin with this treatment of the life of Vincent Van Gogh, which, like all his best work, is compellingly readable. *Love is Eternal* (1954) tells the story of Mary Todd Lincoln, wife of the assassinated American president. The life and achievement of Sigmund Freud provide the basis for *The Passions of the Mind* (1971). His other works include *The Agony and the Ecstasy* (1961) on the life of Michelangelo, and *Depths of Glory* (1985), his treatment of the painter Camille Pissarro.

📖 Nigel Tranter, Mary Renault, Allan Massie   *DH*

Stone, Robert (US, 1937–) Stone served in the US Navy and briefly joined Ken Kesey's 'Merry Pranksters', a group of young artists and writers who rejected mainstream society in favour of hallu-cinogenics and communal living. He also worked as a journalist and his second novel, *Dog Soldiers* (1974), draws upon his time as a Vietnam war correspondent. A disillusioned writer returns from Vietnam to an American underworld of narcotics, hippy gangsters, and police corruption. Similarly, *A Flag for Sunrise* (1981) skilfully blends racy plotting and hard-boiled dialogue to suggest that the West is often more barbaric than the countries it sets out to civilize. In *Outerbridge Reach* (1992) Stone casts his critical eye over contemporary America, while the more demanding *Damascus Gate* (1998) plumbs the psychology of religious and political extremism in 1990s' Israel.

📖 Don DeLillo, Ken Kesey, John Irving   *BH*

Storey, David (Malcolm) (British, 1933–) The son of a miner, David Storey was born in Yorkshire. He worked as a professional footballer and teacher before beginning his career as a writer. His first novel, *This Sporting Life* (1960), drew on his experience of professional sport to portray the difficulties faced by a young rugby league player embroiled in a relationship with his landlady. The book established Storey as one of his generation's foremost chroniclers of northern working-class life. Later novels include *Radcliffe* (1963), an ambitious study of class, sexuality, and violence in the vein of D. H. Lawrence, *Pasmore* (1972), an account of a college lecturer experiencing a nervous breakdown, and *Saville* (1976), a portrait of a Yorkshire mining village that won the Booker Prize in 1976. He is also known as a playwright and has published a retrospective selection of poems.

📖 Alan Sillitoe, D. H. Lawrence, Barry Hines   *WB*

Stout, Rex (US, 1886–1975) Choose whichever of Stout's many Nero Wolfe books you come across, since (to the joy of his fans) they are all very similar to each other, but here are two to look out for: *Some Buried Caesar* (1938) and *Before Midnight* (1955). Nero Wolfe is one of literature's great detectives. He is hugely fat (and sits in a specially constructed chair), has his own gourmet cook, takes a lift every day to the roof of his New York brownstone house so that he can cultivate his orchids, and does all he can to avoid working. He won't leave the building, but has a sidekick, Archie Goodwin, who does that for him, hurrying around New York collecting clues and corralling suspects who are then ushered back to Wolfe's study so he can point his fat finger at the guilty party. The combination of Wolfe's scepticism, Goodwin's wisecracks, and the world-weary sarcasm of their ally in the police, Inspector Cramer, becomes compulsive.

📖 Raymond Chandler, Georges Simenon   *RF*

Stowe, Harriet Beecher (US, 1811–90) The publication of *Uncle Tom's Cabin; or, Life Among the Lowly* (1851–2) catapulted Stowe to fame. Undoubtedly the most famous anti-slavery novel, *Uncle Tom's Cabin* became the best-seller of the nineteenth century and was a catalyst in dividing North and South in the American Civil War. Stowe made three tours of Europe where she developed important friendships with, among others, Lady Byron and George Eliot. *Dred* (1856), a lesser-known anti-slavery novel, tells the sensational tale of a slave rebellion. A devout Protestant, Stowe believed slavery destroyed the souls of men and women

and was, therefore, an affront to Christian beliefs. Set in New England, *The Minister's Wooing* (1859) and *The Pearl of Orr's Island* (1862) draw heavily on the virtues of Christian salvation. As well as novels, Stowe wrote books on housekeeping, the 'servant problem', children's stories, and studies of the poor.

📖 Louisa May Alcott, Mark Twain. *See* SOCIAL ISSUES, UNITED STATES OF AMERICA   *EW*

Straub, Peter (US, 1943–) Straub was born in Milwaukee and educated at the University of Wisconsin. He is best known for his horror novels. Begin with *Shadow Land* (1980), in which a young man is drawn into sorcery after attempting to protect a friend from a magician. Twenty years later, he fights for the freedom of his will. In *Ghost Story* (1979) a community struggles against a malevolent spirit taking the form of a beautiful woman. All its victims have guilty secrets concerning women. *Mystery* (1989) is set in a Caribbean resort for the very wealthy. After a brush with death, the young hero looks into a murder committed in 1925, and stumbles upon dangerous knowledge about some eminent residents. The Connecticut town in *Floating Dragon* (1982) is menaced by an evil visitation and the release into the environment of a lethally dangerous drug.

📖 Stephen King, James Herbert, Dean R. Koontz. *See* SUPERNATURAL   *DH*

Styron, William (US, 1925–) Styron's first novel, *Lie Down in Darkness* (1951), was an instant success. It tells the story of Peyton Loftis, a young woman driven to suicide by parental and personal pressures in the American South. *The Confessions of Nat Turner* (1967) had a controversial reception; although highly praised for its fictional re-creation of a slave rebellion, some critics found it relied heavily on stereotypes in portraying its black characters. *Sophie's Choice* (1979) has been his most successful novel, and was made into a film directed by Alan Pakula in 1982. The tale of Sophie, a Polish woman now living in the United States, gradually emerges to the narrator, Stingo, and he is horrified by what he learns of her experiences during the war in Auschwitz.

📖 Philip Roth, Norman Mailer　　SV

Süskind, Patrick (German, 1949–)
Süskind studied and lives in Munich, and was a television writer and playwright before becoming a novelist. In 1992 his play *Double Bass* was performed at the Edinburgh Festival and the National Theatre. His most famous work, *Perfume* (1985), tells the story of Grenouille, an utterly amoral foundling born with a peculiarly intense sense of smell. Grenouille obtains work at a perfume house, and begins the serial killing of young girls in order to extract and bottle their odour. He leaves a trail of destruction behind him until he is eventually caught and put on trial. The book draws us into his world through the most rapturously sensual descriptions of scent ever committed to paper. *The Pigeon* (1987) is an extended short story about a similarly isolated hero, dealing in intense detail with the trauma and havoc wreaked in his obsessively ordered life by the appearance of a pigeon.

📖 Franz Kafka, Will Self.
See GERMANY　　　　　　　　EC

Sutcliff, Rosemary (British, 1920–92)
Sutcliff studied at art school, and was a member of the Royal Society of miniature painters. Early in life she developed the progressively wasting Still's desease which confined her to a wheelchair. Her books, while written for children, have an adult respect for original literary and historical sources, telling stories drawn from legend, and bringing to life—and to vivid action—the magic and mystery of the distant past. *The Sword and the Circle* (1981) recounts the legends of King Arthur and his knights of the round table. *The Eagle of the Ninth* (1954) is an adventure set during the Roman occupation of Britain, and tells the story of how Marcus Flavius Aquila retrieves the lost eagle standard of the Ninth Legion from the wilds of Caledonia (Scotland).

📖 Alan Garner, T. H. White, Mary Renault. *See* HISTORICAL　　EC

Svevo, Italo (Italian, 1861–1928) Born in Trieste to an Italian-German-Jewish family, Italo Svevo (real name, Ettore Schmitz) wrote plays, stories, and criticism as well as fiction. His first novel, *A Life*, appeared in 1893, but Svevo remained largely unknown until he met James Joyce in the early 1920s. Joyce's encouragement and recommendation ensured publication for Svevo's masterpiece, *The Confessions of Zeno* (1923). The novel is a complex, multi-layered account, with no fixed viewpoint, of Zeno's arguments with his psychoanalyst and himself, and a central story-line about his efforts to give up smoking. Widely recognized as the first novel to be shaped by the theories of Sigmund Freud, *The Confessions of Zeno* has been enormously influential. *The Tale of the Good Old Man and the Lovely Young Girl*

(1929) was Svevo's last completed work before his death in a car accident.

📖 James Joyce, Italo Calvino, Georges Perec *WB*

Swanwick, Michael (US, 1950–)

Michael Swanwick is one of several authors who have moved steadily from traditional science fiction towards innovative forms of fantasy. His first novel, *In the Drift* (1984), is set in an alternate world in which the Three Mile Island nuclear power plant did in fact explode, leading to the familiar scenario of a radiation-blighted and quasi-feudal future United States. *Stations of the Tide* (1991) also has the recognizable scenario of a far planet on which advanced technologies are embargoed, but mixes this with suggestions of voodoo and Tantric sex. *The Iron Dragon's Daughter* (1993), by contrast, begins as a fantasy where changeling children are forced to slave in a fairyland munitions factory. The heroine escapes in a war dragon, to go through further rites of passage at high school and at university. The story can be seen as a satire or exposé of much contemporary wish-fulfilment fantasy.

📖 George R. R. Martin, Tim Powers, Michael Shea. *See* FANTASY *TS*

Swift, Graham (British, 1949–)

Swift was born in south London. He studied at Cambridge and York universities, and taught English until 1983, the year that saw publication of his most celebrated novel, *Waterland*. Like all his fiction, *Waterland* is concerned with the impact of the past on the present. Tom Crick, the narrator, is a history teacher, about to be pensioned off; the novel consists of his addresses to his pupils, including a sceptic who believes that history is little better than make-believe in the light of the threat that everything will end in nuclear destruction. Crick's various stories are a desperate attempt to reclaim the value of humanism: he tells of his family, on one side Fenland lock-keepers and on the other brewers, whose ale for the coronation of George V caused anarchy; of the mystery surrounding the death by drowning of a near childhood contemporary during the Second World War; and of the lasting effects of that death during the present day. Swift's prose, with its restrained lyricism, hauntingly evokes the Fenland landscape, and conveys the disturbing undercurrents of human behaviour. *Waterland* was shortlisted for the Booker Prize, and won the *Guardian* Fiction award. Swift won the Booker with *Last Orders* (1996), in which four south Londoners drive to the Kent coast to scatter a friend's ashes. Perhaps because of his intimate knowledge of the area from which his characters come, the author pulls off the rare feat of re-creating the thoughts and language of superficially ordinary people without any hint of force or pretension. Of Swift's earlier novels, *Shuttlecock* (1981) is highly recommended; in which the alienated, near-paranoid narrator uncovers his father's wartime past. Whilst being a serious exploration of forms of guilt, this is also very funny.

📖 Rose Tremain, Julian Barnes, Ian McEwan *NC*

Swift, Jonathan (Irish, 1667–1745)

Born in Dublin, and a cousin of the poet John Dryden, Swift was educated at Trinity College. After working in various positions for the household of Sir William Temple in England and Ireland, he was ordained and given the prebend of St Patrick's

Cathedral, Dublin, where he later became dean. The author of numerous political pamphlets, he is best remembered for *Gulliver's Travels* (1726) which follows the fantastical journeys of its eponymous narrator, Lemuel Gulliver, a shipwrecked surgeon. These travels take him to Lilliput (an island of six-inch-high people), Brobdingnag (a land of giants), the flying island of Laputa (occupied by impractical philosophers), and eventually to the land of the Houyhnhnms (a society ruled by horses endowed with reason). These societies force Gulliver, and the reader, to re-evaluate our human world. Both the pomp of the Lilliputian emperor and the civil feuds among his people are made to look ridiculous in their diminutive scale. And compared to the rational, clean, and simple lives of the Houyhnhnm horses, the humans of Europe seem filthy and positively 'beastly'. So alienated is Gulliver from his own species that by the time he returns to Europe he recoils from his own family in disgust. Although it is widely known as a simplified story retold to children, *Gulliver's Travels* is most powerful as a stinging moral satire which was originally read, as Alexander Pope put it, 'from the cabinet council to the nursery'.

📖 François-Marie Arouet Voltaire, Charles Dickens, Aldous Huxley.
See HUMOUR, CLASSICS, SCIENCE FICTION   *RP*

Syal, Meera (British, 1962–) Meera Syal's cultural background is Indian but she was born and brought up in the Midlands. She works as an actress and script-writer as well as writing fiction. Her first novel

was *Anita and Me* (1996). The heroine is the plucky 9-year-old Meena, who lives in the defunct mining village of Tollington in the Midlands in the 1970s. Although of Punjabi descent, her aspirations centre on becoming the friend of Anita Rutter, English, and the roughest girl around. The novel is therefore an exploration of a girl navigating her way through two cultures. The story is told with great humour and vivid period detail, and succeeds in creating a believable childhood perspective.

📖 Harper Lee, Hanif Kureishi
(*The Buddha of Suburbia*)   *SA*

Symons, Julian (British, 1912–94) Born in London, Symons was an advertising copywriter before becoming a full-time writer in the late 1940s. *The Thirty-First of February* (1950) is a good introduction to his prolific output of sophisticated crime novels. It concerns an advertising man who is wrongfully accused of his wife's murder. Although he escapes prosecution, career stress and police harassment drive him to insanity. *The Blackheath Poisonings* (1978) is one of a number of his books with Victorian or Edwardian settings. Following the death from alleged food-poisoning of businessman Roger Vandervent, his son Paul conducts investigations which lead to revelations of secret vice and blackmail in his family. The murder of a prostitute in *A Sort of Virtue* (1996) begins a chain of events involving disclosures of corruption at senior government levels and the suspicious death of a home secretary.

📖 Patricia Highsmith, John Creasey
                                                              DH

T

Tamaro, Susanna (Italian, 1957–)
Tamaro's *Follow Your Heart* (1994) is an intensely personal narrative which explores the lives of three generations of women within one family. The story is narrated by Olga, a woman in her eighties living as a virtual recluse in Trieste, and is in the form of an extended epistle to her estranged grand-daughter who has moved to America to study. Olga's narrative is dated 1992, but covers earlier periods of the twentieth century, when women's lives were more repressed and circumscribed. She writes her missive to free her grand-daughter from the binds of earlier generations and to suggest spiritual and philosophical routes towards a life based upon individual choice. *Anima Mundi* (1998) traces the possibilities of a life well lived through the viewpoint of Walter, a shy young boy.

📖 Isabel Allende, Robert M. Pirsig
DJ

Tan, Amy (US, 1952–) Amy Tan was born and educated in California and Switzerland, but her parents were immigrants from mainland China. Her interest in her own roots and identity forms the inspiration for her fiction, and has made Amy Tan one of the foremost of Chinese-American novelists. Her first novel was *The Joy Luck Club* (1989), a collection of interlocking narratives told by four Chinese mothers and their daughters, some contemporary, others set in semi-feudal and Communist China. The Joy Luck Club itself is four mothers who meet regularly to play mah-jong, eat good food, and raise their spirits. The novel has been made into a successful feature film. *The Kitchen God's Wife* (1991) is equally concerned with the relationships between mother and daughter, and particularly the secrets they withhold from each other. In this novel it is the aunt who brings about the revelation of these secrets. In *The Hundred Secret Senses* (1996) Tan looks instead at the relationship between two half-sisters, one culturally American, the other an immigrant from China who can communicate with ghosts—yin people. The novel ends with both sisters visiting China.

📖 Maxine Hong Kingston, Timothy Mo, Isabel Allende
SA

Tanizaki, Junichiro (Japanese, 1886–1965) Tanizaki combines in his work a nineteenth-century love of Romanticism with the utmost modernity. In his youth, he was much influenced by such writers as Baudelaire, Poe, and Wilde, and interested in stories about corruption and decadence. A novel such as *Quicksand* deals frankly with sexual matters. It was first published in serial form 1928–30, and in book form in 1947. English readers had to wait until 1993 to discover an elegant and fascinating work. Tanizaki's undoubted masterpiece is *The Makioka Sisters* (1948). It was written during the Second World War as a way of reminding the author of a happier past, and it takes the reader into the lives of the Makioka family. We learn so much about the sisters that it is something of a shock to realize at the end of the book that ordinary life is still going on, in the real world. Every possible detail of clothes, food, customs, furnishings, and landscape is there, together with a strong plot that deals with love, marriage, and the loving and complicated relationships between four very different women. Readers should be prepared to become for ever part of the Makioka family. It is a great shame that this author is not better known and more widely translated.

📖 Anita Brookner, A. S. Byatt, Thomas Mann (*Buddenbrooks*)   AG

Tartt, Donna (USA, 1963–) Donna Tartt's first and only novel to date, *The Secret History* (1992), was both a commercial and literary success. It has been described appropriately as a 'highbrow chiller'. The novel is set in a small college in Vermont, based on Tartt's own Bennington College. An élite group of Greek classics students murder a farmer for reasons both erudite and fantastical, and are driven to kill again. The story is told by Richard Papen, an impoverished student, awed by this inner circle. The book is both gripping and intelligently written, exploring the nature of evil and the differences between modern and classical values.

📖 P. D. James, Ruth Rendell (writing as Barbara Vine)   SA

Taylor, Elizabeth (British, 1912–75) Elizabeth Taylor described herself as someone to whom nothing sensational had ever happened, who appreciated routine. This perhaps accounts for the quiet brilliance of her writing. The ironically titled *The Soul of Kindness* (1964) is a study of emotional blindness in which Taylor dis-

plays a devastating ability to illuminate the secret interstices between image, self-image, and psychological truth. In *Angel* (1957) this is taken to an amusing extreme but Taylor is too subtle merely to lampoon her characters—the astoundingly arrogant central character is humanely rendered making the book moving as well as funny. *Blaming* (1976), Taylor's final novel, written while she was herself dying, is a study of guilt—the title reflects the trick of deflecting self-criticism by blaming others. Taylor was also a consummate short-story writer. Her appreciation of the ordinary coupled with an instinct for the absurd give a wry brilliance to the stories in *The Devastating Boys* (1972).

📖 Barbara Pym, Antonia White, Elizabeth Jane Howard. *See* SHORT STORIES   LG

Tennant, Emma (British, 1937–) Emma Tennant was brought up in Scotland and England, and has worked as both a writer and a journalist, founding the literary magazine *Bananas*. Tennant is well known for her continuation of several of Jane Austen's novels, which are fun to read if you enjoyed the original. Have a look at *Pemberley* (1993) and *Emma in Love* (1996). Tennant's main contribution, however, has been to a body of women's writing which emerged in the 1970s and was concerned to explore different writing styles and feminist ideas. Her best novels include *Queen of Stones* (1982), a Goldingesque story about some children who disappear in mysterious circumstances, and *Wild Nights* (1979) which addresses fantasy and childhood and is an important example of a feminist adoption of the magic realist mode.

📖 Susan Hill, Bernice Rubens, Angela Carter   SB

Tey, Josephine (British, 1897–1952) Elizabeth Macintosh wrote plays as Gordon Daviot and mysteries as Josephine Tey. She is generally regarded as one of the most interesting crime writers of her generation. In her explorations of unconventional relationships and sexuality, she is a clear predecessor of Ruth Rendell. Begin with *To Love and Be Wise* (1950), featuring the hero of five of her books, Inspector Alan Grant, who is investigating the disappearance of a handsome young photographer. In a triumphant display of smoke and mirrors, Tey produces an astonishing conclusion as she also does in the non-Grant novels, *Miss Pym Disposes* (1946), set in the hothouse environment of a women's college, *Brat Farrar* (1949) where a missing heir allegedly returns to the family fold, and *The Franchise Affair* (1948), the story of two women accused of abducting a young girl. *The Daughter of Time* (1951) re-examines of the story of the Princes in the Tower from a modern viewpoint.

📖 Ruth Rendell, Margery Allingham, Minette Walters   *VM*

Thackeray, William Makepeace (British, 1811–63) Thackeray was born in India where his father was a senior civil servant. He was sent to England to be educated at Charterhouse, which he hated, and Trinity College, Cambridge, where he lived dissolutely. As a young man he suffered from bad luck as well as bad management. He lost most of his inheritance. His wife suffered an incurable mental breakdown after the birth of their children.

His greatest novel is the best place to start. *Vanity Fair* (1848) is a big book set in the early nineteenth century, when Britain was at war with Napoleonic France. This is Victorian literature at its best. The charac-ters are rich and full; the plot has satisfying twists and turns. *Vanity Fair* begins with two young women finishing at a rather fraudulent ladies' school. Amelia Sedley is rich, gentle, and not terribly bright. Becky Sharp is poor, ambitious, and clever. The novel traces Becky Sharp's ruthless progress through society as she sometimes succeeds and sometimes fails in seducing or, occasionally, marrying men who will be useful to her. Thackeray was mocking the middle classes of his own day, as well as an earlier generation, and the book contains many brilliant comic moments. Less famous, but also a cracking good read are the autobiographical *Pendennis* (1850); the historical novel *The History of Henry Esmond* (1852); and a broad view of mid-Victorian social life and marriage, *The Newcomes* (1855). Thackeray was second only to Dickens in his day, and in some ways he is even better, especially if you like dry, satiric, and witty writing.

📖 Charles Dickens, Henry Fielding
TT

Theroux, Paul (US, 1941–) Theroux, the author of over twenty-five books (several of which have been adapted for film) is a best-selling travel writer. His accessible and often witty novels tend to have a sharply sinister undercurrent, centring on extremely realistic but complicated, evasive heroes, who continually wrestle with contradictory inner impulses. Begin with *The Mosquito Coast* (1981), the disturbing story of Allie Fox, an inventor, and his attempts to create a private utopia with his family in the Honduran jungle. Move on to *My Secret History* (1989), the story of a writer's life, his loves, and betrayals. Also try Theroux's energetic, honest travel writing, especially *The Great*

Railway Bazaar (1975), an account of a haphazard, frustrating train journey from London Victoria to Tokyo Central.

📖 Philip Roth, Bruce Chatwin   *SR*

Thirkell, Angela (British, 1890–1961) Thirkell was born in London, educated at St Paul's School, and began writing during the 1920s when she lived in Australia. Begin with her memoir of Victorian childhood, *Three Houses* (1931), which entertainingly sets the upper-class rural tone of much of her fiction. She is best known for her long series of novels depicting the lives and times of the gentry of Barsetshire, a fictional location adopted in tribute to its originator, Anthony Trollope. *Cheerfulness Breaks In* (1940) surveys activity among the county folk as the shire prepares for the Second World War. *County Chronicle* (1950) reflects on the changing post-war order as Mrs Brandon, a dominant presence throughout the series, re-evaluates her life following the marriage of her son. Published to coincide with the centenary of Queen Victoria's coronation, *Coronation Summer* (1937) is a historical novel evoking the imperialistic optimism of that era. Her other works include *Trooper to the Southern Cross* (1934), the story of a near-mutiny that ensues on a troopship to Australia when failed refrigeration results in bad food.

📖 E. M. Delafield, Lettice Cooper, Anthony Trollope   *DH*

Thomas, Audrey (Canadian, 1935–). *See* CANADA

Thomas, D(onald) M(ichael) (British, 1935–) Thomas shot to fame with his novel *The White Hotel* (1981). This tells the story of Lisa Erdman, including her sexual fantasies and analysis by Freud in Vienna, ending with her horrific death in the Ukraine during the Holocaust. The novel has a magic realist feel, and mixes together poetic and historical discourses. Among Thomas's later novels, *Ararat* (1983) concerns a search for poetic inspiration among the mountains of Russia, while *Pictures at an Exhbition* (1993) treats the Holocaust again, but in a more realist vein.

📖 William Golding, Martin Amis
SV

Thomas, Dylan (British, 1914–53) Born in Swansea, Thomas worked as a journalist and broadcaster, earning a reputation as much for his flamboyant personality as his exuberant writing. Best known for his poetry and his verse play, *Under Milk Wood*, he was also an entertaining and affirmative story-teller. *Portrait of the Artist as a Young Dog* (1940) is a collection of largely autobiographical stories, recalling his boyhood immersion in make-believe, his interpretations of the urgent rituals of courting, and his wild aspirations as a neophyte reporter and a budding poet. *Adventures in the Skin Trade* (1955) includes the stories 'The School of Witches' and 'The Burning Baby', which evoke his inheritance of Welsh mythology, as well as chapters of the unfinished title story. Composed in shrewd, wry, deadpan prose, this tells the story of a young Samuel Bennet running away from home to seek his fortune in London, where he becomes involved—all the time with his finger stuck fast in an ale bottle—with a fantastical cast of characters.

📖 James Joyce, Caradoc Evans   *RP*

Thomas, Rosie (British, 1947–) Rosie Thomas (pseudonym of Janey King) was born in Denbigh, North Wales, and educated there and at St Hilda's College, Oxford. She worked as a journalist and in publishing before writing full time. She writes good quality romantic fiction such as the historical saga *All My Sins Remembered* (1991), with its three heroines who live through the two world wars. Her later novels are contemporary, such as *Other People's Marriages* (1994), about a widow affecting the marital relationships in a cathedral town and *Every Woman Knows a Secret* (1996), a darker novel about a family tragedy which propels the heroine into a love-affair with someone twenty years younger than herself. *Moon Island* (1998) tells the stories of some summer visitors to the coast of Maine.

📖 Joanna Trollope, Elizabeth Buchan, Sue Gee. *See* GLAMOUR   SA

Thomas, Ross (US, 1926–) Thomas (who also writes as **Oliver Bleeck**) was born in Oklahoma City, where he was educated at the University of Oklahoma. He worked as a political adviser before becoming a full-time writer in 1966. Begin with *The Seersucker Whipsaw* (1967), which draws on his behind-the-scenes experience of American politics. It concerns a campaign manager working with the CIA in an African state to ensure a suitable outcome to elections. His other novels centring on dubious political practices include *The Fools in Town are on Our Side* (1970) and *If You Can't Be Good* (1973). In *Twilight at Mac's Place* (1990) the death of a former CIA agent finds his son offered $100,000 for a memoir left by his father. As a web of deceit and treachery unfolds, events in the dead man's past make clear the extent of the security risk posed by the memoir.

📖 Ted Allbeury, Lawrence Block

DH

Thompson, E. V. (British, 1931–) After a career in the police force at home and abroad, E. V. Thompson moved to Cornwall to be a full-time writer. Some of his novels are based on incidents from his own life, like *Wychwood* (1992), or inspired by his knowledge of Hong Kong, like *The Blue-Dress Girl* (1992), set in the colony in the 1850s. His *Retallick* series, beginning with *Ben Retallick* (1980), follows the fortunes of a family in nineteenth-century Cornwall. *Lottie Trago* (1990), sixth in the series, tells of lives affected by the closures of the tin-mines. *The Tolpuddle Woman* (1994) concerns two brothers whose lives are touched by the activities of the rick-burning Captain Swing in the mid-1800s. The author's interest in history shows in the background of his books, but the emphasis is on the everyday lives of the characters as they fall in and out of love.

📖 Winston Graham, R. F. Delderfield   FS

Thompson, Flora (British, 1876–1947) Oxfordshire-born, Thompson went to work at 14, married a fellow post-office worker, and began writing essays and poems. Her autobiographical evocation of a country childhood, *Lark Rise to Candleford* (1945), was first published as three books: *Lark Rise* (1939), *Over to Candleford* (1941), and *Candleford Green* (1943). Here she fictionalizes herself as 'Laura', and tells, unsentimentally and with precise recollection, of growing up at Juniper Hill, the reality of life in a hamlet, 'bare, brown and windswept for eight months out of twelve', the hardships and pleasures of the farm labourers and their families, and visits to the nearby town, Candleford. She chronicles a vanished world of rural and seasonal customs in the late nineteenth century. Go on to read the posthumously published *Still Glides the Stream* (1948) in which she again fictionalizes her childhood experience.

📖 Laurie Lee, H. E. Bates   GC

Thompson, Hunter S(tockton) (US, 1939–)

Thompson worked for magazines and newspapers from the late 1950s onwards, becoming a seminal figure in the 'New Journalism' along with Tom Wolfe and Norman Mailer, introducing subjectivity and fictional techniques into reportage. Thompson's so-called 'Gonzo' writing used unrestrained language and deadpan commentary to capture an increasingly bizarre era of drugs, rock music, and political reaction, and he became a counterculture hero. His books evolved from magazine assignments, often with *Rolling Stone*, and from his experience of alternative lifestyles in San Francisco with the Hippies and the Hell's Angels. His most widely read book is *Fear and Loathing in Las Vegas* (1971), which begins as coverage of a motorcycle race and a district attorneys' conference. The book turns into the hallucinatory misadventures of Raoul Duke and his drug-crazed Samoan lawyer, a manic and very funny clash between the drug culture and representatives of the silent majority. Thompson's reporting on the American Nightmare continued with *Fear and Loathing on the Campaign Trail* (1973), about the Democratic Presidential primary elections, reflecting widespread public cynicism as well as his own personal excesses. A number of subsequent books have collected together fiction as well as Gonzo journalism, notably *The Great Shark Hunt* (1979). A 'lost' novel, *The Rum Diary* (1998), written in Puerto Rico during 1959, has been published. It concerns a young writer and his beach friends, with a menacing atmosphere of sexual and racial tension.

📖 Tom Wolfe, Ken Kesey, Jack Kerouac   JS

Thompson, Jim (US, 1906–77)

Jim Thompson, often cited as a dime-store Dostoevsky, is the archetypal poet of modern noir writing. A hack of the original heyday of American paperback publishing, and an alcoholic, Thompson managed to imbue even his lesser commercial efforts with a deep sense of fatalism reminiscent of Greek tragedies, and, unsung in his lifetime, is now recognized as a major voice in American writing, well beyond the parameters of crime. Born in Oklahoma, he went to the University of Nebraska and later had a variety of jobs including oil pipeline worker, steeplejack, and gambler, and collaborated with Stanley Kubrick on his earlier films. *The Killer Inside Me* (1952) is the chilling first-person narrative of a psychopathic lawman on a murder spree and is a frightful portrait of evil in its day-to-day ordinariness. This familiarity with the banality of the darkness of the soul is a Thompson trademark and shines unhealthily in his best books, *Savage Night* (1953), *The Grifters* (1963), *Pop. 1280* (1964), the last two having been the object of cult movies, respectively about low-life California scam artists and the murderous wrath of a deranged Texas lawman set on revenge. Thompson wrote twenty-nine novels; even at his sloppiest and most rushed, they all bear witness to a dark, fascinating talent.

📖 James Ellroy, James M. Cain   MJ

Thorpe, Adam (British, 1956–) Thorpe was brought up in India, Cameroon, and England, and now lives in France. A strong sense of place pervades his writing, particularly his brilliant first novel—and the one to start with—*Ulverton* (1992). The novel consists of twelve stories connected by their setting—the fictional, archetypal English village of Ulverton. The first story is set in 1650 and subsequent stories cover dates up to the final one (in the form of a film-script) dated 1988. One of the joys of the novel is the range and authenticity of narrators' voices in the stories, particularly the letters in 'Leeward 1743' and the peasant stream-of-consciousness story 'Stitches 1887'. The ways in which people love, use, and exploit the land are important here; and Thorpe's sense of history is exhilarating. His second novel, *Still* (1995) was less successful; at 584 pages, and with a jaundiced, self-lacerating, middle-aged male narrator, it is hard work. *Pieces of Light* (1998) opens wonderfully, with the story of Hugh's early childhood in Cameroon; when the novel moves to England, and to his reminiscences as an old man, the voice is less engaging, although the rich plot and scope of the novel are still rewarding. Thorpe is also known for his poetry.

📖 John Fowles, Thomas Hardy   *JR*

Thubron, Colin (British, 1939–) Thubron was born in London and educated at Eton. He was a film-maker before becoming a full-time author in 1965. Begin with *A Cruel Madness* (1984), in which a member of staff in a mental hospital meets a former girlfriend who is a long-term patient. A painful re-engagement with the past ensues. In *Falling* (1989) a journalist in prison tells the story of his love for a circus performer, whom he assists in dying after she is chronically disabled by a trapeze accident. *Turning Back the Sun* (1991) is set in a town on the edge of an African desert where a European doctor feels a growing sense of exile. Drought and disease force him to choose between leaving or remaining with the woman he loves. Thubron's books as a leading travel writer include *Jerusalem* (1969) and *Among the Russians* (1983).

📖 Paul Theroux, Michael Ondaatje, Robert McCrum   *DH*

Thurber, James (US, 1894–1961) Thurber was a diplomat in Paris before turning to journalism and becoming a regular contributor to the *New Yorker*. His collection of humorous sketches, *My Life and Hard Times* (1933) depicts a moneyed middle-class world of problems with servants and old college friends. *The Middle-Aged Man on the Flying Trapeze* (1935) found Thurber's authentic manner, escapist fantasy, imagining an alternative Civil War, 'If Grant Had Been Drinking at Appomattox'. *My World—and Welcome to it* (1942) introduced Thurber's most famous creation, Walter Mitty, the timid man from the suburbs beset by his domineering wife, who lapses into hilariously heroic fantasies while carrying out shopping tasks. Whimsical cartoons were an integral part of Thurber's humour, often showing the irrational bursting through dull domesticity. *The Thurber Carnival* (1945) is a much-reprinted selection of his best stories, fables, and drawings.

📖 Dorothy Parker, Keith Waterhouse, Flann O'Brien, Laurence Sterne   *JS*

Tinniswood, Peter (British, 1936–) Born in Liverpool and educated at

Manchester University, Peter Tinniswood became a full-time writer in 1967. Begin with *Uncle Mort's North Country* (1986), a collection of bizarrely entertaining stories demonstrating his talent for black humour in northern English settings. The stories follow outings taken by the henpecked Carter Brandon and his misanthropically blunt Uncle. The two feature in Tinniswood's novels of the Brandon family's fantasy-ridden existence on a northern housing estate. These include *I Didn't Know You Cared* (1974) and *Call It a Canary* (1985). With unrelenting deadpan humour, they range through the family's obsessions with sexuality, personal hygiene, and social status. In *Winston* (1991) the bored Nancy Empson diverts herself with passionate pursuit of poacher, rogue, and womanizer Winston, a grotesque embodiment of brute vitality and unscrupulous self-interest.

📖 Spike Milligan, P. G. Wodehouse, Tom Sharpe   *DH*

Toibin, Colm (Irish, 1955–) Novelist and journalist, Toibin has edited a collection of Irish fiction and written a travel book about Europe's Catholics. His writing deals with universal themes of death, loss, and the family but the rapid changes in Irish mores over the last fifty years inevitably influence his writing. Shortlisted for the Booker Prize in 1999, *The Blackwater Lightship* focuses on the dying Declan Devereux, a gay man, and his sister Helen. He summons his friends and family to his grandmother's house and this is the catalyst for revisiting the generational grudge between the women of his family. *The Heather Blazing* (Encore award, 1992) looks at the gap between principle and the messy reality of human lives. Judge

Eamon Redmond is close to yet curiously remote from his wife Carmel and his adult children, preferring the intellectual clarity of the law. The novel moves back and forth between his childhood, family deaths, and the post-civil war politics of Ireland. Redmond experiences a deepening of his relationship with his children after Carmel's death. *The Story of the Night* (1996) is set in Argentina and examines issues of sexual identity against the changing political climate.

📖 John McGahern, Brian Moore.
See IRELAND   *TO*

Tolkien, J(ohn) R(onald) R(euel) (British, 1892–1973) Born in South Africa, Tolkien came to Britain at the age of 3 and was educated in Birmingham and then at Oxford, where he later enjoyed a long and distinguished career as Professor of Anglo-Saxon (1925–45) and Merton Professor of English (1945–59). During the 1930s Tolkien was a member of the literary society 'The Inklings' whose other members included fellow Oxford academic and children's writer C. S. Lewis.

His book *The Hobbit* (1937) originated from stories Tolkien had told his children at bedtime and follows the adventures of the hobbit (an amiable type of gnome) called Bilbo Baggins, who is reluctantly recruited by a gang of dwarves to defeat a dragon. On his journeys he encounters both friends and foes drawn from northern European folklore and epic poetry. These include the Orcs, a vicious breed of goblin, and the benign if manipulating wizard, Gandalf.

The book's setting, Middle-earth, and many of its characters reappear in *The Lord of the Rings* (3 vols., 1954–5), a much longer and more ambitious work that more or less invented the genre of sword and sorcery fantasy. It tells of a fellowship of dwarves, elves, men, and hobbits (including Bilbo's nephew, Frodo Baggins) and their endeavours to stop the Ruling Ring of Power from falling into the hands of evil. It is an epic tale in which seemingly insignificant creatures change the fate of an entire world, and is engaging as adult allegory as well as a children's fable.

📖 C. S. Lewis, David Eddings, Mervyn Peake. *See* FANTASY   *RP*

Tolstoy, Leo (Russian 1828–1910) Tolstoy is arguably the greatest novelist of the nineteenth (or any other) century but his most famous work, *War and Peace* (1863–9), is a byword for that heavy tome you know you ought to read but never get round to. Which is unfair because Tolstoy's prose is crystal clear, the compulsive agonizings of his characters are superior soap opera, and his narrative techniques anticipate the best Hollywood screenplays. *War and Peace* follows the fortunes of several aristocratic Russian families caught up in the Napoleonic Wars of 1805–12. Natasha Rostov, young, eligible, and inexperienced, falls in and out of love with three older men: the arrogant but virtuous Prince Andrei, the caddish Anatole, and Pierre whose bumbling search for purpose and meaning takes him through debauchery and good works, via a disastrously failed marriage, to the bloody battlefield of Borodino and final fulfilment with Natasha. The simple questions he asks are Tolstoy's own lifelong obsession: what is life, and how should I live it? The canvas is vast, the set pieces—balls, battles, births, deathbeds, weddings, peasant uprisings, and guerrilla wars—are magnificent, and though the cast is enormous each character is distinctly drawn, most are psychologically complex, and, astonishingly, the majority are based either on his long-suffering wife Sonya and their family or Tolstoy's own wayward, contradictory, self-obsessed personae (Agonised Compulsive Gambler, Guilty Debauchee, War-hating Soldier, Communistic Serf-Owner, Uxorious Wife-Hater, Marital Rapist, Lecherous Celibate, and self-proclaimed Christian Prophet, to mention but a few).

If *War and Peace* is the greatest war novel, *Anna Karenina* (1873–7) remains the most profound, psychologically penetrating story of adultery, sexual passion, and marital love. Anna is a beautiful, accomplished, and devoted mother who leaves her emotionally desiccated husband and only child for the virile but limited Vronsky. She gains sexual satisfaction but loses, successively, her friends, her status in society, her child, and Vronsky himself. She descends into impotent, clinging jealousy and, ultimately, suicide. In counterpoint to this is the story of Levin and Kitty (Tolstoy and Sonya in thin disguise). Soul-searching Levin woos and weds a much younger bride, takes her from Moscow to his isolated country estate where he hopes for a biddable handmaid for his philosophical, sexual, and agricultural passions but discovers the girl has a will of her own. Tolstoy cuts grippingly back and forth between the poisoned relationship of Anna and Vronsky and the marital power struggles of Levin and Kitty as they try to find a way of living together that is fulfilling to both.

His last novel, *Resurrection* (1898), a savage satire on pre-Revolutionary Russian society, was damaged by obsessive religious didacticism but *The Death of Ivan Ilich* (1886), *The Kreutzer Sonata* (1889), and

Master and Man (1895), shorter, narratively compelling meditations on, respectively, death, sexuality, and class, are undiminished masterworks.

📖 Fyodor Dostoevsky, Maxim Gorky, Charles Dickens, George Eliot. *See* CLASSICS, FILM ADAPTATIONS, HISTORICAL, RUSSIA, SEXUAL POLITICS, WAR·   *MH*

Toole, John Kennedy (US, 1937–69) John Kennedy Toole's second novel, *A Confederacy of Dunces*, was published posthumously. His mother fought to bring out the book, without success until she found Walker Percy, another Southern writer, who championed it and published excerpts in the *New Orleans Review*. It was finally published in 1979 to critical acclaim, and won the Pulitzer Prize for fiction in 1981. Toole committed suicide at the age of 32, due at least in part to discouragement over his own failure to publish his work. His first novel, *Neon Bible*, was published in 1989. Ignatius J. Reilly, the shambolic comic hero of *A Confederacy of Dunces*, suffers a series of disasters and misadventures alongside which he airs his philosophy of life in an entertaining rant. The title comes from Jonathan Swift: 'When a true genius appears in the world, you may know him by this sign, the dunces are all in confederacy against him.'

📖 Saul Bellow, Flannery O'Connor, Carson McCullers, Eudora Welty   *AT*

Torrington, Jeff (British, 1935–) Torrington published his first novel, *Swing Hammer Swing*, in 1992 having worked on it for thirty years. It is an inventive, comic account of a few days in the life of Tam Clay, an unemployed Glaswegian with novelistic aspirations, during the early 1960s just as the Gorbals slums are being demolished. *The Devil's Carousel* (1996), Torrington's second novel, also unites linguistic and dialect playfulness with working-class concerns: it is about union action in a Glasgow car factory, structured as a series of character sketches.

📖 James Kelman, James Joyce   *SV*

Tournier, Michel (French, 1924–) Tournier has won international acclaim, and literary prizes within France for his novels and stories. In his fictional world myths, legends, religious and philosophical beliefs, and bizarre coincidences of plot are employed to reveal unexpected insights into events in the real world. Begin with *The Erl King* (1970) which traces the life of Abel Tiffauges, a huge French garage mechanic, from his childhood memories —of which the most potent is being carried on the shoulders of his friend and protector Nestor—to his 1940–4 experience as a prisoner of war, ending up working at a training camp for young boys at Kaltenborn. Tiffauges interprets his life in terms of signs and symbols, and is happy in Germany, 'the country of pure essences, where everything that passes is symbol, everything that happens is parable'. He ranges the countryside securing boys for the camp but it is only as Germany crumbles, the Red Army advances, and concentration camps are evacuated, that he encounters a half-dead Jewish boy, who shows him the real meaning of the symbols he has interpreted (wrongly, oppositely) in his own life. Tiffauges is a compelling creation, and there are moments of sudden illumination, and a yoking of ideas which is more often associated with reading poetry than prose. *Friday* (1967) tells the Robinson Crusoe story from Man Friday's point of view. *The Fetishist and Other Stories* (1978) contains stories of transformation, delusion, and obsession, again often based on old tales, fairy-tales, and the Bible.

📖 Gunter Grass, Primo Levi, Albert Camus   *JR*

Townsend, Sue (British, 1946–) Townsend lives in Leicester, and writes plays and novels; since she created her comic hero Adrian Mole in 1982, she has written a number of best-sellers. Begin with *The Secret Diary of Adrian Mole Aged 13³/₄*, a wonderfully funny teenage diary. Adrian Mole is anxious and self-conscious but hilariously lacking in self-knowledge; his reports on his parents' marriage, his spots, his girlfriend Pandora, and his own intellectual prowess have an innocence and honesty which makes him utterly endearing despite his terrible priggishness. This book was followed by a number of other successful Mole books, charting his progress to adulthood and middle age. *The Wilderness Years* (1993) finds him in his early twenties with an unpublished novel, a job (which he loses) protecting newt colonies, and a disastrous sex-life.

The Queen and I (1992) imagines a republic in which the Royal Family are forced to live in a council house on a sink estate. The Royals are treated with humour and humanity, but it is difficult to be funny about poverty and deprivation, and in places this feels faintly embarrassing. Adrian Mole makes a successful reappearance in *The Cappuccino Years* (1999).

📖 Nigel Williams, Keith Waterhouse, Richard Francis.
See CHILDHOOD, HUMOUR   *JR*

Tranter, Nigel (British, 1909–99) Tranter was born in Glasgow, educated at

Herriot's School, Edinburgh, and worked in insurance before becoming a full-time writer in 1946. Begin with *The Wallace* (1975), one of his many novels about Scottish history, which recounts William Wallace's rise from obscurity. Betrayal leads to defeat when, fired by injustice, he takes on Edward I's forces. In *Unicorn Rampant* (1984) King James I makes his only return to Scotland after becoming king of England. He returns to London with a young Scottish courtier who cuts a dash in the English court and meets Ralegh, Bacon, and the future Charles I. *Children of the Mist* (1992) deals with hostilities between the MacGregor and Campbell clans in the early seventeenth century. Bonnie Prince Charlie's time of flight through the highlands after Culloden is the subject of *Highness in Hiding* (1995).

📖 Jean Plaidy, Bernard Cornwell, Walter Scott   *DH*

Trapido, Barbara (British, 1941–) Trapido was born in South Africa and has lived in England since 1963. In her first novel, *Brother of the More Famous Jack* (1982), Katherine finds herself living in the bohemian family home of Jacob Goldman, her philosophy professor, and in love with his son. The affair ends badly and she flees to Rome, returning ten years later to discover that her life is still inextricably bound up with the Goldmans. Trapido writes witty romantic comedies, yet explores the tragedies of ordinary human lives with some tenderness. Many of the characters in earlier novels turn up in later ones, suggesting that life continues beyond romantic resolutions. *The Travelling Hornplayer* (1997) is an unravelling of the mysterious circumstances under which a young woman is killed running across a road, and tells of her sister's struggle to make sense of her loss. Trapido inspires affection for her characters, and her plots have the quality of a playful dance.

📖 Amanda Craig, Jane Gardam, Jane Austen   DJ

Traven, B. (1882 or 1890?–1969) B. Traven's identity was a closely guarded secret. He was probably either Ret Marut, born in Poland in 1882, or Berick Traven Torsvan, born in 1890 in Chicago. What is certain is that his stories first appeared in German in Berlin, that he spent his final years in Mexico, and left a legacy of novels and stories all concerned with the corrupting influence of money. His finest is *The Death Ship* (1926), about the wanderings of an American seaman with no papers or status after the First World War. *The Treasure of the Sierra Madre* (1927), his famous adventure story of fatal greed, was filmed in 1947 by John Huston, and *The White Rose* (1965) is about the ascendancy of profit over human lives after oil is found on a Mexican ranch. Traven had Marxist leanings and was banned by the Nazis as a Communist, but his work attacks power structures of all kinds.

📖 Jack London, John Steinbeck   CB

Treece, Henry (British, 1911–66) Born in Wednesbury, Treece was educated at the University of Birmingham and worked as schoolteacher until 1959. Formerly a noted poet, he wrote only historical novels from 1952 onward. Begin with *The Dark Island* (1952), the first of numerous vivid re-creations of life among the ancient Britons. It concerns Caractacus' struggle against the Romans while internal disorder divides the Britons. *The Last of the Vikings* (1964)

finds Harald Hardrada of Norway at the Battle of Stamford Bridge in 1066. He looks back over his warlike life before dying in battle against King Harold, who goes on to defeat at Hastings. Treece also wrote historical fiction for teenagers. *Legions of the Eagle* (1954) deals with a 13-year-old whose idyllic boyhood in a peaceful community of Britons ends when the Romans attack.

📖 Nigel Tranter, Mary Renault   DH

Tremain, Rose (British, 1943–) To read a Tremain novel is to be moved through a process; she will make you see something one way and then move you to see it differently. Start with the short stories in *The Colonel's Daughter* (1984) to appreciate her ability to change perspective. *Restoration* (1989) sweeps you through the turbulence of the seventeenth century. *Sacred Country* (1993) moves to rural Norfolk in the 1950s and explores what it feels like to grow up knowing your body is the wrong gender. *The Way I Found Her* (1997) is written from the point of view of a precocious 13-year-old boy on holiday in Paris, enjoying his first taste of independence and its consequences. The real treat in a Tremain novel is the sensuous description of food, of landscape, of period, experienced through the distinct consciousness of the main character.

📖 Jane Gardam, Jane Rogers, Michèle Roberts   RV

Tressell, Robert (Irish, 1870–1911) Robert Tressell (pseudonym of Robert Noonan) was born in Dublin, but settled in Hastings, England, after a brief time in South Africa where he married and had a daughter. He was a member of the Social

Democratic Foundation, a Marxist group, and made a living from housepainting and signwriting. His political beliefs and his experiences on the breadline were the inspiration for his first and only novel *The Ragged Trousered Philanthropists* (1914). He started writing this in 1904, failed to find a publisher, attempted to burn the manuscript, and later emigrated and died in a workhouse in Canada. The novel was not published in its unabridged form until 1955. It tells the story of a group of painters and decorators in Edwardian Sussex, and graphically illustrates the hardships of their working lives. Decorating Mayor Sweater's house, they have to cut corners in order to boost the profits of their bosses. They are joined, however, by the journeyman and prophet-figure Owen, who introduces them to socialist ideas, and they begin to see that the capitalist system is the cause of their privations. *The Ragged Trousered Philanthropists* is unashamedly sympathetic to the workers, heavily didactic in parts, but it is also a moving, detailed, funny, and honest evocation of a section of society not often portrayed in fiction. It is a seminal political novel.

📖 George Orwell (*Down and Out in Paris and London*), George Gissing   *SA*

Trevor, William (Irish, 1928–)
A highly respected short-story writer, novelist, and editor, Trevor has received numerous literary prizes and is a member of the Irish Academy of Letters. His work features the seemingly ordinary, explored from an off-beat angle. His characters are often eccentric or borderline psychopaths. In his novel *Felicia's Journey* (1994), now a film, Hilditch preys on the pregnant Felicia who has lately stepped off the boat from Ireland to search for her feckless boyfriend. In Hilditch, Trevor creates a penetrating psychological portrayal of a serial killer, whilst writing with a lyricism that prevents simple genre classification. *Death in Summer* (1998) deals with emotionally stunted characters, Thaddeus and Pettie. Their capacity for doing good or ill is almost arbitrarily based on the chance presence or absence of love. Trevor's account of Pettie's obsession with Thaddeus does not permit the reader the comfort of smugness. In the short story, Trevor's skill lies in the astute economy of his prose: a character can be revealed in one sentence. The collection *The News from Ireland* (1986) reveals Trevor's intimacy with Irish and English culture, picking up the nuances of hierarchy in an Irish town or the recognition of an unbridgeable gap between an English father and daughter. *After Rain* (1996, short stories) covers familiar territory between England, Ireland, and Italy, illuminating the foibles and appetites of his characters with quiet compassion, and the novella *Reading Turgenev* (1991) is one of the most beautiful in the language.

📖 Elizabeth Bowen, John Banville.
See IRELAND, SHORT STORIES   *TO*

Trollope, Anthony (British, 1815–82)
Trollope was a prolific writer who enjoyed outstanding popularity in his own time. He worked for the Post Office and travelled extensively in the course of his work; he also introduced the pillar box to Britain. He published forty-seven novels and several works of non-fiction.

Trollope was a realist who addressed the tensions and difficulties of nineteenth-century society, exploring topical issues such as feminism, the class system, the social effects of money, and electoral reform. His novels deliberately expound his own beliefs, but he was also an astute psychologist, whose account of his characters' conflicting moral outlooks is extremely convincing. His best-known work includes the character-based *Barsetshire* sequence (1855–67), set in a fictional cathedral town and its county. The six novels depict local society, its intrigues and conflicts, centring on the temperamental Archdeacon and his father-in-law, the Revd Septimus Harding. Begin with *The Warden* (1855), the first volume of the series, which considers the tension caused between Harding's younger daughter Eleanor and her suitor, Dr John Bold, when Bold accuses Harding of mismanaging money left to the hospital of which he is warden. Move on to Trollope's later sequence of *Palliser* novels (1864–80), which begin with *Can You Forgive Her?* (1864–5). Set in London, they follow the political career of Plantagenet Palliser and the lives and relationships of those around him.

Also recommended is *The Way We Live Now* (1874–5), the psychologically acute story of Augustus Melmotte, who, having gained social prestige and political office on largely false grounds, attempts to marry his daughter Marie to rich men and eventually faces political disgrace. You may also enjoy *An Autobiography* (1883), Trollope's account of his difficult early life and successful career.

📖 George Gissing, Charles Dickens, William Makepeace Thackeray.
See CLASSICS   SR

Trollope, Joanna (British, 1943–) Joanna Trollope was born in Gloucestershire, educated at Oxford, and is a descendant of Anthony Trollope. Initially, she began writing historical romances such as *Parson Harding's Daughter* (1979), set in eighteenth-century India. However, she only began to achieve mass popularity when she moved to contemporary novels. Her first, *The Choir* (1988), is set in a socialist-run city where the fate of the old cathedral choir hangs in the balance. *A Village Affair* (1989) followed, telling the story of a female friendship that develops into an affair, and rocks the society in the village where the events take place. *The Best of Friends* (1995) deals with adultery and its effects, while *A Spanish Lover* (1996) is self-explanatory. Trollope is a perceptive chronicler of the English middle classes and has enjoyed tremendous popular acclaim. She is credited with the invention of the sub-genre, 'Aga saga'.

📖 Katie Fforde, Angela Lambert, Mary Wesley   SA

Turgenev, Ivan (Russian, 1818–83) After the radical press criticized him for his unflattering portrayal of the nihilist student Bazarov in *Fathers and Sons* (1862), and the right wing accused him of glorifying nihilism, Turgenev exiled himself to Europe, spending most of the rest of his life in Paris. Abroad, he longed for reform, for the 'westernization' of Russia. He was the first great Russian writer to find success in Europe.

Fathers and Sons examines the conflict between the generations; the older, the landowners wishing to conserve traditional systems, and the younger having revolutionary tendencies. Turgenev intended Bazarov to be a sympathetic character, but he appears rude and abrupt, often ridiculing the simplicities of the peasants. Visiting his friend's father and uncle during the holidays, he causes problems in the family, flirting with the father's mistress, and fighting a duel with the uncle. He also falls in love with the nearby female landowner, the fascinating and chilly Anna.

Sketches from a Hunter's Album (1847–51) describes life in the evocatively drawn Russian countryside. Turgenev demonstrates his fascination with different types —thinkers and doers, whom he calls 'Hamlets and Don Quixotes'. In 'Bailiff' he describes the repressive relationship between the serfs and the corrupt eponymous official, and though the message is not spelt out, the need for reform is clear. 'Bezhin Lea' begins with a wonderful description of the sky during a July morning, and tells of a night spent listening to boys recounting superstitious stories. Turgenev also wrote plays, his most often performed being *A Month in the Country*, admired by Chekhov.

📖 Nikolai Gogol, Boris Pasternak, George Moore. *See* RUSSIA   FS

Turow, Scott (US, 1949–) Turow's work is several cuts above your usual legal thriller. If you like lots of plot twists dependent on legal niceties, you won't be disappointed in *Presumed Innocent* (1987) and *The Burden of Proof* (1990), as Turow draws on his experience as a partner in a Chicago law firm. But it's the moral and political intricacies which will really hook you. These are big, satisfying books (500-plus pages) which are easy to read because Turow's ear for dialogue is so sharp. Where John Grisham gives you fast-paced action, Turow's strength is the slow pressure of the accumulation of plot detail which becomes just as nail-biting. The approach is oblique and sophisticated; the truth is seen from multiple viewpoints and only gradually, if at all, uncovered. *The Laws of Our Fathers* (1996) unravels

thirty years of American history, asking if the 1960s had any lasting impact.

📖 Tom Wolfe, T. Coraghessan Boyle
RV

Tutuola, Amos (Nigerian, 1920–97) *The Palm-Wine Drinkard* (1952), Tutuola's most celebrated work, adopts the storytelling tradition of the Yoruba people to create a magical and fantastical tale. Following the death of the palm-wine tapster, the protagonist, (with an insatiable thirst for palm-wine) sets out on a mythical journey to rescue him from limbo. Among many feats he narrowly escapes death, rescues a woman, and on returning home, relieves a famine with a magic egg. *My Life in the Bush of Ghosts* (1954) is a bewitching and imaginative tale describing a young man's journey in the land of the dead. Tutuola's ability to translate the Yoruba oral tradition onto the printed page makes his story-telling unique.

📖 Chinua Achebe, Wole Soyinka, Ben Okri   EW

Twain, Mark (US, 1835–1910) 'Mark Twain' was the pseudonym of Samuel Langhorne Clemens, taken from the call of Mississippi river pilots. His two most famous books, *The Adventures of Tom Sawyer* (1876) and *Adventures of Huckleberry Finn* (1884), are both based upon Clemens's own boyhood in Hannibal, Missouri, before the Civil War. *Tom Sawyer* is a children's classic, detailing adolescent Tom's scrapes involving drunks, criminals, and buried treasure. Huck Finn appears as a fairly minor character. But in the later novel, one of the most influential in American literature, Huck is both narrator and the main protagonist in a wonderfully rich story, its comically offhand manner disguising a great depth of social commentary and incisive folk wisdom. Huck is caught between his own conscience and the claims of society, especially when floating down the river on a raft with runaway slave Jim, and he eventually resolves to escape civilization by 'lighting out for the territory'.

Life on the Mississippi (1883) is a rewarding collection of travel sketches and stories set in the territory that Twain knew best. Many of Twain's later books show him as an increasingly bitter satirist. In *A Connecticut Yankee at King Arthur's Court* (1889), a blow on the head suffered by Hank Morgan sends him back to sixth-century England, where his attempts to introduce modern American practices and gadgets cause disasters. The title story in *The Man That Corrupted Hadleyburg* (1900) concerns the ownership of a mysterious bequest of gold coins, dishonestly disputed by the leading citizens of a small town.

📖 Jack London, J. D. Salinger, Jack Kerouac, Charles Dickens. *See* UNITED STATES OF AMERICA

JS

Tyler, Anne (US, 1941–) Tyler is a popular writer, whose novels about ordinary American families are fresh, funny, and sad. There is often a misfit in the family, whose point of view is explored and validated; Tyler has sympathy for a wide range of characters. *A Slipping Down Life* (1969) shows a teenage girl becoming obsessed with a local rock singer, and marrying him; the fatalism here, the sense of inevitability carrying people onwards towards unlikely ends, is present in all Tyler's novels. *Dinner at the Homesick Restaurant* (1982) tells the story of a family —single mother, two sons, and a daughter —from the children's early days to middle age, revealing the powerful connections, rivalries, and antagonisms between them and exploring each character's point of view. In *Ladder of Years* (1995) the heroine walks away from her husband and teenage children, and attempts to make a life on her own. For a while she finds herself in a housekeeping role to a divorcee and his son, but does eventually return to her own family; the insights gleaned along the way are bittersweet. *The Accidental Tourist* (1985) tells the story of a travel-guide writer who is addicted to routine, trying to cope with life after the loss of his son and departure of his wife. *A Patchwork Planet* (1998), narrated by black sheep Barnaby Gaitlin, sympathetically and humorously explores the world of old people as Barnaby does odd jobs for them; and offers insights into delinquency as a rejection of stifling materialistic attitudes. Tyler's dialogue always rings true, as do the settings and events of her novels; occasionally she is a touch sentimental.

📖 Richard Ford, Carol Shields, Roddy Doyle. *See* UNITED STATES OF AMERICA

JR

U

Undset, Sigrid (Norwegian, 1882–1949) Undset had to relinquish her ambitions to be a painter after her father's death left her having to support herself from the age of 16. Her early novels, of which the most successful was *Jenny*, caused controversy through their frank portrayal of sexual love and infidelity. She is best known for her historical trilogy *Kristin Lavran's Daughter* (1920–2), the first part of which has been made into a film directed by Liv Ullmann. In these novels, set in medieval times, she draws on the language and style of the sagas to tell the story of Kristin's dramatic life, combining a richly detailed description of the period with a deep psychological insight as Kristin struggles with her feelings of love and guilt, and the need for self-fulfilment set against social and religious conventions and responsibilities. Undset won the Nobel Prize for Literature in 1928.

📖 George Eliot, Theodor Fontane, Robert Graves   *KB*

Unsworth, Barry (British, 1930–) Unsworth was born into a mining family in Durham, and travelled and taught English as a foreign language before and during his early writing career. He currently lives in Italy. His novels are set in a wide range of historical and geographical locations, although they always grapple with current issues and ideas. He chooses the past because, he says, 'You can shed a lot of contemporary clutter'. Begin with his 1992 joint-Booker prize-winning *Sacred Hunger*,

about the mid-eighteenth-century slave trade. The *Liverpool Merchant* collects slaves from Africa but, during a crossing beset by sickness and bad weather, the captain decides to jettison his living cargo to claim the insurance money. Twelve years later the ship (assumed lost) is discovered in wilderness Florida, where runaways—both black and white—live in a utopia 'where no man is chief'. *Morality Play* (1995) is set in the north of England in the fourteenth century, and tells of a group of travelling players who depart from their time-honoured roles and begin to incorporate story details from a recent real-life murder, hunting down the truth by play-acting it. Richly and poetically written, this vividly conjures the Middle Ages, in a plot which works at many levels, from suspenseful whodunit to masterly exploration of illusion and reality. *Stone Virgin* (1985) is set in Venice, and shifts in time from the 1970s (and the conservationist working on the statue of the title) to the 1400s, when the original sculptor was at work.

📖 William Golding, Thomas Keneally, Joseph Conrad   *JR*

Updike, John (US, 1932–) Updike is a great American novelist; he's written over forty books, including stories, poems, essays, and autobiography, but his reputation rests chiefly on the *Rabbit* sequence. This quartet of novels is about Harry (Rabbit) Angstrom, teenage basketball star of little education and no vocation, tracing his life from his early twenties through four decades to his death. Updike's achievement in these novels is unrivalled, and epic in scale, telling the intimate story not just of one man's life but of America in the second half of the twentieth century. *Rabbit, Run* (1960), the first book, opens with Rabbit in his fictional home town fifty miles outside Philadelphia. He butts into a kids' basketball game, goes home to his small, blurry, alcoholic wife Janice in their squalid flat, sets out to pick up their 2-year-old son, and decides on the spur of the moment to make a break for it. He spends the book running; south, away from the narrow trap of his life and his job as a magi-peel demonstrator; away from Janice into the arms of big red-haired Ruth. Not idealistic, not responsible, not rich, not clever, not thoughtful beyond his own pleasure, Rabbit is nevertheless one of the most intensely likeable and human characters in fiction. His relation to the world is intensely physical, so that his thoughts are peppered with memories of basketball shots, of climbing splintering telegraph poles, of the feel of women's skin, of golfing strokes. The world of smells and sounds and sight shimmers around him, and at each misfortune, buoys up and distracts him into optimism again. *Rabbit, Run* ends terribly, as Janice in an alcoholic stupor drowns their baby daughter in the bath, and Ruth falls pregnant. Rabbit is down but not out; he runs again. In *Rabbit Redux* (1971) Rabbit meets politics (physically, the way he experiences everything else); he's now working as a 'linotyper' (soon to be redundant) and involved with rich hippy Jill and her friend, black activist and Vietnam veteran on the run, Skeeter. *Rabbit is Rich* (1981, Pulitzer Prize) takes Rabbit into the 1970s, a patched-up marriage, a secure job as a car salesman, and affluence;

Rabbit at Rest (1990) brings him into the 1980s and a curious reversal, as Janice becomes sharp and competent while he gets old and ill, jealous of his drug-dealing son, still never losing his hunger for life. That the American Dream is cracked and dirty is exposed to the full in these novels and yet—through the loving detail of Rabbit's life and optimism—its vigour is reasserted.

Of Updike's other novels *The Coup* (1978), about a revolutionary dictatorship in Africa, is fascinating by way of contrast, and for the world it creates. In *Couples* (1968), as in the *Rabbit* books, Updike writes wonderfully well about sex.

📖 Russell Banks, Norman Mailer, George Eliot, Leo Tolstoy   JR

Upward, Edward (British, 1903–   ) Born in Romford and educated at Cambridge, Upward was a schoolteacher from 1928 to 1962 and a member of the Communist Party from 1928 to 1962. Begin with *Journey to the Border* (1938), in which a young tutor's stifling middle-class surroundings drive him to hallucinatory breakdown. He reconstructs his identity by committing himself to socialist ideals. The political dimension is also prominent in *The Spiral Ascent* (1977), a trilogy consisting of *In the Thirties* (1962), *The Rotten Elements* (1969), and *No Home But the Struggle* (1977). The novels follow the career of schoolteacher Alan Sebrill, who sacrifices his talent as a poet to the Communist cause but returns to writing after becoming disillusioned with politics. *The Mortmere Stories* (1994) collects the bizarre satires on English middle-class life in the village of Mortmere written by Upward and his friend Christopher Isherwood.

📖 George Orwell, John Berger   DH

Ure, Jean (British, 1943–). *See* TEEN

Uris, Leon (US, 1924–) Uris, born in Baltimore, Maryland, was the son of Jewish parents of Russian-Polish origin. He spent most of his youth in a poor suburb but left by joining the Marine Corps. His experiences are conjured in a vivid account of the Second World War entitled *Battle Cry* (1953). His most famous work is *Exodus* (1958), an epic novel which is both an intimate love-story and a harrowing and gripping account of the Jewish struggle to establish the homeland of Israel. The novel also focuses on the international treatment of Jews during the Second World War. In *Mila 18* (1961) Uris takes one episode from *Exodus*, which deals with the Warsaw ghetto during the Holocaust, and expands this terrible segment of Jewish history into a novel.

📖 John Steinbeck, Howard Fast   *CJ*

Urquhart, Jane (Canadian, 1949–) Urquhart is a novelist, short-story writer, and poet. She won the Governor General's award for fiction in 1997 with *The Underpainter*. The story is told from the perspective of the American Austin Fraser, a celebrated modernist painter. His voice is disturbingly narcissistic. He appropriates the body of Sara, his model and lover, and the stories of his friends, and uses their richer emotional lives in an attempt to fill the moral emptiness at the centre of his own. His vanity allows him to claim credit for the deaths of his friend George and his companion Augusta. In *Away* (1994) the narrative follows Mary, a young Irishwoman, to Canada after a strange encounter with a dying sailor on the west coast of Ireland. The novel picks up Urquhart's themes of memory, history, and abandonment.

📖 Anne Michaels, Margaret Atwood. *See* CANADA   *TO*

V

Valenzuela, Luisa (Argentinian, 1938–). *See* MAGIC REALISM

Vance, Jack (US, 1916–) Jack Vance is the most consistently successful of fantasy writers in the American or non-Tolkienian tradition, and has also written many works of 'space opera', adventurous science fiction often set in quasi-medieval worlds. Vance's fantasy career began with *The Dying Earth* (1950), a collection of stories set in a very distant future where science has become indistinguishable from magic, and where the Earth is populated by ghosts and monsters as well as humans: this has had several sequels. A much later fantasy sequence is the *Lyonesse* trilogy begun by *Lyonesse I: Suldrun's Garden* (1983), this time set in a pre-Arthurian land, now drowned beneath the sea, but once more populated by creatures of incomparable diversity. Successful works of science fiction by Vance include *Big Planet* (1952) and *Star King* (1964). Their strength lies in his ability to create societies and cultures of bizarre plausibility.

📖 Avram Davidson, Michael Shea. *See* FANTASY   TS

van der Post, Laurens (South African, 1906–96) Van der Post spent most of his life undertaking official missions abroad for the British Government and the Colonial Development Corporation. Many of these missions became the subject of his fiction and travel writing. Although criticized for his conservative and individualistic politics,

his early novel, *In a Province* (1934), is a scathing attack on South African racism. *A Far-Off Place* (1974) with its religious overtones and its quest for wholeness and communion with nature is representative of van der Post's work. *The Seed and the Sower* (1963) is based on van der Post's imprisonment in a Japanese prisoner-of-war camp during the Second World War. In 1983 it was made into the film, *Merry Christmas Mr Lawrence* starring Tom Conti. Much of van der Post's work is influenced by the psychoanalytical theories of Carl Jung.

📖 Henry Rider Haggard, André Brink
EW

Vargas Llosa, Mario (Peruvian, 1936–) Mario Vargas Llosa is a journalist, essayist, and politician as well as a novelist, and ran as a Conservative candidate for the office of the Peruvian presidency. He began his career as a leftist, and early books like *Time of the Hero* (1962), a novel about the indoctrination process endured by military students in Lima, reflect these political concerns. He is best known for the humane and sophisticated comic style of his later work, represented in *Aunt Julia and the Scriptwriter* (1977), a witty and entertaining story about a soap opera writer who uses the scandalous affair of a young man and his cousin, an older woman, as raw material for his scripts. As the factual and fictional versions of the same events become increasingly entangled and the soap opera's melodramas unfold, the characters' lives are transformed. *The War at the End of the World* (1981) is an epic novel based on a historical episode from the late nineteenth century, when an apocalyptic cult took hold in north-eastern Brazil. *In Praise of the Stepmother* (1988) is a short novel in which a boy's sexual yearning for his stepmother is interwoven with the boy's fantasies about erotic paintings, while the same boy reappears as an adult in *The Notebooks of Don Rigoberto* (1997), the explicit tale of a Lima businessman's inseparable cultural and sexual lives told as a sometimes bawdy, sometimes poetic comedy of human desire.

📖 Isabel Allende, Guillermo Cabrera Infante, Gabriel García Márquez.
See MAGIC REALISM   WB

Vassanji, Moyez (Kenyan, 1950–) Vassanji was born to Indian parents in Nairobi, and was educated at the Massachusetts Institute of Technology and the University of Toronto, where he lectured until 1989. Begin with *The Gunny Sack* (1989), in which an assortment of curios left to a boy forms the source of stories about the coming of Indians to East Africa from the late nineteenth century onwards. *No New Land* (1991) takes up where the previous book ends, as political conditions force the Asian population to flee. Those who head for Canada establish a new Indian community in Toronto. In *The Book of Secrets* (1994) a retired teacher edits the diary of a British colonial officer in Dar es Salaam in 1913–14. It records interactions between the British and Indian communities and a mysterious relationship with a visionary native woman.

📖 V. S. Naipaul, Rohinton Mistry
                                    DH

Verne, Jules (French, 1828–1905) Jules Verne refused to take over his father's business, at one stage running off to sea and only being prevented after the boat had set sail. In the end, his father was indulgent enough to let him go to Paris where he wrote drama and poetry. Under the influence of Edgar Allan Poe, Verne turned his attention to escapist adventures in prose. His characteristic technique is to set a straightforward adventure yarn in an exotic world and lace it with science. These 'voyages extraordinaires' were taken up by the children's publisher Hetzel who needed a regular author for a children's magazine he was producing. A book to start with might be the early success, *Journey to the Centre of the Earth* (1864), in which Verne's three protagonists travel to a dormant volcano from which they descend to the earth's core. In *Round the World in Eighty Days* (1873) Phileas Fogg embarks on a wild ballooning journey in order to win a bet. Verne has a highly evocative, descriptive style which makes his work attractive and accessible to younger readers, and of course many of his books have been made into films. In *Twenty Thousand Leagues under the Seas* (1870), Verne presents a slightly darker vision. The hero, Captain Nemo, is an Indian prince who has rebelled against the British empire by creating a life for himself in a submarine.

📖 H. G. Wells, C. S. Lewis, Henry Rider Haggard   LM

Vidal, Gore (US, 1925–) Born in Washington to a distinguished political family, Vidal has made great play with history and politics in his fiction. His major achievement is the quintet of historical novels tracing the United States from the

War of Independence to the McCarthy era, mixing real and invented characters. Outstanding amongst them are *Burr* (1973), which re-creates the flamboyant life and times of soldier Aaron Burr, *Lincoln* (1984), a gripping fictional account of his country's greatest Presidency, and *Washington DC* (1967), convincing in its insider's view of senatorial political intrigue. Vidal is, however, also a novelist of social satire and sexual themes, and his lighter books are most enjoyable. *Myra Breckinridge* (1968) is a satirical novel about movie people, with a narrator who turns out to be transsexual. Its gossipy details draw upon Vidal's period as a Hollywood scriptwriter. In *Kalki* (1978) a lesbian test pilot called Teddy brings about the end of the world as the unwitting agent of Kalki, a Vietnam veteran turned Messiah. Told from a deserted White House, the story ends as a plan to repopulate the world fails and the planet is left to the animals. A recent novel, *The Smithsonian Institution* (1998), takes one of Vidal's main interests, dead Presidents, and applies the 'What If' genre, mixing political asides with fantastical physics.

📖 Norman Mailer, Christopher Isherwood, Don DeLillo *JS*

Vincenzi, Penny (British, 1939–). *See* GLAMOUR

Vine, Barbara. *See* **Rendell, Ruth**

Vollmann, William T(anner) (US, 1959–) Born and educated in California, William T. Vollmann became known for an obsessive attraction to violence and danger, and his research has involved seeking out drug barons, torturers, and terrorists in war zones like Afghanistan and Bosnia.

His first novel, *You Bright and Risen Angels* (1987), was a sprawling portrait of contemporary American life held together by a voice that reflects the strangeness and turmoil of the landscape around it. *The Rainbow Stories* (1989) interweaves real-life stories of homelessness, drug addiction, and combat trauma to create a tapestry-style portrait of the American underclass, while *The Butterfly Stories* (1993) describes the lives of prostitutes in Cambodia and Thailand. Vollmann is a hugely prolific and uneven writer, but at his best the difficult and painful stories he uncovers are filtered through a style that is by turns compassionate, strange, and redemptive.

📖 Thomas Pynchon, William Faulkner *WB*

Voltaire, François-Marie Arouet (French, 1694–1778) Poet, thinker, dramatist, satirist, critic, and moralist, Voltaire was a giant of letters whose name is virtually synonymous with the eighteenth-century Enlightenment that prepared the ground for the French Revolution. Successively fêted by French society and then imprisoned in the Bastille for his satires, Voltaire exiled himself to Prussia (where he became Frederick the Great's pet *philosophe*) and then to England (whose constitutional monarchy he much admired). His novella-length 'philosophical tale' *Candide* (1759) is the work for which he is most remembered and which has had the most influence on subsequent authors. It describes the picaresque adventures of an engaging innocent abroad whose encounters with characters from all walks of society provide opportunities for wicked satire.

📖 Jonathan Swift, Jaroslav Hašek, Henry Fielding *MH*

Vonnegut, Kurt (US, 1922–) Vonnegut's writing has been much influenced by science fiction. His work repeatedly attacks the way the human race is desecrating the planet. However, he refuses to create scapegoats and he uses an ironic humour which both allows the reader to pity the human condition and to acknowledge the absurd and the irrational. *Slaughterhouse-Five* (1969) captures the flavour. The hero, Billy Pilgrim, like Vonnegut a survivor of the bombing of Dresden in the Second World War, is captured by aliens. From the aliens, who see all time as simultaneous, Billy learns that the secret of life is to live in the happy moments only. In *Cat's Cradle* (1963) Vonnegut contrasts the obsessively scientific attitude of Felix Hoenikker, one of the original creators of the atomic bomb, with the myth-making of Boronen, the creator of a religion which protects its adherents against the problem of too much reality by offering them a diet of unashamed lies. In *Galapagos* (1985) a bomber pilot fantasizing about sex inadvertently triggers nuclear holocaust. A group of survivors gathered on the Galapagos Islands has to set about survival with no technology apart from a computer that has only linguistics and a million quotations from the world's great literature in its memory.

📖 Ray Bradbury, J. G. Ballard, Roger Zelazny. *See* UNITED STATES OF AMERICA *LM*

W

Wain, John (British, 1925–94) Born in Stoke-on-Trent, Wain studied at Oxford and lectured in English literature before writing full-time. His first novel, *Hurry on Down* (1953), was a significant landmark in post-war British fiction, being the first appearance of the irreverent, anti-establishment hero-as-clown figure, a precursor of the Angry Young Men. The picaresque, low-life adventures of Charles Lumley are still fresh and funny today. *Strike the Father Dead* (1962) is another take on youthful rebellion against stuffy middle-class morality; set in 1942, the black-sheep son outrages his classics professor father by sinking to the ultimate depths of playing piano in a seedy jazz cellar, and—horror!—befriending a black horn-player. *Where The Rivers Meet* (1988), *Comedies* (1990), and *Hungry Generations* (1994) is a trilogy set in Oxford which takes brothers Peter and Brian Leonard from 1930s' adolescence to the drab 1950s. As well as several volumes of poetry, Wain published literary criticism and biographies and a youthful autobio-graphy, *Sprightly Running* (1962).

📖 Kingsley Amis, Iris Murdoch, J. P. Donleavy   *TH*

Wakefield, H. R. (British, 1890–1964). *See* SUPERNATURAL

Walker, Alice (US, 1944–) Walker's subject is the racial repression and segregation of black women. She was born into a sharecropper family in Georgia and uses that as a background to many of her more important works. In *Meridian* (1976) Walker first developed her strategy of 'writing as quilt-making'. The novel is not a straightforward narrative but a series of short episodes told by different characters. The central figure, Meridian Hill, leaves her teenage marriage and child to go to university and join the civil rights movement. Walker questions official attitudes to the movement, whether white American or male African-American, and the nature of political involvement. In *The Temple of My Familiar* (1989) Walker explores the theme of an ancestral African spirituality, which is also one of the concerns of her most famous book, *The Color Purple* (1982) Pulitzer Prize 1983. In this novel the central figure, Celie, is abused by her stepfather and her husband and learns to value herself through a lesbian relationship with her husband's mistress, Shug, a singer. In *The Color Purple* Walker demonstrates that it is possible to make political and social change by changing the nature of sexual relations. *Possessing the Secret of Joy* (1992) explores the horrors of female circumcision.

📖 Maya Angelou, Toni Morrison, Gloria Naylor. *See* UNITED STATES OF AMERICA   *LM*

Wall, Mervyn (Irish, 1908–). *See* IRELAND

Walpole, Horace (British, 1717–97). *See* SUPERNATURAL

Walpole, Hugh (British, 1884–1941) Walpole was socially well-connected, a prolific and highly popular author of historical fiction, school stories, and comical Gothic tales. Many of his works now appear contrived and sentimental, but his best draw on personal experience and remain readable and moving. *The Dark Forest* (1916) has documentary detail from Walpole's own wartime Red Cross service in Russia, allied to a tragic love-story between an Englishman and a nurse. *The Cathedral* (1922) is set in the fictional town of 'Polchester', telling of the progressive disintegration of a proud churchman as his marriage and ecclesiastical life fall apart; he is unable to adapt to changing moral and social values. Walpole's school books, notably the *Jeremy* series and *Mr Perrin and Mr Traill* (1911), make light-hearted reading but describe public-school life evocatively. Similarly, the *Herries Chronicle*, set in eighteenth-century Cumberland, starting with *Rogue Herries* (1930), still rewards the reader.

📖 W. Somerset Maugham, Simon Raven   JS

Walters, Minette (British, 1949–) Each of Minette Walters's books is an intricate and compelling psychological thriller which leaves the reader guessing right to the end. She creates credible and fascinating characters and although her novels are often situated in the English village they explore disturbing territory far removed from that of traditional crime novels. The central character of *The Sculptress* (1993) is Olive Martin, convicted of killing and cutting up her mother and sister. Journalist Roz Leigh begins to believe in her innocence and to campaign for her release. In *The Ice House* (1992)

Walters explores guilt, innocence, and identity as a corpse discovered in the ice house leads to the reopening of an old case. *The Scold's Bridle* (1994) is a brilliant story which opens with the death of unpopular Mathilda Gillespie, found in her bath, wrists slit and wearing the scold's bridle over her mouth. Her considerable estate is to be left to Sarah Blakeney who believes Mathilda has been murdered.

📖 Ruth Rendell, Frances Hegarty. *See* THRILLERS   CS

Warner, Marina (British, 1946–) As a historian and critic Warner is largely concerned with the power of myth and fantasy in shaping women's identities. These concerns are extended into her novels. *The Lost Father* (1988) is a semi-autobiographical account of a woman living in England who sets out to discover her family roots in southern Italy. Warner's prose has a slow, dreamy quality and she captures the rhythms of peasant life and religious observance in early twentieth-century Italy in great detail. *The Skating Party* (1982) depicts a skating party on the English Fens and draws together fragments of myth, painting, and tribal custom to create a picture of people at odds in their need for love and in their ways of obtaining it. *Indigo* (1992), inspired by Shakespeare's *The Tempest*, rewrites the drama in a Caribbean setting, exploring the colonial conflicts of an imaginary island and one family.

📖 Angela Carter, Lisa St Aubin de Teran, A. S. Byatt   DJ

Warner, Sylvia Townsend (British, 1893–1978) Warner was born in Harrow, the daughter of a master at a public school. With her lifelong companion, Valentine

Ackland, she went to Spain during the Civil War, then returned to Dorset where she spent most of the rest of her life. Original and ironic, Warner is an inventive story-teller with wide-ranging subject matter and a brilliant style. Begin with *Lolly Willowes* (1926), her most popular and straightforwardly enjoyable novel. It is the tale of a London spinster who absconds to a village in the Chilterns to meet the Devil and find her calling as a witch. Next read the witty and touching *Mr Fortune's Maggot* (1927), about a bank clerk turned South Sea missionary, whose vocation proves a failure. Warner later turned to historical themes, as in her own favourite, *The Corner That Held Them* (1948), a worldly and affectionate account of life in a medieval convent. She also had 140 short stories published in the *New Yorker* over four decades.

📖 T. F. Powys, Dorothy Parker, Radclyffe Hall   JN

Warren, Robert Penn (US, 1905–89) Penn Warren was a distinguished man of letters, one of the pioneers of the New Criticism, who also became the United States' first Poet Laureate. He was born in Kentucky, and his fiction reflects upon the history and psychology of the South; it tends towards the melodramatic, and often employs richly poetic prose. *Night Rider* (1939) is set at the turn of the century, and concerns conflict between Kentucky tobacco farmers. Several of his novels deal with business and political corruption. *At Heaven's Gate* (1943) depicts Bogan Murdock's efforts to conceal financial irregularities while his daughter slides into alcoholism; and Warren's best-known work, *All the King's Men* (1946), shows the charismatic governor Willie Stark draw-

ing everyone around him into corrupt obligations. The latter won the Pulitzer Prize, and was based on the career of the assassinated Louisiana demagogue, Huey Long; it was made into an Oscar-winning movie starring Broderick Crawford.

📖 William Faulkner, Frank O'Connor   JS

Wassermann, Jakob (German, 1873–1934). *See* GERMANY

Waterhouse, Keith (British, 1929–) As a young man Waterhouse left his native Leeds to work in Fleet Street, and has since combined journalism with novels, stage and television plays, and film-scripts (many of these in collaboration with Willis Hall). In Waterhouse's first novel, *There is a Happy Land* (1957), he captures the giddy joys and shuddering terrors of working-class childhood in a northern town; you can smell the tar bubbles bursting. Billy Fisher is the Ruler of Ambrosia in *Billy Liar* (1959), but in drear reality he's an undertaker's apprentice with aspirations to write gags for television comedians. The scrapes his fantasies land him in are very funny, leading to a poignant finale. *Our Song* (1988) is the story of a middle-aged man's obsession with a gauche young woman, part of whose charm is ordering Torremolinos in an Italian restaurant. Page Three girl Debra Chase tells Her Own Story in *Bimbo* (1990), stoutly declaring that the stuff we've previously read about her is a virago of lies from start to finish.

📖 Stan Barstow, John Wain   TH

Watson, Colin (British, 1920–82) Watson was a journalist who produced consistently successful comic crime novels set in the East Anglian market town of

— 475 —

Flaxborough. His witty squibs never teeter over the line into farce and all his novels have the additional bonus of being intriguing and well-plotted mysteries. Begin with *Hopjoy Was Here* (1962), a spoof about a James Bond-style secret agent investigating the disappearance of one of his men. Like all Watson's novels, it's hard to read without laughing out loud. Other notable Flaxborough novels include *One Man's Meat* (1977), a tale of mayhem and dog food; *Lonelyheart 4122* (1967), where ladies of a certain age go missing; and *Blue Murder* (1979) where those who play with pornography and blackmail get more than they bargain for. Watson also wrote an acclaimed critical study of the English mystery, *Snobbery with Violence* (1971).

📖 Edmund Crispin, Margery Allingham   *VM*

Watson, Ian (British, 1943–) Watson was born in North Shields, educated at Oxford, and lectured in Dar es Salaam, Tokyo, and elsewhere before becoming a full-time science fiction writer in 1976. Begin with *The Jonah Kit* (1975), in which human consciousness is experimentally implanted in whales. The creatures become channels for alien intelligences, who help humanity through a crisis in scientific knowledge. *God's World* (1979) begins with the appearance of angelic beings at holy sites around the world. A spacecraft is built to carry explorers to their place of origin in God's World, where the sinister truth about the angels emerges. In *The Flies of Memory* (1990) a pyramidal spaceship arrives bearing insect-like aliens. Monuments, buildings, and eventually whole cities begin disappearing as they are transported to protective storage on Mars.

📖 Arthur C. Clarke, Larry Niven   *DH*

Waugh, Evelyn (British, 1903–66) Evelyn Waugh's first wife was also called Evelyn. To distinguish between them, they were known to their friends as He-Evelyn and She-Evelyn: this risible situation, so ripe for muddle and farcical misunderstanding, might have been taken straight out of a Waugh novel—or put straight into one.

Born in Hampstead to a middle-class literary family, Waugh read modern history at Oxford, where he cheerfully admitted to doing very little except getting drunk with his chums, Harold Acton and Cyril Connolly. This period was given a golden mythological gloss in *Brideshead Revisited* (1945), which thirty years later was turned into a lavish and hugely popular television series. Waugh combined satire, farce, and broad comedy in a witty and elegant manner in his early novels *Decline and Fall* (1928) and *Vile Bodies* (1930). They made him an instant celebrity, the darling of the Mayfair society he mocked in his books, yet to which he aspired. While giving his characters such fatuous names as Lady Circumference, Mrs Ape, Mr and Mrs Outrage, and Lady Throbbing, Waugh is none the less wickedly accurate and unsparingly vicious in his portayal of the giddy young things, dowagers, and crusty old buffers. These novels set a high standard, being exceptionally skilful for such a young writer, and also very funny.

A Handful of Dust (1934) is Waugh at his best. The backdrop is still that of smart society (parties at Lady Cockpurse's, chaps dining at Brat's club), but the novel presents a darker and far bleaker view of human nature. Tony Last prefers to live in his grand but decaying house in the country while his wife, Lady Brenda, is drawn to the meaningless pursuit of amusement on the cocktail circuit. Her affair with John Beaver, a feckless, self-seeking wastrel, brings destruction to her decent if dull husband, her family, and herself. The scene where she confuses the name of her young son, also called John, with that of her lover, is truly shocking. *Scoop* (1938) is a swingeing, full-blooded satire on Fleet Street. It features the hapless and hilarious William Boot, a reclusive writer of a nature column, who by mistake gets sent to cover a foreign war. The phrase 'Up to a point, Lord Copper' has entered the language, used by a fawning minion who never dares to openly disagree with the tabloid proprietor of *The Beast*.

In 1930 Waugh became a Catholic, and later served as an ageing army officer. He combined these experiences in the magnificent *Sword of Honour* trilogy, *Men at Arms* (1952), *Officers and Gentlemen* (1955), and *Unconditional Surrender* (1961), which follows Guy Crouchback through many escapades during the Second World War, when Guy's faith is put to the test on the field of battle and in his own intimate relationships. No finer fictional testament of that conflict has appeared by an English writer.

Towards the end of his life Waugh became a caricature of the curmudgeonly country squire, fulminating in all directions. It was perhaps his finest creation; certainly no one but Waugh himself could have done it justice in fiction.

📖 Christopher Isherwood, Muriel Spark, Ronald Firbank. *See* HISTORICAL, HUMOUR, WAR   *TH*

Webb, Mary (British, 1881–1927) Mary Webb was born and educated mostly at home in Leighton Cressage, Shropshire, a place which she loved and used as a setting in all of her novels. She is best known for *Precious Bane* (1924), which is typical of her writing and describes the countryside in lush, memorable detail. The story is narrated by the heroine, Prue Sarn; her 'precious bane' is her harelip, which has made her an outcast in her rural society, where she is stigmatized as a witch. The novel is concerned with her romance with a local weaver but also tells the story of her ambitious brother, Gideon. Other novels by Webb include *Gone to Earth* (1917) and *Seven for a Secret* (1922). *Precious Bane* was satirized in Stella Gibbons's *Cold Comfort Farm* (1932).

📖 Emily Brontë, Thomas Hardy   *SA*

Weidman, Jerome (US, 1913–) Of Jewish descent, Weidman was born in New York, where he graduated in law and worked in the garment industry in the 1930s. Begin with the slangy realism and hard-hitting dialogue of *I Can Get It for You Wholesale* (1937), arguably his best novel. Set like most of his fiction in New York, it concerns a ruthlessly ambitious clothing manufacturer. *The Enemy Camp* (1958) tells of a Jewish accountant's confrontations with institutionalized anti-Semitism. *Other People's Money* (1968) uses the formula of triumph over adversity common to a number of Weidman's novels. Its hero, Victor Smith, orphaned by the sinking of the *Lusitania* and adopted by his father's boss, overcomes family rivalries to achieve business success. In *The Sound of Bow Bells* (1962), Sam Silver, a successful writer of magazine stories, undergoes a crisis over the quality of his work and the shabbiness of his personal life.

📖 Saul Bellow, Philip Roth   *DH*

Weldon, Fay (British, 1933–) Fay Weldon has been for nearly thirty years a prolific novelist, playwright, and polemicist. She used to work in an advertising agency, and is credited with inventing the slogan 'Go to work on an egg'. She turns her gaze on women: their lives, emotions, and problems; their search for happiness. This chimed well with the rise of feminism and the foundation of publishing houses such as Virago, recently satirized in her novel and television series *Big Women* (1998). She speaks wittily and directly to the reader, having perfected a technique in her early work of short paragraphs in the present tense which allows her to take us into and out of her characters' thoughts. There is about this writer something of the fairy-tale narrator. She is a wise woman who enchants her audience, while warning them about the world. Weldon's books always have a strong moral purpose and people's actions bring consequences. *Praxis* (1978) is one of her best novels and was shortlisted for the Booker Prize in 1979. The new reader could begin with *Remember Me* (1976), a dazzling account of the revenge of a ghostly first wife. *The Life and Loves of a She-Devil* (1983) was very well adapted for television and is a story about reinventing yourself: a recurring theme in Weldon's work. More recently novels like *Affliction* (1993) are about the pitfalls of psychotherapy.

📖 Beryl Bainbridge, Alice Thomas Ellis, Margaret Forster   *AG*

Wells, H(erbert) G(eorge) (British, 1866–1946) Known as the father figure of British science fiction, Wells foresaw many of the technological advances that we have now made. As a result he mapped out much of the territory which science fiction has now made its own; time and space travel, alien invasions, and the desecration of the world and its resources. Begin with *The Time Machine* (1895) in which Wells foresees a world divided into those with a pacific outlook, the Eloi, and those who want to wage war, the Morlocks. Both these species decay and become extinct as does life as we know it. Wells wrote many of the great classics of early science fiction including *The Invisible Man* (1897), *The War of the Worlds* (1898), and *The First Men in the Moon* (1901). *The Island of Doctor Moreau* (1896) is a shocking dystopia about life on an Island where a god-like vivisectionist surgically transforms animals into human form, creating the Beast People, wretches with human aspirations and animal instincts. Alongside his science fiction, Wells wrote social comedies which deal with the pretensions of the lower middle classes. In many of these books men in lowly professions decide to break away from the constraints of their daily grind and 'go for it'. These novels had their origins in both Wells's lower-middle-class background and also his social idealism —for a while Wells was influential in the socialistic Fabian Society. Of these works, the best to start with is *Kipps* (1905).

📖 Jules Verne, Arnold Bennett, E. M. Forster, J. B. Priestley.
See SCIENCE FICTION   *LM*

Welsh, Irvine (British, 1958–) Raised in Edinburgh, Welsh left school at 16 to become a television repairman and then a housing officer, moving eventually to Amsterdam. Himself a former user, he authentically depicted heroin abuse in *Trainspotting* (1993), which explores the experiences, both blissful and devastating, of a group of unemployed Edinburgh youths as they veer in and out of addiction. Packed with rich Scottish argot, the fragmented narrative portrays a lifestyle sometimes shocking, sometimes genuinely funny, which involves them in everything from opium suppositories to cot deaths and HIV infection. Rooted in the blasted council estates of Edinburgh and Leith, the book gave a voice to an entire Scottish under-class, and through highly successful stage and film adaptations became a cultural touchstone for a generation.

Welsh's second full-length novel, *Marabou Stork Nightmares* (1995), is a tour round the skull of Roy Strang: comatose in hospital, still able to sample the outside world but rejecting it. We follow Roy as he examines his violent childhood, his family's brief emigration to South Africa, his forays into football hooliganism and office life, and the circumstances leading up to his retreat into a hospital bed. These instalments are broken up by his quest for the Marabou Storks, a twisted safari of the imagination.

📖 James Kelman, William Burroughs, Alex Garland, Roddy Doyle. *See* TEEN
RP

Welty, Eudora (US, 1909–) Eudora Welty won the Pulitzer Prize for *The Optimist's Daughter* (1972). A young woman, Laurel, returns to the Mississippi town where she grew up after her father's death, and gains some perspective on her father's remarriage, soon after her mother's death, to a much younger woman; and also on her own past. Many of Welty's books are centred on the theme of returning to one's origins and seeing them through different eyes, like *Delta Wedding* (1946), in which Laura McRaven takes the Yellow Dog train to Shellmound in the Mississippi Delta, to attend the marriage of her family's prettiest daughter to a man from the mountains, and *Losing Battles* (1970), in which an entire family reunites to celebrate Granny Vaughn's ninetieth birthday in Banner, Mississippi. In *The Ponder Heart* (1954) Uncle Daniel Ponder marries some-one much younger, with hilarious reactions and results. Eudora Welty is one of the greatest writers of American short stories. *The Golden Apples* (1949), in particular, brings her acute perceptiveness and close attention to human peculiarities to bear on American Southern life in a linked col-lection of stories. Her *Collected Stories* was published in 1982. She worked as a photo-grapher in Mississippi, where she has spent her life, during the Depression, and her photographs are collected in *One Time, One Place: Mississippi in the Depression* (1971).

📖 William Faulkner, Flannery O'Connor, Carson McCullers   AT

Wentworth, Patricia (British, 1878–1961) Patricia Wentworth's genteel style of crime writing was so quintessentially Eng-lish that it is an irony that, in the last twenty years of her life, her work was significantly more popular in the United States than in Britain, and that her primary publisher was based in Philadelphia. Wentworth is remembered today as the creator of Miss Maud Silver, a retired schoolteacher who became a private detective. When Miss Silver first appeared, in *Grey Mask* (1928), Wentworth was already a well-established novelist. Oddly, it was more than a decade before she returned to the character on whom she eventually was to concentrate all her energies. Wentworth's books seem dated to many modern readers, but retain a quiet appeal for fans of 'cosy' crime writing.

📖 Elizabeth Ferrars, Agatha Christie
ME

Wesley, Mary (British, 1912–) Born in Englefield Green, Surrey, Mary Wesley was educated at the London School of Economics and worked at Bletchley Park during the war. She was 70 when she published her first novel, *Jumping the Queue* (1983). Begin with this blackly comic account of a well-to-do widow's obsession with suicide. She postpones the act after meeting a fugitive who is also on the point of killing himself. After a revelatory survey of her past, she takes her life in the tragically absurd conclusion. *The Camomile Lawn* (1984) opens on the eve of the Second World War, which brings excitement and sexual liberation to the cousins whose lives the novel entertainingly follows through four decades. Hebe, the heroine of *Harnessing Peacocks* (1985), flees her home to escape demands for her to undergo an abortion. She brings up her son in unconventional circumstances, well maintained by her talents for cookery and lovemaking. *A Sensible Life* (1990) offers a further treatment of unorthodox morality. The opening finds its heroine, who is undergoing a painful adolescence, meeting three boys during a holiday at Dinard in Brittany. Over many years, she maintains separate relationships with each of them before deciding she must choose one to remain with. Laura Thornby in *Second Fiddle* (1988) has lost the capacity for lasting relationships through her self-protective emotional detachment. Her secret past and her need for independence are at issue when she moves in with her young lover and his mother.

📖 Marika Cobbold, Jane Gardam, Muriel Spark. *See* ROMANCE   *DH*

West, Dorothy (US, 1912–) West is a born-and-bred Boston lady. She began to write at a young age and went on to become one of a group of influential black writers and artists of the 1930s known as the Harlem Renaissance. Her most famous novel, *The Living is Easy* (1948), set at the turn of the century, deals with Cleo Jericho and her aspirations to become one of the Boston black social élite. The novel tackles the precarious situation of the black middle class and its relation to the white community, through issues such as the importance of the exact shade of a black person's skin. This is a major anxiety for Cleo as her daughter, Judy, 'suffers' from a very dark complexion. *The Wedding* (1995), written after a forty-five-year gap, is set in Martha's Vineyard, a middle-class resort in East Coast America. It is the 1950s and again West addresses the difficulties facing the black bourgeoisie. This time the story revolves around a society wedding which is being jeopardized by a lower-class womanizing black jazz musician who decides he wants the black society bride for himself.

📖 Zora Neale Hurston, Toni Morrison, Margaret Forster   *CJ*

West, Morris (Australian, 1916–99) West is famous especially for three books which became films, *The Devil's Advocate* (1959), filmed with John Mills in 1977, *The Shoes of the Fisherman* (1963), the first of his *Papal* trilogy, and *Vanishing Point* (1996), a psychological thriller. His novels tackle ethical and moral questions in the well-researched international fields of finance, corrupt government, and the Roman Catholic Church. Having almost become a priest, West retained a lifelong interest in the paradoxical life of the Church, in which the flesh and the spirit have to coexist. Start with *The Devil's*

Advocate, an investigation into the ways a priest has to be both a part of and apart from life. 'Everything in the Church is political . . . Man is a political animal who has an immortal soul' says the Cardinal, summing up the theme of the novel and of much of the work of Morris West.

📖 Graham Greene, Brian Moore, Somerset Maugham   *FS*

West, Nathanael (US, 1903–40) Born in New York (real name, Nathan Wallenstein Weinstein), West was the original loner of contemporary American fiction, his work too savage and bleakly despondent —and too fantastical—to gain wide appeal during the Depression. His most accomplished novel, *The Day of the Locust* (1939), focuses on the lonely misfits drawn by the golden glitter of Hollywood, whose unrequited dreams of fame and success lead to a frenzy of hatred and self-destruction. *Miss Lonelyhearts* (1933) is the story of a cynical hack journalist hired to write an agony column, but who then finds himself stricken by the despair of these sad, empty lives; a short novel of compressed poetic power. *A Cool Million* (1934) is a crude, all-out assault on the myth of America as the land of opportunity, while in *The Dream Life of Balso Snell* (1931) the hero takes an allegorical time-trip through western culture and finds it all a pitiful sham. West was ahead of his time, which is perhaps the reason why his entire literary output earned him little more than a thousand dollars. Eight months after his marriage, he and his wife were killed in a car crash.

📖 Flannery O'Connor, J. P. Donleavy, Joseph Heller.
See UNITED STATES OF AMERICA
                                                                        TH

West, Rebecca (British, 1892–1983) Born in Ireland and educated in Edinburgh, Rebecca West (real name Cicily Isobel Fairfield) first wrote witty, irreverent journalism. Her novels explore women's lives from a psychological perspective. Begin with *The Fountain Overflows* (1957), an autobiographical novel telling the story of her journalist father's abandonment of his family and the subsequent fortunes of herself and her sisters. The ambiguities of the sisters' relationships are explored in detail, and West's re-creation of her youth is skilfully sustained. In *The Birds Fall Down* (1966), a novel of the Russian Revolution, she creates another character based upon her father, and in *The Return of the Soldier* (1918), her first novel, about a soldier suffering from shell-shock after the First World War, there is little or no authorial distance. *The Judge* (1922), focusing on the effects of the suffrage movement on women's lives, reflects West's involvement in the early feminist movement.

📖 Elizabeth Taylor, Ivy Compton-Burnett, Elizabeth Bowen   *CB*

Wharton, Edith (US, 1862–1937) Wharton is one of America's greatest novelists. She got off to a late start (like many women writers), for personal reasons; she was 38 when she published her first short novel. But by her death she'd published over forty books, novels, collections of stories (including some terrific ghost stories), poems, and books on travel, fiction, gardens, and architecture.

Edith Newbold Jones grew up in genteel 'old' New York society, with a society wedding in 1885 to a 'suitable' man, the wealthy Bostonian Teddy Wharton. But the young Mrs Wharton had also been writing and reading compulsively since childhood. During her marriage she began to publish, moved into literary circles, and travelled a great deal, especially in Italy and France. The Whartons had a grand house, The Mount, designed and built for them in Lenox, Massachusetts. As her marriage began to fall apart, she had a passionate affair, in her mid-forties, with Henry James's attractive, unreliable friend, Morton Fullerton. Teddy Wharton became depressive, unfaithful, and reckless with money, and the marriage finally ended in divorce in 1913. By this time Edith had left America for a life in France, and only returned once, in 1923, though she went on writing about America all her life. In the war, in Paris, she worked with formidable energy setting up hostels, refuges, and rest homes, and writing books explaining France to Americans. After the war, she bought two houses in France, one near Paris and one in the Mediterranean.

Wharton's fictions reflect her enormous reading and wide cultural range, the painful marital and emotional conflicts of her early years, her mixed feelings about America (part nostalgia, part horror at post-war brashness, and part admiration of its energies), and her fascination (not uncritical) with European traditions and ways of life. But they are never confessional. Wharton writes with a wonderful controlled mixture of sharp humour, disenchanted observation, and dark passion, and she can do a great range of characters, from the New York society types of her childhood, to French aristocratic families, to the bleak, narrow lives of New England farmers (in *Ethan Frome*, 1911) or the American urban poor (in *Bunner Sisters*, 1916).

Her ironical love-stories are always painful and frustrated. And it's usually the woman who pays. Though far from being a feminist, she wrote with deep feeling and intelligence about the limitations and problems of women's lives in the late nineteenth and early twentieth centuries (especially for poor Lily Bart, the doomed heroine of *The House of Mirth*, 1905), about emotional treachery and inadequacy, especially in men, and about the constrictions of married life. Witty, stylish, and unflinchingly realistic, she is also a writer of profound and complicated emotions. Start with *The House of Mirth* and *Ethan Frome*; go on to *The Custom of the Country* (1913) and *The Age of Innocence* (1920); by then you'll be hooked.

📖 Henry James, Jane Austen, George Eliot, F. Scott Fitzgerald, Alison Lurie. *See* UNITED STATES OF AMERICA, SUPERNATURAL   HL

Wharton, Thomas (Canadian, 1963–   ). *See* CANADA

Wharton, William (US, 1925–) William Wharton (a pseudonym) is a shadowy figure like J. D. Salinger and Thomas Pynchon. His first novel, *Birdy* (1979), tells the story of two boys growing up in the 1930s in a working-class area of Pennsylvania and eventually going off to fight (as Wharton himself did) in the Second World War. One of the boys breeds canaries, and becomes more and more obsessed with the behaviour of birds and even with the possibility of being a bird himself. Very few writers can ever have portrayed an alien world as convincingly and memorably as Wharton does here: it's not only Birdy who imagines himself being a canary but the reader too. The novel works equally well as a study of mental disturbance in the face of the trauma of adolescence and of going to war. A later novel, *A Midnight Clear* (1982), is also a powerful read.

📖 J. D. Salinger, Kurt Vonnegut   RF

Wheatley, Dennis (British, 1897–1977) Wheatley worked in a family wine firm then, at the age of 33, sold it to become a writer. He fought in the First World War, and in 1941 he became a wing commander in the RAF reserves. *The Quest of Julian Day* (1939) is typical of the adventure stories which earned him the title 'the Prince of Thriller Writers', featuring a dashing hero, exotic temptresses, and glamorous locations. His hugely influential occult thrillers, featuring resolute heroes battling with Satanists, paranormal phenomena, and the supernatural are masterpieces of gripping, and chilling, horror fiction. *To the Devil a Daughter* (1953), filmed in 1976 with an all-star cast, tells the story of an excommunicated priest's plot to bring to power a child dedicated to the service of the Antichrist.

📖 Bram Stoker, Anne Rice, Stephen King   EC

White, Antonia (British, 1899–1980) Antonia White (real name, Eirene Botting) was born in London and educated in a convent school, from which she was expelled. Later she worked as a journalist. Her first novel, *Frost in May* (1933), is strongly autobiographical, telling the story of 9-year-old Nanda, who is sent to a convent school and begins to write a novel about some spectacular sinners who will repent at the end—but the unfinished manuscript is discovered. The vicissitudes of convent school life are powerfully con-

veyed. Clara Batchelor, the heroine of White's next novel, *The Lost Traveller* (1950), is a thinly-veiled Nanda, now 15, coming to terms with adolescence. Her story is continued in *The Sugar House* (1952) and *Beyond the Glass* (1954), in the last of which Clara is admitted to Nazareth hospital, suffering from insanity, as did White herself. It is a harrowing novel, and begs comparison with Sylvia Plath's *The Bell Jar*. She published a volume of stories, *Strangers*, in 1954.

📖 Virginia Woolf, Sylvia Plath, Janet Frame   SA

White, Edmund (US, 1940–) Edmund White's subject is male homosexuality in American society. His novels are often autobiographical, and can be read as a series covering each stage of the author's life. *A Boy's Own Story* (1983) is a sensitive account of an adolescent coming to an awareness of his own sexuality in an inhospitable environment, while its sequel, *The Beautiful Room is Empty* (1988) follows the same character to the birth of the gay liberation movement. *The Farewell Symphony* (1997) is a lament for those who died of AIDS during the 1980s. *Caracole* (1985) is the story of a young gay man finding his way through the rituals of adult life, and *Skinned Alive* (1995) is a collection of stories. White has also written a biography of Jean Genet, and two collections of essays.

📖 Jean Genet, Alan Hollinghurst, Adam Mars-Jones   WB

White, Patrick (Australian, 1912–90) Patrick White's style is slow-moving and repetitive, heavy with detail; but once a reader is submerged in the vast world of one of his novels, any sense of effort is forgotten. Start with *The Tree of Man* (1956); Stan and Amy Parker clear the native bush and build their own farm, have children, grow old. Each hopes for revelation and meaning; around them the daily triumphs and tragedies of life proliferate. Their neighbours, the Quigleys, have a simple-minded son, Bud, who is looked after by his saintly sister, Doll—until the day Doll's patience snaps, and she comes in to tell Amy she has murdered Bud. The Parker children grow up disappointing—the son vicious, the daughter emotionally sterile. In its portrait of the rhythms of a lifelong marriage *The Tree of Man* is reminiscent of D. H. Lawrence's *The Rainbow*.

Voss (1957), based on a true story, describes an epic and terrible expedition, undertaken in 1845, to cross the Australian continent. *Riders in the Chariot* (1961), White's greatest book, tells the story of four outcasts whose lives are touched by visionary experience. Himmelfarb is a refugee Jewish professor who ends up working in a bicycle-lamp factory; his experience of persecution and the murder of his wife in Germany lead him to believe that the intellect has failed humanity, and he seeks another meaning in the Australian town of Barranugli. But his foreign-ness again singles him out for unwelcome attention. White's dialogue reveals with scalpel sharpness the graduations of snobbery, racism, ignorance, and hypocrisy amongst Himmelfarb's acquaintances. In later novels like *The Twyborn Affair* (1979) White confronted his own homosexuality. Besides the novels he wrote plays and short stories. White was awarded the Nobel Prize for Literature in 1973.

📖 Leo Tolstoy, Henry James.

See AUSTRALIA AND NEW ZEALAND

JR

White, T(erence) H(anbury) (British, 1906–64)

White, by profession a history teacher, achieved major success with his Arthurian tetralogy, *The Once and Future King* (1958). The first volume, *The Sword in the Stone* (1939), is an enchanting account of Arthur's boyhood education by Merlyn. *The Queen of Air and Darkness* (1940; originally *The Witch in the Wood*) moves into a more haunted world where Arthur unwittingly sleeps with his half-sister and literally sows the seeds of his own destruction. *The Ill-Made Knight* (1941) provides a unique and touching interpretation of the love-affair between Sir Lancelot and Queen Guinevere by making Lancelot grotesquely ugly. *The Candle in the Wind* (1958) is an elegiac meditation on the collapse of Arthur's world. The tetralogy is characterized by its mixture of wit, wonder, and regret. *The Book of Merlyn* (1976) is a posthumously published reprise of these themes.

📖 J. R. R. Tolkien, C. S. Lewis, Ursula Le Guin. *See* FANTASY   GK

Wiggins, Marianne (US, 1947–)

Marianne Wiggins was born in Pennsylvania and has lived in Paris, Brussels, Rome, New York, and London. She was married for a while to the novelist Salman Rushdie. Her own writing is lyrical, erudite, and disturbing. *John Dollar* (1988) is about an English schoolteacher widowed in the First World War, marooned with some pupils and the sailor John Dollar on a remote island. It is both a love-story and a tale of brutality. *Eveless Eden* (1995) tells the story of the passionate love-affair between Noah, a foreign correspondent, and Lilith, a professional photographer, against a backdrop of the world's trouble spots, with echoes of the myth of the

Garden of Eden. *Almost Heaven* (1998) is also about a foreign correspondent who returns to America and meets Melanie, who is suffering from traumatic amnesia.

📖 A. S. Byatt, William Golding, Martha Gellhorn   SA

Wilde, Oscar (Fingal O'Flahertie Wills) (Irish, 1854–1900) The son of an Irish surgeon and a political writer and journalist with literary connections, Wilde studied at Trinity College, Dublin, and Magdalen College, Oxford, where he first established his reputation for flamboyance. He travelled on a successful lecture-tour of America in 1882, and edited women's magazines in London. His only full-length novel is *The Picture of Dorian Gray* (1890), a story about a man granted his wish that his portrait should age in his place, leaving his youthful looks intact during a life of debauchery and final degradation. *Lord Arthur Savile's Crime* (1891) is a collection of stories, and *The Happy Prince and Other Tales* (1888) is a collection written for children, though widely read by adults. Wilde is better known as a playwright (*The Importance of Being Earnest*, 1895), and was also a poet and essayist. He was imprisoned for homosexual acts in 1895 and went to France after his release in 1897.

📖 Ronald Firbank, Evelyn Waugh, Max Beerbohm   WB

Willans, Geoffrey (British, 1911–1958). *See* HUMOUR

Willeford, Charles (US, 1919–88) Charles Willeford, who served and was decorated in the Second World War, and who also wrote two volumes of military memoirs, was one of the most original of the American crime writers to emerge in the 1970s. His earlier books were gritty, hard-boiled noir tales full of *femmes fatales* and assorted grifters set amongst the dregs of America's subculture (*High Priest of California*, 1953, *The Burnt Orange Heresy*, 1971, *Cockfighter*, 1972) but it was his first Miami-set Hoke Moseley mystery, *Miami Blues* (1984), which established his ironic and gritty reputation. A toothless and often grotesque loser of a cop, Moseley often finds himself confronted by unlikely and sometimes darkly comic as well as essentially evil psychopaths and his final triumphs are just an inch short of unmitigated disaster. In his dissection of the Miami shadow world, Willeford's excesses highlight the worst sociopathic elements of his characters and make for uncomfortable reading at the best of times, but the effect is gripping.

📖 Carl Hiaasen, Jim Thompson, Elmore Leonard   MJ

Williams, Nigel (British, 1948–) Williams has worked in television arts journalism and has written travel books as well as a series of comic novels. Begin with *The Wimbledon Poisoner* (1990), in which suburban husband Henry Farr makes increasingly desperate attempts to get rid of his feminist wife. The Wimbledon setting is common to a number of Williams's novels including the delightful *They Came from SW19* (1992), narrated by a teenage boy whose father has just died and whose mother becomes involved with spiritualists claiming to be receiving messages from the other side. *Fortysomething* (1999) is the private diary of a middle-aged man (Wimbledon again), attempting to make sense of his newly successful wife, his near-adult sons (he is concerned they may be drug dealing until the consignment of 'white goods' he has heard about materializes as a load of fridges needing storage in his kitchen), and transsexual shenanigans at the BBC where his job as an actor in a radio serial is under threat. The narrator's pompous, self-obsessed, yet endearingly innocent voice will make you laugh aloud.

📖 Sue Townsend, Douglas Adams, James Thurber. *See* HUMOUR   JR

Williams, Tad (US, 1957–). *See* FANTASY

Williamson, Henry (British, 1895–1977) Born and educated in south London, Henry Williamson joined the army during the First World War, an experience vividly described in his novel *A Patriot's Progress* (1930), in which a City clerk named John Bullock suffers the hardships of trench warfare. Williamson's hatred of war led to him supporting Oswald Mosley and Hitler in the 1930s, for which he was interned at the outbreak of the Second World War. Williamson remains best known for *Tarka the Otter* (1927), a minutely observed and unsentimental account of an otter family in the Devon countryside, and *Salar the Salmon* (1935) which is in a similar vein. Williamson's later output is dominated by a series of fifteen semi-autobiographical novels under the collective title *A Chronicle of Ancient Sunlight* (1951–69), which trace the life of a writer, Phillip Maddison, from the 1890s to the early 1950s.

📖 Richard Adams, Anthony Powell, Erich Maria Remarque   WB

Wilson, A(ndrew) N(orman) (British, 1950–) As well as an author of fiction, Wilson is a prolific biographer, journalist,

media pundit, and controversialist. His most ambitious work of fiction is the five-volume sequence *The Lampitt Papers* (1988–97), which records the relationship of the narrator, Julian Ramsay, with a charismatic and well-connected family. At the heart of the sequence is the mystery surrounding the death of the belletrist James Petworth Lampitt, and the possible role in it of a meretricious writer called Raphael Hunter, whom Julian comes to regard as his dark angel. *Dream Children* (1998) is a work that takes on the subject of child abuse, daring to encourage the reader to sympathize with the abuser before exposing his moral poverty. Wilson is one of the few writers with the nerve to tackle this subject ironically.

📖 Anthony Powell, Iris Murdoch, Barbara Pym   NC

Wilson, Angus (British, 1913–91) Born in Bexhill, Sussex, Angus Wilson was educated at Oxford and served in intelligence during the war. In addition to his career as a leading post-war novelist, he worked in the reading room of the British Library and from 1966 was Professor of Literature at East Anglia University. Begin with *Anglo-Saxon Attitudes* (1956), which brilliantly displays Wilson's sharply satirical lightness of touch. The complex plot and extensive cast of characters cover four decades of English middle-class life. The novel centres on an alienated professor of history who belatedly searches for the truth behind an academic fraud. In *Hemlock and After* (1952) famous writer Bernard Sands calls into question the value of his life's achievement as his attempt to found a libertarian writers' colony fails. Further stress results from his decision to accept his homosexuality and he is driven to breakdown and death. *The Old Men at the Zoo* (1961) is a satire of bureaucratic attitudes set in an imaginary near future. Disagreements among administrators delay plans to set up an animal reservation while the country is gradually engulfed in European war. The delusions behind both scientific and spiritual searches for easy access to human happiness are satirized in *As if by Magic* (1973). Hamo Langmuir, who has developed a new type of rice, and his god-daughter Alexandra Grant, who seeks mystical enlightenment, travel together to the East. Their self-centred expectations founder when he finds his rice cannot relieve food shortages and she discovers her guru is a phoney.

📖 Anthony Powell, J. B. Priestley, Evelyn Waugh   *DH*

Wilson, Robert (British, 1957–) Robert Wilson has worked in shipping, advertising, and trading in Africa. His novels are set on the west coast of Africa and feature fixer Bruce Medway whose work brings him in contact with shady characters and dodgy deals. The books depict a vivid world of steamy heat, lies, flies, political turmoil, and corruption. Medway is an anti-hero with a rich stock of one-liners which give a comic edge to the stories. In *Instruments of Darkness* (1995) expatriate Steven Kershaw is missing and when Medway tries to find him he becomes embroiled in the world of drug running, bribery, and murder. In *Big Killing* (1996) Medway is asked to deliver a video for a porn dealer and also to act as minder for a spoilt playboy who is looking for diamonds on the Ivory Coast. When Medway delivers the video a shoot-out results and a mutilated corpse is discovered.

📖 Lawrence Block, James Lee Burke. *See* THRILLERS   *CS*

Wilson, Robert McLiam (British, 1964–). *See* IRELAND

Winterson, Jeanette (British, 1959–) Winterson's first novel, *Oranges are Not the Only Fruit* (1985, Whitbread award), which was later adapted for television, draws on her own upbringing by Pentecostal Evangelists in Lancashire. The central character, Jess, is raised to become a successful preacher but in her teens falls in love with a young woman from the church community. The discovery of their sexual relationship by her mother and the Pastor leads to Jess being exiled from her church and family. The main story is interwoven with allegorical fairy-tales. In *The Passion* (1987) two stories are interlinked. Henri, a poor farm-boy joins Napoleon's troops and ends up as the general's personal chicken-cooker, never killing anyone in his eight years as a soldier. Villanelle, a female transvestite with webbed feet, becomes prostitute to a high-ranking officer in Napoleon's army, meets Henri, and the two desert together. Winterson's prose is sometimes intensely poetic. In her later novels, she increasingly rejects traditional linear narrative and experiments with theme and idea, using poetic prose, legend and even scientific theory to link characters and stories. *Sexing the Cherry* (1989) shifts between contemporary times and a colourfully depicted England in the reign of Charles II. Jordan and his mother, the huge 'Dogwoman', live on the stinking Thames in a London about to face the Plague. Jordan encounters a series of fantastical adventures via Winterson's reworking of well-known fairy-tales such as 'The Twelve Dancing Princesses'.

📖 Angela Carter, Isabel Allende. *See* CHILDHOOD, SEXUAL POLITICS

DJ

Winton, Tim (Australian, 1960–) Born in Perth, Winton has lived in France, Ireland, and Greece as well as Australia. Family, and relations between children and parents are central to his writing. Start with *The Riders* (1995, Booker Prize-shortlisted). Scully's wife disappears, and he drags his daughter Billie from Ireland across Europe in a desperate search for her, feeling himself bereft and incomplete. During their journey Billie becomes ill and Scully irresponsible and half-crazed; the novel's resolution, as Scully recognizes that he will not be one of the Riders, 'faithful in all weathers and all worlds, waiting for something promised', but rather that he can be happy in the present with Billie, is satisfying and moving. Next read *Cloud Street* (1991), a wonderful saga about two neighbouring families, one respectable, one feckless; a big, ambitious novel which is heart-warming without being sentimental. *That Eye the Sky* (1986) powerfully charts a young boy's troubled adolescence.

📖 Peter Carey, Christina Stead, Anne Tyler. *See* AUSTRALIA AND NEW ZEALAND

JR

Wister, Owen (US, 1860–1938). *See* WESTERN

Wodehouse, P(elham) G(renville) (British, 1881–1975) Wodehouse is the greatest English comic writer of the twentieth century. Starting with *The Pothunters* in 1902, he wrote more than ninety novels and collections of short stories, as well as journalism, plays, and musicals. All his work shows an exuberant capacity for humorous invention, and a brilliant command of language—fans enjoy swapping examples of Wodehouse's funniest similes. A genial man, whose work was designed to do no more than bring amusement and delight, Wodehouse is an unlikely figure of controversy: but, as a result of being interned by the Germans during the Second World War and injudiciously making broadcasts for them, he was unable to return to Britain thereafter, and spent the remainder of his life in America. Political naïvety is the most likely explanation for his behaviour—the appeal of his work lies in a blithe sunniness. Certainly, no one who has read *The Code of the Woosters* (1938), which has great fun at the expense of a character based on the British fascist Oswald Mosley, could suspect Wodehouse of having been sympathetic to Hitler's regime.

Wodehouse's most popular works are those featuring Bertie Wooster, an amiable goof, and his preternaturally able butler Jeeves. Delightful, too, are the stories—among them *Summer Lightning* (1929)—set at Blandings Castle, the proprietor of which, Lord Emsworth, is besotted with his prize pig; and *The Clicking of Cuthbert* (1922) and *The Heart of a Goof* (1926), short stories reflecting Wodehouse's love of golf.

📖 Jerome K. Jerome, Stella Gibbons, George Grossmith. *See* HUMOUR

NC

Wolf, Christa (German, 1929–) Born in Poland, Wolf moved to East Germany in 1945 where she joined the Communist Party. She spent three years working in a factory, believing that the experience would ground her fiction in contemporary society. Her first novel, *Divided Heaven* (1963), is a

Marxist exploration of the working class in a divided Germany. Wolf received huge international success with her mythological novel, *Cassandra* (1983). Captured by Agamemnon, the eponymous seeress awaits her fate in Mycenae. Through her diary entries and letters, a broader narrative unfolds which questions, among other things, the role of women throughout the ages, male domination, and nuclear war. Set in a small East German village, *Accident: A Day's News* (1987) is a thought-provoking meditation on the nuclear disaster at Chernobyl. Although Wolf left the Communist Party in 1976, she has remained a committed socialist.

📖 Günter Grass, Virginia Woolf.
See GERMANY   EW

Wolfe, Tom (US, 1931–   ) As a young man, Wolfe shunned a promising career as a literary critic to become a journalist, and his work consistently bears the stamp of his passion for the classics, notably Charles Dickens, Anthony Trollope, and Émile Zola. His cult book, *The Electric Kool-Aid Acid Test* (1968), mixes the techniques of reportage and fiction to create a memorable account of the psychedelic era. Since the 1960s Wolfe has been an outspoken critic of contemporary American fiction, arguing that it has come adrift from its realist roots. His best-selling debut novel, *The Bonfire of the Vanities* (1987), tells the story of a Manhattan yuppie millionaire who becomes embroiled in New York's furious racial tensions. His second novel, *A Man in Full* (1998), again satirizes new wealth, corrupt politics, and racial sensitivities, this time in Georgia.

📖 Hunter S. Thompson, Norman Mailer, Gore Vidal. *See* UNITED STATES OF AMERICA   BH

Wolff, Tobias (US, 1945–   ) Wolff's extraordinary childhood is vividly recreated in his memoir, *This Boy's Life* (1989). In 1993 the book was made into a film starring Ellen Barkin, Leonardo DiCaprio, and Robert De Niro. Wolff's equally fine autobiographical volume, *In Pharoah's Army: Memories of a Lost War* (1994), tells of his tour of duty in Vietnam, but he is perhaps best known as a short-story writer. The first collection, *Hunters in the Snow* (1982), established his reputation as a master of the form: his sharply focused stories capture significant moments in the humdrum lives of American working people. The quality of his writing, with its sparse simplicity and unerring feel for the rhythms of everyday speech, has remained consistently high throughout his next three collections.

📖 Raymond Carver, Richard Ford
                              BH

Woodhouse, Sarah (British, 1950–   ) Born in Birmingham, Woodhouse was educated at Reading University. Begin with *A Season of Mists* (1984), the first of a series of novels set in Norfolk during the Napoleonic era. Anne Mathick inherits a decaying farm and rises to the challenge it poses. Her self-possession is shaken by the advances of the intimidating Sir Harry Gerard. *The Native Air* (1990) finds Dr French, disappointed in his love for Anne, about to depart for India. His ensuing hunt for a kidnap victim uncovers a plot for a French invasion. *Meeting Lily* (1994) centres on an hotel in Italy run by an Englishwoman. The death of a guest throws her affairs into comic upheaval. *Enchanted Ground* (1993) concerns a woman who longs to break free of the ancestral home she has inherited, along with the long-standing enmity of her neighbours.

📖 Angela Thirkell, Joanna Trollope, Pamela Oldfield   *DH*

Woolf, Virginia (British, 1882–1941) Born and brought up in Kensington, the daughter of Leslie Stephen (later knighted), Virginia Stephen suffered her first nervous breakdown at the age of 13, following the death of her mother. She was to be plagued by debilitating depressions the rest of her life, perpetually in dread of what she called the old devil. Her marriage to Leonard Woolf was long and happy. Together they founded the Hogarth Press, and became the focal point of the Bloomsbury Group, a radical and close-knit circle of writers and intellectuals that flourished between the wars.

In a famous essay, 'Mr Bennett and Mrs Brown', published in 1924, Woolf set down her artistic manifesto. In it she rejected the tedious surface realism of the old guard (the works of Wells, Bennett, Galsworthy), insisting that the nature of reality was more transitory and elusive—a luminous halo—which she tried to snare in her fiction. This led to technical experiment and the method known as stream-of-consciousness, and so her novels do demand effort and concentration, which she repays.

Her fourth novel, *Mrs Dalloway* (1925), is perhaps the best place to start. It takes place during a single day as society hostess Clarissa Dalloway makes preparations for a dinner-party. Within this simple frame Woolf plunges into Clarissa's inner life, laying bare the multitude of impressions —trivial, fantastic, evanescent, or engraved with the sharpness of steel—which make

up her core being. An ominous thread is woven into the narrative in the form of a tragic young man, Septimus Smith, who is haunted by his experiences in the First World War. He hears birds speaking Greek (as did Woolf during her illness) and slides terrifyingly into madness and suicidal despair. *To the Lighthouse* (1927) centres on Mrs Ramsay, radiating out to her family and friends as they spend a holiday at the seaside. Little happens in the way of plot, everything in the senses and perceptions of the characters, as Woolf evokes her own idyllic childhood holidays in St Ives, Cornwall, and explores the conflicting roles open to women, through Mrs Ramsay (wife and mother) and Lily Briscoe (artist). *The Waves* (1931) is a prose poem for six voices in which experience is distilled to its essence as they speak directly to the reader, moving with the seasons from bright youth to reflective maturity. *Between the Acts* (1941), published posthumously, is about a pageant of Olde Englande held at a country house on a warm summer night. But the year is 1939, invasion threatens, and an elegiac note sounds through this short novel that a thousand years of history, epitomized by this peaceful pastoral scene, is about to end in brutal violation.

Woolf was an ardent champion of women's rights, protesting especially against the denial of educational opportunity and the injustices of a patriarchal society in *A Room of One's Own* (1929) and *Three Guineas* (1938). She was a perceptive critic, essayist, and biographer; her six volumes of letters and her wonderful diaries (five volumes) are fascinating, indispensable reading. No English writer of the twentieth century has grown more in stature and importance after death than Virginia Woolf.

On 28 March 1941 she put stones in her pocket and walked into the River Ouse and drowned.

📖 James Joyce, E. M. Forster, Katherine Mansfield. *See* HISTORICAL, SEXUAL POLITICS, SOCIAL ISSUES

TH

Wouk, Herman (US, 1915–) Wouk is a best-selling author whose works have been adapted for film and television, notably the huge novels recapitulating events of the Second World War, *The Winds of War* (1971) and *War and Remembrance* (1978). They use traditional, panoramic fictional techniques, switching locations in the portrayal of battles, personal conflicts, and the Holocaust, but also freely mix real and imaginary characters. Wouk is unusual as a twentieth-century writer in his emphasis on a morality based on his Orthodox Judaism and conservative politics. His Pulitzer Prize-winning novel *The Caine Mutiny* (1951) concerns conflict aboard a US naval ship between the irrational Captain Queeg and a junior officer, leading to a court martial with powerful cross-examination scenes. *Marjorie Morningstar* (1955) finds a young woman attempting to escape her background, only to find the pull of Jewish family values too strong.

📖 Bernard Malamud, Gore Vidal. *See* THE SEA

JS

Wren, P(ercival) C(hristopher) (British, 1885–1941) Wren was born in Devon, and after graduating from Oxford his varied life included periods in the French Foreign Legion and the Indian Educational Service. Begin with his best-known book, *Beau Geste* (1924), in which Michael 'Beau' Geste enlists in the French Foreign Legion after being wrongfully suspected of a jewel theft. He is joined by his brothers Digby and John, and the book recounts their adventures in the searing Sahara and describes conditions in the Legion in realistic detail. *Beau Sabreur* (1926) and *Good Gestes* (1929) are sequels. Wren's other books include *Dew and Mildew* (1912), a collection of stories based on his Indian experiences which celebrate the resourcefulness of the expatriate Englishman. *Two Feet from Heaven* (1940) deals with a man who becomes a killer when his wish to help the underprivileged involves him in sordid entanglements.

📖 Rudyard Kipling, Henry Rider Haggard

DH

Wright, Richard (US, 1908–60) Wright was born in Mississippi but brought up in an orphanage in Memphis, Tennessee. His work is strongly autobiographical and was a powerful influence on black writing in the 1930s. *Uncle Tom's Children* (1938) won him a Guggenheim Fellowship, and was followed by the best-selling *Native Son* (1940) in which a black youth is executed for the murder of a white girl. The novel was described by James Baldwin as 'the most powerful and celebrated statement we have yet of what it means to be a Negro in America'. Unflinchingly controversial, Wright's work contains highly evocative if slightly lurid accounts of life for poor blacks in the Southern states and demonstrates the depths to which people can sink as a result of racial oppression. At the same time, Wright emphasizes the spiritual and emotional power which such conditions can produce.

📖 James Baldwin, Alice Walker, Toni Morrison. *See* BLACK AND WHITE, UNITED STATES OF AMERICA

LM

Wright, Ronald (British, 1948–).
See SCIENCE FICTION

Wyndham, John (British, 1903–69)
Wyndham tried a variety of careers—
farming, law, commercial art, advertising
—while trying to make headway as a
writer. He learnt his craft by contributing, under different names, pulp fiction
to American magazines. His first novel,
The Day of the Triffids (1951), had an
immediate impact, and established him as
the most skilful and imaginative English
writer of science fiction since H. G. Wells.
The triffids are seven-foot-tall intelligent
plants with a deadly sting which go on the
rampage against a population blinded by a
freak meteor storm. This outlandish premiss is made terrifyingly plausible thanks
to Wyndham's rounded, believable characters, his concern for moral implications,
and a polished prose style. *The Chrysalids*
(1955) is a prophetic tale of genetic mutation in animals and plants, and examines
the fragility of civilized values when
threatened by the strange and unknown.
In *The Midwich Cuckoos* (1957), filmed
as *The Village of the Damned*, the threat
comes from the children of a quiet rural
village who appear to be the progeny of a
race of telepathic aliens. *The Kraken Wakes*
(1953), about a mysterious force stirring in
the ocean depths, is slower paced but still a
good read. Wyndham also produced two
collections of short stories, *Consider Her
Ways* (1961) and *The Seeds of Time* (1969).
📖 Philip K. Dick, Isaac Asimov,
Brian Aldiss   *TH*

Y

Yeates, V. M. (British, 1897–1934). *See* WAR

Yerofeev, Venedikt (Soviet/Russian, 1938–1990). *See* RUSSIA

Yorke, Margaret (British, 1924–) Margaret Yorke began her career writing family-problem novels. Turning to fictional crime, she created an amateur detective, Patrick Grant, a don who appeared in five novels. *No Medals for the Major* (1974) was a turning-point: Yorke had gained the confidence to allow plot to flow from character and the result was a much-admired novel about the persecution of an innocent man. Yorke's interest lies more in the effects of crime than in describing how it has been carried out and in novels such as *Devil's Work* (1982) her understanding of human behaviour and ability to build suspense combine to memorable effect. Later books often examine aspects of the English criminal justice system. Yorke's accomplished stories are collected in *Pieces of Justice* (1994). Her contribution to crime fiction earned her the award in 1999 of the CWA Diamond Dagger.

📖 Minette Walters, Frances Fyfield
                                        ME

Yourcenar, Marguerite (French, 1903–87) The first woman to be elected to the Académie Française (in 1980), Marguerite Yourcenar felt that the characters in her novels were also companions she communed with in the garden of her home in Connecticut. This is strikingly apparent in *Memoirs of Hadrian* (1951). The Roman Emperor Hadrian, near death, reflects on his own life, most poignantly on his love for the young Antinous who took his own life, apparently in the belief that by dying he would enable Hadrian to live on. *The Abyss* (1984) takes up the tale of Zeno, an alchemist who commits suicide rather than recant or be burnt at the stake, and *Oriental Tales* (revised edition 1983) is a magical little book of retold myths and folk-tales from China, India, Greece, the Balkans, and Japan.

📖 Toni Morrison, Gabriel García Márquez, Isabel Allende   *AT*

Z

Zamyatin, Evgeny (Soviet/Russian, 1884–1937) Zamyatin was born in Lebedyan, and studied naval architecture in St Petersburg. He began writing following his imprisonment and subsequent deportation for taking part in the unsuccessful Revolution of 1905. A senior literary figure after the 1917 Revolution, his writing made him suspect and he emigrated to Paris around 1930. Begin with his only novel, *We* (1920–1), a futuristic account of a totally regulated society which influenced Orwell's *Nineteen Eighty-Four* (1949). The story's doomed lovers embody irrational urges towards which the state is hostile. Zamyatin's picture of stagnation under a benevolent dictator was taken as an allegory of Stalinism and the book remained long unpublished in the Soviet Union. *Dragon* (1966) is a collection of his short stories, which range from social satires to the science fiction of 'The Most Important Thing'.

📖 George Orwell, H. G. Wells, Aldous Huxley. *See* RUSSIA   DH

Zelazny, Roger (US, 1937–) Zelazny was born in Ohio and educated at Columbia University. He worked for the US Social Security before becoming a full-time science fiction writer in 1969. Begin with *The Dream Master* (1966), in which unforeseen hazards await a therapist who has become capable of entering patients' minds. In *Lord of Light* (1967) space travellers on a remote world impose an hierarchical order by installing themselves as Hindu gods. *This Immortal* (1966) is set on Earth after a devastating catastrophe. The immortal Konrad Nomikos has custody of the planet and conducts an extra-terrestrial visitor through many bizarre dangers. The escaped alien in *Eye of Cat* (1982) uses telepathic powers to track down the man who originally captured him. The latter seeks refuge in the homeland of his Navajo ancestors and enters a protective shamanistic trance.

📖 Larry Niven, Frederick Pohl, Robert Silverberg   DH

Zobel, Joseph (Martiniquan, 1915–). *See* BLACK AND WHITE

Zola, Émile (French, 1840–1902) The son of a French-Italian engineer, Zola is widely regarded as one of the founders of the modern 'naturalistic' novel. His output is dominated by twenty novels known as the *Rougon-Macquart* series, which follow the various members of a single family through all the different levels of nineteenth-century French society. *Germinal* (1885) is an account of a mining community that stages a strike, and its detailed settings are balanced by a symbolism that presents the mine as a womb from which the social revolt of the community is born. *Nana* (1880) tells the story of a prostitute whose personal destruction mirrors that of the society through which she moves, and *L'Assommoir* (*The Boozer*, 1877) tells the story of the prostitute's mother, a laundress who descends into alcoholism. Zola's friendships with the Impressionist painters inform *The Masterpiece* (1886), the story of an artist striving to complete a great work against the background of dealers, salons, and collectors of Paris. Zola was an enormously controversial figure in his time, and the publication of his open letter 'J'accuse' in 1898, as an intervention in the notorious Dreyfus Affair, led to a temporary exile in London to avoid imprisonment. Zola's British publisher had himself been imprisoned for distributing the author's works, and their often graphic realism meant that many of his books remained unavailable in translation until the 1960s.

📖 Honoré de Balzac, D. H. Lawrence, Theodore Dreiser, George Gissing   *WB*